This is the fourth volume of *A History of the University of Cambridge*: it explores the extraordinary growth in size and academic stature of the university between 1870 and 1990.

In 1870 the university was a provincial seminary enhanced by a traditional prestige, by expertise in a small range of disciplines, and by a few academic giants. Today it comprises disciplines almost past counting and high international fame in many of them. Yet it is also the home of tradition: a federation of colleges, one over 700 years old, one of the 1970s, the rest of almost every century between, preserving buildings and institutions with a very varied history. This book seeks to penetrate the nature of the colleges and of the federation; and to show the way in which, especially from the 1920s, university faculties and departments came to vie with the colleges for this predominant role. It unravels a fascinating institutional story which is also a piece of social history – of the society of the university and its place in the world. It explores in depth the themes of religion and learning, and of the entry of women into a once male environment. There are portraits of seminal and characteristic figures of the Cambridge scene, Henry Sidgwick, Emily Davies, F. W. Maitland, Gowland Hopkins, Ernest Rutherford, and many others; there is a sketch – inevitably selective but wide-ranging – of many disciplines, an extensive study in intellectual and academic history.

A HISTORY OF THE UNIVERSITY
OF CAMBRIDGE

GENERAL EDITOR
CHRISTOPHER N. L. BROOKE

A HISTORY OF THE UNIVERSITY
OF CAMBRIDGE

General Editor: CHRISTOPHER N. L. BROOKE

Dixie Professor of Ecclesiastical History, University of Cambridge, and Fellow of Gonville and Caius College

This four-volume series will comprise the first substantial history of the university of modern times. Each of the volumes will carry extensive original research and a synthesis of modern scholarship, and will explore the institutions, studies, scholarship, society, sports and buildings of the colleges and university, without neglecting the schools and social context from which the students came. Although not planned on the massive scale of series such as the current *History of the University of Oxford* or the *Victoria History of the Counties of England*, the series will chart afresh and in detail a remarkable passage of history, bring current scholarship into the light of day, and inspire a new generation of students and scholars to fresh endeavour.

Volumes in the series:

1 The University to 1546
   DAMIAN RIEHL LEADER

2 1546–1750
   VICTOR MORGAN
   Forthcoming

3 1750–1870
   PETER SEARBY
   Forthcoming

4 1870–1990
   CHRISTOPHER N. L. BROOKE

A HISTORY OF
THE UNIVERSITY
OF CAMBRIDGE

VOLUME IV
1870–1990

CHRISTOPHER N. L. BROOKE

CAMBRIDGE
UNIVERSITY PRESS

Published by the Press Syndicate of the University of Cambridge
The Pitt Building, Trumpington Street, Cambridge CB2 1RP
40 West 20th Street, New York, NY 10011–4211, USA
10 Stamford Road, Oakleigh, Victoria 3166, Australia

First published 1993

Printed in Great Britain at the University Press, Cambridge

A catalogue record for this book is available from the British Library

Library of Congress cataloguing in publication data

A History of the University of Cambridge.
Includes bibliographical references.
Includes index.
Contents: v. 1. The university to 1546 / Damian Riehl
Leader – v. 4. 1870–1990
1. University of Cambridge – History. I. Brooke, Christopher Nugent Lawrence. II. Leader,
Damian Riehl.
LF109.H57 1988 378.426'59 87-25586
ISBN 0 521 32882 9 (v. 1)

ISBN 0 521 34350 x hardback

CONTENTS

List of illustrations   xiii
Preface   xv
Abbreviations   xxiii

I   PROLOGUE   I
    Cambridge in 1870   I
    From clergyman to don: F. J. A. Hort – Henry
    Sidgwick   7

2   THE UNIVERSITY AND THE COLLEGES   20
    The university   20
    The colleges – Three samples: King's, Jesus, Gonville
    and Caius – The smaller colleges: St Catharine's,
    Magdalene, Corpus Christi, Sidney Sussex, Peter-
    house, Downing, Queens' – The middle ground:
    Emmanuel, Christ's, Trinity Hall, Clare, Pem-
    broke – The giants: St John's, Trinity

                                                                    32
    Epilogue: college finance   73

3   THE SECOND ROYAL COMMISSION AND UNIVER-
    SITY REFORM, 1872–1914   82
    The Royal Commission and the Statutory
        Commission   82
    The Adullamites   90
    Cavendish College and Selwyn College   91
    The debates of 1907–14   95

4   RELIGION 1870–1914   99
    The abolition of religious tests   99

vii

Contents

College chapels   106
Compulsory chapel   111
The agnostics   121
CICCU and SCM   131

5   THEOLOGY   134
Lightfoot   134
Westcott   138
The Divinity School and the theological colleges   141
The early twentieth century   146
Charles Raven   147

6   THE NATURAL SCIENCES   151
Prologue: the Mathematical Tripos   151
Museums and laboratories   153
Geology and earth sciences   157
Botany   160
Physiology   164
The School of Medicine   166
The Cavendish – Foundation – The marks of the Cavendish – Its progress from Clerk Maxwell to J. J. Thomson – Ernest Rutherford – the new Cavendish   173
Chemistry – Frederick Gowland Hopkins – Alexander Todd   194
Archaeology and anthropology   201

7   CLASSICS, LAW AND HISTORY   210
A. E. Housman and the classics   211
Law: Frederic William Maitland   216
Buckland, McNair and Winfield   224
History   227

8   THE SOCIETY   240
I The background of students and teachers   240
II Wives   252
III The masters   257
IV The fellows and the coaches – Two kinds of teacher: Goulding Brown and Welbourne – The economics of the academic profession, 1918–39   267

Contents

V Students – Reading men and rowing men – Sport – Triposes – Women, May Week and the Footlights   287

9   WOMEN 1869–1948   301
Preparation   301
Girton   306
Newnham   311
Girton and Newnham as colleges   316
The admission of women   324
Epilogue   328

10   THE GREAT WAR 1914–18   331

11   SIR HUGH ANDERSON, THE ASQUITH COMMISSION AND ITS SEQUEL   341
The Commissioners   341
Sir Hugh Anderson   343
The Royal Commission   349
The Commissioners at work   364

12   THE UNIVERSITY LIBRARY   370

13   THE DONS' RELIGION IN TWENTIETH-CENTURY CAMBRIDGE   388

14   RELIGION AND LEARNING: C. H. DODD AND DAVID KNOWLES   407
C. H. Dodd   409
Dom David Knowles   418

15   A DIVERSITY OF DISCIPLINES   427
Prologue: on philology and oriental studies   427
From medieval and modern to modern and medieval languages   431
Philosophy and English   436
Art, architecture and music in Cambridge   455
Education and extra-mural studies   463

Contents

Economics and social sciences   467

Geography and HPS – history and philosophy of science   473

Engineering   475

Mathematics   482

Radio astronomy and cosmology   486

Computers and computer science   491

Some biological sciences – Prologue: zoology and veterinary science – Sir Ronald Fisher and genetics – Molecular biology – Sir Frederic Bartlett and psychology – Sir Vincent Wigglesworth   492

16   THE SECOND WORLD WAR   505

17   THE UNIVERSITY AND THE WORLD, 1945–1990: A COSMOPOLITAN SOCIETY   511

I Anthropology – Research – Religion, exams and sport – Cosmopolitan Cambridge – Student attitudes – 'Trade union' attitudes among the dons, and student action – The role of women – Bureaucracy   512

II Politics   538

18   THE NEW COLLEGES   567

Fitzwilliam and Churchill   567

New Hall and Lucy Cavendish   569

The Bridges Report   573

Hughes Hall, Homerton, St Edmund's, Wolfson, Darwin and Clare Hall   575

Robinson College   582

19   EPILOGUE   585

Appendix 1 Fellows and undergraduates of the men's colleges, 1869–1919   593

Appendix 2 Student numbers by college, 1990–1   596

Appendix 3 College incomes, c. 1926   598

Contents

Appendix 4 A note on schools   599
Appendix 5 Professions and status of Cambridge students   601

Bibliographical references   604
Index   625

ILLUSTRATIONS

The map is by Reginald and Marjorie Piggot. Figures 2–5, 8–10, 15, 17, 21–2 are by Wim Swaan, with his kind leave; for figures 6, 18–20, we are indebted to the Curator of Aerial Photography, Mr David Wilson, and his staff; for figures 13–14 to the Syndics of the University Library and Dr Patrick Zutshi; for figures 1, 7 and 16 to the Syndics of the Fitzwilliam Museum; for figure 11 to the Principal and Fellows of Newnham College, for figure 12 to the Mistress and Fellows of Girton College.

Modern Cambridge xxiv–xxv

1 Portrait of A. C. Benson, by Sir William Nicholson, in the Fitzwilliam Museum *page* 47

2 Pembroke College, library and chapel 65

3 Selwyn College, court and chapel 94

4 Sidney Sussex College, chapel 120

5 New Museums Site, Mond Laboratory, now Department of Aerial Photography: the crocodile by Eric Gill 192

6 The new Cavendish Laboratory in west Cambridge 194

7 Drawing of Sir Frederick Gowland Hopkins by Edmund Kapp, in the Fitzwilliam Museum 197

8 Town and gown: Magdalene Bridge 253

xiii

List of illustrations

9 Girton College, Emily Davies Court   312

10 Newnham College, Sidgwick Hall and Clough dining-hall   315

11 Portrait of Miss Jane Harrison, by Augustus John, in Newnham College   321

12 Portrait of Dame Mary Cartwright, by Stanley Spencer, in Girton College   322

13 Sir Giles Scott's first design for the University Library: watercolour by Cyril A. Farley, 1924   380

14 The University Library: an artist's impression of 1931   384

15 Portrait of Joseph Needham, by James Wood, in Gonville and Caius College   401

16 Drawing of M. R. James, by William Strang, in the Fitzwilliam Museum   461

17 The Mullard Radio Astronomy Observatory, Lord's Bridge   489

18 The Backs from the air: the History Faculty, Harvey Court and Queens' new building from the west   548

19 The Backs from the air: the Queens' new building, Harvey Court and the History Faculty from the south-east   549

20 St John's College, new buildings of the nineteenth and twentieth centuries, and the Backs   552

21 Wolfson College, façade   578

22 Robinson College   584

PREFACE

It might be said, with some exaggeration, that in 1870 the University of Cambridge was a provincial seminary; in 1990 it is a major academy of international repute. It would be a half truth, for the dominance of the clergy among the alumni was already in decline in 1870; there had been giants in the land, and in mathematics, botany, geology and theology Cambridge had a high reputation already in the 1860s. Nor could the university which had bred Newton in the seventeenth century, endured Bentley in the eighteenth, and trembled before Whewell in the nineteenth be thought wholly provincial. The reputation of Cambridge today, furthermore, owes much to its history: it learned the art of attracting talent from every corner of the globe in the late nineteenth and early twentieth centuries partly because a prejudice was abroad – not often related to the facts – that Cambridge was a distinguished university. Nor is it in all respects a cosmopolitan university today. In many fields it is a part of the academic cosmos; it draws its students from far and wide; a proportion of its staff and a high proportion of its postgraduate students come from distant lands. But it is also profoundly inward-looking. A scholar can step in a moment from international discussion in his seminar or lab to the parochial atmosphere of his college's Senior Combination Room – or vice versa, from lofty discourse in the SCR to instant coffee in the lab.

None the less, there has been a remarkable transformation. In 1870 the university was a federation of colleges. There was a medical school of a kind and some museums; but as late as the 1850s John Venn could discern no provision for the specialist teaching of science except 'a small table, such as two people might take their tea at; a table not in constant use, but brought into the

Arts School three times a week during the May term', so that Professor Stokes might expound physical optics.[1] By 1990 a vast array of faculties and departments has slid into place beside the colleges, competing with them for power and influence. They are not a federation, but the servants of a hierarchy of small committees – faculty boards, councils of Schools, General Board, Council of the Senate – representative in a sense but so small as to be oligarchical in practice. It is true that over the whole structure presides the governing body of the university, the Regent House, a democracy of all the teachers in the university – and of senior administrators too; and that the Regent House regularly debates and occasionally votes on reports and motions – 'graces' – laid before it. But in the university there is a large, and growing, element of managerial government, more than in the colleges. It could be said that two quite different systems of government are in conflict here – a strange warfare in which the same protagonists sit in both camps, for most of the academic teaching staff of faculties and departments are also fellows of colleges and members of their governing bodies.

It is a fascinating theme for a historian, but profoundly difficult. First of all, a history of the university should be securely based on scholarly histories of colleges and faculties alike; but few exist. I had the extraordinary good fortune, at an early stage, of a generous invitation by Brian Harrison to view his team at work on the *History of the University of Oxford*, VIII; and to many of them, and especially Mark Curthoys and John Prest, I owe invaluable help, advice and insights. I have greatly benefited from the general surveys by John Roach in *VCH Cambridgeshire*, III (1959), and in T. E. B. Howarth, *Cambridge between Two Wars* (1978). Nearly every college in Oxford and Cambridge had a place in the series of histories published by Robinson about 1900, and some are good. But the best stop about 1850, and give only perfunctory outlines of the events of the author's own time. A striking example is John Venn's history of Caius, for he was one of the great pioneers of college history, and had no doubts about its value.[2] But he could not view the events of his own lifetime as history nor see their importance to historians of the future; so

---

[1] Venn 1913, pp. 263–4. For the context, see Brooke 1985, p. 219.
[2] Venn 1901; see Brooke 1985, pp. xiii–xiv.

when I came to write *A History of Gonville and Caius College* a
few years ago I was amazed to discover that of all the periods I
had to cover the least studied, and in some respects the most
obscure, was the age of John Venn himself, from the 1850s to
1923. A new era has dawned: we have modern histories of St
John's, Girton, St Catharine's, Trinity Hall and Queens', and
others are on the way.[3] But many more are needed; and the
same is even truer of the faculties. There is a wealth of literature
on the Cavendish and on its remarkable offshoot, the molecular
biology lab – though this is funded by the MRC and is not,
strictly speaking, a part of the university.[4] There are many
articles on the history of science and individual disciplines. But
there are enormous gaps. For chemistry we depend in some
measure, significantly it may seem, on the reminiscences of
Gowland Hopkins and Lord Todd.[5] Yet it is vital in such a book
as this to give a genuine impression of the variety of the scene –
the different characters of the colleges, so like and so unlike one
another; the differing fortunes of the many disciplines. Such is the
state of scholarship, such are the limits of my own knowledge,
such are the restrictions of space, that my view of any one college,
of any one discipline, must be selective and impressionistic. It is
easy to make such a book a pile of facts, a heap of sawdust. That
above all I have tried to avoid; and it may be that it is too
personal, too idiosyncratic. But I have become increasingly aware
as the work went forward of a paradox: it is easier to see the
wood than the trees – that is to say, it is difficult to see the rich
and varied elements in the University of Cambridge as living,
fruitful organisms. I have dwelt at length on some seminal
figures – Sidgwick, Lightfoot, Hort, Maitland, Housman, Gowland Hopkins, Rutherford and so forth – and on some crucial
buildings and institutions which have moulded the character of
Cambridge – the Cavendish and the University Library are
examples. Perhaps their share is disproportionate; but if we are to
understand anything of a very complex subject we need from

3 Miller 1961; Bradbrook 1969; Rich 1973; Crawley 1976; Twigg 1987; the History of Caius is
  Brooke 1985. Mr D. J. V. Fisher is writing a new History of Jesus; Professor Patrick Collinson,
  Dr Sarah Bendall and I are writing a History of Emmanuel. For the younger colleges, see chap.
  18.   4 See pp. 173–94, 497–9.
5 Needham and Baldwin 1949; Todd 1983.

time to time to go deeply into this or that person or institution; and I hope the effect will be to make the book more interesting and more challenging to our thoughts about how universities in general, and Cambridge in particular, have evolved.

I have deliberately made religion a central theme, for I think this essential to understanding the subtle shades of an era in which a constellation of religious institutions became secularised, without losing all their religious character. While I was engaged in my task the master and College Council of Trinity generously invited me to give the Birkbeck Lectures in ecclesiastical history for 1990–1; and I took this as an opportunity to give shape and colour to some chapters of the book. To them and to many in Trinity who helped me in the making of the lectures I am deeply indebted, and especially to Professor Patrick Collinson, Dr Robert Robson and Mr Alan Cuccia. The result is that religion may seem to some to have a disproportionate share; even so, there is still a great deal missing. On student religion, on the CICCU and the SCM, for instance, there is much less than there should be.[6]

If one contemplates the geography of Cambridge, then one might reasonably say that it was more affected by the growth of playing fields than of labs in the late nineteenth and early twentieth centuries. For the undergraduates in particular Cambridge was above all a great sporting centre. This is inadequately reflected in my pages. Undoubtedly it needs to be stressed; but sport played a small part in making Cambridge a great academy. By the same token my chapters on the social history of Cambridge may seem impressionistic and inadequate. For this I plead a more particular excuse. There has been some analysis of the origin and destiny of Cambridge alumni; but most of it is based on slender foundations, and all of it ultimately depends on matriculation registers and the like. For most colleges little work has been done on them; and I learned from my attempts to provide statistics for Caius, one of the best documented and best published of colleges, that the material is nothing like so lucid or accurate as one would wish. Even for the schools from which the alumni came, for which information is plentiful, there is a major

---

[6] This is partly because the current literature – such as Pollock 1953 on CICCU – provides little searching analysis of its role among students.

difficulty: no serious study has been given to ways of comparing the very different pattern of schools of the 1880s with that of the 1960s or 1990s.[7] Meanwhile I have given in the appendices such tables as I could collect.

I have tried in a measure to balance the themes which are essential to understanding the history of a university: science and scholarship; the institutions – the very peculiar institutions of Cambridge which have shaped its destiny in all sorts of unexpected ways; ideas, religious and academic, notions of the function of a university or a college; and the social setting and the inner anthropology. I have striven to do justice in particular to three areas of change: the transition to a major international centre of scholarly and scientific teaching and research; the transition from an Anglican academy to a secular university; the transition from a male society with two women's colleges attached in some measure to a mixed university in which women are equal partners in principle if not yet in practice. I have tried to analyse the nature and inwardness of these changes while not wholly neglecting their outward form and history.

A wholly intractable problem has been the arrangement of the book. Many themes must be treated analytically; and it would be tedious and tiresome – or take far too much space – to have two or three separate discussions of heads of houses or theology or physics or the role of the colleges in different parts of the book; there is indeed a strong advantage in treating some of these topics so that the contrast between their condition in 1870 and in 1970 is immediately apparent. Yet there must be some chronology, some sense of the movement from 1870 to 1990 which is the central purpose of the book. The result is a chronological frame, with caesuras at the two World Wars, yet with analytical chapters laid out within it. Most puzzling of all have been the chapters on the academic disciplines, now almost beyond counting. Those most central to the earlier decades have been grouped in chapters 5–7; the rest are gathered in chapter 15. The division is often a trifle arbitrary, but if they were all grouped together, they would be wholly indigestible.

I am a medievalist whose life has been spent in the central

---

[7] See pp. 245–9 and Brooke 1985, pp. 308–9.

Middle Ages. As a trespasser in very modern times I have been particularly aware how like and unlike historical scholarship is in the contemporary world; how much I needed help – and the generosity and excellence of the help I have received.

The modern world is full of documents, beyond a medievalist's dreams. But they have been very unequally preserved. Venn and his generation treated the medieval records of university and colleges with loving care, but had little notion of preserving the more intimate records of their own work. In the twentieth century paper has grown to alarming proportions, and in the University Archives and in some colleges it has been deftly handled by professional archivists. Contrary to what is sometimes alleged, the attitude to archives in the Cambridge colleges has greatly improved in the last twenty years, and several have professional archivists. But much of this is very recent, and college memory is peculiarly vulnerable, since the custom in most is to record only the baldest of decisions from college governing body or council meetings. Thus the debates which preceded the admission of women in all the male colleges are only recorded (so far as I know) in a small number in which one or other fellow made a private archive. If we look a little further back, the Royal Commission and the Statutory Commissions of the 1920s have left little record; most of their archives have been lost. I have been alternately overwhelmed by the wealth of material and baffled by its absence. When documents survive in reasonable quantity, however, the techniques of research are much the same in the twelfth and the twentieth centuries, for human nature applied to drafting documents alters little over the centuries, and those of the twentieth century as often intend something quite different from their surface meaning as those of the twelfth. In particular, effective documentation (or more crudely, adequate footnotes) – not always provided by contemporary historians – are as important as ever. One type of source is wholly new to a medievalist, and that is oral evidence and human memory. I have made much use of both – and I recall as striking examples invaluable advice on the Statutory Commission of the 1920s from the late Tressilian Nicholas, its Assistant Secretary, from Richard Eden on the foundation of Clare Hall, and from Charles Brink, Lord Lewis and Martin Brett, on the foundation of Robinson College, in which they were deeply involved, and many of the kind on individual disciplines, for example David Phillipson on arch and anth, Nicholas Brooke on English, Brian Harland on geology, John Baker and Peter Stein on law, Elisabeth Stopp on modern languages, Dame Elizabeth Hill on Russian, Anthony Hewish on radio astronomy, and so forth. I am very much aware that I could have been more systematic and effective, had time and opportunity allowed. Meanwhile it has been fascinating to observe how often memory and archives are at variance – not always due to error and fallibility, but sometimes to a natural difference: archives tend to record formal decisions, the memory the informal processes which lay behind them.

The plot from which this volume emerged was originally laid by Michael Black and William Davies in the Cambridge University Press, and I am deeply indebted to their advice and enthusiasm. In its final preparation and production I am especially indebted to Margaret Sharman and Lyn Chatterton. Damian Leader started the series and the idea owes much to him; I have had many discussions with Victor Morgan and Peter Searby, authors of volumes II and III, and Peter Searby has generously commented on my drafts. Rosalind Brooke, as so often in the past, has revised my drafts and helped to shape the book – and steered the book and its author past many shoals. I have had invaluable advice and help from Denis Bartlett, Peter Bayley, Owen Chadwick, Donald Charlton, Barrie Dobson, Anthony Edwards, Ronald Hyam, Yao Liang, Christopher Morris, Valerie Pearl, Harry Porter, Graeme Rennie, Peter Robinson, Robert Robson, Frank Stubbings, Gillian Sutherland, Simon Szreter, David Thompson, John Twigg; and from Patrick Zutshi and Elisabeth Leedham-Green in the University Archives, and from many college archivists, including Catherine Hall and Anne Neary at Caius, Sarah Bendall at Emmanuel, Malcolm Underwood at St John's, Christopher Parish and Nicholas Rogers at Sidney, and Alan Cuccia at Trinity. To Elisabeth Leedham-Green I am also deeply indebted for reading the proofs. All have been generous in encouragement and must bear their share of credit for the enterprise; its failings are all my own.

For permission to quote reserved or copyright material, and the photographs included in this book, I am deeply indebted to

Dorothy Atcheson, author of the life of Tressilian Nicholas (see p. 155), to Michael Brooke (see p. 283n), to Janet Whitcut (see p. 288n.), the University Registrary (Appendix 2), the College Council of Trinity College and especially the Secretary to the Council, to Lord Bonham Carter, to the Curator of Aerial Photography, David Wilson, to the Syndics of the Cambridge University Library; and in particular to my friend and fellow-worker in another enterprise Wim Swaan for his photographs, and to Sir Trenchard Cox, to whom I owe the use of the delectable memoirs of his late wife Maisie Anderson, 'Time to the sound of bells', now, by his generosity, lodged in the Caius archives.

I owe much generous help to Gonville and Caius College and its staff, and especially to Mrs Edna Pilmer, the Fellows' Research Secretary. The college has provided research grants and a computer, the college library books, Edna Pilmer has brought order out of the chaos of my drafts.

One kindly reviewer of my book on Caius observed that it might be better if a college history was never written by a member of the college. By the same token it might be well for university histories to be written from outside. I confess that my own position is equivocal. I was brought up under the shadow of Cambridge and served college and university for a spell in the 1950s; I returned to Cambridge in 1977. Thus far I write as a devoted alumnus and Regent master. But between 1956 and 1977 I was a professor in Liverpool and London – at Westfield College; and I have looked at Cambridge from the outside too, not always with a friendly eye. I hope that both points of view have contributed to the book. If history is to be interesting and meaningful the historian must be both critical and committed. I have been highly critical of some features of Cambridge – especially of the divorce between colleges and university – but at the end of the day it has been one of the supreme privileges of my life to serve it, and I doubt if any imaginative reader will fail to realise that I feel it to be so.

Gonville and Caius College, Cambridge   C.N.L.B.

ABBREVIATIONS

BMFRS	*Biographical Memoirs of Fellows of the Royal Society*
CUA	Cambridge University Archives (in CUL)
CUC	*Cambridge University Calendar*
CUL	Cambridge University Library
DNB	*Dictionary of National Biography*
DSB	*Dictionary of Scientific Biography*
	ed. C. C. Gillespie, 16 vols., New York, 1970–80
PBA	*Proceedings of the British Academy*
RCHM	
Cambridge	*Royal Commission on Historical Monuments for England, City of Cambridge*, 2 vols., London, 1959
Reporter	*Cambridge University Reporter*
VCH	*The Victoria History of the Counties of England*

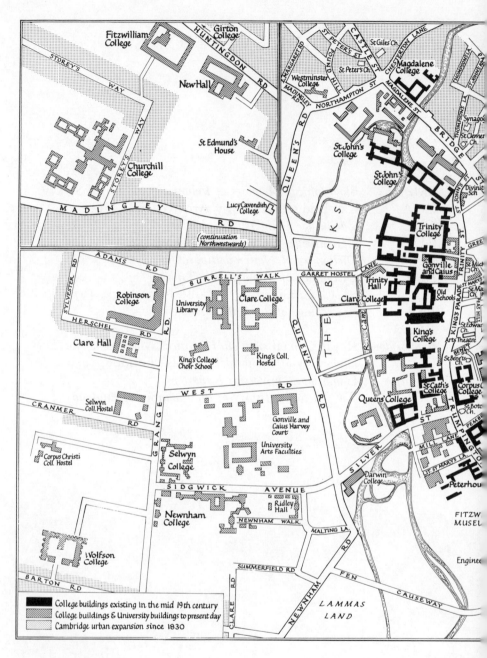

Modern Cambridge

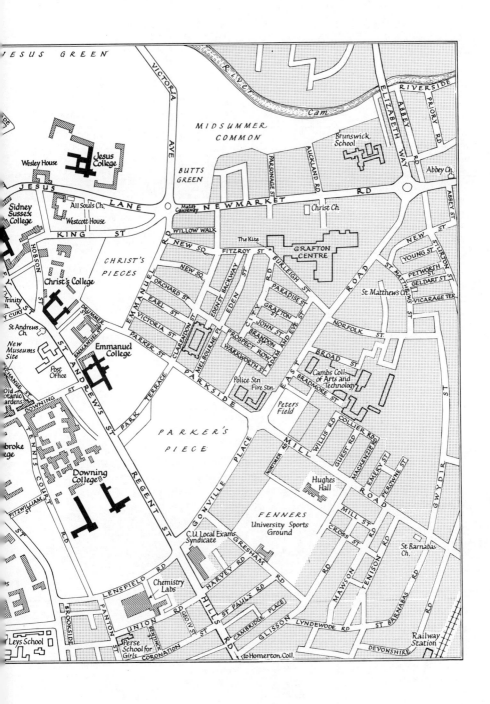

Chapter 1

PROLOGUE

CAMBRIDGE IN 1870

In the years 1869–71 there could be seen a series of dramatic harbingers of change. In 1869 Henry Sidgwick, who had become a devout agnostic, made protest against the survival of religious tests in Cambridge by resigning his Trinity fellowship.[1] In 1870 Joseph Barber Lightfoot refused to be translated from the Hulsean to the Regius Chair of Divinity in the hope – rapidly fulfilled – that this would enable his friend Brooke Foss Westcott to return to Cambridge in the Regius Chair.[2] In the same year, both of them, with F. J. A. Hort, joined the panel which produced the Revised Version of the Bible. Thus was cemented the alliance which made the late nineteenth century the golden age of Cambridge theology; a movement by no means checked by the abolition of religious tests in 1871.[3] In the same year 1870 Lightfoot endowed a fund 'for the encouragement of the study of history, and more especially ecclesiastical history';[4] this helped to establish history as a serious subject and was to support a succession of notable young historians in the century which followed. The endowment was more significant than the career of Charles Kingsley as Regius Professor of Modern History – thronged as his lectures were – which came to an end in 1869, when he was succeeded by J. R. Seeley.[5] In 1870 the duke of Devonshire announced the benefaction from which the

[1] Sidgwick 1906, p. 198; cf. Schneewind 1977, pp. 26–52.
[2] Chadwick 1963, pp. 10–11; Eden and MacDonald 1932, p. 4; Westcott 1903, I, 366. For what follows, Chadwick 1970, pp. 46–50.
[3] On the tests see Winstanley 1947, chap. 3; for theology, below, pp. 134–46.
[4] Clark 1900, p. 329.
[5] Chadwick 1975; Wormell 1980, esp. p. 73.

I

Cavendish Laboratory came forth.[6] In 1869 Frederic William
Maitland arrived in Trinity as an undergraduate and in 1870 or so
wandered into Henry Sidgwick's lecture room.[7] Meanwhile the
movement for reviving college teaching was under way. Trinity
had already set a notable example. In 1868 Augustus Austen Leigh
became tutor of King's; Ernest Stewart Roberts became a college
lecturer in Caius in 1870, tutor in 1876 – and so one could go on,
almost without end.[8] Most portentous of all, the nucleus which
was to become Girton gathered at Hitchin in 1869; the five
students and Miss Clough, who later moved to Newnham, settled
in Regent Street in Cambridge in 1871.[9]

Yet in a very deep and very true sense Cambridge altered little
in these years; and the roots and inspiration of such change as
came lay far back in the past. Some of the leaders of late
nineteenth-century Cambridge looked back to the first half of the
century as the age of the giants. Writing of Robert Willis on his
death in 1875, J. W. Clark, himself a notable scientist, antiquary
and later University Registrary, called him 'almost, if not quite,
the last of those great men who by their brilliant reputation in
studies the most diverse – theology, mathematics, classics, science
– made the first half of the present century the golden age of
Cambridge'.[10] The sentiment seems absurd to us, and yet he
could have provided a remarkable list going back to the great
classical scholar Richard Porson, who died in 1808. He probably
had chiefly in mind, apart from Willis, the giants of Trinity. First,
there was Adam Sedgwick, a craggy Yorkshireman who took his
BA degree in 1808, and by 1818 was professor of geology.[11] He
was one of those who made geology a fundamental science, and
helped materially on the path which led to Darwin's *Origin of
Species*. But when Darwin published his book in 1859, Sedgwick
– who regarded Darwin still as a young man of bright promise
not quite on the right lines – gave it an ambiguous reception.
'Parts of it I admired greatly, parts I laughed at till my sides were

[6] Cavendish 1910, p. 4.
[7] Fisher 1910, p. 7. Maitland became a pensioner in October 1868 and matriculated in January 1869.
[8] Austen Leigh 1906, chaps. 6–7, esp. p. 92; Brooke 1985, pp. 234–6.
[9] Bradbrook 1969, chaps. 1–2; Hamilton 1936, chaps. 5–6; Sidgwick 1906, pp. 205–9.
[10] *Cambridge Chronicle* 6 March 1875, quoted in McKitterick 1986, p. 704.
[11] Clark and Hughes 1890.

almost sore; other parts I read with absolute sorrow, because I think them utterly false and grievously mischievous'; and at the end 'believe me . . . your true-hearted old friend: A. Sedgwick'.[12] For he was in many ways a don of the old school, a cleric and prebendary of Norwich Cathedral, deeply suspicious of the tendency of modern thought to undermine the Christian faith. Next, there was William Whewell, the master of Trinity from 1841 to 1866, a formidable character who struck terror into many who encountered him.[13] Whewell was an original thinker who revolutionised several sciences and even has a niche in the history of moral theology and philosophy;[14] a little more reluctantly, he played an active part in university reform, helping to establish the new triposes in moral and natural sciences. But in Trinity nothing might change: he stood firm against the impertinent enquiries of the first Royal Commission, even though Sedgwick was a Commissioner; he built Whewell's Court for Trinity as an enchanting echo of the gothic past.[15] His death in 1866 made possible at last a movement for college reform in which Trinity could play a leading part.[16] Finally, there was Robert Willis himself, one-time fellow of Caius, but almost a Trinity man since he was a close friend of Whewell and uncle of J. W. Clark. He was a notable mechanical engineer, a leading figure in the development of railway engineering, and for many years Jacksonian Professor of Natural Philosophy. His engineering skills are still remembered, though probably not so widely now as his fundamental work in architectural history. When students engage today in the serious study of English cathedrals, there is usually a study by Willis from which they start.[17]

Whewell died in 1866; Willis lived on to 1875, but in failing health. His great *Architectural History of the University of Cambridge and of the Colleges of Cambridge and Eton* was left to his nephew Clark to complete.[18] The university was a very different place

[12] Clark and Hughes, 1890, II, 356–9; cf. Garland 1980, pp. 105–12.
[13] See esp. Clark 1900, pp. 1–76; also Robson 1967; Robson and Cannon 1964; summary in Brooke, Highfield and Swaan 1988, pp. 270–1.
[14] Robson and Cannon 1964; Schneewind 1977, pp. 101–17.
[15] On which he shared some expertise with his friend Robert Willis. Brooke 1985, p. 204 and n. 59.
[16] Winstanley 1947, chap. 6.
[17] Brooke 1985, pp. 204–5, and see esp. Willis 1845a and b, 1869.
[18] Willis and Clark 1886/1988; and see esp. David Watkin's introduction to the edition of 1988.

from what it had been in 1800: there were new triposes, new museums, professors who lectured, even a few married dons.[19] But the colleges were only very slowly feeling the winds of change, and the old world lived on beside the new in all manner of surprising ways. Perhaps the end of this epoch is most fittingly portrayed by the passing of Sedgwick in January 1873.

'We buried poor old Sedgwick today,' wrote Alfred Newton, professor of zoology, to Clark, at that time curator of his museum, on 1 February:

> the funeral was very well conducted, but the weather was bitterly cold. However, I dressed myself *à l'arctique*, and am none the worse ... [At the Trinity Lodge] all the 'swells' assembled in the big dining-room, and we were *ex necessitate* rigged out in gloves and scarves. The minor dignitaries met in the Combination Room, and fell into the procession as it came round the court. I have no idea how many people joined – perhaps 300. We had the Bishops of Ely and Norwich; Stanley [Dean of Westminster], who looked as if he should have liked to carry off the corpse to his own collection at Westminster ... sundry Deans, a few Lords, masters of public schools and the Mayor of Cambridge. My own order [the professors] ... was of course very strongly represented, in fact I think Vernon Harcourt [professor of international law and an eminent politician] was the only absentee ... So we walked round the court in a shower of sleet ... [20]

The ceremony and the weather speak of a Cambridge which never changes; nor was the old order wholly buried with Sedgwick. At the heart of that procession must have walked a clergyman in his late forties, who combined the roles of University Registrary, vicar of the university church, Great St Mary's, and fellow of Trinity; a very notable figure of the *ancien régime*, a scholar indeed, but equally a cleric – Henry Richards Luard. He lives for us in the charming memoir J. W. Clark wrote of him after his death in 1891.[21]

> He passed his youth and many years of his manhood in the old University, and though he was compelled, intellectually, to admit

---

[19] On married fellows, see pp. 252–7.
[20] Shipley 1913, pp. 115–16. On Sedgwick see esp. Clark and Hughes 1890.
[21] Clark 1900, pp. 328–43; the passage which follows is from pp. 329–30.

the advantage of many of the changes which have taken place in recent years, I doubt if he ever cordially accepted them ... As his older friends passed away, he found a difficulty in making new ones; he felt out of his element; he was distracted by the multiplicity of tastes and studies; and vehemently disapproved of the modifications in the collegiate life which the new statutes have brought about. Though he himself, by a strange irony of fate, was the first Fellow [of Trinity] to take advantage of the power of marrying and still retaining the fellowship, he bitterly regretted that such a clause had ever become law; and it is hardly too much to say that he predicted the ruin of the college from such an innovation.

Luard dearly loved his fellowship, and dearly loved his wife, and he thought it calamitous that he was allowed to have them both. 'And yet he was by no means an unreasoning or unreasonable Conservative. In many matters he was a reformer; I have even heard him called a radical; but, when his beloved college was concerned, the force of early association was too strong, and he regarded fundamental change as sacrilege.'

Like most of his generation, he had been a wrangler in the Mathematical Tripos; but he was at heart a dedicated classic. 'He spoke of Bentley, Porson' and others 'as though they had been his personal friends ... He resented any slights on Porson as almost a personal affront ... He had a particular dislike for English notes [to classical texts]; and I had rather not try to remember what I have heard him say about English translations printed side by side with the original text.'[22] Thus far Clark.

As Registrary Luard had charge of the University Archives, and did his share, as did several of the nineteenth-century Registraries, in ordering and listing them. More than this, he played a leading part in the completion of the catalogue of manuscripts in the University Library.[23] Above all, he is remembered today as the most prolific editor of medieval texts in the Cambridge of his time. Eighteen volumes of the Rolls Series bear witness to his industry, all adorned (strange as it may seem) with notes in English. He seems to have taught himself as he went along. His first endeavour, the Lives of Edward the Confessor, is

---

[22] Clark 1900, pp. 331–2.
[23] Clark 1900, pp. 336, 338–9; McKitterick 1986, pp. 546–51.

one of the worst in the series; his last, the great editions of Matthew Paris' *Chronica Majora* and the *Flores Historiarum*, are among the best – though admittedly he never achieved the stature of William Stubbs. 'His labours in this field of research', Clark claimed, 'have been better appreciated in Germany than in England' – a sort of refrain in memoirs of medieval scholars of this and the next generation – but Stubbs and his disciples greeted his best work with 'cordial appreciation' and his Matthew Paris has been in our hands ever since.[24] It was not a difficult task, since a part of Matthew's own autograph lay to hand in the Corpus library; but it is monumental. Luard was inspired to his love of the Middle Ages by reading S. R. Maitland's works;[25] and it is a strange and sad irony that although Maitland's greater grandson, Frederic William, was an undergraduate at Trinity – and at the end of Luard's life reader and professor in law – there is no evidence of any link or influence between them. None the less Luard's books must often have been in Maitland's hands. This helps to explain how Luard could perform so many roles. A fellow of Trinity need have no personal dealing with undergraduates, though a few had much; a Registrary, if a quick and efficient worker, could himself master all the business of the university now undertaken by innumerable full-time officials and clerks. There was infinitely less paper-work within the university, and no University Grants or Funding Committee without dedicated to sending endless requests for answers to questions of doubtful meaning. He was a conscientious clergyman of an old-fashioned character.

> He was an eloquent preacher, and his sermons in the College chapel used to be listened to with an interest which we did not always feel in what was said to us from that pulpit. They were plain, practical, persuasive; the compositions of one who was not above his congregation; who had nothing donnish about him, but who spoke to the undergraduates as one who had passed through the same temptations as themselves ... On the same principles, for the twenty-seven years during which he was Vicar of Great St

[24] Clark 1900, p. 337; on the quality of Luard's work on Matthew Paris, see Vaughan 1958, pp. 155–7, and for some weaknesses, esp. ibid. p. 31. Luard (in good company) failed adequately to identify Matthew's autographs, and wrongly denied Matthew's authorship of the *Flores Historiarum*: see Vaughan 1958, pp. 39–41.
[25] Clark 1900, p. 336; on F. W. Maitland, see pp. 216–24.

Mary's, he laboured in the parish in a spirit of true sympathy. There was no fussiness about him; he did not take part in movements; he did not 'work' a parish as a modern clergyman does, on the principle of perpetual worry, leaving neither man, nor woman, nor child at peace for a moment; he led his people to better things by gentle measures; he sympathized with their troubles; he relieved their necessities . . . Those who know best tell me that his labours among the poor were unremitting, and that his generosity knew no limits.[26]

He was an old high churchman, not a ritualist. Clark goes on to underline his honesty and fearlessness; set in his ways, he yet understood that others held different views; and his sermon after the death of Frederick Denison Maurice was evidently a model of charity. He had a keen sense of humour and a deep memory from which countless tales of Cambridge life would well up. 'He delighted in society, and few men knew better how to deal with it, or how to make his home an agreeable centre of Cambridge life. In this he was ably seconded by his admirable wife, *qui savait tenir un salon*, as the French say, more successfully than is usual in this country'[27] – and who lived, we may add, in St Peter's Terrace, where one might find, at one time or another in the 1870s, F. D. Maurice, Westcott, Hort and Luard, and which was perhaps, even more truly than the Trinity high table or the Divinity School, the centre of Cambridge religious discourse.[28] Clark lamented at Luard's passing; yet much of him remains. His catalogue, his Matthew Paris, and the Victorian restoration of Great St Mary's, are his living monuments still.

FROM CLERGYMAN TO DON

Luard lived through major reforms, and regretted them. None the less he harboured in himself some of the elements – love of learning, love of the college – which were to remain fundamental through the great changes of late nineteenth-century Cambridge. Beside the college the university began to grow, and labs and departments to achieve a measure of independent life crucial for

[26] Clark 1900, pp. 339–40. For what follows, see ibid. pp. 331–2.
[27] Clark 1900, pp. 342–3.
[28] For St Peter's Terrace, see esp. Hort 1896, ii, passim, esp. pp. 167, 172, 193, 370.

the future, even though the full development of Cambridge's strange constitution – the effective divorce of university and colleges – had to wait for the 1920s. This dual growth, in colleges and in the university, lends a marked ambivalence to the history of Cambridge between 1870 and 1926. By the same token, in the equally crucial changing view of the academic profession, old and new were mingled in an ambivalent way which lends a special interest to the theme we are now pursuing.

This changing view has been labelled by A. J. Engel, for Oxford, the transition *From Clergyman to Don*; and Sheldon Rothblatt has described the process, for Cambridge, as *The Revolution of the Dons.*[29] As a stereotype, Engel's picture is very revealing. The characteristic figure of mid-nineteenth-century Oxford – and Cambridge too – was the old-fashioned unmarried clerical don, whose whole life lay within the college, devoted to its preservation though often lacking in any academic aim we could easily recognise as such – neither directed to research nor to teaching. By 1900 he had been in large measure replaced by the professional academic, lay, learned, and married, whether he was a man of the labs and the libraries or of the towpath.[30] But like all stereotypes it dissolves the more it mingles with the crowd.

We have already studied one admirable example of the old-fashioned clerical don in H. R. Luard. Closer to the formula was the Reverend Dr E. H. Perowne, the master of Corpus, who in his later years certainly regarded himself as cast in the image of Cambridge tradition: he was a clergyman and bachelor and thought of his college as a clerical seminary. But the Corpus of his youth had been liberal in politics and more open to the new fashions of the age; he was one of those who had created the conservative, evangelical model there.[31] There is a sense in which Perowne and his colleagues in their later years were consciously forming the image of the clerical don which was under attack.

Nor were all the clergy arrayed on the conservative side. It is significant that the young tutor and bursar of Caius, E. S. Roberts and J. B. Lock, deeply involved in leading Caius into the new

[29] Engel 1983; Rothblatt 1981.
[30] We have no precise statistics for Cambridge dons to show how many married by 1900.
[31] Bury 1952, esp. pp. 55–9, 84–9, 114–18.

world, both felt it right or incumbent on them to seek orders in the late 1870s.[32] The leaders of reform in the university included Bateson, master of St John's, and Phear, master of Emmanuel; and by Phear's side stood A. T. Chapman, celibate clerical fellow of Emmanuel from 1862 to 1913, when he left his Hebrew books and his wine to the college, twin memorials of what appear to have been the foundations of his life – his devotion to the college, and its common life, and to scholarship.[33] He was a staunch supporter of the remarkable scheme to amalgamate Emmanuel with Christ's, and was evidently involved, with Phear, in the election of Hort as fellow, and, with Hort, in the foundation of the Dixie Professorship – two significant steps designed to give Emmanuel a more professional image in education, religion, learning and research, all four.[34]

F. J. A. Hort

Hort himself had a link with almost every movement of the mid and late nineteenth century. A pupil of Dr Arnold at Rugby, an undergraduate and fellow of Trinity, an Apostle and disciple and personal friend of F. D. Maurice, he held firmly together in his lively, searching, penetrating mind the fervour of traditional Anglicanism with an enthusiastic welcome for the new learning, both in biblical scholarship and in science. In religious sentiment, he came of evangelical stock and gradually assimilated more liberal ideas and a modicum of high-church practices: he rejoiced in the adornment of Trinity chapel with murals and glass inspired by Lightfoot and Westcott and took pains to fill the windows of Emmanuel chapel with glass similarly portraying the glory of the Christian tradition.[35] His son would not allow that he was eclectic, yet he clearly grasped something of value from almost every aspect of the Christian tradition.[36] He rejoiced to say of Cambridge, 'we have no sharply-defined camps', in contrast to Oxford.[37] In 1850 he took part I of the Mathematical Tripos

---

[32] Brooke 1985, pp. 231–2 and 231 n. 30.   [33] See p. 58.

[34] See pp. 58–9. On Hort see esp. Hort 1896; Rupp 1977, chap. 10.

[35] Pevsner 1970, p. 167 and n.; Willis and Clark 1886/1988, II, 587–600, esp. p. 588; Hort 1896, II, 258–9, 293; Stubbings 1977, pp. 16–23.

[36] Hort 1896, I, 43.   [37] Hort 1896, II, 276–7, letter of 1879.

(only one part owing to illness) and was third in the Classical Tripos – Perowne was first; in 1851 he took firsts in moral sciences and natural sciences.[38] We may reflect that rather less preparation was needed then than now; but also admire the universal scope of Hort's interests. Throughout his life he was a passionate botanist – a hobby he was particularly happy to indulge when despatched to the Alps to repair his precarious health; from his days in the Apostles he had formed a lifelong friendship with Clerk Maxwell, who was to be the first Cavendish Professor of Physics;[39] his first reaction to Darwin's *Origin of Species* was of fervent delight – 'In spite of difficulties, I am inclined to think it unanswerable. In any case it is a treat to read such a book' – a little tempered later on when *The Origin of Species* had to face some stony criticisms from Westcott.[40] As a scholar he lives still in his immortal introduction to Westcott and Hort's Greek New Testament, in which scientific and philological criticism of texts was combined with human insight into the interests and vagaries of editors and scribes which brought the whole complex subject onto a higher plane.[41]

Hort is an exceptionally good witness, because in early life he had made a spirited defence of the old-fashioned clerical don in a pamphlet addressed from his county living to his former colleagues in Trinity.[42] Though acknowledging matrimony, on which he had recently embarked, to be the 'greatest of human blessings', he thought temporary celibacy good for young men. He looked forward with abhorrence to the prospect of a Theological Tripos, replacing by a narrow specialism the broader theological training of former times – a bizarre comment (some might think) on an education dominated by the Mathematical Tripos. He deplored the growth of professional theology, and protested against the separation of theology from pastoral work: it was good for the young clergy to serve their celibate apprenticeship, and then seek wives and livings.

Thus Hort in 1857. In 1872 he returned to Cambridge to be the first married fellow of Emmanuel, just in time to embark with

---

[38] Hort 1896, I, 92–4.   [39] Hort 1896, I, 240, II, 230–1.
[40] Hort 1896, I, 414, 431.
[41] Westcott and Hort 1881; Neill and Wright 1988, pp. 74–81.
[42] Hort 1896, I, 362–8.

fervour on teaching the first students of the Theological Tripos.[43] He was to exemplify all that he had protested against; yet the debate was not over. The effects of the radical changes of the late nineteenth century were not self-evidently all gain.

Hort's scholarship was brought to life in Gordon Rupp's entrancing inaugural lecture of 1969, in which he did honour to the founder of the Dixie Professorship.[44] As a philologist Hort 'brought to single words the loving attention which he gave to his Alpine flowers . . . As a daisy by the river's brim held mysteries for him beyond the wisdom of Solomon to conceive, so for him a Biblical word was something [from] which you might extract layer under layer of meaning.'[45] The man and the scholar were all of a piece. 'Devoted to Maurice – he coined the word "Maurikizein" – and to Kingsley, he was never swept into the Christian Socialist camp. But in [Cambridge], where a Chartist demonstration failed to compete with the cricket balls on Parker's Piece, he helped found the first Working Men's College in a room behind the Market Place.'[46]

Thus his friends recalled him:

> 'the familiar sight of the man, with the quick, nervous step, the left arm folded across books and papers, the right swinging vigorously across the body as he hurried down Trumpington Street – or as he rounded at full pace some buttress of books in the University Library.' At closer quarters 'the wonderful blue eyes, piercing keenly beneath the penthouse of ashy brow, the worn emaciated cheek, the noble forehead, the bright glee of his merriment, the tremendous energy.'[47]

'Even more remarkable than the extent of his knowledge was his accuracy,' wrote Armitage Robinson. 'He never seemed to trust to memory. Book after book came down from the shelves in the course of conversation: fact after fact was verified.'[48] Closely linked with this was the strange mixture of distrust with trust – of criticism mingled with warmth of appreciation and

[43] Hort 1896, II, 172ff.
[44] Repr. in Rupp 1977, chap. 10, with notes attributed to chap. 8 on p. 180; Whitney 1919, p. 10.
[45] Rupp 1977, p. 158.
[46] Rupp 1977, p. 154; for 'Maurikizein', see Hort 1896, I, 85.
[47] Rupp 1977, p. 154, quoting H. E. Ryle, *Cambridge Review*, 8 December 1892.
[48] Quoted in Rupp 1977, p. 157.

devoted friendship – with which he viewed Lightfoot and
Westcott. There was a moment in 1860 when he doubted the
possibility of collaborating with them, since he suspected that
they would hesitate to follow scholarly enquiry wherever it led
them.[49] All three had profound reverence for holy writ; Westcott had a deep vein of conservatism in his make-up;[50] Lightfoot
a robust scepticism of flights of fancy coming out of Tübingen.
But to Hort it seems almost to have been a matter of divine
revelation that scholarly enquiry and his faith in the scriptures
must work together to help God's purpose and the pursuit of
scientific truth.

His crowning triumph was to publish his great introduction to
the Greek New Testament just before the emergence of the
Revised Version of the Bible in 1881.[51] He had spent innumerable hours in the Jerusalem Chamber in Westminster Abbey
during the revision: Dean Burgon, the doughty critic of the RV,
'calculates that "Dr Hort talked for three years out of the ten"'
during which the revisers were meeting, and Hort's son observed
that 'it is estimated that he was present at 88 per cent of the
whole number of sittings.'[52] Small wonder that his chosen
projects – his commentaries and his history of the Church –
never saw the light.[53] Devoted committee men are not always
gratefully remembered, but we have many testimonies to his
'generous and inspiring enthusiasm' on boards and syndicates, in
Henry Jackson's words.[54] He certainly had plentiful opportunity. He was conscientious in attending college meetings in
Emmanuel as well as constant in his visits to the Jerusalem
Chamber; from 1878 he was a member of the university's
central committee, the Council of the Senate.[55] The list of
university committees attended in 'these earlier years' – the
1870s and early 1880s – as reported by his son reminds one
irresistibly of Mrs Pardigal. 'General Board of Studies, Law and
History Tripos Syndicate, Natural Science Board, Botanical
Gardens Syndicate, Select Preachers Syndicate, Geological
Museum Syndicate, Historic Studies Board, University Press

[49] Hort 1896, I, 417–23. [50] See p. 137.
[51] Westcott and Hort 1881, II. [52] Hort 1896, II, 236–7.
[53] Cf. Rupp 1977, p. 156 quoting Hort 1896, I, 233–5. [54] Hort 1896, II, 174.
[55] Hort 1896, II, 175.

Syndicate, Board of Theological Studies, Local Lecture Syndicate, University Library Syndicate, Election of Officers Syndicate, Teachers Training Syndicate.'[56] As was said of Coutts Trotter, vice-master of Trinity, no syndicate was complete without him, he was indispensable.

Yet he was a shy man who found it difficult to talk to his own children; and this makes his letters to them all the more moving. 'You will know that one great blessing of our being children of the Heavenly Father is that it keeps us in childhood all our life long,' he said in a moment of profound self-awareness.[57] Such a man destroys the delicate fabric of the historian's constructs and the stereotypes of the social scientist. He was every inch both clergyman and don.

But the abolition of religious tests and of clerical fellowships had left the way clear for a growing element of self-confessed agnostics among the new professional dons. Of these Henry Sidgwick and F. W. Maitland are outstanding examples.[58] Sidgwick and Maitland were professional academics in the fullest sense: we have nothing important to teach them about the nature of our profession in the 1990s which they did not practise in the 1890s. This is not to say that there has been no progress. They were giants, and there were very few who could match their standards or their qualities; but if we wish to know what a professional don might be, then Hort and Sidgwick and Maitland were perfect models. We should also expect to find the new model in the labs, and Clerk Maxwell, an old mathematician turned new physicist; or J. J. Thomson, who came from a relatively humble home and from Owens College in Manchester to the Cavendish in the late 1870s and was Cavendish Professor from 1894, master of Trinity from 1918 till his death in 1940; or Sir Michael Foster, the physiologist, represent the professional scientist-don who has flourished and multiplied in Cambridge under their and other folk's inspiration in the last 120 years.[59]

One cannot contemplate the transition from clergyman to don,

---

[56] Hort 1896, II, 173. On Coutts Trotter, see Clark 1900, p. 316.
[57] Hort 1896, II, 199; cf. esp. ibid. p. 451.   [58] For Maitland, see pp. 216–24.
[59] See pp. 164–5, 180–7.

nor its close neighbour, the transformation of an Anglican
university to one in which Christians and non-Christians of every
faith and none freely mingled, without encountering Henry
Sidgwick.

Henry Sidgwick

Henry Sidgwick has always been reckoned a central figure in the
Cambridge of the late nineteenth century: in the eyes of many
observers, the key to its understanding. This was partly due to his
spiritual progress from simple faith to reverent agnosticism; partly
to his success as a teacher with a small group of disciples who
worshipped him; partly to his fervent support for every liberal
cause and especially for the entry of women to Cambridge; partly
to the width of his interests which compassed everything from
Hebrew to ghosts. Sidgwick Avenue leads to Newnham, and his
most lasting role may seem to us now to be as founder of
Newnham and husband to one of its most remarkable
principals.[60]

In a once-famous passage the poet Horace dates his fervent,
angry youth to the consulship of Plancus, *consule Planco*.[61] 'Henry
Sidgwick . . .' wrote F. W. Maitland,

> dated the 'consulship of Plancus' in A.D. 1860–5; and in 1895 he
> retrospectively spoke of 'the *forward* movement' of the thought of
> those hopeful years when 'Hebrew old clothes' were being
> discarded. Then it was 'that he took service with Reason'. That
> Forward Movement, with reason as recruiting sergeant, may not
> yet have found its historian: but, if less picturesque upon the
> surface, surely it was not less worthy of remembrance than the
> Catholic Revival, which without offence – none is intended –
> might, I suppose, be called a backward Movement.[62]

Sidgwick had sought out the grounds of the Christian faith with
all the earnestness of a great Victorian and a deep philosopher, and
found them wanting. He came with excitement and sorrow to

---

[60] See pp. 303–5. In what follows I have made particular use of Sidgwick 1906; Maitland in Fisher
1910, pp. 7–9; Maitland 1911, III, 531–40; and among recent commentators and interpreters,
Schneewind 1977.
[61] *Odes* iii.14.28.
[62] Maitland 1911, III, 531–2; on the development of Sidgwick's thought, see Schneewind 1977,
chap. 1.

the conclusion that he could not subscribe to the faith; he became a devout agnostic, and carried many of his disciples with him. The hesitations of his agnosticism, the nostalgia for the faith, which he showed throughout his life lend a certain pathos to the progress of his mind; there was undoubtedly suffering as well as the thrill of discovery. To his younger pupils, such as the youthful Apostles of the Edwardian decade, his uncertainties and yearnings were merely tiresome; his profound morality a bore. Thus Maynard Keynes, on reading his *Memoir* in 1906: 'he really ought to have got over [his religious doubts] a little sooner; because he knew that the thing wasn't true perfectly well from the beginning. The last part is all about ghosts and Mr Balfour. I have never found so dull a book so absorbing.'[63]

Yet it was precisely the doubts, the desire to avoid offence, the deep interest in the roots of faith and in other folk's viewpoint, which made Sidgwick so important a figure. To understand his urbanity it is perhaps well to remember that one of his brothers-in-law – his sister's husband – to whom he was devoted was his former teacher E. W. Benson, archbishop of Canterbury from 1883 to 1896; another – his wife's brother – was Arthur Balfour, the conservative politician.[64] Furthermore, Sidgwick truly grappled with the problem of faith. He learned Hebrew so as to study the Old Testament in the original language; and he struggled with the enigmas of the New Testament. Although his doubts sprang up in the years immediately following the publication of Darwin's *Origin of Species* in 1859, it was the challenge of biblical criticism which really concerned him; and above all the miraculous element in the New Testament.[65] Like many Victorians, he was deeply (if very sceptically) interested in spiritualism and ghosts; and he and Mrs Sidgwick were leading members of the Society for Psychical Research.[66] Although this proved pretty much a cul-de-sac, he perceived that the simple rationalism that entirely dismissed such events as Jesus' miracles as impossible did not answer to the experience of the world we live in. 'I still hunger and thirst after orthodoxy,' he wrote in 1862: 'but I am, I

---

[63] Harrod 1951, p. 117.
[64] His relations with both are expounded in Sidgwick 1906 and Sidgwick 1938.
[65] Cf. Schneewind 1977, pp. 24–31.
[66] Sidgwick 1906, esp. pp. 284, 288–94, 296–300, 361–5; Sidgwick 1938, chap. 4.

trust, firm not to barter my intellectual birthright for a mess of mystical pottage.'[67] But though he lost his faith he lost none of his respectability: he resigned his fellowship but continued to live and to teach in Trinity; he was a pillar of the Moral Sciences Tripos and from 1883 was Knightbridge Professor of Moral Philosophy. He was deeply influential in making churchmen like Benson – or his Cambridge colleagues Lightfoot and Westcott – tolerant of the kind of agnosticism he represented; and in return in helping his agnostic disciples like Maitland to take a not unfriendly view even of bishops.[68]

Maitland found Sidgwick to be

> a supremely great teacher. In the first place I remember the admirable patience which could never be out-worn by stupidity, and which nothing but pretentiousness could disturb. Then there was the sympathetic and kindly endeavour to overcome our shyness, to make us talk, and to make us think. Then there was that marked dislike for any mere reproduction of his own opinions which made it impossible for Sidgwick to be in the bad sense the founder of a school. I sometimes think that the one and only prejudice that Sidgwick had was a prejudice against his own results. All this was far more impressive and far more inspiriting to us than any dogmatism could have been ... I believe that no more truthful man than Sidgwick ever lived. I am speaking of a rare intellectual virtue ... [69]

Against this it has to be said that some, even of the notable philosophers who sat at his feet, grew weary of his self-denials and found him dull; and that the Moral Sciences Tripos never attracted large numbers of students.[70] The history of Oxford and Cambridge is a saga of mutual imitation; and yet there have been some things which Cambridge has failed to copy from Oxford, to

---

[67] Sidgwick 1906, p. 90; Schneewind 1977, p. 44. For what follows, Schneewind 1977, pp. 14–15. For his election as professor, Sidgwick 1906, pp. 368–70.

[68] Or so we may reasonably suppose. For Maitland on bishops, see Maitland 1911, III, 495–511. On Sidgwick and Lightfoot, who were colleagues in Trinity for many years, see esp. Sidgwick 1906, p. 198.

[69] Fisher 1910, pp. 7–8.

[70] Schneewind 1977, p. 16. But the list for 1872 in moral sciences, in which William Cunningham and F. W. Maitland were bracketed first, is a warning against judging by quantity (Tanner 1917, p. 709). Cf. Harrod 1951, p. 114: J. M. Keynes to G. L. Strachey (1906) 'I even begin to agree with Moore about Sidgwick – that he was a wicked edifactious person [builder of edifices?]'. For the numbers taking the tripos in Sidgwick's lifetime, see Tanner 1917, pp. 703–26.

its loss. By linking philosophy to classics in Mods and Greats the Oxford tutors ensured that numerous undergraduates studied history and philosophy as well as classical literature; and although no Oxford moral philosopher of the age now seems to us to hold a candle to Sidgwick, far more Oxford students studied philosophy than sat at Sidgwick's feet.[71] His best books were good and lasting; but they have not the literary quality of his most remarkable, and most discerning pupil, the historian Maitland.

Thus Maitland wrote in his review of the *Memoir* of Henry Sidgwick published in 1906:

A man who seemed less self-conscious or less self-centred than Sidgwick was not to be met; nor one who, to all appearance, so steadily and easily kept himself at an objective point of view. There are, for example, in this memoir, paragraphs . . . which . . . will give the right idea of Sidgwick's ceaseless activity in the affairs of the University of Cambridge; but it should, I think, be added with some emphasis that whatever he did was done with ungrudging cheerfulness, and most of it with apparent enjoyment. One wondered whether there was any practical question that he would not study with zest; one wondered whether he could be bored, whether he could be irritated . . . Sidgwick was a wonderful talker: a better I have never heard . . . Sidgwick's talk never became . . . a monologue. He seemed at least as desirous to hear as to be heard, and gave you the impression that he would rather be led than lead. Even more than the wit and the wisdom, the grace and the humour, it was the wide range of sympathy that excited admiration when the talk was over . . . His irony never hurt, it was so kindly; and, of all known forms of wickedness, 'Sidgwick-edness' was the least wicked. Good as are the letters in this book [the *Memoir* by Sidgwick's widow and brother], I cannot honestly say that they are as good, or nearly as good, as their writer's talk . . . [72]

In choosing to be a philosopher, he had chosen a thorny path . . . Whether it requires better brains and harder labour to write a good book on philosophy than to write a good book on physics, I cannot say. But if you take philosophy very seriously, it may distress you in a manner in which you will never be distressed by chemistry or philology or jurisprudence.

---

[71] On Greats see Brooke, Highfield and Swaan 1988, pp. 277–8.
[72] Maitland 1911, III, 533–5.

Sidgwick was distressed by the uncertainties with which he wrestled, yet not cast down.

> We read of a very happy life ... We may hope with some confidence that, even when many years have gone by, this book [the *Memoir*] will still have for a few discerning readers some part of the charm that it has for many of us now. The whole of that charm they can never know; but they may at least see that one of the acutest, profoundest and most influential thinkers of our time was a true and good and noble man; and in some degree they may feel that he is even for them an encouraging master, a wise counsellor, and a delightful companion.[73]

To this we may add that Sidgwick's approach to moral philosophy has enjoyed a modest revival in recent years. His basic aim was to reconcile the two great strands of non-religious Victorian ethics – the morality based on intuition and the utilitarian tradition. A series of eighteenth- and early nineteenth-century philosophers, some ignorant of Kant, some deeply influenced by him, had attempted to sustain ethics essentially based on intuition. Meanwhile the utilitarian principle – that 'the conduct which is objectively right is that which will produce the greatest amount of happiness on the whole'[74] – had been developed and sophisticated by Bentham and the Mills. Such a summary does little justice to the complexities of great philosophic traditions – and it says nothing of the philosophy of common sense, already raising its head before Sidgwick's day; but J. S. Schneewind has summarised a part of Sidgwick's approach most helpfully thus:

> Philosophers, whom he took to be the counterpart in questions of ethics to scientists, had come to no agreements on theoretical issues, but they seemed to be willing to treat common-sense morality as providing the data against which their theories might be tested. To begin at this point would therefore be to begin with the nearest thing to uncontested matter in ethics. Sidgwick's methodological views support the conclusion thus suggested by historical developments. A complete rational system requires intuitively evident starting-points. Now the dictates of common-sense morality are taken by many, including some philosophers,

[73] Maitland 1911, III, 538–40.
[74] I quote the definition in Schneewind 1977, p. 329.

to be self-evident. It is therefore possible that they provide what is needed, and this possibility must be scrutinized. The ecumenical test, requiring that a theory should elicit wide agreement among those competent to judge it, leads us to the same conclusion.[75]

By such means Sidgwick came to see the reconciliation of what was valid in the ethics based on intuition, common-sense and the principle of utility as the constructive approach to morality, both in terms of its inner coherence and credibility, and in its relation to scientific method. As he was writing, the Cavendish Laboratory was getting under way, and Mrs Sidgwick was to work there in the 1880s with Lord Rayleigh, her brother-in-law.[76] It is characteristic of Sidgwick and his generation to seek a common basis with scientific enquiry.

Yet for all this the problems and the attitudes he represented seemed to his younger pupils quintessentially Victorian. The radical criticism of traditional ethics, and of Victorian morality, represented by the *Principia Ethica* of G. E. Moore and the philosophy of Bertrand Russell, cast a shadow over Sidgwick's teaching very shortly after his death. Philosophy became a more technical exercise; ethics a study of logic (in spite of Moore's high moral intent) rather than of morality. But Sidgwick is now recognised once again as a great moral philosopher: J. S. Schneewind's fine study, published in 1977, sets him in context but places him high. And we may allow Sidgwick himself to comment on Moore: 'So far as I have seen his work, his *acumen* – which is remarkable in degree – is in excess of his *insight*.'[77] It is not only for the grand sweep of ethical thought that Sidgwick is admired; nor only for his deep understanding of what was valuable and lasting in the work of the utilitarians; but for his insight, which time and again illuminates his pages and gives him a lasting quality as a moral philosopher. And he is of special interest as the representative of a lofty morality unsupported by Christian faith.

[75] Schneewind 1977, p. 193.
[76] Sidgwick 1938, pp. 71–2; Cavendish 1910, pp. 81, 333.
[77] Schneewind 1977, p. 17.

Chapter 2

THE UNIVERSITY AND THE COLLEGES

THE UNIVERSITY

The University of Cambridge has a very strange constitution. In the course of the fifteenth and sixteenth centuries, the colleges of Oxford and Cambridge grew in number and acquired a monopoly: by 1600 no students could enter the university save by the colleges.[1] Gradually, too, the balance of teaching shifted from the university to the colleges, so that by the eighteenth and early nineteenth centuries teaching was almost wholly in the hands of colleges and private tutors. Some professors were appointed, but few gave any lectures.[2] The great revolution of the late nineteenth century saw college teaching become very much more effective, and a whole structure of university institutions and laboratories grow up beside the colleges. By the First World War the two existed side by side; but the university structure was very unequally financed and housed. The time was ripe for discovering new harmony between university and college, and for seeking finance to make the university structure worthy of the reputation of Cambridge. This was the purpose and aim of the Royal Commission on Oxford and Cambridge which was set up in 1919 and issued in the Oxford and Cambridge Act of 1923, and the elaborate restructuring of university and college statutes which followed.[3] But it had very different consequences in Cambridge from those in Oxford.

What is so unusual about the constitutions of Oxford and Cambridge? They are federations of colleges; yet that by itself

---

[1] Brooke, Highfield and Swaan 1988, pp. 40–1, 118–19 (abolition of 'chamber deacons') and chap. 6 passim ('the colleges take over').
[2] Winstanley 1935, chap. 3.   [3] See chap. 11.

does not answer the question. It is true that most universities in the world, whether ancient, like three out of four of the Scottish universities, or modern, like the English civic universities, have more unitary structures. In St Andrews and Aberdeen the university consists of colleges, but they have no real independence. The universities of London and Toronto are truly federations; but they lack some of the features which are especially characteristic of Oxford and Cambridge. London, for example, is a bizarre accumulation of numerous institutions, including multi-faculty colleges which are in effect small universities in their own right – such as University College and King's College from which the whole agglomeration grew in the nineteenth century; one great Technische Hochschule called Imperial College; a group of medical schools attached to large hospitals; and small schools and institutes which are sometimes world-famous centres of teaching and research – the Courtauld Institute, the Warburg Institute, the Institute of Historical Research, and the School of Tropical Medicine, for example.[4] Like the leading continental Hochschulen, Imperial College is a major centre of research and teaching in the natural sciences and technology, with a good deal else besides. The university was set up to provide an academic umbrella for these various bodies, above all to provide recognised examinations. But time has reversed this role: the various elements are often quite independent of one another – and in everything but name independent of the university – in academic affairs. The university grants degrees to students who have followed courses wholly within this college or that, in which the university has had only the most nominal say. But the University Court controls all finances, and a whisper from it can lead to the destruction or amalgamation of colleges and institutes.[5] This reversal is the product of modern circumstances: since the state became the major paymaster of British universities in the mid-twentieth century, and the colleges of London were ill-endowed, the University Court, through which government funds spread down to the colleges, has come to have almost total economic control over their destinies.

---

[4] The grant to Imperial College has long been specifically indicated in the UGC grant to the University of London (Carswell 1985, p. 176). For the University of London, see Harte 1986.
[5] As has recently occurred with Westfield College.

In Oxford and Cambridge the colleges are much closer to the university in academic affairs. The courses are all designed by university faculties under the university's General Board; the students are wholly dependent on the university for their courses – however much they may enjoy personal tuition within the colleges. The colleges have no meaning without the university in which they live. Yet they are quite independent of it in government and (in most respects) in finance.[6] It is often said that this is because they are independently endowed – that the colleges are rich in endowment though the university is poor; and the endowments of the colleges are an important factor in the story. But they hardly explain it; for many colleges have little endowment, and in this century a number of new colleges have been founded with virtually none at all. If New Hall or Darwin College had been set up in London, they would have been at the mercy of the Court like Bedford College and Westfield College, which have foundered because the Court would not or could not save them. But in Cambridge the umbrella is of a different nature; and although a world of educational finance in which most of the students and most of the staff and their equipment are supported by government grants has much diminished the difference between Cambridge and London, it remains fundamental. This cannot be explained by any simple formula of endowment or tradition, though it certainly grows out of historical circumstances. But it will take the whole of this book to explain it – if it can be explained.

In 1870 the constitution of Cambridge was much like that of Oxford: both were dominated by colleges and by the heads of colleges, though both had witnessed moderate but important measures of reform which gave more influence to the rank and file of the teachers.[7] But in Oxford the tradition that tutors taught had survived, less impaired than in Cambridge where they now do no teaching of their tutorial pupils; they make a virtue of not being academic tutors. The consequence was that in Oxford

[6] See pp. 73–81. The chief exception is that the richer colleges are taxed; but the 'University Contribution' has in recent years gone to support poorer colleges, not the university itself.
[7] In Oxford the weekly meeting of heads, the Hebdomadal Board, had been established by royal decree in 1631; in the mid-nineteenth century it was restructured as the Hebdomadal Council, and became much like the Council of the Senate (Brooke, Highfield and Swaan 1988, pp. 185, 277; cf. ibid. p. 163).

teaching lay more within the colleges than in Cambridge and the college tutors remained a great power in academic affairs. They battled with the old authorities of the Church and the new professors for dominance, and, broadly speaking, they won.[8] When the universities were reorganised in the 1920s, there was less change in Oxford than in Cambridge. The colleges remained the chief centres of teaching in Oxford; very few university teachers were not college fellows. This has made for greater harmony, but slower change. So great have been some of the agonies in bringing colleges to accept shifting academic patterns and fashions that some Oxford professors have thought that Cambridge took a wiser course. In Cambridge a whole structure of university faculties, departments and lectureships was set up quite independent of the colleges; since the mid-1920s Cambridge has had a split personality. Every teacher has had to seek his fortune quite separately in university and college. If he is a professor, he may bob about in the 'professorial pool' for months, even possibly years, waiting to be caught in the fellowship net of some college or other. If he is a university lecturer, he may be gladly snatched by a college or wait for ever. Immense efforts have been made to mitigate the ill-effects of this divorce; but as I write this page there are still virtually no joint appointments made by college and university – though new plans are now afoot and the generosity of a few colleges amid the recent financial holocaust has led them to finance some university posts. Oxford moved slowly and with many groans. But it moved; and all academic appointments in Oxford are now joint appointments, in which both a college and the university are involved.[9] In the 1920s Cambridge seemed to have won an immediate advantage; financially the changes of the period from 1926 to the late 1960s were easier to grasp and plan in Cambridge than in Oxford. But few objective observers would doubt that the end product is far more satisfactory in Oxford – though it goes hard for a dyed-in-the-wool Cambridge author to admit it. It is a fascinating story for a future chapter.[10] We need immediately to observe that Oxford and Cambridge are exceedingly similar – more similar

---

[8] Engel 1983, esp. pp. 45–9, 77–81, 122–55.
[9] See Brian Harrison's forthcoming chapter in *The History of the University of Oxford*, VIII.
[10] Chap. 11.

than their inmates have usually cared to admit: twins, but not identical twins. We shall see, as a general principle as the story unfolds, that this similarity is in large measure due to constant imitation one of the other; and, by the same token, although there is much variety among the colleges – and more now, in many respects, than in 1870 – in fundamental ways the colleges also imitate one another and so have helped to preserve the special character of the Cambridge collegiate structure.[11]

In 1870 the ultimate power to make decisions in the university lay with the Senate, which in effect consisted of all MAs of the university who wished to be members – though it was only on major issues that non-residents were brought in to swell the ranks of the factions. Cambridge, like Oxford, has for many centuries been in principle a democracy of its teachers, and has become so in practice since 1870 through two very significant changes. In 1870 only a minority even of the resident members of the Senate had formal teaching duties or were engaged in any other serious academic activity.[12] By the 1920s a majority were university teachers in some sense or other. And in the reforms of the 1920s the Senate was replaced by the Regent House – an ancient name for an entirely new body, the whole corpus of resident teachers. Like so many Cambridge reforms, it did not quite achieve what it claimed. Between 1926 and the 1990s the Regent House included many retired teachers, for example. But it is more recognisably, in principle, a teachers' democracy than it was a hundred years ago; and, apart from Oxford, no other such structure exists in any university in the world. But if the constitution of Oxford and Cambridge is unique, their influence has been none the less deep and decisive among the British universities.[13]

In January 1879 Professor J. B. Lightfoot, the eminent Cambridge theologian and academic reformer, revisited his native Liverpool, where the University College was struggling into existence, and made a speech to the Liverpool Council of Education. He maintained with fervour that the college would provide the culmination of all that the Council was trying to

---

[11] See chap. 18.
[12] But an unknown number were engaged in private tuition. See Peter Searby, forthcoming. (vol. III of this *History*).
[13] For the changes of the 1920s, see chap. 11.

foster; and he described a dream he had of Liverpool as it might be in 1914. He stood before 'a stately pile of buildings' with private hostels or colleges gathered round it. 'I entered then the central building with my guide, and passed through long suites of museums, libraries and lecture rooms, all well arranged and suitably furnished.

'And, seeing room after room assigned to some different Professor I could not refrain from asking' how they were paid for. The answer came that some were endowed by public subscription, others 'by the munificence of individual benefactors, whose names they bear ... All the citizens are proud of University College. Along with their shipping, they regard it as the great glory of the place.'[14] Among his audience was William Rathbone, head of a great patrician family in Liverpool, who himself recorded his response to it.

'The moment I heard this speech, I said to myself "The thing is done, he has given us the lines on which to raise the money"' – and he not only endowed, with his brothers, the King Alfred Chair – named after another celebrated patron of education, and soon to be adorned with the most eminent Shakespearean scholar of the day, A. C. Bradley – but he played a leading part in inspiring the merchant princes and the local nobility to do likewise.[15]

It is piquant to witness a Cambridge professor inspiring the formation of a civic university, tracing a pattern so different from the one he knew, helping to erect a rival which might have laid Oxford and Cambridge low. To many men of learning of the age, both within and without the ancient universities, the model of the German universities in particular, in which academic leadership lay in the hands of a group of eminent men of learning, seemed far more appropriate than the democracy of idle and ignorant fellows which seemed to some learned professors (however unjustly) to be the character of Cambridge. Furthermore, it was inconceivable that the men who had founded University College or King's at London, and were to found the civic universities in the late nineteenth and early twentieth centuries, would leave their direction to a democracy of the teachers. The

[14] Kelly 1981, pp. 45–6.
[15] Kelly 1981, pp. 47–8. On Bradley, see ibid. pp. 54, 111, 482, 525.

Liverpool patricians who loved their college and their university, and poured their resources into it, none the less reckoned the professors their employees, as did the German states and Lände.[16] They deeply respected them but kept in their own hands the power of the purse. Thus the pattern of University Senate – the academic oligarchy consisting of professors presided over by the Vice-Chancellor – and Council, the governing body of the university dominated by the patriciate – was formed; and after 1903, when the University College was elevated into a university, the University Court, its highest body, met in formal session in Liverpool Town Hall with the lord mayor of Liverpool in the chair.

Cambridge in 1870 was only just beginning to grow once again into a distinguished academy of learning. That was hardly its main character in 1870; and if we could examine the motives of the growing numbers of students who flocked to it, we should hardly find many of them who thought it was so. There was much to be said for the view that a university run by professors would be a more effective learned body than a university run by all the teachers. Nor is it fair to adjudicate in this debate too readily, for Cambridge and Liverpool were swept into a tide of academic progress which put both of them into very different regions in the mid-twentieth century from those which either had inhabited in the 1880s or 90s. The great strength of the more hierarchical system is that it allows an inspired academic leader more freedom of decision and initiative, the opportunity to guide and direct a growing scientific enterprise. Its great weakness is that the junior staff may be deprived of the chance effectively to participate; may have no role in decision making; may feel left out. When I moved from Cambridge to Liverpool in 1956 I found much, very much, to admire; but I was deeply impressed by the inefficiency of departments in which some or many of the staff felt themselves hired labourers.

Rule by professors offers basically an authoritarian model; and

---

[16] The classical exposition of this aspect of the relations of lay and academic members of a university council is in Bruce Truscot's *Redbrick University* (Truscot 1943). But there were many nuances, and I encountered several deeply committed lay members in my Liverpool days who had no such attitude as is here described.

authority has played its part in Cambridge, sure enough. From the sixteenth or early seventeenth century to the mid-nineteenth the heads of houses were in possession of great authority: they could exert discipline within their colleges, and they could make decisions when they met together.[17] From the 1620s and 1630s they had met weekly after the university sermon, and they still met in the early nineteenth century. It was still reckoned that their common action in nominating the Vice-Chancellor and other leading officers, and the control they could exercise over the Caput – the quaint little body, theoretically of faculty representatives, which prepared graces for the Senate and could veto them – gave them a decisive voice.[18] In the eighteenth century they had tended to form caucuses, whig and tory, and their common voice may have been rarely heard. But it was still a fundamental ground for complaint down to the 1850s that there was no more representative body to prepare business for the Senate.[19] The most contentious element in the Royal Commission of the 1850s and the statutes which followed it was the provision for the Council of the Senate – how many heads it should contain, and how the heads and other members should be chosen. In the event, the contention went away, for once the Council was formed, the heads ceased to regard their own meetings as having any constitutional function; if they needed to exert pressure they did it through the Council or through their colleges. Only very much later did the Colleges' Committee come into existence: the twentieth century has proliferated intercollegiate committees of tutors and bursars and so forth, which have now great influence in ensuring that there is some communication between the colleges; but none of an executive character.[20] The colleges are more independent of one another than they were before 1850.

All this has greatly mitigated the authority of the heads in Cambridge. Until 1992 it was the practice to choose the Vice-Chancellor from among them; but he was chosen by the Council of the Senate and not by vote as he was until the mid-nineteenth

---

[17] Winstanley 1935, pp. 18–21, 276–95.
[18] Winstanley 1940, chap. 4, esp. pp. 29–31.
[19] See Winstanley 1940, chap. 4 passim, for this, and also for what follows.
[20] See p. 363.

century.[21] The heads carry great respect – except when their younger colleagues or students are actually in rebellion against them – and the office remains extremely prestigious; something of the prestige traditionally accorded to the master of Trinity or St John's also now attaches to the president or warden of the youngest and newest of the colleges. And this very easily deceives those who have not lived long within the colleges into imagining the office more authoritarian than it is. In the modern world the head of a Cambridge college is *primus inter pares*. College statutes vary endlessly in the details of their prescriptions; but it is common for a head to have more than a casting vote – sometimes he has as many as two votes and a casting vote.[22] Yet that is all. His voice carries the prestige of the person and the prestige of the office; nothing more. The governing body decides. If one wishes to find a post of real authority in Cambridge it can only be found in the chief officers of the university, Vice-Chancellor, Registrary, Secretary-General of the Faculties and Treasurer, and above all in the heads of the large scientific departments. The hierarchy has been headed by a Vice-Chancellor since the Chancellor ceased to be normally resident in the late Middle Ages; his traditional henchmen are the proctors and Esquire Bedells who hold more venerable offices than he, stemming from the thirteenth century. The proctors retain a little of their ancient function in government, a little of their longer-lasting function in discipline, much of their ceremonial functions on university occasions of a formal kind; and in the ceremonies of the university the Esquire Bedells (no longer beadles in any other sense) still participate. Since 1506 the Vice-Chancellor has been supported in all university administration by the Registrary; and since 1522 formal addresses to royalty and foreign universities and eminent visitors (especially since the nineteenth century to those receiving honorary degrees)

---

[21] Formally, the Council has nominated two candidates for election by the Regent House, under the statutes of 1926, D III 2–4; in practice one of them has been pre-elected. A new statute is in the making which will end the intimate link between the Vice-Chancellorship and the colleges.

[22] In King's the provost has two votes at a Congregation (a formal general meeting of fellows), and, if present and presiding, a casting vote besides (*King's Statutes* 1952, p. 12); at St John's the master has no additional vote in the College Council, but if the master or acting chairman differs from the majority, the proposal is adjourned to another meeting; then the majority prevails (*St John's Statutes* 1948, p. 12).

For what follows see Tanner 1917, pp. 14–62; *Cambridge University, Historical Register, Supplement, 1921–30* 1932, p. 13; *Supplement, 1931–40* 1942, p. 2.

have been composed in elegant Latin by the Public Orator. The Registrary is still the senior officer after the Vice-Chancellor, and his authority has been enhanced in very recent times by the Wass Report. But the complexity of modern administration, and its changing nature, have been recognised in the offices of two new major dignitaries, the Treasurer and Secretary-General. In the early 1920s the Financial Board had a Secretary and in 1926 his dignity was marked by the title Treasurer, and not long after by the elevation of the first holder, G. H. A. Wilson, to be master of Clare, and of the second, Thomas Knox-Shaw, to become master of Sidney. One of the chief innovations of the 1920s was the formation of the structure of faculties, and their central importance was recognised in 1933–4 when the Secretary of the Faculties was given the title Secretary-General, who in all academic arrangements has reigned supreme.

But the most independent of the potentates of modern Cambridge are the heads of the large scientific departments. Even they are subject to the board of their faculty, the council of their school and to the General Board of the Faculties; but the power they can exercise and the initiative they still enjoy is great. The contrast comes out most piquantly in the memoirs of Sir Nevill Mott, who returned from Bristol to Cambridge in 1954 as Cavendish Professor of Physics, and in 1959 was elected master of Caius.[23] Although he had known Caius for many years, he admits that he had not appreciated the difference between a head of department in Bristol or the head of the Cavendish, and a head of house in Cambridge. In Caius he found every initiative he took, every nomination he made, subject to the scrutiny of the College Council or of the general body of fellows. He expected constitutional monarchy, and found himself chairman of a club.[24]

How had this difference arisen? The Cavendish Chair, the head of department, are creations of the nineteenth century; an alien plant in Cambridge, just as the modern laboratory was – yet quickly absorbed and accepted as part of the rococo structure of

---

[23] Mott 1986, chaps. 11, 13, 16. But contrast Todd 1983, pp. 167–9: Lord Todd describes his role as master of Christ's in much the same terms as his headship of the Organic Chemistry Department. On p. 169 he claims to have appointed a senior tutor, not previously a fellow, without 'even consulting the College Governing Body'.

[24] But see pp. 266–7 on the reign of Lord Todd as master of Christ's.

the university. The head of house enjoys an ancient office. From the sixteenth century on church and state had tried, time and again, to invest him with the authority they reckoned so sadly lacking in the lively, tumultuous community of young fellows and students. Some success they had; and tradition invested the heads of house with a majesty which served their cause. Their authority was preserved in an altered form when it was transmitted in the mid-nineteenth century to the Council of the Senate. The structure of university government has remained an extraordinary mixture of democracy and oligarchy. The democracy was represented by the Senate – all the MAs on the colleges' books – which was replaced for all practical purposes in 1926 by the Regent House, the whole body of university teachers and college fellows. With them lie ultimate decisions. But most of the business is handled by the hierarchy of councils and boards – the Council of the Senate, the General Board of the Faculties (1882), the Councils of the Schools (of the 1970s and 80s) and the Faculty Boards (1926). The Regent House is far larger and more democratic than its equivalent in any other British university save Oxford; the other bodies, by a strange paradox, are (relatively at least to the size of the staffs they represent) far smaller and, though elective, more oligarchical than any equivalent body in other universities, save perhaps London.

But tradition had equally consecrated the notion that all fellows were equal, at least at the moment of voting. In practice there were plenty of inequalities: in several of the colleges, especially the larger ones, statute or convention had placed all power into the hands of a group of senior fellows, who ruled it with the master. This took root first in the statutes of Henry VI for King's though they envisaged that the whole body be consulted on major issues.[25] He founded a community of seventy scholars, and, after some vicissitudes, a community of seventy entered the nineteenth century. They began their Cambridge careers – by coming from Eton – when they were sixteen or seventeen; and by the time they were twenty, after three years' residence, they were fellows, and so could vote in the election of the provost. But the founder, and tradition, had ensured that

---

[25] *VCH Cambs*, III, 383; and for what follows, see below pp. 33–7.

democracy went no further in this case. Most colleges had quite small groups of ten, a dozen or up to thirty fellows, whose duties were minimal and whose stipends or dividends were far from princely; so that by the mid-nineteenth century many were non-resident. Even when they were there, a social hierarchy mitigated any democratic tendency in the constitution. It was a common practice – in some cases surviving as late as the mid-twentieth century – for the fellows to sit at dinner in order of seniority, a custom which cemented some friendships and hardened some enmities, and much reduced the opportunities for serious discussion. The head by custom might marry; the fellows by statute might not; the head remained till death, the fellow till marriage. This meant that there was often a great difference in age between the head and most of the fellows – one of many possible excuses for discord. In 1860 some colleges swept celibacy away; more or less all followed in the late 70s or early 80s, and the community of dons' wives was considerably increased.[26] But the same happy event gradually eroded the resident community – not quite so fast or so far as was feared by the pessimists, since at first a few tutors managed to find themselves houses within the precincts. The senior tutor of Caius even had part of Gonville Court converted into a house.[27] And in the mid-twentieth century the number of fellows rose steeply, so that there came some revival in the number of resident bachelors. But in general the head of the house has remained the sole married resident, the master's lodge the domestic centre, or the domestic anomaly, of the college.

Let us for a moment go through the deceptively traditional gothic arch which leads to the old Cavendish.[28] There we will find in early days the distinguished innovative mathematical physicist Clerk Maxwell and a small group of assistants and students; there, from 1879 to 1884, the precise and efficient Lord Rayleigh, a professor of private means who was later to finance a new building and die Chancellor of the university, but was for the time a dignified if friendly director. After Rayleigh for well over thirty years J. J. Thomson presided over the Cavendish – a very characteristic Cambridge character of this epoch, from an

---

[26] See pp. 252–4.   [27] Brooke 1985, p. 249.
[28] Pevsner 1970, p. 206. For what follows, see Cavendish 1910, esp. chaps. 2–4.

impoverished home in Manchester, formerly a pupil at Owens College (which was to grow into the Victoria University and the University of Manchester): most of the undergraduates in Cambridge of this epoch came from comfortable homes, many of the leading dons did not.[29] Thomson was one of the boys; he led by erratic and informal genius, not by the authority of his office.[30] Admittedly, as professor, within the means at his disposal, he could appoint assistants, direct research, choose students – do very much what he liked. He was unencumbered by bureaucracy or tradition. He was a fellow of Trinity, but it might seem that the Cavendish, to which aspiring scientists flocked from every corner of the globe, had nothing in common with the remote, traditional world of the Trinity lodge. Yet J.J. ended his days master of Trinity. Herein lies the fascination of our story: for the interaction of these two very different worlds created the Cambridge of the mid-twentieth century.

THE COLLEGES

Cambridge is a federation of colleges: in 1870 there were seventeen; and in addition Girton and Newnham were already struggling into existence, even if they had to wait until the 1940s for full collegiate status in the university. There are now over thirty. Some recent historians have desperately tried to rationalise the picture, and reduce the area of research to make it manageable, by observing that Trinity contributed one-third – and Trinity and St John's between them nearly one half – of all the students coming to Cambridge in the mid-nineteenth century.[31] In these two, moreover, were concentrated many of the leading characters of Cambridge of the age – just as Trinity has always led the field, to this day, in Nobel laureates.[32] Surely one can view the whales and ignore the minnows? But Cambridge is a true federation and the picture is badly distorted if one resorts to this

---

[29] See pp. 249–52. [30] See esp. Wilson 1983, pp. 83–4.
[31] In 1870 there were 2,019 undergraduates in all, 548 in Trinity, 361 in St John's. See pp. 593–4. These figures are for *men*: for the women, see chap. 9. At the latest count, there are 31 colleges, approved societies and approved foundations. For Girton and Newnham, see chap. 9; for Selwyn, chap. 3; for the new colleges of the 1950s, 60s and 70s, chap. 18.
[32] See index, s.v. Nobel Prizes.

kind of simplification; it also destroys all the magic of the place. In a similar way Switzerland is a federation of cantons.[33] One might think that in recent times most of its wealth and population had been concentrated in and about the great cities of Zürich, Berne and Basel; but it would wholly distort the character of federal Switzerland to attend to the cantons in which these cities stand and ignore the rest. If one really wishes to understand both the character of Cambridge and the movements of our period the colleges must be seen in their individuality as well as within the university which is their home.

Three samples

King's

In 1870 King's was still one of the least populous of the colleges; yet in our period it was to count among its fellows Henry Bradshaw the University Librarian, M. R. James the antiquary, Maynard Keynes, economist, man of affairs and college bursar, Sir John Clapham the economic historian, Sir James Gray the zoologist, and among its honorary fellows the novelist E. M. Forster.[34] Like New College, Oxford, it was founded for seventy scholars and fellows; all came from Eton and they had endowment sufficient for their needs.[35] King's had for a time commoners who had not known Eton, but by the mid-nineteenth century they were no more. Under its original statutes the fellows were sworn not to tamper with the statutes, and the provost could prevent any proposal he disapproved being discussed by the governing body; in the years immediately before 1850 Provost Thackeray vetoed every project for reform.[36] In 1850 the first Royal Commission was under way; and in that year he died. In 1851 the college abandoned its privilege of exemption from

[33] For a penetrating introduction, see Steinberg 1976.
[34] See pp. 37, 229, 236, 272–4, 341–2, 460–1, 467–72, and *DNB*.
[35] On New College, see Buxton and Williams 1979, esp. pp. 72–106 (Alan Ryan). King's is exceptionally well covered in recent literature: there are general surveys by John Saltmarsh in *VCH Cambs*, III, esp. pp. 400–6, and by Christopher Morris 1989; a very useful study of the period 1873–1972 in Wilkinson 1980a; and a galaxy of biographies, of which I have made particular use of Austen Leigh 1906 (Augustus Austen Leigh, the founder of modern King's); Prothero 1888; Pfaff 1980 and Cox 1983 (M. R. James); Anstruther 1983 (Oscar Browning); Harrod 1951 (Maynard Keynes); Wilkinson 1969 (Sir John Sheppard).
[36] Saltmarsh in *VCH Cambs*, III, 400.

university examinations – which had in fact prevented its scholars from competing in the tripos.[37] In 1857 the governing body voted to admit some non-Etonians. 'The revolution had come.'[38] Perhaps it was so; but it was to be many years before King's became an effective teaching college; many more before the Etonians and the non-Etonians met and mingled on equal terms. The really radical changes, which destroyed the ancient character of the community, and prepared the way for the members of King's to become an academic élite among the colleges, were primarily the work of Augustus Austen Leigh, one of the unsung heroes of Cambridge history, who has had little honour from King's historians because he was overshadowed by more colourful characters, led by the preposterous Oscar Browning.[39] To the O.B., we are told, the ethos of King's owed more. It may be so, but Leigh was the true revolutionary. He was an Etonian, one of three brothers, all fellows; he was deeply loyal to Eton, to King's and above all to King's chapel; he was a man of quiet charm, with no pretence to scholarship, but an effective teacher with a vision of a better college. In this respect he illustrates a theme repeated again and again until we meet its culmination in Trinity: the efforts in many colleges, and eventually in all, to make the college a true centre of university teaching once again by appointing college lecturers, alias teaching fellows. Austen Leigh was universally loved and trusted. Few of the old guard really believed that he could do mischief; most of the young knew what he was at and admired and respected him. He became a tutor in 1868 and gathered a cadre of teachers about him; the non-Etonian element in the college steadily expanded.[40] He continued to rule

---

[37] Ibid.

[38] Saltmarsh in *VCH Cambs*, III, 401.

[39] Wilkinson 1980a, pp. 10–11 (justice is done to Leigh in Morris 1989). Wilkinson truly observes that Austen Leigh had many old-fashioned notions: only such a man would have been trusted to see through the far-reaching reforms which made King's an intellectual élite, and a college with a very active social life. Thus was formed the basis on which the O.B. and others could build. It would be foolish to lay too much emphasis at any point in this book on the influence of a single person; but Austen Leigh 1906 – though written by a brother devoted to the provost's memory – is a very careful, largely factual, record of a remarkable achievement. On the O.B. see Anstruther 1983, a book which perhaps underestimates O.B.'s creative work in the college: see Morris 1989, pp. 49–51, and cf. Wilkinson 1980a, pp. 11–16 – and esp. below, pp. 464–6, and Searby 1982, for his best work.

[40] Austen Leigh 1906, chap. 7; Saltmarsh in *VCH Cambs*, III, 403–4; Wilkinson 1980a, pp. 5–6; Morris 1989, pp. 51–3.

the college as vice-provost and provost till his death in 1905; but it is significant for the future that his election in 1889 was far from unanimous. Many of the younger fellows sought in Henry Sidgwick of Trinity a provost of real academic distinction, an Apostle not wedded to the chapel.[41] The election passed off quietly enough: Leigh was elected and he was not the man to resent what had happened. But it was a harbinger of divisions to come. For the 'ethos' of King's is founded on argument, dissension and division, which have often proved of a thoroughly refreshing and fruitful kind, often indeed producing social harmony out of religious and political friction. But the divisions have been real. In 1903, not long before Leigh's death, a great debate was held in a meeting of undergraduates with many dons, and the provost, among them, to discuss the form a college mission or settlement in London should take. The young produced a very urgent plea that it should have no religious bent or bias, and the agnostic case was eloquently presented by Maynard Keynes, then nineteen, and J. T. Sheppard, later provost. By about 75 votes to 25 they won the day;[42] in matters religious and ideological King's was and is deeply divided.

The tiny resident community in which Provost Leigh had lived as an undergraduate in the early 1860s only counted one resident fellow of intellectual pretensions; but he was Henry Bradshaw, whom Leigh's elder brother Edward and his friends inspired to become the friendly centre of a society in which – as time passed and Leigh recruited more fellows seriously interested in teaching – fellows and undergraduates came to mingle more freely and more naturally than in most colleges.[43] At the same time King's was sufficiently well endowed that it had no need to tout for students; and Leigh and his colleagues were able to insist that only undergraduates seriously bent on honours entered the college – thus producing an intellectual élite in Cambridge when the prevailing tone was anti-intellectual, even philistine – though even King's was able in the end to hold its own on the river and on the playing field.[44]

[41] Sidgwick is not named in Austen Leigh 1906, pp. 225–7; see Morris 1989, p. 51.
[42] Harrod 1951, pp. 93–4.
[43] Austen Leigh 1906, chap. 4, esp. pp. 65–8; cf. Prothero 1888; and below, pp. 272–4.
[44] The first volumes of *Granta* (1889ff) are dominated by the King's connection and show no lack of interest in sport; much the reverse.

In this expanding society O.B. played a remarkable part.[45] He had become a fellow under the old regime and gone on to Eton, where he was for a time a successful housemaster. But his arrogance, and the suspicion that he was too familiar with some of his boys, led to his dismissal, and he returned to King's to live, rather sparely, off his fellowship. But by teaching history, and writing very bad books about history and other things, he made enough to live in comfort and entertain royally. In the process he helped to bring Cambridge history to life: King's was one of its notable centres in the 1880s and 1890s, for it had a serious historian of considerable gifts in G. W. Prothero, and Prothero and the O.B. were a fine combination of solidity and vigour.[46] Browning actually knew almost everybody and pretended to know the rest; so that he was able to erect name-dropping into a principle of life. In the process he enabled the young men of King's to meet a wide range of genuinely interesting people as well as the great and dull. In 1896, for example, he encountered the young New Zealander, Ernest Rutherford, who was taken by an eminent scientist, an admirer of Rutherford's early work in the Cavendish, to dine in King's.

'Seated opposite me', wrote Rutherford to his fiancée in New Zealand, 'was a Mr Browning – a lecturer at King's – and he made himself very agreeable. He seemed an extremely well informed man – in appearance he was a good deal like the typical John Bull one so often sees in *Punch*' (to Max Beerbohm he rather resembled Mr Punch himself)[47] – and Browning invited him to lunch. He describes with less enthusiasm the rich and aristocratic persons he met there. 'Browning is quite a character here. He is a bit snobby. From what I have heard he professes to know all the people worth knowing in Europe. It is a common yarn about him that he said "the German Emperor was about the pleasantest emperor he had met".'[48] Yet for the undergraduates of King's Browning's parties – in which one might meet the stars of many academic disciplines as well as an occasional prince (if not an emperor) – must have been extraordinarily interesting, and at

[45] On the O.B., see n. 39; Anstruther 1983.   [46] On Prothero, see esp. Crawley 1970.
[47] Beerbohm's cartoon of Mr Oscar Browning entertaining a mixed gathering of great men and students is reproduced in Anstruther 1983, pl. 9, opposite p. 118.
[48] Wilson 1983, pp. 103–4.

times intellectually stimulating, for those not too shy or too insecure to participate. In his way he genuinely tried to draw in the non-Etonian and the Etonian alike. It seems that with many of the newcomers he failed; that some continued for many years to feel excluded from the élite if they had not come from Eton. But the O.B. and, in his very different way, Monty James, who succeeded Leigh as provost, seriously tried.[49]

James was in his own way a genuine scholar: his catalogues of the manuscripts of the college libraries are full of learning and scholarly perception; if he had troubled to proof-read them, they might have been accurate too. Yet there was an element of dilettante about him: litterateur, ghost-story writer, an amateur in many fields. He fostered a tradition similar to the O.B.'s, that intellectual and aesthetic pursuits – ideas and literature – were the stuff of King's men, not the mechanical details of scholarship. In point of fact King's produced or attracted many scholars of extremely varied interests. It is characteristic of the traditions it formed in the time of Oscar Browning that in the 1940s and 50s the young King's men, and a few very privileged from other colleges, could enjoy the society of E. M. Forster,[50] who was invited by the college to spend his declining years there, a remarkable adornment to the college and to Cambridge.

Jesus

Jesus College presents a contrast. It is not that Jesus lacked interesting men: early and late some of the notable Cambridge scholars of these generations spent some time in Jesus. But it was also the leading rowing college for much of the time, and several of its deans and tutors worked to keep it that way. The story is told that the Jesus alumni opened their *Times* at some date in the late 1940s, and found that Jesus was no longer head of the river – and that Jesus men were getting firsts; and they organised a deputation to the master to protest. The story is apocryphal in

---

[49] On James, see Pfaff 1980, Cox 1983. The text is partly based on long acquaintance with his ghost stories, his catalogues, and his admirable edition and translation of Walter Map (see James, Brooke and Mynors 1983).

[50] I speak from personal gratitude as a Caian who enjoyed this privilege. On Forster see esp. Furbank 1977–8.

detail, but it harbours a truth: as John Buchan said of nineteenth-century Brasenose, 'it is preeminently a sporting record' but 'there was . . . always a respectable sprinkling of firsts'.[51]

The contrast between King's and Jesus has been the theme of a brilliant paper by J. A. Mangan;[52] for Jesus he has used a number of memoirs and *The Chanticlere* – so named in reminiscence of the cocks which adorn the college in honour of its founder, Bishop John Alcock – as well as Freddy Brittain's edition of the *History* by Arthur Gray, who was master from 1912 to 1940.

> Few things depict better the similarity between the Victorian and Edwardian public school and Jesus than the College magazine of the period, *The Chanticlere*. In the main it is hearty, philistine, considerably taken up with athletics and preoccupied with the associated issues which so greatly concerned the English public school boy of the period – athletic heroes, successes and regalia. In 1889 the editors of *The Chanticlere*, with a certain perspicacity and some irony, amused themselves by speculating on the eventual fate of the volume which they had produced; 'We can picture the joy of some learned professor of English on finding this priceless treasure, a relic of the remote past. Aided by this work he will prove that the Universities of the ancient English were really devoted to athletic pursuits.'[53]

He goes on to quote Shane Leslie, writing of a Jesus man who was a serious reader and felt out of tune with the society, that 'Jesus was a medieval foundation which in the course of modern progress had passed from the housing of religious women to the production of less devout but highly trained oarsmen.'[54] This aspect of the college's adventures was largely the result of the creative work of the two Morgans – H. A. and E. H. – both former masters at Lancing, where they had fostered the vigorous plant of athleticism in its native clime, the English public school; both were central figures in late nineteenth-century Jesus, though they were neither friends nor relations. Mangan says of them that 'H. A. Morgan was a glorified headmaster with a taste for sport', while 'E. H. Morgan was a glorified games master with an

---

[51] Buchan 1898, p. 76.   [52] Mangan 1984.   [53] Mangan 1984, p. 58.
[54] Leslie 1923, pp. 43–4, cited Mangan 1984, p. 59. For what follows, see esp. Mangan 1984, pp. 60–6; cf. Gray and Brittain 1979, pp. 185–94.

obsession for it'.[55] The college multiplied in numbers under Black Morgan (H.A), and began a new building; but when Red Morgan (E.H.) ruled the college as dean it became notorious as the home of ignorant, ill-disciplined athletic louts and declined. Arthur Gray was to destroy the image of Red Morgan, but not the prowess of the college boat club; for in 1904 Stephen Fairbairn returned to coach the boat – on the first lap of his triumphant career as the most celebrated of Cambridge coaches – and Dr Foakes-Jackson, the dean, assured him that 'the position of the college boat on the river was an index of the prosperity of the college'.[56] From then on decent college life and successful boating could progress together.

In both King's and Jesus in the late nineteenth century the ideal of muscular Christianity, the union of manliness and godliness, was powerfully represented; and this much complicates the picture of philistine athleticism so vividly portrayed in Mangan's study. In Jesus itself an austere theologian like Dr Corrie, master from 1849 to 1885 – who resisted every effort at reform and told the Royal Commission of 1877 that 'the present chief want of the University is exemption from the disturbing power of Royal or Parliamentary Commissioners'[57] – none the less fostered the boat club, presumably because he saw in it an instrument of manly Christian education.[58] Foakes-Jackson – Foakes or Foakesie as he was affectionately known to his colleagues and students – was a distinguished Church historian, who saw nothing incompatible between scholarship and rowing.[59]

Gonville and Caius

Less distinguished than King's in intellectual enterprise, and less successful than Jesus on the river, was the Caius of the 1880s and 1890s. In the 1850s college teaching was perfunctory; no attempt was made to provide honours students with serious instruction; as in most colleges before the 1870s, they sought out their own

55 Mangan 1984, p. 66.
56 Mangan 1984, p. 61; cf. ibid. p. 74 n. 65; Fairbairn 1931. On Gray's attitude to Red Morgan, Mangan 1984, p. 65.
57 Gray and Brittain 1979, p. 168.
58 This is denied by Brittain in Gray and Brittain 1979, p. 172; but see Mangan 1984, pp. 61–2.
59 Mangan 1984, p. 61; Gray and Brittain 1979, pp. 187, 195.

coaches, at their own expense, and prospered if they chose well. In 1870 E. S. Roberts became a fellow of Caius and a college lecturer in classics; in 1876 he became a tutor, and from then on, with much encouragement from a group of reforming fellows of whom John Venn, philosopher, mathematician and college historian, was the most distinguished, he set to work to perform for Caius the role that Austen Leigh was so successfully filling in King's.[60] As an undergraduate, 'he was a hard-reading man who had little time at first for relaxation; but once he had secured his fellowship in 1870, he took to the water – it was not uncommon then for fellows to row – and stroked the second boat in the Mays of 1872, by which time he was already Senior Treasurer' of the college boat club.[61] His life was dedicated to teaching and pastoral care; but he was a scholar too who found time to write a substantial treatise on Greek epigraphy. 'In research and teaching and sport he fervently believed and played his role in each according to his strength and opportunity.'[62] He was a moderate exponent of muscular Christianity – for 'manly' he substituted 'wholesome'; the boat club was preeminent in the wholesome regions of college life; no freshman entered the college (we are assured) while he was tutor (1876–1903) and master (1903–12) without being encouraged to join the boat club. Yet all the while he was fostering the academic work of the college too. At the very end of his life he welcomed to Caius two young college lecturers, Zachary Brooke and Edward Bullough (1908, 1912), who were to make Caius a place in which the serious study of history and modern languages could grow. They came to compete with the medical and natural sciences already powerfully represented, Roberts' own classics, and law, which enjoyed in W. W. Buckland and Arnold McNair the most distinguished Roman lawyer and international lawyer bred in Cambridge in the nineteenth or early twentieth century.[63] The boat club was Roberts' first love; but under his kindly rule playing fields were acquired and other sports found their home. Caius was not in his

---

[60] Brooke 1985, pp. 218–22 (Venn), 234–6 (Roberts), and chap. 12 passim.
[61] Brooke 1985, p. 234, esp. refs. in n. 41.
[62] Brooke 1985, p. 234; cf. esp. *Caian* 1912.
[63] Brooke 1985, pp. 282–3; Grierson 1946 (Z. N. Brooke); Moriarty 1988 (Bullough); *PBA* 33 (1947), 283—91 (Buckland by A. D. McNair and P. W. Duff); Brooke 1985, pp. 229–30, 282 and refs. in n. 5 (McNair).

period a particularly athletic community; nor had it begun to achieve the academic distinction of the mid and late twentieth century. Roberts sought a mixed community of hard reading men who lived wholesome lives, alongside the hearty philistine medical students – as some though far from all the traditional medical students of Caius were in that era. As late as 1920, when Thomas Okey became a professorial fellow of Caius, entering academic life for the first time in his late sixties, he was struck that discussion in the Combination Room with a visiting headmaster about possible recruits wholly 'related to their prowess at Rugby . . . Not a word was said as to their learning' – though he gathered that they all worked when they came up and some 'gained double firsts . . . but this is not talked about'.[64] He evidently heightened the colours a bit; but this reflects a fundamental fact of Cambridge life down to the 1930s, that the wholehearted dedication to sport was not necessarily incompatible with lofty academic standards. Even to this day the Senior Combination Room can be thronged with television viewers on a Saturday afternoon.

The smaller colleges

St Catharine's

Between 1870 and 1900 the undergraduate population of Cambridge rose from just over 2,000 to just under 3,000.[65] Broadly speaking it was the colleges of medium size like Caius which accounted for most of the growth, but the figures hide some remarkable fluctuations. Trinity rose by over 100 to 676; but St John's fell by 124 to 237; Jesus after a sensational rise had fallen again to 112; Corpus fell from 141 to 59. Caius, Pembroke, Christ's, Trinity Hall, Clare and King's all rose to levels between 140 and 230.[66] The smaller colleges remained small – though Queens' was poised for a remarkable increase in the 1900s. The rapid rise in the university's hinterland in the late nineteenth century – in secondary schools at large and in the public schools in particular – provided plenty of recruits; but the schools and

---

[64] Brooke 1985, pp. 283–4; Okey 1930, pp. 139–41.
[65] 2,019 to 2,985 according to *CUC* 1870, p. 532, 1900–1, p. 944. A detailed check shows that *CUC* slightly underestimates the figures for 1870: see p. 593.
[66] See pp. 593–4.

through them the parents of these new recruits were very much aware that colleges differed one from another and that their reputations and their fortunes fluctuated accordingly. We cannot trace these differences in detail in the present state of knowledge; but we can discern in a rough and ready way the distinction between the small, the medium and the large.

The small colleges, having relatively few alumni, were little known: they were to enter into their own when Cambridge came to mean more in the world than any of its colleges; in the late twentieth century there has been much more parity between different societies. But some colleges were acutely aware that the expansion of the late Victorian era had passed them by. St Catharine's in retrospect has tended to attribute its lack-lustre career between 1870 and 1914 to the election of C. K. Robinson as master in 1861. 'The scandal caused by the election was probably the greatest disaster that ever happened to any College in either University,' wrote the college historian W. H. S. Jones in 1936.[67] One cannot help feeling that college legend has greatly enlarged the unhappy story of Robinson's vote to excuse an uninspiring epoch in college history.[68] St Catharine's was a small society of five fellows, two of whom, Robinson the bursar and Jameson the tutor – both good evangelical divines – were reckoned likely candidates for the mastership. The wind was set fair for Robinson when two of the younger fellows, to his evident chagrin, announced that they would after all vote for Jameson. A non-resident senior was for Robinson; so the election was bound to be settled by the votes of the protagonists themselves. They had discussed the matter and come to a misunderstanding – at least that is the only reasonable conclusion we can draw. Jameson voted for Robinson, and Robinson, following what had been the normal tradition at St Catharine's and in some other societies, voted for himself, and so secured the mastership, which he was to hold for nearly fifty years, till 1909. At first Jameson accepted defeat and offered warm and effusive congratulations. But then, according to the story later told by

---

[67] Jones 1936, p. 148.

[68] Jones 1936, pp. 139–48, has useful material, but the best account of the election, with a careful sifting of all the contradictory evidence, is in Winstanley 1947, chap. 1. For a balanced view of St Catharine's in this period, see Rich and MacDonagh in Rich 1973, pp. 164–265.

E. H. Perowne, the master of Corpus, Jameson discovered that
Robinson was engaged to be married: as a fellow he could not
marry, as master he could – and he promptly went off to
Scotland to claim his bride. Jameson concluded that Robinson
had stolen the mastership for unworthy motives, and proceeded
to denounce his victorious rival in a series of noisy pamphlets.
From these blows Robinson and his reputation never recovered.
The protagonists continued to contradict each other's account of
the arrangement between them; but a fuller disclosure of the
evidence has seemed to make clear that there was a genuine
misunderstanding, natural in an extremely embarrassing circumstance. Yet Robinson became a recluse, ostracised, or imagining
himself ostracised, from the society of Cambridge heads, and the
reputation of St Catharine's suffered while he ruled. In 1892 some
effort was made to rouse the college by appointing two new,
young tutors, but after two or three years of lively activity they
'began gradually to sink into inefficiency. They had shot their
bolt, and the success of their efforts was small; the Robinson
cloud grew darker still.'[69] In the small societies all the work fell
on a tiny group of men; and it must have been especially
disheartening to them to observe a master 'sinking into a soured
and embittered old age ... The Bursar retired to the country
living of Little Shelford. Spratt [dean and tutor] gave himself up
to his private coaching, and Southward [the other tutor] devoted
himself to music.'[70] All was not black, however, and W. H. S.
Jones paints an attractive picture of Spratt, at once kindly and
formidable and hopelessly unpractical with money; the music of
Southward was uncommonly good. A serious revival began after
1909; and meanwhile, St Catharine's went steadily on, modest in
numbers but far from negligible, producing worthy ordinands
and schoolmasters, most of whom still had to be content with
pass degrees.[71]

But the truth is that if we look at the shape of the university
in 1900, St Catharine's, with 6 fellows and 73 junior members,
was by no means the smallest or most insignificant of the Cambridge colleges. Corpus, Peterhouse and Downing all had fewer,

[69] Jones 1936, p. 152.   [70] Jones 1936, pp. 151–2.
[71] Jones 1936, p. 158; cf. O. MacDonagh in Rich 1973, pp. 255–9.

and Queens' had only recently risen above it.[72] It was rather one of a group of small colleges whose future seemed precarious in the later years of the nineteenth century, as the agricultural depression eroded their rents and the revival of teaching stretched their resources. The Oxford and Cambridge Act of 1877 gave power to the Statutory Commissioners to unite two or more colleges – a revolutionary clause now largely forgotten. A plan was formed to unite Emmanuel and Christ's, and another to merge St Catharine's and King's. Neither succeeded, and the second foundered in 1880, owing (it is said) to the difficulty of accommodating Robinson in the united colleges.[73] Many colleges, and many fellows, were deeply divided in mind on this clause in the act of 1877. If the university was to live up to its vocation, the resources of the colleges would have to be much more efficiently deployed. Since the sixteenth century teaching had largely centred in the colleges; even granted that the new world of the 1870s and 80s inexorably demanded a larger role for university teaching once more, it could only be supported if the colleges themselves contributed generously to the university, and at the same time built up a cadre of lecturers, that is college teachers, within their fellowships.

Magdalene

To the tiny fellowship of Magdalene, presided over by a master who had been slumbering in the lodge since 1853, these arguments must have seemed remote: the college could scarcely contemplate either contributing to the university or providing any range of teaching from its own resources. In any case, for many the college was a sacred trust, whose corporate life was eternal: the first duty of its fellows was to preserve it. If they could have looked forward a hundred years, the fellows of Magdalene might have found quite a different justification for their survival; for as the twentieth century went on the college grew, and after the Second World War every college increased its numbers of undergraduates and fellows until it was bursting at the seams. The existence of so many colleges has been the salvation of Cambridge

---

[72] See pp. 593–4.
[73] Rich 1973, pp. 226–9; Jones 1936, p. 150. For Emmanuel and Christ's, see pp. 86–7.

in the late twentieth century, for they have been able to expand without losing all sense of community.[74] But in the process they have considerably altered their nature; and had the fellows of Magdalene altogether foreseen the college of the 1980s, secularised, expanded, teeming with women as well as with men, one or two of them might a little have wondered if they were right to preserve it.

Every small college sought its own salvation by different means. King's was small only in undergraduates; it had ample fellows and broad acres, so that once it had the will for expansion, it could find the way. St Catharine's sought (for a time) an unequal marriage with King's. Failing that, it had to be content to teach a narrow range of subjects, and it could not compete with the larger colleges who could offer an abundance of labs and lectures. Slowly the university came to provide the labs, and lectures in history, law, modern languages and other newfangled subjects.[75] The teachers plotted together to provide intercollegiate lectures. By such means a semblance of effective teaching could be mounted in most colleges; though it must be admitted that in the present state of knowledge we cannot document how this was done, or how effectively, in all.

By 1900 the resources of Magdalene supported a master and three fellows only.[76] The master was appointed by Lord Braybrooke; and in 1900 he was the patron's brother, the Reverend and Honourable Latimer Neville, who had presided over the college since 1853: his only known contribution to the debate was a determined devotion to the college's traditions. When the Statutory Commissioners in 1881 insisted that the new statutes provide for the possibility of a master who was not a clergyman of the Church of England, he protested with solemn dignity to a 'contravention of the intention and will of the founder'.[77] In 1904 he enjoyed a new lease of life in an unexpected role, as the

---

[74] This much simplifies a complex story: for some, especially bursars, with an eye on the financial advantages of large numbers of students, it has seemed that there could be advantages in having fewer, larger colleges even today. But most governing bodies have seen a balance of arguments – larger numbers fill the coffers and make for economies, but they overfill the buildings and public rooms and may threaten the sense of community.

[75] Law was not new in a sense, but there was little in common between the old Faculties of Canon and Civil (i.e. Roman) Law and the new Law School of the late nineteenth century.

[76] See p. 594.

[77] Quoted in Winstanley 1947, p. 356.

Lord Braybrooke; he rose from master to patron.[78] The next oldest was the token professorial fellow, Professor Newton, an ancient zoologist, and a noted eccentric, untidy, difficult, absurd, yet 'a real old gentleman' for whom the young A. C. Benson, when he became a fellow of Magdalene in 1904, felt an instant liking.[79] The business of the college was thus entirely in the hands of the two remaining fellows: the tutor, A. G. Peskett, who had been first classic and Chancellor's Medallist in 1875, and the bursar, later also tutor (and ultimately president) A. S. Ramsey, who was to be a central pillar of the college for more than a generation to come, and father of one of Magdalene's most eminent alumni, Michael Ramsey, later archbishop of Canterbury.[80]

In most colleges the election of the master has been the most treasured symbol of the democratic rights of the fellowship at large. In Trinity the master is appointed by the crown; in Peterhouse and Jesus he was chosen by the bishop of Ely from candidates put forward by the fellowship until the mid-nineteenth century; in Magdalene he is appointed by the representative of the founder, Lord Braybrooke.[81] Within the patron's family, the college seems to have been regarded as the close relative of a boarding school. Although there have been many cases of schoolmasters turned fellows and masters – or fellows and tutors turned headmasters – in the twentieth century, the link between Magdalene and Eton is unique. In 1904, 1915 and 1925 Lord Braybrooke presented former Eton housemasters as masters of Magdalene – Stuart Donaldson, A. C. Benson and A. B. Ramsay. Ramsay died during the Second World War and a reaction followed with the appointment of an eminent public servant and politician, Lord Willink; then the schoolmaster tradition was revived for a time in Walter Hamilton,[82] who

78 See below, and n. 81.
79 Newsome 1980, pp. 157–8.
80 See Chadwick 1990, pp. 16–26, for Michael Ramsey's career at Magdalene.
81 Down to 1926 this was defined as the owner of Audley End, the home of the founder, Lord Audley, in 1542; and this meant, in recent generations, Lord Braybrooke. In the statutes of 1926 the provision was altered so that the choice now lies with Lord Braybrooke *eo nomine: VCH Cambs*, III, 452.
82 Hamilton had been a master at Eton, fellow of Trinity, and headmaster of Westminster and Rugby; Howarth had been head of King Edward's, Birmingham and St Paul's and second master of Winchester (*Who's Who* 1988, pp. 750, 870).

Fig. 1 Portrait of A. C. Benson, by Sir William Nicholson, in the Fitzwilliam
Museum

brought with him as senior tutor another eminent ex-headmaster,
T. E. B. Howarth. This succession has suggested to some observers that if a college has not the resources of a fellowship to
support academic distinction, it may rather be viewed as a kind of
boarding school; and this notion was not wholly false at least to
Ramsay's view: he attempted to revive compulsory chapel in
Magdalene; and he treated the Cambridge classicists much as if
they were sixth-form Etonians.[83] But it does very much less than
justice to the character of the college in which that man for all
seasons A. C. Benson lived and flourished from 1904, when he
became a fellow without stipend, to 1925, when he died master of
Magdalene.

Few men have left more hostages to fortune than A. C.

[83] So I was informed by the Reverend G. K. Tibbatts, former chaplain of Magdalene. Ramsay
was a kindly man, as I can testify from personal experience. Cf. p. 113.

Benson. In his lifetime he published innumerable books by which he amassed a substantial fortune – volumes of meditative philosophical reflections and light, whimsical novels: his novels earned him one of the most cruel, yet also affectionate, of Max Beerbohm's parodies.[84] He left for others to publish a vast series of diaries in which the doubts and anxieties and passing thoughts which trouble us all, enhanced by the shadows of mental illness which afflicted him severely from time to time, were laid out in inexorable detail, and for which he reserved the caustic comments and the sharp flights of wit which he carefully kept out of his urbane conversation.[85] For Benson was a great master of conversation, and made the Magdalene high table and the college rooms in which he lived, for a time, notable centres of good talk. Thus Maisie Anderson:[86]

> my recollections of taking tea with A. C. Benson are pictured in soft undertones, as gracious as the skill with which he would lift the banal remarks of a dinner table companion to a level far above their merits. He told Mamma once that, in his home, they had all been taught to converse well, being criticised and schooled by their father [Archbishop Benson] after every party. Certainly I never met anyone in whom the art of conversation, as opposed to brilliant monologue, was carried to such perfection.

When Benson became master of Magdalene in 1915 he was given the higher doctorate offered to all heads of house until the 1920s, and he rejoiced in his scarlet robes. But he was no scholar and had little idea of what scholarship might be. He was good friends with M. R. James but thought James idle – which doubtless he appeared to many who viewed him as director of the Fitzwilliam Museum or provost of King's and took no account of the marvellous detail of his studies and catalogues of manuscripts.[87] Nor did Benson have much idea of the Cambridge curriculum save as it impinged on a highly successful schoolmaster. But he made friends easily among young and old alike and

---

[84] 'Out of harm's way', *A Christmas Garland*, London, 1912, pp. 21–30.

[85] Extracts from the diary have been printed in Lubbock 1926, and Newsome 1980 is a biography based on them; for all the author's skill and insight he does less than justice to Benson and to the interest of his diaries.

[86] Anderson 1988ff, chap. 8.

[87] On James see pp. 341–2, 460–1.

helped immeasurably to create a sense of community in his college, and in Cambridge at large. He was by training a classic who had rebelled – in the mild and gentlemanly fashion in which his rebellions were conducted – against the narrowness of the traditional classical curriculum; and he was one of those who took pains to introduce a broader interest in literature into Cambridge in the years when the English Tripos was making its uneasy debut.[88] He had an inveterate dislike for the O.B.: doubtless he realised that he too as a dilettante and an ex-Eton housemaster appeared to many to be tarred with the same brush; but he avoided the O.B.'s most notorious faults. His snobbery was not obtrusive and his dilettantism was shot through with shrewd insight and understanding of many of the needs of Cambridge students beyond what most of his colleagues could grasp. Above all he showed Magdalene a path to salvation: by his presence, his generosity and his encouragement he helped to build the new society there of the 1920s and 30s, which had many features of the old world, of Eton and Audley End, but also many of the new, in a wider variety of fellows and disciplines.

Corpus Christi

The speed of change in the smaller colleges is clearly illustrated in a comparison of Corpus and Pembroke. Corpus had been one of the leading evangelical colleges in recent generations and had prospered while Dr Pulling was master and Dr Perowne tutor. In 1879 Pulling died and Perowne succeeded him as master; and in 1880 there were 122 undergraduates, and the identical number in Pembroke. By 1900–1 Pembroke had 226, Corpus 59.[89] In Patrick Bury's admirable *History* this marked decline is attributed in part to the rigid conservatism and evangelical fervour of Perowne at a time when change was in the wind and the Cambridge evangelicals no longer so popular as they had been: a revolt against the narrow kind of evangelicalism which had been prevailing in Corpus led to the replacement of a tutor in 1892 –

[88] See p. 446.
[89] My figures are from *CUC*; Bury 1952, p. 86 n. gives rather different figures from the dean's book – 70 in 1900 and 58 in 1901. Since the college officials in Corpus must have provided the figures in *CUC*, the discrepancy is probably due to the time of year when the figures were calculated.

and this led to a decline in the college's reputation in the very regions where it had before been strongest. It lost for a time both kinds of recruits, non-evangelicals and evangelicals.[90] When Pulling died the *Cambridge Chronicle* observed that he 'did all in his power to render his own College a seminary of religious education' and had opposed all moves 'to dethrone Christianity from its paramount authority in the teaching and discipline of the place'.[91] In this he had been supported by Perowne long before Perowne became master, and the old-fashioned clerical college survived until the turn of the century.

When the Statutory Commissioners in 1881 insisted that in future a master of Corpus might be a layman, Perowne entered 'my most solemn protest' against their intention to allow the election of 'any person wholly irrespective of his religious belief and profession, so that the mastership may be held by a professed atheist' – and he invoked the intention of the founder and benefactors, acts of parliament and the history of the college, calling it an act 'to the grievous detriment of . . . [the college's] efficiency as a place of education, and as an act tending to the dishonour of Almighty God'.[92] Winstanley called this the protest of 'an angry, unbalanced man'; but that was hardly fair. Perowne was a learned man in his way, and he could be a charming, warm-hearted friend and a kind host. But he had a very fixed and, as we should think, narrow, view of a college. Two very different views were in conflict. To Perowne it was a seminary of devout clergy. To the Commissioners, who were far from atheistical in purpose, it was a place of 'education, religion, learning and research' for all who might seek it, irrespective of creed or intellectual discipline, in the academic world of the 1880s.

When change came, however, it did not involve a full measure of secularity. By a sleight of hand Corpus was transformed, not only into a twentieth-century academic community, but into a society now high church in its ecclesiology though as conservative as before in its politics. This was accomplished by E. C. Pearce, dean from 1901, and the group of lay colleagues who had in their

---

[90] Bury 1952, chap. 39, esp. pp. 85–6.   [91] Cited Bury 1952, p. 55.
[92] Winstanley 1947, p. 357.

different ways stood in opposition to Perowne. First of these had been the gentle scholar E. B. Cowell, a noted orientalist, whose example and personal efforts helped to make Corpus a centre of scholarship.[93] Next there was the ebullient tutor, Henry Fanshawe, the architect of the palace revolution of 1892: a man determined to convert Corpus from an evangelical seminary into a multi-faculty college in the new mould. Beyond a certain age he resisted further change; he stood out against the telephone and electric light and other innovations. But he had let in a new dawn to Corpus.[94] Presumably the most influential figure in altering the religious complexion of the college was the dean, E. C. Pearce,[95] but the full extent of his influence was kept in check while Perowne lived. Finally, when Perowne died in 1906, he was succeeded by R. T. Caldwell, the 'Major', a man of genuinely military background who shared E. S. Roberts' devotion to the University Rifle Volunteers, and had been bursar of Corpus from 1871 to 1899.[96] The first two new fellows elected in his mastership were Will Spens, first director of studies in natural sciences and an eminent high-church layman, and E. G. Selwyn of King's, a high-church divine.[97] Selwyn was to leave Corpus in 1913 to become warden of Radley – and at the end of his life he was dean of Winchester; but his mark was deep in Cambridge, where he and Spens and other like-minded scholars had issued *Essays Catholic and Critical* (1926), the manifesto of a group devoted to high anglicanism combined with contemporary scientific and historical thought.

Sidney Sussex

Sidney, like Corpus, had retained into the late nineteenth century something of the character of a modest-sized seminary; and like St Catharine's, a curious reputation not altogether deserved for being an intellectual backwater.[98] In 1876 Lord Edmund Fitzmaurice had suggested that the endowments of Sidney should be

---

[93] Bury 1952, pp. 100, 221–3.   [94] Bury 1952, pp. 85, 213–15, esp. p. 214.
[95] Bury 1952, pp. 123, 126, 137–54. Pearce was later master, 1914–27, and bishop of Derby, 1927–35.   [96] Bury 1952, chap. 40, esp. p. 119.
[97] Bury 1952, pp. 155–74, 239–40. Spens was master 1927–52.
[98] Scott-Giles 1975, esp. p. 103.

transferred to the university.[99] Sidney had been founded, like Emmanuel, as a seedbed for puritan, or anyway protestant, preachers at the end of the sixteenth century; but its character had been permanently affected by Samuel Taylor of Dudley, an ardent devotee of mathematics of the age of Newton, who left the college a handsome property in 1723 for the support of mathematics, especially for a fellowship. But the Sidney statutes prescribed that the fellows study divinity, so a special order in Chancery was made to convert Taylor's fellow into a lecturer, and the seminary of theologians, spiced with a little mathematics, survived until the statutes of 1882. At that epoch the college was presided over by Dr Phelps, who had been a reformer in the 1840s and was by 1882 the most reactionary of heads, Perowne only excepted.[100] Meanwhile there was already diversity of talent in the fellowship, and the fellows and the Commissioners produced statutes which ensured that the college became more diverse. The Taylor bequest became the foundation for notable growth in natural sciences as well as mathematics; and from 1882 there were college lecturers in theology, classics, mathematics and natural sciences.[101] Meanwhile growth was slow – there were 10 fellows but only 72 undergraduates in 1900–1.[102]

Peterhouse

The least variable in number of the smaller colleges was Peterhouse. In 1880 it comprised a master, 10 fellows and 57 undergraduates; in 1900 a master, 10 fellows, one research fellow, and 55 undergraduates.[103] In practice, the community of fellows was smaller than these figures might suggest. Several were non-resident, and a small group of three or four divided the college offices – tutor, assistant tutor, dean, praelector, librarian and chaplain – among themselves. It was a very intimate society, but not without distinction. The theologian W. E. Barnes was to claim in the 1920s that Peterhouse 'at no period in its history

[99] Winstanley 1947, p. 272; Sidney, by implication, was 'comparatively useless', like the heads of house whom he also proposed to abolish.
[100] Scott-Giles 1975, pp. 78–9, 99–101.   [101] Scott-Giles 1975, p. 101.
[102] *CUC* 1900–1, pp. 911, 944.
[103] *CUC* 1880, pp. 375–6, 642; *CUC* 1900–1, pp. 677, 944.

probably had a greater display of genius and talent among its living fellows, past and present, than in the quarter of a century between 1845 and 1870.'[104] William Hopkins, the great mathematical coach, teacher of innumerable wranglers, had been a fellow down to the mid-nineteenth century. Adolphus Ward, a distinguished expert on history and literature, was a fellow from 1861, from 1866 a professor at Owens College, Manchester but still a fellow – or after marriage an honorary fellow – of Peterhouse. Later in the century the fellows of Peterhouse commonly elected one or two men eminent in research or learning to the fellowship, and so acquired the experimental physicist Sir William Thomson, Lord Kelvin – professor in Glasgow but a not infrequent visitor to Cambridge – and Richard Shilleto, the doyen of classical coaches.[105]

In the succession of its masters the year 1900 marked a change of direction. Both H. W. Cookson (1847–76) and James Porter (1876–1900) were clerical dons of the old school. Cookson had been godson to William Wordsworth and a pupil of Hopkins. He was a man of wide interests with a genuine zeal for the natural sciences, and skill and experience in university affairs matured through five years as Vice-Chancellor between 1848 and 1873. He had an unerring eye for the bye-paths of university business which earned him the nickname 'the artful dodger' – he seems to have been a worthy successor to the celebrated sixteenth-century master Andrew Perne; but on the abolition of the tests he came forward openly to defend Anglican privilege.[106] James Porter was a moderate defender of ancient ways, and a man little known outside his college and the university.[107]

But in 1900 Adolphus Ward was summoned back to Cambridge, at the age of 62, to embark on twenty years of benevolent activity as master. He had been professor of History and English at Manchester, and had had two spells as Vice-Chancellor of the Victoria University of Manchester, Liverpool and Leeds. He had

---

[104] Barnes 1924, p. xii, in the appreciation of Adolphus Ward by Peter Giles and W. E. Barnes: this passage may be attributed to Barnes.

[105] For the fellowship see e.g. *CUC* 1870, pp. 299–300; *CUC* 1880, pp. 375–6; *CUC* 1900–1, pp. 677–8. On Lord Kelvin see e.g. *DSB* XIII, 374–88 (J. Z. Buchwald).

[106] On him there is a kindly account by A. W. Ward in *DNB*; Winstanley 1947, pp. 79–83, 278–9 (esp. 278 and n. 3 for his nickname), is less kind.

[107] See e.g. Winstanley 1947, pp. 232–3, 321–2, 326–7.

been a creative figure in the civic universities; and in Cambridge –
while his benevolent, bearded figure was a constant reminder of
the Victorian past – he laid the foundations for the serious study
of history and literature in university and college: English a little
remotely, by launching *The Cambridge History of English Literature*; history more immediately, by editing *The Cambridge Modern
History* and by inspiring its Medieval successor. *The Cambridge
Modern History* is forever associated with Acton, who laid its
foundation at the behest of the Syndics of the Press. But he
abandoned the task owing to ill-health, and it was Ward as chief
editor (1901–12) and chairman of the Press Syndics (1905–19)
who saw the *Histories* came to fruition. And it was Ward who
presided over the election of Harold Temperley, the first professional teaching fellow Peterhouse contributed to the History
Tripos, a central figure in the Junior Historians from 1911 on, one
of the creators of Cambridge history.[108] Ward and Temperley
prepared the way for the apotheosis of history between the 1920s
and the 1940s when Herbert Butterfield, Munia Postan, Denis
Brogan and David Knowles all entered the fellowship.[109]

Downing

'A certain Jarndyce, in an evil hour, made a great fortune, and
made a great will': thus did Mr Jarndyce of *Bleak House* summar-
ise the opening of a great Chancery suit.[110] In an hour held in
blessed remembrance in Downing College Sir George Downing,
who had inherited a noble estate, also made a great will, in which
he left his properties to various relatives, if they or their legitimate
heirs should survive him; and failing that, his estate was to form a
trust for the foundation of a college in Cambridge called Downing's College. The will was made in 1717; Sir George died in 1749,
and, contrary to all reasonable expectation, all his family who
might inherit had died before him. So the will went into
Chancery, and the Court of Chancery proceeded with customary
despatch, finally settling the case in 1800. In that year Downing
College received its charter as a college for 'law, physic and the

---

[108] See below, pp. 235–6; Barnes 1924, esp. p. xviii; *DNB 1922–1930*, pp. 881–3 (G.P. Gooch).
[109] See pp. 236–9.
[110] *Bleak House*, chap. 8.

other useful arts and learning', with a governing body comprising the master, a professor of law, a professor of medicine and sixteen fellows; but the endowments only allowed for three – by 1900 there were six.[111] The pursuit of useful arts marked a new departure, and the incorporation of professors into the society was a forward-looking move, anticipating the efforts of the Commissioners of the 1870s, though in the end frustrated by the Commissioners of the 1920s, who unloosed the ties between professors and colleges.[112] But the long suit in Chancery and the claims of the family[113] had grievously reduced the estate – though not to extinction, as in Jarndyce v. Jarndyce; and the Court of Chancery continued till the late nineteenth century to hold a portion of it as a building fund. Meanwhile Francis Annesley, who had campaigned ceaselessly for the college and become first master, was able to preside over the acquisition of a splendid site and the choice of William Wilkins, a young, relatively unknown fellow of Caius, as architect; and the first buildings went up.[114] Throughout the century it remained a very modest foundation and in 1900 still had only 52 undergraduates.[115] But the presence of the professors as resident members of the community gave it a certain lustre, and Downing at the turn of the century will always be remembered as the home of F. W. Maitland.[116] Meanwhile the master from 1888 was Alex Hill, a noted anatomist and a man of vision, who sought for some special role for his college in a Cambridge then apparently only too well provided with small and struggling communities of undergraduates. He proposed that it should become a graduate college financially linked to the university, and resigned when this was rejected by the governing body in 1907.[117] He was evidently given to circulating memoranda and not skilled at avoiding clashes in the fellowship. 'I am hoping that there will be no great rumpus at Downing while I am away,' wrote Maitland to Henry Jackson in 1902. 'If only A[lex] H[ill] would keep his

---

[111] For all this see French 1978, esp. pp. 34, 41, 82–3; *CUC* 1900–1, pp. 919–20.
[112] But see p. 354 n. 33.
[113] Although Sir George's named heirs were extinct, widows and more distant relatives survived to dispute the will.
[114] Sicca 1987; Liscombe 1980, pp. 46–50; Bicknell 1982.
[115] *CUC* 1900–1, p. 944. [116] See pp. 216–24.
[117] French 1978, pp. 130–1, 138.

fingers from the ink pot! But mind you that man is a saint and will go straight to heaven without questions asked.'[118] In return, Hill paid tribute to Maitland after his death in 1906. 'The older members of the Society, knowing his attachment to Trinity, doubted whether he would feel himself naturalised in the smaller College. From the moment of his admission all misgivings vanished. With characteristic chivalry he assumed and almost over-acted his new role.'[119] Meanwhile the central figure in the college was the tutor and bursar, John Perkins, a man equally at home in the hunting field and at the bump supper – yet a real Cambridge tutor who delighted above all in the number of first classes his pupils scored. 'He once declared', writes the historian of Downing, Stanley French, 'that he believed his best memorial to be the great increase in the number of Downing undergraduates whilst he was Tutor and the fact that whilst he was Bursar no fox was shot on the College estates.'[120] His career ended sadly in 1901, when 'he shot himself, perhaps because he was afraid of approaching blindness'.[121]

Queens'

It is not surprising that Downing was (in spite of Perkins' efforts) one of the smallest colleges; but it is strange to find Queens' smaller still – in 1880 recording only 45 undergraduates.[122] In 1851 J. N. Peill had reported to the Royal Commission that 'Our college staff of lecturers is sufficiently complete' for all purposes 'excepting some provisions of the new triposes; hitherto we have not had any student reading a subject beyond the usual subjects for the BA degree, and so soon as the necessity arises we shall provide ourselves with efficient lecturers in the newly introduced subjects.' In 1877 the old president, George Phillips, was singing the same song, as an excuse for not contributing to the cost of new university professorships. 'Every college is able to provide adequate instruction for its pupils, not only in the old subjects of

---

[118] Fifoot 1965, no. 345, p. 269.   [119] Fisher 1910, p. 68.
[120] French 1978, p. 131.   [121] Ibid. p. 131.
[122] Either the figure was exaggeratedly low or there was a sudden upturn in the early 1880s. Twigg 1987, p. 234, cites evidence for 84 in 1883, 100 in 1900 (98 in 1900–1 in *CUC*, p. 944), 212 in 1913.

study . . . but also in the new.' 'Peill and Phillips were probably bluffing to a large extent,' comments Twigg[123] – and the Cambridge reformers of the 1870s took a very different view from theirs. We may suppose that Queens' had remained narrow in its teaching and old-fashioned in its ways. Yet W. M. Campion, a moderate reformer and a reasonably enlightened man, had been tutor for many years. From the late 1870s there was a group of young fellows growing up in the college who were to transform it rapidly in the next thirty years. The central figure was Arthur Wright, who became assistant tutor in 1878, and worked in the closest amity with Campion, who was increasingly prepared to leave the college in his hands or to follow Wright's initiatives.[124] It was Wright who proposed the 'New System' of college fees, which simplified charges and helped to ensure that rooms were properly furnished and cared for. This was in 1883; and in 1886 a new building was opened to enable more of the growing numbers to enjoy rooms in college.[125] By such means, by receiving a better press in the students' guides of the period and above all by the rapid expansion – not of the fellowship, for Queens' had always enjoyed a large fellowship – but in those with a vocation to teach, Queens' rapidly became more attractive and its student body passed from being the smallest to one of the largest in Cambridge within thirty years.[126] The outward and visible sign of its growth at that date is the new chapel of 1888–91; characteristically, it provides for greatly increased numbers in a college with a strongly marked religious emphasis, and the idea for it was conceived on a walk by Wright and Campion.[127]

The middle ground

Emmanuel

If we turn now to the colleges occupying the middle ground – fluctuating between 100 and 230 undergraduates – as well as Jesus and Caius, we may contemplate Emmanuel, Christ's, Trinity Hall, Clare and Pembroke. Emmanuel had been founded, like

---

[123] Twigg 1987, p. 293.   [124] See esp. Twigg 1987, pp. 227–8 on Wright.
[125] Twigg 1987, pp. 233–6.   [126] Full details in Twigg 1987, chaps. 16–21.
[127] Twigg 1987, pp. 277–8; below, pp. 110–11.

Sidney, as a seminary of protestant clergy in the late sixteenth century, and had flourished exceedingly in the seventeenth. After some marked fluctuations it had recovered by the 1870s to be reasonably prosperous and exceptionally forward-looking. The master from 1871 to 1895 was Samuel Phear, who had been a fellow from 1853 and whose career might suggest he was an old-fashioned clerical don; equally so might that of A. T. Chapman, who lived in college as a bachelor fellow from 1862 till his death in 1913, and is held in remembrance for 'Chapman's garden' to this day. But it is evident that both of them were fervent supporters of reforming causes in the 1870s; and Phear was a man of scientific as well as religious interests who had been a member of the Syndicate which led to the formation of the Cavendish Laboratory.[128]

In 1861 a new college statute had permitted the election of one married fellow; but no action was taken on it until 1872 when Fenton Hort was elected and made lecturer in theology. Over the next twenty years the college established teaching, and found distinguished teachers, in some scientific subjects as well as in classics, mathematics and theology. It embarked on an imaginative scheme for union with Christ's which would have greatly strengthened the teaching resources of both colleges – however destructive in other ways it must seem to us now.[129] The election of Hort not only brought to Emmanuel one of the outstanding characters in its history, and the best documented fellow of the nineteenth century;[130] it also laid out the path which Emmanuel was to follow: in an age of increasing diversity the college none the less lived up to its vocation as the home of future clergy. Its theological teaching became and remained exceptionally distinguished; and when Phear and others were seeking means to serve the university in the 1870s, it seems to

[128] See p. 173. On Chapman see Stubbings 1984–5; on Phear, Venn, *Alumni*, Part II, v, 104; *Cambridge Review*, 14 Feb. 1919, pp. 211–12 (P(eter) G(iles)); Winstanley 1947, pp. 229–30, 278–9, 288, 294–5. He is an obscure figure: he unfortunately died in 1918 when the *Emmanuel College Magazine* was in limbo owing to the war, and there is no obituary notice of him there. Venn recorded that Perowne had referred to his retirement as 'a most immoral proceeding', but one suspects that this simply reflects Perowne's own refusal to retire.
[129] See Emmanuel Coll. Archives COL. 18.15C, pp. 30, 34, 36, 70, 72, 80ff; 19.10a–f; etc.
[130] Above, pp. 9–13, and esp. Hort 1896 – his son's fine memoir, a goldmine of information about the Cambridge of his age, though there is relatively little about the inner life of Emmanuel itself.

have been Hort who suggested that it should establish a chair of ecclesiastical history. With alacrity and zeal the college set up the Dixie Professorship, to which Emmanuel contributed from the endowment given by Sir Wolstan Dixie in the reign of Elizabeth I, and in 1884 Mandell Creighton was elected first holder, bringing from Oxford – and a country parish – an added lustre to the Cambridge historians.[131]

Christ's

In Emmanuel we can discern the influence of a group of enlightened men bringing the college gently into the new world of the late nineteenth century, but arousing doubts and anxieties when they planned a merger with Christ's.[132] In the present state of knowledge Christ's must be represented for us by John Peile, a remarkable man who combined the love of the old and the new to a quite exceptional extent. He was the central figure in Christ's in the negotiation for a merger which would have hidden his own college under a strange name, even though he himself might have been its master; yet he also stands with John Venn as a supreme devotee of college history, author of histories of Christ's large and small.[133] Like Roberts of Caius he was a classical scholar, oarsman, much loved tutor, and leader in liberal causes. But Peile was the larger man; and although he was very closely identified with Christ's in his time his monument lies elsewhere, in Peile Hall in Newnham: he was one of Henry Sidgwick's first allies in the foundation of Newnham and the cause of women in Cambridge; and at the end of his life his many services to both were recognised by Mrs Sidgwick and the Council of Newnham in the naming of the hall.[134]

Christ's and St John's were founded in the early sixteenth century by the Yorkshireman, John Fisher, under the patronage of Lady Margaret Beaufort, countess of Richmond, and they retained their north country links. John Peile was born in 1837, appropriately enough for the sound of his name, in Cumbria; and

[131] See pp. 140, 231–2; Whitney 1919, p. 10.   [132] See pp. 86–7.
[133] Peile 1910, 1900.
[134] For all this, see *Christ's College Magazine* 1910, pp. 143–57.

when he came to Christ's 'both the Master, Dr Cartmell, and the Tutor, Mr Gunson, were from Cumberland'.[135] John Seeley, future Regius Professor of Modern History, and W. W. Skeat, were contemporaries. With Skeat, the foremost English philologist of his day, Peile's links were very close.[136] Peile 'studied comparative philology at Göttingen ... and was largely instrumental in introducing the subject at Cambridge'. In his day he represented for classical philology and etymology what Skeat so preeminently offered for English studies; and both were among the earliest fellows of the British Academy.[137] As the years passed, Peile's energies – great though they were – came increasingly to be diverted into college and university business. He was a kindly, genial, entertaining man; but a firm leader withal. As stroke of the first college boat, he had already shown his mettle. 'The stroke rowed with quick and untiring firmness, and the men behind him recognised that they were expected to stick to their work. He appreciated thoroughness in others, and set the example himself.'[138] These were the qualities which he was to show as tutor and as master; these and a genial sympathy. 'The poll-man [a student for the general degree, not for honours], as well as the brilliant scholar, knew that John Peile, as we always affectionately called him, was ever ready to help him with counsel, sympathy and encouragement.'[139] These sympathies were not narrowly conceived. Under his mastership were forged the links with the Catholic community and especially with Downside; the first Benet House lay within the precincts of the college.[140] 'His Sanskrit studies led to his interest in the education of our Indian fellow-subjects, whom Christ's was the first College to welcome as students.'[141] He was close to Henry Sidgwick and Henry Jackson, and felt the new wind of inspiration to college teaching and tutorial care coming out of Trinity. 'The whole tone of his mind and character was liberal, with a liberalism based on an exceptional knowledge of and reverence for the past.' He was also

[135] Ibid. p. 143.
[136] See Skeat's appreciation of Peile, ibid. pp. 149–53. On Skeat see K. Sisam in *DNB 1912–1921*, pp. 495–6 and refs.
[137] Cf. ibid. pp. 147–8. Skeat was a founder-fellow, Peile was among the first elected after the foundation.
[138] Ibid. p. 150.   [139] Ibid. p. 154.   [140] See p. 391.
[141] *Christ's College Magazine*, 1910, p. 147.

'a staunch churchman of a liberal type' who 'rarely missed a chapel service'. 'A progressive in University politics, he played a leading part with his friends Dr Henry Sidgwick and Dr Henry Jackson in framing the new Cambridge in which we live. The widening of College and University teaching, the encouragement of the newer studies and the promotion of research were among the movements that he helped to forward.'[142] As a long-standing member of the Council of the Senate, and as Vice-Chancellor from 1891–3, 'he was wise, tolerant, appreciative', but also a firm guiding hand.[143] It is the outlook of men of his stamp which helps to explain how the spread of college teaching came so quickly in the late nineteenth century, and why – for all his readiness to consider a merger with Emmanuel – he was also a devout student of the traditions of Christ's. The lesser colleges are as necessary as the greater for an understanding of the history of modern Cambridge.

Trinity Hall

Emmanuel and Christ's sought to harness the old world and the new – to bring diversity and strength in other fields while restoring the tradition of the college as the home of notable divines. In a rather different way the least clerical of all the colleges, Trinity Hall, was also entering the modern world. The Hall was founded in 1350 to foster the study of canon and civil (that is, Roman) law; and in the mid and late sixteenth century, in spite of the notional condemnation of the study of canon law by Henry VIII, it was still a home of civil and church lawyers.[144] By a curious twist of fate it became the rule that advocates in Doctors' Commons in the city of London – which was the Inn of the church lawyers and a unique centre for the courts of church and admiralty (strange bedfellows), and closely linked with Trinity Hall – should always be laymen; and this seems to have encouraged the fellows of Trinity Hall to avoid ordination. In the eighteenth century over 30 per cent of the fellows were advocates

---

[142] Ibid. pp. 144–5.   [143] Ibid. p. 145.
[144] Crawley 1976, esp. p. 57; for what follows, Squibb 1977; for canon law after the Reformation, Helmholz 1990.

in Doctors' Commons, and a far greater proportion (so it seems, for the records are imperfect) non-resident. The two clerical fellows kept the chapel and, for the most part, cared for the small community of undergraduates.[145] In the early nineteenth century, as Charles Crawley observes, 'breezes of change were beginning to blow, gently'; the number of undergraduates increased.[146] In 1848, the year of revolutions, Henry Latham came from Trinity as tutor; from 1856 he was senior tutor, and by the time he was promoted master in 1888 the undergraduate numbers had grown 'from under 40 to nearly 180'.[147] The college kept its legal fame: Henry Maine, an assistant tutor in the 1840s, returned to be master from 1877 to 1888. But neither he nor his predecessor as master, T. C. Geldart, 'in whom "the courtesy of a country gentleman, the frankness of a sportsman and the education of a scholar were agreeably combined"',[148] gave the college its character. Latham was evidently a supremely successful tutor, and he was ably complemented by the two most celebrated fellows of the mid-nineteenth century, Leslie Stephen and Henry Fawcett. Stephen was a fellow from 1854 to 1868 and during part of the time a very popular tutor, a pioneer among the eminent Cambridge men who scaled the Alps, and an exceedingly active rowing coach.[149] From this time forward the Hall was as famous in the schools for rowing as for law. But Stephen lost his faith and felt constrained to resign first his tutorship and then his fellowship. His closest friend, Henry Fawcett, fellow from 1856, remained. Fawcett had the terrible misfortune of losing his sight in a shooting accident in 1858; but his strength of purpose was such that he remained an active and sociable fellow, a successful academic – he was elected first professor of political economy in 1863 – and in the end a thriving politician. He was Postmaster General in the Liberal ministry of 1880–4, and patron of the first parcel post. But in academic politics he was neither liberal nor given to innovation. Even though he and Stephen had been allies in forcing the senior fellows to accept a substantial mitigation of

---

[145] Crawley 1976, p. 79. [146] Ibid. p. 143.
[147] Crawley 1976, pp. 152–4.
[148] Crawley 1976, p. 147, quoting H. E. Malden.
[149] Crawley 1976, pp. 158–60; on Stephen see also pp. 121–2.

the laws of celibacy in 1860,[150] he defended the old-fashioned prize fellowships based on the Mathematical Tripos, not on learning or research or for potential teaching, and he resisted the movement to tax the colleges in support of the university.[151] None the less he gave valuable support, as Stephen had done, to the work of Henry Latham, and the college became in due course larger and more diverse: one of the most active and successful of the houses of medium size in the last quarter of the nineteenth century.

Clare

No college, perhaps, has a history more obscure in the late nineteenth century than Clare.[152] When the story is told it seems likely that it will prove to be a striking example of the mingling of continuity and change. In the mid-nineteenth century the Reverend Edward Atkinson had revived its fortunes and was duly elected master in 1856. He lived until 1915, to be succeeded by W. L. Mollison, the senior tutor, and he by G. H. A. Wilson, formerly bursar; then Henry Thirkill, senior tutor, was master until 1958. Atkinson was a conscientious, hard-working master according to his lights, 'who lived to see an old order replaced by a new', but continued to portray 'the old traditions of aloofness and Olympian dignity so long associated with the Head of a House'.[153] The seventeenth-century fellows had provided Clare with some of the most beautiful stone buildings in Cambridge, and in contrast to Pembroke the Victorian age left them untouched. When new building came in the 1920s it lay beyond the Backs, leaving one of the loveliest Cambridge gardens similarly intact.

In 1870 there were 16 fellows and 70 undergraduates; in 1880 the figures were 18 and 123. By 1900-1 the undergraduates had

---

[150] Stephen 1885, pp. 108–10; cf. Brooke, Highfield and Swaan 1988, p. 272; Crawley 1976, pp. 160–1.

[151] Crawley 1976, p. 162.

[152] The article in *VCH Cambs* scarcely reaches the late nineteenth century, nor does the volume in the Robinson series. The two stately volumes celebrating the centenary of 1926, *Clare College 1326–1926* (1928), are rich in material on earlier history and are helpful on the history of sport in this period, but have little to say on recent academic history.

[153] *Clare College 1326–1926*, I, 198.

risen to 183, while the fellowship had been slimmed down to 15.[154] The student body had grown; it had acquired a modest presence in the tripos lists and a more distinguished role in the playing fields and the river.[155] The fellowship had declined in numbers but was rapidly growing in academic reputation. By 1900–1 there were two FRSs, Thomas McKenny Hughes, one of the creative figures in the School of Geology,[156] and Walter Gardiner, botanist and, in later years, a noted eccentric. Gardiner celebrated Queen Alexandra's birthday every year by delivering 'a choice bouquet of flowers from the University Botanic Gardens' at Buckingham Palace; he is also probably one of the creators of the Clare Fellows' Garden; he was certainly a distinguished figure in the School of Botany.[157] The humanities were represented by a small group of classics; more notably by James Rendel Harris, university lecturer in palaeography, and Hector Munro Chadwick, then junior fellow, later professor of Anglo-Saxon. Chadwick was to become one of the great Cambridge polymaths, making notable contributions to Anglo-Saxon studies based on a deep knowledge of historical texts, philology, anthropology and archaeology. He led his own disciples into arch and anth, though he was himself to be one of the architects of the English Tripos, and is perhaps most widely remembered as the co-author, with his wife, Nora Kershaw Chadwick, of a vast encyclopedic study in comparative literature, *The Growth of Literature*.[158] Clearly much was astir in Clare in 1900; but it is not till the 1920s, in the present state of knowledge, that it comes into the light of day, in the golden age of Manny Forbes, English don, the kindly host of Finella, the house on Queen's Road which he adorned with spectacular decorations of the 1920s, and Henry Thirkill, physicist and tutor – the quintessential tutor of the 1920s.[159]

[154] See pp. 593–4.
[155] For tripos lists see Tanner 1917; for the playing fields, *Clare College 1326–1926*, II, 603–31.
[156] See p. 159; for the fellowship in 1900–1, *CUC* 1900–1, pp. 686–7.
[157] Godwin 1985, pp. 58–9.
[158] Chadwick 1932–40; see pp. 444–6.
[159] On Forbes, see Carey 1984; on Thirkill, below p. 262.

Fig. 2 Waterhouse in Pembroke College: the library, 1875 with a corner of the chapel

Pembroke

The story of Pembroke is revealed to an exceptional degree by its buildings. At the northern end a medieval nucleus is encased in Victorian dress; at the southern, a red and yellow block proclaims the presence of Alfred Waterhouse. Between stands Wren's enchanting chapel, enclosed and beleaguered. In 1870 John Power was elected master, a man who believed in progress. The master brought back C. E. Searle to be senior tutor and the college community grew and flourished under Searle's guidance. The college was ripe for revival. 'In 1858, there was but one freshman, and he went off to Caius.'[160] By 1870 there were 44 undergraduates, by 1880 122.[161] The master looked with envious eyes on the new buildings of Caius and Jesus and summoned Waterhouse to prepare a plan for Pembroke. Waterhouse was a man of high imagination, but ruthless in his treatment of more modest predecessors.[162] The tiny fourteenth-century court was almost intact when he arrived; when he had gone only a fragment of it survived. A new master's lodge to the north-east, a new residential block to the south replaced some of it; and a grander hall grew up out of the foundations of the old. It is amazing to us that a college of modest resources could contemplate such an expensive scheme, and it is said that one major motive was the fear that a future generation – perhaps they feared the next Royal Commission – would carry off the handsome building fund already accumulated to support the university.[163] Meanwhile a fervent protest by a number of the alumni of the college failed to impress the master, whose faith in Waterhouse remained unshaken. It was the ambition of Waterhouse to add an apse to the chapel – as he was allowed to do, most incongruously, at Caius – and to build a campanile 'high enough to be the most conspicuous tower in Cambridge'.[164] At last the fellows rebelled, and Waterhouse was prevented from any assault on Wren's exquisite chapel. In 1878 George Gilbert Scott, the discreet and intelligent son of the celebrated architect of St John's chapel, was called on to enlarge the chapel, a task he performed with notable sympathy. He also completed the work of enlarging and remodelling the original buildings.[165]

---

[160] *VCH Cambs*, III, 351.   [161] See p. 593.
[162] Pevsner 1970, pp. 127–8.
[163] For all this *VCH Cambs*, III, 352. The article was the joint work of Sir Ellis Minns and John Roach.
[164] Quoted ibid.; see also Willis and Clark 1886/1988, I, 152–3.
[165] Pevsner 1970, pp. 127–8.

By such means a tiny group of ancient buildings was converted into a Victorian college. Pembroke is perhaps the most striking monument to the growth of the smaller colleges in the late nineteenth century. It had 44 undergraduates in 1870, 122 by 1880, 226 by 1900–1.[166] This spectacular expansion was made possible, in part at least, by the ambitious designs of Power and Waterhouse. The buildings prepared the way, but did not guarantee this growth. Something may be attributed to Pembroke's standing in the academic world, of which Sir George Stokes, 'almost the last of the great Newtonian physicists', was the chief embodiment.[167] But more credit belongs to C. E. Searle, tutor under Power, and master from 1880 to 1902, who gathered round him a cadre of teachers of classics and a range of other disciplines, 'producing not so much distinguished men as sound evangelical clergymen and various servants of the state especially in the Indian Civil Service'.[168]

The giants

St John's

There remain the two giants, Trinity and St John's. In the eighteenth century St John's had sometimes led Trinity both in numbers and distinction. Such movements for reform as the eighteenth century gave birth to tended to impinge on St John's.[169] In the nineteenth century their roles were reversed. Leadership in the reform of college teaching and in academic distinction came to be concentrated in Trinity. In 1870 St John's had 54 fellows and (after a rise in the 1860s) 361 undergraduates; Trinity had 56 fellows and 548 undergraduates. By 1900 the distance was much greater: Trinity had 75 and 676, St John's 44 and 237.[170] St John's was one of the colleges which had suffered most from the agricultural depression – or thought it had, at least, for it had a large fellowship and an expensive establishment to maintain. But so had Trinity; and it is not clear why this should affect undergraduate recruitment. It is true that St John's was not able to

---

[166] See pp. 593–4.   [167] *VCH Cambs*, III, 351.
[168] *VCH Cambs*, III, 352.   [169] Miller 1961, pp. 66–9.
[170] *CUC* 1870, pp. 388–9, 420–2, 532; *CUC* 1900–1, pp. 809–11, 851–3, 944.

sustain all its plans for wider teaching, and that the scholarship funds were for a time severely restricted.[171] But there was increased diversity of support and a growing variety of subjects studied. Mathematics and classics retained their supremacy and the large majority of students still avoided honours and either took no degree or were content to be 'poll men'.[172]

Yet there is a paradox in this, for St John's was presided over from 1857 to 1881 by the leading university reformer of the day, W. H. Bateson. It is clear that Bateson had a rough ride, anyway in his early days. In both St John's and Trinity all authority was concentrated in the hands of the master and eight seniors, and the eight were described by a younger colleague at St John's as 'a narrow minded and bigoted clique'.[173] The new statutes of 1860 were radical in many respects, especially in clearing up the confusion of ancient endowments, and opening the way for electing professors and university lecturers as fellows. But the rest of the fellowship still had to be celibate clergy until the second reform of 1882, completed just after Bateson's death, which cleared away these restrictions too. Evidently the fellowship was much divided about its future role, and although there were scholars of distinction to support Bateson in his efforts, there was nothing like the galaxy of young fellows in Trinity at this time. It was said of the years around 1870 that they were 'the golden age of Johnian classics', but Edward Miller comments that 'if so, the gold came chiefly from a single mine: from Shrewsbury, the

[171] Miller 1961, p. 98, gives: £6,700 in 1880, £3,900 in 1896, £4,700 in 1910.
[172] Miller 1961, p. 87; for a slightly later period, ibid. p. 99 gives the following distribution of scholars and exhibitioners:

	1886–7	1909–10
Mathematics	30	21
Classics	12	24
Hebrew	0	1
Natural Sciences	12	19
Theology	2	3
Law	0	1
History	0	3
Modern Languages	0	5
Economics	0	2

[173] Miller 1961, p. 85.

school which produced Heitland, Henry Wace (like Heitland senior classic, but also a rugby "blue" and a soccer international) and T. E. Page', later editor of the Loeb classics.[174] It seems that the vital links with the northern grammar schools, which had been the strength of St John's recruitment in earlier days, and were to be so again, had for the time faltered somewhat, though the story is not fully known. Meanwhile in the third quarter of the century Bateson himself, ably supported by G. D. Liveing, pioneer of Cambridge chemistry, J. E. B. Mayor, professor of Latin, for a time University Librarian and a noted eccentric, and another distinguished classic, H. J. Roby, had struggled through many years to bring the college into the modern world.[175] Bateson was the central figure in schemes for university reform, starting as Secretary of the first Royal Commission in 1850–2; later as a leader in the agitation to abolish religious tests; finally as the elder statesman in the plans and achievements of the 1870s.[176]

Trinity

Throughout our period Trinity has been the undisputed giant, enlarging its lead in the number of fellows over King's and St John's – 53 at King's, 54 at St John's, 56 at Trinity in 1870; 46, 44 and 75 in 1900;[177] and compassing a third of the student population of Cambridge in 1870, 548 out of 2,019, and still a quarter in 1900, 676 out of 2,985.[178] Not only so, but its academic distinction made it a university within the university. In the old subjects, it was the home of eminent mathematicians from Arthur Cayley to G. H. Hardy and beyond; in classics, of Verrall and Jebb and Housman;[179] in theology, it was the college of Lightfoot and Hort – though Hort was later to be a principal ornament of Emmanuel;[180] in the new subjects, an array of Cavendish Professors of Physics, Clerk Maxwell, Lord Rayleigh,

[174] Miller 1961, p. 87.
[175] Miller 1961, esp. p. 84; on Mayor, see McKitterick 1986, esp. chap. 16.
[176] Miller 1961, p. 83; Winstanley 1947, pp. 70–1, 81–2, 289–91.
[177] *CUC* 1870, pp. 349–50, 389, 420–2; 1900–1, pp. 751–2, 809–11, 851–3.
[178] *CUC* 1870, p. 532; *CUC* 1900–1, p. 944.
[179] See pp. 211–16, 483–6.   [180] See pp. 9–13, 134–40.

J. J. Thomson and Rutherford, were fellows of Trinity, as was the founder of the new School of Physiology, Michael Foster.[181] Later on, Trinity was to rescue the creative genius of Cambridge biochemistry, Gowland Hopkins, when he had suffered a collapse in 1910.[182] Some of these impinged little on undergraduates, some much; but they all played their role in Trinity. There was space in that large society for much else – for conservative clergy like H. R. Luard,[183] for numerous gentlemen commoners, some of them, perhaps, reading men, many of them layabouts; and for all sorts and conditions of men. But the special place of Trinity in the history of the university was marked by a group of reformers of the 1860s and 70s, determined to make it an effective teaching college once again. In early days the central figure in this group was Henry Sidgwick. When he felt compelled to resign his fellowship in 1869 owing to religious scruples and doubts he could no longer play an active part in the deliberations of the fellows.[184] But he was rapidly appointed a college lecturer; his role in Trinity was only slightly diminished, and his influence was in some ways enhanced. For it seems likely that friendship with Sidgwick played an important part in convincing Lightfoot and other clerical fellows that the religious tests must be abandoned, that the church and clergy must find their own place in a university and college in which different opinions mingled.[185] Perhaps the most energetic of all the younger fellows over the 60s and 70s were Henry Jackson and Coutts Trotter. Trotter was the archetypal university reformer, a member of almost every syndicate, a notable pioneer in scientific education, a tireless deviser of schemes, of infinite ingenuity in finding paths through the jungle of university law and statute; immortalised above all in his modest proposal in 1877 to rescue badly needed funds by abolishing the heads of houses.[186] Henry Jackson was a fellow from 1864, and an assistant tutor from 1866 – one of the first appointments made by W. H. Thompson when he succeeded Whewell as master.[187] Thompson was a reserved man best

---

[181] See pp. 164–5, 180–91.   [182] See pp. 195–9.   [183] See pp. 4–8.
[184] See pp. 16, 100.   [185] See p. 100.
[186] See Winstanley 1947, p. 348; Clark 1900, pp. 314–18.
[187] On Jackson see Parry 1926, esp. pp. 24–6.

known for his devastating sarcasms – 'we are none of us infallible, not even the youngest';[188] and he was overshadowed by the ferocious grandeur of Whewell, his predecessor, and the ebullient if sometimes ludicrous charm of his successor, Montagu Butler.[189] But behind his rather forbidding exterior he was a humane man who quietly gave his support to the reformers while not losing the respect of the more conservative seniors with whom he had to rule the college.[190] In 1875, when he knew Jackson was wanting to get married, and marriage was still incompatible with a fellowship of Trinity, he appointed him praelector in ancient philosophy, a teaching post which enabled him to give what were in effect university lectures on Plato and Aristotle, and to marry while retaining his fellowship.[191] Jackson's biographer, R. St John Parry, thus describes the consequences of this appointment:

> In cooperation with Henry Sidgwick, Richard Jebb and 'Pat' Currey, he extended to all classical students the provision of individual teaching in translation and composition, which had hitherto been provided only for the fourth year men who were shortly taking their Tripos. It was in appearance a small reform: but in fact it was the first and decisive step in a fundamental change in the ideal of the position and duties of a College Lecturer, not in Classics only but in all branches of study. Hitherto the formal lecture had been regarded as his sole duty: individual teaching had been left to the private coaches.[192]

The real difficulty, as Parry goes on to emphasise, was to convince the candidates that the college lecturers could compete with the coaches in winning them a high place in the tripos; and this was not finally achieved until the 'order of merit' and the 'fetish of the Senior Wrangler' were abolished in 1910.[193] But the quality of the teaching in Trinity, and the warmth of Jackson's personality, in the end won over undergraduates and

[188] Thomson 1936, p. 273.
[189] On Whewell, see esp. Clark 1900, pp. 1–76; on Butler, *DNB 1912–1921*, pp. 78–80; on Thompson, Thomson 1936, pp. 267–73; Winstanley 1947, pp. 241–62.
[190] Winstanley 1947, p. 255 and n. 2 quoting Jackson in Parry 1926, pp. 294–5.
[191] Parry 1926, p. 25. Many years later his son, H. A. Jackson, used to recall in his classroom at Winchester while reminiscing on his father's Cambridge, the kindness Thompson had shown.
[192] Parry 1926, p. 25.   [193] Parry 1926, p. 26.

colleagues alike. Trinity was a very large society, and all was not peace and happiness in it, then or later; at the very end of his life Jackson himself was to play a divisive part in the unhappy affair of Bertrand Russell's lectureship.[194] But by his inspiration and dedication to teaching, and by his central role in the social life of the college, he showed that a married layman could be as dedicated a tutor and scholar as any of his clerical predecessors.

> His rooms in Nevile's Court were a centre of unceasing hospitality. The oak was never sported except when he was out. His habit of sitting up very late made him accessible at all hours of the evening and far on into the early hours of the morning, and there were few evenings throughout those more than thirty years when he was alone. It was his regular practice to give a general invitation to the table in the Combination Room to adjourn to his rooms to smoke: and at the larger parties and feasts he would walk round the tables inviting the hosts to bring their guests ... On the Commemoration Day in December ... the College [entertains many guests including scholars, prizemen and other junior members,] and from very early days in the tenure of his fellowship Jackson made a practice of inviting all to his smoking party after the dinner in hall.

He had to use two large lecture rooms in Great Court for the purpose. 'Here Jackson, a cigar box in hand, met his guests, old and young, and by midnight the cloud of smoke and the din of talk culminated.' Speeches and songs followed, 'and the new day was well advanced before the last card players had finished their games and Jackson returned to his rooms'.[195] Jackson was a considerable scholar, but his habit of life left little time for writing; none the less his fame as a critic and teacher, and a sheaf of articles on Plato, won him a fellowship of the British Academy and the Regius Chair of Greek; and the adoration of his pupils, who included royalty, won him the O.M. In his last years the Trinity fellowship included both Jackson, the Regius Professor of Greek, and Housman, the professor of Latin.[196] A greater contrast could hardly be imagined between the unsociable, austere, difficult, brilliant, immortal Latin scholar,

[194] See pp. 339–40.   [195] Parry 1926, pp. 32–3.   [196] On Housman, see pp. 211–16.

and the outgoing, ebullient, universal friend who won at last the chair of Greek. Of such contrasts was the society of Trinity composed.

EPILOGUE: COLLEGE FINANCE

In earlier centuries the colleges' benefactors had given their largesse for a variety of commonly quite specific purposes: for fellowships, scholarships, chaplaincies, to support the college lights, the college porters, the hall fire, for occasional feasts or 'exceedings'; and if the benefaction was large, a special feast might be ordained after the audit. To the Perse Feast in Caius come the Vice-Chancellor and the Esquire Bedells, and they receive, in accordance with the will of Stephen Perse, a small fee for their pains as well as their dinner. It is clear, however, that there was a time when they failed lamentably to perform their role, for the intentions of Stephen Perse were less than perfectly fulfilled in the eighteenth and early nineteenth centuries.[197]

Perse had died in 1615, leaving the master and four senior fellows of Caius as his trustees; and he left £5,000 in their care, from which they were to draw an income of £250 a year in perpetuity, and to distribute it among numerous charities – with various college purposes and the Perse School the most lavishly supported. Time passed, and inflation put into the hands of the trustees ever larger sums of money, while the real value of £250 fell in proportion. Since they were fellows of a college and accustomed to the normal arrangements of college finance, they assumed that the surplus was for their benefit; and the junior Perse fellows, and the headmaster and second master of the school, suffered accordingly. In the 1830s some enraged citizens of Cambridge who wished the school to prosper took the trustees to court, and won their case. A distribution more in accordance with Perse's intentions was enforced; and in the 1860s and 70s, in an era of more radical reform, a portion of the Perse estate was taken away from the college to form a separate trust. The endowments of colleges were frequently tied up in formulas which made no allowance for inflation, and had often to be

---

[197] Brooke 1985, pp. 98–103; for what follows see Brooke 1985, pp. 201–3.

interpreted by later generations – who commonly placed upon them the gloss most favourable to their interests. Sometimes the whole process seems to us reprehensible; but the outcome in one vital respect was entirely commendable. It was in the interests of masters, bursars and fellows to keep their colleges' endowments in good health, and on the whole their record is not a bad one. The reformers of the 1860s and 70s took the investment of the Perse trust right out of the hands of the Caius seniors and placed it with the Official Trustee of Charitable Funds, who invested it so cautiously it is now worth, in real terms, a small fraction of the noble sum Perse himself bequeathed.

In one sense the task of the colleges in managing their endowments was straightforward. Down to the agricultural depression of the 1870s it was taken for granted that the bulk of their endowments should be invested in land – and not until the 1950s were most of them even permitted to invest in industrial shares. Already by 1600 the colleges had devised a bizarre variety of methods of payment to the masters, bursars, tutors and fellows. Over the centuries which followed some variety survived; but the colleges shared a common task and often imitated one another, so that a common pattern is visible. It has been most fully revealed in E. J. Gross' *Chronicle of the College Estates* for Caius (1912), and H. F. Howard's lucid *An Account of the Finances of the College of St John the Evangelist* (1935) for St John's.[198] Rapid inflation in the late sixteenth and early seventeenth centuries led to a whole series of additional payments to the fellows, and especially the bursar, of St John's, to save them from penury and ensure that they had a share in the prosperity of their manors. Privileged fellows also farmed some of the estates themselves, enjoying such profit as they could make. Meanwhile a special attempt had been made to beat inflation by the Corn Rent Act of 1576, which insisted that a third of any corn rents due to Oxford and Cambridge colleges came in kind. This was distributed unequally to the master and senior officers, and the rest equally to the fellows, and thus the principle of a dividend was established.[199] In due course it was reckoned more equitable and more

[198] Venn IV, pt. 2; Howard 1935.
[199] Howard 1935, chap. 3, esp. pp. 32–40; Gross in Venn IV, pt. 2, pp. iii–x; Brooke 1985, pp. 102–3. On the act of 1576, see now Collinson, McKitterick and Leedham-Green 1991, p. 19.

conducive to the peace of the house for other surplus revenues to be distributed as dividends. The old payments based on the wills of founders and benefactors were covered by fixed rents which rarely altered; the additional value of the estates was garnered through ever more princely entry fines at the expiry of leases, which were fixed (from the seventeenth century) at reasonable intervals. These fines came to be distributed to the fellows and to form the core of the dividends, and similar practices spread throughout the colleges. The consequence was that even rich colleges like St John's, or moderately rich colleges like Caius, had no reserve funds, no regular income from which, for example, new buildings could be funded. Instead they often supported very large numbers of absentee fellows, or accumulated balances in funds which no one knew how to use.

It had been one of the tasks of the first Royal Commission of the 1850s to clear up a good deal of the lumber of college statutes and financial arrangements.[200] But the Commissioners were prudent men and – though some were ardent for reform – many heads and fellows were extremely reluctant to countenance change, so that much of the old world survived. It is fascinating to observe the way in which the colleges first overcame the impediments their financial systems put in their path, then accepted a measure of reform – and gradually embarked on very radical reforms which converted them in the end into efficient twentieth-century business enterprises, though their opportunities for speculation are still quite closely circumscribed by law. But through all these changes the central notion of the fellow's dividend long survived, though now a shadow of what it had been; and the accounts follow a pattern devised by the Statutory Commissioners of the 1920s, fully as complex as the colleges' ancient accounts, intended to convince the fellows that the old ways had not entirely departed, while hiding from them their opportunities to profit from the new.[201]

The most obvious weakness of the old systems was that they made no allowance for reserve funds or building funds. Both St John's and Caius engaged in major building enterprises in the nineteenth century before any substantial revision of the account-

---

[200] Winstanley 1940, chaps. 11–15.   [201] See pp. 359–60.

ing process had taken place. St John's used special funds, appeals to old members, and borrowing from the more buoyant of the college funds intended for other purposes.[202] Both in the 1820s and in the 1870s – in the wake of the New Court and of the new chapel – a rich college loaded itself with debt which took many years to clear, partly because agricultural depressions came in the wake of both campaigns. The fellows of Caius built a new hall in the 1850s, and a large new residential block, the Waterhouse building in Tree Court, in the late 1860s.[203] They had been plotting to build since the 1820s and the Perse scandal had taught them that it was unwise to convert tied funds to other ends. So the generous practice of masters and fellows giving lavishly towards the building fund was established, and this laid a foundation which made the adventures of the 1850s and 1860s possible, when supplemented by generous giving by alumni and some revision of the accounting system in the 1860s.[204] But the basic logic was clear: all the college's disposable surplus went to the fellows in dividends, and so it was reasonable to ask the fellows to return some of it when building was needed.

But building was not the only function ill-provided for. In former centuries the majority of the fellows had been tutors, and the tutors had taught their younger colleagues and the undergraduates. This system had withered away long before 1800, far more in Cambridge than in Oxford where a tutor was still a teacher and remains so to this day. By the 1870s the more enlightened colleges in Cambridge were strenuously seeking to ape their Oxford rivals and revive the colleges' teaching function; they sought to absorb or outbid the free-lance coaches who had filled the gap. There were indeed some college lecturers – men with specific teaching appointments within a college – and in one or two colleges, most notably in Trinity, they had kept, and could readily revive, a teaching function.[205] But the college lecturers in other colleges tended to be paid sixteenth-century salaries and to be perfunctory in their lecturing in proportion. The colleges, one after another, revived college teaching and

[202] Howard 1935, p. 212.   [203] Brooke 1985, pp. 215–17.
[204] Cf. Brooke 1985, pp. 208–9, 214.   [205] See esp. pp. 71–2.

created the modern supervision system. Since the surplus revenues of the college went (after ample payment to the college's administrative officers) in equal shares to the fellows, most of whom had no discernible duties to perform, teaching had to be rewarded in some other way. This is not entirely fair, since the junior fellows were increasingly expected to engage in learning and research, and a period of up to six years free from teaching duties was an essential preliminary for many of them to the life of the new-style don. The reforms of the 1860s, 70s and 80s had converted the old clerical fellow, who was put out to grass in a country living when he married, into the lifelong teaching fellow who might marry and rear a family without resigning his fellowship or giving up his teaching.[206] It seems that the dividend was still in 1870 a reasonable wage for a bachelor enjoying free meals in college; but from the late 1870s, as the estates became less profitable, the dividend tended in most colleges to decline; in Downing no dividend at all was paid for three years in the 1890s.[207] It was not, and was not regarded as, a reward for teaching, or an ample stipend to support a growing family. So teaching fellows had to be paid out of fees. Even university lectures were funded in the main by fees from those attending; and as late as the early 1920s, a busy college lecturer giving major courses for the university might have a precarious living as he received a fluctuating income dependent on the university courses assigned to him. But college and university teaching from the 1870s, and university teaching from the 1920s, could not be paid for out of college endowments. The former was made possible by much increased college fees; the latter by government grants supplementing income from fees.[208] The consequence of rising fees was that it became increasingly difficult for impoverished undergraduates to support themselves, and this is part of the reason for the notorious fact that the rapid increase in student numbers in the late nineteenth and early twentieth centuries was fed from the relatively well-to-do families who had sent their sons to public schools.[209] In former centuries boys of modest

---

[206] See pp. 7ff.
[207] Dunbabin 1975, p. 641. This will be more fully dealt with in Peter Searby's vol. III, chap. 3.
[208] See pp. 352–4.   [209] But see pp. 245–52.

means could earn their keep by service to fellow commoners, to fellows or to the college. There was nothing demeaning in such service, any more than in its twin, fagging in public schools.

> Who sweeps a room, as for thy laws
> Makes that and th'action fine

sang George Herbert in the early seventeenth century.[210] His main experience of life had been in Cambridge: he originally wrote 'chamber' for 'room' and very likely had the college chamber in mind. But in the eighteenth and nineteenth centuries snobbery prevailed: the sizar, the servant, was thought of as a social inferior; and in the nineteenth century he was extinguished, and his work done by professional servants. The lot of the poor scholar became harder in the process. It was always a major preoccupation of enlightened tutors to ease the financial burdens on poor students and to improve the scholarship funds available to them – and this was one of the principal motives for the rearrangement of college accounts in the 1920s.[211]

There has been a lively debate in recent years as to how deeply the colleges were affected by the agricultural depression of the 1880s, and how much this affected the efforts of reformers and commissioners to encourage the colleges to support the university and rebuild its faculties. No one doubts that the colleges were hard hit: they were deeply involved in the fortunes of their estates. 'The college is a landlord; a steady-going, careful, impoverished landlord, vitally interested in wheat and barley, in roots and artificial grasses, in pigsties and farm-buildings, and all the paraphernalia of rural life.' Thus H. A. L. Fisher in 1896, in a passage which John Dunbabin has taken as a text for his study of college finances between 1871 and the Great War.[212] Some colleges suffered more than others. In Oxford, Merton, Magdalen, Brasenose and St John's were able to develop urban properties and enjoy handsome and improving rents; and St John's in particular flourished on the profits of developing north Oxford. In Cambridge the old east field, the Barnwell field, had been enclosed in the opening years of the nineteenth century, and a

---

[210] Cf. Brooke, Highfield and Swaan 1988, pp. 169–70.
[211] See pp. 358–62.
[212] Quoted in Dunbabin 1975, p. 631. For the debate see Dunbabin 1975; Engel 1976; Dunbabin 1976.

group of colleges had properties well placed for urban development – Bateman Street tells of a Trinity Hall development of the 1860s, and a swathe in south-east Cambridge from Harvey Road to Willis Road not only commemorates the worthies of Caius but its enterprise in the 1880s in developing urban houses both large and small to check the effects of agricultural depression.[213] At the same epoch prosperous dons with private means could build houses in west and south Cambridge; the more modest prosperity more widely spread that followed the reforms of the 1920s is reflected in St John's developments in the west – Wilberforce and Clarkson Roads for instance, whose names commemorate the centenary of the slaves' emancipation, fostered by St John's men, in 1933[214] – and Trinity's in the south, Bentley, Newton, Barrow, Porson and Rutherford Roads. In both Oxford and Cambridge it is difficult to determine whether the developments of the 1880s were inspired more by the need to replace falling agricultural rents, or by the happy chance that the two towns were ripe for development in these regions at that time. Indeed it is clear that they were cooperant factors. What is much more obscure is whether the efforts of the University Commissioners of the 1870s to stir the colleges to put their revenues at the disposal of the universities were seriously hindered by the depression. There can be no doubt that the depression was a heaven-sent excuse to heads and fellows who wished to see their colleges drag their feet. It evidently helped to frustrate some enlightened schemes. But over the years from 1880 to 1914 there was in fact substantial support from colleges in both universities – partly by means of a compulsory tax, partly by the expression of good will and cooperation – to fund university projects.[215]

Thus it has been alleged that the great reluctance of some colleges to support professors was due to poverty. But the dispute whether professors were needed at all was not new; and many a don in Oxford – and Cambridge too – must have been delighted to read the outburst from the young Hensley Henson, recently departed from All Souls, in 1889:

[213] See Crawley 1976, pp. 221, 226; Brooke 1985, p. 252.
[214] See pp. 283–5.　[215] See pp. 86–9; Dunbabin 1975.

It is not unnatural that in times of severe agricultural depression,
... academic economists should regard with suspicion ... the
secure and comfortable stipends of the professors and readers ...
nor is it surprising that ... busy college tutors and lecturers should
chafe against the existence of well-paid professors, whose lectures
nobody attends, and whose researches nobody cares about ...[216]

Henson was jumping on a bandwaggon: the professors had always
been drones, and the workers now had a golden excuse to drive
them from the hives. But, in truth, although the teaching fellows
of Oxford and Cambridge colleges have never ceased to regard
professors as drones, they have tolerated their presence with a
remarkably good grace.

By the same token attempts have been made to argue that
Oxford was slow to develop science because the resources were
lacking at the crucial moment. But precisely at the same moment
science in Cambridge, where resources were equally depleted,
was entering its first golden age. The difference is striking, though
often exaggerated: if Oxford lacked Nobel laureates in physics, it
was soon to find them in physiology.[217] But there was a marked
difference sure enough, and the causes go further back and lie
deeper: the teaching cadre formed by the Oxford tutors was a
much more effective academic force than Cambridge could
muster in the last quarter of the nineteenth century, and partly for
this reason was stronger to preserve the old world. Both
universities acquired new museums at about the same time. But
in Cambridge the paths towards the future were laid by a galaxy
of Cavendish Professors in particular, led by Clerk Maxwell,
Lord Rayleigh and J. J. Thomson.[218] In Oxford from 1865 to
1915 R. B. Clifton was professor of experimental philosophy,
which meant physics if it meant anything, and 'held up the
development of physics at Oxford for fifty years'.[219] But he was a
man of merit compared with his opposite number among the
chemists, William Odling, who 'considered it beneath the dignity
of a professor to appear in a laboratory' or to soil his hands with
experiments or research;[220] not that his laboratory, which had

---

[216] Henson 1889, p. 318, quoted in Engel 1976, p. 444.
[217] Especially Sir Charles Sherrington (on whom Cohen 1958 is a good introduction).
[218] See pp. 180–5.   [219] Brooke, Highfield and Swaan 1988, p. 309.
[220] Ibid.

been modelled with loving care on the abbot's kitchen at Glastonbury, was a natural habitat for research. The marvel is that Oxford was able to catch Cambridge up in so many fields in the twentieth century.

I have presented a desperately simplified version of college finance, but the final word must be of its complexity. Through all the many changes of this period we can follow that thread: the men who made and administered college accounts in the 1920s, as in the 1870s, loved its intricacies and bye-ways, which their successors in the 1990s find absurd.[221] But our purposes are different.

---

[221] See pp. 359–63.

Chapter 3

THE SECOND ROYAL COMMISSION AND UNIVERSITY REFORM, 1872–1914

THE ROYAL COMMISSION AND THE STATUTORY COMMISSION

In January 1872 Gladstone launched the second Royal Commission on Oxford and Cambridge 'to inquire into the property and income belonging to, administered, or enjoyed by the Universities of Oxford and Cambridge, and the colleges and halls therein . . .'[1] At first sight it seems narrowly conceived: only finance was involved. But as finance touches most of the sensitive points in ancient corporations and as it was followed by Statutory Commissions appointed to rewrite all the statutes of the universities and colleges, there was nothing superficial about its plans and achievements. The story of these two Commissions reveals with remarkable clarity how powerful were both the radical and the conservative voices in Cambridge. They formed two divergent poles; but between them every shade of opinion was held, and the division between the passion for tradition and for reform often came within a single mind.

The rub of the matter was that university and colleges were struggling to revive their teaching functions, and new subjects for teaching and research were crying for attention, each more expensive than the one before. In 1913 John Venn, president of Caius, looked back to his experience as an undergraduate in the 1850s. 'The elder Mr Weller . . . rather prided himself on the educational advantages which he had conferred upon his . . . son; he had . . . let him run about the streets and pick up information for himself. The College authorities of my day adopted a

[1] *Parliamentary Papers* 37 (= *Reports from Commissioners*, 20, 1873–4), i, p. 5; Winstanley 1947, p. 264.

somewhat similar plan.'[2] There were college lectures, but of a perfunctory character; the hard reading man, ambitious to score high marks in the tripos, sought his own private coach. Venn paid for the services of William Hopkins and Isaac Todhunter, who represented an older and a younger generation, without whose help few reached a high level in the order of merit.[3] There had always been some who thought it was the duty of college tutors to arrange teaching; and voices were raised, especially in Trinity, suggesting that the colleges should not only arrange it but pay for it out of the fees undergraduates provided.[4] This was a revolutionary doctrine attempting to recreate a distant past, in this case the Cambridge of the early seventeenth century – or, nearer at hand, of Oxford and Oriel of the 1830s, of Balliol of the mid and late nineteenth century.[5] Most fellows of most colleges were dedicated to other pursuits; many were not resident in Cambridge. The colleges' resources were generally harvested to give the fellows the maximum available dividend; but the dividends were not providing teaching. There were many opinions; but a number of would-be reformers wished to see the example of Trinity spread around Cambridge, that is to say, serious college teaching, with supervision at its heart, replacing the work of the old coaches – and wished to see it as part of the normal life of every college.

To provide adequately for mathematics and classics would have stretched the resources of some colleges severely enough. But the air was full of new triposes: moral sciences, natural sciences, theology and history – or of old triposes come to life, like medicine and law.[6] The real conservatives, like Robert Phelps, the master of Sidney, and E. H. Perowne, the master of Corpus, saw such schemes as the damnable intrusion of modern secular civilisation, tending to the destruction of all that was most precious in Cambridge. Perowne, in particular, had a vision of Corpus as a tiny community of dedicated clergy and ordinands,

---

2 Venn 1913, p. 262.
3 Brooke 1985, pp. 219–20; cf. Winstanley 1940, pp. 411–12.
4 See p. 71.
5 Brooke, Highfield and Swaan 1988, pp. 272–5, 285–6; Jones 1988, chap. 15.
6 For the old triposes, mathematics (1748) and classics (1824), and for moral sciences (1851) and natural sciences (1851), see Peter Searby, forthcoming, in vol. III of this History; for law (1858), theology (1874), history (1875), see Tanner 1917, pp. 812, 854, 895; medical science only achieved independence of natural sciences in 1974–5.

devoted to the evangelical cause.[7] From this point of view, the reformers' plans must be beyond the resources of the college, and tend to its destruction.

To the radicals it seemed a scandal that Cambridge should have such resources of talent and money, such a tradition of academic leadership, and yet be in many respects an academic backwater. They saw London and the new civic universities growing up to challenge the unique standing of the ancient foundations; and they heard voices from Germany and elsewhere describing what true scholarship, what genuine academic communities, could be. They were particularly hard hit by the example of Oxford, in which college teaching had never entirely died, and where it was being revived in a way peculiarly threatening to the waning reputation of Cambridge.

In Oxford, the brilliant study of A. J. Engel has shown that there were three parties, considerably overlapping one another.[8] There were those who thought the function of the university was to teach, the party of the tutors, many of whom wished to keep Oxford a mainly humanist university, and to foster and preserve the remarkable tradition of college teaching, enjoying a lively renaissance in the mid and late nineteenth century in the first heyday of the Oxford tutorial. In Cambridge each college rarely had more than one or two tutors and their function was administrative and pastoral; they also lectured, but could not cope with serious individual teaching; by contrast the Oxford tutors were more numerous and they organised the whole of undergraduate life, especially the teaching function. Opposed to the tutors was the less numerous, but often very eloquent, group who thought that the university's main function was to foster learning and (as the century wore on) research; who looked to Germany for their model and saw there universities run by the most learned men, the professors, and sighed for a similar recognition for learning in Oxford. The tutorial view has been traditionally associated with Benjamin Jowett, the tutor and master of Balliol under whose magic wand a college of modest resources but growing fame enjoyed for two generations the

---

[7] See pp. 49–52.
[8] For what follows, see Engel 1983, esp. pp. 45–9, 77–81, 122–55.

undisputed hegemony of Oxford.[9] The professorial case has been associated with the rector of Lincoln, Mark Pattison, a notable figure whose less amiable features were cruelly caricatured by his friend George Eliot in Dr Casaubon in *Middlemarch*.[10] Those who have studied Jowett and Pattison most deeply have very reasonably observed that Jowett was more of a scholar and Pattison more interested in teaching than this caricature suggests; and the Cambridge theologians regarded Jowett the scholar with considerable respect – the references to him in Hort's letters seem to portray him very reasonably as a careless giant.[11] Meanwhile in Cambridge J. B. Lightfoot displayed many of Pattison's characteristic views: he was deeply sympathetic with college ideals, and a resident fellow of Trinity for over twenty-five years. As a tutor he had many pupils, as a professor few, and he complained bitterly of the change. His marvellous evocation of the future University of Liverpool – when he joined in the movement to promote higher education in his own native city in 1879 – strikingly anticipates the German, professorial model which came to rule in the civic universities.[12] There was also in Oxford a third party, whose spokesman or pamphleteer was the Reverend Charles Dodgson, otherwise Lewis Carroll, dedicated to defending the privileges of the Anglican communion and of the clergy.[13] This too had many echoes in Cambridge. But it is noticeable that many of the natural leaders of the clergy in Cambridge followed the lead of men like Bateson and Lightfoot in accepting conversion to the abolition of tests even before 1871. The Cambridge Commissioners of the 1870s, of whom Lightfoot was one, firmly rejected the view that any Cambridge head of house should have by statute to be an Anglican clergyman.[14] They accepted, however, and fostered the notion that there should still be a small number of clerical fellows and some ties between divinity chairs and the established church. If Ely

[9] See above, n. 5.
[10] A case has often been made against the identification, but some of Casaubon's characteristics and his name, which was the title of Pattison's best known early writing, must always have reminded readers with any knowledge of Oxford of Pattison. On Pattison see Green 1957, 1979.
[11] See esp. Hort 1896, I, 313, 315, 322, 326, etc.
[12] Winstanley 1947, p. 184; Kelly 1981, pp. 45–6; see pp. 24–5.
[13] Engel 1983, pp. 120–1, 150.
[14] Winstanley 1947, pp. 356–7. They made an exception for St Catharine's, whose master had a canonry of Norwich annexed to his office.

cathedral had been a few miles nearer Cambridge it is very likely that (as at Oxford) closer ties would have been preserved over a longer period. As it was, the canonry of Ely hitherto attached to the professorship of Greek was transferred to the new Ely chair of divinity and the Regius Professor of Divinity (by a special act of parliament, not by the work of the Commissioners) was divested of the rectory and the tithes of Somersham, whose souls the conscientious Professor Westcott felt he could not cure.[15] Meanwhile in Oxford the dean of Christ Church and the canon professors retained their dual role.

The question was urgent: how could the university or the colleges provide teaching in physics, chemistry or physiology? A variety of answers was forthcoming. First of all a few colleges built or devised laboratories for their students.[16] But they were obvious makeshifts; and a new hope dawned when the Chancellor, the duke of Devonshire, provided the money needed to build the Cavendish Laboratory in 1870, and the university scraped round to pay the professor.[17] These demarches made clear – what was obvious enough to reformers contemplating the humanities – that colleges must combine their resources of men and money if real progress was to be made. The idea which was doubtless most horrifying to conservative minds was that colleges should be merged. To this end the Oxford and Cambridge Act of 1877 empowered the Statutory Commissioners to set in motion such mergers if they saw fit. It is hardly surprising that nothing came of the idea; but it had an active life for at least thirty years. An attempt to unite King's and St Catharine's foundered in 1880.[18] In February 1878 William Chawner – senior tutor and later to be master – raised in the governing body of Emmanuel the question how a union of Emmanuel and Christ's could be accomplished. It must have been well canvassed before the meeting, since the fellows, though far from united, set seriously to work on a scheme; and a joint committee of the two colleges drew up heads of proposals. It must have had the support of Phear, the master of Emmanuel, a leading reformer, since he

---

[15] Winstanley 1947, pp. 329–31.
[16] For St John's, Miller 1961, pp. 84–5, etc.; for Downing, French 1978, p. 132; Caius (1871: Brooke 1985, pp. 232, 253).
[17] See p. 174.   [18] See pp. 44–5.

seems to have agreed that the first master of the joint college should be the master of Christ's; but the moving spirits in Emmanuel appear to have been Chawner and two theologians, the older of them the Hebrew scholar, A. T. Chapman, and the younger the New Testament scholar Fenton Hort. We know less of the involvement of Christ's in this adventure, but the central figure is likely to have been the future master John Peile. The scheme rapidly foundered – James Cartmell, master of Christ's, was its chief opponent; but Chawner and Peile were sufficiently interested in it to stage a revival in about 1890, which once again failed, as we know from a moving letter from Peile to Chawner of June 1893, expressing his appreciation that he had been thought of as a possible master of the joint college. It is very likely that there were other schemes not yet unearthed; and the idea remained active in men's minds, to be revived in 1906–7.[19] Chawner and his allies in Emmanuel were prepared to embark on a plan which might have ended in the virtual disappearance of their college. It was even suggested that the united college might have an entirely new name, 'St Andrew's College', though 'the New College of Christ's and Emmanuel' was slightly preferred. Between such notions and the view of Phelps and Perowne that their primary duty was to preserve their colleges, in accord with their founders' intentions, free from the contamination of modern liberal reforms, a great gulf was fixed. One hardly dares contemplate what they must have thought of the notion that their own office, of heads of house, was grandiose, costly and redundant, and that much useful money might be saved by abolishing it.[20]

If the university was to command larger resources, it must seek outside help or depend on the colleges. Although the timely aid of the duke of Devonshire was particularly welcome, it was generally assumed that the first and only major step which could be taken was to tax the colleges: government aid still lay far in the

---

[19] This is based on notes in Emmanuel College Archives, COL.18.15C, 19.10a–f, very kindly communicated to me by Dr Frank Stubbings. For Cartmell see Peile 1910–13, II, 437. For 1906–7, see below, p. 96.

[20] Winstanley 1947, p. 348, cited Coutts Trotter's pamphlet to this effect; but he was not alone in looking in this region for valuable economies. Their purpose has been fulfilled in ironic fashion in recent times by the common practice of colleges electing as heads professors, who are paid by the university, often saving the colleges substantial sums.

future. The difficulty was that most colleges were poor; that their incomes were declining; and that all had most of their available funds tied to non-teaching fellowships. The Commissioners were not hard-faced revolutionaries from outer space; they included leading academics like William Bateson, master of St John's.[21] But they recognised that fairly radical measures were required to give the university the resources it needed; hence the invitation to colleges to merge – to which in the event none succumbed. Income was declining because of the agricultural depression of the 1870s and 80s: this was a misfortune which the Commissioners could not check, and which was only finally reversed when the colleges took to investing extensively in equities, and supporting themselves on other sources of income than rents, in the mid-twentieth century.[22] Meanwhile it was a golden excuse for the colleges to grumble and resist taxation. Although the Commissioners pursued other measures, the heart and core of their plan was to reform the existing system of fellowships and ensure that college dividends were diverted from fellows' pockets to university tax. It was bound to be a painful process. The university, wrote Henry Sidgwick, 'has for years been struggling and starving in the most pitiable manner, unable to provide decently for the most indispensable functions; while what are commonly talked and thought of as "her rich endowments" have been distributed among thriving schoolmasters, school inspectors, rising journalists, barristers full of briefs, and barristers who never look for briefs.'[23] The point was that down to the reforms of the 1850s most fellowships were for life, the only conditions being celibacy and (for many) the taking of orders. The new statutes of the late 1850s and early 60s had restricted many fellowships to periods of ten years or so, and some had lifted or mitigated the rule of celibacy.[24] But no serious attempt had been made to end non-residence or tie fellowships to research or teaching or administrative work for the college. The Statutory Commissioners set their faces to limit normal tenure to six years, but encouraged the union of fellowships to college offices not confined to six years;

---

[21] *Parliamentary Papers* 37, i, 5–6.   [22] See esp. Dunbabin 1975.
[23] Quoted Winstanley 1947, p. 266.
[24] See Brooke 1985, pp. 223–7, esp. 224 n.1.

and also, by ending the rule of celibacy and the insistence on orders, to make teaching fellowships more attractive to a wider variety of men with no vocation to the Church, and with a variety of belief or disbelief, seeking to make a lifelong profession of university teaching.

In other words, the reforms were harnessed to a changing view of the academic profession, which we have already explored in Hort and Sidgwick.[25] Once men of this calibre were established in chairs – and once the Cavendish and the Physiology Department were growing in size and fame – professional scientists multiplied.[26] But there was still ample space in Cambridge, and especially in the humanities, for the teacher, the man of broad culture, and the dilettante. We have met them in King's and Magdalene: Oscar Browning, for all his preposterous egotism and his flabby approach to scholarship, yet contributed much to the teaching of history in Cambridge and to the tradition of professional teaching combined with amateur learning.[27] In M. R. James the mixture was curiously different; he was a man of culture as broad as the O.B.'s, though he lacked the panache of the O.B.'s teaching; but he was also a scholar – careless, unequal, even lazy in his methods; yet extraordinarily penetrating too. In James the amateur and the professional mingled in the 'antiquary', and it was in that sense that he called his best known book *Ghost Stories of an Antiquary*.[28] A. C. Benson had nothing of the scholar about him; yet he brought to Magdalene a broad view of the teacher's craft, and found and helped to advance in Cambridge a civilised attitude to conversation and a broad culture, in which professional specialism was put in its place.[29] Yet even Benson found a place in his scheme for scholarship: one of his closest friends was the American Gaillard Lapsley of Trinity,[30] a medievalist who fired many of his pupils with a sense of the interest and value of medieval constitutional history, while inspiring those to whom the subject was alien with a notion that it was a branch of theoretical history akin to quantum physics.

[25] See pp. 9–19.   [26] See chap. 6.
[27] See above, pp. 36–7 and below, pp. 464–6.
[28] See Pfaff 1980.   [29] See pp. 47–9.
[30] Newsome 1980, index s. n. Lapsley.

THE ADULLAMITES

When F. M. Cornford analysed 'the parties in academic politics' in chapter 2 of *Microcosmographia Academica* in 1908, he listed five: 'Conservative Liberals, Liberal Conservatives, Non-placets [i.e. those who opposed all reforming graces in the Senate], Adullamites, and Young Men in a Hurry'.

> The *Adullamites* are dangerous, because they know what they want; and that is, all the money there is going. They inhabit a series of caves near Downing Street. They say to one another, 'If you will scratch my back, I will scratch yours; and if you won't, I will scratch your face.' It will be seen that these cave-dwellers are not refined, like classical men. That is why they succeed in getting all the money there is going.

If we contemplate today the tumble of buildings in the New Museums Site of the later nineteenth century and the first decade of the twentieth, and the first large group in the Downing Site of the period 1900–14, we can see dramatically revealed the achievements of the Adullamites, and the reason they sought 'all the money there is going'.

There have been three high periods in university building since about 1870: the first mounted steadily from 1870 to 1914, but reached its peak in the Edwardian era. The second reflected the great endowments from Rockefeller and other benefactors in the 1920s, and the first inflow of government funds, and culminated in the University Library, completed in 1934. The third came as part of the national building explosion of the 1960s. In some ways the first is the most remarkable, since it came at a time when resources were exceedingly limited, and without government aid. We may lament the character of much of the building that was done, but we cannot withhold admiration from the persistence, energy and skill in fund-raising of the builders. A mere catalogue gives an impression of the achievement: on the New Museums Site, the Salvin buildings of the 1860s; then the old Cavendish in three campaigns, 1870–4, 1896 and 1908; then the old chemical lab of 1886–8, the old engineering lab (now physical chemistry) of 1893–4; also the School of Medicine, now zoology; and finally the Examination School and the Arts School of 1909–10. South of Downing Street lies the Downing Site acquired from Downing

College in the opening years of the century: here between 1904 and 1914 grew up the Law School (long since departed to the Old Schools, and now on its travels again) and the Museum of Arch and Anth; and beside it the Sedgwick Museum and the geology labs. Behind these, botany and the former Department of Agriculture; and beyond botany, physiology and old pharmacology. It is the astonishing achievement of a generation confident that the natural and medical sciences held the future in the palms of their hands – and ready to allow a little space to law, which had a special endowment, to the arts in general, and, rather belatedly, to the supreme monument of Victorian educational beliefs, the Examination School. The sciences and law will have their separate histories explored in chapters 6 and 7; but separate treatment tends to obscure the massive growth dramatically revealed by the buildings. They housed museums, especially of geology and ethnology; they housed libraries, especially the Squire Law Library; they housed labs beyond counting. But they also housed professors and lecturers; the university was beginning, on a shoestring, to acquire academic staff in many disciplines.

CAVENDISH COLLEGE AND SELWYN COLLEGE

A major preoccupation of the late nineteenth and early twentieth centuries was to provide higher education – every kind of education indeed – at more reasonable cost than was currently available. Winchester and New College and their like had been founded for the poor or moderately poor in the fourteenth century; the inflation of five centuries had made them havens of the well-to-do and the moderately rich. Before 1870 there had been a great movement for the foundation of primary schools in which the clergy had been especially involved: there was a close link between clergy of all denominations and the schools of the nineteenth century, which only declined as secularisation set in at the turn of the century.[31] After 1870, the state provided what private enterprise had not accomplished; but it was not till after 1900 that the state played an effective role in secondary education; and however true it may be that secondary schools,

---

[31] See pp. 246–7.

especially boarding schools, tended to serve the offspring of the well-to-do, the most strenuous efforts were made to prevent them becoming only accessible to the rich. Though some clergy were comfortably off, most were relatively poor; and scholarships were provided and schools founded to educate their sons at reasonable prices.[32] Nor did the founders of schools think only of the clergy: they often sought to widen the entry to all of modest means. It is probably true to say that this commonly meant the 'middle classes' in the late nineteenth century; and that it was only at the turn of the century that many voices were raised saying that Oxford and Cambridge colleges, founded for the poor, should be open to those from every kind of home.

Practical steps were taken in Oxford and Cambridge by opening their gates to non-collegiate students[33] and by the founding of Cavendish and Selwyn Colleges. The story of Cavendish is a tragi-comedy, in some ways a sort of parody of the collegiate scene of the 1870s and 1880s. It was founded by a Dickensian character named Joseph Brereton, a devoted disciple of Thomas Arnold who wanted to see the extension of middle-class education in all directions: his adventures have been delightfully brought to life by Peter Searby.[34] He founded boys' schools; he founded girls' schools; he plotted the founding of county colleges, intended to provide for those who could not profit from – or could not afford – a full university education. When one scheme was precariously afloat, without waiting to collect the money it needed he set off on another. His projects were grandiose; his debts enormous. But he was an entrepreneur with an extraordinary talent for persuasion. His noblest venture, a college in Cambridge, won support not only from his habitual friends but from major figures of the Cambridge establishment, including the duke of Devonshire himself, in whose honour it was named – not Arnold College as Brereton had wished but – Cavendish.[35] It was founded at a difficult time: the agricultural depression was beginning to hurt the pockets of some of those who might have supported his ventures, and many of the older colleges were preparing for rapid expansion, and so to plunder his

[32] See pp. 246–7. [33] See Grave 1983. [34] Searby 1982–3.
[35] Searby 1982–3, p. 113.

markets. It was visibly a poor relation from the start. The rooms were cold and austere – a special narrow bed was patented to fit the specially small rooms[36] – its site remote from the main centres of the university beyond the Hills Road railway bridge. Brereton made estimates based on a student population of 300, but he built rooms for only 100, and recruitment faltered. Searby has shown by careful analysis that Brereton's aim of opening Cambridge to a new type of recruit was not fulfilled. Unfortunately, the origin of less than half the Cavendish boys is known; but of these not much more than a quarter came from other than public schools, while in the same period 38 per cent in Christ's, 40 per cent in Peterhouse, were thus recruited.[37] By 1892 it was hopelessly bankrupt and closed its doors. None the less, 358 students had matriculated in the university from Cavendish College; and its buildings were taken over in 1894 to form the nucleus of a much more successful venture, Homerton College.[38]

Bishop G. A. Selwyn was the brother of Professor William Selwyn, founder of the Divinity School, and one of the remarkable characters of the Victorian church, bishop successively of New Zealand – where he 'helped to create not only the Church in, but the Dominion of New Zealand' – and Lichfield.[39] He died in 1878, and his suffragan in both his sees, C. J. Abraham, led a campaign to raise a monument to him in the shape of a college in Cambridge. Evidently Keble College at Oxford, which opened in 1870, was the model, for it was to be founded on principles of economy and simple living; that was its heart and essence – 'an ordinary college, not a theological college; a college to educate everyone, not simply a college to educate future clergymen'.[40] Like Keble, it was inspired by Anglican devotion and aimed not only to instil simple living, but 'the Christian character'. In practice this meant, as Arthur Lyttelton, the first master (Glad-

---

[36] Searby 1982–3, p. 117.
[37] Searby 1982–3, p. 114: this comprised 11 per cent of the total intake at Cavendish, but the origin of 57.5 per cent is not known. If the 11 per cent form a representative sample, there were still less than 30 per cent from other than public schools, including those privately educated or from abroad.
[38] Searby 1982–3, pp. 114, 117, 119; see pp. 464, 576.
[39] Chadwick 1973, p. 1.
[40] Abraham, as cited by Chadwick 1973, p. 2; for Keble, cf. Brooke, HIghfield and Swaan 1988, pp. 290–3.

Fig. 3 Selwyn College, court and chapel, 1880–95, designed by Sir Arthur
Blomfield

stone's brother-in-law), announced, that only Anglicans would
normally be admitted; and although this was not formally
enshrined in the original charter, the college was limited to
Anglicans by the statutes of 1913, and remained so till the late
1950s, when Selwyn changed its statutes, abandoned its Anglican
chains, and became a full college of the university,[41] under the
leadership of one of its most eminent Anglican masters, Professor
Owen Chadwick.[42]

In 1879 the founders bought six acres from Corpus, and from
1880 set Blomfield to work to build a college – by slow paces,
since funds were short and times were hard. In 1882 the college
opened, and in 1883 was accepted by the university, like

[41] Chadwick 1973, pp. 22, 26.
[42] It was still the case in the 1950s that a Selwyn student converted to Roman Catholicism had to
be discreetly deemed a non-collegiate student, however benevolent an eye the tutors might cast
on him.

Cavendish, as a public hostel where students of the university might live.[43] A succession of 'young, and often brilliant scholars' ready to work for the college 'in return for a microscopic stipend' helped it survive while Cavendish foundered.[44] It suffered from many disadvantages: it had no hall until 1907–9;[45] it seemed cut off from other colleges; its staff were not called fellows, nor did they govern the college, so that it was not easy to keep pace with change and movement in Cambridge at large – impossible for some to avoid feeling they were poor relations; and it was easily mistaken for a seminary. Yet in early days its separate character was far from being wholly detrimental. It attracted good and earnest young men, and in the 1880s and 90s sent forth a remarkable number of Christian missionaries.[46] Yet as time passed the subtle alchemy of the Cambridge colleges – all eager to preserve their separate characters while constantly imitating one another – took its toll. The hall was built; the court came to resemble a Victorian version of a traditional college. From 1913 there were fellows, and most affairs were managed by the master and fellows, even though the old external council did not finally disappear till 1957.[47] The third master, A. F. Kirkpatrick (1898–1907), was a very notable scholar, and research was given a place in the statutes of 1913. In the 1960s the college received a new court from Sir Humphrey Cripps – one of three which commemorate his generosity in Queens', St John's and Selwyn; and university and colleges crept westwards so that Selwyn was no longer set apart.[48]

THE DEBATES OF 1907–14

In 1906 a Royal Commission discussed the future of Trinity College, Dublin, of which Henry Jackson was a member. To Jackson himself – now growing old and no longer the young Turk of the 1880s, though still fervent and vigorous – the moral of it

[43] Chadwick 1973, p. 3; Searby 1982–3, p. 113; *Reporter* 1882–3, pp. 85–9, 157, 213, 215.
[44] Chadwick 1973, p. 7.
[45] Chadwick 1973, pp. 13–14. The delay had happy consequences, for it is a fine hall, richly adorned with panelling of *c.* 1700 possibly designed by Wren, presented by A. C. Benson. Chadwick 1973, pp. 14–15.
[46] Chadwick 1973, p. 8.   [47] Chadwick 1973, pp. 13–14, 19–20.
[48] Chadwick 1973, pp. 20, 26.

seemed to be that reforms must be planned within a university.[49] To others (we may conjecture) it gave fresh hope that a new Commission might solve some of the problems of the old universities in England. In 1907 a group of Oxford friends encouraged Charles Gore, bishop of Birmingham and formerly fellow of Trinity College, Oxford, to raise up his voice in the House of Lords for the cause of university reform. In a famous speech he voiced some of the anxieties of the day: the university sector was still less well provided than the colleges; and, in particular, the great foundations of Oxford and Cambridge were closed, by virtue of their high fees, to folk from humble homes in Birmingham and elsewhere. He called for a Royal Commission, and his cry was heard with mingled hope and fear in both the ancient universities.[50] But the prime minister, H. H. Asquith, played for time. Meanwhile in the same year, in Cambridge and Magdalene, A. C. Benson sent on its way one of his most popular books, *From a College Window*.

> My college is one of the smallest in the University. Last night in Hall I sate next a distinguished man, who is, moreover, very accessible and pleasant. He unfolded to me his desires for the University. He would like to amalgamate all the small colleges into groups, so as to have about half a dozen colleges in all. He said, and evidently thought, that little colleges are woefully circumscribed and petty places; that most of the better men go to the two or three leading colleges, while the little establishments are like small backwaters out of the main stream. They elect, he said, their own men to Fellowships; they resist improvements; much money is wasted in management, and the whole thing is minute and feeble. I am afraid it is true in a way; but on the other hand, I think that a large college has its defects too. [He argues that smaller colleges care more for the less privileged and less able] . . . The only cure, said my friend, for these smaller places is to throw their Fellowships open, and try to get public-spirited and liberal-minded Dons. Then, he added, they ought to specialise in some one branch of University teaching, so that the men who belonged to a particular department would tend to go there.[51]

Benson's 'friend' reflected the widespread dissatisfaction of

[49] Parry 1926, p. 91.
[50] Cf. interesting comments by Henry Jackson in Parry 1926, pp. 86–91.
[51] Benson 1907, pp. 6–7.

university reformers in the years before the war, when informal committees of considerable weight were formed in 1904 and 1908 and 1911, plotting the refurbishment of the university.[52] In 1906 the master of Downing had proposed the conversion of his college into a society of postgraduates with its finances run by the university; and when this was rejected by his governing body, he resigned. Subsequently an urgent, reasoned plea came from the Special Board for Economics and Politics for a revision of the financial arrangements between university and colleges.[53] In 1910 specific proposals were made for a House of Residents – a governing body of resident MAs similar to the Regent House of 1926 – and other changes. The discussion reveals many anxieties, especially that proposals for change would stimulate parliament to intervene: Bishop Gore had spread terror among the more timid or suspicious or conservative minds. The proposal for a House of Residents was rejected by 340 votes to 241.[54] In 1913 a modest proposal was made to apply to the government – to the Board of Education – for a grant to support medical education, as it was supported in other universities. This provoked a massive discussion, in which J. J. Thomson, the Cavendish Professor, was a leader among the opponents; he made a powerful plea for freedom from government control. In this he followed the Disney Professor, Ridgeway, always a prophet of doom: 'Oxford had got into the snare and been inveigled. Let them take warning . . .'[55] He seemed to think the university almost as much under threat of parliamentary or government intervention as from the entry of women. In 1913–14 his warning was not heeded; but the debate provokes now a wry smile – and has indeed been quoted in the Senate House in the 1980s when the doom he prophesied struck.[56] On 14 March 1914 a cartoon appeared in the *Cambridge Magazine* of a scarecrow bearing the message 'Beware the Ides of March . . . Government Inspection and Control', with Sir Clifford Allbutt, Regius Professor of Physic, haranguing it thus: 'My good man, you will find bank-

52 CUA Comm. B.7; Oxford Bodleian Library MS Asquith 139, fos. 213–14. For the crisis in Downing, see p. 55.
53 Bodleian Library MS Asquith 139, fo. 214.
54 *Reporter* 1910–11, pp. 106–10, 236–44, 321.
55 *Reporter* 1913–14, pp. 209–10. On Ridgeway see pp. 204, 375–6.
56 A. W. F. Edwards in *Reporter* 1988–9, pp. 192–3.

ruptcy much more alarming.'[57] On that day the Senate voted by 267 votes to 235 to ask for the grant.[58] Thus the way was paved for the much more extensive proposals for state aid of the 1920s.[59] Soon all these schemes were to be shelved, for a time, during the war of 1914–18.

Meanwhile, in 1906 F. W. Maitland had died, and his brother-in-law H. A. L. Fisher, fellow of New College, Oxford, prepared in sorrow a fine memoir of him.[60] In 1912 Fisher was elected Vice-Chancellor of Sheffield; in 1916 an MP and a minister, president of the Board of Education; and in that role he was to launch the Education Act of 1918 and the birth of state scholarships, which paved the way for a successful answer to Gore's complaint – and the summoning back of the aging Asquith from retirement to preside over the Royal Commission on the Universities of Oxford and Cambridge from 1919 to 1922.[61]

[57] Ibid.   [58] *Reporter* 1913–14, p. 753.
[59] See below, chap. 11.   [60] Fisher 1910.
[61] *DNB 1931–1940*, pp. 275–8 (Gilbert Murray); below, chap. 11.

Chapter 4

RELIGION 1870–1914

In 1856 among the provisions of the Cambridge University Bill it was enacted that no religious test, no declaration of faith, need be attached to any degree save in divinity; but it expressly added that membership of the Senate, the governing body of the university from whose ranks all its officers were drawn, was restricted to masters and doctors 'who had declared themselves to be *bona fide* members of the Church of England'.[1] In the fifteen years which followed, one of the fiercest battles in the history of the university was fought over the remaining tests – it was fought in Cambridge, it was fought in Oxford, it was fought in parliament; and in all three places there were those who thought that the abolition of the tests would prove a mortal blow to the religious life and vocation of the universities; and there were others who thought the exact opposite – and many no doubt who fluctuated in between. Charles Longley, archbishop of Canterbury,

> recalled the far off ... days when he had been a Tutor of an Oxford college, and referred affectionately to his pleasant memories of the society of the Common Room, where 'with the eight or twelve others [a rather modest picture of Christ Church], who were engaged in the same work, he had ever held friendly council with men whose common object was to instil with their teaching the truest principles of religion and morality.'

If the new bill was passed, the Common Room would 'be occupied by "eight or twelve men of all religious denominations"

[1] Winstanley 1947, pp. 37–8; for what follows, see Winstanley 1947, chap. 3.

or of none; and consequently cease to be a temple of harmony'.[2] One cannot help suspecting that the archbishop's memory was distant and rosy, and that his knowledge of Church history was relatively superficial. None the less, his was a deeply held and intelligible position: the colleges had been founded to sustain religion as well as learning and education; and by the 1860s religion had by long prescription meant the religion of the Church of England.

There was also a very strong tide flowing in support of these brave measures. Petitions are notoriously unsatisfactory instruments – many people find it easier to sign them than not; names have a way of joining them by accident; but it is noticeable that petitions came to parliament in 1868 in support of the abolition of tests from 80 university officers and 123 fellows and ex-fellows of Oxford colleges, and no less than 227 'present and past officers and fellows at Cambridge'.[3] The signatories included 32 of the 60 fellows of Trinity, probably including both J. B. Lightfoot, most eminent of Cambridge theologians, who had become a convert to abolition in the course of the 1860s and regarded the tests as a stumbling-block to serious religion, and Henry Sidgwick, who was to resign his fellowship in 1869 on account of his scruples about the 39 Articles.

In the end the tests were abolished, after eight years of parliamentary argument, by an act proposed by Gladstone himself as prime minister, and passed in 1871. Gladstone's own views, as burgess for Oxford, had been for many years ambivalent; but he had gradually come to be convinced that the voice of the dissenters – and their supporters in the establishment – must be heard. Doubtless, when his bill became law, it owed much to the support of other interests: of many men who wished to see the universities centres of a more secular learning; of those who prized tender consciences more than conformity; of those who thought that Oxford and Cambridge were hotbeds of clerical privilege.

The story is full of paradoxes. It represented both the deep interest in, and the profound ignorance of the outer world

[2] Winstanley 1947, pp. 60–1; on Longley at Christ Church, see Bill and Mason 1970, pp. 34, 36, etc.
[3] Winstanley 1947, p. 61.

towards the ancient universities. Thus it was proposed and nearly carried that a number of college officers should be pledged not to 'teach anything contrary to the teaching or divine authority of the Holy Scriptures', though it was not made clear by what steps this teaching was to be made known to college officers trained (as the majority were at this time) in the Mathematical Tripos; and the final act states that 'Morning and Evening Prayer, according to the order of the Book of Common Prayer, shall continue to be used daily as heretofore in the Chapel of every college subsisting at the time of the passing of this Act.' That saving clause rescued Newnham (which did not subsist when the act passed) by the skin of its teeth.[4]

To us looking back from the late twentieth century, the Cambridge of the 1860s seems a place of modest academic attainment. We might well think that the ardent aspiring young of the late nineteenth century were not gravely disadvantaged by being excluded from it if they could not subscribe to religious formulas. Doubtless such a view was held by many at the time. But the pursuit of education was a very deep urge in mid-Victorian England; the aspiration to provide for the formation or instruction of oneself and one's family a central feature of the culture of the age; and there was a very large body of opinion which looked to Oxford and Cambridge, with all their faults, as the foundations of learning – or at any rate as the places where higher education must be sought. These were not the only motives for entering Oxford and Cambridge. 'Nobody comes to the University in order to learn', wrote Leslie Stephen in his *Sketches from Cambridge* of 1865. 'If that is too strong a statement, I may at least say that no one comes with a view to learning chiefly.'[5] Yet the pursuit of learning was in the air; and even the new centres of learning depended heavily on the old.[6] In this world the issue of religious tests was everywhere crucial, and University College, London had earlier set the tone for the new universities by excluding them. In the north the pathfinder was Owens College, Manchester, core of the Victoria University of

---

[4] Winstanley 1947, pp. 88–9 and 89 n. 2; *Public General Statutes* 34 and 35 Victoria (1871) chap. 26, pp. 191–3.
[5] Stephen 1865, pp. 39–40.
[6] Two-thirds of the early non-medical professors at Liverpool came from Oxford or Cambridge, nearly a third from Trinity alone. Kelly 1981, p. 92.

Manchester, Liverpool and Leeds and of the later University of Manchester; and when University College, Liverpool received its first charter in 1881 it contained the formidable clause that:

> It is a fundamental condition of the constitution of the College that no Student, Professor, Teacher, or other officer or person connected with the College shall be required to make any declaration as to his religious opinions, or to submit to any test whatsoever thereof; and that no gift or endowment for theological or religious purposes, or having any theological condition attached thereto, shall be accepted on behalf of the College.[7]

The founders of University College, Liverpool had some close links with Cambridge; and in 1879 they had been inspired by a celebrated lecture given by that eminent Liverpolitan, Professor Lightfoot of Cambridge, in which he recounted a dream of Liverpool thirty-five years hence, with a fine college run by a group of distinguished and well-endowed professors. The dream doubtless reflected the frustrations of a professor in Cambridge in the 1860s and 70s, where they were very much second-class citizens – as they still are in the eyes of right thinking Cambridge folk – but it also reminded the leaders of Liverpool enterprise of the ambivalence of Cambridge, where religious tests had officially been abolished in 1871 but many vestiges of sectarian privilege still clung to the colleges and chapels and divinity professors. The clause forbidding theological or religious endowment was attributed to the powerful and eloquent Unitarian minister, Charles Beard – a man of real culture and vision and author of a notable book on the Reformation. He presided over the main Unitarian church in Liverpool and his congregation included great and beneficent Liverpool patricians such as William Rathbone and George Holt.[8] Liverpool was already a city in which sectarian strife was naturally seen as the prime enemy of peace and cultivated life; but such evidence as we have strongly suggests that it was the Unitarian circle which inspired the exclusion of religious endowments. When the college became a university in 1903 the clause was replaced by one which still made the exclusion of any religious test 'a fundamental condition of the

---

[7] Kelly 1981, p. 53.
[8] Kelly 1981, pp. 37–53 (for Lightfoot's lecture, pp. 45–6).

constitution of the University' – but equally banned all teaching of theology – though allowing Semitic languages, Hellenistic Greek and ecclesiastical history to slip through its net.[9] I was myself a witness, as a professor in Liverpool, of the demise of this clause in the new charter of 1961; and proposals for a theological department were favourably received, but no money was forthcoming.

There were many in parliament and government in 1871 who were deeply concerned that the abolition of tests should not lead to the abolition of religion in the colleges; and this was spelt out in the act of 1877, which gave the University Commissioners their instructions for drafting new statutes for the universities and colleges.[10] Here for the first time, so far as I know, a public airing was given to the celebrated definition of the purposes of university and college: 'education, religion, learning and research'. The two surprising words in this list are religion and research. For some it was eminently fitting that in the decade which had seen the opening of the Cavendish Laboratory and – to balance atoms with archives – the advent of the great legal historian F. W. Maitland, research should enter the list of purposes. It may well be that some of those who used the word reckoned that it meant enquiry more generally than original investigation. However that may be, research remained, or became, a word of scorn on the lips of many Oxford and Cambridge dons (often men of learning themselves) for nearly a century after it was promulgated by act of parliament. The presence of religion could have been even more divisive. The formula was duly incorporated into the statutes of all colleges save one in the early 1880s – and that one conformed in 1926. True, it appears in a variety of different contexts. In the current statutes of Caius, for example, it is only used of the election of the master, who shall be the person most suitable to preside over the college 'as a place of education, religion, learning and research'.[11] But though the colleges might have religion among their purposes, the university, so far as its statutes revealed, did not. It is a curious fact that the full formula,

---

[9] Kelly 1981, pp. 130–1.

[10] What follows is based on Burnaby 1953, esp. pp. 1–2. See also *Public General Statutes 1877*, p. 236 (40 and 41 Victoria, chap. 48, c. 15).

[11] *Statutes of Gonville and Caius College* (edn of 1926), chap. 6, 1.

including religion, was only introduced into the University Statutes in 1949.[12] And when John Burnaby became Regius Professor of Divinity in 1953 he took the formula *Education, Religion, Learning and Research* as the title for his inaugural lecture and meditated on what meaning religion might have among the stated purposes of a university which many thought entirely secular.

Noone doubts that the university was a religious institution in its origin; nor that the early colleges were set up with religious worship and service as one of their chief purposes. But the older colleges have lived long enough to see religion change its face many times; and there is a deep ambiguity in the word which we shall presently explore.

The medieval colleges had been founded as academic chantries: they had a dual function, to educate poor scholars and sustain daily prayers and masses for their founders and benefactors. Thus King's and its chapel are a chantry for Henry VI, Henry VII and Henry VIII, an impressive witness that the author of the English Reformation did not doubt his own need for masses and prayers. Nor are prayers for the dead condemned by the 39 Articles. But the dominance of the Calvinist doctrine of election in late sixteenth-century Cambridge and England – in the world in which John Whitgift was master of Trinity and archbishop of Canterbury – made them seem redundant and offensive, if not superstitious to many, and they were discontinued. A pale reflection of the original function of the college chapels remains in the benefactors' services, which should be weekly or daily events. Meanwhile the other elements in the medieval tradition continued and flourished.

Furthermore, the colleges were originally in large measure communities of clergy; and it was still expected in the early and mid-nineteenth century that the high tables would be largely peopled with clergy. There were plenty of exceptions. From the days of Dr Caius the masters of Caius had as often been laymen as clerics. The fellows of Trinity Hall expected to practise in the church courts – and under the curious sixteenth-century rule that only laymen could practise in the church courts they mostly had

---

[12] Burnaby 1953, pp. 1–3.

to remain laymen – preserving only a skeleton staff of chaplains down to the time of the Reverend Leslie Stephen – the very briefly Reverend Stephen, for he rapidly lost his faith and became the apostle of late Victorian agnosticism.[13] Yet the production of clergy had always been one of the prime functions of the ancient universities. In the first great age of university expansion in the late sixteenth and early seventeenth centuries indeed laymen had come greatly to outnumber the clergy, but only in a purely numerical sense; for many of the laymen came for a year or two to acquire something of the learning or other blessings of the place before going on to the Inns of Court or the grand tour. Those who stayed the full course and became fellows remained predominantly clerical; and in the eighteenth century some colleges produced almost nothing but clergy. So it would be natural to assume if we approach the study of Cambridge history without presuppositions that the core of the curriculum was theological. But this was not so. Here we enter one of the deepest paradoxes of our subject; for it was precisely in the era of secularisation, when the old clerical monopoly was being rolled away, that Cambridge became a major centre of theological scholarship. The Theological Tripos opened in 1874; to this same era belong the major works of Lightfoot, Hort and Westcott.[14] It was not impossible to study some theology before, and everyone in the early nineteenth century was expected to make some acquaintance with Paley's *Evidences of Christianity* and other forgotten masterpieces. But there was no systematic study of theology or any aspect of clerical duty or pastoral care; no possibility of it save in the give and take of personal dealings between pupil and tutor – and not much evidence of it there. Here as in so many realms of life the old professors and the new alike were becoming much more professional. It is not entirely a coincidence that the foundation of Girton and Newnham, which opened the path to more professional careers for women, and the foundation of the Theological Tripos, are so close in date.[15]

It was assumed that the colleges were places of religious education in some sense of the term, but it would be very hard to

---

[13] Crawley 1976, pp. 57, 79, 107, 158–60; Brooke 1985, p. 85.
[14] Winstanley 1947, pp. 159–63; Tanner 1917, p. 812.
[15] See chap. 9.

define the sense. It could have a purely institutional force; it could be the heart and core of a lively community. One has only to think of Oriel College, Oxford in the late 1820s, with Newman and Robert Wilberforce among the tutors, or Balliol in the best days of Jowett, to realise that the highest ideals, the most refined thought, of an age – be it conservative Anglican or liberal – could flow round the quads or be heard Sunday by Sunday in the chapel.[16]

COLLEGE CHAPELS

There is no doubt that deep religious conviction was widespread in Victorian Cambridge; and of this the most visible criterion is the money spent on building, rebuilding, and furbishing college chapels. It is not quite so crude as might appear, for expensive building schemes in nineteenth-century Cambridge were felt instantly and sharply in the fellows' own pockets; and even so they could only be realised if a wider community joined in zealous and generous giving. There had been no generation in the history of the colleges which had not contributed some new chapel or some major work to one or other of the existing chapels. Even the eighteenth century had witnessed the major refurbishment of the chapels of Caius, Magdalene and Trinity Hall.[17] In the early nineteenth century Corpus acquired a new chapel; and in the 1840s Jesus embarked on a spectacular restoration of their ancient and splendid chapel, the church of the nuns of St Radegund, in which the fellows of Jesus retained a strong and evident pride.[18] The church of the Holy Sepulchre had recently been restored, almost rebuilt, by Anthony Salvin acting on the brief provided by the Cambridge Camden Society – it was a celebrated turning point in the history of church furnishing, and in attitudes to the layout of a church. So Jesus turned first to Salvin too.[19] But after a while, on the advice of their fellow-commoner John Sutton, they laid Salvin off and put themselves into the hands of Pugin. The structural work he supervised was

[16] Newsome 1966, pp. 84–96; Hinchliff 1987.
[17] Brooke 1985, pp. 172–3; Pevsner 1970, pp. 116, 179.
[18] For Corpus, Pevsner 1970, p. 64; for Jesus, Willis and Clark 1886/1988, II, 147–54 (Pugin and Sutton), 154–60 (Bodley and Morris); see also *RCHM Cambridge* I, 48–51, 83–4, 86–91.
[19] On the Cambridge Camden Society and Pugin, see esp. Crook 1987, pp. 59–68; White 1962.

not altogether satisfactory and some of it had to be redone. But the screens and stalls and wood carving form one of the glories of Cambridge; and his windows – Pugin made a special visit to Chartres in search of inspiration for them – are a charming addition.[20] Pugin's woodwork has ensured that the collegiate community worships in a very small space within a large chapel: it is perfectly medieval in inspiration, as is usual with Pugin; yet it provides for a small inward-looking college: not in the manner of the medieval parish churches which enshrined college chapels within them, like St Michael's or Little St Mary's, or in the manner of the great chapels of New College and King's; but much more reminiscent in scale and attitude of Matthew Wren's chapels at Peterhouse and Pembroke of the seventeenth century, private oratories for inward-looking communities. The devotion of the fellows of Jesus did not cease with the departure of Pugin: twenty years later they called in Bodley and Morris, and the Morris decorations and the windows by Burne-Jones and others would make Jesus chapel a marvellous monument of nineteenth-century Cambridge even if Pugin had not been there before them.[21]

The works at Jesus gave an atmosphere and setting suited to the fashions of the age; and they included the gorgeous organ given by John Sutton in 1849.[22] In King's and Trinity and St John's the choir had always sung and there had long been organs. But in most college chapels by the early nineteenth century the services were said; and the revival of church music was one of the deepest influences on the college chapels in mid and late Victorian times.

In the 1850s the bursar, later master, of St John's, William Bateson, started a movement to provide a new chapel. The essential urge seems to have been for more space. In the 1860s the college was to feel the brunt of the second great wave of expansion in nineteenth-century Cambridge. Its old hall and chapel – once the chapel of the medieval hospital of St John – could not house anything like the whole community. Bateson and a number of his colleagues felt the need for drastic action. In the early sixteenth century John Fisher, recently

---

[20] Willis and Clark 1886/1988, II, 152 n. 1, quoting a letter from Pugin to Sutton (?1849).
[21] Willis and Clark 1886/1988, II, 154–60.
[22] See esp. Thistlethwaite 1983, pp. 15, 44–5.

president of Queens', had presided over the building of the glorious Tudor red-brick front court, which in its day – in company with the old court at Queens' – must have been one of the supreme beauties of Cambridge. In the eighteenth century the fellows of St John's reflected the whimsical switches of fashion and summoned James Essex to face (or deface) the southern side of the court; in the 1860s Bateson's dream came true and they utterly destroyed the northern side, carrying away the perfectly preserved chapel and hospital buildings of the early to mid-thirteenth century. In their place Sir Gilbert Scott provided, between 1862 and 1869, a large French gothic church of the late thirteenth century; designed – however one may admire many of its qualities – with an extraordinary disregard for its setting. It contains ninety-eight stalls and seating for about 400, a very ample provision for a large Victorian college in which some pretence or hope that the whole community attended chapel was taken to be fundamental to its being.[23]

The sermon at a special commemoration in 1861 which helped to launch the enterprise, and the sermon at the laying of the foundation stone in 1864, were both preached by William Selwyn, former fellow and Lady Margaret's Professor of Divinity – of all the divinity professors of that age the one who made the greatest mark on the face of Cambridge and the least on the study of theology. To his munificence we owe the Selwyn Divinity School; to his inspiration in a fair measure we must impute the new chapel of St John's.[24] For the sermon of 1861 he took his text from Haggai:

> Yet now be strong, O Zerubbabel, saith the Lord; and be strong, O Joshua, son of Josedech, the high priest; and be strong, all ye people of the land, saith the Lord, and work: for I am with you, saith the Lord of hosts. The silver is mine, and the gold is mine, saith the Lord of hosts. The glory of this latter house shall be greater than of the former, saith the Lord of hosts: and in this place I will give peace, saith the Lord of hosts.

The date is significant. St John's was enjoying some of the fresh

---

[23] On St John's new chapel see Willis and Clark 1886/1988, II, 324–44, esp. 342; plan on p. 329; on Bateson's initiative, and the financing of the chapel, Howard 1935, pp. 183, 209–12.

[24] On the Divinity School, see pp. 141–2. For the sermon, Willis and Clark 1886/1988, II, 324–5.

breezes of religious renewal characteristic of the age. The fellows were ready to forego a part of their dividend to allow for these ambitious building projects – for a new master's lodge and a great extension to the hall accompanied the new chapel. They contributed quite extensively from their own pockets. The 1860s was a time of financial euphoria. The cold winds of agricultural depression in the 1870s and 1880s help to explain why the debts incurred in building the chapel were not paid off till 1896.[25] They also very likely explain why so few Cambridge colleges destroyed their old courts and built new chapels in the last quarter of the century. This makes it the more commendable that the fellows of Queens' built a fine new chapel in the 1880s and 1890s without any destruction in their old court.

In the present state of knowledge, we know more of the religious temper of Queens' as it set about building a new chapel than of any other Cambridge college of the 1880s and 1890s, owing to the admirable account in John Twigg's *History of Queens' College*.[26] In St John's the common enterprise of building a chapel hid many differences of opinion and outlook among the fellows. But in Queens' a group of clerical dons and sympathetic laymen – of widely different personal views – seems to have worked harmoniously together. Queens' had shown its interest in current ecclesiological fashions by employing G. F. Bodley to restore its old chapel in the late 1850s. Bodley was also to play a leading part in the decoration of the old hall at Queens', today a gorgeous palimpsest of nineteenth and eighteenth and fifteenth-century tastes. His role indicates how deeply Queens', like Jesus, had come to be influenced by the Cambridge Architectural Society, heir apparent of the Cambridge Camden Society. In the chapel, this meant colour and the beauty of holiness. In its origin in the 1830s and 40s this Cambridge movement had tried to add medieval splendour and ritual to the high-church theology and austere practices of the Oxford movement. But long before 1858 it had split, and the Cambridge Architectural Society went forward as an aesthetic movement not linked or chained to high-church doctrines.[27] Thus it was possible for a group of dons of

[25] Howard 1935, p. 211.
[26] What follows is mostly based on Twigg 1987, pp. 277–86.
[27] White 1962, esp. p. 153; Thompson 1990, pp. 23–4.

varied outlook – with an evangelical tendency perhaps slightly predominating in their personal views – to unite in offering Bodley patronage and in building the new chapel.

First, there was W. M. Campion, a veteran of the 1850s, already a fellow when Bodley refurbished the old chapel; a stalwart of moderate educational reform who ended his days president of Queens' in the 1890s.[28] In 1867 he was joined in the fellowship by Arthur Wright, who after a spell as a parish priest in London became dean in 1872, and the very type of the devoted college fellow till his death in 1924.[29] In due course they were joined by R. H. Kennett, later Regius Professor of Hebrew, and (after the chapel was completed) by H. E. Ryle, president from 1896 till he became bishop of Exeter in 1901. Wright was a fervent proponent of New Testament criticism and Campion a firm supporter of critical enquiry applied to the Old; Ryle and Kennett were biblical scholars of some distinction, if not of the first eminence. Ryle sprang from an evangelical family, and was himself of central churchmanship with low and high church sympathies; Kennett was a liberal evangelical; they were both supporters of CICCU in its early days, when liberal evangelicals felt as much at home in it as the more conservative. But their evangelical temper caused no rift or division that we can discern in the furbishing or use of the new chapel: Kennett became a college lecturer in 1888, when the chapel was begun, Ryle president in 1896 when it had been recently completed.[30]

The old chapel of Queens' was designed for a modest medieval community and was far too small for an expanding nineteenth-century college which still hoped to see all its undergraduates at prayer.[31] But times were hard, Queens' was far from rich, and nearly twenty years elapsed after the completion of the new chapel of St John's before any drastic measure was conceived in Queens'. Arthur Wright was a self-confident man who knew his own mind; and in later years he claimed (in Twigg's words) that

the idea of building a new chapel came from a walk in the country

[28] Twigg 1987, pp. 224–5, 227, 274–7, 286, etc.
[29] Twigg 1987, pp. 227–8, 277–8, 285–6, 330n., etc.
[30] Twigg 1987, pp. 229, 283–4, 298 and n. (Kennett), 229–30, 280n., 283–5 (Ryle). On Ryle cf. *DNB 1922–1930*, pp. 733–5 (M. H. FitzGerald).
[31] Cf. pp. 56–7.

which he took with Campion: Wright suggested enlarging the existing chapel, and although Campion thought this an impractical idea, he offered to subscribe £1,000 towards the cost of a new chapel if Wright would take the responsibility for arranging its construction. Bodley was invited to draw up plans in January 1887, and a formal decision to build the chapel was made in January 1888. The necessary funds were raised by subscription, several fellows giving generously, and the chapel was consecrated in 1891.[32]

The fellows of St John's of the 1890s may have thought the new chapel of Queens' a poor relation of their own: it is less exuberant and far less expensive. But Bodley's thought and experience and taste created a building whose solemn red-brick exterior blends harmoniously – unlike some of the more recent buildings of Queens' – with the ancient court behind it; and whose tall and slender proportions give character and dignity to a building which combines a measure of simplicity with a measure of adornment, now greatly enhanced by the exquisite fifteenth-century triptych on the altar. It was successfully completed in a remarkably short time; and it is a fitting monument to a devoted generation.

COMPULSORY CHAPEL

A theme most fashionable among social historians at present is popular religion; but it is of unpopular religion that I have now to speak – of the decline of compulsory chapel. Compulsory chapel seems to us infinitely remote. It requires a powerful effort of historical imagination to recover that world, not far away in time, in which it was thought by many men of good will that regular attendance by all undergraduates was essential to the preservation of discipline and the survival of the Anglican religion in the colleges of Cambridge. But not by all. Thus the agnostic F. M. Cornford, in *Microcosmographia Academica* in 1908, could make satire of it.

> There must be some rules. If you enquire the reason, you will find that the object of rules is to relieve the younger men of the

<hr />

[32] Twigg 1987, pp. 277–8.

burdensome feeling of moral or religious obligation. If their energies are to be left unimpaired for the pursuit of athletics . . . they must never be troubled with having to think whether this or that ought to be done or not: it should be settled by rules. The most valuable rules are those which ordain attendance at lectures and at religious worship. If these were not enforced, young men would begin too early to take learning and religion seriously; and that is well known to be bad form.[33]

Or, from a less prejudiced (though also a sceptical) witness, the saying attributed to A. J. Balfour, later Chancellor of the university: 'There is one pleasure that never palls, and that is the pleasure of *not* going to church.'[34]

Compulsory chapel was no Victorian novelty; it lay at the heart of all the early colleges. All on the foundation were expected to join daily in the round of prayer. By definition it was the fellows who had the highest obligation; but it was they who first forsook the strait and narrow path. By 1860 a high proportion of college fellows were non-resident, and (though some were men of the highest integrity and conscience) they totally ignored their obligation. Nor were the resident fellows necessarily as assiduous as they had been two or three hundred years earlier. When in 1838 the Seniority of Trinity tightened the rules a group of undergraduates formed The Society for the Prevention of Cruelty to Undergraduates, and made up their own roster of the attendance of master and fellows, which they proceeded to print and circulate over a period of six weeks or so.[35]

The Reformation had abolished masses for the dead, but provided no excuse for absence from chapel. In or about 1860 every college acquired new statutes, most of which were silent on the matter. But undergraduates were still expected to attend a good number of services during term. The abolition of the Test Acts in 1871 started the colleges on a new tack. On the one hand it was deeply felt that a special effort was needed to preserve the Christian character of the colleges, and therefore chapel attendance must be defended. On the other hand it was accepted that the nonconformist and the Jew, now accepted members of these

[33] Cornford 1908, pp. 18–19 (edn of 1987, p. 10).
[34] Ex inf. the late A. H. Warr, but I have never traced it to a written source.
[35] Shipley 1913, pp. 35–8.

societies, could not be compelled to join in chapel worship – the nonconformist at least was told he was welcome, but not bound by the rules; and the agnostic set a new and worrying problem. It was not that agnosticism itself was new: there had been plenty of unbelievers before and doubtless an infinite number to whom religion was a matter of indifference, as in all ages of recorded history. But the college authorities did not have to recognise them; now, perhaps, they did.

It is peculiarly hard for us to grasp the issue because the assumptions of college tutors in the late nineteenth century were in large measure compounded of two notions alien to us. The tutor was *in loco parentis*; he was much more like a housemaster in an early nineteenth-century boarding school than like a modern tutor – that is to say, he reckoned some measure of discipline essential to the education of his charges, though he left them most of the time very much to their own devices and asked few questions as to how they conducted themselves. But the tutors were Victorians, so there came to be a growing sense of moral earnestness in their views of discipline, anyway for a time. They also believed that forced attendance at church services was salutary; that some good must come of it; that only so could the message of the gospel enter into the consciousness, and so the memory, of their charges. This is not a problem which can entirely be forgotten: churchgoing parents must always live with it as their children pass through phases of reluctant piety. But we now think of undergraduates as adults; and compulsory religion for adults seems to us a contradiction in terms.

In most Cambridge colleges, I fancy, compulsory chapel survived until 1914, and quietly died with the First World War. It is hard to be sure, for with few exceptions its demise was peaceful, and not even marked by a College Order. In Magdalene alone, so far as I know – I am assuredly open to correction – it survived into the 1930s; at some Oxford colleges even longer. Dr Ronald Hyam informs me that an attempt was made to revive it in Magdalene in 1928-9, but it seems to have died peacefully in the 1930s. I have had descriptions of its dying phase at Worcester College, Oxford in the 1950s from Mr H. G. Pitt, whose task it was, as lay dean, to enforce it; and from an American postgraduate of that era who described the liberal spirit in which it could be interpreted away. But Worcester was the supreme home of lost causes; in the same college at that time, though a fellow might marry, he still had to ask the permission of the governing body to do so, and the answer was by no means a foregone conclusion. One of the great fascinations of Oxbridge history is the way in which the assumptions of totally different worlds overlap and coexist over surprisingly long periods of time.

Early in March 1890 the anxious and frustrated dean of Caius wrote to the governing body saying that the rules on chapel attendance were in disrepair and urging that they be clarified. Soon after, the same man, in his role as Registrary of the college, wrote a College Order revising the rules, but reaffirming that they were to be obeyed. They included, for example, attendance twice on Sundays. But the discussions continued, and in May the senior tutor, E. S. Roberts, circulated a list of suggestions, asking for comments from his colleagues who formed the governing body.[36] From this remarkable document, comprising his questions and his colleagues' answers, three points emerge with special clarity. Compulsory chapel must be maintained: that is assumed. Roberts was a man of considerable liberality, a devoted college man, at the centre of the movement to make Caius a serious educational establishment, and a scholar too. In the wake of the abolition of tests, as a tutor, he had thought it right to take orders on the title of his fellowship. Roberts was a moderate exponent of muscular Christianity. He avoided the excesses of Kingsley, but he dearly loved the Caius Boat Club, and wrote an appendix on it for John Venn's great *Biographical History* of the college, affectionately terming it the 'wholesome' region of college life.[37]

'I assume that the G[overning] B[ody] or a majority of it approves a certain amount of obligatory or disciplinary attendance, and I have very strong reasons for believing that, especially for our college and for a long time to come, the abolition of the rule requiring attendance would be simply disastrous.'[38] The Reverend John Venn, mathematician, philosopher and college historian, had some years earlier renounced his orders owing to

---

[36] I owe my knowledge of this document, Gonville and Caius College Archives, Roberts Papers, 1890, to Anne Neary. On Roberts, see Brooke 1985, pp. 234–6, 290.
[37] Brooke 1985, p. 235.
[38] Gonville and Caius College Archives, Roberts Papers, Discussion of Compulsory Chapel, 1890, p. 2.

some difficulties with the 39 Articles and the creeds; and he was in general a staunch supporter of what we would call (in the widest sense of the term) liberal positions. On Roberts' proposition he commented: 'Accepted: not so much from decided agreement as from total inability to suggest any other course.' Roberts gives no grounds for his general position, because he says it is agreed; more's the pity from our viewpoint. The governing body knew that compulsory chapel was being challenged; but they saw no alternative.

In King's some years before this the reforming provost Augustus Austen Leigh – the man more responsible than any other for the silent revolution which brought King's into the nineteenth century – had none the less written to all junior members not long after his election saying that regular attendance at chapel was to him the foundation of college life;[39] even so, a rule had come to be established in the 1870s that men might sign a book rather than attend, an alternative which became widespread (I fancy). But by 1912 the lay dean, J. H. Clapham, found himself left high and dry with what had by then become 'more paternal than the rules of most places'. He explained that the rule was intended to ensure that the men got up in the morning; and clearly the young men of King's objected to being made to get up four mornings a week, which was the rule.[40]

The second point which emerges from Roberts' questionnaire is that the real problem was that the young men were bored, and misbehaved. 'There is no more trying time in the whole day for policeman-tutors than the five or ten minutes on a non-choral evening before the curtain is drawn' – that is, before the service begins.[41] One scholar has recently asserted that the majority of Cambridge students of this epoch were noisy and philistine and cared only for sport; and that true intellectuals were a tiny minority.[42] I am not convinced that the evidence exists for such a view; and my own impression is that it takes far too little account of the many dons and undergraduates, like E. S. Roberts himself, who devotedly combined scholarship and sport. No doubt there

[39] Austen Leigh 1906, pp. 248–50 (31 October 1889: he was elected on 9 February, ibid. p. 226).
[40] Letter of Clapham to the dean of St John's, St John's College Archives, Tanner Papers 14.16.
[41] See n. 38 (p. 3).   [42] See esp. Mangan 1984.

have always been noisy undergraduates, such as those who booed William Whewell in the Senate House when he was Vice-Chancellor, or those who broke down the gates of Newnham in 1921 to celebrate the vote against the admission of women to the university – not to mention the events of the late 1960s and early 70s;[43] and philistine groups there were in fact and legend. Evidently rowdy behaviour in chapel was (in student eyes) an acceptable form of protest – or simply a natural reaction to boredom.

The key words in Roberts' comment on the tutors' anxious minutes are 'a non-choral evening'; and much of the paper is given over to plans for shortening and enlivening the services, and above all to providing them with music. The most crucial step had already been taken: Charles Wood had been imported from Selwyn as 'organist scholar' in 1889;[44] he was to stay till his death, by then professor of music, in 1926, and to create a new tradition of music in the college. Many colleges made similar appointments about the same time.

The best records of chapel attendance known to me were rescued and preserved in the archives of St John's by Malcolm Underwood. Attendance was noted – as in college hall still in the 1940s in Caius – by markers, and some of the markers' sheets survive. Their message was then transferred into large attendance books, in which the record was noted with sophisticated detail, distinguishing whether they had actually been seen or only sent messages, when they read lessons and so forth.[45] The end of all this elaborate administration, for those who failed the test, was a visit to the tutor, with penalty of gating (in other colleges fines) for stubborn offenders. These records are the more piquant since St John's was one of the colleges which had felt the need of a new, much larger chapel in the 1860s. All this sets in perspective the fierce arguments which issued from the pulpit of the new chapel in the 1870s on the abolishing of tests. Edward Miller writes:

> It need hardly be said that the change did not meet with universal approbation. J. S. Wood, who became president at the very time

[43] See below, pp. 326, 557–9.   [44] Brooke 1985, p. 243.
[45] St John's College Archives, DS 3.2, 3.5, 3.7 (Junior Dean's Books), DS 6 (Chapel Marker Sheets, 1896–9). For the whole passage I am much indebted to Malcolm Underwood.

that the act of 1871 became law, thundered against a measure which turned colleges into 'chance medleys of churchmen, dissenters and unbelievers . . . bodies alien to the Church of England, alien to the Church of Christ'. Religious passions were stirred and T. G. Bonney and G. F. Reyner swapped sermons in the chapel in defence of latitudinarian and more traditional views respectively, creating an atmosphere which made it necessary for sermons to be discontinued for some years.[46]

In Trinity, as no doubt in other colleges, the idea had been in the wind that compulsory attendance might not last for ever. The Trinity reformers of the early 1870s led, among others, by the young Henry Jackson, had avoided the issue when they drafted new statutes;[47] and it lay dormant, so far as we know, until 1905, although as out of many a volcano molten lava occasionally dribbled from its crater. The young mathematician G. H. Hardy, as a boy, had found pleasure in church 'by factorizing the numbers of the hymns'; but his experience of compulsory chapel at Winchester did not disincline him to reject belief in God. When he came to Trinity in the 1890s he explained to the dean that he could not conscientiously attend chapel, and he was compelled to write to his parents for their consent – a letter which he knew would be hurtful to them, and was infinitely hurtful to write. He was to be a fellow of Trinity for most of his life, but he never entered the chapel, even for the admission of a new master. 'He had clerical friends', wrote C. P. Snow of him, 'but God was his personal enemy'.[48]

In 1905 the College Council approved a minute ending the gating or other penalties for those who failed to attend chapel, but the tutors continued to circulate a notice saying 'students, who are members of the Church of England, are expected to attend Divine Service in chapel, on Sundays both at Morning and Evening Prayers and on weekdays twice in the week'.[49] By 1913 there was a natural disquiet about the meaning of 'expected' and the tutors proposed in 1913 that it be altered to 'required', but that the services stipulated be reduced to one each Sunday for all

[46] Miller 1961, p. 89.
[47] A draft proposal was made, but withdrawn: Winstanley 1947, chap. 6, esp. pp. 245–6.
[48] Hardy 1940/67, pp. 14, 20.
[49] Council Minute 10 of 16 June 1913: I am indebted to Robert Robson for knowledge of these minutes, and to John Easterling and the Trinity College Council for permission to quote them.

'except those who profess a conscientious objection to attendance'.[50] The Council replaced the clause about conscientious
objection by one referring to receiving exemption from a tutor or
a dean. There was evidently a good deal of disquiet among the
seniors, for two amendments were carried, one to say that the
Council 'agree generally with the motion', the other 'that no
action be taken until an opportunity has been given for consider-
ation of the matter by a College Meeting'. On 15 November a
Special College Meeting was held at which, after various
manoeuvres, it was resolved, on the motion of Henry Jackson,
himself a fervent believer, seconded by the eminent agnostic
philosopher M'Taggart, 'That attendance at the College Chapel
be not enforced by gating or other penalty'.[51] From then on,
chapel was no longer in any sense compulsory. A legend quickly
grew that the forces of liberalism had overcome 'the clerical
party'. Since 1910 Bertrand Russell had been a college lecturer in
philosophy, and in 1914–15 he was nearly re-elected a fellow. In
due course his election was not proceeded with, and later on,
notoriously, he was removed even from his lectureship on
account of his wartime activities.[52] Writing in the 1920s, Russell
himself suggested that 'The reason for not offering me a Fellowship was that the clerical party did not wish to add to the anti-
clerical vote. The result was they were able to dismiss me in 1916,
when they disliked my views on the war . . .' With characteristic
fair-mindedness, Hardy himself gave this view the lie.

> There is always something in a large society like Trinity which,
> though actually it will include very few clergymen [how far
> Trinity had come since 1860!] can be described by a stretch of
> language as the 'clerical party'. There is a 'religious' and an
> 'irreligious' party, though the boundary between them is shifting
> and ill-defined . . . but the feeling against [Russell] after 1914 was
> almost entirely political, and there was no sort of correlation
> between 'political' and 'religious' dislike . . . There had been one
> 'religious' controversy in the College . . . when the Council . . .
> had attempted to restore compulsory chapel. In this event the
> 'clerical party' had been decisively defeated, and the opposition

[50] Ibid.; and Tutors' Memorandum signed W. M. Fletcher from Report Book vi. 52.
[51] Trinity College Archives, Council Minute 10 of 16 June 1913 and Minutes of Special College
Meeting on 15 November 1913.
[52] Hardy 1942, pp. 25–46; see pp. 337–40.

had been led by the very men (Jackson and M'Taggart) who were Russell's most bitter opponents later.[53]

When the tutors reduced obligatory Sunday attendance from two services to one, we may suspect that they were partly moved by the increasing pressure on the chapel. Even Trinity chapel could hardly cope with the growing numbers; and on Sunday evening visitors were carefully restricted. By 1913 it is not at all likely that any college chapels save King's and Trinity and St John's could really have held the whole student community if all had attended at once. The only college to embark on a new chapel at this time was Sidney; and ample as the chapel must have seemed when completed in 1923, it can hardly have been intended to hold more than 100, whereas the college by then comprised roughly 150 fellows and undergraduates – it had been 200 strong in 1919–20. During the First World War the students were reduced to a trickle, and when the flood came in in 1919–20, it brought far too many for most colleges to fit their whole communities in chapel, and men too mature to be dragooned to worship. Compulsory chapel survived patchily here and there, but on the whole the 1920s seem, in Cambridge, to have witnessed its demise.[54]

The generation which had witnessed the abolition of tests in 1871 doubtless felt that chapel attendance, as well as being a healthy discipline for the young, was also the last chance to preserve the Anglican character of the colleges. In this they were partly justified, partly not. College chapels became increasingly ecumenical; after the Second World War most of them opened their altars to members of all the churches prepared to participate; and the churches of the town, as before, sometimes drew students away, sometimes helped to strengthen their loyalties within the colleges. In very recent times we have seen a free churchman as a college dean; I have seen a mass being celebrated in Polish in Caius chapel. The conservatives of 1871 would see in all this their worst fears confirmed; for most of us it is a small message of a large hope. On attendance, we have very little precise evidence of how mattins and evensong fared; no doubt they declined in the years

[53] Hardy 1942, pp. 30–1; for what follows, see Trinity College Archives, Senior Dean's Book 1880–1900, fo. 3.
[54] Caius attendance records of the period after 1918 show attendance faltering.

Fig. 4 Sidney Sussex College, chapel, 1911–23, by T. H. Lyon

between the wars. But, in compensation, the number of communicants increased. In large measure this may be attributed to the changing pattern of worship in all the churches: the parish communion or eucharist has become for many of very various persuasions the centre of their worship. In part it may be attributed to the greatly increased number of students in Cambridge, especially since the 1950s. I can myself bear witness that the great increase in communicants, in some colleges at least, in the years following the Second World War, was in considerable measure inspired by a very notable generation of college deans and chaplains – it was the age of the Chadwicks in Trinity Hall and Queens', and of Ian Ramsey at Christ's, of George Woods in Downing, of John Robinson at Clare, of Stephen Neill at Trinity, of Eric Heaton and Hugh Montefiore at Caius – though even in that period in most college chapels communicating fellows seemed an endangered species. I have no doubt there were other reasons for the flood which came to the altar deep in the religious sentiment of those decades. But it ran counter, evidently enough, to the normal experience of most parishes. Whatever the causes, if we are to ask the question, in the present state of knowledge, when in the history of the Cambridge colleges were the largest numbers of communicants, then the answer must be, in the 1950s and 60s. Indeed in some chapels the numbers have not fallen far below that peak in the 1980s and 90s. I do not put much faith in such figures. But I am sure that the notion that the act of 1871 ushered in a century of unmitigated decline in the fortunes of the established church in Cambridge is a myth.

THE AGNOSTICS

In 1862 the Reverend Leslie Stephen, fellow and tutor of Trinity Hall, lost his faith and resigned his tutorship; not long after, he left Cambridge and became a professional author and journalist. Leslie Stephen discovered in 1862, three years after the publication of *The Origin of Species*, that something was wrong with the book of Genesis. It could not be literally true; and so, he reckoned, his faith was void.[55] It says little for the state of theological teaching in Cambridge that a highly intelligent college tutor should have known so little of recent studies of Genesis as to wait till 1862 to find out this obvious truth. What Darwin completed, Lyell and the geologists had most fully prepared. After Lyell, it was impossible seriously to believe in Genesis as history. But why should one? It does not take a very sensitive reading of Genesis to see that its authors were not concerned with literal history, but with a theological mythology which would do justice to God's personal creative work. There were plenty of theologians who saw this clearly long before 1862.[56] In fairness to

[55] Maitland 1906, chap. 8, esp. p. 134; Annan 1951, p. 47; on Stephen, see Maitland 1906; Annan 1951/1984.
[56] See p. 10.

Stephen, there were plenty more who did not, who reacted to Lyell and Darwin by disbelief, or sought other meaning in the sacred text which would make it possible for it to remain literally true.[57] Stephen had accepted ordination as a natural prologue to his pastoral work in the college. By the same token he was a keen oarsman, a dedicated teacher and the life and soul of the college's modest social life. But the new learning was quite foreign to him; and when his real intellectual life began, it drove him from Cambridge, and from the Church. Stephen was an attractive, gifted man, with strange quirks and quiddities. His *Life and Letters* by Maitland, his closest friend, is a moving and convincing portrait with a few warts removed; these – and the eddies of his intellectual influence – were added in Noel Annan's studies of 1951 and 1984.[58] In later life Stephen dedicated himself above all to two intellectual adventures, to the dissemination of agnosticism and to the *Dictionary of National Biography*, a very notable achievement. In promulgating agnosticism Stephen was on the crest of a wave; he must have credit for making what has come to be a creed very widely and deeply held respectable among the late Victorians.[59] On his grasp of philosophy Henry Sidgwick was extremely scathing;[60] but as a dignified exponent of a high morality divorced from any religious basis he is a key figure in the intellectual world of his day. His work lay in London not in Cambridge; and when his family settled in Bloomsbury after his death, they created a circle as essential to the intellectual history of Cambridge as the high tables of Trinity and King's.

Stephen's conversion was a straw in the wind. The pressures of the 1860s are very familiar. Strauss and Baur and their disciples had taught those who were ready to listen that the gospels were full of myth and fiction, and George Eliot had translated Strauss' *Leben Jesu* so that the doctrine could spread around the English-speaking world.[61] Darwin had shown – what many had long known in part – that the world we know was not the product of instant creation, but had evolved over an immense space of time, under the pressure of natural, scientific forces, rather than by

---

[57] See Chadwick 1970, pp. 1–35, esp. pp. 9–11.   [58] See n. 55.
[59] See esp. Annan 1951/84, chap. 6.
[60] See Schneewind 1977, p. 364 n. 2.
[61] See esp. Neill and Wright 1988, pp. 13–30.

divine intervention. These are superficial phrases for one of the great intellectual revolutions of recorded history. They caused agony in many minds, a mild flutter in far more. Those inclined to deism or indifference were confirmed; those who kept, or found, their faith in the Christian revelation, either sought out new ways to reconcile learning and religion, or retreated into various modes of fundamentalism. In the modern world – and this has been broadly true since the later Victorian age – the great intellectual divide is not between believer and unbeliever, but between those who accept the findings of science and scholarship and those who do not: innumerable Christians are to be found on both sides of it, not a few have stood precariously on the boundary between. None the less, the turn of the nineteenth and twentieth centuries undoubtedly saw agnostic positions more firmly established and more confidently proclaimed than ever before. In many walks of life churchgoing was still an essential ingredient in perfect respectability; in Cambridge it was respectable for a don, if occasionally still a little risky, not to go to chapel – and to proclaim the reason.

Leslie Stephen never seems to have had much grasp of current theological thinking. The same can hardly be said of William Chawner, senior tutor and master of Emmanuel, and a central figure of the Cambridge establishment.[62] He had entered the college in 1867. In the 1880s as senior tutor he had aided the quiet revolution which made Emmanuel a teaching college, and in 1895 he was duly elected master. He was not a notable scholar, though he had published a prize essay in early life on *The Influence of Christianity upon the Legislation of Constantine the Great*; nor was he a man of profound ideas, though he was an intelligent and assiduous student of Christian origins. He had contributed energetically to building up the college in the late nineteenth century; he was a devoted college man; he was a forceful head of house. In 1909–10 two remarkable events took place in Emmanuel. Charles Raven was appointed dean at the age of 24, and the master made it public that he had lost his faith. Raven arrived in January 1910

---

[62] On the Chawner affair, see Cupitt 1970–1; *Emmanuel College Magazine*, 54 (1972), 17–30; Chawner 1909a, b, 1911; Dillistone 1975, pp. 69–76; Emmanuel College Archives, COL.19.7–9, 29 (I owe much help in this context to Frank Stubbings and Sarah Bendall). On Chawner's reforms, see Brooke, Highfield and Swaan 1988, pp. 295–6; Shuckburgh 1904, p. 183.

to find himself at the heart of a violent controversy. Chawner had been immersing himself in the evidences for Christian orthodoxy and had come to the conclusion that they could not be sustained: he had reached approximately a Unitarian position. But more than that, he had come to think that orthodox Christianity, and the institutional structure which sustained it, were doomed. He spoke to a religious discussion society; he published his talk in the pamphlet entitled *Prove all Things*; and he distributed his pamphlet and the responses he received to it with a lavish hand among fellows and undergraduates alike. His basic purpose – to foster candour and openness in religious discussion – must seem to us wholly admirable. To shower pamphlets attacking the orthodox from the master's lodge was distinctly eccentric. And he not only criticised Christian orthodoxy; he condemned compulsory chapel. Charles Raven as dean was responsible for discipline and for the chapel and the religious life of the college. He was not without allies: the senior tutor was F. W. Head, later archbishop of Melbourne; the professorial fellows included the formidable Dixie Professor Gwatkin. But the master had supporters too: the governing body was sharply divided. In later years Raven described Chawner thus. He was 'a layman, unmarried and in ill health, a great administrator, officially something of a martinet, privately a charming host and delightful companion, obviously the strongest member of the Governing Body . . . He seemed like a man who had caught late in life the scepticism that affects most of us at eighteen; and like measles at his age it was a bad attack.' Emmanuel had many links with Anglican schools and a number of ordinands on its books. Its applications declined, and Raven received an enquiry 'from a headmaster . . . whether Emmanuel was a fit place for a candidate for holy orders'.[63] The young dean took this letter to the governing body, to the master's irritation. On 31 May 1910 a letter was sent to the master signed by seven of the governing body (seven out of sixteen, apart from the master himself), who 'wish to represent to the Master their conviction that his recent practice of issuing to the undergraduates pamphlets and circulars dealing with questions of religious controversy is detrimental to the general interests of the College and specifically

[63] Raven 1928a, p. 133; Dillistone 1975, pp. 70–1.

and gravely embarrassing to other officers of the College in the discharge of their statutory duties'.[64] The master could take comfort in that the other half of the governing body did not join the signatories, though two at least wrote their own protests to him; and he was sufficiently worried to take Counsel's opinion. This was to the effect that the master was not in breach of statutes, but had erred in his duty as master 'in publicly deprecating' the regulations on chapel attendance. On this point – to the modern observer palpably the most superficial – he admitted error, but on no other.

In the year before the protest had been sent to the master, the governing body had confirmed L. H. G. Greenwood lecturer in classics.[65] His rival for the post was the brilliant young J. T. Sheppard of King's. Nearly half a century later, so the story goes, as he processed into King's chapel, by now an ex-provost, Sir John Sheppard told the tale to a visitor, a fellow of Emmanuel.[66] He claimed that Emmanuel had rejected him 'as a militant atheist', a charge he strenuously denied. It is a piquant coincidence that this event should have fallen into the midst of the Chawner affair; and it seems improbable in the extreme that the governing body would have engaged in theological debate with the master in the chair. Greenwood was a respectable classic – and not (in the event) one of the master's opponents. Sheppard may have consoled himself at the time with the thought that his failure was due to *odium theologicum*, and it may indeed have affected some of the electors. But he was soon to be consoled in his own college, where already conventional faith and fervent unbelief were powerfully mingled. Through the winter of 1910–11 battle raged in Emmanuel, and the young Charles Raven – recently married, impecunious, full of desperate anxiety – prepared to pack his bags. But in March 1911 the master took a holiday in Provence for his health; and there he died. The passions cooled; the young dean kept his post.[67] The experience of the Chawner affair – which may teach us at the outset how serious was the threat to

[64] Cupitt 1970–1, p. 7. For what follows, see ibid. pp. 8–9.
[65] Emmanuel College Archives, TUT.4.2, pp. 295–7, 317–19; COL.11.3, p. 53. The protest is recorded under 31 May 1910.
[66] Professor Dennis Nineham, to whom I am indebted for kind permission to tell the story, first told me by Dr Frank Stubbings.
[67] Dillistone 1975, pp. 71–3; on Raven see below, pp. 147–50.

religion in the colleges in little more than a generation after the abolition of the tests – helped to form deep in Raven's mind the urgency of reconciling Christianity and the modern world.

Already in 1909 Chawner had been recognised as a leading opponent of orthodox Christianity, and when that celebrated eccentric C. K. Ogden was plotting the formation of the society of Heretics he turned to Chawner for advice. A remarkable letter of 6 December 1909 survives in the Emmanuel archives, in which Ogden canvasses a list of potential honorary members of the Heretics, which is evidently an informed cross-section of those prepared to declare themselves as agnostics or anyway opposed to traditional Christianity.[68] Of the fifteen names, two were already professors and four were later to be heads of house. Some may still have had an aura of *enfants terribles* about them in 1909, but they were not characters from the margin of Cambridge academic society.

In his delightful memoir of Sheppard, Patrick Wilkinson left open the puzzle of his beliefs.[69] Like many who heard him as provost utter the opening of the fourth gospel in the Christmas Eve carol service, Wilkinson felt that some element of belief was necessary to explain the fervour of his utterance. It may be so, and I am sure he was not a militant atheist. He loved to bless young men and evidently thought his blessing had some meaning. There is a sorry tale told of one student who, when addressed with Sheppard's customary 'Bless you, my boy', is said to have answered, 'I am not your boy, I'm from Selwyn.' But he misjudged Sheppard, whose blessings were ecumenical. He loved drama, as I myself witnessed by chance by attending the last nights of two of his productions of Greek plays – *The Frogs* and *Oedipus Coloneus*. After *The Frogs* he joined the final curtain and harangued us for many minutes on the theme that beauty is truth, truth beauty, a romantic faith hardly compatible (in its literal form) with any normal form of Christianity. The *Oedipus Coloneus* was appropriately chosen as his farewell, and we anticipated a speech without end; but he felt too much, and had too keen a sense of drama for that, and positively said nothing. The rest is silence.

---

[68] Emmanuel College Archives, COL.19.9, letter of 6 Dec. 1909.
[69] Wilkinson 1969, pp. 8–9.

The agnostics

Sheppard is one of a group of Apostles in Ogden's list: M'Taggart, Lowes Dickinson, J. M. Keynes, Verrall and G. M. Trevelyan are the others. Some of the greatest names – F. W. Maitland, G. E. Moore, Bertrand Russell, E. M. Forster – are missing, because Maitland had died in 1906 and the others were at this time away from Cambridge.

A society such as the Apostles formed of a group of young intellectuals engaged in intimate and frequent debate may tend to enhance the natural independence of its members, or do the exact opposite. The Apostles of the 1930s, or some of them at least, notoriously formed a cell of left-wing, anti-Christian, anti-capitalist friends, from whom spies and heroes were strangely formed.[70] On the other hand Henry Sidgwick reckoned the central quality of the Apostles as he had known them over many years in the 1850s and 60s, 'a belief that we *can* learn, and a determination that we *will* learn, from people of the most opposite opinions'.[71] That was certainly the chief lesson I myself learned from them in the late 1940s and early 50s: we had at one time a communist and a Catholic in the society together; I was myself one of a tiny group of one or two Anglicans who learned a deep respect for a variety of agnostic and anti-Christian positions, while imparting, to the whimsical entertainment of E. M. Forster, in whose rooms we met, to a group of young sceptics, a faint impression that the Christian faith might earn some respect even among the Apostles. In the twenty years before the First World War the Apostles lay between these two tendencies. G. E. Moore hammered out his own philosophy on the anvil of apostolic debate, but remained a man of profoundly independent mind.[72] Come 1914, most were pacifists: Rupert Brooke evidently was not, nor was Trevelyan, though a non-combatant – he was a very active leader of a team of ambulance drivers. One or two may have been believers, but the dominant ethos was agnostic. M'Taggart is now remembered as the architect of an idealist metaphysic of such amazing complexity that Hegel seems elementary beside him. In it he found no place for God. G. E.

---

[70] On the Apostles, see Allen 1978; Levy 1979/81; on their relation to the spies the books are legion – see e.g. Annan 1990, chap. 15. I owe much to conversations with Professor W. Lubenow, who is preparing a major study of the Apostles.
[71] Allen 1978, p. 4.   [72] For what follows, see esp. Levy 1979/81, chaps. 5–9.

Moore as a boy had a brief phase of intense dedication to an evangelical sect which seems to have inoculated him against religion for life.[73] He was deeply concerned for truth, but it was the truth of things we can grasp and understand which gripped and absorbed him; common sense and common experience were especially convincing to him. God and the Christian faith did not come within his experience or understanding, nor did they interest him. Lowes Dickinson was a Platonist and romantic. When he was an undergraduate in the 1880s, he tells us,

> It was exciting, to a degree that no modern young man of intelligence could comprehend, to discover that Christianity was not, as it were, an inextensible box, very small, in which the whole world was packed, but that an immense world extended quite outside of it ... It was exciting, then, to conceive that perhaps Jesus was not God but only an exceptional Being. It still seemed shocking at first that anyone should conceive him as only man. Then interest in him ... began to fade.[74]

The predominant view of the Apostles, among whom only a generation before Hort himself had been a central figure, came to be indifference; Christianity was no longer interesting. J. M. Keynes was more aggressively agnostic, and he and Sheppard as undergraduates led the remarkable debate in King's in 1903 on the formation of a college mission in London. 'During the last week', wrote Keynes on 5 February,

> the whole of King's has been turned upside down by a religious controversy – as to what lines a mission, which it is proposed that the College should start, is to be run upon. It was, at one time, to be high church, but Sheppard and I and several others helped to organise a regular opposition and we finally carried in the College meeting by a majority of some 75 to 25 that the scheme should be on a purely *secular* basis. It was a tremendous triumph ... I had to make a speech before the Provost, almost the whole College ...[75]

– but he hardly spared a thought for the feelings of the provost, Austen Leigh, the old, deeply conventional Victorian reformer, to whom the debate and its outcome must have been infinitely

---

[73] Levy 1979/81, pp. 39–41; on Moore, see below, pp. 438–42.
[74] Lowes Dickinson 1973, p. 61; on him see esp. Forster 1934.
[75] Harrod 1951, p. 93.

wounding.[76] Yet we can savour too the excitement of the young Apostles: Christianity was dead; the world was full of new ideas. Later that year, they could rejoice in a new gospel, Moore's *Principia Ethica*.

Russell and Moore were immortal philosophers, and Keynes had a range and depth of insight to enable him to talk their language. Sheppard was a romantic who seems never to have been quite on the same wavelength as Moore. Bob Trevelyan, Apostle and poet, was among Moore's closest friends.[77] Not so his brother G.M., perhaps because he lacked a speculative dimension. Like Lowes Dickinson and Rupert Brooke, he was a romantic, not a logician. Trevelyan in early life coupled agnosticism to a virulent anti-clericalism.[78] But he was a man of great depth of kindness curiously obscured by a dog-like tendency to bark. Astringent as his mind was, it was mellowed in later life by a warm charity, even towards the clergy – speeded by the remarkable discoveries that his daughter was engaged to (and soon married) a clergyman, and that his chair had fallen into the hands of a monk. For Bishop John Moorman and Dom David Knowles he came to have lively admiration and warm friendship – in Knowles' case fostered by their common love of the romantic poets. The copy of Mary Moorman's life of Wordsworth [vol. 1] given to David Knowles 'with much gratitude' by Trevelyan in 1957 is among my treasured possessions. Charity and faith are not the same, but the remarkable address he gave in Trinity chapel while he was master on 'Religion and Poetry' shows that he had travelled further than Sheppard.[79]

Among the unapostolic Heretics one name particularly attracts the historian's eye: Francis Darwin, later Sir Francis and one of the central figures of the greatest of all Cambridge dynasties. He must for the moment represent the distinguished body of natural scientists in Cambridge who regarded the Christian faith as a dying superstition. He was a botanist and naturalist, and his father's research assistant: his *Life and Letters of Charles Darwin* formed the principal monument to the founder of the dynasty before larger basilicas were undertaken in more recent times. He

[76] See pp. 34–5, 115.   [77] Levy 1979/81, pp. 48–9, 52–3, etc.
[78] Trevelyan 1943, p. 22; and the memoir by Mary Moorman, his daughter and wife of Bishop John Moorman (Moorman 1980, esp. p. 243). What follows is partly based on personal reminiscence.
[79] Trevelyan 1943, pp. 149–57.

will always be remembered as Gwen Raverat's Uncle Frank, that enchanting combination of fun and wit and gloom. Cambridge station is still haunted by him, for even though at home at 12.15 (five minutes before the cab was due) he 'said bitterly: "I have now given up all hope of catching the train" ', he still 'had to wait 35 minutes [for it] at the station'. Mrs Raverat made clear that he was also the most entertaining of her uncles. And she says of the Darwins as a family:

> They were sometimes very blind about things which lay outside their own particular world . . . For instance, they had no feeling at all for philosophy or religion. They accepted the Christian ethics, and would have liked to be ordinary Christians themselves, if they could have believed in the dogmas. In fact, they might well be called *Christian Parasites* (which is what most of us are, in reality). They were tolerant of the religion of others; only all religion seemed equally strange to them; and the rites and ceremonies were just curious survivals of magic and paganism: mumbo-jumbo.[80]

Francis and his second wife, Ellen Crofts, former fellow of Newnham, were consistent agnostics, and their children were not baptised. Gwen's father, Sir George, shared their agnosticism, but allowed his wife to direct the religious upbringing of their children which included fairly regular churchgoing, by which Gwen herself was inoculated against religion. 'I went to church cross, and got crosser all the time.'[81] 'When we were both between nine and ten years old, Frances [daughter of Francis and Ellen, and the future Mrs Cornford] took me to a very private place under the wooden bridge on the Little Island, and told me there, in confidence, that it was not at all the thing nowadays to believe in Christianity any more' – we are in the mid-1890s. 'It simply wasn't done. I felt at once that this was what I had always thought, though I had not been quite able to express it.'[82] It came as a great relief and Gwen gave up saying her prayers; though she admits that her mentor was not perfectly consistent, because she began soon after to be troubled in mind about not being baptised. Frances was also troubled when she read 'that she ought to love Christ more than her own mother . . . Believing what you can't

---

[80] Raverat 1952, pp. 188–95, esp. pp. 188–90. [81] Raverat 1952, p. 225.
[82] Raverat 1952, p. 219.

believe is a kind of exercise which some people like. Others don't. I don't. This is however the religious temperament, and it got Frances in the end.'[83] In this debate I am on the side of Gwen Raverat; none the less, I believe. She quite mistook the borderline of faith and doubt; but her insight was very characteristic of her family and her age, and not her own age alone, for she brought her thoughts to publication in 1952.

Let the final word be with M'Taggart. Shortly before Ogden's letter of 1909 was written, M'Taggart had sent a message of comfort to Chawner on his pamphlet. 'I am convinced that in twenty years those who remember 1909 will realise how much your action has done to promote in Cambridge, not only true learning, but also true religion.'[84] A far cry from Raven's attack of measles; and it is hard to think that either of them had quite taken the measure of the event.

CICCU AND SCM

Most of this chapter, like chapters 13–14, tends to gravitate to high table. We have observed students in chapel, and something of their diversity of belief; we have met them as agnostics. But student religion has tended to evade us. This is not wholly true, for all the dons had once been undergraduates, and many or most of them had formed their religious views, sometimes to considerable depth, before they took their degrees. Yet there is a large gap, which research one day will fill as the material revealed, for example, in J. C. Pollock's history of CICCU, *A Cambridge Movement* (1953), or T. T. Tatlow's *Story of the Student Christian Movement of Great Britain and Ireland* (1933), well illustrates. Both the CICCU and the SCM showed in their origins the creative vitality of student religion in Cambridge in the late nineteenth century. Both have long been part of national and international movements which owed much to Cambridge in their origins; both have had numerous vicissitudes such as student movements are especially prone to. At one point in the First World War CICCU 'was reduced to one registered member'.[85] Yet both

[83] Raverat 1952, p. 221.
[84] Emmanuel College Archives, COL.19.9, letter of 11 Nov. 1909.
[85] Pollock 1953, p. 193.

have had a measure of continuity and deep roots in Cambridge: the CICCU or the Cambridge Inter-Collegiate Christian Union, as it was called from the start, was founded in 1876; among the precursors of the SCM were the Cambridge Student Volunteer Missionary Union of 1892 and the national Student Movement, which became the Student Christian Movement in 1905. In early days they were closely linked – the Student Movement for a time was the national body of which CICCU was a limb. CICCU was always evangelical in spirit, but not narrowly so: it appealed to a wide variety of churchmen, and it related to a wide range of religious activity. Some of it found a home in the Trinity master's lodge, where Montagu Butler held highly successful Bible meetings, some in the Henry Martyn Hall, built for the University Church Missionary Union in memory of a great Cambridge missionary in 1886–7, soon the home of CICCU too.[86] There were other societies, such as the Church Society refounded by the high Anglican Gordon Selwyn of Corpus in 1906 – just as there were later to be other religious groups and societies claiming their share of undergraduate allegiance, such as the Sanctae Trinitatis Confraternitas, the high-church society of inter-war years. There was a variety of missions too, including the university and college missions in London – later to be joined by the long vacation missions to the fruit-pickers of north Cambridgeshire and the hop-pickers of Kent. But in early days the evangelicals claimed a preponderance among the undergraduates of Cambridge, and CICCU appealed to the liberal and conservative evangelical alike. There were signs already in the 1900s of a polarisation, which became much more marked as the societies revived in the 1920s. By then the SCM had become still more comprehensive, more inclined to accept liberal opinions, as much concerned with debate as with prayer. CICCU had become the preserve of the conservative, fundamentalist, evangelical. This meant for a time accepting relatively small numbers; but they were greatly strengthened by the formation of the Inter-Varsity Fellowship – later to become the Vatican of the conservative evangelical students – and the women's wing, the CWICCU, formed in 1920 and long since merged in the parent body. They also had a close relation for a

---

[86] Pollock 1953, pp. 113–14.

time in the early 1920s and again in the early 30s with Dr Frank Buchman and the so-called Oxford Group, though his highly personal methods quickly aroused a measure of suspicion. In the 1940s and 50s the SCM was much more in tune with the opinions of the leading college deans and chaplains than CICCU – even though some of them tended a little to keep both at bay in the attempt to make the colleges flourishing centres of religious discussion as well as worship. But in the mid and late twentieth century fundamentalist evangelicalism has been a major growth area in the protestant churches, and the CICCU has flourished again. It lives now in a much more variegated religious world than that of the 1870s and 80s in which it was born. In the twentieth century there have been centres of high church influence in the Oratory of the Good Shepherd and the Society of St Francis.[87] College chapels are centres of spontaneous worshippers no longer dragooned by deans and tutors, and outside the colleges, the CICCU and the SCM, a whole spectrum of groups and societies flourish, especially those associated with the leading parish churches, with the Catholic Chaplaincy in Fisher House and the free church chaplaincies and colleges.

[87] See Tibbatts 1988.

Chapter 5

THEOLOGY

LIGHTFOOT

Joseph Barber Lightfoot was born in 1828 and went to school at the Royal Institution at Liverpool and King Edward's, Birmingham – where he just missed Westcott but was contemporary with Edward White Benson, later to be archbishop of Canterbury and Henry Sidgwick's brother-in-law.[1] A close bond with Benson was to be important to them both, and to help Sidgwick and Lightfoot to influence one another.[2] From 1847 to 1879 he lived in Cambridge as a member of Trinity, from 1852 a resident fellow. He was a man of exceptional stature, who felt many of the conservative impulses of his kind, but grew out of them; yet in the process, so deeply did he understand both the old world and the new that he could be a peacemaker between young and old, conservative and radical. G. F. Browne regarded Westcott as conservative, Lightfoot as progressive; 'but . . . the men were too great for anything like party action. As I learned more of the ways of the Council [of the Senate], I learned that the whispers of Professor Lightfoot to Dr Westcott . . . not infrequently neutralised Dr Westcott's vote . . .'[3] At one time or another Lightfoot defended celibacy and religious tests for fellows. But his voice was to be decisive in the abolition of celibacy[4] – though himself remaining a lifelong bachelor – and in reconciling the clergy of Trinity and Cambridge to the events of 1871.

[1] For what follows see Eden and Macdonald 1932; Robinson 1981; and esp. Chadwick 1970, pp. 69–71. For Lightfoot, I am much indebted to a lecture by David Thompson, now Thompson 1992.
[2] It seems likely that his change of mind on religious tests was influenced by Sidgwick, as Sidgwick's plans in the late 1860s were by Lightfoot (see Sidgwick 1906, p. 198).
[3] Hort 1896, II, 94; Browne 1915, p. 132 (David Thompson first drew my attention to these references).   [4] Browne 1915, p. 161.

Lightfoot

Lightfoot loved an argument, and his controversial writing is lively and robust.[5] But he was a kindly, friendly person, a great peacemaker in the Cambridge of the 1860s and 1870s. We are told that in early years he was somewhat reserved and shy in private, but blossomed in larger gatherings; as bishop he was to be noted for his geniality,[6] whether addressing miners' rallies, confirming the young in remote parishes, instructing his devoted pupils and chaplains, or marching across the Durham hills with his lively dog – a St Bernard we are told it was, giving to worrying the sheep Lightfoot had come to save; and we may well believe that a man who had spent all his life in Trinity, where dogs may not go, knew little of their ways, however much he delighted in their company.[7] He was a tireless professor and rapidly wore himself out as bishop; he died in 1889 aged only 61. But he lives on in his portrait in the Lightfoot Room, a warm if disconcerting presence in the heart of the Divinity School he helped to create – disconcerting, as only a bad portrait of an extremely ugly man can be, but also because those who sit at his feet are constantly reminded of such consummate scholarship, which may inspire us but may also lead us to despair.

St Paul's Epistle to the Galatians, which Lightfoot published in 1865, is my favourite among his books.[8] One does not go to it for the most subtle or profound theological exposition of the mind of St Paul. Lightfoot was a modest man who knew well he lacked the theological depth – and the sensitivity to language – of Hort and Westcott; and in any case major discoveries such as the marvellous rubbish heap of papyrus from the Cairo Genizah, much of which came to the Cambridge University Library a while after Lightfoot's death, have greatly enriched our knowledge of the thought world in which St Paul worked.[9] There are elements in Lightfoot's historical understanding which are antiquated: of such was his belief in national character, which led him to seek in the epistle the natural contours of the Gaulish people in

---

[5] For Lightfoot's controversial writing, see Lightfoot 1889.
[6] Eden and Macdonald 1932, pp. 5, 35–6; Chadwick 1970, p. 69. A. C. Benson regarded him as not so much shy as naturally silent (Benson 1911, esp. p. 189).
[7] Eden and Macdonald 1932, pp. 29, 134.
[8] I use here the third edition of 1869.
[9] For the biblical work of Lightfoot, Westcott and Hort and its limitations, see the admirable summary in Neill and Wright 1988, chaps. 2–3.

Galatia[10] – though in fairness one may recall that similarly absurd notions were still current among eminent scholars down to the mid-twentieth century. But when that has been said, and notice taken of all that we have learned since 1865, it remains a masterpiece of historical exposition. There has been constant argument ever since whether the epistle was addressed to 'north' or 'south' Galatia, and on the whole Lightfoot's preference for the north has not prevailed. But the arguments on this side and on that have never been laid out with such clarity and force, nor the evidence for the date and authenticity of the epistle set in so clear a light, nor its character and content so clearly expounded.[11] And if we seek today a lucid exposition of the different views which have been held about Jesus' family – 'the brethren of the Lord' – Lightfoot's masterly appendix is the first place to find it.[12] The clarity of his mind was united to a breadth of learning, and a sanity of exposition, which make his commentaries matchless.

In forming the Greek text which he prints and glosses, he acknowledged the help of Westcott and Hort.[13] From 1863 till 1881 this celebrated pair of intimate friends were at work on the text of the Greek New Testament, and its publication marked a great step forward. It was rapidly followed by the discovery of much early papyrus material which has altered the whole complexion of the subject since 1881; but it laid sure foundations for later work. Hort was much more the pure scholar than Westcott, though they shared a deep interest in words and a strong feeling (not so marked in Lightfoot) for their theological significance. 'In a whole term's lecturing', it has been said of Hort, 'he would cover perhaps ten verses of an Epistle.'[14] Westcott had a deep knowledge of Greek, especially patristic Greek, and a loving affection for every word in the New Testament. His learning, and his friendship for Lightfoot and Hort, kept him in scholarly paths. But he had a strong strain of mysticism and a natural flair for the obscure – 'A critic once said', wrote A. C. Benson, 'that Westcott's writings resembled the French definition

---

[10] Lightfoot 1869, pp. 1–17.   [11] Lightfoot 1869, pp. 18–68.
[12] Lightfoot 1869, pp. 247–82.
[13] For what follows, see Neill and Wright 1988, pp. 74–81.
[14] Neill and Wright 1988, p. 98.

of metaphysics as the art of bewildering oneself methodically'.[15] He was naturally an optimist, so that he felt sure the end of the religious tests in Cambridge would be good for Christianity and the Church of England; but he was also deeply conservative by instinct, and worried by the possible outcome of scholarly enquiry. In 1860, early in his friendship with Hort, he had written anxiously 'for a guarantee in advance that the results of the investigations would be satisfactory from the point of view of orthodox convictions'.[16] Hort wrote to Lightfoot, addressing them both. 'If you make a decided conviction of the absolute infallibility of the N.T. practically a *sine qua non* for cooperation, I fear I could not join you.'[17]

But we should probably be wrong to take this too seriously. Hort wrote in almost identical words to Lightfoot and Westcott; and in spite of the depth and purity of their friendship, Hort seems to have retained a certain reserve as to his colleagues' qualities of mind.[18] At times one wonders if he was in his heart a little jealous of Lightfoot, so much more prolific, extrovert, capable of expressing himself in print. Hort felt in himself a depth of theological insight which he could not discern in Lightfoot; but Lightfoot laid more weight on solving historical problems than theological – and it is characteristic of him that his most substantial foray into theology should be on the origins of 'the Christian ministry' and especially of episcopacy, which shows remarkable subtlety and insight.[19] Hort was doubtless painfully aware that his colleagues were more productive than he. He may also have a little resented the concentration of his own energies on textual criticism, which he thought only a preparation for greater studies to come.[20] The truth seems now to be that all three flourished most (as is common in the history of scholarship) in collaboration; and that it was his common work with Westcott

[15] Benson 1911, p. 25; Chadwick 1963, p. 15.
[16] Neill and Wright 1988, pp. 95–6, citing Hort 1896, I, 418–22, esp. 419–20.
[17] Hort 1896, I, 420; Neill and Wright 1988, p. 96n.; cf. Barrett 1959, pp. 7–13.
[18] For what follows, see esp. Hort 1896, II, 35, 79; and see p. 12.
[19] Lightfoot 1868, pp. 179–267. David Thompson has drawn attention to a very searching passage in an address by Lightfoot of 1873 on the theological needs of the age, ranging from its answer to utilitarianism (shades of Sidgwick!) to contacts with other religions, relations with science, and approach to social questions (Thompson 1992, pp. 13–14). This reflects a much wider and deeper theological consciousness than appears in *Galatians*.
[20] Cf. e.g. Hort 1896, I, 233–5.

which drew out Hort's unique genius as a textual critic. Of the three, it seems to me that Lightfoot had the best judgement: he saw most clearly where their true quality, and the possibility of achievement, lay; Hort the textual critic would in any case very probably have outlived Hort the systematic theologian. Nor is it likely that even the textual criticism would have seen the light without Westcott's constant help. Hort suffered much from ill-health and somewhat from perfectionism; but his son's *Life* is packed with evidence that he had no sense of time. He accepted commissions for new books or articles – he accepted new committees – with wild abandon.

WESTCOTT

There is a rock-like quality about Westcott's faith which is impressive in its way; but perhaps his convictions had come too early and too easily to him for perfect comfort in the unfolding revelation of scholarship. There is a charming story told of how Westcott first met his future wife. He encountered a schoolfriend beset by a bully, whom he sent packing; the friend took him home to tea, and introduced him to his sister; this led to a romantic friendship which blossomed many years later into marriage.[21] At the very end of his life, when he was bishop of Durham, his wife died, and with her a great part of his life departed; it was a heroic effort which carried him through a few months more of active pastoral work before he rejoined her. At the time that the friendship began, she was about twelve and he seventeen. Many of his convictions were as early formed and as lasting as his bond with Mrs Westcott. Human friendship was also very deep in his nature, and the example of Lightfoot and Hort kept him firmly in the path of scholarship.

Westcott was born in 1825, and was fellow of Trinity from 1849: in the years which followed both Hort and Lightfoot were to be among his pupils. From 1852 to 1870 he was a master at Harrow, and found time to write a series of books on the New

---

[21] Westcott 1903, I, 7–11, 32. There were various versions of the story; what seems certain is that Westcott formed this romantic friendship when she was 12 or so, he 17 (cf. esp. ibid. I, 32, II, 404). For what follows, ibid. II, 336–44.

Testament – his work on the social gospel belongs to the 1880s in particular, his systematic theology to a later epoch still.[22]

In 1870 Westcott returned to Cambridge as Regius Professor; in 1871 the religious tests were abolished, and after mighty efforts the Theological Tripos was approved in the same year.[23] The first class list was issued in 1874, comprising three firsts, six seconds, eleven thirds and one aegrotat.[24] Since then the numbers have modestly risen and modestly fallen again, but the standards are a good deal higher; as throughout the Cambridge triposes, the thirds have been almost obliterated. Also in 1871 there was a thorough reformation of the higher degrees in divinity, once freely distributed by Richard Bentley to enlarge the whig vote in the Senate, and in 1871 'acquired by anyone who could print a few sermons and pay the fee'.[25] Westcott was in fact distinctly harsh in his judgement of DDs; standards rose instantly.

The Oxford honours school dates from 1870, and in many ways the two universities moved forward hand in hand. But the emphasis was more narrowly historical in Cambridge; and since these events coincided with the golden age of historical influence on theology – Adolf Harnack was a student in the early 1870s – Cambridge theology could be in the forefront of world endeavour at this time. The triumvirs were natural leaders of the enterprise which produced the Revised Version of the Bible in 1881.[26] All the stars of British biblical scholarship had gathered month by month in the Jerusalem Chamber in Westminster Abbey. Of Hort it was said that he talked 'for three years out of the ten years during which the revisers sat . . .'[27] Lightfoot was not a textual critic after the fashion of Hort but a historian. 'Yet', writes Owen Chadwick, 'he was the greatest scholar in the Jerusalem chamber, and his cautious utterances were weighty beyond all others.'[28] They all served in other spheres: Hort was a country parson, Westcott a canon of Peterborough for a time, then of Westminster, and Lightfoot a canon of St Paul's – both

[22] Westcott 1903, passim.
[23] Winstanley 1947, pp. 85–90, 158–63; Chadwick 1963, pp. 22–4.
[24] Tanner 1917, p. 812.
[25] Chadwick 1970, pp. 450–1; cf. Chadwick 1963, pp. 22–3.
[26] Chadwick 1970, pp. 45–50.   [27] Above, p. 12; Chadwick 1970, p. 49.
[28] Ibid.

the last two while holding their Cambridge chairs. In St Paul's Lightfoot worked side by side with the great conservative tractarian and Oxford professor Canon Liddon – so like in his devotion to the cathedral and to preaching, so unlike in Liddon's refusal to come to terms with current scholarship.[29] In 1879 Lightfoot left Cambridge, and London, for Durham – to be followed by Westcott in 1890; and it was Hort who pressed on Emmanuel College the opportunity and the duty to fulfil Lightfoot's work in fostering the study of 'history and more especially of ecclesiastical history' by founding the Dixie Chair in 1878–84.[30]

As with Hort, so with Westcott, the most lasting elements in his scholarship lie in his textual work on the Greek New Testament. Hort brought out the best in him: his learning, zeal for words and warmth of desire to find theological depth in their meaning. Unlike Hort, he was immensely prolific, and his standing as a scholar perhaps suffers from this. It is not easy to define precisely what it is that separates Lightfoot from Westcott, but whereas much of Lightfoot's *Galatians* can be read and reread today without the discomfort of feeling that over a century has passed, Westcott's Commentary on St John's Gospel (1881), immensely popular for over half a century, now gathers the dust.[31] Westcott's impressive books on social problems perhaps wear a little better, but are obviously of their time.[32] Owen Chadwick cites some remarkable figures for lecture attendances in the 1880s: Westcott's most popular course gathered over 300, his most specialised 10–20; Hort's classes comprised 11 or 9.[33] I hope none of us may be judged by such evidence; but it is a salutary reminder of the immense success of Westcott's labours, which reached far beyond the Divinity School where he lectured – far beyond Bishop Auckland where he died – to innumerable parsonages and libraries throughout the English-speaking world. The Clergy Training School he founded was renamed Westcott

[29] Chadwick 1970, pp. 378–9, 385–7.
[30] For early discussions of the Dixie Chair, see Emmanuel College Archives, COL. 18.15c, esp. p. 89; cf. Whitney 1919, p. 7. The quotation is from the Council's Report preparing for the setting up of the Lightfoot scholarships: Clark 1904, pp. 329–30.
[31] For a sympathetic view of Westcott as commentator, see Barrett 1959.
[32] Westcott 1887, 1901, 1903.
[33] Chadwick 1970, p. 453 n. 2.

House with good reason.[34] Yet it is primarily in his New Testament studies, and for his textual criticism, that Westcott's scholarship survives today.

THE DIVINITY SCHOOL AND THE THEOLOGICAL COLLEGES

Meanwhile the least distinguished of the divinity professors of the 1860s had laid the foundations for the most substantial monument of this era in Cambridge theology. The building of the Selwyn Divinity School has a curious history, brought into the light of day by Gordon Rupp in his delightful centenary lecture.[35] The Lady Margaret's Professor of Divinity had for centuries been chosen by all the BDs and DDs in the university, and as a majority of these had long been members of St John's, it had tended to provide outdoor relief for worthy Johnian divines. In 1855 there was a movement for reform: Harold Browne of Emmanuel was put up against the candidate from St John's, the amiable, undistinguished William Selwyn, brother of the better known George Augustus Selwyn, bishop of New Zealand, in whose memory Selwyn College was founded. Browne might have prevailed by a single vote, but Dr Whewell became impatient with the proceedings, went for a walk, and returned to find that there had been a tie, and the Vice-Chancellor had given Selwyn his casting vote.[36] Selwyn was a kindly man and well-to-do; and the Lady Margaret's Chair had long been the best endowed in the university. Of the £1,500 a year at which it was then assessed he gave £700 to Browne until he became bishop of Ely in 1864.[37] Meanwhile Selwyn had urged the Divinity Board as early as 1858 to minute its need for a new Divinity School – its ancient room in the Old Schools was small and dark and overrun with other business. From 1864 Selwyn's surplus income was transferred from Browne to a building fund, which steadily accumulated until in 1874 it stood at nearly £9,000.[38] The time was ripe for building, and Selwyn himself favoured the vacant site across the grass from the Senate House; but as Rupp says with

---

34 See below, p. 144.   35 Rupp 1981.
36 Rupp 1981, p. 421.   37 Rupp 1981, p. 421.
38 Rupp 1981, pp. 418, 421.

relish, 'the 1870s were not congenial to emphasising the temporal estate of the clergy'; and eventually the site opposite St John's was chosen.[39] In competition with Gilbert Scott and Blomfield, Basil Champneys was selected as architect, and he designed a building in Tudor gothic red brick to stand its ground opposite the Tudor red-brick front of St John's. It was intended to provide space also for the 'literary professors' of law and history and the like, who had no new museums to expand in;[40] but it was mainly and primarily for divinity, and its character was ecclesiastical, in marked contrast to the charming villas of the 'Queen Anne' revival which Champneys provided for the secular foundation of Newnham. Gradually the Faculty of Divinity has spread to every corner of the building and beyond; and learned to sigh for a large lecture room in which current theology may make itself heard. In fairness to Champneys, it must be said that the smaller lecture rooms, though not ideal for their purpose, are fully as good as most of those provided to the arts faculties in the 1960s. If professors of divinity and history fail to attract or hold audiences, they may apportion (if they wish) a part of the blame to their predecessors who failed in the briefs they gave in the 1870s and the 1960s.

I have called the late nineteenth century the golden age of Cambridge theology; and such it was in the sense that in the smaller academic world of the 1870s and 1880s it had few rivals outside Germany in stature and fame. It has had far more in the twentieth century; but the school which Burkitt and Raven and C. H. Dodd and the Chadwicks have adorned can hardly be said to have suffered decline. In the 1870s the Divinity School reflected not only the generosity of Selwyn but the panache of his faculty. The same decade had seen a more modest building, also in Tudor gothic, by a lesser architect, W. M. Fawcett, provide a home for the Cavendish Professor and the growth of Cambridge physics.[41] Only a little expanded, it was to encompass the atoms of Rutherford and his disciples well into the twentieth century.

[39] Rupp 1981, p. 422.
[40] Rupp 1981, p. 422; for the Divinity School and Newnham, see Watkin 1989; Pevsner 1970, pp. 37, 194, 205; cf. also ibid. p. 210.
[41] See p. 176.

These two buildings are notable documents of the aims and methods of the leaders of university reform in the 1870s.

Thus it is abundantly clear that theology, like physics, benefited from the advance of scientific enquiry, the general raising of academic standards and the more cosmopolitan outlook of British scholars in the late nineteenth century; that in some sense these disciplines were climbing the same stairs – were allies. Yet is there not a great paradox here? Is it not notorious that the decades from 1860 to 1900 witnessed a mighty conflict between science and religion, that very many Englishmen lost their faith – or never acquired it – that in Oxford and Cambridge the church lost its monopoly and most young fellows no longer sought ordination?[42] Recently A. G. L. Haig has produced some fascinating tables showing the pattern in the decline of Cambridge first-class honours graduates entering orders: from 65.2 per cent in 1841–3 to 18 per cent in 1881–3.[43] Yet contemporary witnesses, though fully aware of the advance of unbelief, were not always convinced that this reflected a decline in religious fervour. 'Many capable observers', Owen Chadwick reports from a wide and deep knowledge of contemporary comment, 'believed that the two universities, regarded less as institutions than as groups of men, were more religious in 1884 than before 1871.'[44] Needless to say, we cannot measure religious fervour, and all the statistics are unsatisfactory. If we ask – was the standard of theological instruction and so, for example, of university sermons, rising or falling? – we have seen that this question can be answered very firmly: there was little theology in Cambridge in the mid-nineteenth century, and it was one of the supreme centres of the subject in the world from 1870 on. If we enquire into clergy training in the new professional sense, we see a similar advance. The most ancient theological college to try its fortunes in Cambridge was Cheshunt College, founded by the countess of Huntingdon in 1768, but this only came to Cambridge in 1906, by then Congregational, later United Reformed.[45] Meanwhile an active movement within the established church had produced

---

[42] On the conflict of science and religion in general, see Chadwick 1970, pp. 1–35.
[43] Haig 1986, esp. p. 190.
[44] Chadwick 1970, p. 448.
[45] Orchard n.d., esp. p. 16; *VCH Cambs*, III, 139. On Cheshunt, see now Welch 1990.

the twin colleges named after Wycliffe in Oxford and Ridley in Cambridge: Ridley Hall opened its doors in 1881. Lightfoot and Westcott had been warm supporters of this scheme until they discovered that one of the founders, Bishop Perry, had written some theological stipulations of an evangelical character into the trust deed for Ridley Hall; and so – rather in the fashion of Henry Sidgwick and his friends founding a second women's college ten years earlier – they founded the Clergy Training School in the same year, 1881, to represent the Anglican church, as they saw it, in a fuller sense.[46] The Clergy Training School was renamed Westcott House after its chief founder's death. In 1892 the redoubtable pair of learned sisters, Mrs Gibson and Mrs Lewis, who had built Castle Brae in Chesterton Lane as a memorial to the Scottish baronial homes of their native land, offered to endow a Presbyterian training school, and Westminster College opened in 1899. Wesley House was to follow in 1921.[47]

Yet there are many other signs of religious health. 'At Cambridge over 150 undergraduates taught in the Jesus Lane Sunday School during Lent 1877. Religious societies flourished as never before – the Confraternity of the Holy Trinity, the Christian Union, the Church Society at Cambridge.'[48] But there were naturally some at the end of the century who 'thought Oxford and Cambridge to be less religious than they seemed to be in the eighties'.[49] Among the intellectuals, we are moving into the era of Moore and Russell – of a generation of young graduates to whom religion was totally irrelevant.[50] But for many it counted as much as ever, and our answer to the paradox must be ambiguous.

Let us look a little more closely at Haig's figures. A fundamental difficulty is that most of our other evidence relates to a small élite: those who studied theology were always few in number, the serious theologians a tiny minority of the graduates of the later nineteenth century. It was in any case an age of specialisation in the professions as well as in academic disciplines; and the bishops looked to theological colleges as much as to universities to fill

[46] *VCH Cambs*, III, 139–41. On Ridley Hall see also Bullock 1941–53.
[47] *VCH Cambs*, III, 139, 141.
[48] Chadwick 1970, pp. 448–9.
[49] Chadwick 1970, p. 449.
[50] See pp. 127–9.

their parishes – however much some might retain their devotion to trained theologians, as did Lightfoot at Durham.[51] Then again, the schoolmaster and the don of the 1840s were characteristically clergymen; by 1900 they were laymen. In some cases this represented a change of faith and vocation. But in how many? We cannot tell. Nor can we tell how many of the clergy of the mid-century were engaged in teaching. Haig has indeed been most scrupulous in sorting out the known schoolmasters, and distinguishing the clergy from the laity.[52] But many clergymen of the nineteenth century, like Jane Austen's father in the eighteenth, held informal schools in their parsonages.[53] From the mid-nineteenth century on the land was filled with village schools, many of them church schools, in which the parson spent some of his time teaching.[54] The professions were related in a way no figures can disentangle; and the entries in Venn's *Alumni*, on which the investigator must rely, cannot be expected to tell us about informal schools or teaching. Then again there is a large proportion of college fellows among the clergy of the 1840s. Some fellows already did not have legally to be in orders, and the fashion was already declining from the middle of the century; some changes in college statutes helped to speed this decline in the 1860s. Meanwhile there were some dons who entered orders still as a matter of course.[55] This practice had virtually ceased by 1900; and a major reason for its decline was precisely the increasing sense of vocation. An ordinand expected, and a bishop demanded, a special vocation and vocational training before he became deacon or priest. Like everyone else, the clergy were becoming more professional. A college fellowship is still a title to orders: that is to say, if a fellow feels a vocation and a bishop is willing, he can be ordained without seeking a curacy. But the practice has been rare in this century, and that has as much to do with fashion, with rising standards of clerical specialism, as with declining fervour. Haig's statistics are extremely interesting and revealing; but as with all such figures, their interpretation leaves

51 Eden and Macdonald 1932, chap. 3.
52 Haig 1986, pp. 196–8.
53 Thus my grandfather, the Reverend A. H. Stanton, kept a small school when he was a curate at Bournemouth *c*.1890.
54 Chadwick 1970, pp. 186–92; for town schools, ibid. pp. 299–308.
55 Brooke 1985, pp. 231–2 and 231 n. 30.

many puzzles. It would be excessively sceptical, however, at the end of the day, to doubt that agnosticism and indifference had made substantial progress in Cambridge by 1900 – just as it would be to doubt that there was much and varied fervour too.

THE EARLY TWENTIETH CENTURY

Meanwhile, after Westcott had departed for Durham in 1890 and Hort had died in 1892, the study of theology continued and flourished. One could dwell on the Regius Professor, H. B. Swete, worthy successor to the triumvirs, or the early Dixie Professors, Mandell Creighton and H. M. Gwatkin; or one could hasten forward to Bethune-Baker and Burkitt. Creighton was one of the true founders of Cambridge history; and Gwatkin – who laid his mark on Charles Raven and in a certain measure on my father – was a brilliant, if almost inarticulate, polymath. The dust has gathered on his work on the early church, but his influence remained. I resist the temptation to dwell on that delectable eccentric, Joseph Armitage Robinson, who spread a sharp mind of a naturally discursive tendency over the Epistle to the Ephesians, as he was later (while dean of Westminster and Wells) to ramble in the tenth and twelfth centuries and among the medieval deans and archdeacons of Wells.[56] Bethune-Baker stayed longer in Cambridge and grew to be a central figure in the Anglican modernist movement, and to leave a fund of money and entertaining stories behind him. He especially delighted to recall the little girl of five who declared in her Cambridge school that there were four bad persons in the Bible beginning with B, Bathsheba, Beelzebub and Bethune-Baker.[57] From Bethune-Baker's writings it is difficult now to recapture any of the excitement he inspired; and in his later years young high church-men came to regard him as an autocratic liberal.[58] But this is not so with F. C. Burkitt (1864–1935), layman, orientalist, Syriac scholar – and the author of *The Gospel History and its Transmission*

[56] On Creighton see esp. Creighton 1904; on Gwatkin there is an incomplete MS Life in the Emmanuel Archives. I hope to say more of them in the forthcoming *History of Emmanuel* by P. Collinson, C. N. L. Brooke, and S. Bendall. On Armitage Robinson, see Taylor 1991 and esp. Robinson 1903, 1921, 1923.

[57] Dillistone 1975, p. 57, n. 5. On Bethune-Baker, see *DNB 1951–60*, pp. 57–9 (H. Chadwick).

[58] Cf. Chadwick 1990, pp. 27–8.

(1906), an incisive and exceedingly readable evocation of the state of synoptic studies in the generation before the form critics came to power.[59] I press on to Charles Raven.[60]

CHARLES RAVEN

Charles Raven was born in 1885 and came up to Caius in 1904, too late to have known the triumvirs personally, though their memory and their books were very much alive. At Caius he was cured of his affection for the Classical Tripos by W. T. Lendrum (one of those teachers who separates the strong from the weak by ferocious criticism), and wooed and won the master's niece.[61] He also transferred his interest to theology, and fell under the spell of J. H. A. Hart of St John's and H. M. Gwatkin. By Gwatkin and Bethune-Baker he was inspired to a deep interest in the early church, and a disdain for the Middle Ages which never left him. From Hart he learned an approach to the New Testament which fostered his best and worst instincts as a scholar.

In commenting on Schweitzer's *Quest of the Historical Jesus* – that most celebrated and seminal study above all of the Odyssey of nineteenth-century scholarship – Hart had sharply observed:

> Wheat and tares alike are rooted up and dried and pressed and labelled and discussed – and you learn as much about the living plant as you can of a fox by contemplating its mask and pads and brush, each cured and mounted for display as the relics of an animal worthy to be hunted or shot or trapped according to the custom of the country. For scientific observation of living things, the systematist must wait upon the biologist. You must go to the earth and hide and wait if you want to see the vixen play with her cubs.[62]

As a call to read the gospels as living texts – to study history as a revelation of life – this is wholly admirable; and as Raven was already a devoted naturalist it enchanted him. But it also perhaps a little explains a curious crevasse in his scholarship, an impatience

---

[59] On F. C. Burkitt (1864–1935) see *DNB 1931–1940*, pp. 124–5 (J. F. Bethune-Baker); Ratcliff 1935.
[60] What follows owes something to personal knowledge; far more to Dillistone 1975.
[61] Dillistone 1975, pp. 40–1, 47–8.
[62] Quoted Dillistone 1975, p. 51.

with the depths and the details of scholarly fields which did not appeal to him. It was in part the penalty he paid for being a polymath. He learned in the Cambridge Divinity School what real scholarship can be, and his early work on Apollinaris comprises solid and serious scholarship.[63] Much later, in the 1940s, he was to publish his *John Ray: Naturalist*, which is an immortal masterpiece in the history of science.[64] To it he brought a deep knowledge of scientific research as it impinged on the world of a naturalist, and an understanding of the mental world of the seventeenth century of exceptional depth and insight. But when his whole mind was not gripped and engaged by a scholarly problem, he could be remarkably inadvertent and even superficial. He followed *John Ray* with a wider sweep, *English Naturalists from Neckam to Ray*; and while he dwells in the Middle Ages he shows little of the penetration or depth of learning and understanding which are so conspicuous when he reaches the seventeenth century.[65]

Raven was a man of great power of mind and charm and eloquence. The first lecture I heard him give, on bird-watching, was an unforgettable experience for a ten- or eleven-year-old schoolboy. He was a man of quite remarkable moral and physical courage, yet dependent to an exceptional degree on human support – on his wives and his friends, on the approval of his colleagues and on public acclaim – a sad necessity for a man who deliberately stood out for unpopular causes, above all for pacifism and for the ordination of women.[66] Raven travelled widely and his influence was felt all over the world; but for most of his career he was based in Cambridge, first as dean of Emmanuel from 1910 to 1920 – with a long break when he was an army chaplain; then from 1932 to 1950 as Regius Professor of Divinity and fellow and master of Christ's. He lived through two mastership elections: in the first he was the unsuccessful, in the second the successful candidate. A part of him lives in the character of Jago, the defeated candidate in C. P. Snow's *The Masters* (1951): the fire and warmth, the deep dependence on others, the mercurial

---

[63] Raven 1923.   [64] Raven 1942.

[65] Raven 1947. It has the significant subtitle 'a study of the making of the modern world'. For an example of superficiality, cf. the 'bad attack' of measles, above p. 124.

[66] Dillistone 1975, chaps. 13, 15; Raven 1928b.

temperament are his. But Snow made no attempt to portray the scholar, nor to sketch the stature of the man. An extraordinary trick of fortune made this eminent pacifist Vice-Chancellor just after the end of the Second World War, from 1947 to 1949, and it fell on him to greet Field-Marshal Smuts as Chancellor in his own and Smuts' college, and to entertain war leaders and Churchill himself as they came collecting honorary degrees.[67] Less improbably, it was he who conferred the first degree Cambridge offered to a woman, when he made the Queen (now Queen Mother) a doctor of the university in 1948.

His pacifism, in a strange and powerful way, linked Raven the man of his age with Raven the prophet. He came to it by no easy path, for he had struggled in 1914 already with a call to war and a call to peace; and it was not until the 1920s that he finally made up his mind. It was partly the mode of the twenties – the Great War must have ended all wars in right-thinking folk's minds; like so many of his generation, he had no presentiment of Hitler before he came to power. But he also had a deeper and more penetrating insight into the nature and the horror of war, and into what must now be recognised as a tragic dilemma facing all serious Christians.[68] He was strongly ecumenical in outlook, and mingled freely in the 1920s and 30s with communions in which women ministers were coming to be an accepted part of the scene. Towards the end of his life he was a central figure in a remarkable Working Party set up by the British Council of Churches to discuss the theology of ordination and the future of women in the churches. I was myself invited to one of their meetings to offer historical evidence; but when I arrived Raven had had a characteristic change of mind and decided that history (as it related to women) was bunk; so I had in the event a pleasant weekend observing this group of female ministers and male Anglican converts (if that is the word I want), who took it for granted that the ordination of women would come even to the Anglican Communion. That was nearly thirty years ago, and Raven had already been an advocate in the cause for a quarter of a century.[69]

---

[67] Dillistone 1975, pp. 318–21.   [68] Dillistone 1975, chap. 13.
[69] See esp. Raven 1928b.

In these regions he was a prophet; in the common study of theology and science he was a major prophet. His own views on the origins of life and on natural religion would not command wide assent today; but his insistence that it was perhaps the most urgent and hopeful task for Christian theologians in the twentieth century has lost none of its force, nor his assurance that theologians must accept as axiomatic God's blessing on the endeavours of pure scholarship.[70] His own theology tended to a moderate liberalism: he was a supporter of the Modern Churchman's Union, but not a devoué of it. He sought a new reformation and did not find it; and there was a strong element of disappointment and discouragement in him in his later years. To us it seems unfounded; for by his example and inspiration he had helped to breed a new generation to whom the total integrity for which he stood – the utter refusal to allow dogma to build compartments in the mind, the assurance that all valid academic enquiry took place on common ground blessed by God – is a secure faith. There are many things in our world which would alarm him: the growth of fundamentalism and the widespread justification of force in religious and political argument above all. But his was a powerful and beneficent voice which can still be heard.

If he was a pessimist when contemplating his own achievement, his approach to natural religion had an element of optimism in it which brought him into unavoidable conflict with many of the great continental and American theologians of his day. Reinhold Niebuhr's theology was more deeply imbedded in the hard facts of human conflict than his; Karl Barth in crisis human and divine; Bultmann dissolved the gospels into a thousand fragments, leaving a deep assertion of faith linked to history and reason by the slenderest of threads. Raven believed deeply in a theology of evolutionary process; and these lines of thought were profoundly antipathetic to him.[71] His own particular constructions have hardly survived the passage of time. But his approach – the union of reason, scholarship and science in the service of science and theology – lives on.

[70] Dillistone 1975, esp. chap. 14.
[71] See esp. Dillistone 1975, pp. 80–1, 215–18, 250, 302.

Chapter 6

THE NATURAL SCIENCES

The first and the mother of all triposes was the mathematical, and down to 1909 – when the tripos list (part I) appeared for the last time in order of merit – the position of senior wrangler was the most distinguished an undergraduate could attain: he was the equivalent, in the smaller world of pure academic success, of the captain of the University Boat Club. Mathematics was the foundation of learning in Cambridge in the late eighteenth and nineteenth centuries, and the mother of the sciences as well as of the triposes. So it might be logical to open this survey of the natural sciences with the history of maths. In a more detailed, technical history, this should be attempted. It has often been noticed, however, that in the late nineteenth and early twentieth centuries the Maths Tripos lost its preeminence – it declined, first relatively, then absolutely – in numbers. But in considerable measure this was due to the expansion of the sciences: much of what had once been maths became physics. The historian is constantly bemused by the shifting boundaries of all disciplines, above all of the natural sciences. Thus Sir William Hardy (1864–1934) was made a university lecturer in physiology in 1913, but was later famous for his contributions to colloid chemistry and the physics of friction and the like; the *DNB* sums him up as a 'biologist'.[1] These shifts were partly due to changes in Hardy's interests – and his growing conviction that the way of the future, as he urged on the young Joseph Needham, lay in 'atoms and molecules, atoms and molecules, my boy'[2] – but equally to the

[1] *DNB 1931–1940*, pp. 397–8 (A. V. Hill); on him cf. Brooke 1985, p. 241. On the history of mathematics, see pp. 482–6.
[2] Quoted Brooke 1985, p. 280.

fundamental links between the different regions of the natural world which he studied. The sciences are for ever breaking into a thousand fragments and reassembling in different groups and patterns. Already in the late nineteenth century there was a fairly plain distinction between mathematics pure and applied, and a professorship for each.[3] Even the purest mathematics of one generation has had the disconcerting habit of becoming the foundation of other sciences in the next; and in the mid-twentieth century the speed of the transition has accelerated. In the 1950s topology was admirably pure, by the 1980s it had come to be applied to sciences beyond number. Still, the distinction through most of the period of this book between pure and applied maths is a great deal clearer than that between applied maths and other sciences. The dominating figure in Cambridge maths in 1870 was G. G. Stokes, Lucasian Professor from 1849 to 1903, later Sir George Stokes, Bart., MP and master of Pembroke and much else besides. Much of his original work falls before 1870, much after; and it ranged as widely as the spectrum he did so much to illuminate, to fluid mechanics, to optics, to light, to astronomy.[4] Early in life he laid the foundations of physical geodesy. In its traditional form as the study of the measurement of the earth geodesy had a great future in Stokes' lifetime as the British empire expanded, and with it, especially in India, new lands to measure. His own work provided techniques for studying the inner structure of the earth, and so provided, in the long run, a theoretical foundation for modern geophysics. But we are already in the region of geology, one of the sciences well established in Cambridge in the age of Adam Sedgwick; and his work was not far removed from mineralogy, one of the special interests of William Whewell. By a series of historical accidents geology came in the first half of the twentieth century to be represented by three departments working in separate, if adjacent, labs: geodesy and geophysics, mineralogy and petrology, and geology itself. In the late 1970s an ecumenical movement led to their reunion, and from 1980 they have become a single Department of Earth Sciences.[5] The range of Stokes' interests, and the adven-

3 The Lucasian for applied, the Sadleirian for pure.
4 *DNB*, 2nd suppl. III, 421–4; *DSB*, 13, 74–9 (G. M. Parkinson).
5 See below, p. 160.

tures of geology, are allegories for our incursion into the history of science. But Stokes has another interest for us: he was one of the central figures in the syndicate whose discussions led to the foundation of the Cavendish. There had been experiments before, but the Cavendish was their first major centre in Cambridge; and the growth of experimental science is the great difference between old mathematics and new natural sciences. This is what we chiefly have to explore, and in the process mathematics will get less than its due. For the best of Stokes will be in the previous volume; and his successor, Sir Joseph Larmor, must wait for J. J. Thomson and Rutherford, since his most notable scientific work lay in developing Thomson's discovery of the electron, and his greatest service to the university was to bring Rutherford back to the Cavendish Chair. And pure mathematics will do well to wait for G. H. Hardy.[6]

MUSEUMS AND LABORATORIES

By 1850 the University of Cambridge had the Observatory, a fine monument of the 1820s, the Fitzwilliam Museum, a stately home for many good pictures and other antiques, assorted accommodation in and out of the Old Schools – that is to say, mingling with the old University Library – and a Botanic Garden in part of the old precinct of the Austin Friars, the core of what is now the New Museums Site to the east of Free School Lane. Beside the Botanic Garden a Botanic Museum and some rudimentary labs had grown up. But between 1846 and 1852 the Botanic Garden departed to its present, more ample site, and in 1851 the Natural Sciences Tripos was born. These two events concentrated the minds of the rulers of the university.[7] A masterly plan was devised by Robert Willis and others, and Salvin was chosen as architect. But the scheme encountered every hazard: shortage of funds, arguments of taste, arguments about its uses; and above all an underlying divergence of view about the future of science. In the end, in the mid-1860s, a dispirited architect completed a shadow of his first design;[8] and as one

----

[6] See pp. 185–6, 483–6.
[7] Willis and Clark 1886/1988, III, chap. 2, esp. pp. 157–8.
[8] Ibid. pp. 179–81.

contemplates the shapeless development which came to fill the old Botanic Gardens – or the New Museums Site as it came to be called – one witnesses the heroic struggle of Cambridge science to find space, first to house its notable collections of stones and bones, then to provide lecture rooms for the advancing numbers of natural scientists and medical students, and finally to create the environment in which many of the greatest discoveries of modern science came to birth. Romantic architects have been offended by the disproportion between the meanness and muddle of the buildings and the splendour of their achievements.[9] Nor did the planning much improve before the 1960s, and tastes much differ as to how Cambridge fared in that era when university planning first became a national issue. Meanwhile in 1895 Downing College, after much debate, began to surrender a part of its campus to the university; by 1901 it had agreed to give up the whole of what is now the Downing Site. Here, unlike in the New Museums Site, there is a plan of a kind. But it is very hard to grasp on the ground, and the overall impression is of confusion of planning and diversity of styles.[10] Some of the most dramatic developments of the period of this book have been the growth of science students and the growth of scientific research. Neither was foreseen in the 1850s and 60s. Willis' master plan seemed rather to be making a small segment of the university receive an extravagant share. The muddle and confusion of the New Museums Site reflects a university not inclined to master plans, only prepared for individual decisions piece by piece, as the tide of battle flowed this way and that. It was not a fight between old and new, for those who wished to see Cambridge humanities grow were as revolutionary as the scientists: the reigning queen, the Mathematical Tripos, was nicely balanced between them. The humanists, furthermore, needed new books, while the scientists in large measure were trying to house collections of material as old as the hills. Nor did anybody win. At the turn of the nineteenth and twentieth centuries, when the sensational growth of natural scientists was the most striking single feature of the examinations, and the Medical School was struggling into existence again, it was widely canvassed, especially in Oxford, that the future of Cam-

---

9   See quotation in Rawle 1985, p. 192.
10   French 1978, p. 132; Pevsner 1970, pp. 207–9; Rawle 1985, p. 192.

bridge lay with science, the future of the humanities in Oxford. In 1906 or 1907 a schoolboy called on the headmaster of Berkhamsted School to discuss university entrance; and the conversation went something like this: 'I have entered you for Trinity College, Cambridge,' said the headmaster. 'Oh sir! Please, I don't want to go to Cambridge. Oxford is my family university. My grandfather and great-grandfather were both at Wadham College.' . . . 'My boy, you are to be a scientist. I have entered you for Trinity College, Cambridge,' came the answer; and in Cambridge the hero of this story, Tressilian Nicholas, lived for some 80 years – only broken by service in the First World War – until his death in 1989 aged 101.[11] Since then the world of assumptions has changed: in the generation which followed, Oxford became a great scientific university – without losing Classical Greats or its humanist eminence – and Cambridge has become a powerful rival to it in the humanities. Indeed the large majority of students in both, in contrast to the majority of British universities, have studied arts subjects.[12]

The growth of science at Cambridge in the two generations following 1870 is a fascinating case study in academic and intellectual history. It cannot be explained by simple formulas nor can any one group of causes explain all the sciences at once. Nor can we grasp the whole spectrum: a few sciences must serve as illustrations of a subject of infinite wealth and as complex as the New Museums Site itself. When Professor Roy MacLeod and his colleagues have completed their survey of the early history of the Natural Sciences Tripos much that is now dark will be clear. Their preliminary studies have shed light on many paths. The remarkable growth of science students in the last decades of the nineteenth century presupposes some interest and improvement in the schools and, even more, a growing interest in the colleges through whose portals all but a handful of students came. MacLeod and Moseley note the way in which Coutts Trotter and Michael Foster used their college base in Trinity to further their deep designs for the growth of science.[13] Enlightened governing

---

[11] Atcheson 1986, p. 71.   [12] Cf. Carswell 1985, pp. 8–9.
[13] On all this see MacLeod and Moseley 1980 (esp. for Trotter and Foster, pp. 185–6; and above, pp. 69–70, and below, p. 165); and MacLeod and Moseley 1979; MacLeod 1982.

bodies elected young fellows who engaged in scientific research, and, more gradually, promoted them to be college lecturers; in their turn they sought pupils by offering scholarships and by fostering wider links between colleges and growing scientific interest in schools. All this may one day be fully documented; meanwhile the general lines are becoming clearer. The growth of natural sciences was particularly closely linked with the revival of the School of Medicine.[14] MacLeod and Moseley find in the graduates of the Natural Sciences Tripos the formation of a new élite, scientifically trained, secular in outlook.[15] There is truth in this, but we are in deep waters; I am reminded that the rise of this scientific élite coincided with the eclipse of British industrial pre-eminence, for example. The Reverend Adam Sedgwick, the Reverend Coutts Trotter and the Reverend Fenton Hort – who secured a first in the Natural Sciences Tripos in 1851 – would have been surprised to learn of its role in secularising the university. There is no simple cause and effect here: both are cooperant factors in a larger world.[16] What can more readily be grasped is the way scientific disciplines grew, as time passed, in unequal measure.

By the 1880s some sciences, such as geology, already flourished; others, like chemistry, had at least the framework of an existence. None of the prehistory explains the particular form progress was to take, save that early starters like geology and botany greatly profited from the foundations already laid, and chemistry (very popular with the students) would scarcely have existed but for the heroic efforts of journeymen like Professor Liveing to provide courses and meet growing demand.[17] There is a sense in which the growth was student-led. McKenny Hughes in geology and Michael Foster in physiology provided a framework for the rapidly growing demands of students; and some of these students were to reveal talents for research beyond those of the professors. This the two entrepreneurs quite realised; their function was not to lead a great research team, like the founders of the Cavendish in physics or – rather later – Gowland Hopkins in biochemistry, or, much later still, Alexander Todd in organic chemistry; but to

---

[14] See pp. 164–73.   [15] MacLeod and Moseley 1980, pp. 186–90.
[16] See pp. 2–3, 9–12.   [17] Roberts 1980.

provide the means, the framework, and choose the teachers who could make their disciplines flourish. The massive Sedgwick Museum and the Department of Geology are monuments to Hughes, the lasting repute of the Physiology Department to Foster. Hughes presided over the evolution of one discipline until in his later years the Cambridge School of Geology was the leading school in Britain. Foster inspired at least eight disciplines and set his pupils and disciples and friends to develop them all. But these are superficial statements: we need to look deeper.

The Natural Sciences Tripos was first sat in 1851, but it was then confined to BAs who had already made their mark in mathematics and classics. From 1861 it was open to students for a BA. It still attracted small numbers until the later 1870s, when they began to climb. New regulations, dividing the tripos into two parts, in 1881–2, led to a rapid increase, to 54 men and 6 women in part I in 1882; by 1910 about 200 men were taking part I, between 10 and 20 women. In other language, 'less than 2% of Cambridge undergraduates read for the NST in 1861, the proportion had doubled by 1880, and had reached 18% by 1910. From 1883 the NST had annually more graduates than the Mathematical Tripos.'[18] Only relatively small numbers went on to the more specialised part II; and the great expansion perhaps owed most of all to the rapid growth of the Medical School between 1870 and 1900.

GEOLOGY AND EARTH SCIENCES

In a fascinating paper Roy Porter has put Cambridge geology between 1850 and 1914 in its historical setting.[19] The late nineteenth century saw a growth in geology teaching in many universities; yet with this was combined a decline in original thought and intellectual fertility: it was as though the growing number and size of classes actively discouraged research. Most really original work was done in the Geological Survey and elsewhere, outside the universities. Yet in considerable measure Cambridge was an exception. The period from the 1870s to 1914

---

[18] MacLeod and Moseley 1980, p. 181; Tanner 1917, pp. 737, 740, 750–1, 799–800.
[19] Porter 1982.

was a golden age in Cambridge geology, even though Cambridge was subject to many of the same stresses as other universities, and witnessed a similar process of professionalisation of the discipline, such as had proved debilitating elsewhere. Whereas Sedgwick had set – for a tiny number of pupils – exam questions which revealed geology as a part of a liberal education, or its relation to his philosophical views, including his opposition to Darwin, after his death the pupils became more numerous and the questions drier, more factual – rarely analytical, more often descriptive. But as time passed a more analytic approach entered in; the school became noted for the freshness of its teaching. It produced a notable outcrop of good geologists; Tressilian Nicholas was one of many inspired by it to lifelong devotion to geology; and it became the centre of a significant research effort, culminating in the establishment of the Cambrian Revolution – the definition, that is, of a key moment in the earth's history.[20]

Roy Porter discusses some of the reasons why the Cambridge school did not suffer the fate of other departments which in 'becoming academic [were] strait-jacketed by examinations, [which] stultified and stereotyped' their approach to geology.[21] He observes that Cambridge was 'privileged in wealth and resources'; the growth of college fellows dedicated to personal teaching, to college supervision in the subject, helped to counteract the effects of the exam system; and the combination of faculty and college organisation 'played crucial roles in generating competitive excellence'. Yet this wealth was not easily mobilised for the support of the sciences, and reasonable complaints of poverty filled the air then as now; the collegiate system could fossilise as well as stimulate teaching. What seems to me to set geology apart is the combination of a traditional role which could be enhanced and exploited with the appearance of a group of exceptionally gifted teachers, and the recruitment of students and teachers of remarkable talent. Porter stresses the role of T. G. Bonney, who created a School of Geology within St John's which greatly fructified the university department.[22] Here the traditional reputation of Cambridge geology doubtless counted, and the general

---

[20] I owe this, and much help in this section, to the kind advice of Dr Brian Harland.
[21] Porter 1982, p. 202.   [22] Porter 1982, pp. 202–3.

attractions of Cambridge for all sorts of other reasons, as a centre of sport, for example, or lively debating in the Union, not obviously related to geology itself. From 1873 McKenny Hughes was professor. By then Bonney was already well established in St John's; and although he worked in London for a time as professor in University College, that helped to foster links between Cambridge and London vital in the growth of this, as of other, sciences. Hughes (who has perhaps had less than his due)[23] worked hard to build up the department, to win money for new appointments; above all he built the Sedgwick Museum, which gave geology a substantial share in the first building campaign on the Downing Site. In some measure not easy to define he played the role in geology Michael Foster was playing in physiology and related sciences. They were alike in this, that neither was a notable creative scientist: their research papers were relatively few and not of lasting significance. But both knew how to match university departments and college fellowships in the creation of an enhanced and lasting cadre of teachers, and to provide a framework within which others could do research.

All this came to an end with the Great War, and in the 1920s and 30s geology made little headway; it became for a time 'stultified and stereotyped'. Meanwhile there grew up beside it, especially in the 1930s, independent and flourishing departments both of geodesy and geophysics, and of mineralogy and petrology. These subjects had been relatively dormant in the ascendancy of Hughes and geology; in the 1930s they took the lead while geology slumbered. Sir Harold Jeffreys and Sir Edward Bullard made Cambridge a centre of world renown in geophysics, and from 1931 to 1961 C. E. Tilley, as professor of mineralogy and petrology, presided over its transformation from the old world of minerals and crystals to the new modes of crystallographic and paragenetic research into rocks and minerals.[24] But in the 1970s there was a remarkable ecumenical movement between them: joint courses in teaching became common; lines of research converged; professors and lecturers were seen linked in earnest

[23] He is neither in *DNB* nor in *DSB*, and it is difficult to find significant material on him.

[24] For an outline of these events, see *Reporter* 1979–80, pp. 322–3, 389, 438: I owe my knowledge of this valuable report to Brian Harland and to Margaret Johnston, administrator of the Department of Earth Sciences.

debate. To show that they had jointly discovered a new world, they were united, at their own wish and request, into the single Department of Earth Sciences on 1 August 1980.

BOTANY

Botany, like geology, owed its place among the Cambridge sciences in the first instance to earlier tradition. There had been a professor of botany since 1724; but he did little or nothing. As a rebuke to the idleness of professors, Dr Walker, vice-master of Trinity, generously provided the first Botanic Garden in 1760–2.[25] His spoken purpose was to provide a real opportunity for the study of botany such as the professor had neglected, and to provide plants for medicinal study as well as botanical; his unspoken intent, no doubt, was to emulate the delightful Botanic Garden which is still one of the ornaments of Oxford. The chair of botany was held from 1825 to 1861 by the Reverend J. S. Henslow, a keen, skilled botanist who inspired some of his pupils, but who often felt more at home in his Suffolk vicarage, advancing knowledge of the flora of Suffolk, than in his lecture room in Cambridge. He was a man equally of the new world and of the old; an ally of Adam Sedgwick in founding the Cambridge Philosophical Society as well as in his devotion to the church. He has won immortal fame by stimulating the delight and curiosity in the natural world of Charles Darwin and by helping Darwin, first, to his appointment as naturalist on the *Beagle*, and then in caring for the specimens gathered on the voyage.[26]

In Henslow's last years the old Botanic Garden was moved to its new, more ample site, along the Trumpington Road. A far-sighted scheme led to the provision of a really large garden between 1846 and 1852. By 1856 it was complete with glass-houses; in 1858–9 the lake was dug and the gardens had achieved something like their present physiognomy. Its fundamental purpose was scientific, but its designer 'consulted an ornamental appearance whenever it did not interfere with the main object'.[27]

[25] Willis and Clark 1886/1988, III, 145–52; Tanner 1917, p. 90; Walters 1981, p. 72. What follows owes much to the helpful survey in Walters 1981.
[26] On Henslow, see *DNB*.
[27] Walters 1981, pp. 72–3, 100–3; Willis and Clark 1886/1988, III, 137–8.

Its curator in the late nineteenth century, R. I. Lynch, was one of the many friends of Michael Foster – himself a keen amateur gardener. Foster inspired him to write *The Book of the Iris* (1904), which is dedicated to him.[28] The Botanic Gardens had the exceptional fortune of receiving a major benefaction in the 1940s, which enabled a considerable enlargement and extension of its range of scientific activity. Mr Reginald Cory died in 1934, and under his will a handsome endowment came to the garden at the height of the Second World War in 1943.[29] To those accustomed to great gardens set among hills and valleys, a garden in Cambridge must seem sadly flat. But the Botanic Garden has long been one of the notable amenities of city and university, and has set its mark on the study of botany in Cambridge.

From 1861 to 1895 the chair was held by C. C. Babington, an active teacher and a devout botanist of the descriptive mode, an unreconstructed Linnaean. He thought ill of the efforts of S. Vines of Christ's, a disciple of Michael Foster, to introduce new scientific notions into the school, and Vines departed for Oxford. But the mantle of Darwin was laid on Cambridge botany by his son Francis Darwin, who settled in the department not long before Babington died, there to complete his work on his father's papers and advance his own scientific study of botany. Babington was succeeded by another of Foster's friends, Marshall Ward, a devoted pupil of T. H. Huxley and a great enthusiast for the botany of the lab.[30]

Marshall Ward may be reckoned the creator of the department as we know it today; in 1991 the current generation has consummated his tradition by renaming it the Department of Plant Sciences. Ward lived to see it a centre of study and teaching in several disciplines – though the physiology and biochemistry of plants have made enormous strides since then. He lived to see the botany lab built, among the first to be completed on the Downing Site in 1903. When he died in 1906 it was firmly set in its role as a major element among the Cambridge natural sciences.

To the outside observer one of the most remarkable features of Cambridge botany has been the development of palaeobotany, a

---

[28] Walters 1981, p. 77.   [29] Walters 1981, pp. 100–3.   [30] Walters 1981, p. 67.

mingling of botany, geology, archaeology, geography and economic history which has transformed our knowledge of the
history of the world and its resources in the last hundred years.
Ward's successor was A. C. Seward, later Sir Albert Seward,
professor from 1906 to 1936, master of Downing, 1915–36, a
scientist as well known among geologists as among botanists, a
great master of fossils. One of the most eminent of Seward's
pupils was Sir Harry Godwin, whose charming autobiography,
Cambridge and Clare,[31] is a major source for Cambridge botany
and much else of Cambridge life besides. Godwin immediately
felt the inspiration of Seward's lectures when he heard them as a
freshman in 1919–20. He was partly impressed by the manner of
his lectures, so that when he himself began to lecture, 'I made my
way to listen beneath the floor of the lecture theatre to hear ...
the delivery and style he employed, his pace, emphasis, measured
pause and change of pitch.' He was also impressed by the way he
came to know all the students by talking to them at their practical
classes. But above all the mingling of plant science and the
evidence of evolution, especially the evidence of fossils on which
Seward was a leading international authority, caught his imagination, and directed his life. It rapidly became enriched by the
ecological interests of another notable figure of the School of
Botany, A. G. (later Sir Arthur) Tansley. Tansley's work was
little regarded by Seward, and after some shifts of fortune he
went to be professor of botany in Oxford. But the fascination of
his work lingered in the minds of Godwin and his wife and fellow
worker, Margaret Godwin.[32] In due course the Godwins became
historians of the botanical past; and in the 1930s they became
actively engaged in pollen analysis from archaeological sites –
establishing the history of plants and crops and diet in historic and
prehistoric periods. In the 1930s this was a novelty; now every
archaeologist has to be a bit of a botanist among the bewildering
variety of his skills. In 1932 these historical studies acquired a new
dimension in the work of the Fenland Research Committee,
whose chairman was Seward and whose central figures were
Grahame Clark, the prehistoric archaeologist, and the Godwins.

[31] Godwin 1985; on Seward, esp. ibid. pp. 40–1; H. Hamshaw Thomas and F. O. Bower in *RSO*
3 (1939–41), 867–80.
[32] On Tansley, see Godwin 1985, chap. 13.

Archaeology, geography, geology and zoology were involved as well as botany, and the frontiers of many disciplines partially redrawn.[33]

> Considerably aided by the chronological scale provided by our pollen-analyses, we were enabled to fit into one broad sequential pattern the major features of evolution of the Fenland, recognising the stages of infilling of the shallow basin by alternate beds of brackish and fresh-water deposits, the latter culminating in deep peat fens, bearing at their margins fen-woods whose traces remain as buried forests, along with giant bog-oaks of the former forest floor now water logged and buried in peat. Former waterways were recognised in the 'roddons', low winding banks of silt meandering across the present-day black fens, and shell-marl deposits were identified as fresh-water meres adjacent to the roddons in their active phase. The contemporary fauna of the past was recovered and referred to the habitat of the time, as for example by whale vertebrae in the roddon silts, the giant aurochs from the buried high forest, and fossil foraminifera from the brackish-water Fen Clay. The deepest parts of the ancient rivers we were able to confirm as holding deposits from the transitional Late-glacial time, and on the banks of the streams there were recovered, stratified into the deposits, remains of successive human cultures. In particular in carefully organised deep excavations at Shippea Hill, the Fenland Research Committee proved no less than four distinct archaeological horizons, Mesolithic, Neolithic, Early Bronze Age and Roman.[34]

From this has stemmed Godwin's own particular contribution to the Botany Department, the Godwin Lab for Quaternary Research, set up in 1948 under his direction, physically part of botany, but responsible also to the Departments of Arch and Anth and Geology. Its disciplines spread even wider, from early days drawing in physics, as Godwin became one of the first scientists in Europe to become interested in the technique of dating by radiocarbon first tried out in Chicago in the late 1940s.[35] The function of the quaternary research sub-department has been to investigate 'what happened in this

33 Godwin 1985, chap. 15; Clark 1989, pp. 80–1; cf. p. 207.
34 Godwin 1985, pp. 174–5.
35 Clark 1989, pp. 84–9; Godwin 1985, pp. 207–10.

country and elsewhere from the time when the first ice-sheets began to invade temperate Europe to the time when historical records effectively begin.'[36] This work has had many fruits, some of which we shall observe in arch and anth.[37] For the historian and naturalist, some of the most exciting work which has come from the historical approach so characteristic of Cambridge botany can be observed in the studies of Dr Oliver Rackham. On the one hand he has been a leader among palaeobotanists in several countries who have studied tree-rings in timber buildings, and so brought a new precision to the dates of many structures by determining when the trees from which they were made were felled – a technique of like importance to radiocarbon dating. On the other hand he has by a kind of magic revealed the history of Hayley Wood and other natural habitats by investigating the archaeology of the living trees and shrubs and plants.[38] He has performed for ancient woodland what Harold Taylor and many others have performed for the archaeology of standing buildings.[39] The links which Godwin forged with archaeology – and with history – are very much alive; but the Department of Botany is also aware of its shifting frontiers with biochemistry and other sciences; and it has determined, in 1991, that it will take a new name, and be henceforth Plant Sciences.

PHYSIOLOGY

As in so many fields of science and scholarship, the great masters of nineteenth-century physiology were German. Towards the end of the century this pre-eminence passed to Britain. Cambridge lies near the centre of this story, and the key to the success of Cambridge, as is very well known, was Sir Michael Foster. His work and influence have been brought into the light of day in the fundamental book by M. F. Geison.[40] At first sight this is a paradoxical view, since his own original contributions were slight, and although he started teaching in Cambridge in 1870 and

---

[36] Godwin 1985, p. 203.   [37] See p. 207.
[38] Rackham 1975.   [39] See pp. 208–9.
[40] Geison 1978, on which what follows is chiefly based. There is a useful summary in Weatherall 1990; see also Rook 1971.

died professor of physiology in 1907, his last original paper was published in 1876.[41]

Michael Foster illustrates numerous features of nineteenth-century Cambridge. First of all, he was a sceptic of nonconformist background – the son of a Baptist deacon – and so ineligible for a Cambridge fellowship before 1871. Henry Sidgwick resigned his fellowship at Trinity in 1869 owing to religious doubts; in 1870 Michael Foster was given a praelectorship in Trinity; in 1871 the religious tests were abolished, and Foster was one of the first to receive a fellowship in Trinity after the end of the Test Acts.[42]

It had been natural for him to seek his education in University College, London, where he took a medical degree and fell under the spell of T. H. Huxley, then lecturer at the Royal School of Mines, a lineal ancestor of Imperial College; Foster was inspired by Huxley's example, by his genius as a lecturer and as a propagandist for natural science and scepticism.[43] He also mingled with teachers imbued with the latest German scholarship; like so many of the central figures in late nineteenth-century Cambridge – Sidgwick, Trotter, and J. W. Clark for example[44] – he was deeply influenced by German books and articles. Above all he brought from London the fervour of Huxley's devotion to natural science, and a firm belief that science and medicine must be close allies.

From 1858 those who held the degree of MB enjoyed the right to practise: it was a crucial step in establishing medical training and the dominance of medical schools. When Foster moved to Cambridge, George Paget of Caius was the central figure in the medical establishment. Though often allies, they did not always see eye to eye, for both were eagerly in pursuit of scarce resources for their own departments.[45] Paget had been in practice in Cambridge since the 1830s, and a leading physician in Addenbrooke's Hospital; he was a very popular figure in Cambridge, and by the 1870s an elder statesman. Round Paget and Foster gathered the growing numbers of medical scientists who recreated the Cambridge School of Medicine.

[41] Geison 1978, p. 7.   [42] See pp. 99–106.
[43] Geison 1978, p. 67.   [44] Cf. Geison 1978, p. 111.
[45] Weatherall 1990, pp. 38–40. On Paget see also Brooke 1985, pp. 206–7 and references.

THE SCHOOL OF MEDICINE

In 1870 Cambridge had a small Medical School; by 1883–4 the intake of 90 was second only to St Bartholomew's among the medical schools in Britain; from then it remained among the largest in the land.[46] But the curious paradox is that while Cambridge grew as a place to study the basic medical sciences, its clinical school, after a promising revival in the 1880s, steadily declined and virtually disappeared – only to be partially revived after the Second World War, and fully established in the late 1970s.

In 1864 George Paget had told the BMA that 'We do injustice to medicine if we treat it as a mystery. It is a science, and entitled to rank as such ... and we should be ready to show that its maxims are founded in truth and reason.'[47] Paget was equally at home in both parts of the Cambridge establishment: he had been a senior fellow of Caius till his marriage and narrowly avoided the mastership; he was a deeply respected figure in the university, and was to be Regius Professor of Physic from 1872 till his death in 1892.[48] He was perhaps the most influential of the three triumvirs who dominated Cambridge medicine in the nineteenth century; the other two were John Haviland, Regius Professor from 1817 till 1851, and Sir George Humphry, professor of human anatomy till 1883, then of surgery. The switch was significant: Humphry was determined to see the serious study of surgery as a central feature of the rising school; clinical work and science must go hand in hand. This was the more striking since Humphry did not himself believe that students should complete their clinical studies in Cambridge. In 'the great debate' of 1878 he alone of the leaders of the Medical School stood out against a complete clinical school. None the less he strongly supported a substantial clinical element in Cambridge teaching.[49] Paget and Humphry were in a privileged position: they belonged equally to the establishment of the hospital world and to the university. They could rise serenely above the intense jealousies between scientists and practitioners; but they could not quell them.

46 Weatherall 1990, p. 49.
47 Quoted by R. G. Hodgkinson in Rook 1971, p. 101.
48 On him, see Rook 1971, pp. 101, 111–13; Brooke 1985, pp. 206–7 and refs.
49 Weatherall 1990, pp. 43–6.

The problem arose from an ancient feud. By the eighteenth century the once noble School of Medicine in Cambridge was moribund: students came to garner the ample scholarship funds and the blessings of a Cambridge degree; but they had to go elsewhere to study medicine.[50] By 1800 there was some change: Sir Busick Harwood was an active professor of anatomy and first Downing Professor of Medicine (1800–14). A witness to some small revival is the *cause célèbre* in the opening years of the nineteenth century when Mr Thackeray, a surgeon of Addenbrooke's, was refused a medical degree on the ground that this was incompatible with the pursuit of a trade or a profession – that is, not open to a practising surgeon.[51] It is evident that professional jealousies were deeply affected: between physicians and surgeons and between academics and clinicians there were wars and rumours of wars. In the course of time the immense progress both of professional standards and of academic medicine in Cambridge made these jealousies seem antiquated and absurd; but time moved slowly; the full force of the change was not felt until 1976, when the modern Clinical School was founded. Meanwhile, in the late nineteenth century, there was intense suspicion within the university of the Medical School as an expensive tradesmen's entrance to the academic world – expensive, that is, to the university. There was equally intense suspicion in Addenbrooke's of the university's efforts to use its facilities without giving the hospital the financial support it needed nor its staff the academic recognition they craved.

These jealousies came to a head in 1892, when Paget died and Sir Clifford Allbutt was elected Regius Professor.[52] Allbutt was a Caian who had studied briefly under Paget and Humphry, but sought his clinical training at St George's Hospital in London. He had been a classic before he caught from Auguste Comte the addiction to science which made him a medical student; yet he remained all his days a man of the widest culture; he achieved immortality by giving some of his qualities to Lydgate in George

50   Cf. e.g. Brooke 1985, p. 197. This period in Cambridge medical history is being studied by Dr J. Kendall.
51   Brooke 1985, pp. 198–9 and refs.
52   On Allbutt see esp. Lord Cohen in Rook 1971, pp. 173–92; cf. Brooke 1985, pp. 238–9 and refs.; and the very attractive portrayal of him in Anderson 1988, chap. 20. For what follows, see esp. Cohen in Rook 1971, pp. 173–7. On Latham see also Tanner 1917, p. 95 and n. 9.

Eliot's *Middlemarch*. For twenty years he was a consultant in Leeds, then briefly a Commissioner in Lunacy. Allbutt and his work were known to Sir Michael Foster, and he strongly backed him for the Regius Chair in 1892. The university might elect, but the hospital refused the new Regius Professor entry to its doors, or at least to its clinical facilities. It is said that this was chiefly due to the personal jealousy of P. W. Latham, Downing Professor of Medicine and physician at Addenbrooke's. But it is clear that the *amour propre* of the hospital and its governors was also at stake. While Paget lived these anxieties were kept at bay; when he was gone they flared up. In the end, after Latham's death, a compromise was reached: the university greatly increased its contribution to the hospital, and in return it was accepted that the Regius Professor of Physic, as of right, had his share of the hospital's beds and clinical facilities.

But a peace treaty between university and hospital could not rescue or preserve the clinical element in the Medical School. The students voted with their feet. They came in throngs to study the preliminary, pre-clinical medical sciences, and then set off, mostly for London, for more prestigious or just more distant centres of clinical experience. London in the late nineteenth century was one of the most disease-ridden cities in Europe, and in its teaching hospitals gathered many of the most successful and the most ambitious of the great physicians and surgeons of the century. To them flocked the students who wished to achieve the best experience, or to attach themselves to the most effective patrons. We are accustomed in the late twentieth century to contrast the stable British student, who normally spends his whole undergraduate career – and quite often his postgraduate too – in one university, with the wandering scholars of the continent; especially those of Germany, who until quite recent years moved on from year to year in search of better teachers or other attractions further afield. But the British medical student of the nineteenth century was accustomed to travel. Early in the century he might come to Cambridge for funds and (from the 1820s) for rowing; then go on to Edinburgh for medical science or London for medical experience. As medical training became more formalised and more scientific, this wandering declined. But it never wholly ceased. Some distinguished teaching in anatomy there had long been in Cambridge, and in the late nineteenth century pathology revived and physiology enjoyed its apotheosis under Foster. So students came thronging to Cambridge for basic science, for medical science, for medical degrees – and for rowing. They went on to seek the patronage of St Bartholomew or St Thomas or St George or St Mary – or the like – when the time came for clinical experience. Not all went to London; some went elsewhere in Britain, some went to Vienna, Berlin, Paris and other medical schools on the continent;[53] down to 1914 a spell on the continent was part of many serious students' education in almost all faculties.

For these – and no doubt for other – reasons the Medical School flourished but the Clinical School declined. The Medical School was one of the segments of the university which the Commissioners of the late 1870s most earnestly sought to enhance. Under the statutes of 1882 professorships were established in physiology, surgery and pathology.[54] Physiology was Foster's chair, and from it he reigned supreme for many years – not without jealousy and backbiting from those who envied his success or belittled the value of his science.[55] But his chair and his achievement survived, and his students multiplied. Surgery was founded for Humphry and he adorned it till 1896; it was briefly revived in 1903 for F. H. Marsh, who held it for a time with the mastership of Downing. But the need for teaching in surgery melted away after Humphry's death, and slender resources had to be absorbed elsewhere. The first professor of pathology, C. R. Roy, was a disciple of Foster; his appointment ensured that science rather than medicine should prevail in the work of his department, and he began with exceedingly small apartments and narrow resources, a circumstance little remedied until the coffers of Rockefeller were opened in the 1920s.

Space and funds remained extremely limited: students expanded, colleges took on college teachers; but classrooms refused to grow and the staff of most medical departments were heavily engaged in teaching. In 1913 occurred a large and fateful debate in the Senate House. Other medical schools in the land

[53] Weatherall 1990, pp. 49–50.   [54] Ibid. pp. 47–8; Tanner 1917, pp. 105–6.
[55] Geison 1978, p. 366.

already received government grants, and the Medical School, led by Sir Clifford Allbutt, made urgent representations that the university should apply for help. After long debate the Senate agreed by a narrow majority.[56] But the Great War came to put paid to all new schemes for a while. After the war new winds blew. The Royal Commission was specifically set up to investigate the need, and provide a framework for, substantial government aid to the ancient universities. Its chief interpreter in Cambridge, Sir Hugh Anderson, was a medical man. In earlier life he had made a name for himself as a neurophysiologist. He took a wide view of the university's needs and he is chiefly remembered for his work for the new University Library.[57] But the Medical School was never far from his thoughts, and when in the early 1920s he began to make contact with the Rockefeller Foundation, its officials sought him out precisely because his involvement in it was well known. In 1923 John D. Rockefeller Jr set up his Education Board to administer a vast scheme for the endowment of medical, human, and animal sciences – not excluding agriculture. Richard M. Pearce, director of the Division of Medical Education for Rockefeller, approached Anderson, and in September 1924 they had a crucial meeting in Cambridge. First of all, the Rockefeller Foundation agreed to provide ample new resources for pathology: for a new building and for new staff.[58] The principal beneficiary was Professor H. R. Dean, later also master of Trinity Hall. In his last years in the 1950s he was said to prescribe good claret as the best cure for many minor ailments (his views were not hampered by large clinical experience); but in his heyday he had been a notable pathologist, and one of the creative figures in the Medical School of the 1920s. Nor was this all: in the second wave of Rockefeller endowment in the late 1920s many of the other medical and biological sciences were greatly helped. Between the government and the Rockefeller Foundation, a wholly new scale of financial support was provided for the Medical School. Its close ally biochemistry, meanwhile, was flourishing under the most celebrated of Foster's

---

[56] See pp. 97–8.   [57] See chap. 12.
[58] Rockefeller Foundation Archives, 401A/UC/P, Historical Record, University of Cambridge – Pathology, 1922–1929, 1933–1934.

disciples, Sir Frederick Gowland Hopkins, and benefiting in a similar fashion from the munificence of Sir William Dunn, city magnate and noted philanthropist.[59]

But Dean was an academic, not a clinical pathologist. The layman may doubt whether such a distinction can have any scientific meaning; but it certainly had great practical significance in the Cambridge of the 1920s. The standard of medical care and scientific knowledge in Addenbrooke's was variable. 'Nursing, diet, investigation and treatment', Leslie Cole tells us, 'were well below the standards of a London teaching hospital which were much lower than today.'[60] But it had some notable physicians and surgeons within it, including J. F. Gaskell, a distinguished bacteriologist who was an honorary assistant physician at Addenbrooke's and director of the hospital's pathology lab – the John Bonnett Laboratory, opened in 1914.[61] But between Gaskell and Dean, and between their labs, there was relatively little contact. At this date there was little pressure from the established departments of the university for a Clinical School, and not a great deal for a Medical Studies Tripos.

Hitherto many medical students had taken an Ordinary BA accompanied and followed by the specific exams for the various parts of the MB (Bachelor of Medicine) examinations; the more ambitious had taken the Natural Sciences Tripos, specialising in those courses which gave exemption from parts I and II of the MB. Academic medicine was reckoned a scientific study: it was this which had given it respectability in the late nineteenth century; and the old prejudice against the tradesmen's entrance and the empirical approach of the clinician died very hard indeed. But from 1929 to 1933 there was a running debate on whether Cambridge should not follow the practice of many other universities and have a special exam structure for medical students, a Medical Sciences Tripos. It was only finally achieved in 1966. Meanwhile, in 1929, Dr Archibald Clark-Kennedy, who significantly combined the posts of fellow and director of studies in medicine in Corpus with a clinical post in the London Hospital, laid an elaborate complaint before the Regius Professor,

[59] See pp. 195–9.   [60] L. Cole in Rook 1971, p. 268.
[61] L. Cole in Rook 1971, p. 270, cf. pp. 263–4.

Sir Humphrey Rolleston, and other heads of department. This led to earnest discussion and a Syndicate; and in 1932–3 it proposed a Medical Sciences Tripos no longer under the control of a variety of Natural Science Boards. Equally revolutionary – or reactionary, for in large measure it harked back to the days of Paget and Humphry – was the proposal that clinical work should be included in the tripos and taught by the physicians and surgeons of Addenbrooke's in cooperation with the relevant university departments. The discussion of the Report in the Senate House took several hours and twenty-five pages of the *University Reporter*.[62] After anxious deliberation the Regent House rejected the scheme for a tripos and most of the plan; but some significant changes were accepted, notably that honours in natural sciences were to be necessary for the MB. Little more than lip service was paid to the proposal for clinical teaching.

None the less the forces of change had been unleashed, and in Cambridge, as more conspicuously elsewhere, clinical and academic studies were drawing closer together. In 1944 the Goodenough Committee reported on the future of British medical schools at large, and a blueprint was prepared much in accord with medical thinking in Cambridge itself. This foreshadowed the building of a regional hospital for East Anglia in Cambridge, which saw the light twenty years later as the new Addenbrooke's on the edge of the hill country south-east of the city. It proposed the setting up of a postgraduate school of clinical research in Cambridge; and it explored the possibility of a Clinical School of the normal kind.[63] Soon after came the Labour government of 1945 and the National Health Service, inaugurated in 1948. By slow steps the Goodenough Report was implemented. Clinical studies developed, including haematology under the Regius Professor, Sir Lionel Whitby. One of the new chairs, of human ecology, failed to survive its first holder, Leslie Banks (1949–71); but foundations in this as in other sciences were laid. In the Medical School, as in so much else in the British academic world, the sixties were the creative era. In 1966 the Medical Sciences Tripos was finally established; and in 1969 – following the Report

[62] *Reporter* 1932–3, pp. 294–318; see Cole in Rook 1971, pp. 271–3.
[63] Weatherall 1990, p. 70; Cole in Rook 1971, p. 279; for what follows, ibid. pp. 279–84; Weatherall 1990, p. 70.

of a Royal Commission in 1968 – the decision was taken to form a Clinical School, which opened its doors in 1976. Many medical students still take their BA – their three undergraduate years, that is – in Cambridge, and go to London or elsewhere for clinical studies; but many more do not. In little more than ten years the school came to the front among British clinical schools, and in the fearful judgement day of the UGC, the selectivity exercise of 1988–9, it scored a top rating. The hopes of Paget and Humphry had finally, in substantial measure, been realised.

THE CAVENDISH

Foundation

In 1868 the Clarendon Laboratory began to rise in Oxford, and the response from Cambridge – where the lack of adequate space for research and teaching in experimental physics had long been felt – was instant.[64] In the same year a Syndicate was appointed to report on the need for experimental physics and the means to compass it. It comprised a wide range of those interested in science teaching in Cambridge, including G. G. Stokes, later Sir George, Lucasian Professor of Applied Mathematics, G. D. Liveing, professor of chemistry, E. J. Routh, the celebrated mathematical coach, who had reared many senior wranglers without encumbering them with practical experiments, W. M. Campion, tutor of Queens', an enlightened man with no particular scientific bent, and S. G. Phear, tutor of Emmanuel, an ardent reformer who had in his early years shown a special interest in the teaching of science.[65] The list of names shows clearly that the need for much enhanced facilities for the natural sciences was widely felt. In the 1850s John Venn reckoned that the specialist provision for the teaching of science was Professor Stokes' small table. True, there was a Medical School, just beginning to unfurl its wings in the 1850s, and Sedgwick's Geological Museum in the Cockerell building of the University Library.[66] But hitherto, here and elsewhere, laboratory experiments had commonly been confined to professors' houses and the

[64] Larsen 1962, p. 14; Crowther 1974, p. 4.
[65] Crowther 1974, pp. 23–7; see pp. 58, 110–11.
[66] Venn 1913, pp. 263–4; Brooke 1985, p. 219; Willis and Clark 1886/1988, III, 121n.

like, although there were some academic laboratories in Germany and France – as was well known to some at least in Cambridge.[67] The New Museums Site at Cambridge is a monument to a period in the history of science when great progress was made on a shoestring. In spite of the cold wind blowing from Oxford in 1868, doubtless a spur to efforts elsewhere,[68] there was still in that year little in Cambridge to suggest the extraordinary expansion in experimental science which was to come. By 1914 the Cavendish and a swarm of satellites had grown up on the New Museums Site in Free School Lane; and the Downing Site across Downing Street, comprising a substantial part of the college's original precinct, had been acquired and colonised and was rapidly filling.

In 1869 a second Syndicate appointed to raise the necessary funds recommended the purchase of apparatus for £1,300, a new building for £5,000, and the appointment of a professor of experimental physics, a demonstrator and an attendant, to cost in aggregate £660 per annum.[69] But they had no idea how the money would be raised and could only suggest that another Syndicate be appointed. Their report was not well received 'and the University separated for the Long Vacation without arriving at any conclusion'.[70]

In October 1870 the Vice-Chancellor received a letter from Holker Hall in the Cartmel Peninsula, from the Chancellor of the university, the duke of Devonshire. He notes the report of the Syndicate and expresses his desire 'to assist the University in carrying this recommendation into effect, and [I] shall accordingly be prepared to provide the funds required for the building and apparatus, so soon as the University shall have in other respects completed its arrangements for teaching Experimental Physics, and shall have approved the plan of the building.'[71] This was immediately welcomed by a meeting of heads of colleges, who accepted an ingenious means of providing the professor's salary – propounded by the resourceful Coutts Trotter – without raiding the University Chest or consulting the Senate.[72]

[67] Crowther 1974, p. 5 describes J. C. Adams' visit to Germany and France 'to collect ideas on what Cambridge should do'.
[68] Crowther 1974, p. 4.   [69] Crowther 1974, pp. 28–31.
[70] Willis and Clark 1886/1988, III, 182.
[71] Willis and Clark 1886/1988, III, 182; Crowther 1974, p. 31.
[72] Willis and Clark 1886/1988, III, 182; Winstanley 1947, pp. 194–8.

The Cavendish

William Cavendish had become duke of Devonshire after the death of his cousin the sixth duke in 1858. He inherited enormous estates and a mountain of debt; and he set to work with zeal and energy to put his estates and his fortune to rights. Cartmel is adjacent to Furness in what was then Lancashire north of the sands – now south Cumbria – and between Furness abbey and the sea he and his allies built the town of Barrow with an immense Bessemer plant and a port to harvest the haematite iron ore which his family had in their turn inherited from the monks of Furness in the Coniston hills. They built the railway line from Coniston to Foxfield, and the seventh duke, among many other enterprises, was the patron of the Furness railway, which ran from Carnforth, through Barrow and Foxfield, eventually to Maryport. He was a strange mixture of entrepreneur, academic and aristocrat. He had been a fellow commoner of Trinity, second wrangler, first Smith's prizeman, eighth classic. From 1861 he was Chancellor of the university – and encouraged it to take an interest in agriculture while he improved his estates. A like interest in the development of the physical sciences came naturally to a great Victorian industrialist, and Holker Hall near Barrow was of all his palaces the one most appropriate as the address on his letter founding the Cavendish Laboratory. He was a man of exceptional intelligence and wide interests, with a deep moral earnestness that led him to spend much of the great fortune he amassed in the earlier, successful period of his enterprises, in trying to save Barrow from extinction when the iron ore failed.[73] He was also a strange, reserved, eccentric man, who attributed his failure as a statesman to an excessively academic upbringing and so refused to allow his heir to go to Cambridge. The old Cavendish Lab with its mean proportions and gothic gateway feebly aping the great gates of the Tudor colleges seems a strange symbol of Victorian splendour; but its building was a notable act of inspired munificence; and the Cavendish was to do more than any other building before the new University Library of the 1930s to make Cambridge a centre of international research.

[73] See esp. Pollard 1955–6; also Crowther 1974, pp. 18–22.

The natural sciences

The marks of the Cavendish

This was the work, first and foremost, of the extraordinary dynasty which has ruled the Cavendish: Clerk Maxwell, Rayleigh, J. J. Thomson, Rutherford, Bragg, Mott, Pippard and their successors. It would be superficial to lay it all to the credit of the giants, though the history of the Cavendish – which at one time or another has been the history of Cambridge and the history of physics alike – is unimaginable without them. But the story raises fascinating problems for the historian. Thus we are often told that modern science needs an immense investment of resources; but the Cavendish was ruled from 1884 to 1937 by J. J. Thomson and Ernest Rutherford, both notorious for their reluctance to seek money and to spend it. Thomson was not an eloquent man, but he spoke with almost prophetic fervour against seeking government financial aid as late as 1913.[74] In the 1920s and 30s Chadwick as Rutherford's second-in-command combined a fervent respect for Rutherford with ceaseless frustration at his devotion to 'string and sealing wax'.[75] But by the time of Rutherford's death in 1937 – still more after the war of 1939–45 – even the Cavendish had learned extravagance.

Of the regime of J.J. and Rutherford the old Cavendish remains the outward sign: it was built in 1871–4 by W. M. Fawcett, one of the least inspired of Cambridge architects, and he extended it in 1896 when numbers were rapidly swelling.[76] In 1908 it was extended again by a generous gift from Lord Rayleigh, once Cavendish Professor, now Chancellor. Meanwhile chemistry, engineering, zoology and other sciences pitched their tents here and there about the site; and along its northern shore the examination hall and the Arts School added to the gloom in 1909–10.[77] Much later the Cavendish broke its bounds and in 1933 an enchanting addition, the Mond Laboratory (now Aerial Photography), was set up in the middle of the site by three men of great imagination, Peter Kapitza the Russian scientist, H. C. Hughes the architect, and Eric Gill; to this was added in the late 1930s the large Austin wing, generously funded by Lord

[74] See p. 97.   [75] Brooke 1985, p. 270; Wilson 1983, pp. 421–5.
[76] Crowther 1974, pp. 47–60, 125, 152–3.
[77] Pevsner 1970, pp. 206–7; Willis and Clark 1886/1988, III, 183.

Austin the car manufacturer in imitation of the benefactions of Lord Nuffield in Oxford. But the Cavendish was already crowded, and after the Second World War it had to shed some of its most notable elements to survive the expansion of its research interests and its students. It was only in the 1960s that Brian Pippard was allowed to prepare the brief for the new Cavendish in west Cambridge in a precinct considerably larger than the whole of the New Museums Site.[78]

Just as the buildings seemed too slight to reflect the human throng which gathered in honour of the rising fame of the Cavendish, so was the apparatus for two generations extremely modest in cost and scale and outward show, though anything but modest in its display of human ingenuity. J.J. had great reluctance to spend money and seems to have thought that small apparatus was of the order of things. When Rutherford came back to Cambridge in 1919, like many a new broom he spoke out for the need for more expensive apparatus. But the great triumphs of the 1920s and 30s were achieved without it, and he soon developed a reluctance to proceed beyond 'string and sealing wax' akin to J.J.'s. In the mid-twentieth century nuclear physics entered a phase in which large machines – cyclotrons and nuclear accelerators among them – were needed for progress in many regions. These were chiefly developed elsewhere, in government laboratories such as Harwell, and above all in the United States; and when the discoveries of Rutherford and his colleagues were harnessed to the creation of the atom bomb in the 1940s an army of research workers gathered under the direction of General Groves. Rutherford had died in 1937, but his genius was among them, and his principal lieutenant, James Chadwick, led the English contingent; yet to compare the tiny works of the Cavendish and the mighty Manhattan project is like setting a bicycle beside an articulated truck; only in the narrow streets of Cambridge is the bicycle obviously the better means of transport.

The third mark of the Cavendish and its history has been its international character. Those who chose the first professors were aware that experimental physics must be studied and viewed in a European dimension, and it was not long before its leaders were

78 Crowther 1974, pp. 412–30.

looking yet further afield. In 1895, under pressure from the scientific community, the university recognised the need to provide for research students who could not afford the time to become wranglers. A special grace was established in that year and they were allowed to proceed to a BA in less than the usual time. One of the first to benefit from this scheme was Rutherford himself, from New Zealand; it is improbable that he would have considered coming to Cambridge but for the change.[79] Those who worked in the Cavendish in the 1890s simply accepted it as a fact of life that science was international. Some of the most crucial discoveries of the first Cavendish Professor, Clerk Maxwell, were crowned by a very elegant experiment made by Heinrich Hertz in Germany – and because it was so closely related to the work of Maxwell, immediately acclaimed in the Cavendish.[80] The story goes on in the same way: Cambridge can be very inward-looking, and the old Cavendish wears a forlorn, parochial look; but there has been nothing parochial about the work inside it or the inspiration of its best minds. When Rutherford returned to Cambridge in 1919 after long service in Montreal and Manchester, he found that the battle to establish the Ph.D. degree in England and especially in Cambridge was on the verge of being won. Already in 1916 J.J. had been pressing the case in a discussion of the Senate, against opposition from such as William Ridgeway, who urged that native Cambridge students should be fostered rather than invaders from America.[81] In 1917 Arthur Balfour, Chancellor both of the Exchequer and of the university, joined H. A. L. Fisher, the Oxford don now president of the Board of Education, in gathering a Standing Conference of imperial universities to investigate the need. By 1920 the Ph.D. degree had arrived, a few months after Rutherford.[82] He was soon one of those on the newly founded Board of Research Studies (now the Board of Graduate Studies – a board and an office unique to Cambridge, an interesting reminder of the events of the early 1920s) urging yet further research degrees, M.Litt. and M.Sc. Research students were coming from all over the world to

---

[79] For the circumstances, see Wilson 1983, pp. 62–6; Crowther 1974, pp. 121–2.
[80] Larsen 1962, p. 21; Crowther 1974, p. 114.
[81] Wilson 1983, p. 418.   [82] Wilson 1983, p. 419.

the Cavendish and to other departments of the university, though their numbers seem comparatively modest now, looking back from the 1990s.[83]

One of the unanswerable questions in the history of scholarship and science is whether research flourishes more abundantly in a teaching university or a research institute. On the one side there is abundant testimony to the stimulus many academics have received from their pupils, to the deep and abiding value of being constantly made to explain the basis and roots of their ideas to intelligent, ignorant audiences – or to the sceptical. The professor who is neither subjected to the discipline of explaining himself nor to the cut and thrust of debate with his students easily takes to living in a dream world, or rests too readily content with his own thoughts. But it may be equally true that much teaching – and the administration which must accompany it – absorb time, and elementary teaching can distract from serious enquiry at the frontiers of knowledge. The Cavendish has always been a teaching department of a university dedicated to education as well as to learning; its standing and success have depended very much on its place in Cambridge and its role as the workplace of students as well as professors; but its greatest successes have been won in collaboration with scientists in other laboratories, some of them research institutes.

Then, again, its success has owed much to its contact with new talent – with its capacity to attract ambitious and able students, and especially research students, from far and wide. Yet students cost time and money and equipment and space, and there is a fascinating reminiscence by James Chadwick of 'a difference of opinion [with Rutherford] about how the laboratory should be run. I thought we were having too many research students, because we did not have the room for them and because certain things, some points, were not being looked into because they might give a negative answer' – and in any case could not provide exactly the right amount for work for a Ph.D. Every leader in research has found the Ph.D. a straitjacket and a hindrance to research as well as a much valued passport for students entering

[83] Total Ph.D. students 1920–1, 72 (*Reporter* 1920–1, pp. 648–50); 1925–6, 276 (*Reporter* 1925–6, p. 924); 1986–7, 1463 (out of a postgraduate total of 2941, *Reporter* 19 August 1987, Special No. 19, pp. 2, 3, 5).

academic life. 'What I wanted to do was to have a few rooms set aside in which various pieces of equipment could be ready for any examination we wanted to make in a hurry, such as a cloud chamber ... which only meant a few rooms, but it meant shutting off these rooms from the occupation of these research students.' But Rutherford insisted on giving the students their head, and Chadwick, looking back, grudgingly admitted he may have been right.[84]

The leaders of the Cavendish have been men of varied background. There has been a small element from one of the notable Cambridge dynasties. The second Cavendish Professor, Lord Rayleigh, was married to a Miss Balfour, sister of the future Chancellor, and also of Mrs Sidgwick, wife of Henry Sidgwick the philosopher, founder of Newnham. Mrs Sidgwick began her academic career as assistant to Rayleigh in the Cavendish and ended it as principal of Newnham. But far more characteristic of the history of the Cavendish have been the newcomers: J.J. and Chadwick from comparatively humble origins in and near Manchester; Rutherford from the New Zealand bush; Kapitza from the Russia of Lenin and Stalin. If the whole catalogue were unrolled it would take us to many parts of America and Europe, to Japan and China and Indonesia; Luard and Perowne would be astounded, and their successors in the late twentieth century may reasonably be proud. Cambridge can be parochial; but it is also extremely cosmopolitan: had it not been so, the Cavendish might have been founded but could never have flourished.

Its progress from Clerk Maxwell to J. J. Thomson

The modest resources of the university in the 1870s and the good sense of Syndics and electors dictated that the Cavendish should evolve slowly at first, but with very sure steps. Since William Thomson (Lord Kelvin) would not leave Glasgow, the electors chose as first Cavendish Professor James Clerk Maxwell, a distinguished senior wrangler best known in Cambridge as a mathematician. He had been one of the many distinguished pupils of William Hopkins, one of the most successful of the private

[84] Interview quoted in Wilson 1983, p. 424.

coaches; and Hopkins had lectured, 'in addition to differential and integral calculus ... on mechanics, gravitational theory, hydrostatics, hydrodynamics, sound, light, and astronomical instruments'.[85] Maxwell was a Scottish laird, and it has been supposed that his physics owed much to Scottish metaphysics; but it seems now accepted that he owed more to his training in Cambridge. His philosophical arguments were partly derived from Whewell; his 'use of physical-geometrical theory' – or, more broadly, of the relations of mathematics and physics – was 'characteristic of the work of his mentors, Stokes and Thomson'.[86] Maxwell was a man of wide scientific interests whose special qualification to be professor of experimental physics lay in his brilliant success in shaping the experimental discoveries of Faraday into mathematical form. Thus he himself wrote: 'As I proceeded with the study of Faraday, I perceived that his method of conceiving the phenomena was also a mathematical one ... For instance, Faraday, in his mind's eye, saw lines of force traversing all space where the mathematicians saw centres of force attracting at a distance ...' and so forth.[87] He thus devised the Faraday–Maxwell theory of electromagnetic waves. 'He concluded that light was an electromagnetic phenomenon; that light and electromagnetic waves are identical in kind, though different in wavelength.'[88]

Maxwell was not a dynamic person, and suffered from frequent ill-health – he was under fifty when he died. But he set the Cavendish going and won it a reputation within and without Cambridge for serious original work; and his lively mind and dedication to science were infectious. 'He was high-spirited and entertaining,' wrote C. P. Snow. 'His only vice was the writing of indifferent light verse with an obsessive facetiousness', which became for a while a Cavendish tradition.[89]

Maxwell had been a laird, though of modest estate. By a curious chance, his successor was also a landowner. Many of the ills of Cambridge in the late nineteenth century have been blamed on the agricultural depression; but the falling rent rolls which

---

[85] D. B. Wilson in Harman 1985, p. 17.
[86] Harman 1985, p. 9, summarising ibid., chap. 8.
[87] Quoted Larsen 1962, p. 20.   [88] Summary in Larsen 1962, p. 20.
[89] Snow 1981, p. 22.

inclined John William Strutt, third baron Rayleigh, to seek a profession, proved one of the kindly gifts of providence. He solved his financial anxieties in the long run by developing dairy farming; meanwhile he had transferred his private research for a time from Terling in Essex to the Cavendish. His is not a great name in the history of physics; but he is honoured for at least three contributions to the Cavendish. First, he and his colleagues devised apparatus (still preserved there) comprising a spinning coil with which the ohm, the standard unit of electrical resistance, was first accurately measured in 1882;[90] for this and for a wide range of scientific enquiries he was later awarded the Nobel Prize for physics in 1904. He 'raised the standard of electrical measurement', wrote J. J. Thomson, 'to such a high level that it may be claimed that here he has changed chaos into order.'[91] Maxwell had admitted women students only during the vacation, when he was himself away from Cambridge; Rayleigh brought intellectual women with him in his own family circle, and the future Mrs Sidgwick had forged a place for them among the students of the Cavendish long before she became principal of Newnham. Most of all, perhaps, Rayleigh set the studies of the Cavendish on a more organised and secure footing, and supplied it with much more adequate – if still, to our view, surprisingly modest – apparatus, for much of which he paid out of his own pocket. After only five years in office, he departed for the Royal Institution in London; but his work continued. In 1896 the first substantial addition to the Cavendish was completed, and in 1904, when Rayleigh won the Nobel Prize, he offered part of it to Cambridge. In the event he distributed it between the Cavendish and the University Library – showing a fine instinct for the current needs of the university – and out of the £5,000 granted to the Cavendish the Rayleigh wing was built. It was opened in 1908 in the same year that Rayleigh became Chancellor.[92]

Meanwhile, in 1881 a research student called J. J. Thomson had published his first papers; in 1884 – to the surprise and indignation of some of his older colleagues – a 'mere boy' still in his twenties,

---

[90] Larsen 1962, pp. 23–5.   [91] Thomson 1936, p. 112.
[92] Crowther 1974, pp. 125, 152–3.

Thomson was elected Cavendish Professor.[93] He was to be Cavendish Professor till 1919, master of Trinity from 1918, a notable Cambridge figure till he died, still master of Trinity, in 1940. In that year tramps were a less familiar sight in Cambridge than they are in the 1990s, and the tramp-like master of Trinity was a well-known figure in its streets. Long before then, 'his rather straggling aspect (his razor seemed always a little blunt), his shuffling walk, the little touches of his native Lancashire accent' led to his being likened to a 'grocer's errand boy', according to one obituary notice.[94] He was a product of the Mathematical Tripos, and too clumsy with his fingers to be at ease with apparatus; none the less he had an intuitive sympathy with it.

> When hitches occurred and the exasperating vagaries of an apparatus had reduced the man who had designed, built and worked on it to baffled despair, along would shuffle this remarkable being who, after cogitating in a characteristic attitude over his funny old desk in the corner and jotting down a few figures and formulae in his tidy handwriting on the back of somebody's Fellowship Thesis or an old envelope or even the laboratory cheque book, would produce a luminous suggestion like a rabbit out of a hat, not only revealing the cause of the trouble, but also the means of the cure.[95]

His easy, informal relationship with his colleagues and students, and his growing fame as a scientist, rapidly led to a great expansion in the Cavendish. In 1896 he was able to provide £2,000 out of savings from students' fees intended for new apparatus towards the building of the first extension.[96] But it was at once his weakness and his strength to undervalue the need for space and equipment. 'It is a weak point in the universities overseas', he wrote in 1912 after visiting Canada, 'that so much value is attached to buildings. The buildings and laboratories make one's mouth water, but with all that there is a great dearth of any means of enabling poor students to continue their work and education after they leave university' – and by implication in the fruitful advance of research by young and old.[97]

---

[93] Larsen 1962, p. 261; Crowther 1974, pp. 106–9.
[94] Wilson 1983, p. 86, from *Country Life*.
[95] F. W. Aston quoted in Wilson 1983, pp. 83–4. [96] Crowther 1974, p. 125.
[97] Quoted in Wilson 1983, pp. 189–90.

J.J.'s early work as professor involved

> experiments on the passage of electricity through gases ... My
> view was that whenever a gas conducts electricity, some of its
> molecules must have been split up by the electric forces acting on
> the gas, and that it is these which carry the electricity through the
> gas. On this view, a gas in which all the molecules are in the
> normal state cannot conduct electricity.

So far we are still in the world of Maxwell; but not for long.

> My idea at that time was that some of the molecules were split up
> into two atoms, one of which was positively, the other negatively
> electrified, and my first experiments were intended to test this
> idea. It was not until 1897 that I discovered that the decompo-
> sition of the molecule was of quite a different type from ordinary
> atomic dissociation; then I found that one of the bodies into
> which the molecule split up, the one carrying the negative
> electricity, is something totally different from an atom, and that
> its mass is less than one-thousandth part of that of an atom of
> hydrogen, the lightest atom known.[98]

Thus was the electron discovered, and with it the way into the
heart of the atom. Meanwhile in 1895 had come Röntgen's first
detection of X-rays in Würzburg. The significance of the discovery was immediately apparent both to J.J. and his new research
student, Ernest Rutherford, in Cambridge, and to Becquerel and
his disciples, the Curies, in Paris.[99] The two decades before the
First World War were a period of great fecundity in the
development of X-rays and nuclear physics. J.J. himself never
again, perhaps, rose to such heights as in 1897; but he fostered a
group of young scientists of an extraordinary range of talent:
Rutherford; C. T. R. Wilson, 'Cloud Wilson', who had a vision
on the summit of Ben Nevis and created the cloud chamber in the
Cavendish to simulate its effect and study its causes; R. J. Strutt,
who carried research begun in close collaboration with Thomson
and Wilson in Cambridge to Imperial College, London; John
Townsend, who similarly developed a branch of the Cavendish
tradition in Oxford – and many others.[100] J.J. might be clumsy

[98] Thomson 1936, p. 118; partly quoted in Larsen 1962, p. 28.
[99] There are brief summaries in Larsen 1962, pp. 31–6; Snow 1981, p. 25.
[100] Crowther 1974, esp. pp. 133–51.

with his fingers and unimpressive in dress and presence, but his brilliance and width of knowledge, his enthusiasm and readiness to listen and to help, made him a notable leader. He was so absent minded that he sometimes appropriated other men's ideas believing them his own; but most of his victims accepted this as a part of the genius of the place.[101] Rutherford had departed for Montreal in 1898;[102] he passed on to Manchester in 1907;[103] there, with the aid of Charles Darwin, later master of Christ's, and Harry Moseley, soon to be killed in the war, he elucidated the structure of the atom. By 1918–19 he had disintegrated the nucleus of the atom.[104] Thus when J.J. agreed to resign the Cavendish Chair – after his appointment to the mastership of Trinity – in 1919, Rutherford must have seemed the inevitable successor.

Ernest Rutherford

Rutherford's life and achievements and personality are exceptionally well documented; happily so, for he is one of the most notable characters in the history of Cambridge. His career was marked by extraordinarily good fortune. His appointments were no doubt inspired by his exceptional gifts; but we now know that they were immediately procured by very determined human agents working for him. Thus in 1906–7 Sir Arthur Schuster, professor of physics at Manchester, embarked on a campaign to establish Rutherford in his chair: he took early retirement and offered ample financial inducements to the university from his own resources, and the translation was quickly effected.[105] In 1919 the master mind was that of Sir Joseph Larmor, Lucasian Professor of Applied Mathematics and a leading figure in the Cambridge scientific establishment. He had done important work on the electron in the wake of J. J. Thomson's discovery of it. But he found much of the new theoretical physics of the twentieth century distasteful, and doubtless saw in Rutherford a great experimental physicist not too deeply influenced by theory.[106]

[101] Crowther 1974, p. 144.   [102] Wilson 1983, pp. 166–72.
[103] Ibid. pp. 216–23.   [104] Wilson 1983, chap. 13.
[105] Wilson 1983, pp. 166–72, 216–23.
[106] On Larmor see A. E. Woodruff in *DSB* 8, 39–41.

He was described by Lady Rutherford, in her homely and candid style, as 'like a nice old hen with one chick to find a nest for'.[107] With great tact and energy Larmor squared both the Rutherfords and the electors. The ground of his energy is abundantly clear: Rutherford had capped an immensely distinguished early career by splitting the atom in Manchester, and if the Cavendish was to recover its former greatness after the caesura of the First World War, it required no very great discernment to discover in Ernest Rutherford the man to take over from J.J. – or to settle by his side, for J.J. remained a research professor till his death.

Rutherford retained something of the simple directness of the young New Zealander all his life; his biographer David Wilson describes him as a 'simple genius'. A genius he was, and a man who cultivated simplicity: most great scholars and scientists have an ultimate simplicity which enables them to see the root of an immensely complex problem or field of enquiry. The discoveries of Rutherford's pupil James Chadwick have the simplicity of a great artist: C. P. Snow wrote of him, 'Chadwick, under a repressed façade, had the most acute of aesthetic senses and was an artist among the experimental physicists.'[108] To the lay observer there is nothing aesthetic in Rutherford's triumphs; but his extraordinary capacity to see quickly through to the heart of a problem, to worry it like a dog with a bone, to know by instinct when to transfer his attention from experiment to mathematics and from maths to experiment, suggest the direct insight of a man of superhuman gifts. Doubtless it was not so: his success was the combination of very exceptional human and intellectual gifts. As a man he was warm, kindly yet ambitious: he found the simplicity of the 'colonial' well received by those whose approval he coveted in the Cambridge of the 1890s and preserved it.[109] As a scientist he learned very early that immense concentration and wide knowledge, and the readiness to listen to colleagues far and near, were essential parts of a scientist's equipment. As

[107] Wilson 1983, p. 413; for what follows, Wilson 1983, pp. 408–14.
[108] Snow 1981, p. 85.
[109] Wilson 1983, chap. 3, esp. pp. 67–8, cites evidence of opposition to Rutherford and of early social and professional difficulties in Cambridge. But they are no more than what any ambitious, and not too tactful, young scientist must encounter; a historian may be impressed with the rapidity with which he formed a niche in the Cambridge of the 1890s.

F. W. Maitland said of the very different world of legal history, 'Simplicity is the outcome of legal subtlety; it is the goal not the starting point.'[110] One of Rutherford's most notable discoveries, 'of the scattering of alpha particles by the nucleus', which formed the basis of the nuclear theory of the atom, has been described as 'very simple and very beautiful'.[111] Scientists are prone to use the word beautiful in a rather different sense from art historians; but few would challenge its appropriateness here.

Rutherford's 'first love' had been radio transmission;[112] but he had already in the 1890s transferred his main interest to J.J.'s atomic research, and especially to exploring the consequences of the discovery of X-rays and radium. In a celebrated confrontation of two very different generations in the Royal Institution in 1904, the aged Lord Kelvin, aided by refreshing slumber during most of Rutherford's lecture, was made to accept that radium had altered the age of the earth – and many other things besides.[113] From his work on radium many consequences ensued; and in the years that followed he concentrated on the structure of the atom. He had an exceptional combination of scientific skills and the readiness to listen and encourage able colleagues. It has often been said that neither in Manchester nor in the Cavendish was Rutherford's regime entirely satisfactory for the run of the mill; that his own and his colleagues' lectures to the novices were far from inspiring; and his biographer David Wilson testified that in the Cavendish in the late 1940s elementary lectures were still 'not likely to arouse enthusiasm'.[114] But he also produced evidence pointing to a different view, of a relatively modest Manchester student, for example, who remembered with gratitude the interest Rutherford took in her class, recalling him as 'a fatherly figure, very approachable and generous . . .'[115] The truth is that most eminent academics seem inspiring to some of their pupils, dull and remote to others; all evidence of this nature must be treated with caution. The cumulative impression is that Rutherford was anything but simple: he might be noisy and direct in manner, hearty and encouraging by instinct; but his successes

---

[110] Maitland 1897, p. 9. [111] Blackett in Larsen 1962, p. 45.
[112] Wilson 1983, pp. 200–1. [113] Wilson 1983, p. 206.
[114] Wilson 1983, pp. 271, 609. [115] Ibid. p. 271.

were won by a very complex mixture of mental power, intense concentration, and an uncanny gift to seek out and help very gifted colleagues. Among the most significant examples is his early contact with the Dane Niels Bohr, who came to him in Manchester in 1912 after failing to make his mark in the Cavendish.[116] C. P. Snow thus describes their meeting.

> Rutherford was loud-voiced and explosive and liked to have his own way in a conversation. With Bohr ... he was unlikely to get it. For Bohr, though one of the deepest minds of his century, and the incarnation of altruism, was a talker as hard to get to the point as Henry James in his later years. One qualification sprang out of another. He had to dig down for the final, the perfect word, and on not finding it, had pauses, minutes long ...[117]

Rutherford listened, and gave him the encouragement he needed; a strange alliance was formed between the great master of experimental physics and one of the founders of quantum theory, a region almost as aetherial – as much the home of the theoretical physicist – as the relativity theories of Einstein, the one great physicist of the age with whom Rutherford had little contact. They respected without much understanding each other's genius. In the end, by an ecumenical process characteristic of the story we are telling, it was to be one of Rutherford's pupils, P. A. M. Dirac, who in what Snow calls the golden age of theoretical physics – 'a bit like the Elizabethan–Jacobean theatre' – with towering figures such as Einstein, Max Born and Heisenberg scattered about the world, brought into a common theoretical frame the quantum principles of Bohr and the relativity of Einstein.[118]

Rutherford's disciples comprised a galaxy of talent. There were John Cockcroft and E. T. S. Walton, who were to develop the nuclear accelerator, and Cockcroft was later to carry his skills as scientist and administrator to the founding of Harwell – and of Churchill College.[119] There was Patrick Blackett, later professor at London and Manchester and a Labour peer. But the central place belongs to James Chadwick and Peter Kapitza, two great

---

[116] Wilson 1983, pp. 325–7.   [117] Snow 1981, p. 56.
[118] Snow 1981, pp. 74–5.   [119] See pp. 586–9.

experimental physicists of opposite temperaments who managed to share Rutherford's most intimate patronage and remain close friends. Kapitza was Chadwick's best man – he has left on record a remarkable description of how an English wedding impinged on a young and observant Russian. They rode a motor bike together, Chadwick driving, and had a dangerous spill.[120] But they managed somehow to share Rutherford's inspiration and friendship, and to carry his work to new horizons.

Chadwick was reserved, pessimistic, beset with fears of ill-health, which did not in the end prevent him from living into his eighties. David Shoenberg, one of the most talented of his pupils, describes 'the traditional introduction to research in the Cavendish' in the early 1930s, 'a few weeks of practical work . . . under Chadwick's supervision. The equipment provided was rather primitive . . . and it was easy to get discouraged, but Chadwick would come by occasionally and encourage us with some gloomily sympathetic remark.'[121] Chadwick's relations with Rutherford were not always easy: the younger man was compelled to run the Cavendish on what he regarded as a shoe-string; they were temperamentally very different. But Rutherford was warm-hearted and trusting, and appreciated Chadwick's stature; and in return Chadwick deeply admired Rutherford and gave him unwavering loyalty. Behind an undemonstrative façade Chadwick was a warm-hearted, kindly man; he was also by temperament an artist.[122] In 1932

He calculated just what effects would distinguish a neutral particle from radiation. And then he set up experiments of classic beauty and simplicity to look for these effects. Like the Joliot-Curies, he shot alpha particles at a target of the light metal beryllium; and out came the mysterious 'radiation'. But Chadwick intercepted it with paraffin wax. The 'radiation' hit the nuclei of hydrogen atoms within the paraffin wax, and ejected *them* at high speed . . . By his measurements on the ejected protons, Chadwick proved that what was hitting them was not radiation: it was a neutral particle, almost identical in mass to the proton.

---

[120] Boag and Shoenberg 1988, pp. 210, 222–3, with photograph of bridegroom and best man. On Kapitza see now Boag, Rubinin and Shoenberg 1990.

[121] Shoenberg in Williamson 1987, p. 106.

[122] On Chadwick see Gowing 1964; Venn et al. 1978, pp. 485–502; Massey and Feather 1976; Brooke 1985, pp. 269–75; cf. also the moving account in Gray 1988, pp. 27–9.

Thus was the neutron discovered.[123] Chadwick went on to be professor of physics at Liverpool, head of the British mission to the Manhattan project – and so a leading figure in the development of the atom bomb, and master of Caius. But though he was able to gather fine equipment and a splendid department at Liverpool, and deploy a cast of thousands in America, he never enjoyed quite the same opportunity again as in 1932 in the Cavendish.

Kapitza was in most ways the opposite of Chadwick: lively, mercurial, informal, impertinent: they were united by their devotion to physics, by depth of insight and imagination, and by loyalty to Rutherford.[124] There are many stories of Kapitza's debut in Cambridge, and of how his impudence roused Rutherford's hasty temper and lasting affection. For Kapitza alone Rutherford showed something like favouritism; but it was based on warm admiration for the lively and varied talents of the young Russian. Kapitza's work in Cambridge produced no dramatic breakthrough comparable to Chadwick's discovery of the neutron; but he greatly advanced knowledge of high magnetic fields and low temperatures, of the methods of producing them and working in them, and their properties. Since his departure Shoenberg and other distinguished disciples in the Cavendish have spent long and fruitful years 'in the cold'. Kapitza broke through the formality of British scientists by forming the very informal Kapitza club – where Chadwick's discovery and many others were first reported; it was characteristic of him that he presided and gave it his name. His panache and skill – especially, it seems, his engineering skills[125] – inspired Rutherford to rare extravagance, which came to a peak when in 1933 the Mond Laboratory was built and equipped by the Royal Society, and Kapitza installed as director and Royal Society Professor. Here, in the midst of the New Museums Site, may still be seen the most remarkable monument to this era in the history of Cambridge. The architect H. C. Hughes, who adorned Cambridge with many fair houses, devised this building with its delightful apsidal end;

---

[123] Snow 1981, p. 85.
[124] What follows is chiefly based on Badash 1985, Boag and Shoenberg 1988, and Boag, Rubinin and Shoenberg 1990; and I am much indebted to the kind advice of David Shoenberg.
[125] Badash 1985, p. 9.

and Kapitza arranged for Eric Gill to carve on its face a crocodile, symbol of Rutherford. Much scientific learning has been put to the question how Rutherford earned this title; all that is certain is that Kapitza gave it to him within a few months of his first arrival and enjoyed mystifying his colleagues with its origin. The best recorded version goes: 'In Russia the crocodile is the symbol of the father of the family and is also regarded with awe and admiration because it has a stiff neck and cannot turn back. It just goes straight forward with gaping jaws – like science, like Rutherford.'[126] But Kapitza could not go straight forward: in 1934 he visited Russia and was prevented from returning. After immense international effort to reclaim him for Cambridge, Rutherford accepted defeat and arranged for his equipment to be sold to the USSR; and Academician Kapitza embarked on a new career. It was a warning that high-level physics, as an international science, cannot escape the hazards of international politics – as was to be only too abundantly proved during and after the Second World War, in the world of the atom and hydrogen bombs. Chadwick helped to invent the atom bomb, and Kapitza strove hard to resist the hydrogen bomb – in very different ways, both were to be trapped in the world of nuclear catastrophe.

The new Cavendish

Meanwhile, in 1937 Ernest Rutherford died. He was succeeded by Sir Lawrence Bragg, best known for his work on crystallography; and he by Sir Nevill Mott (1954–71), an eminent theoretical physicist with yet other interests. Though the Cavendish has retained its central role in international physics, it has achieved this by change and diversification. Above all, as the frontiers of the sciences have shifted, it has given birth to some distinguished children, of which one of the most celebrated is molecular biology, which was to find a new home near Addenbrooke's and open a new era in genetics.[127] Another is radio astronomy, which still lives in the Cavendish, though its observations are made in telescopes ranging from Lord's Bridge to Hawaii.[128] One of the

[126] Boag and Shoenberg 1988, p. 208 and n., quoting Ritchie Calder; cf. Badash 1985, p. 16 and n.
[127] See pp. 497–9.
[128] See pp. 486–90. The Mullard Radio Astronomy Observatory is at Lord's Bridge near Barton.

Fig. 5 New Museums Site, Mond Laboratory, 1933, designed by
H. C. Hughes, now Department of Aerial Photography: the
crocodile, symbol of Lord Rutherford, by Eric Gill

most interesting has been the Energy Research Group, led by
Professor Richard Eden, which has converted physics into
economics in its enquiries into the future pattern of the earth's
resources. Eden's career is significant: he began on the frontiers of
mathematics and physics, and moved from applied mathematics
to the Cavendish in Mott's later years, when theoretical physics
took a larger hold there. Mott's special skill has lain in brilliant

speculation on the frontiers of theoretical and experimental physics, which have aided progress in several different fields. Thus the citation of one of his numberless honorary degrees: 'His research on insulation, his study of dislocations, and, from the 1950s onwards, his interest in liquid metals, impurity bands in semiconductors, and the glassy semiconductors – all these things, and many more, have left ineffaceable traces on the scientific history of our time.'[129] The departmental structure of the present Cavendish reflects his interest in semiconductors and (following his friendship with Philip Bowden) the physics and chemistry of solids. It reflects the interests of his colleagues and successors in high energy physics, in low temperature physics, in microstructural physics, in superconductivity, and what-have-you: a rich and varied tapestry. One looks in vain for some of the great machines of modern nuclear physics – such as the linear accelerator which Mott shut down.[130] But the new Cavendish is a very impressive and complex organism, as is reflected in the great new building of the 1960s. There could hardly be a greater contrast than between the old Cavendish of the 1870s, cramped and gothic, a Dickensian presence in Free School Lane, a kind of museum of Victorian science in the 'New Museums Site', and the extensive, graceful, functional buildings of the new. The master planner was Sir Brian Pippard, who was to be first president of Clare Hall in the late 1960s and to succeed Mott as Cavendish Professor in 1971. In Clare Hall the project was devised before he joined it; yet one may see there, in microcosm, something of the concept of modern academic life and work represented in the Cavendish in macrocosm. The heart of Clare Hall is a common room, a meeting place, through which a rich variety of human personality and academic interest passes and pauses a while, exchanging greetings and ideas. The Cavendish provides flexible space for lab, workrooms, lecture rooms, tea rooms and offices; it also provides ample space for circulation and a large common room – too large perhaps ever to capture the intimacy of Clare Hall. But the new Cavendish was designed for conversation, for the exchange of ideas, as well as for experiments.[131]

---

[129] Mott 1986, p. 144.   [130] Mott 1986, pp. 100–1.
[131] See Crowther 1974, pp. 412–30.

Fig. 6 The new Cavendish Laboratory in west Cambridge

CHEMISTRY

The history of chemistry clearly illustrates the shifting pattern of scientific frontiers. The great master of biochemistry, Frederick Gowland Hopkins, was one of Michael Foster's discoveries: he came to Cambridge in 1898 to teach chemistry, under the aegis of physiology, to medical students. Such was his genius that biochemistry grew up around him; in 1914 he was a professor; in the 1920s, with Sir William Dunn's munificent endowment, a new lab and enlarged department was built for him.[132]

Chemistry, meanwhile, had flourished as an undergraduate

[132] On Hopkins see *DNB*; *DSB*; and especially the memorial volume Needham and Baldwin 1949. On Liveing see above, p. 156.

discipline under the genial baton of G. D. Liveing, professor from 1861 to 1908, when he retired at the age of 81. He was followed by a much more considerable scientist, Sir William Pope, an autocrat aptly named. In his last years occurred 'the break up of the Papal State';[133] physical chemistry spawned colloid science; after Pope's death (1939), and after the Second World War, some physical chemists followed Philip Bowden to the Cavendish, while others became chemical engineers. Meanwhile the war delayed the appointment of Pope's successor and brought chaos to the decaying papal state. Thus it was its crumbling fragments which were offered to Alexander Todd, the Napoleon of Cambridge chemistry, who came from Manchester in 1944 to be professor of organic chemistry and head of the department.[134]

At first glance the division is clear: biochemistry on the one hand, organic, inorganic and physical chemistry on the other. But it is not only that the frontiers of physical chemistry and physics are uncertainly defined – whether the science of skiing is physics or chemistry was a very real question in Philip Bowden's studies, since some of his most original practical work was conducted in the Swiss Alps, in the snow.[135] Even more obscure are the frontiers of biochemistry and organic chemistry: Todd has worked extensively on vitamins, the jewel in Hopkins' crown; and shortly before he accepted the papal throne he had turned down the chair of biochemistry.[136] Yet, if their work overlapped, two more contrasting characters could hardly be imagined; and the contrast is of exceptional interest in the history of science and Cambridge.

Frederick Gowland Hopkins

In Hopkins there dwelt two men at least: one a timid, insecure, sensitive, kindly, homely person, a man who had worked his way up from a relatively lowly position as a hospital chemist at Guy's, by slow stages acquiring academic degrees, until Foster had laid hands on him in his late thirties. His move to Cambridge came

---

[133] I take the phrase from Tabor 1969, p. 5.   [134] Todd 1983, esp. pp. 64–76.
[135] Tabor 1969, pp. 9–11.   [136] Todd 1983, pp. 61–2.

very shortly after his marriage, and his wife brought courage and some measure of efficiency and organisation into his life.[137] A fellowship at Emmanuel gave him a secure base; but a breakdown in 1910 nearly ended his career. He was rescued from disaster by generous admirers in Trinity led by Walter Morley Fletcher – later Sir Walter and founder of the Medical Research Council – who brought him to Trinity to a praelectorship in biochemistry with nominal duties. Its income was presently absorbed into a professorship, largely at first financed by the college. 'For twenty-six years', he wrote in 1937, 'I have received all the great privileges that membership of the College [a fellowship, that is] confers and have been asked for no single service in return' – save that of adding to the immortal fame of that eminent society.[138] Yet the Hopkins of the 1920s retained many signs of his early timidity. Among his greatest admirers was Sir Hugh Anderson, master of Caius, the mandarin of the university in the 1920s, who, as a neurophysiologist with a special interest in developing human and medical sciences, was well placed to appreciate Hopkins' greatness and the significance of his work. Anderson's daughter recalled their friendship thus:

> When Professor (later Sir Frederick) Gowland Hopkins came to lunch we also prepared to laugh for Father's real devotion to him found expression in the most outrageous banter. He rarely called him anything but 'The Worm' because, for all his great brain and his international reputation among men of science, he was quite incapable of fighting his own battles. According to Father, his gentleness and sympathy led his pupils to take up all his time telling him about their love affairs, and as for standing up for himself and his Department on University Boards, well . . . he just *was* 'the Worm' who must be fortified by the best claret and the most ribald insults before an important meeting 'to put some spunk into him'. The famous 'Worm' would bow his head, with its magnificently moulded narrow forehead and drooping white moustache, before this storm of raillery, and the naturally mild expression of his pale face would take on a slightly burlesqued expression of humility as he watched for an opening through which he might hit back at his tormentor . . . Surely never was so

---

[137] Needham and Baldwin 1949, p. 20 (from Hopkins's autobiographical sketch).
[138] Needham and Baldwin 1949, p. 23.

Sir Frederic Gowland Hopkins O.M., aet. 82   Kapp '43

Fig. 7 Sir Frederick Gowland Hopkins, by Edmund Kapp, in the Fitzwilliam Museum

much abuse heaped upon one man by another with such mutual enjoyment and deep affection.[139]

Yet there was another Hopkins, the brilliant scientist with a gift for close analysis helped by his early training, and the intuitive

[139] Anderson 1988ff, chap. 11 (*Caian* 1990, pp. 102–3).

insight, the capacity to see the simple core of an immensely complex problem, and the tremendous tenacity of purpose which marked his genius. The Needhams summarised thus:

> the course of his researches; first on gout and uric acid and the pigments of butterflies, then on amino-acids with the discovery of tryptophane (with Cole),[140] then on the accessory food factors now called vitamins [outstandingly his most celebrated investigation] next to muscle contraction and lactic acid (with Fletcher); and, finally, to oxido-reductions and the discovery of glutathione – a subject which kept his interest during most of the period between the two world wars – until at the end he returned to his earliest interest, the pterine pigments of lepidoptera, now with much wider significance and more precise analysis.[141]

In due course he became conscious of his own powers, and exerted a natural leadership among his colleagues all the more effective because they knew his warmth and simplicity and kindliness.[142] Joseph and Dorothy Needham characteristically quoted the Taoist paradox of him: 'The Sage has no personal wishes, therefore all his desires are fulfilled.'[143] Assuredly his colleagues did not think he was ineffective; and there is a clarity and an authority in his addresses which make some of them thrilling reading even to a historian who knows nothing of biochemistry.[144] One can perceive a natural progression from his early days in which he had to convince the organic chemists that the study of human and animal tissues was capable of the same kind of chemical analysis they were engaged in, to the eloquent plea in his Linacre Lecture for 1938 that chemists and biologists should tread a common path, understand each other's minds.[145] Equally characteristic in the Linacre Lecture is the generous catalogue of his colleagues' contributions to science: he was the father of a family rather than the head of a department – gentle, warm, inspiring, guiding.

'I think we may say', observed Hopkins about 1930,

---

[140] S. W. Cole, one of his earliest collaborators, and a colleague for most of his working life.
[141] Needham and Baldwin 1949, p. 113.
[142] See esp. M. Stephenson in Needham and Baldwin 1949, pp. 27–38; and the Needhams, ibid. pp. 111–19.
[143] Ibid. p. 119.
[144] There is an admirable selection in Needham and Baldwin 1949.
[145] Needham and Baldwin 1949, pp. 302–18.

that organic chemistry, moving closer to physics, is now passing from its classical period into a romantic one. It is becoming intellectually more adventurous in its concepts, more dynamic, in its dealing with evidence more subtle. This it owes largely to the marvellously refined methods of modern physics as applied to the problem of molecular structure . . .[146]

Alexander Todd

Alexander Todd's apprenticeship was served in Glasgow, Frankfurt and Oxford, and each contributed something to his deep knowledge of science and experience of the world. There seems little of the romantic in his approach to organic chemistry, and he revealed none of Hopkins' insecurity when, as a research student, he refused an invitation from a German *ordentliche Professor* to his seminar on Saturday at 8 a.m.: 'I am afraid I told him in my very blunt German that I was busy on Saturdays, and that in any case 8 a.m. was far too early for me.'[147]

His marked ability and drive won early recognition, and after relatively brief spells in Edinburgh, London and CalTech he became – in 1938 at the age of 30 – professor at Manchester and director of the Chemical Laboratories there. Manchester at that time had (as Todd reckoned) the third largest School of Organic Chemistry in Britain, after Oxford and Imperial College. Cambridge meanwhile was languishing, and declined even more during the war. It was only with extreme reluctance, and after exacting draconian conditions, that he consented in 1944 to follow the path from Manchester to Cambridge that Rutherford had taken nearly a quarter of a century earlier. He came at an ideal time: after the war, and particularly in the 1950s and 60s, finance for universities, and especially for large scientific departments, steadily expanded; and with strong support from the university guaranteed at the outset, and a growing reputation able to inspire financial support from Rockefeller, Hoffman La Roche and elsewhere from without, Todd was able to gather a galaxy of talent and finance rapidly expanding programmes of research under his own direction. Even the antiquated premises worked in

[146] Needham and Baldwin 1949, p. 203.   [147] Todd 1983, p. 18.

his favour, since he was able to insist that the university gave the highest priority to new chemical laboratories. They were constructed in the 1950s on a scale which seemed prodigious. His success depended on a remarkable combination of brilliant scientific gifts – learning, insight, theoretical grasp, experimental flair – and exceptional energy, drive and self-confidence. He tells us himself that probably 'most people' regard his work on vitamins

> as my main contribution to research – the chemistry of vitamins, of nucleosides, nucleotides, coenzymes and nucleic acids. Such a view is entirely reasonable, since there can be little doubt that our nucleotide work and the establishment of the chemical structure of nucleic acids form the base on which molecular biology and modern genetics have developed in such spectacular fashion during the past quarter of a century. Yet, in addition, I have always had a deep interest in natural colouring matters – an interest triggered by my association with Robert Robinson [in Todd's early life in Oxford] in research on the beautiful red and blue colouring matters of flowers known by the generic name of anthocyanins. As a result, I have, during my career, done a good deal of work on natural colouring matters and especially on those remarkable pigments found in aphids, those well-known sucking insects which are the bane of many gardeners' lives.[148]

To this impressive list might be added that he nearly inspired the abolition of chemistry as a science, for his pupil V. M. Clark, setting up a new department in the University of Warwick, renamed it molecular science: this faithfully reflected a fundamental shift in the nature of science, but the name chemistry has been preserved in conservative Cambridge.

This brief summary represents only a part of Todd's work, even for Cambridge. Not only did he lead a spectacular research programme, which brought him the Nobel Prize for chemistry in 1957, and set the fashion for massive modern laboratories; he played a key role in the founding of Churchill College; he was also master of Christ's; he was chairman of the University Press Syndicate and helped to rescue the Press from a desperate crisis; he has been a politician, a member of the House of Lords, nearly a

---

[148] Todd 1983, p. 83.

minister; chairman of government committees; first Chancellor of the University of Strathclyde in his native Glasgow.[149]

Yet all these achievements illustrate above all his capacity to select and work with other men – at least with those of his own choosing. As master of Christ's, he found a new bursar and a new senior tutor to run the college for him; his main task at the Press was the choice of Geoffrey Cass as chief executive. In the wider world, he was evidently on the best of terms with R. B. Woodward of Harvard, his chief imperial rival in the world of organic chemistry.[150] Above all, the success of his work in Cambridge depended on the marvellous team of younger chemists whom he trained or attracted to his lab. Nor is all this talk of organic chemistry a fair summary of the adventures of Cambridge chemistry. The redoubtable R. G. W. Norrish was deeply entrenched in physical chemistry before Todd came. Todd himself records among his earliest achievements in Cambridge tempting the inorganic chemist H. J. Emeleus from Imperial College.'[151] In later years he has been joined in the House of Lords by his inorganic colleague Lord Lewis, who is also warden of Robinson College. A modern spectrometer applied to Cambridge chemistry would detect an immensely complex structure.

ARCHAEOLOGY AND ANTHROPOLOGY

It will be uselessly debated till the end of time whether archaeology is more properly considered a science or an art. In Cambridge it is numbered among the social sciences, as befits its union with social anthropology; and it has liens with history which ought to be closer. But many of its most remarkable links have been with geology and botany; and its leading practitioners in recent years have tended to emphasise its place in the sciences. There we will place it, not without qualms. For arch and anth grew up in a museum most notable for its ethnological collections; and ethnology, in which the study of skulls, or physical anthropology, had a central role in the late nineteenth century, was a branch of the natural sciences.

---

[149] See pp. 264–7, 568; Todd 1983, p. 172.   [150] Todd 1983, pp. 136–7, 153, 165–7.
[151] Todd 1983, p. 75.

The natural sciences

To visitors from other continents it is simply of the order of nature that anth and arch should dwell together; but it is not so in England. Their union in Cambridge is exceptional in Britain. The other special feature of the Cambridge school is that it is the home of *prehistoric* archaeology. There has been good work done on historical archaeology from its midst; it has counted some first-rate historical archaeologists among its staff; it has bred some of the leaders in that field. In the 1920s it seemed to H. M. Chadwick, professor of Anglo-Saxon and one of the founders of the English Tripos, that arch and anth was his natural habitat; and Saxonists have flourished in arch and anth since then, even though Anglo-Saxon studies were led back to the English fold by Dorothy Whitelock in the 1960s.[152] It might seem that there was an ever-present challenge in a historic town like Cambridge to the local archaeologists; and they have indeed done some notable work here and formed from within the department an Archaeological Unit. But only in 1990, many years after the Oxford Unit came to being. Oxford did not think of teaching undergraduates archaeology until the 1990s, yet it has been a notable centre of medieval archaeology for many years. Cambridge has been supreme in prehistory.

If we had to say in a sentence how these two basic features have come to dominate Cambridge arch and anth, then we might say that they grew out of a Museum of Ethnology and came to maturity in the age of Sir Grahame Clark. The truth is more complex, but the museum and the influence of Professor Clark are central to the story.

The Cambridge Antiquarian Society had been founded in 1839 as the local expression of developing interest in the study of antiquities in Britain at large.[153] From the start its members gathered local antiquities and it made various shifts to find space to preserve them. In 1875 the society offered its collections to the university on the condition that they were housed and cared for. The link between society and university had always been close, and became intimate. But it took some years to find the right mode of collaboration. In 1883, Sir Arthur Gordon, first governor of Fiji, announced the offer of his own collection of Pacific

[152] See p. 445. I have had generous help in this section from David Phillipson.
[153] Thompson, M. W. 1990. For what follows see also Ebin and Swallow 1984; Cumming 1981.

material, coupled with that of his friend Alfred Maudslay – and with the collections they offered also a curator. For Gordon stipulated that they should be cared for by his close friend Baron Anatole von Hügel, who had recently been living and working with him in Fiji. These offers were passed on to the university by J. W. Clark, president of the Cambridge Antiquarian Society, and at the time superintendent of the Zoological Museum; but also a leading Cambridge antiquary of universal learning, nearing the completion of his own and his uncle's masterpiece, Willis and Clark's *Architectural History*. Thus the museum and Cambridge acquired one of the remarkable characters of the age, for, in spite of some serious bouts of ill-health, Baron Anatole remained an active curator, setting his mark on the museum and the school until his retirement in 1921–2. Clark told him that he was probably the first Roman Catholic to hold a university post since the end of the Test Acts in 1871; and Baron Anatole, who was brother of the more famous Baron Friedrich, theologian and mystic, was one of the founders of the Catholic community in Cambridge.[154]

At the same time plans were under way for the construction of the Arc, the Museum of Classical Archaeology, which was to dwell for the 99 years of its lease on the site of the old malthouse of Peterhouse. The end of the lease was to stir the Faculty of Classics and the university to provide a new museum and a new department on the Sidgwick site in the 1980s. Meanwhile, in the 1880s, extra space was provided for a Museum of General and Local Archaeology and of Ethnology.[155] Under the benign and enthusiastic rule of Baron Anatole, the collections rapidly outgrew their first home. In 1900 plans were laid for the new museum, to be designed by T. G. Jackson, who had given Oxford its Examination School,[156] and in due course building started in 1910. It was not to be completed until after the Great War, and collections grew so rapidly that space has always been a problem, though much less apparently so after the complete restoration and reorganisation begun when Peter Gathercole was curator and

---

[154] See pp. 388–91; for J. W. Clark's letter to von Hügel, Cumming 1981, 'Catalogue', p. 5.
[155] Ebin and Swallow 1984, p. 10; Cumming 1981, pp. 1–2. It is now the Museum of Archaeology and Anthropology.
[156] Brooke, Highfield and Swaan 1988, pl. 181.

continued under his successor David Phillipson in the 1980s and 90s.[157]

The main proponent of teaching in anthropology was A. C. Haddon, who had begun his career as a zoologist, curator in zoology under the superintendence of J. W. Clark. He went to the Torres Straits in 1888–9 in search of tropical fauna, fell in love with the people of the islands, and returned an anthropologist.[158] He gradually became less and less of a natural scientist, more of a social scientist; and eventually, from 1904, was able to teach anthropology under a new Board of Anthropological Studies.[159] He was assisted by two remarkable men who were simultaneously engaged in developing the study of psychology in Cambridge, W. H. R. Rivers, who had accompanied Haddon on his second expedition to the Torres Straits in 1898–9, and C. S. Myers, who was the true founder of Cambridge psychology.[160] But the success of the course was due to Haddon's appeal for candidates aspiring to the Indian Civil Service. The ICS and the Colonial Service supported Cambridge arch and anth for a generation, and many a sahib or colonial judge was bred on it.

Apart from Haddon, the chief props of the museum and of the growing interest in anthropology which it fostered were the Disney Professor of Archaeology, Sir William Ridgeway, and J. G. Frazer, Sir James Frazer of *The Golden Bough*. Frazer was a fellow of Trinity from 1879 until his death in 1941, and resident in Cambridge save for a brief spell in Liverpool as honorary professor.[161] Frazer's armchair methods of anthropological study have been deeply unfashionable in recent decades, but his application of Darwinian evolution to human societies, and his literary skill, greatly enhanced the reputation of social anthropology as a science. Ridgeway was no field archaeologist; but he combined an immense range of learning in classical antiquity and current anthropology with a considerable knowledge of ancient coinage and other artefacts. His interests are well reflected in the titles of

---

[157] Cumming 1981, pp. 5–10.
[158] Ebin and Swallow 1984, p. 17. On him see Quiggin 1942.
[159] For what follows, see Ebin and Swallow 1984, pp. 21–2.
[160] See p. 499; Ebin and Swallow 1984, pp. 17–22.
[161] He was honorary professor of social anthropology at Liverpool from 1907 to 1922, but he only resided there briefly in 1907–8, returning for a time at least to give occasional lectures (Kelly 1981, pp. 142–3); for his career as a whole, see *DNB*; Ackerman 1987.

his best-known books – *The Origin of Metallic Currency* ..., *The Origin and Influence of the Thoroughbred Horse*, *The Origin of Tragedy*.[162] He was almost blind in later years and could not see ordinary things, like a bowl of soup – to the undoing of inexperienced waiters; but he could still see a Greek coin held close to his eye. He was eccentric, belligerent, the fervent opponent of several movements of reform, but the steadfast support of arch and anth. To him they were a single discipline.

The world of ICS and the sahibs came to an end with the Second World War. In its wake first India, then most of the rest of the empire, melted away, and a course on native customs for their future rulers ceased to make sense. But in the meantime both anthropology and archaeology had changed. In the 1950s and 60s the social sciences were at the height of fashion, and in Cambridge this spelt new life for social anthropology as well as for the newer social and political sciences.[163] Anthropology as a social science was inimical to the evolutionary approach of Frazer, and had little interest in history; concentration on living specimens as social organisms led its pratiquants to spurn the museum. The fashion for a functionalist approach to these studies had already weaned many students away to LSE and Malinowski in the 1920s and 30s; now the more advanced approaches flourished in Cambridge under Sir Edmund Leach. Once again, change was in the air; and by the 1980s anthropology was led by Professor Jack Goody, who showed how far his tribe has moved from the contempt for history rampant in the 1950s and 60s by writing on *The Development of the Family and Marriage in Europe* (1983), a book which combines anthropology and history in a manner profoundly important to both disciplines. Thus it is a chastened social anthropology which flourishes beside archaeology in the 90s – and one of broader cultural interests, devoted once again to the Museum of Arch and Anth.

Before the Second World War archaeology was a modest discipline in most British universities. Its most notable centre was the Institute of Archaeology in London, which grew up between the wars under the inspiration of Mortimer Wheeler, most

---

[162] Ridgeway 1892, 1905, 1910; on him see pp. 97, 375–6, 393. What follows is partly based on personal information from the late Z. N. Brooke and others.
[163] See p. 472–3.

brilliant of field directors and archaeological showmen, and Gordon Childe, who gave prehistory a simple Marxist frame which helped the young science to learn to walk. In Britain at large, archaeology grew and flourished very rapidly in the 1950s, and especially in the 60s and 70s, and the rapidly expanding departments in English universities – joined from the late 1960s and 70s by those offshore islands of academic archaeology, the archaeological units – were in considerable measure, though not exclusively, peopled with graduates from Cambridge.[164] There were notable teachers of archaeology already in Cambridge in the 1920s and 30s. Ridgeway's successor as Disney Professor, Sir Ellis Minns, was a polymath who did notable work 'on the region between the Carpathians and the Caucasus'; but like Ridgeway he was not a field archaeologist.[165] Nor was his successor Dorothy Garrod, though an eminent prehistorian, engaged in field work by the time she became Disney Professor.[166] The presence of a galaxy of men and women with trowels in their hands is a phenomenon of the last forty years. Meanwhile, in the 1920s and 30s a relatively young discipline had to establish itself both in the university and in the colleges, and arch and anth had at first a considerable struggle for survival in both. But it is one of the subjects which the colleges tended to favour before the university; and Grahame Clark, in his magisterial study of *Prehistory at Cambridge and Beyond* (1989), has emphasised the role of the colleges in supporting many of the leading figures in Cambridge archaeology: Peterhouse in particular supported Clark himself – he was eventually to be its master – and among his more celebrated pupils, David Clarke; and St John's supported Glyn Daniel and several younger men.[167] Glyn Daniel combined original scholarship among the megaliths with a flair for presenting archaeology to a wider world, in his lectures, in *Antiquity*, which he edited for many years, and on television. He was the best known of all in the public eye. The least widely known was David Clarke of Peterhouse, who died still a relatively young man in 1976; but among practitioners of his craft his is a name to

---

[164] The story is told in considerable detail in Clark 1989.
[165] Clark 1989, pp. 30–4, esp. 32–3.   [166] Clark 1989, pp. 42–8, etc.
[167] See esp. Clark 1989, p. 53.

conjure with, for his *Analytical Archaeology* (1968), compact with mathematics and archaeologico-sociological jargon, foreshadowed the 'new archaeology' of the 1970s and 80s, the attempt, that is, to fashion an exciting new science only intelligible to the initiated – playing the role for archaeology that structuralism has had for literature.[168]

But the most influential of all has been Grahame Clark himself. He presided over the department in its most critical years of expansion; and the growing appeal of the subject to some of the brightest younger scholars of the 50s and 60s, and the reputation of Cambridge and Clark, brought him a galaxy of pupils. A part of his strength has lain in his readiness to trespass in other scholar's territories – or rather, to seek their collaboration, be they botanists, geologists, or anthropologists; his role in the Fenland Research Committee was crucial.[169] Furthermore, his outlook has never been insular: he was first drawn to archaeology by a relic fished from the North Sea which revealed an epoch when Britain was not yet an island; his pupils and colleagues have been active in Africa, Asia and the New World; and some of his own most influential books have a European dimension.[170] In *Prehistoric Europe: the Economic Basis* he laid foundations of vital interest for the whole of economic history; and he showed with a new clarity and insight how the advanced techniques of his generation could make history – the history of whole cultures – out of a period innocent of documents. Thus he gave prehistory a free-standing historical image of its own – made it a period or cluster of periods in its own right – and at the same time drew prehistory and history closer together. It was not for nothing that he was a fellow of Peterhouse in the heyday of Postan, Knowles and Butterfield.[171] It is perhaps the free-standing image which has been most influential, for it helps to explain the dominance of prehistory in Cambridge archaeology since. The department has worked shoulder to shoulder with a flourishing group of classical archaeologists in the Classics Faculty and Egyptologists in oriental

---

[168] Grahame Clark emphasises that David Clarke 'was himself fully convinced of the humane nature of archaeology' (Clark 1989, p. 97), which is also true of some, not all, of the exponents of the new archaeology.

[169] See pp. 162–3.   [170] Clark 1989, pp. 53–4, 86.

[171] See p. 238.

207

studies; it has reared some of the most notable historical archaeologists of our day – Martin Biddle and Peter Addyman were undergraduates there in the 50s – and some of them teach within it. Its view is world-wide; it has fostered the Centre of African Studies and played its part in other regional adventures. But its emphasis, and its bias, is emphatically prehistoric, as now symbolised by the current Disney Professor, one of Grahame Clark's most eminent disciples, Colin Renfrew (Lord Renfrew), master of the prehistoric cultures and societies of the Aegean and the Orkneys, director of the newly formed McDonald Institute of Archaeological Research – the gift of a rich benefactor, specially impressed by Renfrew and the Cambridge school – and master of Jesus.

Yet that is not the end of the story, for Cambridge archaeology does not live by the trowel or the computer alone. In the 1930s Kenneth St Joseph, then a geologist, was inspired by the celebrated pioneer of archaeological techniques O. G. S. Crawford to sample aerial reconnaissance. The war of 1939 kept him in the air, and he returned to Cambridge deeply experienced in aerial observation and determined to establish aerial photography there. In the event arch and anth, classics, history, geology, geography and other disciplines supported him; and the department he created – still flourishing under his successor, David Wilson – quickly won an international reputation for its aid to a variety of sciences. His own interests became primarily archaeological; but the first of his notable series of surveys, *Monastic Sites from the Air*, written with the monastic historian David Knowles (1952), established the value of his techniques for standing buildings as well as for hidden foundations; and some of his most successful work was done on medieval cities. By the same token the archaeology of standing buildings came to be the special interest of Harold Taylor, successively University Treasurer and Secretary General of the Faculties in the 1940s and 50s, and so a central figure in the restructuring of the university in the postwar expansion. Taylor was in origin a mathematician, and the work that he and his first wife Joan brought to fruition in *Anglo-Saxon Architecture* was (in his own view) an amateur interest; but it is a striking example of the highly professional work out of the normal course, and across the frontiers of disciplines, which the academic breezes can encourage, and departmental professionalism does not wantonly stifle, in the heart of a university.[172]

[172] See pp. 591–2.

Chapter 7

CLASSICS, LAW AND HISTORY

The study of classics is the lineal descendant of the most fundamental component in medieval education, the study of grammar. 'Civil' or Roman law had been a branch of higher study in the Middle Ages. But they only achieved triposes in the nineteenth century, classics in 1824, law in 1858.[1] Classics had suffered from being on the ground floor of a building of which the upper storeys were occupied by maths. Civil law had a Regius Professor and a modest shadow existence; for the laws of England were taught in the Inns of Court not in Cambridge. But from 1800 there was a Downing Professor of the Laws of England, and from 1858 a tripos.[2] The foundation of the chair had been anticipated in 1788 by the appointment of Edward Christian as Professor of the Laws of England: he became the Downing Professor in 1800. Meanwhile history, though studied by a very respectable line of antiquaries and historians, was a parvenu as an undergraduate discipline. It had had a Regius Professor since 1724; but it had only become a serious study when Charles Kingsley departed from the chair in 1869 and J. R. Seeley reigned in his stead.[3] It had had a ghostly existence among the moral sciences, from which it was summarily ejected in 1867. It took its first steps as a tripos in 1870–4, when it was yoked to law. From 1875 the History Tripos stood alone, at first very modestly supported by staff and students. This was the heyday of the classics, though part II of the Classical Tripos was so exceedingly specialised – and so much dominated by philology, which was

---

[1] Tanner 1917, pp. 602, 854.
[2] The Downing Chair was formally founded, with the college, in 1800, after a Chancery suit of infinite length (see pp. 54–5). See Tanner 1917, pp. 94–5.
[3] Tanner 1917, pp. 88–9; see below, pp. 231–2.

caviare to the general – that many good students felt impelled or encouraged after part I to seek their destiny in other fields, such as law and history. At the turn of the century both these were mounting in popularity; by 1910 law was a large, history a giant, tripos: 90 men took the two parts of law, 175 men and 41 women the two parts of history.[4] In the same year 104 men and 16 women took part I classics; 8 men and 3 women part II – though in compensation, 5 of the men and 2 of the women got firsts.[5]

These subjects pose to the historian the familiar dilemma: should one dwell on the heights, study the patron saints of law and history and classics; or should one take a middle ground and explore the men and women who laid the foundations of teaching and scholarship on which these disciplines have been built; or should one study syllabuses and libraries and undergraduate programmes? A part of the answer is inescapable: a history of Cambridge which had little to say of Maitland and Housman would be a shadow of a book. Both law and history live still in the afterglow of Maitland; and Housman remains a name without compare among modern Cambridge classics. But only in law was Maitland's influence and teaching directly felt: he had few pupils and not many friends among the historians. And Housman is associated with a very distinguished, but now very select, element among classical scholars: the burgeoning study of ancient history, ancient philosophy and literature owes nothing directly to him. Maitland and Housman remind us of the paradoxes as well as the glories of our theme.

A. E. HOUSMAN AND THE CLASSICS[6]

'If a man will comprehend the richness and variety of the universe, and inspire his mind with a due measure of wonder and of awe, he must contemplate the human intellect not only on its heights of genius but in its abysses of ineptitude', said the poet Housman, 'and it might be fruitlessly debated to the end of time whether Richard Bentley or Elias Stoeber was the more marvel-

---

[4] Tanner 1917, pp. 894, 936–7.   [5] Tanner 1917, pp. 701–2.
[6] For this section I have found Brink 1986 especially helpful; on Housman see ibid. chaps. 8–9; Gow 1936.

lous work of the creator.' Stoeber's edition of Manilius 'saw the light in 1767 at Strasbourg, a city still famous for its geese'. Thus Housman adorned the trail which led from Scaliger via Bentley to Housman himself as editors of the classical Latin poet Manilius.[7] By the same token it might seem wise to approach the study of classics in Cambridge through its lesser lights; Housman has a way of dazzling us. But his career and his genius sharpen the edge on so many problems in the history of Cambridge, and of scholarship at large, that in a book which must of its nature be highly selective, I have deliberately set him beside Maitland as examples of what the great, and only the great, can teach us. Housman himself was a student in the Oxford of Benjamin Jowett and Mark Pattison. Between them lay a famous argument: was the university a place of teaching and education, or of learning and scholarship?[8] It is apparent now that neither took a simple view. Jowett, the great educator, was a notable exponent of the virtues of scholarship, a leader among those who sought to bring England back into the main stream of classical learning, and to naturalise on British soil the biblical scholarship of Germany. Pattison did not undervalue education; rather he denied that Oxford was geared to offer the best it had or could have to rapidly increasing numbers of inferior students. Jowett's influence was central in creating the immense prestige of Greats as the breeding ground of the Oxford élite of the late nineteenth and early twentieth centuries – a course which became immensely popular with able students never destined to become classical scholars; though a professor himself, he was not enthusiastic about his kind.[9] Pattison saw more clearly the inferior nature of British scholarship and wished above all to raise it; in the long run his message was also to prevail. In contemplating modern Oxford and Cambridge we shall not be wise to make a peremptory judgement between them.

Housman viewed them with a like impartiality, rather differently founded. Of Jowett he said: 'Jowett's Plato: the best translation of a Greek philosopher which has ever been executed

[7] Housman 1903–30, I, xix.
[8] For what follows, see Brooke, Highfield and Swaan 1988, pp. 284–5; Brink 1986, pp. 129–33; Green 1957, esp. pp. 260–1; Jones 1988, chap. 15, esp. p. 219.
[9] Ibid. p. 219.

by a person who understood neither philosophy nor Greek.'[10]
And in writing to Lord Asquith about Scaliger's mighty commentary on Manilius, he observed: 'Pattison had never read the
book: he was a spectator of all time and all existence, and the
contemplation of that repulsive scene is fatal to accurate
learning.'[11]

Housman kept a notebook in which he prepared his poisoned
arrows for use as occasion might demand; he was not a contemporary of Oscar Wilde for nothing.[12] The brilliant wit makes
the prefaces to Manilius delicious reading; but the cynicism and
the cruelty of his comments have sometimes made him seem a
negative influence, crushing lesser scholars into silence, driving his
Cambridge pupils away from the classics. This is not wholly fair:
his teaching, and far more his writings, have inspired generations
of scholars; and his criticism of his predecessors and colleagues –
for he was impartial in his punishments and no respecter of
persons – bring into sharp focus the history and some of the
problems of classical scholarship. Housman was born in 1859, and
took a first in Mods twenty years later.[13] But his interest already
lay in classical literature and textual criticism; he totally neglected
history and philosophy and failed to obtain honours in Greats.
His recovery was amazingly rapid. After ten years working in the
Patent Office – and in the British Museum in the evenings – he
became professor of Latin at University College, London, in
1892, and went on to the Latin chair at Cambridge in 1911. Sir
Frank Adcock used to say of Manilius that he was 'a lesser light,
who shines in the reflected glory of a greater poet than himself',[14]
which was faint praise perhaps for Housman the poet. Yet
Housman was an accomplished poet, as well as a textual critic of
genius; but strangely, he was not a literary critic at all. His famous
Leslie Stephen lecture, *The Name and Nature of Poetry* (1933),
shows that at the end of a long life he had no sense of the
intellectual content of great poetry – poetry culminated, for
Housman, in a feeling in the pit of the stomach – an astonishing

[10] Page 1983, p. 146, quoted in Brink 1986, p. 130.
[11] Housman 1971, p. 236, quoted in Brink 1986, p. 132.
[12] See Page 1983, p. 145.
[13] For this and what follows, Gow 1936, pp. 5–14, etc.
[14] In lecture courses in Cambridge which I heard in the late 1940s. Adcock was a notable ancient
historian, professor from 1925 to 1951 (Hammond 1968).

failure for one of the immortal students of classical Latin poetry. His work on Horace shows that he had much more real understanding than he would admit, even to himself. But his achievement remains a *tour de force* of specialised scholarship, unaware of its neighbourhood.

Yet he grasped the history of textual criticism with the shrewdest insight. In the person of Richard Bentley, British scholarship had led the world in the early eighteenth century; but though much lip service was paid to Bentley in the Cambridge of the later nineteenth century, the scholarship of Oxford and Cambridge was greatly inferior in depth of learning and critical acumen both to the world of Bentley and to contemporary Germany.[15] German scholarship in the age of Lachmann, the early and mid-nineteenth century, was incomparable; but its very success had bred the cult of 'streng wissenschaftliche Methode', a scientific method which became formal and wooden in the hands of lesser men; and it was this which led Housman to express contempt for some German critics. His attitude was not chauvinist – he thought most English critics beneath contempt – and his views were shared, in moderation, by the best of the Germans, such as Ulrich von Wilamowitz-Moellendorf, who was just over ten years his senior (1848–1931).[16]

Classical scholarship in late nineteenth-century Cambridge had been dominated by Sir Richard Jebb and Henry Jackson, O.M., successively Regius Professors of Greek, both fellows of Trinity.[17] Jebb was a notable figure in the English classical world and in Cambridge society – he was the husband of Gwen Raverat's Aunt Cara[18] – but in international scholarship he was respected as a journeyman editor of Greek texts, and not at all as an original or penetrating critic. Jebb was an appalling lecturer; but through his books and personal contacts he greatly improved the reputation of Cambridge classics and prepared the ground for better scholars to thrive after him. Henry Jackson was not a productive scholar at all; a few notable articles on Plato are almost all he published. But he was a man of exceedingly acute mind and a

---

[15] For all this, see esp. Brink 1986.
[16] See Brink 1986, pp. 6–7, 79, 145–8 etc.; Wilamowitz 1985.
[17] On Jebb, Jebb 1907a, b; cf. Brink 1986, pp. 143–8; on Jackson, Parry 1926.
[18] See pp. 254–5.

central figure among the Cambridge reformers of the later
nineteenth century, the life and soul of Trinity in its heyday; a
bon viveur who gathered all the guests at a feast to smoke with
him at its conclusion; tutor to all the great and good; one of those
who, without being creative themselves, help to foster scholarship by incisive conversation, wise counsel, and admirable choice
of colleagues.[19] Thus Trinity and Cambridge were uncreative in
classical scholarship, but not at all uncongenial to it, when
Housman, now well over fifty, came there in 1911.

Housman's fame is securely based on his great edition of
Manilius. He wrote much else besides, but nothing so far-reaching
or so fundamental to his craft.[20] He chose Manilius because the
manuscripts were bad and most of the editions worse, and
because a deep knowledge of ancient astronomy, not an enlivening subject to most Latinists, was essential for his understanding;
and so he provided an excellent field for Housman's critical skills.
Housman was not fond of manuscripts and on the whole left
others to read them for him. He loved to exercise learning – he
knew what all the critics had made of the passages he glossed; he
made a close study of the working of Manilius' mind, of his use of
metre and language; and of his astronomy, which had been
beyond the patience or the understanding of most former editors.
Above all, he worked his way into the author's mental processes.
By his work and his example he raised current textual scholarship
to the level of Bentley and Lachmann and beyond; and his best
disciples have maintained the standards he created. Not for
nothing did Shackleton Bailey dedicate his first major book, his
Propertiana (1956), to Housman's memory. It is quite false to
accuse Housman of sterility. Yet the skills he exercised can only
be acquired by the very few; and it is not clear that there will be
work of this kind for many more generations to perform. His
achievement raises in a very acute form one of the fundamental
questions of this study. Cambridge between 1870 and the late
twentieth century has witnessed academic progress, scholarly and
scientific advance, without parallel in its history. But this is not a
process which can be guaranteed to go on for ever. The sciences,

[19] See pp. 70–3.
[20] Housman 1903–30; his other major works were his Juvenal and his Lucan (Housman 1905, 1926).

chameleon-like, change their nature and their name, and university departments are not always quick to grasp the significance of the changes. In the humanities, some goldmines can be worked out, and at best the paths which scholars of genius cleared have to be kept open by ordinary mortals. The textual criticism of the Latin classics is far from concluded; modern critics can work in the much wider field of literary and historical criticism which Housman ignored. The Faculty of Classics has found new life in the work of ancient philosophers, archaeologists and historians; in particular Moses Finley and Keith Hopkins and their colleagues have opened vistas of historical enquiry scarcely conceived in the days of Adcock.[21] Furthermore, not all Latin is classical Latin, and in the world at large a number of leading Latinists have seen the light and penetrated the deep forests of medieval Latin. None the less, there is a problem; the sense of pioneer achievement which makes some of the most abstruse passages of Housman's Manilius thrilling reading will soon be gone: how can an original scholar practise the art of textual criticism in a field already fully cultivated?

Yet that must not be the last word. Housman's scholarship was specialised, but not narrow or sterile. He brought a new light of reason into a major field of study; it was the mingling of deep learning and high reason which made his scholarship so lasting and so exciting; he lifted the achievement of the Cambridge humanities onto a new and higher plane. It is that which makes it necessary to see him in the same perspective as Maitland.

LAW: FREDERIC WILLIAM MAITLAND

Although there had been teaching in law in Cambridge since the thirteenth century, and it had bred eminent lawyers in every century since, there had been little legal education for many generations before its revival in the 1870s. It was in one sense the supreme example of a great profession seeking academic respectability when professional qualifications came once more to count. Many voices had been raised to say that the eating of dinners by barristers in the Inns of Court – and sitting at solicitors' desks in

---

[21] On Adcock, see n. 14.

other parts of the Inns – was no substitute for the academic training which by then was so conspicuous a feature of the continental law schools. Wider opinion represented by such bodies as the Royal Commission on the study of law in the Inns of Court of the 1850s came to have an increasing influence in Cambridge.[22] But when the Law Tripos was first conceived it was not intended to replace the practical training in the London offices. 'I have heard it said to me by well-disposed persons', wrote F. W. Maitland in 1901, addressing the Cambridge Law Club and looking back over twenty-five years as a teacher of law in Cambridge,

'Now you at the Universities teach the theory – then we in London will see to a working knowledge of English law.' That sounds plausibly, and I think it very possible that there are among us here some who think that a sort of theory of law – the *generalia* of jurisprudence – can be profitably taught to those who as yet know nothing of any concrete system ... My own opinion is that we get our men too young for us to be able to deal with them in the manner that is thus suggested. I won't say but that a man who has seen a little of the world and taken in law through the pores might not intelligently read what we call general jurisprudence before he studied the law of Rome or England or Germany. Our freshmen are too ignorant of life. When I lecture to them I adjure them to read the newspapers, more especially the *Times*. If I could have quite my own way with them I would plunge them at once into Dr Kenny's *Case Book of Criminal Law*. All this I know to be a disputable point, but you will see how my opinion about it affects my opinion about some other matters. To a very large extent our Tripos must be an elementary examination in very concrete English law ...

But he went on to seek a more advanced and a more adequate space for principles – especially to argue that jurisprudence should hold an honoured place in part II rather than be an introductory course in part I.[23] The Law Tripos had been devised partly by Trinity Hall lawyers who still studied civil, that is, Roman law,

---

[22] For what follows see esp. Stein 1992. In studying the Law Faculty I have had valued help from Peter Stein and John Baker. Most students of the Law Tripos have aimed to be solicitors rather than barristers.
[23] Maitland 1911, pp. 427–8.

and at their head was Sir Henry Maine, master of Trinity Hall from 1877 till his death in 1888.[24] In 1887, soon after his return to Cambridge to teach, Maitland had written to a distinguished American legal historian: 'I send you a list of the Law Lectures delivered in this University. I am sorry to say that at present we have a great deal of Roman Law and of what is called General Jurisprudence in our scheme – but I hope that a projected alteration may give English law a fairer chance.'[25] Anyone glancing at Law Tripos exam papers of the 1870s and 1880s will immediately be impressed by the number and technical difficulty of the questions on Roman law. Gradually this was subdued, though some knowledge of it is still an essential ingredient for most students of the tripos. Gradually too crime and tort and the other mysteries of the English law crept in. The English law comprises many statutes and an infinite quantity of case law. The twentieth-century undergraduate has tended to see the law as an immense pile of cases which have to be learned; his teachers see it as a structure of principles which can be discerned and illuminated by their application to cases. Gradually the element of English law in the tripos expanded, accompanied at first by an ingeniously devised paper entitled 'Problems'. Roman law remained a powerful presence, if somewhat remote to many of the students; but a distinguished line of Roman lawyers from W. W. Buckland to Peter Stein has ensured that it has a notable place among the scholarly adventures of the Law Faculty. Maitland's own achievement was to make Cambridge a leading centre of the study of legal history – and among historians to help to embed law (for a time) and the constitution deeply in the History Tripos. Though regarded with equal veneration by lawyers and historians today, his heart was with the lawyers. 'No, I don't think that I would give up law for history if I had the chance,' he wrote to Henry Jackson answering a suggestion he might succeed Acton in the Regius Chair of Modern History; and when the offer came he firmly rejected it. The reason he gave Mr Balfour, the prime minister – and future Chancellor of Cambridge – was his health. But to Jackson he had said: 'We are a peaceful lot at the Law Board and my colleagues are exceedingly kind to me. I

---

[24] See esp. Stein 1992; also Crawley 1976, pp. 146–52.
[25] Fifoot 1965, no. 27, pp. 30–1.

have not to contend with a Gw-tk-n, a M-rs-ll, an O.B. and a couple of archaeologists.'[26] So he stayed among the lawyers.

Maitland was an artist in prose.[27] It may seem a little paradoxical so to describe a scholar whose writings are full of legal terminology and Domesday arithmetic. But he was a magician with words, and turned the driest of scholarly material into a kind of fairyland: his writing is like a ballet – an elegant dance twisting and turning through the labyrinth of medieval law so gracefully, so charmingly, so wittily that the modern reader may still be entranced by half an hour in the wastelands of Domesday who would find the broader canvas of Freeman or Froude dull and unpalatable. Maitland in his maturity reveals at every turn an ingenious mind constantly at work like a drill – yet transformed by a wit and humanity which turns every abstraction into human shape. He can tramp over the fields and yet the carpet in his Victorian drawing room is unsoiled. 'It is manure that the lord wants; the demand for manure has played a large part in the history of the human race.'[28] Or of the depression of the peasantry, of the question, can a villein quit his land? – 'Men may become economically so dependent on their lords, on wealthy masters and creditors, that the legal question whether they can quit their service has no interest. Who wishes to leave his all and go forth a beggar into the world?'[29]

To comment on Maitland is a sorry task for ordinary mortals; we reveal the clay on our boots at every word. Yet he is a crucial witness; for if we wish to understand how a university may gain and lose repute, he has much to teach us. He came of a Trinity family and for most of his life he was a Cambridge don; and yet he left few pupils in Cambridge and his legacy was more appreciated in Oxford – H. A. L. Fisher wrote his life, A. L.

---

[26] Fifoot 1965, no. 323, p. 251; Maitland's letter to Mr Balfour is ibid. no. 343, p. 268. Of the members of the Board of History and Archaeology, H. M. Gwatkin was Dixie Professor (see p. 147), Alfred Marshall the founder of Cambridge economics (pp. 467–72); for Oscar Browning, see pp. 36–7, 464–6; the archaeologists must have included the belligerent William Ridgeway (see pp. 204–5, 375–6).

[27] This study of Maitland is based on Smith 1908 (with bibliography); Fisher 1910; Fifoot 1965 (the collected letters; Patrick Zutshi is preparing a supplementary volume); Buckland 1921–3; Cam 1957; Bell 1965 and Milsom 1980 (the most penetrating assessments); Maitland 1957; Fifoot 1971 (the most complete biography); Elton 1986 – and long acquaintance with Maitland's works, especially Pollock and Maitland 1895; Maitland 1897, 1898a, b, 1906, 1911.

[28] Maitland 1897, p. 76.   [29] Maitland 1897, p. 51.

Smith wrote the earliest commentary on him, and one of the best;[30] the Maitland Memorial Library is in Oxford. His greatness was recognised in many parts of Europe and his books and friendships secured him a deep influence in America too.

He was born in 1850 and came to Trinity in 1869. In or about 1870, in his own words, 'some chance – I think it was the idle whim of an idle undergraduate – took me to Sidgwick's lecture-room, there to find teaching the like of which had never come in my way before'.[31] Maitland always revered Sidgwick as 'a supremely great teacher', and ardently aspired to be a philosopher; he was top of the university in the Moral Sciences Tripos in 1872, and wrote a dissertation – which failed to win him a fellowship – which comprised 'A Historical Sketch of Liberty and Equality as Ideals of English Political Philosophy from the time of Hobbes to the time of Coleridge'.[32] Yet it was not in Cambridge that he became a historian, but in Lincoln's Inn. There he concentrated his brilliant wits for nearly a decade on the subtleties of conveyancing and equity drafts; and in his spare time he encountered Stubbs' *Constitutional History* in his club and started to translate Savigny's *Geschichte des Römischen Rechts*.[33] The Public Record Office was at his elbow and he pottered in it; he began to transcribe *Pleas of the Crown for the County of Gloucester*. The year 1884 transformed his life. He met Paul Vinogradoff, and from the lips of a Russian he learned what historical science could mean to one who had sat in Mommsen's seminar in Berlin.[34] The work on which he had embarked took on new meaning; he had entered the world of continental historical scholarship in which he ever after dwelt. Later in the year a generous gift from Henry Sidgwick financed a readership in law in Cambridge which enabled Maitland to return there, and from 1888 he was Downing Professor of the Laws of England.[35] But in 1887 we have the first intimation of serious illness; and as the years passed it grew worse. From 1898 on he spent every

---

[30] Fisher 1910; Smith 1908.
[31] *Reporter* 1900–1, p. 318; quoted Fisher 1910, pp. 7–9; and elsewhere.
[32] Fisher 1910, p. 10; Tanner 1917, p. 709; Maitland 1911, I, 1–161.
[33] Fifoot 1971, p. 53; Fisher 1910, p. 18; Maitland 1911, III, 503.
[34] Fisher 1910, pp. 24–5, corrected by Powicke 1955, p. 10 and n., and Bell 1965, pp. 3–4.
[35] Fisher 1910, pp. 29–35; Fifoot 1971, pp. 63, 91–2.

winter in the Canary Islands, and on 20 December 1906 he died there, aged 56.[36]

Maitland was happily married and attentive to wife and daughters; he was generous in giving time to syndicates and good causes; he gave his stint of lectures when not ordered off the scene by the doctors. Yet it is clear that he spent the greater part of his later life in the study, writing.[37] No doubt the death sentence which he already feared from 1889 on concentrated his mind; no doubt he had quite exceptional gifts of concentration and speed in writing; no doubt a Victorian paterfamilias did not spend long hours in the nursery or any hours at the kitchen sink. He was for ever editing texts and the Selden Society is his monument. But in his golden years from 1895 to 1898 he published two volumes of *The History of English Law before the Time of Edward I* (1895, 2nd edn 1898) – ostensibly with Pollock, but there was mighty little Pollock in it; over 500 pages on *Domesday Book and Beyond* (1897); and for good measure his Ford Lectures on *Township and Borough* and his papers on *Roman Canon Law in the Church of England* (1898). He worked fast; he made some mistakes; his vivid imagination, which made possible so many of his intellectual adventures, sometimes led him astray. Yet not one of these books has the dust upon it; all are part of the immortal literature of historical scholarship. They speak eloquently of a dedicated life; and for all his charm and kindness and conscientious service to his university, they speak of a man who was allowed the privilege of living his days out in large measure in his study.

It is very much to the credit of his colleagues that this was possible. Henry Sidgwick had financed a readership to lure him back to Cambridge; the electors to the chair made him a professor long before his famous books were written; in later years he was given leave of absence again and again almost before he asked for it. There were some, even notable scholars, who did not care for him;[38] but for the most part he was appreciated by his contem-

[36] Fifoot 1971, pp. 279–80; for his illness see ibid. pp. 181–3, 202–3, 274–5; Bell 1965, pp. 5–6.
[37] See esp. the bibliography for 1895–1906 in Smith 1908, pp. 62–7; and cf. Fisher 1910, p. 278. Although interrupted by his illness, his work on editing Year Books and the memoir of Leslie Stephen forms an eloquent coda. For the notion expressed in 1889 that his time was limited, see Bell 1965, p. 6, quoting Fifoot 1965, no. 62.
[38] See Fifoot 1971, p. 109, on the antipathy between him and H. B. Swete, the saintly Regius Professor of Divinity. There was doubtless an anti-clerical streak in Maitland – his agnosticism was discreetly expressed, but savours more of Leslie Stephen than of Sidgwick (see pp. 121–2);

poraries as he is by us. On 17 October 1900, early in the Michaelmas Term, he wrote to R. L. Poole, 'Yesterday my lecture room overflowed, but, as I told the boys, I never knew the room I could not empty'[39] – words which have brought comfort to some of us who lecture in Cambridge; and even if many attended his lectures and a small number of his pupils became distinguished, he was caviare to historians and lawyers alike and his greatest influence in Cambridge and elsewhere came long after he was dead, through his books. In the 1920s Helen Cam and Gaillard Lapsley made Cambridge once again a centre of medieval legal history. But the young medievalists of the Edwardian era who created medieval history as a serious subject in Cambridge, Z. N. Brooke and C. W. Previté-Orton, had little or no personal contact with him. The contrast with J. J. Thomson – approximately his contemporary – is very striking: generations of physics students from all over the world worked under J.J.'s eye in the tiny old Cavendish Laboratory.[40] Cambridge cherished Maitland, but was not ready for him. It lacked the tradition of scholarship, the pool of graduate students and the seminars, to make adequate use of his genius.

None the less his achievement was parallel to J. J. Thomson's, for his reputation gave Cambridge a world-wide fame among historians and lawyers, a fame which will not die. For a decade or so I myself wrestled with urban history; and for those who struggle to make sense of the English towns of the eleventh and twelfth centuries and of the boroughs of Domesday, Maitland's pursuit of the boroughs in *Domesday Book and Beyond* was prophetic utterance of unparalleled brilliance.[41]

> Dark as the history of our villages may be, the history of the boroughs is darker yet . . . The few paragraphs that follow will be devoted mainly to the development of one suggestion which has come to us from foreign books, but which may throw a little light where every ray is useful. At completeness we must not aim, and

---

there is no evidence of any debt to Lightfoot or bond with him. His memoir of Stubbs (Maitland 1911, III, 495–511 = Maitland 1957, pp. 266–76) breathes charity in every line; but it is evident they belonged to different worlds – save in their dedication to medieval scholarship. See also Armitage Robinson's tribute, quoted in Taylor 1991, pp. 24–5.

[39] Fifoot 1965, no. 274. [40] See p. 183.

[41] What follows is from Maitland 1897, pp. 172–219, esp. 172–3, 190–1, 217. On *Domesday Book and Beyond*, see the Foreword by J. C. Holt to the reprint of 1987.

in our first words we ought to protest that no general theory will tell the story of every or any particular town.

He proceeds to cast his lively eye about the medieval borough, to determine what it was: he seeks for legal definitions, but with a marvellously concrete vision of what a town was like, what it was for. His enquiry was prejudiced by dwelling on the defensive needs which had helped to inspire Alfred and his successors in building towns at the turn of the ninth and tenth centuries – and the analogy of what Henry the Fowler achieved in Saxony in the early tenth. He proceeded with inexorable skill towards his celebrated theory that towns were essentially garrisoned fortresses – and to explain the peculiarity of borough tenures by the fashion in which they were garrisoned. But he shed all manner of light by the way.

> We have it in our modern heads that the medieval borough is a sanctuary of peace, an oasis of 'industrialism' in the wilderness of 'militancy'. Now a sanctuary of peace the borough is from the very first. An exceptional and exalted peace reigns over it. If you break that peace you incur the king's *burh-bryce*. But we may strongly suspect that the first burg-men, the first *burgenses*, were not an exceptionally peaceful folk. Those *burhwaras* of London who thrashed Swegen [in 994] and chose kings were no sleek traders . . . In all probability these burg-men were of all men in the realm the most professionally warlike. Were we to say that in the boroughs the knightly element was strong we might mislead, for the word *knight* has had chivalrous adventures. However, we may believe that the *burgensis* of the tenth century was very often a *cniht*, a great man's *cniht*, and that . . . he was kept in the borough for a military purpose . . . These knights formed gilds for religious and convivial purposes. At Cambridge there was a gild of thegns, who were united in blood-brotherhood. We can not be certain that all these thegns habitually lived in Cambridge. Perhaps we should rather say that already a Cambridgeshire club had its headquarters in Cambridge and there held its 'morning-speeches' and its drinking bouts.

He went on to survey the other functions of boroughs, as market centres and mint centres and so forth; but the argument which keeps the whole chapter alive drives on to the conclusion that the borough was a military place in its essence. 'We have thought of the typical borough as a fortified town maintained by a district for military purposes.'[42]

The book was reviewed in the *English Historical Review* by the young James Tait, and it helped to make his reputation.[43] Tait was a far duller writer than Maitland, but he had spent longer hours with the impenetrable documents of the medieval borough, and was able to show how much more deeply the towns were founded on their markets than their ramparts. Tait was to be the chief lieutenant of T. F. Tout in forming the Manchester History School, where the tradition of teaching historical documents combined with Tout's devotion to the Public Record Office helped to make Manchester the creative centre for the study of medieval history in Britain.[44] But noone who ponders these pages of *Domesday Book and Beyond* at all seriously can fail to be struck by the brilliance of historical logic, however false the conclusion, or by the floods of light the author shed over his path. Maitland may have had few close pupils; but he lifted Cambridge legal studies and Cambridge history onto a higher plane, and has inspired generations of disciples in Oxford, Cambridge and America.[45]

BUCKLAND, MCNAIR AND WINFIELD

In 1906, when Maitland died, the Law Tripos was well established, and the Law School had a substantial physical presence on the Downing Site: over the arch leading into the first courtyard there one may still read the name of Rebecca Flower Squire, from whose legacy the Squire Law Library came. The Squire bequest came to Cambridge unexpectedly. It had originally been intended for Oxford, but it had some clauses indicating favourable treatment for founder's kin and other restrictions which the high-minded dwellers by the Isis could not agree to, and so it came to rest by the Cam.[46] Its chief fruit was a substantial faculty

---

[42] Maitland 1897, p. 217.   [43] Tait 1897.

[44] On Tout, see esp. Powicke 1955, pp. 21–44.

[45] Cf. e.g. R. Brentano in *Speculum* 63 (1988), 151–2 – compulsory reading for all students of Maitland. For recent appraisals see Milsom 1980 and Elton 1986.

[46] This is based on notes by W. Steiner kindly lent me by John Baker; see now Steiner 1991. See also Clark 1904, pp. 140–50; Lawson 1968, pp. 96–7. On the Downing Site, see Pevsner 1970, pp. 207–9.

library, set up on the Downing Site in 1904–6. In the 1930s it had outgrown its first home, and sought asylum with the Seeley Historical Library in the Cockerell building – the great nineteenth-century addition to the old University Library, now part of the complex of the Old Schools, and soon to become, if current plans mature, the library of Caius. From the 1930s to the 1990s the Law Faculty has had a part of the Old Schools as its quarters; now it is building a new home in West Road, near the Sidgwick Site and the new home of the Seeley Library. Thus it has had a physical centre much longer than have most of the arts faculties.[47] With a cramped site has gone a staff of modest size – originally so, because law expanded rapidly when the university's resources were meagre, and because many brilliant lawyers preferred to practise at the bar or as solicitors. But the stream of notable academic lawyers has never gone dry.

W. W. Buckland suffered many anxieties in his early life – his finances were precarious and his health even more so. As a result he had the good fortune to spend a winter near the Maitlands in the Canary Islands, and the kindness and encouragement of the older man deeply influenced him.[48] Buckland meanwhile was supported by his college, Caius, and became in due course senior tutor and Regius Professor of Civil Law. His crowning achievement was *A Text-Book of Roman Law from Augustus to Justinian* (1921), an amazingly comprehensive and penetrating digest of current scholarship, built to last.[49] 'The compression is extreme', say McNair and Duff, 'but controlled by genius; and though its bulk is formidable, the *Text-Book* is the easiest to read of all Buckland's books.'[50] That was a doubtful comment, since clarity was not one of his virtues; his earlier books, especially his so-called *Elementary Principles of Roman Private Law* (1912), can be made out with the help of the *Digest*. But they add up to a formidable corpus: they ensured Buckland and Cambridge great renown in continental academic circles where Roman law lay

---

[47] Though all faculties once claimed a share in the Old Schools. But this meant little by 1900, and in 1904–6, when law first had its own separate headquarters, history and medieval and modern languages had none.

[48] Fifoot 1965, nos. 304, 369, 413, etc.; Buckland 1921–3; for Buckland see esp. McNair and Duff 1947.

[49] See esp. the 3rd edn by Peter Stein (Buckland 1963), and Stein's Introduction.

[50] McNair and Duff 1947, p. 289. This admirable memoir unfortunately imitates the conciseness of its subject.

much closer to the law of the land. That he made it a popular subject with Cambridge undergraduates is more doubtful still; but his learning and kindliness won him a small coterie of devoted pupils, and his colleagues in Caius – once accustomed to his genial habit of sharpening his wits on his younger colleagues – recognised his genuine humanity and academic eminence by making him president of the college (1923–46).[51]

The most remarkable of Buckland's pupils was A. D. McNair (1885–1975), a man who combined Buckland's sharpness of mind and humane and kindly wisdom with great breadth of interest in the study of law.[52] He is remembered in Caius as tutor and life fellow, deeply admired and greatly loved; in a wider circle as Vice-Chancellor of Liverpool (1937–45); but above all as a great international lawyer, president of the International Court at the Hague and first president of the European Court of Human Rights at Strasbourg (1959–65). His stature depended not only on a deep and instinctive fair-mindedness, but on a unique study of comparative law. Among his most characteristic books is *Roman Law and Common Law* (1936), written in collaboration with Buckland: a precise and factual study with no frills, but showing deep insight based on accurate, wide-ranging knowledge of both laws. As a judge he was able to exercise the learning of a notable academic lawyer in the practical sphere to which his talents specially suited him. But he is remembered in Cambridge as one who never forgot his pupils nor their interests: a plain, humble, friendly, shrewd, delightful, unpretentious man.

Buckland's *Text-Book of Roman Law* was in a great tradition of legal manuals, whose roots may be sought in Gratian's *Concord of Discordant Canons* (more succinctly, the *Decretum*) in the twelfth century, nearer home in Henry William Cripps' *The Law of the Church and the Clergy*, which passed through an infinite number of editions between the 1840s and the recent past. Cambridge has made a notable contribution to these works of authority which instruct budding lawyers and accompany them through life: to an earlier generation belonged Pollock and Maitland's noble treatise on *The History of English Law* (1895) down to the thirteenth

---

[51] Brooke 1985, pp. 247, 306: this is partly based on personal reminiscences of Z. N. Brooke and others.
[52] Wade 1976; Brooke 1985, pp. 229–30, 282 and refs.; and personal knowledge.

century, and Kenny's *Cases on Criminal Law* (1901) and *Outlines of Criminal Law* (1902). In 1921 came Buckland's *Text-Book*, in 1937 Winfield's *Textbook of the Law of Tort*; in recent decades Emlyn Wade and G. C. Phillips on Constitutional Law and Sir William Wade on the Law of Real Property and Administrative Law – a branch of law he in large measure discovered.[53] Percy Winfield is a characteristic product of the Cambridge Law Faculty. Before the Great War he had become indispensable in a growing faculty as lecturer and law coach, though still without faculty or college office. After the war he became a fellow of St John's, and from 1926 university lecturer; from 1928 he was first Rouse Ball Professor of English Law.[54] From editing textbooks and publishing important articles, he graduated in 1937 to his *Textbook* on tort, that central mystery of the common law. For tort had survived from the days of bows and arrows and handloom weaving into the industrial and technological twentieth century, and it either needed a legal reformer to put it down or a brilliant legal mind to set it up again; and that it found in Winfield. 'It is perhaps impossible to give an exact definition of "a tort" ' confronts one at the outset of his *Textbook*, and from that hopeful beginning it never looks back: it reflects the legal mind, sharp, incisive, grappling and tortuous. In later life his powers declined, but till then he remained a kindly, amiable colleague and a master of the common law. Meanwhile the Law Faculty has never lacked eminent leaders, who can instruct the bench and even the House of Lords – as Glanville Williams has done[55] – or devise constitutions for developing nations, like Sir Ivor Jennings and Sir William Wade, or revise Maitland, like S. F. C. Milsom.

HISTORY

It is a curious reflection that a Regius Professor of Modern History at Oxford, Frederick Maurice Powicke, was named after Frederick Denison Maurice, who is the one man known to have abolished the study of history at Cambridge. There had been a

[53] E. C. S. Wade and Phillips 1931; Megarry and H. W. R. Wade 1957; H. W. R. Wade 1961. On Winfield see Bailey 1955.
[54] Bailey 1955, esp. pp. 330–1, 334.
[55] Williams 1985 was instrumental in the House of Lords overruling the decision in *Anderton v. Ryan* (1985) in *Regina v. Shipvuri* (1986).

Regius Professor at Cambridge since 1724.[56] None of the holders of the chair have been more famous, or more ineffective, than the poet Thomas Gray; and none have commanded wider audiences, or done less to win respect for history as a scholarly subject, than the novelist Charles Kingsley. In the early years of the Moral Sciences Tripos history had been a component. But in 1866 Maurice proposed, and in 1867 the university decreed, that history should be removed from the moral sciences exams.[57] The problem was twofold: it was impossible to examine history satisfactorily, since exams consisted of memory tests which could hardly be mental exercises worthy of a tripos; and in any case it was difficult to find teachers. In 1869 J. R. Seeley became Regius Professor and instantly set about gathering the fragments of his subject; from 1870–4 it lived in unequal partnership with law; in 1874 the marriage of law and history was dissolved and from 1875 the History Tripos has had a life of its own. Numbers were very few at first; but they gradually picked up, and from the 1890s steadily increased. Peter Slee, who has studied the early history of the tripos in depth, writes: 'At Cambridge between 1875 and 1895 403 men took honours in history [and 102 women]; 148 were from Trinity and fifty-six from King's. Trinity took eleven firsts, fifty-nine seconds, seventy-eight thirds, King's nineteen [twenty by my count] firsts, twenty-seven seconds and ten thirds.'[58]

It is notable that soon after law and history had parted both disciplines received in F. W. Maitland their outstanding scholar and lecturer.[59] Maitland's posts were in law, and it was to lawyers that he chiefly lectured. He found the History Board and the History Tripos unsatisfying ground. He had few pupils.[60] Yet his presence and his books provided an example and an inspiration which have never flagged; Cambridge historians have known that they worked in a noble tradition. One distant star, however, does not make a galaxy; and the strength of the Cambridge History Faculty has not lain in notable leaders. The Cavendish Laboratory of its very nature has reflected the eminence of a celebrated line of Cavendish Professors – if of many

---

[56] Tanner 1917, pp. 88–9. [57] Slee 1986, p. 36.
[58] Slee 1986, p. 150 n. 8. [59] See pp. 216–24.
[60] But see pp. 318, 320–1.

others as well; and the new Cavendish of the 1960s was most carefully designed to perform a social and intellectual as well as a purely scientific function. The History Faculty has been served by many eminent scholars, and a number of them play their role in this book; but the strength of the faculty lies in their number, not in their individual skills. Nor has the History Faculty building of the 1960s – the celebrated Stirling building admired by architectural students from every corner of the globe, which the university none the less seriously considered demolishing in the 1980s owing to the cost of maintaining it – proved a notable social centre. At a dinner to honour G. M. Trevelyan's 80th birthday in 1956, the other doyen of the faculty, Frank Salter of Magdalene, asserted that the History Faculty was more noted for its friendliness than its scholarship – to the scandal of some of his younger colleagues; but it is true that good companionship and indeed many friendships have been formed in the faculty despite its lack of social focus.[61] It is in the colleges and the University Library that its main work has been done.

The most striking features of the early statistics are the predominance of King's among the firsts and Trinity among the thirds; and the good ranking of the women. Twenty King's men got firsts between 1875 and 1895, and twenty-three women (fourteen of them from Newnham) out of a total of seventy, nearly one in three.[62] These included some notable names: in 1894 G. P. Gooch of Trinity and W. F. Reddaway of King's scored firsts; in 1895 John Clapham of King's and Caroline Skeel of Girton[63] – later to be first professor of history at Westfield College, London. The tripos was recruiting some first-class academic minds. But it has always been difficult to establish a new subject in Cambridge; and an arts subject needs a strong representation among the fellows of colleges. The period from 1875 to the eve of the Great War may be regarded as prehistory. It was also the age of the giants, Maitland and Acton, and there was active debate among enlightened men about its aims. But there were pitifully few professional teachers of the subject, and a

---

[61] The Faculty Board and the Examination Boards meet in the boardroom but its SCR is little frequented.
[62] Tanner 1917, pp. 895–910.   [63] Tanner 1917, pp. 909–10.

glance at a few exam papers shows how far removed it still was from anything we should recognise as serious history. The candidates were expected to answer numerous dull, factual questions in most history papers – even in the special subjects inaugurated, in imitation of Oxford, in 1885.[64] The turning point came in 1911 with the formation of the society of Junior Historians.[65] The number of students had climbed dramatically and the colleges were responding by appointing expert lecturers. A group of able young scholars had formed within the colleges; they were determined to make Cambridge history a fully professional subject, in teaching and research alike; and they were deeply concerned with the structure and content of the tripos. Their efforts were frustrated by the First World War, and it was only in the 1920s that their inspiration bore fruit; by then history had penetrated the colleges, though never quite to the same depth as in Oxford. In the 1960s and 70s there have normally been over 1,000 students of modern history at any one time in Oxford – something between a fifth and a quarter of all those studying single honours history in Britain – and 700–750 in Cambridge.[66] London (a university varying from three to four times the size of either Oxford or Cambridge) followed with 600–650; the rest have been far smaller, though often including very substantial numbers studying history in harness with another discipline.[67]

Caius is a significant example. Although Seeley was a professorial fellow from 1882 till his death in 1895,[68] and the Caius fellowship included notable ancient historians in J. S. Reid and William Ridgeway, there was no fellow to teach medieval or modern history till 1908, and no Caius man scored a first till 1900 – in striking contrast to the late twentieth century, in which Caius has commonly led among the firsts in history. From 1893 to 1908, and in a measure till 1916, history was at the mercy of a schoolmaster, G. E. Green, who was a part-time college lec-

---

[64] Slee 1986, p. 83.   [65] See below, p. 235.

[66] These figures are very approximate; those for the country as a whole are based on notes made when I was a member of the UGC Arts Sub-Committee in the late 1960s and early 1970s.

[67] The structure of the Cambridge tripos, which allows fairly free movement from one tripos to another after part I, means that the numbers taking two honours subjects are entirely hidden in these figures.

[68] On Seeley see esp. Wormell 1980; cf. Brooke 1985, pp. 246–7.

turer.[69] Arthur Sanctuary (a student 1910–14), who died in 1992 aged 100, was the sole known survivor of the Green era. 'My Director of Studies was a dull dog – we had two in College for History, and I got the dud one. The other chap took Scholars and the cleverer fellows.'[70] 'The other chap' was Z. N. Brooke, elected in 1908 and soon to be one of the founders of the Junior Historians. Brooke was on leave, working in Rome, in 1911–12, and that is probably the true reason why he did not teach Sanctuary. With Green, I 'simply presented an essay once a week and he said "Thank you". I was badly taught, really.'[71] Mr Sanctuary went on to a year of theology and (after war service) to be administrator at the Radcliffe Infirmary in Oxford; the Cambridge History Tripos had not called out his real quality.

Seeley's task as Regius Professor (1869–95) was to rescue the tripos from oblivion.[72] He was to a limited extent a creative historian: his life of Stein is a substantial contribution to the history of Germany and Europe in the early nineteenth century. He is best remembered for *Ecce Homo*, a very dated evocation of the Victorian liberal protestant Jesus the moralist; and for *The Expansion of England* (1883), a historical study setting in new perspective the place of expansion and empire in British history, and at the same time a political statement of a moderate and (if such a term is permitted in the late twentieth century) relatively enlightened imperialism. In the long run it started a tradition in Cambridge, represented for many years by a paper called 'The Expansion of Europe', and now by numerous third-world options. Immediately, its importance in the tripos was as a manifesto of Seeley's view that history – however much it might be a serious scholarly discipline – must justify itself as a practical course leading, more rationally and immediately than Oxford Classical Greats, to the colonial civil service – or to teaching or the like. On this basis Seeley rescued the tripos in the 1870s; and in the 1880s found himself entangled in controversy with several of his colleagues. For Mandell Creighton, the first Dixie Professor of Ecclesiastical History, founder of the *English Historical Review*,

---

[69] Brooke 1985, p. 245; Venn II, 529; V, 54.   [70] Sanctuary 1990, p. 87.
[71] Ibid.   [72] Wormell 1980; Slee 1986, chap. 5.

and a distinguished product of the Oxford History School, history was a scientific discipline, and a tripos laden with practical subjects such as Seeley had favoured – economics and political science among them – could hardly give scope to serious enquiry.[73] In the great arguments which ensued a compromise was reached. A special subject was introduced to open the path to the study of original sources, and English constitutional history – also adorned with sources – made its debut. Political economy was converted into economic history by a sleight of hand master-minded by William Cunningham (later archdeacon); and political thought survived as an essential limb of Cambridge history.[74] In the 1890s European history at last began to win its way; and these elements – shaken up and rearranged so as to leave a good deal more space to serious enquiry and to sources by the Junior Historians a generation later – still formed the core of the syllabus I myself attempted in the 1940s, and were not substantially altered till the 1960s. The undergraduate dissertation, which was the inspired contribution of T. F. Tout, who at the turn of the century made Manchester the most forward-looking and original History School in the island, reached Cambridge in the 1970s.[75] Lest it be thought that Cambridge moved with exceptional slowness to meet the challenge of the times, it may be noted that the Oxford History School, the flagship of British history schools in the nineteenth century, and perhaps in the twentieth too, had a new syllabus in the 1870s which was not fundamentally altered till the 1980s. It is possible to think, with Seeley, that syllabuses and exams are the excrescences on the serious study of a subject, not of its essence;[76] it is equally possible to think, with Tout, or with many a German professor of his age, that a well-devised syllabus is needed to make serious study directed towards the sources, at student level, possible.

In 1895 Seeley died and Acton ruled in his place – briefly, but decisively. He lived in Cambridge for less than seven years; he had little share in the changes in the tripos; he had few close pupils. Doubtless his influence has been exaggerated.[77] But Acton

---

[73] This is most fully discussed in Slee 1986, chap. 5; see also McLachlan 1947–9; Kitson Clark 1973.
[74] Slee 1986, pp. 71–2, 82–3, 126.
[75] On Tout see esp. Slee 1986, chap. 8; Powicke 1955, pp. 21–44.
[76] Cf. Slee 1986, p. 80.
[77] As Slee rightly says: Slee 1986, p. 136.

played a crucial part in making history a serious discipline in Cambridge. This was not by any remarkable contribution to scholarship: probably the books he possessed, now a treasured element in the Cambridge University Library, have done more for scholarship precisely defined than he ever did with his own pen. Nor was it by planning *The Cambridge Modern History*; for it seems to have owed more to Adolphus Ward than to Acton, and was never a very remarkable contribution to learning.[78] It was far more that he represented in himself, and emphasised in his lectures, the crucial importance of continental learning – and especially German – for the progress of history. He was himself one of the most learned historians of his day, little as he published; and his scholarship had been formed at Munich.[79] He was a thoroughly cosmopolitan figure, who was born in Naples and died in Germany; he was equally at home in Germany and England – and in many other parts of Europe; he had spent many months in Rome, partly as a scholar working in the Vatican archives, partly as a journalist recording the adventures of the First Vatican Council.[80] The consuming interests of his life were history, liberalism and the Catholic Church: he was a fervent Catholic layman when Catholicism and liberalism were thought by many to be wholly incompatible. His liberalism, and the circles in which he moved, brought close friendship with Gladstone; it was Gladstone's successor, Lord Rosebery, who made him Regius Professor. By then he was over sixty, and himself told Gladstone that 'There is, I think, no great school of history there, and not much studious curiosity about it. And as my predecessor did not awaken it, there is no chance of my doing much.'[81] Perhaps he did not *do* much; but his presence helped immeasurably to establish history as a serious academic discipline, and to make the Cambridge school a branch of European learning.

It has been much debated whether the development of historical scholarship in Britain in the late nineteenth century owed more to the inspiration of the natural sciences or to German

[78] See p. 54.
[79] There is a useful summary of Acton's career in Butterfield 1948. See especially Chadwick 1987, who gives at p. 386 n. 2 the chief books on Acton.
[80] See Chadwick 1978, esp. pp. 53–61, 140–2.
[81] Quoted in Butterfield 1948, p. 22.

historical scholarship – or whether it was a native growth little affected by either.[82] 'The influence of German on English historiography is a highly contentious question.'[83] I would rather say, complex and subtle. In history as in classics and theology, German scholarship dominated the academic world in the nineteenth century, and naturally earned envy and criticism as well as admiration and homage – sometimes from the same scholars. For medievalists homage was inescapable: it was obvious that the *Monumenta Germaniae Historica* had set an example and established standards which all serious scholars must admire and emulate. Something must be accorded to other nations too, especially to the French; for the Germans and Austrians had learned the art of charter criticism, of diplomatic, from the École des Chartes in Paris. The young Cambridge medievalists of the Edwardian decade, Z. N. Brooke and C. W. Previté-Orton, created the study of medieval history within the History Tripos – just as in and after the 1920s they were to edit the later volumes of *The Cambridge Medieval History* together, and to be the first holders of the chair of medieval history. Brooke in early years embarked on a study of Gregory VII and the Investiture Contest, and surrounded himself with all the German literature on the subject, even the most obscure *Inauguraldissertationen* which he could lay hands on. Not the German only, for French and Italian works were of equal interest to him; Giry's *Manuel de Diplomatique* sat beside Bresslau's *Handbuch der Urkundenlehre* on his shelves.[84] By the same token, Previté-Orton modelled his first book, *The Early History of the House of Savoy* (1912), on the *Jahrbücher* of the Holy Roman Emperors. German scholarship was part of the atmosphere they breathed; its pre-eminence was taken for granted. It was not, however, absorbed uncritically, either by the young Cambridge scholars or by Acton himself. There was a notion abroad that it could be too meticulous, too much involved in minutiae; just as, in the phrase of Acton's Romanes Lecture at Oxford, never delivered, 'The dust of archives blots out ideas.'[85] Some Cambridge historians had closer

---

[82] See the vigorous discussion in Slee 1986, pp. 131–2 and 150 n. 14. Cf. also pp. 165, 409, 428.
[83] Slee 1986, p. 131.
[84] As I know from inheriting the greater part of his historical library; the obscurer tracts are in CUL.
[85] Chadwick 1978, p. 142.

links with other parts of Europe: for Harold Temperley, the crucial experience lay in Austria-Hungary, especially in Hungary, and Serbia. But Germany was the natural centre of historical studies, especially for the medievalists, until the Great War broke the links for a generation.

Seeley and Acton could plan syllabuses and bring the History Tripos into wider repute. Maitland could make Cambridge a centre of historical and legal scholarship. But they were none of them college lecturers, and it was in the colleges that the humanities were made. Nor did their syllabuses convert history from a jejune memory test into a searching discipline.[86] The development of history in Cambridge into a major discipline, studied in depth, started with the foundation of the Junior Historians in 1911. By then most colleges had acquired a college lecturer who was both young and had some pretension to be a professional historian; and the younger historians clubbed together to plan a more professional approach to teaching, to the syllabus, and to their common scholarly interests. By 1914 fourteen colleges had come to be represented in the society.[87] At the first meeting on 26 January 1911 Z. N. Brooke of Caius spoke on 'The teaching of medieval history', and he was to be the leader among the medievalists for many years. But the central figure in the society in early days was probably Harold Temperley of Peterhouse, a vivid, dedicated teacher, who became as a result of the Great War something of a politician, master-minding the great history of the Peace Conference of 1919.[88] But he resumed his teaching in Cambridge after the war, and died master of Peterhouse in 1939. The early membership of the Junior Historians comprised a wide range of interests and personalities; but the common theme was the teaching of history as a serious university discipline, interspersed with some views of the wider world – J. B. Bury spoke at the second meeting in March 1911 on *Kulturgeschichte*, with special reference to the work of Lamprecht at Leipzig; Hilary Jenkinson of the PRO spoke in February 1912 on 'Diplomatique and its application to English Archives'. On

---

[86] See *Cambridge University Examination Papers*, passim.
[87] CUL, CUA, Min. IX. 52 (unpaginated), Junior Historians' Minute Book, 1911–1976, on which what follows is based.
[88] Temperley 1920–4; cf. Gooch 1939, esp. pp. 14–19.

3 March 1914, the last meeting before the war, G. M. Trevelyan visited Cambridge to present his celebrated lecture 'Clio a Muse'.[89] In the war five of the Junior Historians – one-third of the total membership – were killed; but the survivors resumed their activities with undiminished energy, and became the central forum for tripos reform. In 1921–2 the Cambridge Historical Society and the *Cambridge Historical Journal* (now the *Historical Journal*) were founded on the initiative of J. H. Clapham, himself too senior to be a member; and the Junior Historians decided to continue their own course and not to merge with the new society. By 1929 the young men of 1911 were young no longer; and it is evident that they were reluctant to admit it. In 1929 Herbert Butterfield and Michael Oakeshott, both very recent recruits, resigned; and legend has it that this was in protest against the refusal of the seniors to withdraw. But in 1931 they returned and soon after, in May 1932, Temperley, Brooke, Benians (of St John's) and Previté-Orton intimated 'their desire to be relieved of some of their duties as members and to become honorary members'. At the same meeting the rule was made that members 'who have passed their fortieth birthday shall become honorary members'. By 1932 history was entrenched in all the colleges; the Junior Historians had completed their original task. They have continued and flourished and multiplied since, for they have come to include women and research fellows; and they remain an important element in the History Faculty.

The Cambridge tripos of the 1930s and 40s still contained a special subject, but almost no other specialised work at all. A student had to study both medieval and modern European history in outline and most of English history, firmly divided into constitutional history, reflecting the legacy of Maitland, and economic history in the Cunningham tradition. But it had a reflective element represented by its general essay papers, and an intellectual element represented by political thought. To the undergraduate of the 1940s these were symbolised above all by Herbert Butterfield and Michael Oakeshott; and the old dried up watercourse of economic history had received a copious flow of fresh water from the fertile genius of Munia (Michael) Postan.

---

[89] Trevelyan 1913. On Trevelyan see pp. 129, 366–9; Plumb 1988, pp. 182–204.

Postan, Butterfield and Oakeshott were to the generation of the 1940s what the three knights – J. H. Plumb, Geoffrey Elton and Owen Chadwick – were to the 50s and 60s. Butterfield had the preacher's gift of depth without clarity. It is true that his most widely read book, *The Whig Interpretation of History* (1931), had a relatively simple message: English historical writing had been dogged by the liberal notions of Macaulay and others that history represented progress, was teleological; this prevented serious study of the doomed elements in any period or civilisation; for the true historian all periods were equal; the historian must never be too conscious of what was to follow. But his other writings, especially his *Christianity and History* (1949), were increasingly difficult to grasp; and his one major contribution to scholarship, *George III, Lord North and the People, 1779–80* (1949) has been variously interpreted and valued. His was a complex character, for with all his moral earnestness he had a great love of gossip. Like Acton he had a profound influence, based less on what he wrote than on what he stood for: a deep Christian faith, and a faith equally devout in the historian's profession.[90] Michael Oakeshott was a philosopher who taught history in Cambridge and Caius from the mid-1920s to the late 40s, and politics in LSE from 1951 on. Though deeply influenced by Hegel, and a fervent and mystical believer in tradition, he had an extraordinary clarity of mind which lent pattern and shape to the most unyielding of political thinkers. His philosophical mode was deeply unfashionable while he taught in Cambridge, and he had the strange experience of first winning disciples and recognition from young philosophers and politicians in his grey hairs. Meanwhile he had a deep influence in Cambridge – as later in LSE – through his lectures, which provided history with precisely that rational, reflective, speculative element which Cambridge history had hitherto lacked.[91] Butterfield and Oakeshott were obverse and reverse of a coin: both made us think, made us see something much deeper in history than mere events and movement; but Oakeshott sparkled and glittered and lit up the patterns of the

[90] On Sir Herbert Butterfield see Cowling 1979; Elton 1984; and the useful introduction in Cannon et al. 1988, pp. 61–2. The text is partly based on personal knowledge: a full biography by Patrick Higgins is in the making.
[91] Brooke 1985, p. 297; on him see Casey 1991.

past, while Butterfield's musings reflected the deep obscurity of human events and human destiny. Of the leading historians of Cambridge of the mid-twentieth century, Postan was perhaps the most paradoxical. Educated in Russia and the LSE, a colleague, later husband, of Eileen Power, he brought to Cambridge in the mid-1930s cosmopolitan culture combined with a vivid, incisive, exciting approach to medieval economic history. He abounded in ideas, with which he attacked and belaboured the most solid and unyielding of medieval evidence. He became the master in a field in which the patient sorting of account rolls and court rolls is of the essence of the scholar's task – and brought to them a naturally impatient temperament. He had a cavalier attitude to dates and figures, yet knew that on them his science was based, and worked extremely hard to make them yield their secrets. He never had the patience to finish the massive work on medieval English agriculture he projected; but his lectures and books and articles revolutionised economic history – and threw floods of light in other fields too – and inspired a generation of younger historians; his brilliance and his kindness never flagged, and he was at work in his seminar into his eighties.[92] Butterfield and Postan were fellows of Peterhouse, where they were joined in 1939 by Denis Brogan, a polymath who wrote mainly on America and France and held (rather strangely) the chair of political science, and in 1944 by David Knowles.[93] In this remarkable galaxy of talent, Knowles alone wrote great books which will outlast the century; but he came 'from another tradition' and belongs on another page.[94] The others illustrate with some clarity the way in which Cambridge history achieved the standing it has had in the second half of the twentieth century. They illustrate it, without telling the whole story. Thus for example the Cambridge Group for the History of Population and Social Structure is an offshore operation under a research council, the ESRC, with the closest links with the History Faculty, first inspired by their brilliant pioneer Peter Laslett, then made closer by the eminent demographers who have worked in it.

---

[92] This account of Sir Michael Postan is mostly based on personal knowledge: see esp. Miller 1983; C. C. Dyer in Cannon et al. 1988, pp. 338–9.

[93] See p. 419; on Brogan, see J. M. Taylor in Cannon et al. 1988, pp. 52–3.

[94] See esp. p. 418.

It is sometimes held that the teaching of history in British universities in the late nineteenth and early twentieth centuries has had a social or political aim more than a scholarly: that men like Temperley and Butterfield were more concerned to instil the intellectual principles of their world than historical scholarship.[95] It is in the nature of history that sharp lines cannot be drawn – should not be attempted – between the historian's faith and his scholarship. It is also true that in contrast to German curricula the Cambridge tripos contained little real scholarship – even in the 1990s the undergraduate dissertation, fostered a century before by the Manchester school, is still voluntary. But this springs from the desire to give ample coverage still to the findings of modern scholarship over a wide area, that is, not from an inadequate concept of the historian's professional status, but in a way from its exaggeration: the spirit of serious, professional history which inspired the men who founded the Junior Historians in 1911 has dominated Cambridge history ever since.

[95] This is most eloquently expounded, for Oxford, in Soffer 1987 a, b; cf. the critical comments in Slee 1987, with which (in the main) I concur.

Chapter 8

THE SOCIETY

I THE BACKGROUND OF STUDENTS AND TEACHERS

If we seek to sketch the university as a social organism – its inner life as a reflection of the society of the wider world – we rapidly encounter a deep thicket of difficulties. Certain fundamentals seem at first sight well established. In the late nineteenth century the vast majority of students, and so of dons, came from the middle class, and many had been to public schools;[1] their successors in the late twentieth century still belong to the middle class, but a much higher proportion come from other kinds of school.[2] In 1870 or 1880 the vast majority were paid for by their parents; in the 1990s those who have lived in Britain long enough have grants, though many parents have to make a contribution. In 1870 Oxford and Cambridge were only beginning to feel the winds of competition from younger universities in England, even if they had long been outclassed by those of Scotland and Germany in academic quality; in the 90s they are only two in a large platoon.[3] These changes are mirrored in the life and organisation of the university. It has grown larger, more meritocratic, in some ways more democratic.

But as soon as we look closer, and try to sophisticate these general statements, determine what class means, what a public school may have been at this epoch and at that, difficulties multiply. We have to work with a set of basic concepts which are

[1] See summary in Anderson and Schnaper 1952, and below, Appendix 5, pp. 61–2. For the shift from a substantial proportion to a majority, see p. 247. Jenkins and Jones 1950 give interesting statistics based on Venn's *Alumni* for the period 1850–99; for our purpose this period is too broad, and the bias of the sources too little regarded – some colleges are much better recorded than others and this is reflected in Venn's *Alumni* – to be of much use in the present context.
[2] See below, pp. 248–9; and cf. esp. Brooke 1985, pp. 308–13.
[3] See p. 540.

unhelpful. We are told that the universities reflect the class changes of the last hundred years. The concept of class is certainly of the nineteenth century – in anything like a modern meaning it is not to be found earlier; but its history is very imperfectly known.[4] In origin 'class' was a synonym for 'group'; a class interest was the interest of a group sufficiently intimate for communication within it to be clear and meaningful. But in the nineteenth century, especially in the hands of Marx, it came to comprise much larger groups sometimes with no visible means of communication between them, which had – or were supposed to have – common interests and common means of expression and action. Men and women in the nineteenth century were very conscious, we are told, not only where they stood in their local groups and communities, but in the broader perspective of class. An income of £160 or £200 or more enabled a family to live in a decent house and have one or two servants at least; and those who enjoyed these privileges – or the affluence of higher incomes and status – formed perhaps 12 per cent of the population as a whole.[5] But if we apply the microscope we find that we rarely know with any precision the income of the parents of Cambridge undergraduates or of the dons themselves.[6] As we move into the mid and late twentieth century it is relatively easy to calculate the salaries of dons and of many professional parents; but to relate income to 'class' becomes impossible.

Everyone is agreed that great social changes took place between 1870 and 1990. They also agree that old class barriers have broken down; but the extent and nature of the breakdown is variously interpreted. The differences start with the very notion of class. For any meaningful definition it must comprise elements of income, status, profession, and the subtle spectra of social attitudes. In most analyses these elements become hopelessly confused. In every age a person's standing has depended in part on economic and in part on social facts and fancies. In the fifteenth century a peer who went bankrupt was demoted; in the eighteenth century he was given a pension or an heiress. Wealth has

4 Briggs 1983 (1st publ. 1967) is a pioneer study, but it hardly touches the semantic history of the word. See also Stedman Jones 1976; Perkin 1969; Banks 1954, esp. chaps. 6–7. I am particularly indebted to Simon Szreter for help on this theme.
5 On all this I owe much to Perkin 1989; for incomes see pp. 29–30, 78–9.
6 For a rare exception see pp. 282–7.

always counted. It would be generally agreed that social attitudes have shifted and softened in the last hundred years, and this must mean that money counts for more in determining a person's place in the world. But the social statistics issued by the Registrar General, on which all our knowledge of modern social organisation depends, tell us nothing of money, for any significant knowledge of income distribution is locked up in the files of the Inland Revenue and cannot be divulged. That is an excellent liberty; but it has to be recognised that it enforces a compulsory ignorance.[7] These statistics perpetuate in a curious way the attitudes and snobberies of the Edwardian era when they were devised: they give status above all to the more respectable professions, especially to the civil servants who devised the categories. They tell us very little of the true state of British society in the modern world.

It is commonly held that two very major changes have overtaken British society in the last hundred years. First of all, it has become more professional – *The Rise of Professional Society* is the significant title of Harold Perkin's masterly recent survey.[8] The better off in early nineteenth-century England were gentlemen, soldiers, sailors, lawyers and clergy; there were many prosperous trades of lesser social standing, and many, such as physicians and surgeons, of ambiguous standing. But one could only become a gentleman by birth, and none of the professions required any very prolonged or special training; they were entered by patronage or apprenticeship. Oxford and Cambridge were only regarded as specific training grounds for clergy, and it is not at all obvious to us today how they contributed to their training.[9] But as the professions became more professional – as they absorbed and stimulated the cult of competitive examinations – schools and universities began to be important since they provided some of the teaching needed. This movement affected women as well as men, so that a major stimulus leading to the founding of women's schools and colleges is reckoned to be the search for professional employment.[10] Here we are on relatively

---

[7] On the history of the Registrar General's statistics I owe much help to Simon Szreter. See now Szreter 1984.
[8] Perkin 1989.   [9] See pp. 10, 143–4.
[10] See p. 304.

firm ground, since the history of the professions can be sketched. But even here the story is far from simple. For many professions mathematics and various kinds of natural science have been an obvious need. But notoriously the dominant public schools of the nineteenth and early twentieth centuries were slow to allow science to compete with classics as the foundation of most boys' curricula. Mathematics fared better, especially as it had been first the only, then the dominant, tripos in Cambridge in the late eighteenth and for much of the nineteenth century. Attitudes varied enormously already in the nineteenth century when mechanics' institutes and the like catered directly for immediate needs, while the ancient universities tended to remain ivory towers reflecting various notions of liberal education. Divergent attitudes also overlap over time: as late as 1966 I asked an experienced preparatory schoolmaster if a boy taking a scholarship would enter for the science exam that was available. 'Good God no', he replied – and a long tradition spoke with him.

The survival of classical education was not just conservatism. Alongside the flowering of professional qualifications there grew very powerful conceptions of a liberal education, with Oxford's Classical Greats as the most prestigious and mystical of all – mystical, since its proponents really believed it to be the ideal foundation for governing India and other improbable tasks.[11] This example underlines the subtleties and ambiguities – and the interest – of our theme, for it combined a theory of education with a social theory of totally different origin. If the concept of class was ambiguous, the notion of gentility was even more so. In Jane Austen's eyes – or at least in her novels – all gentlemen were equal. The aristocracy in her novels are uniformly arrogant and dull; some of her tradesmen are gentlemanly in manners and outlook. But all those who are sons and daughters of gentlemen belong to the gentry.[12] There is a deep union here between the concept of a way of life matched with social obligation and courtesy and one purely genealogical. Both were immensely powerful in the nineteenth century and only survive today in tiny cells remote from the normal centres of life. In its widest sense the

[11] See Brooke, Highfield and Swaan 1988, pp. 286–7; Symonds 1982, 1986.
[12] See esp. *Pride and Prejudice*, chap. 56, Elizabeth Bennet to Lady Catherine de Bourgh: 'He [Darcy] is a gentleman; I am a gentleman's daughter; so far we are equal.'

notion of a gentleman became fused with a vision of service to the community and office in the civil, foreign or colonial service. The old notion that no very precise training could be appropriate for such respectable callings combined with the new pride of the professions to produce the remarkable alliance between Jowett's Oxford and the Indian Civil Service, between a liberal education of a remarkably traditional character and the rising professions most highly regarded by the Registrar General.

In the 1940s it was still possible to hear the phrase 'the top drawer' – especially in the form 'he or she is not out of the top drawer' – meaning 'not well born', 'did not come from a "good" family', which was the last vestigial remnant of Jane Austen's doctrine that all gentlemen were equal. The corollary in her world, though she viewed it with a critical eye – that true gentlemen were men of leisure – also survived, especially among 'young men about town' and distressed gentlewomen. If Jane Austen's gentlemen could be idle – though Mr Knightley and Sir Thomas Bertram were deeply engaged in managing their estates and in the welfare of their dependants – the women remained idle much longer. Elizabeth Garrett Anderson stormed the fortress of medical science in the 1860s; but many women were prevented by habit or parental fiat from seeking serious employment well into the mid-twentieth century.[13] Many had no husbands or wealth to support them; but they sustained their morale, sometimes very effectively, by their faith in the value of their position, in the doctrine of the drawers, at much the same time as Bertie Wooster and the young men about town maintained the fading respectability of idleness. For Bertie, university – Oxford, in his case – is revealed as the nursery of idleness; a remarkable survival of the function noted by the hero of *Sense and Sensibility*: 'I was therefore entered at Oxford and have been properly idle ever since.'[14]

Since the concept of class as it is commonly used comprises many subtle shades of attitudes and assumptions it is always possible to assert that it still exists in Britain or in any country in the universe. That is harmless enough. But if such arguments are used to suggest that social differences are much what they were a

---

[13] See pp. 307–8.   [14] Chap. xix: cf. Brooke, Highfield and Swaan 1988, p. xv.

hundred years ago, then they are being used to cover a fundamental error. A similar, though less dramatic problem afflicts the study of schools and their role in providing Cambridge with students.

In the late nineteenth century secondary education usually had to be paid for.[15] Education was highly regarded by folk in many different walks of life, and especially by the well-to-do. It was the key to the professions, to civilised life; it was fashionable; perhaps above all, paying for children's education was something everyone did, like having servants. There were still free places in old grammar schools, but they were few, and declining. More and more sought out the rapidly expanding boarding schools – or the boarding wings of reviving grammar schools – or the prestigious day schools of the great cities. The public boarding schools had their heyday: 'public' and 'boarding' almost became synonymous outside the catchments of the greater day schools, and some of the day schools, like Christ's Hospital, moved into the country. But they were still not necessarily the resort only of the rich. Christ's Hospital remained a fascinating palimpsest of the history of schools, with a large element surviving right through this period of the children of the genuinely poor mingling with a growing throng of fee-paying boys. Two kinds of public schools reveal the changing pattern with particular clarity. There has been no serious study (so far as I know) of the social history of the Clarendon schools, the most prestigious of the public schools, which were the theme of the Clarendon Commission of 1861–4.[16] But something is known and more may be inferred. Winchester had been founded in the fourteenth century for poor or moderately poor scholars, and in the late nineteenth century still contained a nucleus of scholars who paid no fees. By the 1870s the scholarship examination was a reality so that the poor scholars had had to receive a good, and often an expensive, education before they arrived. They were surrounded by a throng of commoners who paid fees. There had been down to the mid-nineteenth century an element of 'founder's kin' among the scholars, which largely comprised the family of Twistleton-

---

[15] See, in general, Roach 1986.
[16] See Shrosbree 1988. The 'Clarendon' schools were Eton, Westminster, Winchester, Charterhouse, St Paul's, Merchant Taylors, Harrow, Rugby and Shrewsbury.

Wykeham-Fiennes, Lords Saye and Sele, and their siblings.[17] That apart, Winchester was a haven neither for the nobility nor the rich. Scholars and commoners alike seem to have been drawn from sons of the gentry, the more prestigious professions, and from groups of families with a traditional interest in the school. Thus in the 1810s Jane Austen's nephews, sons of gentry and clergymen, 'future Heroes, Legislators, Fools, and Villains', were there in strength.[18] In the 1830s two sons of country clergymen from Gloucestershire were there, first cousins, from whom a large number of Wykehamists have descended between that day and this, some the sons of clergy, some of dons,[19] some of prosperous lawyers, a small number of gentlemen of means. The connection between the clergy – always the most poorly paid of the respectable professions[20] – and the great public schools was as natural in the late nineteenth century as it is forgotten today. For then many schoolmasters were clergy and an infinite number of clergymen schoolmasters, at least for part of their lives. If they held no posts in schools they taught quite regularly in the church schools, so marked a feature of the Victorian landscape, or in the board schools, the newcomers of the 1870s; or they eked out their scanty living by taking in pupils.[21] Very many of their sons went to boarding schools. This was possible, first of all because all public schools had scholars, and the provision for scholars in a few, like Winchester, was lavish. There was a natural tenderness in clerical schoolmasters towards their clerical colleagues, both in the selection of boys and provision of aid. More than that, there were energetic well-to-do clergy engaged in improving the opportunities of their less fortunate brethren; and schools such as Marlborough were founded primarily for clergy's sons. Finally,

---

[17] See Squibb 1972, pp. 36–42, 93–6, 103–5, 115, 124–5, 188–94.

[18] Chapman 1952, p. 458, no. 130, of 9 July 1816: Jane Austen to her nephew Edward, son of the Reverend James Austen, then on holiday from Winchester.

[19] Of whom I am myself one. The two were Henry William Cripps, later a prosperous lawyer; and William Henry Stanton, a poor country clergyman in Gloucestershire.

[20] Although there were still in the nineteenth century a number of well-endowed livings which gave a proportion of the clergy a handsome income; when Mandell Creighton passed from a handsome country living to the Dixie Professorship, he had to face a fall in income (Creighton 1904 I, 248). More recent measures to equalise clerical incomes have removed the plums and left all equally poor. On the Victorian clergy, see esp. Haig 1984.

[21] See p. 145.

there was Nathaniel Woodard (1811–91), who founded a whole string of schools with a very close link with the clergy in mind.[22]

The link between the clergy and the public boarding schools old and new was even closer than this; for in late nineteenth-century Oxford and Cambridge a substantial proportion had been schooled in the Clarendon schools or the younger public schools which imitated them. In 1867, out of 1,154 undergraduates at Oxford whose schools were known to the Taunton Commissioners, 487 had come from the nine Clarendon schools, Marlborough or Cheltenham; 352 from grammar schools; 123 had sat at the feet of private tutors. At Cambridge the figures were less dramatic: 207 from the first eleven; 295 from grammar schools; 116 from the tutors.[23] Thirty years later the element from public schools as a whole was predominant in both. Oxford and Cambridge were rapidly climbing out of the world in which they had been primarily seminaries for Anglican clergy, but the influence of the clergy in their midst and among their alumni and parents was still extremely strong. This helps to make intelligible the anxieties and divisions when the Test Acts were abolished in 1871.[24] It also makes nonsense of most efforts to compare the pattern of British schools in 1870 and in 1970 or 1990. It throws a benevolent light on the social pattern of Victorian Cambridge: it was by no means a preserve of the rich, though they were well represented. Rather the poorer professions had their full share among the parents and alumni. It throws a lurid light on the slow progress of women's education in Cambridge; for notoriously the clerical profession, in the Church of England at least, has been the slowest of all to admit women to partnership. In 1870 Winchester was still deeply under clerical influence and the sons of clergy strongly represented. By the 1940s the clergy were much diminished, but the professions were still in the ascendant, the catchment area as wide as Britain and beyond. By the 1960s and 1970s the catchment area had shrunk: the majority came from within a hundred miles; the parents were people of means,

---

[22] On Woodard see Roach 1986, pp. 167–9 and refs. in p. 173 n. 19. On Marlborough, Roach 1986, pp. 165–6.

[23] These figures are quoted from Roach 1986, p. 255. They do not include the substantial numbers (123 at Oxford, 108 at Cambridge) from proprietary schools, many of which became day or boarding public schools. For what follows see pp. 599–600.

[24] See pp. 99–106.

fewer and fewer were drawn from the teaching professions. It is not so much the case that such schools have become much more expensive,[25] but the young professional teacher or academic – even if not inhibited by the climate of opinion – has little to spare from his house mortgage to save for the secondary education of his children. The Cambridge students of the 1990s come from a very different pattern of schools from their predecessors in 1870; but that by itself does not mean that they come from very different backgrounds, for the schools themselves have changed out of recognition.

I have spoken so far solely of the public boarding schools, which might seem the most stable element in the galaxy. It is obvious enough that the old grammar schools of 1870 have changed their nature many times: some are now public boarding schools, some – Manchester Grammar School, St Paul's – are among the most prestigious academic public day schools in the land. Many became 'direct grant schools' in the 1940s; then, when direct grant schools were abolished in the 1970s, some became independent, some comprehensive. Meanwhile the old grammar schools and the new maintained secondary schools of the early twentieth century were transformed in the 1960s and 70s, when many became comprehensive. 'Comparisons are odorous,' and certainly unscientific. Nor have we many reliable statistics to study. The figures for Caius may be reckoned (in the present state of knowledge) not untypical – though some sampling elsewhere suggests considerable variety; at Peterhouse in the late 1870s, for example, a much lower proportion came from public schools, whereas at Trinity, in 1879, 91 out of an entry of 191 came from Clarendon schools, and 46 from other public boarding schools.[26] In the years 1886–90 43 per cent of Caians came from public boarding schools, 20.1 per cent from day public schools, 23.2 per cent from grammar schools and the like. The public schools were at the height of fashion, and by 1907–11 their proportion had risen to 66.5 per cent, while the grammar schools' had sunk to 10.3 per cent. From the 1930s the pattern began to change, and the pace of change rapidly increased in the 1950s and 60s, so that by

---

[25] For the problems of effective comparison, see below. For the catchment area of Cambridge undergraduates, see *Reporter* 1990–1, Special Issue no. 17.
[26] See Appendix 4.

1967–71 the proportion from the public boarding schools had sunk to 20.5 per cent, that from grammar and comprehensive schools had risen to 51.3 per cent; the day public, alias independent, schools have had their share of the increase – they had fallen to 10.2 per cent in 1932–6, but rose to 26.5 per cent by 1967–71.[27]

If the schools present a crowd of problems, the social background of the undergraduates is more uncertain still. The Caius admission records are as good as any among the colleges; but the forms on which they are based have always been filled in by harassed or reticent parents or applicants, not adequately apprised of the interests of future historians and sociologists. The most we can hope to do is to map the changing pattern of parental occupations.[28] For the period 1886–90 nearly a quarter are unspecified, which renders any percentages meaningless. This figure fell sharply in later decades, to an average of 2.4 (out of 124.4) in 1951–5, but had risen to 7 out of 126.8 by 1967–71. Of the known professions in 1886–90, the clergy come easily first, with 11.2 out of 63; and they have suffered the most dramatic decline, to 0.8 in 1967–71. In the university as a whole, the sons of clergy represented 32.6 per cent in the figures culled by Anderson and Schnaper[29] between 1752 and 1886, 7.4 per cent in 1937–8; while over the same periods the clergy among the alumni fell from 54.3 to 6.2 per cent. In Caius physicians and surgeons – a natural feature of the Caian landscape – (to return to averages) stood at 8 out of 63 in 1886–90 and moved to 11.2 out of 126.8 by 1967–71; but they had peaked at 16.2 out of 124.4 in the early 1950s, the epoch which saw the highest incidence of sons of old Caians. Most of the other figures reflect changing patterns of profession and changing terminology: the decline of merchants etc. from 7.2 to 0.8 is balanced by a rise in accountants, bankers and above all in other types of business (0.4 to 18). The most significant change is among the civil servants, 0.8 to 7.6. But all the figures confirm that the vast majority of students at every point in time have been first-generation Caians. What we cannot tell in the present state of knowledge is what proportion of

---

[27] Brooke 1985, pp. 308–9.
[28] For what follows see Brooke 1985, pp. 311–13, cf. p. 308.
[29] Anderson and Schnaper 1952: see Appendix 5.

students in Cambridge as a whole have been sons of non-graduate parents. In the country at large the statistical growth of student numbers makes clear that in every generation hitherto a large majority have come from non-graduate homes. Cambridge is not likely to be a normal sample; but it would be quite wrong to assume that at any date there have not been very many first-generation university students. Much clearer is the proportion of overseas students in Caius and the university at large, since there were few of them until quite recent times. In the last two decades the number of overseas students has grown from 962 in 1972–3 to 1,590 in 1989–90, of whom 1,022 are 'postgraduate'; the total student population has risen meanwhile from 11,302 to 13,723, the postgraduates from 2,548 to 3,533.[30]

If we pass on to study the destiny of Caians, we find comparisons difficult once again, for the number whose destiny is unknown had risen from 4.8 out of 63 in 1886–90 – and 4.6 out of 87.8 in 1907–11, the heyday of close tutorial relations and of the 'old college tie' – to 32.2 out of 124.4 in 1951–5; the proportion would probably be still higher today. For what they are worth, some figures are stable: future physicians, 17.6 in the 1880s, 18.2 in the 1950s;[31] schoolmasters, 8.8 in the 1880s, 9.2 in the 1950s. The clergy again lead the decline, but only from 7.6 to 3.6: the clerical profession had already lost much of its appeal by the late 1880s. In compensation, 'business' has claimed numbers rising from 3.6 in 1886–90 to 20.6 in 1951–5 – and probably higher still today. University teachers and their like have risen from 2.8 to 15.4 in the same period.[32]

There are many subtler points not touched on by these figures: in the present state of knowledge we have little idea how many Cantabs have followed their fathers' professions; nor for how many Cambridge represented a complete change of outlook and prospect. We can only say that Cambridge was then, as it has always been, a place in which the social pattern of the wider

---

[30] *Reporter* 1972–3, Special No. 19, p. 6; 1989–90, pp. 3, 14. 'Overseas students' means those normally living abroad; in 1989–90 the total not of British nationality was 2,035, of whom 1,266 were postgraduate (ibid. p. 16) – comparable figures for the early 1970s are not available.
[31] For the university as a whole, 3.5 per cent 1752–1886; 11.2 per cent 1937/8: Anderson and Schnaper 1952: see Appendix 5.
[32] Brooke 1985, pp. 314–15, cf. p. 308.

world was imperfectly reflected – that is to say, in which the social hierarchy counted less, ability more, in the opportunities open to the young who came there, than in the world at large. On this theme, from every age, we could gather a cloud of witnesses to bemuse us. Snobbery we have always with us – it is older than the 'class' values of the Victorians by several thousand years, and it is as familiar in egalitarian as in hierarchical societies. So also are its converses, inverted snobbery and social unease of every kind. The problems this raised in the late nineteenth and early twentieth centuries are most fully documented for King's, where the mingling of a community of Etonians with growing numbers of non-Etonians produced divisions and tensions – and remarkable ecumenical movements – over two generations.[33] It was alleged that one provost of King's in the twentieth century invited the Etonians to breakfast, said good morning to the Wykehamists and ignored the rest.[34] I doubt if it was true, but it is significant that it could be thought so: the intelligent young are more credulous in such matters than in almost any other region of human experience. But there was also a significant element in Cambridge from really poor homes, who encountered no such snobberies. Thomas Okey, who became professor of Italian in 1919, was a hereditary basket-maker from the East End of London, proud to be a member of the aristocracy of the working class. He had no previous first-hand experience of Cambridge, and was immediately struck by its equality. 'Money . . . social position as such, count for nothing. . .' He enjoyed 'the consciousness that one stands for what one is worth as a scholar and a man. . . All stand on an equality of worth, from the porter at the gate to the Master in the lodge. . .' But he was aware that it did not apply to women.[35] Not long after, Sir Ernest Barker, who had performed long service in Oxford and London, came to be first professor of political science in 1928 and fellow of Peterhouse. He was an acute and canny and delightful man who gauged his colleagues' reactions to a nicety, and whether in Merton or Peterhouse

[33] Morris 1989, pp. 54–5; Pfaff 1980, pp. 49–53, 143.
[34] The story was told me by a friend who was at King's in the 1920s, and if true it must relate to M. R. James or Sir Walter Durnford, but it is extremely improbable that it is true.
[35] Brooke 1985, p. 283, quoting Okey 1930, pp. 17, 139–41.

cultivated his Lancashire accent at a time when this was not so fashionable as it is today.[36]

But if Cambridge can seem relatively egalitarian compared with the wider world, it has often seemed very hierarchical within. We will contemplate Mount Olympus from its heights to its foothills; but to set it in perspective, let the most unprivileged group of all speak first.

II WIVES

J. W. Clark delighted to describe how isolated the women of Cambridge were in the days of his childhood in the 1830s and 1840s. The heads of houses married, and so did some of the professors, but the heads' wives did not call on the professors' wives – or so an old friend of his mother's had explained when Miss Willis married Professor William Clark.[37] The rest of the community was celibate. There was evidently some exaggeration in the story, for Miss Willis was sister of Robert Willis, the Jacksonian Professor,[38] who had married into the Cambridge patriciate – Charles Humfrey, a leading local architect, developer and one-time mayor, was his father-in-law – and we may be reasonably sure they mingled with town as well as gown. Romilly's diaries show that a formal dinner was not a rare event.[39] But this only serves to underline the point: when the women came to Girton and Newnham, and equally, when they came to marry the once-celibate fellows, they were pioneers and settlers of a new territory.

The 1860s and 1870s witnessed the arrival of Girton and Newnham, and of fellows' wives. The academic women have been a major feature of Cambridge society ever since, but they are the theme of a separate chapter.

There is a nice legend that a special university grace was passed in 1882 to allow fellows to marry, and that its passing was marked

---

[36] Strictly, he was a native of north Cheshire but his accent sounded like Lancashire in Oxford and Cambridge; and though his home was humble and his father a miner, he had studied at Manchester Grammar School and Balliol and had long been a member of the academic élite before he came to Cambridge. On him see summary in Brooke, Highfield and Swaan 1988, pp. 308–9 and references.

[37] Shipley 1913, pp. 17–18, cf. esp. pp. 50–1.   [38] See pp. 2–3, 476.

[39] Romilly 1967: pp. 210–13, 216–17 contain a good sample.

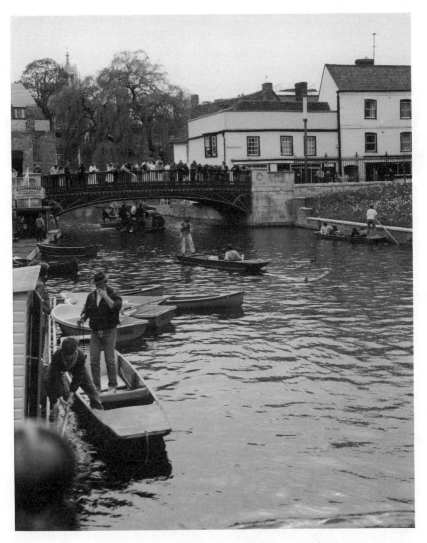

Fig. 8 Town and gown: Magdalene Bridge

'by the arrival of many brides' or 'an army of brides'.[40] The truth is that the university statute of 1570 enjoining celibacy disappeared in 1860, and that college statutes were changed piecemeal,

[40] Fowler 1984, pp. 239–40. Raverat 1952, p. 47, dates the change from new college statutes of 1878 and later.

a few in 1860, more in the late 1870s.[41] The entry of women was slow, but when it came, extremely decisive. When Mandell Creighton came to Cambridge as Dixie Professor in 1884, his wife observed that 'like everyone else we dined out a great deal; and gave many little dinners in return'.[42] By 1886 the fellows of Caius had been allowed to marry for twenty-six years, and the fellows' family homes were well established. In that year the senior tutor, E. S. Roberts, married, and insisted that the college carve a house out for him and his bride in its innermost court and for a decade or two the court was delightfully (or intolerably, as some might think) filled with the prattle of nursemaids and children.[43] More characteristic was the household of Gwen Raverat's Great Aunt Cara, Lady Jebb. She was an American of exceptional beauty, who first came to Cambridge in her late twenties, already a widow: her first husband had been a general in the Federal Army in the American Civil War.[44] Such was her charm – or such the dearth of rivals – that she claimed to have received as many as three proposals of marriage in a single day. In the end, in 1874, she married Richard Jebb, fellow of Trinity, later Regius Professor of Greek, Sir Richard and MP for the university, and they settled in Springfield, at the corner of what is now Sidgwick Avenue, their home till his death in 1905 – Lady Jebb's till after the Great War.

> The Springfield household [wrote Mrs Raverat] consisted of: first, Aunt Cara's Prime Minister and confidant ... Melbourne, the groom-gardener; a perfectly round little man, 'reg'lar Norfolk dumpling', as he justly called himself. Next in the hierarchy came Zoë, the pretty, yellow mare; then Glen, the collie dog, given her by Mr Carnegie; then Darius, the Persian cat; then the three maids, who stayed for ever; and last of all – or so we thought – poor Uncle Dick. I know that he was a scholar of international reputation, but to our childish minds he was a figure of extreme unimportance; a sort of harmless waif, who was kindly allowed to live in a corner of the library, so long as he kept quiet and gave no trouble.[45]

[41] Brooke 1985, p. 224 n. 4. [42] Creighton 1904, I, 300.
[43] Brooke 1985, esp. p. 249.
[44] Raverat 1952, pp. 87–93.
[45] Raverat 1952, pp. 90–1.

Wives

In the syndicate room, to which Aunt Cara never came, or in the Trinity Combination Room, to which no woman ever came, Uncle Dick could reign supreme. The home was his wife's domain, and though few wives were quite so dominant as Lady Jebb, the women of Cambridge carved out their own life, sometimes very much to their satisfaction. Some had little share in college affairs, others had much: they helped their husbands in entertaining and caring for students, they helped to make the fellowship a community, at the least they tended the flowers in the college chapel. Mrs Cameron, wife of the master of Caius from 1928 to 1948, filled this role to perfection.[46] She knew many of the undergraduates better than her husband did; quietly but firmly she knit the fellows and their wives into one communion and fellowship. But it would never have occurred to her that a master's wife was deprived by not being invited to dine at high table, or join in the normal social or academic life of the fellowship – any more than she would have expected to dine in a London club. She was highly intelligent, but deliberately unacademic. When the wives were invited to dine with the fellows of Caius once a year in the late 1940s, it was regarded as an act of singular liberality, though rumour had it that the fellows' Christmas dinner, thus honoured, had previously been a noisy affair, and that the ladies were partly invited to civilise it. Only in the 1960s and 1970s did it become wholly normal for women to dine at some men's high tables; and there are still colleges in the 1990s in which there is discrimination, in fact or supposition, against fellows' wives. Cambridge is a puzzling mixture of social innovation and trackless conservatism.

Meanwhile, from the 1870s on, the role of wives had been mitigated – or confused, according to one's viewpoint – by academic alliances. In 1876 Eleanor Balfour married Henry Sidgwick; in the 1880s she was engaged in research in the Cavendish under the direction of her brother-in-law Lord Rayleigh; from 1892 she was principal of Newnham – of which her husband was the founder – and from 1894 they lived together in the college.[47] Needless to say, the women's colleges always took a more civilised view of men than the men's of women; in a

[46] See pp. 306, 386.
[47] See Sidgwick 1938, esp. pp. 54, 71–3, 118; and below, chap. 9.

255

measure they were bound to, for they were always dependent on male teaching and support. When Francis Darwin (Gwen Raverat's Uncle Frank) married Ellen Crofts in 1883, she gave up her fellowship in Newnham.[48] In early decades Newnham and Girton were mainly served by unmarried women, many of them as dedicated to celibacy as to teaching and scholarship. But from the 1920s there came first a small then a large nucleus of married women fellows – and a much wider coterie of intellectual wives who formed their own social and academic circles. Thus in 1929 Marjorie Tappan, economics fellow of Girton, married Henry Hollond, a leading Cambridge lawyer who was Secretary of the Statutory Commissioners.[49] A more unusual alliance of the 1930s was that between Eileen Power, ex-fellow of Girton and professor at LSE, and Michael Postan, professor of economic history and fellow of Peterhouse. They set up house in Cambridge as the war clouds gathered; and the outbreak of war brought LSE itself to Cambridge for a while, though it also carried Postan off to war work in London. Sadly, Professor Power's early death in 1940 cut short this partnership, though not before it had had deep effect on the scholarly work of both partners, and so on the pattern of medieval economic history, whose lively genius Postan was to remain till his death in the 1980s.[50] By the 1960s and 70s partnerships between male and female dons had become extremely common, and played an incalculable part in the new movements of the age. But if one asks where in Cambridge the model of an academic community in which spouses mingled freely and naturally and equally really took root, the answer is probably in Wolfson and Clare Hall in the 1960s, where it is certain that the non-academic and the academic wives each took their share in fostering it.[51]

Thus Cambridge in the last hundred years has (not surprisingly) provided examples of every kind of relation between woman and man in marriage and other partnerships. In recent decades partnership in a very full sense – in work and society and family life and the rearing of children – has become much more in evidence, though Cambridge opinion still has some way to go

[48] Raverat 1952, pp. 192–5.
[49] See p. 369; *Girton College Register, 1869–1946* (1948), p. 655.
[50] See p. 238; and Power 1922, 1941. [51] See pp. 577, 582.

before it can be seen to face the problems of partnership squarely. A useful barometer of opinion in this field is the degree of support for crèches to enable married women to lead full academic lives. Every shade of opinion may legitimately be held on the pros and cons for parents and children of such arrangements. But it can be reasonably held, and is widely held, that married women with children must be at a permanent disadvantage in academic life if the community does not fully share in the care of children: the slow progress of provision for crèches by the university, and the absence of progress by the colleges (in spite of much talk of helping the academic wife) does not suggest that Cambridge is in the forefront of British opinion; it is undoubtedly well behind practice in some other countries.[52]

But 'before' and 'behind' are emotive words, suggesting a teleological view of human opinion. So let the last word be with an enlightened, but not exceptional, don, preparing his fiancée for marriage to an academic.

'Pray understand I don't say women are the same as men, but I refuse to assume they are different: it seems to me a theory either way is unnecessary, and, more than that, that we have not at present anything like materials for a universal solution of the question. . .'[53] He went on in this and other letters, and in the advice he gave as a married man to younger friends, to outline a doctrine of partnership in marriage which allowed ample scope for the development of the woman's own interests and concerns. The letters were written in 1871 by Mandell Creighton, fellow and tutor of Merton College, who was to be – from 1884 to 1894 – first Dixie Professor of Ecclesiastical History in Cambridge and fellow of Emmanuel. The doctrine that marriage is partnership was not invented in the twentieth century; it existed fully fledged before our period opens. It has had many rivals and companions; it has made some progress; but it is in itself no novelty.

III THE MASTERS

In the late sixteenth and early seventeenth centuries substantial efforts were made to place the government of the university in

[52] A recent development by the university has gone some way to meet this criticism.
[53] Creighton 1904, I, 99; but see also ibid. I, 287, 290.

the hands of the heads of the colleges. They came to meet weekly to discuss essential business, especially (in the 1620s and 30s) to pass judgement on university sermons. They were given every encouragement by external authority to exercise discipline and control, and for the most part they grasped the challenge with reasonable success. When Charles I attempted to impose the duke of Buckingham on Cambridge in 1626 – and succeeded by the narrowest of majorities (if majority there truly was) – the voting figures reveal a most interesting pattern.[54] In some colleges the master and fellows were almost solid, whether for the crown or for the puritan opposition; in four or five the fellows were sharply divided. There was in some colleges and in the university at large – even then – a strong residual feeling in favour of democracy. College elections, college decisions, were made by the governing body, and in the end by a majority, even if the master sometimes had more than one vote or, as in King's, a veto on uncongenial proposals. University decisions were made by the Senate, even if the Senate was only free to vote on motions placed before it by the Caput, a tiny oligarchy of representatives of faculties appointed personally by the Vice-Chancellor, himself always a head.[55] The status of the heads was emphasised by the separate living quarters – sometimes palatial, as in Trinity and St John's – with which they were provided; and the special privilege of being allowed to marry. But in the eighteenth and early nineteenth centuries the dominance of the heads grew less. External pressures to ensure orthodoxy and good order – and exercise patronage – virtually disappeared. Nothing ever entirely disappears in Cambridge, and the privilege of Lord Braybrooke of appointing the master of Magdalene has preserved an element from the age of patronage, just as the veto on legislation not proposed by the Council of the Senate preserved until very recently the tyrannical function of the Caput.[56]

But the Council of the Senate is very different from the Caput which it replaced in 1856.[57] It was deliberately designed to meet a

---

[54] Mullinger 1911, pp. 667–71. The details may not be wholly reliable.

[55] For the system, Winstanley 1935, chap. 1, esp. pp. 8–21. The Vice-Chancellor was not quite always a head, but the last exception was in 1587.

[56] See Edwards 1989; below, p. 565.

[57] For what follows, see Winstanley 1940, chaps. 4, 11, esp. pp. 238–42, 254–7, 315–34.

variety of claims; it comprised a group of four heads and four professors and eight others deeply concerned in the management of the university. Most of its business was exceedingly trivial;[58] but it appointed some professors and made nominations to all syndicates and committees of any importance. Through its discussions small groups of active heads continued to exert great influence. Here one might meet William Bateson, master of St John's (1857–81), John Peile, master of Christ's (1887–1910) and many others, alongside Professors Lightfoot, Hort and Maitland. Bateson was one of the central figures in the reforming movements of the 1870s; Peile of the next generation – and chairman of the Council of Newnham and a leading figure in the campaign for women's education in Cambridge.[59] As master of Christ's Peile was involved in the abortive negotiations for a merger with Emmanuel, intended to save money with which college and university teaching might be financed. One saving would have been the suppression of a head, if two colleges became one. A more radical proposal came from the Reverend Coutts Trotter, who published a pamphlet on university reform in 1877 in which, among other measures, he suggested the abolition of the office: he questioned whether 'an officer in the position now occupied by the head of House appears to be a necessary or desirable part of a body like a college?' A chairman it needed, but not an expensive or permanent chairman. Coutts Trotter was no obscure revolutionary, but a much respected fellow of Trinity, 'too tender-hearted for conflict' according to Henry Jackson, and shortly to be elected vice-master – and a heroic syndicate man as constant on committees as Hort himself. He published little and did no discernible research; but he is a central figure in the campaign to provide effective scientific education in the 1870s and 1880s.[60] What the master of Trinity of his day, W. H. Thompson, thought of his proposal seems not to be recorded.[61]

Behind the leaders, Bateson and Peile and their like, there was a second rank of heads, active in their own colleges and in the

[58] The Minute Books are CUA Min. 1. 2ff.
[59] On both, *DNB*; on Bateson, see pp. 68–9 and Winstanley 1947, esp. pp. 70–1, 81–5, 196–7, 215–16, 289–91; on Peile, *Christ's College Magazine*, 1910–11, pp. 143–57, and above, pp. 59–61.
[60] On him see esp. Clark 1900, pp. 314–18, and the very revealing comments of Henry Jackson, Parry 1926, p. 294; on his pamphlet, Winstanley 1947, p. 348.
[61] On Thompson, see pp. 70–1, and esp. Clark 1900, pp. 302–13.

university too in less conspicuous fashion. Phear of Emmanuel (master 1871–95) was one such: his successor Chawner (1895–1911) was another.[62] In Trinity the formidable William Whewell had been succeeded by W. H. Thompson, and under his moderately benevolent eye the reformers could take action at last: moderately benevolent since he followed every move in the game with his mordant wit, but benevolent since he was a kindly man at heart – he helped to create the marriageable office of praelector in ancient philosophy when he knew that Henry Jackson was contemplating betrothal;[63] and at every crucial stage in the progress of reform in Trinity the master's support, active or passive, was required. Even in his last years, when ill-health made him something of a recluse, J. W. Clark could write of him: 'His very isolation from the worry and bustle of the world gave authority to his advice.'[64] It is a noble epitaph on one model of what a master might be.

There were no pensions, no retiring ages, and so most heads carried on till death, sometimes reaching a very ripe old age. Retiring ages were introduced in the statutes of 1926, but not for existing heads, so that life heads only finally disappeared in the 1950s.[65] On 25 November 1888 died Richard Okes, provost of King's, born in 1797, provost since 1850. His predecessor had used the clause in the King's statutes which allowed the provost a veto on any business he disapproved to such effect that King's men were still exempt from degrees – which meant that they were not eligible for honours or to be senior wranglers. Dr Okes took instant steps to abolish this exemption; but this first move on the path to revolution was enough. He did no more. He was a shrewd and kindly man who allowed others to tread a path he viewed with sceptical eyes. He offered no obstinate resistance to – though he deplored – the decision to enlarge the college and seek recruits from other schools than Eton. It was fortunate for King's that its revolutionary tutor, Austen Leigh, had himself so much in common with Okes: deep devotion to Eton and King's and all the instincts of the old-fashioned clerical don. In his hands Okes felt

---

[62] See pp. 58, 123.
[63] Parry 1926, pp. 25, 28. See also Henry Jackson's very moving tribute, Parry 1926, pp. 294–5. For what follows see also Winstanley 1947, pp. 255, 260–2.
[64] Clark 1900, p. 313.
[65] In Cambridge: in Oxford the dean of Christ Church is still legally exempt from a retiring age.

safe, that he could allow the revolution he hardly sought; 'King's may have had more glamorous provosts', wrote Christopher Morris, 'but probably none wiser'.[66] However that may be, he was singularly inactive in his later years, and lived to be 91.

There were other heads even more hidden from view than Okes. When the first Royal Commissioners came in 1850, the then Vice-Chancellor tried to bar the gates against them; but when he was succeeded by Okes in 1851, the new Vice-Chancellor had welcomed them. Other heads believed it to be their sacred trust to prevent radical men and measures from intruding on their colleges. The idea of Victorian England as a revolutionary – or dangerously radical – world in which every traditional standard and custom was threatened seems a little strange to us; but Coutts Trotter's proposal itself is a reminder that radical suggestions were in the wind. These were enhanced by the debate over the Test Act. Perowne, then master of Corpus, was not by nature inert; but he had a vision of his college totally opposed both to the old world from which he had rescued it, which had been rather liberal in outlook, and to the new which threatened it later in his life, which was somewhat secular, and even high church.[67] Perowne believed deeply that his college should be and remain a haven of evangelical principle in an evil world. He resisted every kind of change; but in the end he and his followers were the victims of a palace revolution, and though he was kindly treated by his colleagues, his last years were without influence in either the university or the college. Some heads like Perowne on principle,[68] others like Ferrers, the master of Caius from 1880 to 1903, who was most of that time crippled by disease, helped to foster the legend that the heads were redundant. 'You live in a picturesque old house', observed Leslie Stephen in 1865, 'haunted by the associations of centuries. You succeed to a long line of dignitaries... In your own little world, you hold indisputably the first place... You have a sufficient salary, and last, not least, you have nothing in the world to do.'[69] Even Stephen admitted that some heads worked extremely hard, and

[66] Morris 1989, p. 46; *DNB*.   [67] See pp. 49–52.
[68] Robert Phelps, master of Sidney 1843–90, was another such: Scott-Giles 1975, pp. 99–101.
[69] Stephen 1865, pp. 123–4.

the picture he paints of anxious celibate fellows electing as master their chief rival for the most desirable college living[70] – which would enable them to marry – was gathering dust even as he wrote.

More characteristic than Perowne has been the tutor turned master who carried his tutorship into the master's lodge. E. S. Roberts of Caius (1903–12) was a distinguished example;[71] another of more recent days was Sir Henry Thirkill, master of Clare from 1939 to 1959. He was a respected member of the Cavendish who could as master still keep a conversation going with eminent visitors like Heisenberg.[72] But from 1920 his life was devoted to his tutorial pupils and college and university affairs at large. He was one of those pre-eminent tutors, like Miss Clough, first principal of Newnham, dedicated to the care of their students, spending long hours talking to them while they studied, and writing to them after they had gone into the world: his holidays were punctuated by forty letters or more a day from old students, duly received and answered.[73] As master he continued to act in all essentials as senior tutor. In similar fashion when, in 1951, the fellows of Emmanuel had the responsibility of making the first election after the publication of C. P. Snow's *The Masters*, they hastened to promote their senior tutor, the celebrated eccentric Edward Welbourne.[74] But this type is now rare.

In Oxford it has been common to elect to headships great men of the world – ambassadors, civil servants, generals, ex-ministers, vice-chancellors, headmasters and the like. There have been many headmasters in Cambridge, some of whom, like Ramsay of Magdalene, carried over the habits of the schoolroom into the lodge[75]; others with greater sensitivity have attempted to disguise their origin. Civil servants and generals have been few. Lord Chalmers, ex-civil servant, colonial governor and University Commissioner, was promoted from undergraduate to master of Peterhouse in his late sixties in 1924; his successor at Peterhouse, Sir William (later Lord) Birdwood, was a field-marshal.[76] Lord Butler, the leading conservative politician, was made master of

---

[70] Stephen 1865, p. 127.   [71] See p. 40.
[72] Godwin 1985, p. 136; see ibid. pp. 134–45 on Thirkill.
[73] Godwin 1985, p. 134.
[74] See pp. 279–81.   [75] See pp. 46–7.
[76] See *DNB 1931–40*, pp. 154–5; *1951–60*, pp. 112–14.

Trinity by another politician contemplating retirement, Harold Wilson. But far more have been distinguished academics, sometimes also active fellows, sometimes strangers. Down to the 1950s it was rare for a head of house to be drawn from the alumni of another college. The ethos of the 1920s – reflected in the probings of the Royal Commission[77] – gradually made the view more widespread that a head should be a person of academic distinction; and in the new salary structures of the 1950s and later, which allowed men to hold both offices but only to receive a single income, it did not escape observation that a college could save much of the cost of its head by appointing a professor who may have been the fellow of another college. In some cases, especially in recent years, the professor has found the combination of offices too burdensome, and resigned the chair. From outside Cambridge this seems a strange plurality of offices, and historically it marks the survival of eighteenth-century practices designed to bolster the income of the poor rich of Cambridge. But it has been most successfully practised by some notable men, and has attracted surprisingly little criticism within the university.

Down to 1870 the heads were the undisputed leaders of Cambridge society, and such in a sense they remain. But there has grown up beside them a group of men often with as great or greater resources at their command, the heads of department, especially of the greater scientific laboratories. Some heads of department have been modest persons, hardly distinguishable from the chairmen of faculty boards in the humanities, who have great responsibility, and a little authority, for two years or so, and pass on. They may lead, but among equals. Then there are the heads of large laboratories, who are like some Indian rajahs under British rule – men in control of great power and large resources only checked by a distant and benevolent authority. Down to 1870 such persons did not exist in Cambridge, and the title 'Head of Department' is more recent still. But once there were university laboratories handling substantial sums of money – which the university had no machinery to manage for them – the head of the Cavendish was a semi-independent prince; and that he is still,

---

[77] See e.g. *Royal Commission* 1922, Appendices, pp. 24 (evidence from Oxford), 43 (evidence from Cambridge), criticising election 'for purely domestic reasons'.

though the growth of bureaucracy within and without the university constrains the manoeuvres of the modern heads. By great good fortune, two of the most notable scientific heads of department of the last generation, Lord Todd and Sir Nevill Mott – both of whom retired from their chairs in 1971 – have published autobiographies, which show their own attitude to their roles to perfection. By still greater fortune, both were also heads of colleges, so that they help us to see the relation between the two offices, and through it, the strange interaction of department and college.

During the Second World War elections to professorships were frozen; but in 1944 a moderate thaw set in, aimed to meet special needs; and one of the most evident was to fill the chair of organic chemistry, vacant for five years. A major work of reconstruction was needed, and for once the university authorities laid plans and prepared to negotiate. Leading chemists had told them that if Cambridge wished to find a place in the sun in this field, they must try to attract Alexander Todd, the tough, brilliant, creative professor at Manchester. Todd agreed to visit the existing lab, and 'I really was appalled by what I saw and at first felt I should withdraw at once,' but instead he decided to offer draconian conditions; seldom can an incoming professor have addressed an august body of Cambridge electors in such Olympian tones.

> I must have complete authority as head of department to reorganise and develop the University Chemical Laboratory ... Queen Mary College and St Bartholomew's [wartime refugees] must go back to London... A post must be provided for A. R. Gilson to act as Laboratory Superintendent in charge of all non-academic affairs. Gas lighting should be abolished and replaced by electricity ... and money provided to equip the laboratories as quickly as possible to modern standards. I would need an undertaking that the university would give the highest priority to building a new University Chemical Laboratory on a fresh site ...

and he also asked for other staff appointments. 'Within a few weeks ... I was informed that all my conditions would be met.'[78] Under Todd's direction, a galaxy of talent gathered in the

---

[78] Todd 1983, pp.67–9.

department, and the new laboratory rose in Lensfield Road, obliterating the home of William Wilkins – and marring the view from Downing which he had created – but setting new standards in laboratory accommodation for Cambridge and the country at large.[79]

In 1954 Nevill Mott came from Bristol to be the head of the Cavendish.[80] Mott is a theoretical physicist with a genius for seeing other folk's problems and solving them. Although the bulk of his work has been done in two fields, solid state physics and non-crystalline semi-conductors, it has not had the monolithic core – nor has he been the centre of an army of experimentalists – such as the Cavendish had comprised under Rutherford or chemistry under Todd. In the Cavendish, furthermore, he found a much livelier tradition than Todd encountered in organic chemistry. He seems more aware of the limitations of his position; he mentions many arguments, for example, on the General Board. But within the Cavendish he speaks as one who had authority. He closed down the old nuclear equipment, legacy of the efforts to keep Cambridge in the forefront of nuclear advance; he cut adrift the Molecular Biology Unit, though he claims to have recognised its creative talent – and it has since become perhaps the most celebrated new laboratory in Cambridge[81] – recognising the rather obvious fact that molecular biology is not a branch of physics, however closely allied all fundamental science must be in its roots. He translated Philip Bowden and his group working on surface science – friction, to the layman – from physical chemistry to physics, providing a home for it where physicists and chemists might work together.[82] In later years he came to accept the view of younger colleagues that the Cavendish must move, and to be the benevolent patron of the inspired planning undertaken by Brian Pippard, later his successor.[83] But Mott's own account of his reign at the Cavendish actually lays more stress on teaching, and on physics in education, than on research.[84]

[79] See pp. 199–201.
[80] Mott 1986, chaps. 13, 14, 16.
[81] Mott 1986, pp. 110, 112; and see pp. 497–9.
[82] Mott 1986, pp. 110–12.   [83] See p. 193.   [84] Mott 1986, pp. 102–10.

In 1959 Mott was elected master of Caius. He had been a fellow of Caius in the early 1930s, and a professorial fellow since 1954; but it is evident from his own account that he was not deeply versed in the ways of the college – 'Caius was a society in which I had never felt at home': he was a man of the lab. 'The Master's duties were not entirely clear. He certainly did not have authority; any contentious issue was settled by the fellows by vote.'[85] But he had been accustomed in Bristol and the Cavendish to make his own decisions and expect others to accept them, and he found the independent methods of a fellowship at that time exceptionally divided impossible to fathom, let alone to master. He confesses that he made mistakes 'in trying to see if a "master's party" existed'.[86] 'My mistake was to assume that a mastership was like running a university physics department.'[87] He resigned in 1965, remaining Cavendish Professor till his retirement in 1971, going from strength to strength in his field, achieving the Nobel Prize for physics in 1977 for work partly done in his seventies.[88]

When Todd came to Cambridge in 1944, he 'knew literally nothing about any of the colleges ... I finally chose to go to Christ's because it was recommended to me as a smallish college with a decent reputation and one which had, in Charles Raven, a notable figure as Master' – and also the then Secretary-General of the Faculties in its fellowship.[89] Other professors have been chosen by colleges; Todd chose Christ's; but he does not mention it again till nearly twenty years had passed. 'In January 1963 I was approached by the vice-master of Christ's College.' Would he become master? He had refused other posts, but this was different. 'For one thing, it was my own college and I knew it and its ways so well that it would not be a great strain to take it over.' His original work in the lab was drawing to a close and he was attracted by the master's lodge, 'most attractive as a place in which to live'. The outcome was as complete a contrast with Mott's mastership at Caius (then drawing to its end) as could be imagined. 'I thoroughly enjoyed my fifteen years as Master of

[85] Mott 1986, pp. 121–2.
[86] Mott 1986, p. 128.   [87] Mott 1986, pp. 128–9.
[88] Mott 1986, chap. 17.   [89] Todd 1983, p.69.

Christ's; living with successive generations of undergraduates in college is a most rewarding experience . . . I was also very lucky in the key appointments I made.'[90] He persuaded C. K. Phillips, Deputy Treasurer of the university, to become bursar – whereas in Caius Mott was overruled in the appointment of the bursar, an event which began 'the end of my . . . mastership'.[91] Todd's idea of college management was to have a full-time bursar and senior tutor – they had been part-time offices (notionally at least) hitherto – and in 1967 he was able to offer the senior tutorship to Gorley Putt, whose post in the Commonwealth Fund had temporarily lapsed: 'without further ado (or even consulting the College Governing Body), I pounced on Gorley, who to my great joy accepted the post of Senior Tutor in charge of admissions, a position which he held with distinction throughout the remainder of my Mastership. With Phillips and Putt, running Christ's was an easy task, and I believe the college thrived as a result.'[92] A budding master would be unwise to make Todd his model; most governing bodies most of the time have been jealous of their privileges. Commonly the head of a college is chairman of a group of equals, each with his own individuality to express and preserve, and the most successful have been those who could find the pulse of that strange community and draw out the best from that large pool of talent. But there is a residuum of dignity and authority in mastership too, which a man of exceptional force of character, self-confidence and adroitness in the handling of men may harness to an authoritarian regime. For those of us who have known many heads of colleges and heads of departments, they seem to dwell in different worlds.

IV THE FELLOWS AND THE COACHES

The Cambridge don of the late nineteenth century might be a professor, a fellow of a college, a university lecturer (a rare bird), an administrator (rarer still) or a coach. These were not water-tight divisions. It had always been the case that a professor might be a fellow if he obeyed the rules and eschewed a wife – or a head

---

90 Todd 1983, pp. 167–8.   91 Mott 1986, p. 128.
92 Todd 1983, pp. 168–9.

of house if he did not. One of the principal reforms of the 1880s was the creation of the professorial fellow, a measure intended to tie the professoriate more closely into the colleges (though it was later discovered that some of them disappeared into colleges to be no more seen by the university at large),[93] and provide the professors with some income. University lecturers might or might not be fellows; most coaches probably were not, though the leading private tutors usually were. But neither then nor later has every don been a fellow; and this has bred class distinctions. At first the chief frontier was between the coach or private tutor who earned his bread from college teaching but was not of the elect, and the fellows, who might or might not teach, but always ruled their little empires.[94] From the 1920s, as the university came to have more staff and more independent life, the number of university lecturers who were not fellows slowly grew. Then in the 1950s, with university expansion, it grew very rapidly and became a major issue of Cambridge politics. In Oxford, after many creaks and groans, a logical solution has been found: all university teaching officers are fellows of colleges, including the professors, who have colleges allocated to them.[95] In Cambridge even professorships are not attached to colleges.[96] When professors are appointed from outside Cambridge a bizarre auction takes place, with rules as complex as some old-fashioned types of football, which ends in the distribution of the professors among the colleges. Since 1960 most colleges have greatly enlarged their fellowships, chiefly by appointment of college lecturers to teach expanding subjects; and a number of new colleges have been founded, partly to cater for postgraduates and other needs, but with the aim very clearly in mind of providing fellowships for university teachers.[97] A comparison with

---

[93] Hence the statute which forbade them to do college teaching, recently abolished.

[94] See p. 267–71, 279–80.

[95] There were three stages in this: professors were tied to colleges in the new constitution of the 1920s; there was a substantial impulse to close the growing gaps in and after the Franks Report of 1966; the gap has been closed by more recent efforts and legislation.

[96] There have been exceptions: the Downing Professors before 1926 were automatically members of the Downing governing body and had houses there; the Regius Professors have always had some link with Trinity; the Dixie is automatically offered a fellowship at Emmanuel. But these links were weakened, not strengthened, by the reforms of the 1920s, when the University Commissioners deliberately advised Oxford and Cambridge to move in opposite directions.

[97] See chap. 18, esp. pp. 573–5.

Oxford shows that Cambridge has not followed the only path open to it. The closer ties between college and university appointments in Oxford doubtless tend to perpetuate the greater influence of the colleges in university affairs, and this has its weaknesses – it is more difficult to float a new subject or phase out an old in Oxford than in Cambridge. But Oxford is in its arrangements more logical, more fair to its staff; and if the colleges have more sway over the university, by the same token the university has in many ways much deeper influence in the colleges. But the very idea of fellowship – which provides within the colleges a unique type of democracy – breeds and preserves a whole series of status distinctions.

With the spread of democracy in Britain at large, the Cambridge fellowships have become more privileged, not less: like the ancient Greeks, they have discovered the charms of democracy based on the services of subject peoples. A trivial illustration of this is the privilege of walking on the grass in college courts. Its history is obscure, but where it is known it seems to be of nineteenth-century invention.[98] Some courts had no grass before then; and the communities which lived in King's, to take a striking example – and the visitors who came from afar – were far fewer then than now. There is some evidence that when first enforced it was in some colleges a privilege of all MAs.[99] But MAs are occasional visitors; fellows are there all or most of the time; and the right to walk on the grass is in most colleges a fellows' privilege which even head gardeners have to respect.

The old-fashioned coach has disappeared, but there are many folk in Cambridge of high academic qualifications who engage in free-lance teaching, especially in college supervision which cannot be supported by often exiguous university staff, or by college lecturers. They preserve the old distinctions, which are evident too among the administrative staff: the more senior are fellows of colleges; the vast majority are not. The 'graduate' staff usually have their names on a college's books, and efforts are made to ensure as much; but this can mean very little in practice; and to a vast number of university staff, technicians, secretaries

[98] For the assumption in 1865 that undergraduates should not walk on the grass but did, see below, p. 271.
[99] So it was in Caius, as I was told on good authority by an MA of the 1920s; so it still is in King's.

and others, it means precisely nothing at all. An academic community can hardly avoid allowing some kind of distinction to academic standing. But the colleges themselves can have highly qualified academics on their staffs – in libraries and archives, for instance – who are not fellows and have no access to the SCR. Viewed from the outside world, Cambridge may appear very egalitarian; at least it has softened and modified and in a measure abolished the distinctions of the wider society. But in their place it has set its own, peculiar creatures of its structure and history.

When Leslie Stephen surveyed Cambridge society in 1865, there were no administrators save heads of houses, the University Registrary – who wrote the minutes of the Council of the Senate with his own hand[100] – and two or three Esquire Bedells, whose main function was ritual, as it still is:[101] to lead the Chancellor and Vice-Chancellor in procession and preside over the ceremonial of the Senate House. The teaching community comprised coaches and college tutors.

> Next above schoolmasters in the scale of misery, I should place what we call a 'poll-coach'; the unfortunate being who undertakes to steer the helpless undergraduate through the shoals and quicksands of the poll degree [the ordinary degree]. He has to deal with human beings who are less restless and more doggedly indifferent than boys; with a trust and a reverence which is really touching, they implicitly abandon all charge of their own thoughts, and surrender their minds to him as passive vessels to be pumped into. They only hope that he will pump in as little as possible, in order that they may discharge it the more readily. To do such a duty thoroughly well demands two qualifications: perfect temper and qualified omniscience; a man's knowledge, that is, must extend over the whole field of University requirements, but need never penetrate beneath the surface.[102]

Stephen went on to contemplate the fate of the honours coach, on whose prowess the general quality of university education mainly depended in the 1860s.

I can see the placid and benevolent face of my old instructor now

[100] See CUL, CUA Min. 1. 2 ff.
[101] Today the Esquire Bedell has a part-time office, commonly held by an Assistant Registrary or the like.
[102] Stephen 1865, pp. 99–100.

[Isaac Todhunter, the maths coach], and listen to his invariable exhortation 'push on'; just as if I had been, as indeed I was, a wearied and disgusted wayfarer. Every morning he appeared in chapel punctually at 7.30. From 8 to 8.15 breakfast. Pupils from 8.15 to 3. Then a constitutional so regular, that we used to believe that the philosophers at the observatory took their time from the instant at which he passed their gates, instead of remarking the sun's transit, which indeed is apt to be invisible in our misty climate. At 4 dinner. From 5.30 to 10 pupils again, with ten minutes' interval for refreshment. He lived in a perfect atmosphere of mathematics ... even his chairs and tables, strictly limited to the requirements of pupils, and the pattern on his carpet, seemed to breathe mathematics. By what mysterious process it was that he accumulated stores of miscellaneous information and knew all about the events of the time ... I have never been able to guess ... Still less can I imagine how it came to pass that he published a whole series of excellent educational works ...[103]

Stephen's portrait of the college tutor is more of a patchwork. First, he tames the parents.

In former days a strong Evangelical tendency was a useful adjunct ... for attracting and suppressing the parent. I should say that at present the best theological mixture was a good safe orthodoxy, strongly opposed to *Essays and Reviews*, but opposed with equal decision to any less noxious eccentricities.[104]

The raw youth is, perhaps, harder to bring into thorough subjection ... No tutor is a hero to his pupils; they exaggerate his weaknesses with unpleasant acuteness, retail small stories of traditional blunders, and represent themselves as treating him with affable contempt ... The struggle ... between dignity and impudence is sometimes severe and protracted, and it is only by degrees that the supremacy of intense respectability asserts itself. When the noise of the untimely cornopean is hushed in the courts, when the grass-plots are left untrampled, when a lively fire is not kept up with saloon pistols at the notices fixed on the chapel door, when supper-parties return home in peace ... when chapels and lectures are regularly attended ... the tutor may feel that he ... has reduced his menagerie to order. He has shown a dignity befitting a

[103] Stephen 1865, pp. 106–7.
[104] Stephen 1865, p. 115. Stephen himself had taken the first, most crucial, steps on the path that led to *An Agnostic's Apology* (1893) when he wrote this passage.

loftier position . . . he may soar towards the congenial atmosphere of the bishop's bench; there, the magnificent repose of manner which once humbled the most unruly undergraduate, may terrify the country clergy, and overawe curates of extravagant tendencies . . .

There are . . . other ways in which a tutor may successfully sway the rod of empire . . . He may go beyond the ordinary routine of lectures and endeavour to teach his pupils something. He may take a pride in the number of first-class or wranglers that he can manufacture out of indifferent raw material, or a humbler pleasure in the number he can save from actual plucking.

There are other and lower expedients . . . He may affect to be on terms of familiarity with his pupils, join in their athletic games, and win glory by coaching the college crew [as Stephen himself had done]. Of such a one a story is told illustrating his performance in a Greek Testament lecture. 'Hallo!' he is said to have exclaimed, 'easy all! Hard word there. Smith, what does it mean?'

'I don't know', says Smith.

'No more don't I', replied the aquatic, but moderately learned, tutor; 'paddle on all!'[105]

Throughout the generations of this book there has been a steady flow of comment from some former undergraduates that they saw little of the fellows. Others have seen much of them, some too much – whether it be that they have recalled an intimacy too demanding for their own development, or only an exigent dean or tutor exerting discipline on the unruly young. But most colleges most of the time have had a nucleus of friendly fellows who ensured some measure of social contact; and this has been especially marked in King's. They have not all been teaching fellows, and the tradition at King's was founded by Henry Bradshaw, an assistant in the University Library, later one of the most celebrated of its librarians.[106] The shape of the community of King's when Bradshaw came back from a brief sojourn in Ireland in 1856 can be gauged from a glance at the Gibbs building, which, with some help from the Wilkins building of the 1820s, comfortably housed the undergraduates and the resident fellows under the matriarchal government of a small group of bed-

---

[105] Stephen 1865, pp. 115–19. The cornopean is (or was) a kind of cornet.
[106] See references in n. 111 below.

makers.[107] In later years he became the life and soul of the community. But if in essence he created the social life of King's, in a truer sense it created him. For in early life he was reserved, more noted for his candour than for charm, 'too honest to be popular'.[108] One day in the late 1850s he was visited by the young Edward Austen Leigh, elder brother of Augustus, later provost, recently arrived from Eton, seeking company; and it was Leigh and his friends who brought out the hidden social gifts in Bradshaw.[109] But already in 1852 Hort had called him 'about the nicest fellow in Cambridge'.[110] From the late 50s on, his rooms were open to any of the young of King's who sought them; and as his wings unfurled, he took to seeking them out himself. A. C. Benson gave a celebrated description of their first meeting in 1874.

> There came into the room, solidly, quietly, and imperturbably, a short, stoutly built, plump, clean-shaven man, in a serviceable suit of grey. His hair, cut very short, bristled over his big round cranium . . . Everything about him was solid and comfortable. . . His small eyes were half-closed, and a smile half-tender, half-humorous, seemed to ripple secretly over his face, without any movement of his small but expressive lips.[111]

Such visits helped numberless King's men to emerge from the chrysalis less painfully than Bradshaw himself had done.

But when in turn they visited his rooms they found not only a friend but a scholar at work. There and in the University Library he dedicated thirty years of selfless labour to make Cambridge a centre of scholarship and the Library something it had hardly been before – a notable home of bibliography and book-collecting of international fame.[112] With the knowledge of hind-sight we can smile at Hort's comment on his first arrival in the Library: '*It* is very lucky to get him; but I cannot help thinking that so affectionate and genial a creature is thrown away on mere

---

[107] Austen Leigh 1906, pp. 63–5, 107.   [108] Clark 1900, p. 295.

[109] Austen Leigh 1906, pp. 66–7.

[110] Hort 1896, I, 227. Presumably as a young man he only showed his charm among his intimates.

[111] Benson 1911, pp. 218–19, quoted in McKitterick 1986, p. 658. I am much indebted to David McKitterick's deep and sympathetic study of Bradshaw. Of contemporary accounts Prothero 1888 and Clark 1900, pp. 292–301, are especially helpful; see also Stokes 1984.

[112] 1856–86, save for a brief interval in 1858–9, when he wearied of the humble administrative work in which he was engaged: McKitterick 1986, pp. 529–30. Thereafter more suitable tasks were found, but he was dogged as a young man by fits of idleness alternating with 'desperate activity', McKitterick 1986, p. 529.

dry bibliography and yet more mechanical work. But he seems at present to like it.'[113] He entered with zest into many projects, and never refused a request for help from a friend. He had 'a memory which never failed him, and an instinct of discovery little short of marvellous'.[114] For the Library this meant ceaseless adventures in the sale rooms of Europe by a man who always knew far more than his rivals what was rare and interesting, what would adorn a great collection of the future. He had dazzling insight too, and his brilliant ideas and suggestions fell like dew on scattered fields, such as medieval liturgy, the history of cathedral chapters, the study of Chaucer and the heritage of medieval Ireland. On any project he set to work with the instincts of a scholar; on none did he ever concentrate enough either to conceive or to write a work of lasting depth; his seminal ideas have often proved wrong.[115] But his zeal, and his friendships within and without Cambridge, played a crucial role in its conversion from a finishing school for clergy – and for the 'upper classes' – to a major centre of academic study. If we look for a rival to Bradshaw among the learned men of Cambridge in the 1860s and 70s we naturally light on Fenton Hort – like Bradshaw a man of learning amazingly wide and deep, though Hort's best work has lasted better. And it is significant that Hort and Bradshaw had been intimate friends since 1851 when Bradshaw joined the Choral Society and the Ghostly Guild, predecessor of the Society for Psychical Research, the first fruits of the long collaboration between Hort and Westcott.[116] The friendship of Bradshaw and Hort is as significant for the academic and scholarly development of Cambridge as Bradshaw's friendship with Austen Leigh was for the development of collegiate society.

After 1860, and still more after 1880, the don may also be sought in his home, with his wife and children. The early married dons live most vividly in the pages of Gwen Raverat's *Period*

---

[113] Hort 1896, I, 350; but see previous note.
[114] Clark 1900, p. 298.
[115] An example is his study of the 'four-square cathedral chapter', an explanation of the constitution of English secular cathedral chapters after the Norman conquest: see Edwards 1967, pp. 13–20; but see also Greenway 1985.
[116] Hort 1896, I, 173, 208, 211; II, 339–41.

Piece, supplemented by her sister Margaret Keynes' *A House by the River*.[117] Charles Darwin never lived in Cambridge after his undergraduate days and rarely visited it; but his genius and his children have played a leading role in its history. We are concerned here with the children, especially with 'Uncle George', Gwen's father, owner of Newnham Grange, now Darwin College. He and the Jebbs of Springfield, a stone's throw away – where Mrs Darwin's Aunt Cara presided – lived in the heart of west Cambridge. Not far away, off the Huntingdon Road, lived Uncle Horace and Uncle Frank. George's son Charles was to be a notable scientist in his own right and the model for the successful master of *The Masters*;[118] his daughter Margaret married Geoffrey Keynes, an eminent London surgeon whose memorial is in Cambridge in the Keynes room in the University Library and in his family. He was himself the son of the Registrary and brother of the economist Maynard;[119] he was father, grandfather and great-grandfather of distinguished dons; and one of his sons, by marrying Anne Adrian, linked the heritage of Darwin and Keynes to that of Lord Adrian, one of the most eminent of Cambridge physiologists, later master of Trinity, Vice-Chancellor and Chancellor of the university.[120] Meanwhile Francis Darwin married as his second wife Ellen Crofts of Newnham, and as his third, 'the strange and beautiful widow of Professor F. W. Maitland'.[121] His daughter Frances married F. M. Cornford the classical philosopher and author of *Microcosmographia Academica*, often quoted in these pages.[122] The Darwins represent the hereditary element in Cambridge at its most prosperous and distinguished.

George Darwin was a mathematician and astronomer, who advanced knowledge of the tides and moon and other regions by a remarkable mixture of brilliant scientific imagination – the hallmark of his family – and patient mathematical drudgery. He was a man of wide interests, especially in history and heraldry, and 'the most romantic man alive', as Gwen Raverat assures us.

---

[117] Raverat 1952; Keynes 1976/1984.
[118] Keynes 1976/84, pp. 243–50. [119] See p. 396–7, 467–72.
[120] On Lord Adrian see *DNB 1971–80*, pp. 7–9 (A. L. Hodgkin).
[121] Raverat 1952, p. 195. [122] Cornford 1908.

'Heraldry had been the unforgotten passion of his boyhood; history and languages remained his chief interests all his life; outside science, of course. Though I should not be surprised to learn that even his scientific interests had had a romantic origin; at any rate, what could be more romantic than the tides or the moon?'[123] Though professor of astronomy, his work lay largely at his desk, and often that meant in his study at Newnham Grange.

> We used to rush in and out of the study, when he was working, to get 'frog-paper' – half sheets of paper for drawing on, which he kept for us, under a green china frog – and he would just wait, with his 'Stylograph' pen in the air, looking disturbed but friendly, till we had banged the door and he could get back to the 'Pear-shaped Figure of Equilibrium' again. My mother, too, always sat in the study, rustling and scrattling about in her heaps of papers, and sometimes talking to us or the servants in whispers, which can't have been very soothing. I am afraid he had very little peace in the study; but though he sometimes looked rather distraught, he never gave us the slightest hint that he would like to be quiet. Indeed, he was so affectionate, that it is quite possible that he did really prefer the human warmth of the interruptions to the coldness of solitude[124]

– as did Sir Hugh Anderson, the master of Caius of the 1910s and 20s, dedicated day and night to university and college business, so that his wife and daughter could only enjoy his company by spending the evening quietly in his study.[125] I fancy many Cambridge studies were less frequented by the family; to my father's, in the late 1920s and 30s, we rarely went as small children, though we could be sure of a warm welcome if we did; as we grew up, companionship in work and play brought us there more often.[126]

The hereditary element in Cambridge, though numerous and influential, has always been a small minority. Of the multitude of the less privileged, let G. G. Coulton speak. He did not come from a poor home: his father was a country attorney who spent all he could on his numerous children's education, and sent his son to a public school and to St John's, though he himself had

---

[123] Raverat 1952, pp. 184–5.   [124] Raverat 1952, pp. 187–8.
[125] Anderson 1988, chap. 16.
[126] And the exigencies of wartime fuel drew us all into a single room, in winter, in the 1940s.

never been to Cambridge.[127] Coulton went to Felsted while the Darwins went to Clapham Grammar School; the names of schools can be a deceptive guide to early privilege. As a young man Coulton made his living by teaching and coaching, and a little by his writings, and from his late twenties he read deeply in the materials for medieval social and religious history. He came back to Cambridge in 1911, aged 53, with his wife and two young daughters, and no settled job. He came first to give the Birkbeck Lectures, which 'were successful, and friends advised me to try my fortune altogether at Cambridge. I might take pupils there, use it as my base for Extension Lectures, and finally, perhaps get a Lectureship at my old College, or elsewhere.'[128] At first all went well and he gave a course of university lectures to a large fee-paying audience: he was able to give up coaching and move to a house in Shelford. But the war came and the students departed, leaving the Coultons to hardship and penury. But they survived, 'and with the Armistice came a rush of prosperity'.[129] In 1919 the new-formed teachers of English found a place for him as a university lecturer, whose task it was to provide the historical background for medieval literature. In the same year St John's made him a fellow, and the learned outsider, living on the fringe of academic society, became a member of the establishment at the age of 60. Warm-hearted if egotistical, kindly, eccentric and pugnacious, Coulton remains one of the notable characters of Cambridge history; something of the flavour of the man – his vivid imagination, his devotion to history and controversy, the anecdotal, discursive nature of his life and of his mind – come out in his *Four Score Years*; for the full flavour one must go to his daughter's biography, where one sees the warts portrayed with angry zeal, and yet in the end the warmth of family affection breaks through.[130] But we have already strayed into the 1920s, and must take a fresh look at the dons of that era, first as teachers, then in their social and economic milieu.

[127] See Coulton 1943, pp. 2–3, 68–90, 111–26: Coulton's grandfather died at the moment when his father was due to go to Cambridge, and he had to take over the business without more ado. On Coulton see esp. Coulton 1943; Campion 1948; Bennett 1947.

[128] Coulton 1943, p. 312.

[129] Ibid., p. 313; for what follows, see Bennett 1947, pp. 5–6 (he was born in October 1858 and so 60 in May 1919 when elected to St John's).

[130] Coulton 1943; Campion 1948.

The society

Two kinds of teacher: Goulding Brown and Welbourne

Twentieth-century Cambridge has been a palimpsest in which many layers of academic tradition can be discerned by archaeological enquiry in a single generation. The old argument between the virtues of the married and the bachelor, which rocked the university between the 1850s and the 1880s, when college statutes were gradually altered to permit the fellows to marry, has persisted. Marriage enables an academic to lead a normal family life and yet devote his lifelong energies to his profession; many married men – and women – have been dedicated servants of their colleges and their students. When E. S. Roberts married he insisted that a tutor's house be formed within the narrow confines of Caius so that he could combine college and family life in the most immediate way.[131] But is there even now any substitute for the fellow who is a permanent member of the community and lives within its walls? To such questions there are no answers; but an infinite variety of human cases to support every view which may reasonably be held.

Equally persistent are the arguments between research and learning, between scholarship and teaching. And what is teaching? Does it comprise, first and foremost, lecturing or demonstrating in lecture rooms and labs; or supervision in colleges, 'college teaching' as it is still called in the mysterious, but fundamental, jargon of the place. Should it be conducted wholly by university or college lecturers? The revolution of the dons of the late nineteenth century was directed, among other aims, to reviving the college's function to teach – to replace the dominance of the private coach in Cambridge education. But the private coach turned free-lance supervisor is with us still, a very vital part of the Cambridge establishment. The old-fashioned coach has perhaps departed – though not so very long ago; but there are numerous experts in Cambridge without formal posts whose teaching is a valued contribution to the work of the university and is often recognised by membership of the Regent House and status as 'affiliated lecturer'.

Some of the layers of the palimpsest were revealed with peculiar clarity in David Newsome's brilliant evocation of 'Two

---

[131] Brooke 1985, p. 249.

278

Emmanuel historians', Bertram Goulding Brown and Edward Welbourne.[132] Goulding Brown represented the unprivileged Cambridge teacher: he was one of the survivors of the ancient order of coaches; he had no fellowship; he had no scholarly reputation outside his immediate circle. He had settled in Cambridge after unsuccessfully competing for a Trinity fellowship in 1906; he lectured for the English Tripos during the Great War on Donne; he became librarian of the Seeley – the History Faculty library; he directed studies for Downing and Emmanuel. His professional income was sparse; his home and family were supported by private means. He was not wholly without privileges: he enjoyed dining rights in Emmanuel, and a room, in which he taught for forty years. 'To enter Goulding Brown's room as a freshman . . . was to imbibe at once the ethos of *semper eadem*' – Newsome writes as one who entered it in the early 1950s.

> Neither furniture nor furnishings had changed since he first took root there during the 1914 war. Perhaps the vast library had increased . . . There were cabinets of various sizes, containing faded letters and spidery notes; old pipes reposing in sombre ashtrays; a mantelpiece cluttered with Christmas cards from ten years back; by the fire, two chairs – one high-backed and ample, from which the frail Edwardian figure, with long thin legs crossed above the knee and at the ankles, surveyed you solemnly as you fumbled for your essay; the other – reserved for pupils – a huge wicker monstrosity, its seat only inches from the floor, so that the act of sitting seemed like dropping into a void.

The Middle Ages were studied according to an established pattern, based on the classics of his own youth; most moderns were dismissed, Gaillard Lapsley as 'ingenious'.[133] Yet the fare was never stale and the lesson was worth learning: the books he admired were of lasting worth.

> By contrast, Welbourne was entirely unpredictable. With Goulding Brown a supervision lasted fifty minutes and not a minute more . . . Welbourne, however, continued a supervision until his next engagement. I normally went to him at 4 p.m. on Fridays . . .

---

[132] Newsome 1984, originally published in 1965–6. What follows is a résumé of Newsome's article, supplemented from personal knowledge.
[133] Newsome 1984, pp. 104–6.

and the supervision lasted until Hall at 7.30. He never set an essay title. 'Bring me another', he would say at the close of each supervision. 'Read away!' would be the first words one heard on entering his room, the following week. In fact I succeeded in reading an essay to him only once, and on this occasion he fell asleep. It was normally sufficient to read just the first sentence to let loose the stream of paradox which flowed on undisturbed... It was always brilliant, but frequently baffling... Looking at some notes which I attempted to take after one supervision (ostensibly on the Counter-Reformation), I find that we covered *inter alia* the childhood of Ribbentrop, the *real* story behind the building of the American railways, why London footmen were usually Irish, the origin of the Lyons Corner Houses, Luther's consumption of liver-sausage and the religious significance of porridge. Somehow it all got back to the Council of Trent.[134]

'He could be mischievous – he could be perverse; he was certainly wonderfully stimulating' – and I have heard the same from those who only knew him from his university lectures on nineteenth-century economic history; yet there were perhaps few who had the patience to follow them. He knew the value of scholarship – to talk with him 'for quite an hour on the history of hat-making' led to something which was 'real knowledge, and to find out the truth you might have to talk with a master-craftsman himself, which to Welbourne was sheer delight'.[135] He sometimes lamented that he himself had never published any books; but the iconoclast in him demolished the professional scholars and despised the Ph.D. – although the postgraduate student had been recognised since the 1890s, the Ph.D. only impinged on Cambridge in the 1920s and only achieved universal regard in the second half of the century. ' "The high medievalists have made their subject into a mystery which will kill it" ... He referred to many of his fellow-historians as "technicians" ... Professionalism led to mystique, and mystique to romance. Too many historians through lack of plain common sense and simple observation, missed the obvious and sold their own rationalisations as truth.'[136] Welbourne was a brilliant, if eccentric and erratic, teacher, a

[134] Newsome 1984, pp. 106–7.   [135] Newsome 1984, p. 111.
[136] Newsome 1984, pp. 110–11.

scholar determined to hide his scholarship under an amateur's cloak, a quintessential college man who was both senior tutor and master of his college. In these two men one sees, as in a mirror, the strange hierarchy of academic society and academic values in Cambridge: the head of house, college tutor, university lecturer, fellow, and the coach and the supervisor who is not a fellow; one sees a devotion to learning and historical truth defending itself against professional research, a dedicated teaching of a deeply personal kind, addressed to one pupil at a time. In the late twentieth century it has become more difficult for a man like Goulding Brown to find a living in Cambridge, though the number of free-lance teachers is still large. In the late twentieth century it has become much more difficult for a teacher like Welbourne who never publishes to carve a career in university and college; yet there are still many who share his preferences and his values. Teaching and research are much more professional activities in the 1990s than in 1900; or rather, they appear so and are practised as such by a larger cadre of university teachers. For Goulding Brown and Welbourne both grew up among historians much more dedicated to professional research than they. It is the balance which has shifted, as history like every other discipline has become more specialised and new avenues of knowledge and research have opened. But the palimpsest is still there, to remind us that 'the revolution of the dons' was no simple affair, that values old and new live long together.

The economics of the academic profession, 1918–39

A stroll through west Cambridge, along Grange Road, through Herschel Road, Sylvester Road and Adams Road to Wilberforce Road and Madingley Road, may give the impression that the Cambridge academics prospered greatly in the two generations before the Second World War when most of the houses were built. Let us observe at once that many of them were not built by dons; that the great houses of Grange Road and Madingley Road, for example, often reflect the prosperity of local business men or are even the town houses of large local landowners. We have encountered clusters of university men in less expansive regions: in terrace houses in Brookside and St Peter's Terrace, for example, or building Harvey Road.[137] Yet the conclusion is not wholly false. The majority of the houses in Wilberforce Road were built for academic families in the 1930s, and are the outward sign of a period of relative prosperity and stable economic prospects. The thirties were overshadowed by war and rumours of war; the stability was an illusion; and we are easily deceived by contemplating houses which few academics could buy, let alone build, in the 1980s, into imagining a greater opulence than really existed.

The material for understanding such a society is very uneven; statistics and general statements are of little use. We probably learn most from a scatter of case histories which reveal its variety. A glance at the published university accounts for the early 1920s shows how varied were the rewards of the Cambridge academic before the Royal Commission and the Statutory Commissioners had brought a measure of uniformity and reason into university stipends. A don might receive his income from a variety of sources: from an old university or college endowment, from a fellowship dividend which still (down to 1926) largely depended on the income to be derived from land and rents; from fees collected more or less directly from students attending lectures; from fees for examining and for a variety of lesser services to faculty or college; and the Regius Professor of Divinity was still expected to gather in person the tithes on which a part of his income depended.[138] Amid this bizarre variety it is abundantly clear that some were relatively prosperous, especially if they combined university income with a modicum of private means or income from outside sources, as a proportion did; others lived from hand to mouth. To determine the precise income of most university teachers is impossible, but the rare survival of a household account book in my own family helps us to penetrate many dark corners of this enquiry.

My father, Zachary Nugent Brooke, had been a fellow of Caius and college lecturer in history since 1908. After four years' war service he returned to Cambridge in 1919 bringing his bride, Rosa Grace Stanton – they were married on 1 July 1919. From that date till his death in 1946 my parents kept a precise monthly

[137] See p. 7; the Goulding Browns lived in Brookside.
[138] See e.g. College Accounts in *Reporter* 1920–1; *Royal Commission* 1922, pp. 48–9.

account – striking a balance every year – of their income and expenditure. In an otherwise happy household its making caused them and their children some discomfort; but today it is a fascinating social document.[139] ZNB had had to be extremely careful in managing his affairs in early life and the precision of the account book reflected an anxious approach to finance: until I came closely to inspect it I had supposed that I had myself been much better off as a don of the 1950s and 60s than he, because I had worried less about money. Prosperity is as much a matter of temperament as of economics, and comparisons are full of traps and pitfalls. Down to 1939 my parents had at least two living-in maids and other help besides; they sent three sons to public schools; and they built a house in the Wilberforce Road which noone who depended on an academic salary could contemplate buying in the late 1980s. They rarely travelled abroad; they did not have a second home; they had one car, which was expected to last, and no television; they rarely dined out; they were not extravagant in food and drink – save that special festivals were celebrated with bottles of exceptionally fine vintage port bought by my father as a bachelor before the Great War for less than three shillings a bottle. One can list many items which they enjoyed and which are beyond our dreams; many too which we take for granted which they would have reckoned they could not afford. The first lesson such an account book teaches us is that there is no answer to the question, were the dons of the 1930s better or worse off than those of the 1960s and 70s?[140] Our prosperity depends in great measure on our aims and aspirations. My parents felt themselves less well off than I do because they assumed that most of what they paid for was simply necessary; it was not the fruit of choice; whereas I reckon to have exercised more selection in my expenses. But the plain fact is that many of the expenses they took for granted have not been within my grasp at all.

To a generation grown accustomed to a fluctuating inflation – particularly to one which has experienced the soaring prices of the 1970s and the leaping house prices of the 1980s – the first

---

[139] I am greatly indebted to my eldest brother Michael Brooke for the loan of the account book and permission to use it.
[140] I have omitted the 1980s since I take it for granted that there was a sharp decline in the 1980s: see below.

impression such an account book makes is one of extraordinary stability. There appears to be no inflation at all. Prices moved this way and that in the 1920s and 30s,[141] but more down than up; and the official statistics of economists are of little help in our enquiry since they hardly relate to the special needs and interests of academic society. My father's income (which included a very small element of private income of my mother) stood at just over £1,150 in 1920–1, the first year for which the summaries have been clearly worked out, and at £1,550 in 1945–6; and a good part of the difference was due to his advancement to a professorship in 1944. Their expenses fluctuated, commonly in the early years showing a modest credit balance, sometimes a deficit; in 1926–7 the income was £1,256-9-9, the expenses £1,256-8-0. In 1934 they built the house in Wilberforce Road, and at the same time their three sons were passing into their teens: school fees were at their height in the late thirties and in 1936–9 there were always deficits, though none of them very large – a shortfall of £218 in 1937–8 was exceptional, and this was the first of the years in which school fees ran over £300 a year.

This stability meant that my father and his generation had a much clearer idea what their money would do from year to year – a clarity which doubtless gave comfort to optimistic minds as much as it fed the pessimism of others. They never had the experience of the 1970s of seeing large mortgages rapidly eroded by the inflation of incomes and house values.

In 1921 they bought a substantial house in Milton Road (the main road to Ely) for £2,300. But in the 1920s and 30s it was reckoned that for peace and quiet and ready access both to town and country – to the old colleges and the new University Library – the region of Grange Road and the land to the west was the most desirable of all for dons to dwell in. Many retailers delivered, so that distance from shops was no disadvantage. In the years following the centenary of the emancipation of the slaves, 1933, St John's recorded the event by naming new roads after Wilberforce and Clarkson; and it may be that my father had some advantage in obtaining a lease from St John's of land in Wilberforce Road because he himself was a member of the

[141] For price movements in the 1920s, see charts in Deane and Cole 1967; Mitchell 1971, p. 726. I owe these references to Dr W. J. Macpherson.

college before he moved to Caius. The college agents, however, showed considerable suspicion of the architect's plans: a visitor to Wilberforce Road today can see at a glance that the fashion for flat-roofed houses was at its height; and my parents put themselves in the hands of one of the most distinguished Cambridge architects of the 1930s, H. C. Hughes, of Hughes and Bicknell, architect of many charming houses of the era, and of Fen Court at Peterhouse, his own college.[142] Their house is now an attractive monument of its age – though I fancy its roof has had to be extensively repaired more than once. At the time it inspired both admiration and amazement: 'Poor Zachary', commented G. M. Trevelyan, 'I cannot think what inspired him to this horror.' It gave the family much pleasure and my father much anxiety; for its cost far outran the sale price of their former dwelling at a time when school fees were threatening. The account book does not give details of the new house, but I believe that the old was sold for almost exactly what it cost, £2,300, and for the new he had to pay something over £3,000, which considerably eroded his private resources. Even so, it seems a remarkable venture to us: a house in the most desirable region of west Cambridge, with what amounts to eight bedrooms, allowing for two maids, the family, a guest room and a dressing room.

The hopeless fate of all attempts at detailed comparison between the economic standing of dons of the 1920s and 30s and of the next generation is well illustrated by two items of expenditure. The cost of 'servants' rose from just under £72 in 1919–20 to £105 in 1921–2 when a children's nurse was first needed, to £141-3-3½ in 1931–2 in the last year when there was a nurse. This sum comprised the wages of the nurse, cook and house-parlour maid, but not of the gardener who came one day a week; beyond this extraordinarily modest figure – which was yet characteristic of its age, for my parents would have been punctilious in paying the going rate – the staff enjoyed board and lodging whose cost cannot be identified in detail in the accounts. As the nanny departed, so the education bill began to mount, from £11–15 in 1926–7, as the eldest entered kindergarten, to £226-8-10 in 1934–5, when three sons were at preparatory school, to

---

[142] See pp. 190, 391.

£358-1-9 in 1938–9, when two were at boarding school and one at preparatory. The current cost of equivalent fees would be in the region of £7,500 per head, which is considerably beyond the inflation in academic incomes: this has been (very roughly) twenty-fold.[143] School fees are a very significant mark of the changes of recent generations. To academic parents who wished to provide appropriately for their children, public school for the boys was almost inevitable – though there were some who thought day school better for their health or their development, or for some other reason preferred to send their boys to the Perse Boys' School. For girls the situation was still ambiguous, but there was a growing body of opinion that girls should be treated the same as boys, and if the boys went to boarding school, so should the girls. For the next generation there was a wider choice, partly affected by politics. To those to whom political allegiance came first it was by the 1950s and 60s dogma that children should mingle in the state system and go to the local grammar school or (as time passed) to the comprehensive. To those to whom the children came first and who were convinced (rightly or wrongly) that the traditional boarding school education was still the best available, public school was to be preferred. For most there was a difficult – for many an agonising – decision in which the pros and cons of both had to be weighed. Cynical[144] politicians made the decision more baffling by separating the two systems even further – the socialists by trying to isolate the public schools and threatening to abolish them, a threat which for economic reasons has never looked very real; the conservatives by spending less and less on the state system and so making it less efficient.[145] But however all this may have been, the young academic could still find means of saving from his income to pay school fees if he thought it was right and wished to do so. The inflation of house prices in the 1980s means that a comfortable house in Cambridge now costs approximately one hundred times what it did in the

[143] A precise and meaningful comparison between the highly variable stipends of 1939 and present scales cannot be made. My father's professorial stipend combined with fellowship dividend in 1944–6 amounted to approximately £1,500 per annum; average professorial stipends are now in the region of £30,000 per annum.

[144] Or idealistic: the consequences were much the same; and in fairness the politicians commonly thought themselves idealistic, while to the troubled parents they naturally appeared cynical.

[145] This of course very much simplifies an extremely complex story.

1930s, and swallows all and more than all the savings from an income only twenty times inflated. If we turn back, and seek to compare the living standards of the 1930s, the 1950s and the 1980s, we face unanswerable questions. There is much that can be bought in the 1980s which did not exist in the 30s or even in the 50s; there were opportunities and services in the 1930s which have been beyond the dreams of postwar dons. If my father, looking forward from 1930, had forecast the way of life of his sons a generation later he would have thought them desperately impoverished; yet in a very real sense the don of the 1950s had more freedom of choice than his predecessor, even if the time to enjoy it was diminished by washing up and washing nappies; and the don of the 1980s or 90s, even if he or she cannot command the servants or the school fees which were 'inevitable' in the 1930s, nor the range of choice open to the don of the 1950s and 60s, none the less has an income which places him well above the majority of his fellow-citizens. But he cannot buy a house in west Cambridge in the 1990s, or perhaps in Cambridge at all;[146] and it is in the artisan dwellings off Mill Road that one now seeks out the aristocracy of young academic Cambridge.

V STUDENTS[147]

Reading men and rowing men

Different men have very different feelings about their years at the University. For many people it is an episode like another, the impressions or memories of which have been wholly obliterated by the more strenuous activities and the more ardent interests of later life. To others again their College life is an unforgettable adventure, every incident of which stands out in vivid colours thirty years afterwards. I belong emphatically to the latter class.

---

[146] Anyway on a single income; for many married academics, a double income is the only route to modest prosperity.

[147] It is widely held that 'student' is a term foreign to Cambridge: they are undergraduates or postgraduates (or graduates). 'In my youth', wrote Lady Keynes (Keynes 1976/1984, p. 114n), 'undergraduates were never referred to as students; that name was reserved for girls at Girton and Newnham. They could not properly be termed undergraduates until they were allowed the BA degree (in 1949 [1948]).' In late nineteenth-century texts, however, the word 'student' occurs in college regulations and the like. Significantly, the commonest use was 'men' – reading men, honours men, poll men, rowing men. My impression is that 'students' revived when Cambridge became less parochial (and less male) in the 1960s and 70s, and aware that 'students' exist universally in the rest of the world; and Cambridge is now full of Students' Unions. I use both words without apology.

Thus Maurice Amos, later Sir Maurice and an eminent lawyer.[148]

For me admission as an undergraduate of Trinity [in 1891] was the transition from a rather solitary and very unconventional life, to the vivacious world of a great national institution, offering in the fullest measure all that I most desired, the delightful companionship of a great variety of young men of my own age, sports of all kinds, a vivid intellectual life, endless conversation, great libraries, learning in floods; the sweet sense of conventionality, discipline, and decorum, symbolised by my blue gown, my surplice in chapel, the bell ringing for hall, the scrutiny of porters, the unirksome rules about gates and exeats, all of which made me feel at every moment of the day that I was a privileged member of one of the greatest of English Societies.

To these advantages I must add one that gave the framework to the whole, namely the great beauty of Cambridge, a beauty which at all times from my first day sang through my mind like counterpoint in music.

And yet, you know, I should never have admitted that I was completely happy at Cambridge. It has always seemed to me that a person who can speak of his University life as being one of unclouded happiness cannot have lived as ardently and as fully as I did. I not only found my place, but I was put in it. I was admitted to the society of gifted young men; new horizons of ambition and attainment opened out to me; but, at the same time I had to learn that the stable, composed as it was of my intimate friends and companions did not regard me as a candidate for any of the big events. I had what would be generally regarded as a successful University career ... but I remember when I left Cambridge agreeing with Ralph Wedgwood that our business in life was to make the best of a bad job ... I of course was a smug,[149] and lived with smugs, and a good half at least of the interest of our lives consisted in trying our teeth on new and manly studies. We got from the University what we were sent there to get – the education of companionship and learning.

Great social freedom reigned at Trinity; and this seemed to me

[148] His career lay mainly in Egypt where he held several leading posts in the Egyptian legal service; he was also for a time professor of law at University College, London. I am deeply indebted to his daughter Mrs Janet Whitcut for lending me his 'Reminiscences for my children', and allowing me to quote from them.
[149] A reading man. Wedgwood was Josiah's descendant and so cousin of the Darwins, later chairman of the LNER.

to be less true of the smaller colleges, it was I suppose partly due to our size.[150] By social freedom I don't of course mean freedom from reasonable college discipline, but that we were free from the social tyranny of any one set of people or of any one kind of tastes. The eminent cricketers and oarsmen did not rule the college; they were merely one set among others, whom many of their fellow undergraduates did not even know by sight. Conversely of course this was equally true of the future Prime Ministers and Astronomers Royal. There is another important respect in which Trinity differs from some other educational institutions, and that is in the preeminence enjoyed among us by young men of comparatively mature mind. The head boys of the great public schools came up to Trinity already better trained in mind, and with wider interests than many so called educated men.[151] By the time they had reached their third or fourth year they were already making themselves felt as men of character and intellect, and were creating throughout wide circles of the college, something of the atmosphere of an adult society. More particularly I am thinking, in my own time, of such men as Theodore Llewellyn Davies, Bertrand Russell, Charles Sanger, George Moore, and Ralph Wedgwood.[152]

It was partly I think this flavour of an almost grown-up aristocracy which prevented the corporate spirit of the college taking childish forms and perpetuating after its due time the extravagantly tribal life of a public school or of some small colleges. Though I confess that when I go back there now, I am amazed at the apparent youthfulness of the happy wearers of the blue gown, I still regard Trinity as a world not of boys but of men.[153]

Maurice Amos was looking back from the 1920s at Trinity in the 1890s; and the friend of Bertrand Russell and G. E. Moore had no ordinary experience of undergraduate life. None the less it is an observant and authentic impression of a successful smug.

In his satirical view of university society of 1865, Leslie

---

[150] It has frequently been observed that smaller colleges give more intimacy, but less range of choice in seeking friends and congenial groups. The shy student has often been more at home in the small college.

[151] Amos himself had never been to school; he had been unconventionally educated by parents and tutors.

[152] For this circle see Levy 1979/1981, chap. 5, esp. pp. 150–1.

[153] M. S. Amos, 'Reminiscences for my children', pp. 73–5. The book is not dated, but on p. 185 he speaks as if 1919 were five years in the past, i.e. as if this, the final section, was written *c*.1924.

Stephen imagines an encounter with a country clergyman come to a vote of the Senate.

> He tries to persuade you that he has come to save the Church, or to secure the adoption of a petition against the abolition of church-rates, or of a scheme for theological education. But, after half a sentence of due wisdom, he inquires, –
> 'How about the University boat?'
> He scarcely knows whether he says *placet* or *non placet* to the inquisitive proctor, who demands his vote; and half-an-hour later you find him puffing gallantly along the tow-path in a crowd of undergraduates, and panting out that nobody now can row such a stroke as Jones of Trinity. He puts aside your feeble efforts to amuse him by a congenial discussion on Hebrew roots or the National Society, and plunges with amazing avidity into half-forgotten details of boating 'shop'. He rows his old races over again, and gives you prescriptions for restoring Cambridge to its old pre-eminence on the river ... Tomorrow he will be again a domestic parson, teaching a Sunday school. Today he has got back into his old life. He resided at the University for, say, 800 days, excluding Sundays and vacations. Of those, he passed 790 on the river, and during nine of the remainder he was laid up with a strain caused by his exertions. The remaining day, which he wasted in lionizing his mother and sisters, he will regret as long as he lives ... He bitterly grudged the hour which he daily devoted to the process of being 'crammed' for his degree ... After all, this is not an exaggerated account of a certain not uncommon type of undergraduates. Their sphere of thought is somewhat limited; but they are very good fellows, and are excellent raw material for country parsons, or for any other profession where much thinking power is not required.[154]

This is satire written by a boating man; fanciful but if read imaginatively not misleading.

Sport

When Wordsworth was at Cambridge in the 1780s, he paid almost as little heed as Stephen's boating parson to his formal course, though he read widely all manner of literature not in the

---

[154] Stephen 1865, pp. 18–20.

syllabus. But his sports were field sports, sought out for himself in the fens and by the river.[155] The rich played real tennis and hunted; they mingled with the not-so-rich at Newmarket. The first college boat clubs were founded in 1825; the University Boat Club followed in 1827.[156] But for a long time rowing was the only organised sport. In 1852 Caius sold a substantial plot of agricultural land to form Fenner's Cricket Ground; and in the 1860s and 70s football began to spread out of Parker's Piece. As the public schoolboys flooded into Cambridge in the late nineteenth century, they brought with them the urgent demand for sport. Charles Kingsley, Regius Professor of Modern History in the 1860s, preached muscular Christianity as well as lecturing on history. But the cult of athletics, so far as we can now discern, was essentially student-led, like many of the revolutions in nineteenth- and twentieth-century Cambridge. The students demanded ground for cricket, rugger and soccer, and specially built courts for fives and squash; they rebelled against daily attendance in chapel; they demanded proper tuition, and even (with a more delayed success) proper college libraries; they rejected the presence of women in the university; and they established entertainments for themselves and their families of great sophistication – they founded May Week and the Footlights. Above all, they thundered at one another in the Union Society – which, founded in 1815 and the seedbed of politicians and preachers past counting, is the most venerable of numberless student societies. Generalisations thus stated must be superficial. The government of college and university was securely in the hands of the dons until the 1960s, though students often publicised their views, and occasionally made their point by rioting.[157] Leslie Stephen himself was a tutor in Trinity Hall in the 1850s and 60s very soon after he had been a schoolboy and a student: he was elected to a fellowship immediately on graduation in 1854, ordained deacon in 1855 (priest in 1859), a tutor in 1856. He made his first ascent in the Swiss Alps in 1857 and in the 1860s was a leading figure in forming the new passion for rock climbing.

---

[155] *Prelude* (1850 edn), esp. III, ll. 64–75, 251–8; Moorman 1957, chap. IV.

[156] Scott 1927, pp. xiv–xv. For Fenner's, below, see Brooke 1985, p. 252.

[157] Or by making a hubbub in the Senate House, as in 1840 (Romilly 1967, p. 204). The Union Society is a purely debating society; the Cambridge University Students' Union represents student opinion and has a role in university government (see pp. 556, 559).

Meanwhile he was fostering his college's prowess in rowing and athletics as well as taking a proper interest in his men's education.[158] It was this rapid transition from student to don and the natural sympathy between like and like which enabled the very rapid influx of public school fashions into late nineteenth-century Oxbridge. Needless to say tutors were not all young, even if they had once been; but many recalled their younger days and the tutor with something of the schoolboy in him was a familiar part of the Cambridge scene. Nor was there any marked division between student and fellow in these activities: the young fellow and the reading man were novices in learning alike; and the young fellow might well row in the college boat till he was well on in his twenties.[159]

The late nineteenth century saw some very marked changes in the topography of Cambridge. The 1880s witnessed a rapid growth of houses, varying from artisan dwellings to substantial middle-class family homes designed to house Victorian families of children and maids. They sprang up on every side, though never on the scale of north Oxford. To the north-east and east they are relatively modest; to the west, especially as the nineteenth turned into the twentieth century, one finds the largest. They were built to house the patriciate of Cambridge, and also the new married dons, especially the more prosperous. But one of the most marked changes in the topography of Cambridge was the spread of sports grounds, both university grounds and college grounds. Most characteristic of all of the new types of building of the late nineteenth century are the boat houses: on a stretch of the Cam from Chesterton Road to the gas works over half a mile in length, with a small number of civic club houses in their midst, the university and college boat houses represent a most impressive monument to a great Victorian cult which still flourishes, hardly abated. Stephen's friend truly regarded Cambridge as a place where one rowed; many a man came there in the late nineteenth and early twentieth centuries to row, to play football, to pursue athletics – paying a modest attention to the academic nature of the place. This is no longer so: everyone comes with a tripos

---

[158] Maitland 1906, pp. 53, 55, 58 and chaps. 5–6 passim; *DNB*.
[159] E.g. E. S. Roberts of Caius rowed till he was 28 (Scott 1927, pp. 83–5, 91, 181; cf. Venn, VI, 505, 510).

ahead and an array of A levels behind. Competition has driven out the professional athlete.[160]

If the cult of sport was a reminder that schooldays were not far behind, the dogma of the tutors that some measure of discipline was essential for the well being of the young was also closely related to the common ethos of school and college. The puzzle was how to exert discipline on a mob of young men used to the self-government of the prefectorial system, who suddenly found themselves in the much greater freedom of Cambridge. The answer lay in the college chapel. The rules for attendance must be rigorously enforced; or so some thought, for there were never wanting those who felt compulsory chapel to be in some sense a paradoxical notion. To the pious don regular attendance seemed the right way to preserve the Christian character of the place; to those who cared little for chapel – or had observed that since 1856 there were Jews and Dissenters, and downright unbelievers, in the place – early morning chapel, or the signing of a register, ensured early rising, which was the heart of the matter. But we have contemplated compulsory chapel in its heyday and in its decline on another page.[161]

Triposes

The first number of *Granta*, 18 January 1889,[162] quoted a worthy governor of Virginia of 1671. ' "Learnyng ... has brought disobedience and sects into the world, and printing has divulged them. God keep us from both." We belong to no sect... Providence and lecturers have kept us from learning. Our print, therefore, is at least innocuous.' Its innocence of these vices hardly deceives us, especially when we find *Granta* constantly revealing the influence of King's, the one college at that date whose recruits all had to be reading men, or at least to be enrolled for triposes.[163] Indeed, it shows sound inside knowledge of King's, offering 2 to 1 on Austen Leigh for provost;[164] he was duly elected.

---

[160] Cf. e.g. Fairbairn 1931. None the less a very high level of quasi-professional athletic standards is characteristic of the 1990s.

[161] See pp. 111–19.   [162] p. 2.   [163] See p. 35.

[164] *Granta*, 25 Jan. 1889, p. 4.

In the middle of the century more than half the students in Cambridge were poll men, reading for the ordinary degree.[165] In the late nineteenth century the proportion slowly declined. Precise figures are difficult to find, but those from one moderately intellectual college, Caius, will show the pattern.[166] Of those entering in the late 1880s between a third and a half left with an ordinary degree or none at all: the yearly average was 15 for the pass, 11.6 for no degree, out of yearly totals averaging 63. By 1907–11 the proportions had actually risen – though perhaps the onset of war affected the careers of the last intake at least – to 27.4 pass men per year, 14 with no degree, out of yearly averages of 87.8. By the 1930s the pass men had fallen to 10 per cent, the failures to less. By the 1950s the pass men are still 10 per cent, the failures now 4 per cent. By 1967–71 the pass men had disappeared – they have been reduced to one a year, the result of examination failure by men entered for a tripos. The failure rate was still roughly 4 per cent; it would be much lower now.

Down to the 1860s there had been no university entrance examination, though all candidates had to sit the Previous examination early in their careers. There was a spectacular gap, furthermore, between the standard of teaching mathematics in most public schools and the first rungs of the ladder of the Mathematical Tripos, still the flagship of the tripos flotilla.[167] Nor was there any college entrance exam, as Winstanley pungently observed:

> One consequence of this failure of the colleges to honour their responsibilities was the domestication of gross ignorance in a home of learning. 'Crammers' did a flourishing trade in pushing young men along the road to a degree, but the journey was frequently slow, and often never finished. And as there was so much ignorance, there was a general reluctance on the part of the authorities seriously to increase the difficulty of the ordinary degree course; it was feared that many young men, better born than educated, might thereby be discouraged from coming to Cambridge, and this was thought undesirable, as the University

[165] Winstanley 1947, p. 147.   [166] Brooke 1985, pp. 308–10.
[167] Winstanley 1947, pp. 144–6.

still attached great importance to its connection with the upper classes.[168]

It may be so; and Trinity still recorded in the University Calendar its representation in the House of Lords down to the 1960s. But in a wider sense the university was expanding rapidly from the 1870s, and one might suppose that the colleges could afford to set higher standards. Standards undoubtedly rose, but slowly; and it is not at all clear whether rising standards in the schools, better teaching in the colleges and the university, rising admission standards or changing fashions among the young had the most to do with it. What is clear is that colleges never felt till very recent times that they were secure of a steady flow of good recruits. Some colleges had more than they could cope with; others suffered alarming declines; the figures show strange and often unaccountable variations.[169] Yet even today, when entry is highly competitive and the word goes round the schools how difficult it is to find a place in Oxbridge, the college admission tutors and directors of studies are in a constant state of fluctuation between anxiety and euphoria. How much more so must it have been in the 1870s and 80s as they looked earnestly to see if the good schools would view them with favour.

For those who pursued honours in a tripos, mathematics was still the highway: in 1870 115 men received honours in mathematics; 66 in classics; 15 in moral sciences, 9 of them from Trinity or St John's; 17 in natural sciences; 23 in law – or law and history, as it had just become.[170] As the years passed, the numbers taking the Maths Tripos did not decline, but they became an ever smaller proportion of the expanding total. Classics grew rapidly, reflecting the prestige of the classical education in the schools and among the country's political élite in the late nineteenth and early twentieth centuries. In the 1880s natural sciences leapt forward and by the 1890s were even with maths. Moral sciences alone stayed small. Meanwhile newcomers were arriving. From 1874, theology, never large but steadily growing, from 20 in 1874 to 35 in 1910.[171] In 1875 the brief union of law and history was

---

[168] Winstanley 1947, p. 147.   [169] See Appendix 1 below.

[170] In these figures, taken from Tanner 1917, I have not counted *aegrotats*, those who were allowed to pass though ill, on the basis of their previous record.

[171] 35 in part I; 15 in part II: Tanner 1917, pp. 812, 844.

dissolved, and both climbed steadily their separate paths. Hitherto the preparation for some triposes had not been lengthy and it was possible for an able man to take two or three or even four; but this became increasingly difficult and was replaced by a new opportunity for combining different disciplines. Triposes were divided into two, so that a candidate might take half of one and half of another. By 1910 almost all triposes had been thus divided; and the popularity of law, especially for those who had not flourished elsewhere, is marked by the figures in 1910: 30 in part I, 60 in part II, 41 of whom scored third classes.[172] The History Tripos opened with 9 successful candidates in 1875. In the late 1880s it began to mount: 28 men and 8 women in 1888; 92 and 23 in part I in 1910, 83 and 18 in part II.[173] In 1878 semitic languages made its debut, with four examiners and one candidate, to whom they awarded a first; an identical statistic was achieved in the Indian Languages Tripos in 1879. From 1895 they were united in oriental languages, but the numbers only once rose above three or four – to five in 1896 – and in 1910 sank to two examiners and one candidate.[174] In 1886 came medieval and modern languages, a late developer, for numbers only began to multiply in the late 1890s, and then chiefly among the women: in 1895 11 men and 17 women, in 1910 29 men and 33 women.[175] These figures illustrate very clearly the importance of college involvement and college teaching in developing new triposes. Girton and Newnham comprised a very small proportion of the student population, but they fostered the teaching of languages and prospered in them. In 1895 6 women got firsts in MML, in 1910 10.[176]

In 1894 7 candidates sat for the new Mechanical Sciences Tripos, in 1910 35. The last newcomer before the Great War was economics, with 5 men and 5 women in 1905; in 1910 11 men and 7 women took part I, 9 and 3 part 2.[177] But economics was still not all it might appear to be; for the solitary first in part II in

[172] Tanner 1917, p. 894.
[173] Tanner 1917, pp. 895, 903, 936–7.
[174] Tanner 1917, pp. 938, 942, 946–50.
[175] Tanner 1917, pp. 951, 956, 970–1.
[176] Tanner 1917, pp. 956, 971; and see below, pp. 431–2.
[177] Tanner 1917, pp. 972, 980–1, 986.

1910, W. G. Constable of St John's, was later to be an eminent art historian and first director of the Courtauld Institute.

Women, May Week and the Footlights

In the early 1870s the new colleges of Girton and Newnham were given a cautious welcome by many of the more enlightened Cambridge dons; and a significant nucleus offered them hospitality in the lecture room and helped them with examinations.[178] One might have expected that as they became a normal and accepted part of the scene, the doubts and hesitations would fade away – but the opposite happened. Support for their claims to membership of the university actually declined in the 1890s, and had not sufficiently revived by the 1920s for them to win full admission then, unlike in Oxford. They had to wait till 1947 for a grace of the Regent House to welcome them formally into the fold. The reasons for declining support at the end of the nineteenth century are not clear. But statistics tell us something. In 1897 a referendum was promoted among the undergraduates on the eve of the formal vote of the Senate. There were about 3,500 in all at the time, of whom 2,137 were reckoned to have voted against any concession to women, 298 in favour. In the Senate 1,707 voted against concessions, 661 in favour.[179] This was a large vote and the old members – the 'country clergy' of legend – turned out in force.[180] It is evident that opinion among senior members was much more evenly divided than among the juniors. This prompts two reflections. First of all, the undergraduates of 1897 included many who were voting members of the Senate in the early 1920s. The second is that it is likely that the student vote carried considerable weight. In the 1970s the admission of women to colleges was a student-led revolution, however little notice many dons took, or thought they were taking, of student opinion. But certainly then, and – one may well suppose – also in the 1890s, college tutors took careful note of student preferences; for they were hungry for good recruits and sensitive to their wishes.

[178] See pp. 303, 309, 316.
[179] Hewison 1983, p. 27; *Reporter* 1896–7, p. 985 and see p. 325; for 1947, see p. 327.
[180] Cf. Cornford 1908, pp. 16–17.

It is not so clear why the student vote in 1897 was so overwhelming. It seems that for many the place of Girton and Newnham was peripheral to their notion of the place of women in Cambridge. In May Week parents, sisters, relatives and friends came in great hordes from the 1880s on. H. C. Porter has traced with delicate precision the growth of these festivities.[181] The May Races began in the 1820s. By the 1860s an American observer noted that 'An army of Amazons take Cambridge by storm in the month of May, and grey old Alma Mater puts on her best dress and sets her parlour in order, to receive her guests.'[182] The first May ball is recorded in 1866, and was 'organised by the Trinity First Boat ... probably in a local hotel'.[183] The balls rapidly spread and were accompanied by other entertainments, especially concerts, by CUMS (the Cambridge University Musical Society, founded in 1843) and in the colleges. The summer festival had in former times been attached to Commencement – the ceremonial entry into degrees;[184] but by the 1870s Commencement was in retreat. Bumps, balls, concerts and parties grew apace; and by the 1880s and 90s May Week had become a notable display of conspicuous consumption, as it has remained ever since, save when eclipsed by war. It was then the one season at which the masculine young men admitted women to their company, with evening dresses and chaperones. Today it is the one season of the year when the impoverished students, women and men alike, discover unexpected resources – many, though far from all – and organise sumptuous balls whose cost would make their elders blench.

Down to 1881 May Week was untroubled by exams; the fact that pass exams tended to start at the end of May seems to have stimulated rather than hampered the hectic jollity of the weeks before. Triposes lay far away, mostly in January. In 1882 the university, hell-bent on educational reform, suddenly moved the main season of exams from January to May, sending May Week flying as they came. But not to a great distance, for May Week has been in June ever since. Nor was the motive of the reformers to put down the excesses of May Week, though some grumbled

---

[181] Porter 1987.   [182] Porter 1987, p. 46, quoting William Everett of Harvard.
[183] Porter 1987, p. 46.   [184] Porter 1988.

at them.[185] Their aim was to ensure that tripos candidates could have three years of study and (normally) no more, ending at the close of the Easter Term of their third year.

From the mid-1880s a new entertainment appeared among the festivities of May Week: the Footlights Revue. The club was founded in 1883, put on its first original operetta, 'Uncle Joe at Oxbridge', in 1885,[186] and was soon established as a major competitor to the examination rooms as the seedbed of fame for Cambridge men. A characteristic product of the pre-war years was Jack Hulbert of Caius (1910–13). In his own reminiscences, written sixty years later,[187] he portrays himself as an ardent rowing man, deeply involved in theatricals, who tried hard but failed to find time for any serious academic work. One of his directors of studies, Z. N. Brooke, told a different story.[188] Hulbert was a hard-working man increasingly involved in the Footlights, the ADC [Amateur Dramatic Club] and so forth, yet never entirely losing sight of the pass BA (including some history) among his goals. He remained all his days – for all the light-heartedness of his roles – an exceedingly hard-working pro-fessional actor. After the war his brother Claude came to Caius to read history, and idled his time alike at his books and in the theatre. It was widely thought that Claude had more natural talent than his brother, as an actor if not as a historian. But his attitude was a worry to Jack, who confided his concern to Z. N. Brooke. For, said he, Claude has to learn that hard work is of the essence of our profession. In spite of what he said in his reminiscences, Jack Hulbert as an undergraduate clearly saw academic work as a stimulus to more serious work elsewhere: the musical comedy of the 1920s and 30s owed a little to the stimulus of a Cambridge degree.

The poll on the place of women in Cambridge took place in May 1897. On 10 June the Footlights presented one of their most elaborate and sophisticated inventions, *The New Dean*, a por-trayal of Cambridge in 2000, with a woman Vice-Chancellor and a female regime. It had clearly been in the making already before

---

[185] Porter 1987, pp. 47–8. [186] Hewison 1983, esp. pp. 9–10.
[187] Hulbert 1975; cf. Brooke 1985, p. 295; Venn, IV, 117; V, 114.
[188] This is based on personal reminiscence.

the vote, and was very much to the taste of many in Cambridge at the time; so much so that it was revived in 1900 and 1904. Its plot owes something to Tennyson's *Princess* and the *Princess Ida* of Gilbert and Sullivan. A rich American has produced a vast subsidy to save the university from ruin, and has set up 'a woman's government'. The Vice-Chancellor marries the benefactor; and the new dean, Emily Bellingham, marries an undergraduate, thus breaking the rules. The Bedmakers' Union stages a strike, and their leader, Mrs Rugginshaw, assumes the role of dean, while Emily Bellingham becomes her maid; the dons, who have no standing in the new regime, are found places among the gyps. The opera ends, a little like *Iolanthe*, with all the women officials of the university marrying men and resigning their posts.

> Now feminine rule is ended, once more to men we bow
> For guidance and light: and acknowledge their right
> To rule us as they know how.[189]

May Week is still with us, a striking symbol of continuity, and so are the Footlights. Indeed, they have won some of their greatest triumphs in the last twenty years. The music at the balls has changed in taste and volume; but many of the trappings would seem not unfamiliar to revellers from the 1890s. Yet one could hardly conceive Jonathan Miller or John Cleese as characters in *The New Dean*. The male society of the 1890s has gone; Cambridge in the 1980s and 90s is a mixed university, however many vestiges of its past remain.[190]

---

[189] Hewison 1983, pp. 27–9.   [190] See pp. 526–33.

Chapter 9

WOMEN 1869–1948

PREPARATION[1]

At the end of *Bleak House* we are told that Mrs Jellyby 'has been disappointed in Borrioboola-Gha, which turned out a failure in consequence of the King of Borrioboola wanting to sell every-body – who survived the climate – for Rum; but she has taken up with the rights of women to sit in Parliament ... a mission involving more correspondence than the old one.'[2] In 1853 the entry of women to parliament and Downing Street was still remote; but even Dickens had noticed that such issues were under discussion. The most earnest and the deepest were the discussions on women's education. It had been widely observed that women novelists had made a unique contribution to English literature; it impinged even on many men that women had much every way to contribute to the nation's culture, if they had but the opportunity. Serious efforts were made to provide schools for girls, first informally, then, from the 1840s and 1850s, on a more permanent base.[3] The provision was exceedingly inadequate, and the opinion that formal schooling was wrong for girls was widely held in Victorian England. The stereotype Victorian attitude portrays the girl as a potential wife and mother, bred to domestic arts, to attracting a husband, to providing him with a well-run home, a decorative wife, and children who might occasionally be seen and never heard. Needless to say this is no more than a caricature, and when one allows for all the fervour of

---

[1] In preparing this chapter I have been especially indebted to Gillian Sutherland: see e.g. Sutherland 1987, 1990; and also to Betty Wood and Rosalind Brooke. For its theme see also McWilliams-Tullberg 1975.
[2] *Bleak House*, chap. 67.
[3] Cf. Sutherland 1987, pp. 92–3 and nn. 2–4; Fletcher 1980.

prejudice which the progress of women's education had to face, it remains abundantly clear that there were many women and men in the 1860s and 70s ready to be convinced and converted to its value once they saw it at work. Girton and Newnham were founded in the years round 1870 against great odds; their first years were full of struggle, disappointment and anxiety. But they survived and very soon prospered. In spite of the fact that the doors of the British universities were opening and competition growing with remarkable speed – in spite of the foundation of three colleges for women in Oxford – numbers at Girton had risen to 180 by about 1900, by which date over 750 students had passed through its corridors, and at Newnham to 165.[4] Two colleges were founded in Cambridge rather than one primarily because Miss Davies and Henry Sidgwick had different approaches, different backgrounds, different philosophies. But they agreed in a fervent belief that women should have education, and university education, comparable to men. They would have accepted the statement of this belief by George Eliot when she heard in October 1869 that Miss Davies had established in Hitchin the college which was later to become Girton.

> I have a strong conviction . . . that women ought to have the same fund of truth placed within their reach as men have; that their lives (i.e. the lives of men and women) ought to be passed together under the hallowing influence of a common faith as to their duty and its basis. And this unity in their faith can only be produced by their having each the same store of fundamental knowledge. It is not likely that any perfect plan for educating women can soon be found, for we are very far from having a perfect plan for educating men. But it will not do to wait for perfection.[5]

It is a striking summary of the faith she shared with Emily Davies, and with some modifications with an immense multitude of men and women of liberal sentiments today. Miss Davies' initiatives were extremely unconventional, and she valued conventional sentiments – where they did not interfere with her

---

[4] Bradbrook 1969, pp. 28 (180 in 1902), 56; *Newnham College Register, 1871–1950* (Cambridge, 1964), I, 145–70.
[5] George Eliot, *Letters*, V, 58, quoted in Sutherland 1987, p. 91; cf. Mandell Creighton, above, p. 257.

views on women's education – all the more for that. She greatly appreciated George Eliot's encouragement; but she knew that George Eliot had reservations about compelling women to sit examinations and about other parts of her scheme, and she took pains to avoid it being too publicly known that she was in touch with anyone so unrespectable.[6] The whole incident is a striking reminder that the foundation of Girton was part of a national movement. It happened in Hitchin and came near to Cambridge in 1873; but it came to Cambridge almost by chance. In contrast, Newnham came from within.

In 1871 Henry Sidgwick invited Anne Jemima Clough to come to Cambridge to preside over the residence he had acquired in 74 Regent Street for women coming from afar to hear lectures organised for them. Next year they moved to Merton Hall – the ancient Cambridge house of which the School of Pythagoras forms the medieval core. In 1875 the first Hall of Newnham College was ready for occupation. Thus the founder of Newnham was Henry Sidgwick, already widely recognised as a pillar, even if an unorthodox pillar, of the Cambridge establishment.[7]

But this contrast hides a more complex pattern. Emily Davies came from without, and remained something of a stranger in Cambridge all her days; yet she knew from the outset that she needed allies within the citadel, and they were very much the same people who helped Sidgwick in his ventures. Miss Clough was already 51 when she came to Cambridge; she was the sister of Arthur Hugh Clough, poet and principal of University Hall, London, who had died in 1861, and she was herself an established educationist who had set up lectures and classes for girls in Liverpool, her home city, Manchester, Leeds and Sheffield. By 1867 she had created the North of England Council for the Promotion of the Higher Education of Women, and this was one of the inspirations which led Owens College, Manchester, to consider admitting women in 1869 – and so to the admission of women to the Victoria University comprising Manchester,

---

[6] See Bennett 1990, pp. 252–4 for Miss Davies' meetings with George Eliot and the areas of agreement and disagreement between them.
[7] See pp. 14–19; Phillips 1979, pp. 3–5.

Liverpool and Leeds when it was formed in 1878.[8] Sidgwick (himself a Yorkshireman) and several of his colleagues had met her through these lectures, and been impressed by her ability and dedication. She represented a very distinct national element in the formation of Newnham.

Thus women's education for its own sake was central to the interests of Miss Davies and Miss Clough; yet there is also a common background to their ventures which perhaps runs deeper still. The professions were astir; and it has been argued in a very persuasive paper by Gillian Sutherland that this is the essential background to the founding of Girton and Newnham. Schools became an increasingly formal and institutionalised preparation for many professions; and girls came to be involved in this as well as boys. 'The century 1780–1880 saw a transformation of attitudes to educational qualifications and to schooling *as a whole*. It was only then that education became a formal institutionalised process, its stages marked by competitions and prizes. The enthusiasts for women's education find places naturally, both in terms of interests and ideals, in this larger development.'[9] These dates emphasise how slowly effective reform came to Cambridge. But by 1870 it was really on the move; and the ringleaders were ready to welcome the arrival of women – to travel all the way to Hitchin to lecture to them or to invite them to attend their own lectures. By 1873 many doors had been opened in Cambridge itself.

Within Cambridge there was another kind of preparation, for the number of university wives who shared their husbands' interests had begun modestly to grow. It was often alleged that before 1860[10] the only academic wives were married to heads of

---

[8] On Miss Clough see below, pp. 311–14; Clough 1897; Hamilton 1936, chaps. 4, 8; Kelly 1981, pp. 35–6; *DNB*. On the admission of women, Hamilton 1936, p. 75, who points out that Newcastle admitted women in 1875; Kelly 1981, p. 58 gives 1871 for Owens and Newcastle. But in practice women entered Liverpool (in large numbers) in 1882, and Owens in 1883 (ibid). Even then they were excluded from the Liverpool Medical School until after 1903 (Kelly 1981, p. 131).

[9] Sutherland 1987, p. 106.

[10] Or some later date: it is a very common error to offer 1872, 1877, 1878 or 1882 as the earliest possible year for the marriage of fellows. See Brooke 1985, p. 224 and n.4. The *locus classicus* for the narrow circles of academic wives is J. W. Clark's account in Shipley 1913, pp. 17–18, 46–51. But Clark's own uncle, Robert Willis, married the daughter of Charles Humfrey, a highly successful local architect, and this was not the only marriage between town and gown (cf. Brooke 1985, pp. 203–5 and refs.; for Humfrey, ibid. p. 204 and n. 58).

houses or professors, and that the two groups never mingled. Female society was never quite so confined; and the number of professors was growing. From 1860 they were joined by wives of college fellows, though many colleges kept their fellows celibate until the 1870s or 80s. Caius alone swept all obstacles to marriage away in 1860; Trinity Hall, after a spirited debate, allowed a few to marry.[11] Thus it was in the drawing room of the wife of a fellow of Trinity Hall – Mrs Millicent Fawcett, no less, the future queen of the suffragists – that the meeting took place in December 1869 which was to lead to the founding of Newnham. The gathering included at least one head of house and several professors – and Mrs Peile and Mrs Adams; the wife of a fellow of Caius, Mrs Venn; and the daughters of the redoubtable Benjamin Hall Kennedy, the scourge of innumerable schoolboys struggling to learn Latin, but one of the heroes of the admission of women to Cambridge.[12] Henry Sidgwick himself was in due course to marry Eleanor Balfour, a highly skilled mathematician and physicist who worked in the Cavendish with her brother-in-law, Professor Lord Rayleigh.[13] Mrs Sidgwick became for a time vice-principal, and later for many years principal of Newnham; and the example of a companionate marriage was visible for the husbands and wives of Cambridge to admire and emulate – or shun. For just as resistance to the admission of women lasted long and ran deep, so that full entry to the university was delayed until 1948, so many wives of dons conserved rather than modified the Victorian stereotype. Partly this was because they and their husbands had no wish to remould the conventions of the society in which they lived; partly it was because the don's wife who lacked university training felt at a disadvantage. Yet it ran deeper than that. Until well past the middle of the twentieth century Cambridge was a male university – however much most dons recognised and welcomed the presence of two notable colleges of women in their midst. The high tables of the men's colleges were male clubs, and vestiges of this status still linger. But the image has been modified more than many women could now readily credit. Down to the 1950s it was extremely rare for women to be

---

[11] Brooke 1985, pp. 223–7, esp. 224 n. 4; Brooke, Highfield and Swaan 1988, p. 272.
[12] Hamilton 1936, pp. 89–91.   [13] See pp. 19, 180.

admitted to high tables or Combination Rooms in men's colleges; and many of the leading women of Cambridge regarded this as part of the nature of things. Many more did not, especially those who participated in the life of the women's colleges. Lady Anderson, wife of the master of Caius from 1912 to 1928, had little education herself and prevented her daughter from enjoying any formal schooling, even though her husband was deeply involved in the service of both Girton and Newnham.[14] Her successor, Mrs Cameron, who presided over the master's lodge and was a central figure in the life of the college from 1928 to 1948, and a woman of high intelligence, sensitivity and charm, whose influence spread into almost every corner of it and who was deeply loved and revered by the community she ruled, would have regarded it as inconceivable that she should dine at high table or mingle in the society or the committees of the college. She was wholeheartedly loyal to a system which seems now, looking back, both chauvinist and archaic.

The role of the wives of masters and fellows remained ambiguous and ambivalent. Yet there came to be an increasing number who were themselves academic in their interests, including a number who were fellows in their own right; and their role and influence – though difficult to define – has been crucial in the reshaping of Cambridge in the twentieth century.

GIRTON

Thus the rise of Girton and Newnham was part of a movement both local and national. To adapt a saying of Gillian Sutherland, if Emily Davies had not existed, we should have to have invented her.[15] Yet she did exist, and in death as in life she cannot be ignored. She is indeed one of the heroic figures in Cambridge history: fiercely determined, firm as a rock, endlessly fertile in plans and schemes, ruthlessly persuasive, all at once friendly and formidable. Some who have written about her have adopted an apologetic tone: nothing could be more unnecessary. She has triumphantly survived attempts to idealise her as she survived her detractors in her lifetime. Henry Sidgwick was her natural ally, as

[14] See pp. 343–4.   [15] Sutherland 1987, p. 91.

they both clearly understood; but there were differences between them. 'I am sure it is generous consistency and not cruel mockery that makes you say you are willing to help us when your scheme is the serpent that is gnawing at our vitals ... ' she wrote in a famous letter to Sidgwick.[16] She had a vivid sense of style and knew well how to alienate her friends. Her own education had been spasmodic; she had little conception of scholarship; she never knew much of Cambridge – she escaped to London whenever she could. Yet Girton is her monument and she laid an indelible mark on the whole university. She was a person of quite exceptional stature.

Miss Davies was born in 1830 and spent her childhood in her valetudinarian father's vicarage at Gateshead, a loyal daughter of a conventional evangelical father. Mr Davies was a man of considerable intellectual gifts and her brothers received a good education: her favourite brother Llewellyn became a leader among the disciples of F. D. Maurice, and vicar of Marylebone for many years – hence Miss Davies' *entrée* to London – and principal of Queen's College, Harley Street. The sister received no formal schooling but much instruction at her parents' hands. Chance brought her early friendship with Elizabeth Garrett, Mrs Fawcett's elder sister, and the two plotted together Miss Garrett's heroic campaign to enter the medical profession. As Mrs Elizabeth Garrett Anderson she became a celebrated doctor and she and Miss Davies were leading figures in the circles of educational reform in London.[17] Her other principal ally was Barbara Leigh-Smith, Mme Bodichon, wife of an eccentric Algerian doctor, who divided her time between Algeria and a cottage in Sussex built to her own design, called Scalands. They formed a remarkable alliance of contrasting characters. Miss Davies was 'small and plain, her manner conventional, her face unrevealing between smooth bands of mouse-coloured hair', as she appeared to Miss Garrett on first encounter;[18] but a marvellous organiser, a first-rate public speaker – with a small voice of perfect clarity – unshakable in integrity and conviction. Miss Garrett was much

[16] Bennett 1990, p.137. This very readable and useful life is inclined to take an apologetic line. Bradbrook 1969 gives a very balanced appraisal of Miss Davies' qualities. Also useful is Stephen 1927.

[17] Manton 1965; Bennett 1990, pp. 16–18 and passim. [18] Bennett 1990, p. 17.

livelier and more intellectual, though she shared Emily Davies'
shrewdness and resolve never to be prevented from doing what
was right by the will of man. Mme Bodichon was charming,
ebullient, and mercurial: she espoused every cause in sight but had
neither the will nor the health to support any with real consistency. She was the perfect foil for Miss Davies, whose reproaches
she shrugged off without a murmur, and she could sometimes
reconcile her to her enemies by a little romancing.[19] She was also
well off and generous, and could save Miss Davies' enterprises
when in desperate need. Miss Davies regarded her as fellow
founder of Girton. It has sometimes been said that her role was
much less than this suggests, and that she was often obstructive
when Emily needed support.[20] Yet it is abundantly clear that her
friendship was necessary to Miss Davies, and that Mme Bodichon
performed the vital role of the friend to whom one could let off
steam. Most of us need a safety-valve, Miss Davies to an
exceptional degree; and Barbara Bodichon was much more than
that – a warm-hearted, impulsive, perceptive, generous supporter. Most visitors found Scalands and its regime extremely
uncomfortable and disconcerting; but for Miss Davies it was a
real home, the one place in which she could wholly relax.

Her first efforts were aimed, naturally enough, at finding a
place for women in the University of London; but it soon
became clear that this was unlikely to succeed. In the event the
portals were to be opened in 1878, when London looked like
being left behind in the growth of women's opportunities.[21] She
next made overtures to examining boards in Oxford and Cambridge, and, after many vicissitudes, made sufficient progress at
Cambridge to determine her to look there for a permanent
home.[22]

Early in her alliance with Miss Garrett, they sat at the feet of an
American physician, Dr Elizabeth Blackwell, who was very
urgent in the view that 'the idea of some separate and inferior
qualifications for women' must be rejected – a principle which

---

[19] The letters cited by Bennett, p. 75, as evidence of her duplicity seem to me rather to show her
romancing in ways she thought would bring the desired result. They prove, surely enough, that
she little foresaw that future historians would be able to read them. Cf. ibid., p. 115.

[20] Thus Bennett 1990, pp. 75–6 and passim.

[21] Harte 1979; Sutherland 1990; cf. Bingham 1987, p. 45.

[22] Bennett 1990, esp. chaps. 7–9; Bradbrook 1969, pp. 15–28.

made much sense in the search for professional qualifications, as in medicine.[23] It was not so obvious to Henry Sidgwick and his friends that it made much sense in Cambridge. To achieve a Cambridge degree three hurdles had to be crossed. The Previous examination or Little-go was a kind of preliminary examination, intended to establish a basic standard in mathematics and classics.[24] The unambitious could then go on to the pass degree, a disorderly collection of fragments of learning, the haven of the 'poll men'. The reading men went on to honours, which by 1870 meant the Mathematics Tripos, classics, moral or natural sciences – under whose wings various satellite subjects like history took shelter.[25] If women were ever to achieve equality of educational opportunity with men, if they were ever to have professional qualifications which men would recognise and admire, if they were ever to be fully admitted to the University of Cambridge, then they must seek and win exactly the same qualifications as men. Hence the attraction of the Little-go, the pass degree and honours. To the pass degree Miss Davies never won access; but by stages she succeeded in winning the consent of the examiners, and of the university, for her girls to sit Little-go and tripos exams.

But these things were secondary to Henry Sidgwick and his colleagues. They included J. R. Seeley, who came back to Cambridge as Regius Professor of Modern History in the year that Miss Davies settled in Hitchin, and brought with him a powerful sympathy for her aims, soon to turn to exasperation, and Fenton Hort, the theologian, so conveniently stationed at St Hippolyts near Hitchin when she arrived.[26] They sought above all to provide serious instruction for women; and that meant lectures and classes on intellectual themes. Examinations might come later – and they reckoned full admission would only come when the women had been so firmly installed in Cambridge as to be readily accepted. The Little-go needed reforming, the pass degree even more so; they were red herrings across the path. These men would willingly lecture for Miss Davies, but on their

[23] Bennett 1990, p. 27.
[24] It was normally taken in the second year, and included an examination in Paley's *Evidences of Christianity*. On it see Winstanley 1947, pp. 144–5.
[25] See pp. 293–7.
[26] Wormell 1980, pp. 58–60; Bennett 1990, pp.89–91, 93–4, 103–4, 114, 119–20; Hort 1896, II, 57–8, 111, 113–15, 117–18; cf. ibid. I, 357.

own terms; and when she dictated to them they were naturally rebellious. To a party of lecturers who had nobly agreed to work for her and totally disregarded her instructions, she cried out: 'I should like it to be understood that I am not ready to carry out any other idea than the ones I have tried to explain.'[27]

In the end, both have proved right – though neither Miss Davies nor Professor Sidgwick foresaw how long the delay would be before their colleges received full membership of the university. Had they foreseen it, they might have despaired. Miss Davies was right that women had to be seen and accepted as full equals and partners with men before a male university could become a mixed university; and Henry Sidgwick was right in believing that Cambridge would accept infiltration much more readily than frontal assault – and that it would have been preposterous to refuse the many who might profit from the lectures which he and Miss Clough could arrange for the sake of the few who could immediately prove that women can achieve high honours.

The other principle which governed all Miss Davies' actions once she and her right-hand man, Henry Tomkinson, the business head of her committee, had chosen the site in Girton, was that every penny she could raise, and a good many more, should be spent on building.[28] She sat in Hitchin with five students, rising to fifteen by the time she moved to Cambridge – and plotted a building for several hundred. After the move to Girton, she wanted endowment, she would have liked research students, she sympathised with those who wanted a garden to civilise the setting of the college and do justice to the magnificent estate she had acquired; but all these things could wait. Not only so, but the building must above all comprise ample rooms for students. She would like to see a chapel and library – and she lived to see them. But they had to wait their turn. First things first: 'We need more schools, not churches,' she had said before the idea of a college came to her;[29] she never doubted the faith of her forebears, but students' rooms came before churches and chapels. She had endless battles with her committee, whose members tried often to

---

[27] Bennett 1990, p. 248, from Girton College Library, Emily Davies Papers, 1868.
[28] See esp. Bradbrook 1969, pp. 56, 59, 61–2, 65; Bennett 1990, pp. 133–4, 198–9, 238, 243.
[29] Bennett 1990, p. 36.

curb her enthusiasm for building, and especially with Lady Stanley, the most munificent of her supporters, who in the end provided the library.[30] Miss Davies lived to see the garden too: it was laid out with great sensitivity by Miss Welsh, one of her favourite protégées who was mistress of Girton for a time.[31] But for many years Miss Davies would not allow a penny of the money she had raised to be diverted to these ends, and was content to see her beloved college, the acme of architectural beauty in her eyes, surrounded by waste land and rubble. Miss Welsh, garden steward from 1883, with the aid of a special benefaction, laid out the hedges and the Honeysuckle Walk. Later on, writes Professor Bradbrook, 'more land was bought to the west, making over fifty acres. Then the full sweep of the Woodlands Walk was designed by Miss Welsh from the top of the new tower, and the beauty of her planting still remains – single trees on the lawns, glades and thickets beyond . . .'.[32] In 1912, long after Miss Davies' retirement, a special celebration was devised fifty years after she had come to London to begin her work for women's education; £700 was collected to mark the occasion, and she instantly handed it over to the secretary of the building fund.[33] She left Girton loaded with debt, but very amply provided with buildings; and buildings, she knew, were of the essence of a college.

NEWNHAM

It is hard to imagine two more contrasting characters than Miss Davies and Miss Clough, first principal of Newnham. Anne Jemima Clough had experience of organising committees and experience of teaching young girls.[34] But she had little of Miss Davies' flair for public meetings, appeals, and organisation. She was only like Miss Davies in her devotion to women's education and in being no academic herself: for formal teaching she depended utterly on friends in Cambridge and, very soon, on the best products of Newnham itself. Yet her own gifts were as rare:

[30] Bennett 1990, p. 198; Bradbrook 1969, p. 61.
[31] Bradbrook 1969, pp. 58, 63.
[32] Bradbrook 1969, p.63; cf. the lyrical passage, ibid. pp. 63–4.
[33] Bennett 1990, p. 238.
[34] For what follows, see Hamilton 1936, esp. chap. 8; Clough 1897; but esp. Holt 1987.

Fig. 9 Girton College, Emily Davies Court, part of the original buildings
designed by Alfred Waterhouse, completed in 1873

while Miss Davies was taking the train to London, Miss Clough
was sitting quietly in Newnham talking to her students. Her
pastoral gifts were quite exceptional. She was a born teacher who
taught her students everything but the maths and classics and

languages they came to Cambridge specially to learn. She taught them other things – for many of them equally precious. What did the apostles teach us, asked St Bernard of Clairvaux in a famous apostrophe? Not the art of tent-making, surely; they taught us how to *live*. If the role of the Cambridge tutor can be justified, a part of its meaning lies here.

Miss Clough was principal from the arrival of the first five in October 1871 in Regent Street and of the first 27 in Newnham in October 1875 until her death in 1892 in her early seventies. Among the last generation of students to complete her three years with Miss Clough was Catherine Holt, daughter of a Liverpool shipowner, niece of Beatrice Webb, and so a member of one of the notable female dynasties of Victorian England, the Potters.[35] Miss Holt was a lively, articulate, critical woman, and her letters home are a vivid source for the history of Newnham in the late 1880s and early 1890s. Her report of the principal's death in February 1892 is deeply moving.

> We are hoping they will not fill the Principal's place in our time, and I dare say they will let everything remain as it is till the Long Vacation. I do not think we could bear to have anyone else over us; it is hard enough to think that there is no one left here to care what happens to one when one has gone down, and welcome one if one came up again. She cared for each of us individually; she never forgot everything we told her about ourselves or our people; she made plans for each of us with wonderful insight into character and unfailing sympathy. During one's first two or three weeks she would come up several times to each new student's room and sit talking till she knew all about them and their surroundings; and after that she would never repeat a question nor get mistaken about any detail.[36]

In another woman such assiduous attention to the newcomer might have been merely fussy, and would have appeared so to the self-possessed young Liverpool patrician. In Miss Clough it evidently sprang from that deep and insatiable interest in other people, especially young people, which is the highest quality a

---

[35] See Caine 1988.
[36] Holt 1987, p.47. For a more critical view of Miss Clough, see Phillips 1979, p. 1.

teacher can possess.[37] Shrewdness and insight and an interest which was totally unselfish saved her from possessiveness or sentimentality; yet she was also human. 'The Principal has no acquaintances: everybody is a friend and a very dear one too. Somebody once told her an unpleasant story about a mutual acquaintance and she said at once "It's not true, my dear – and if it is, I don't believe it." '[38]

Miss Holt, the student, belonged to one of the notable dynasties of the age; Miss Balfour, treasurer of the Newnham Hall Company which had been engaged in building the first hall of the college in the early 1870s, came from another. Lord Salisbury was her grandfather, Arthur Balfour her brother; Lord Rayleigh, second Cavendish Professor, her brother-in-law. In October 1875 she witnessed the opening of the first hall; in December she became engaged to Henry Sidgwick.[39] She and her husband provided much that Miss Clough so evidently lacked: academic distinction and administrative skills. Some of the story is clearly known. Sidgwick Avenue not only records the contribution of the Sidgwicks to the making of Newnham; it was Henry Sidgwick's drive, generosity and diplomacy which made it possible to make the road at all, and so divert the passage of people and traffic so that they pass by and not through the college.[40] They also, and very obviously, provided academic leadership to the community, and gave it – gave both women's colleges indeed – respectability in the eyes of many Cambridge folk. How much the buildings owe to them is not so clear; and it would be fascinating to know. Between them they chose an old acquaintance of Sidgwick, Basil Champneys, who was to design the group of early halls and the gatehouse and gate. The halls are in the 'Queen Anne' or Dutch red-brick style then fashionable; but in notable contrast, in taste if not in colour, to the 'red brick

---

[37] I have once witnessed it myself in a similar degree in perhaps a rather unexpected quarter, in my company commander in the Army School of Education in 1949, the late Major the Earl Wavell. I could claim only a small part of his quality, but I none the less learned more about teaching from him than from anyone else I have encountered, though I have had singularly good fortune in those who have taught me.

[38] Holt 1987, p.48.   [39] Hamilton 1936, pp. 119–20 and passim.

[40] See Hamilton 1936, esp. chap. 9; Phillips 1979, pp. 25–8.

Fig. 10 Newnham College, Sidgwick Hall, designed by Basil Champneys, completed 1880, with Clough dining-hall on left, 1888

and red terracotta imitation Tudor' of Girton.[41] Since Champneys had no aversion to Tudor or Gothic as his Divinity School – or the John Rylands Library in Manchester – reveal, we may presume that the domestic style and the unit, ideal for a principal and tutors to preside each over a group of thirty students whom they could know intimately, and who could form a cell within the larger society of the college, was inspired by those who gave Mr Champneys his brief. The domestic aspect doubtless in part reflects Miss Clough's manner of life; whether the Dutch style owes more to her or to the Sidgwicks we cannot tell.

In 1879 Mrs Sidgwick became vice principal; in 1892 principal. Though Mrs Sidgwick was in some ways equally unlike Miss Davies, she nonetheless was a remarkable complement to Miss

[41] Pevsner 1970, p. 190. Champneys' work for Newnham is set in context in Watkin 1989 and Girouard 1977/84, pp. 70–6. He and Sidgwick were old acquaintances; but a dominant influence may have been that of Miss Mary Ewart, benefactor and member of the building committee (ibid. pp. 71, 73 and nn.25, 29 on p. 234).

Clough. 'Mrs Sidgwick I worshipped,' wrote M. A. Willcox, of the 1880 vintage.

> She was always remote, as I suppose happily married people are wont to be, and one felt in her the long line of privilege ... She was like an exquisite alabaster vase with the soul shining through. I think she came to care for me partly because she divined how very much I cared for her, but we never had the personal chitchat common between friends who are equals ... .[42]

GIRTON AND NEWNHAM AS COLLEGES

It has been the special mark of the colleges of Oxford and Cambridge that they were, and are, autonomous, endowed academic communities – utterly dependent on the universities for their *raison d'être*, yet to an extraordinary degree free-standing in material and intellectual endowment and in their government.

The new women's colleges needed money for building and money for endowment, and this involved a struggle which has never ceased. Neither Cambridge college found a benefactor on the model of Thomas Holloway, who spent over £600,000 on Royal Holloway College.[43] Gillian Sutherland has analysed the sources of support for Girton and Newnham. There were two significant groups: the Lancashire–Liverpool manufacturing and commercial connection, evidently a link with Miss Clough's original home, and the source from which Catherine Holt had sprung; and the liberal intelligentsia, strongly represented in Cambridge, led by Henry and Eleanor Sidgwick, Henry and Millicent Fawcett, Alfred and Mary Marshall, Kennedy, Bateson and J. N. Keynes.[44] Newnham's northern supporters included a strong Unitarian group, doubtless encouraged by the unsectarian nature of the college, in which there was to be no chapel. Girton's supporters contained many individual friends and acquaintances of Miss Davies, led by Barbara Bodichon and Lady Stanley of Alderley, who, after watching Miss Davies invest every penny she had won and a good many more in domestic quarters for students, built them a lab and a library.[45] The other most

[42] Phillips 1979, pp. 14–15.
[43] Sutherland 1987, p. 113 n. 32; cf. Bingham 1987, esp. p. 55.
[44] Sutherland 1987, pp. 97–9.
[45] Bradbrook 1969, pp. 60–1.

substantial of Girton's early benefactors was a case apart. 'In 1852 Jane Catherine Gamble, a wealthy spinster, was pursued to Italy by an adventurer named Henry Winkoff – not altogether without encouragement. He abducted her and held her in a palace at Genoa; but she kept him at bay, avoiding a fate worse than death, and Winkoff was sentenced to imprisonment for eighteen months.' When she died in 1879 she left £19,000 and various effects, including 'several trunks of manuscript plays of her own composition', to Girton, 'so that no man should benefit' from her wealth.[46] Such adventures were rare, and the endowment of the women's colleges was a ceaseless struggle.

For many years Newnham and Girton were governed by external committees of worthy well-wishers a little like boards of governors of schools or the councils of civic universities: perhaps more like the latter, since the staff of the women's colleges in due course came to play a significant role in their councils. In early days the mistress of Girton was not a member of the college committee.[47] To a fellow of any Cambridge college in the late twentieth century this seems unintelligible; yet in our schools the absence of much or any representation of the staff who really run it – and on whom its work and distinction depend – is still often accepted as of the order of things. Miss Davies held robustly to the Victorian view that the committee (which for many years met in London) should entirely comprise worthy people not involved in the day-to-day running of the college; she resisted the intrusion of the mistress on to the committee for thirty years. The secretary of the committee – that is, Miss Davies herself – was in her eyes the natural go-between. In earlier days she had said 'As the college grows it will tend more and more to be governed by the resident staff';[48] but while she remained secretary she became less and less enamoured of staff involvement in its government. She allowed two exceptions: when she herself was mistress and when Miss Welsh was mistress in the 1880s. She even resisted Miss Welsh's appointment to Council; but gave way with a good grace, merely observing it must set no precedent. When Miss Constance Jones became mistress in 1903, it was accepted as a

---

[46] Bradbrook 1969, p. 61; Bennett 1990, p. 198.
[47] Bradbrook 1969, p. 58; Bennett 1990, pp. 206–7.   [48] Bennett 1990, p. 207.

matter of principle that the mistress should be a member. Miss Davies alone resisted the decision; and when she was defeated recognised that her days were numbered. She never lost her fervent interest in Girton; but she no longer attempted to govern it.[49] In 1910 a staff representative was first nominated to the Executive Committee; in 1911 it became the College Council; in 1924 Girton received a charter which made mistress and fellows the nucleus of the governing body, although representatives of men's colleges and old students retained a modest place until full self-government came in 1952.[50] At Newnham a similar evolution had ended in 1917.[51]

Miss Davies looked to men to teach her students. From the first, the founders of Newnham looked forward to providing an element of teaching from within. At Newnham a cadre of young teaching lecturers was formed with remarkable speed. Thus in the 1880s Mandell Creighton, the first Dixie Professor and one of the founders of the History School, was in close touch with Alice Gardner, founder of history in Newnham – and their correspondence reveals Miss Gardner as a highly intelligent, widely read and shrewd interpreter of the needs of her students.[52] Her memory has been somewhat eclipsed by her most brilliant pupil, Mary Bateson, daughter of the master of St John's, himself a leading reformer and a patron of the women's colleges. Mary Bateson had the extraordinary distinction of being almost the only research student of F. W. Maitland but sadly died before her promise could come to full fruition.[53] Newnham was probably one of the best colleges in which to read history long before the subject had seriously penetrated some of the men's.[54] By the same token, it is noticeable that the newly formed Medieval and Modern Languages Tripos recruited in Newnham and Girton – where staff were provided – out of all proportion to their numbers.[55] But though Girton was a little slower than Newnham to develop its own teaching strength, it can in effect be said

---

[49] Bennett 1990, p. 207; Bradbrook 1969, pp. 58–9.
[50] Bradbrook 1969, pp. 59n, 70, 78.
[51] *VCH Cambs*, III, 494; the charter of 1917 was revised in 1951.
[52] Creighton 1904, I, 288–9, 295, 300, 303.
[53] See below. [54] See p. 229.
[55] See pp. 431–2.

that the women's colleges became serious centres of college teaching at very much the same time and by much the same process as the men's. Trinity apart, there was much formal lecturing and no college supervisions in men's colleges before 1870.[56] Many of the pioneers of college teaching were deeply involved in the formation of the women's colleges, from Henry Sidgwick down. In some respects the women were the pioneers whom the men came to imitate, and this is especially evident in their libraries. Once again Trinity was a notable exception.[57] But most men's colleges hardly thought of opening their libraries to undergraduates in the nineteenth century; and some, such as Caius, had to wait till the 1920s before students entered the library as of right.[58] Meanwhile Newnham from 1882 and Girton from 1884 began to form the splendid collections which make them still outstanding among the college libraries today.[59] Only 'a select few third-year students were permitted to use the University Library', so Mrs Quiggin, a student of 1899, was later to observe – and also that she had much later learned from her husband (a respectable fellow of Caius) that it was an acknowledged rendezvous for lovers to which chaperons were not admitted.[60] Even so, access to the University Library was limited; and women came to Girton and Newnham to read.

The transformation of the women's colleges from student hostels to academic colleges was not only a matter of bricks and mortar, of money and recruits; nor could it be accomplished simply by changes in statutes making them self-governing like men's colleges. They needed also to recruit fellows of academic distinction to give them the standing within and without which have made them – irrespective of the precise date when women received formal degrees – equal partners in the community of colleges. Newnham had a head start since its founders were academics; and in early days it won notable distinction in classics and was a pioneer among the colleges in the serious teaching and study of history. Jane Harrison (1850–1928) was a brilliant, flamboyant figure, a very notable student of Greek archaeology

[56] See chap. 2 passim, esp. pp. 70–2, 76–7.
[57] See Brooke, Highfield and Swaan 1988, pp. 244–5.
[58] See Brooke 1985, pp. 214–15, 254.
[59] B. A. Clough in Phillips 1979, p. 28; Bradbrook 1969, p.61.
[60] Phillips 1979, p.46.

and religion, who laid new foundations for the understanding of Greek society at much the same time that the formidable Disney Professor of Archaeology, Sir William Ridgeway (1853–1926), was laying different foundations.[61] It was said of Ridgeway that his friends found it difficult to recall exactly what his theories about drama and religion in ancient Greece comprised, save that they were at all points the opposite of Jane Harrison's.[62] On the whole her scholarship has worn the better; but both were notable pioneers, and Ridgeway has the melancholy distinction of leading the campaign which delayed the admission of women to the university.[63] A student of 1909 in Newnham recalled Jane Harrison as 'a most dramatic figure. In one's first term to be introduced – after dinner – to lectures on Orphic elements in Greek religion was quite an experience . . . Often a visible effect would be produced when a glittering shawl, worn by Miss Harrison round her shoulders and shrugged off at an exciting moment of recital, would fall in shimmering folds about her feet . . .'[64]

In history Alice Gardner laid the foundations, and Mary Bateson quickly won wide professional recognition. She bade fair to join her teacher F. W. Maitland among the immortals in legal and social history; but the fateful year 1906 carried both of them away. Of the second volume of her *Borough Customs* (1904–6) Maitland himself wrote:

> Such a book cannot make its mark in a couple of months, nor yet in a couple of years. It cannot attract the 'general reader'; it can be only a book for a few students of history. Moreover, Miss Bateson, a true daughter of Cambridge, felt such scorn for what she would call 'gas' that it was difficult to persuade her that a few sentences thrown in for the benefit of the uninitiated are not to be condemned by the severest taste . . . It was my good fortune to see this book . . . in manuscript, in slip, and in page. Good fortune it was. The hunger and thirst for knowledge, the keen delight in the chase, the good-humoured willingness to admit that the scent was false, the eager desire to get on with the work, the cheerful resolution to go back and begin again, the broad good sense, the

---

[61] See pp. 204–5; on Jane Harrison, see Steward 1959; Peacock 1988.
[62] Personal reminiscence from Z. N. Brooke.
[63] Cf. p. 376. [64] Phillips 1979, p. 86.

Fig. 11 Portrait of Miss Jane Harrison, by Augustus John,
in Newnham College

unaffected modesty, the imperturbable temper, the gratitude for
any little help that was given – all these will remain in my
memory, though I cannot paint them for others.[65]

If Girton started later it rapidly brought forth its own
harvest, especially in the 1920s and 30s when – lest it be thought
that women shone only in the humanities – it found peculiar
distinction in Dr Ann Bishop, FRS and leader in medical
research, and Dame Mary Cartwright, one of the leading
Cambridge mathematicians of our day.[66] Two scholars very
characteristic of Girton at its best were Eileen Power and Helen
Cam. Eileen Power was a fellow from 1913 to 1921. She helped
to build in Girton and Cambridge a tradition of social and

[65] Maitland 1911, III, p. 542.   [66] Bradbrook 1969, p. 70.

Fig. 12 Portrait of Dame Mary Cartwright, by Stanley Spencer,
in Girton College

economic history inherited from Archdeacon Cunningham; but
her first major book, *Medieval English Nunneries* (1922), rather

reflected the influence of G. G. Coulton and A. Hamilton Thompson of Leeds, the foremost monastic historians of the time.[67] The graceful, penetrating studies of her later years show fresher originality. From 1921 she taught at the London School of Economics; from 1931 she was professor of economic history, and the war brought her briefly back to Cambridge where LSE was evacuated; but all too briefly, for she died suddenly, aged 51, in 1940. Meanwhile she had been a colleague, then the wife, of Michael or Munia Postan of LSE – later professor of economic history at Cambridge;[68] and the incisive charm of her later work is very close to the sparkling brilliance of his. It will be uselessly debated till the end of time which of the two more deeply influenced the other; had they not met, it is reasonable to think, the study of medieval history would have been greatly impoverished.

It is evident that Eileen Power's best and most mature work was achieved after she had left Girton. Helen Cam came from Oxford to succeed her, and taught and wrote in Girton for a quarter of a century.[69] Yet she too had a second summer. For in her mid-sixties she accepted a chair in another Cambridge, was deeply stimulated by the brisk intellectual and social life of Harvard, and in her turn inspired a generation of young medievalists there. In the 1920s and 30s she had fostered the tradition of Maitland – of medieval history tightly bound to legal history, and like Maitland she could see law and society as part of a common whole.[70] Medieval English constitutional history had been taught in Cambridge as an intricate intellectual puzzle-game by Gaillard Lapsley.[71] Though herself a warm-hearted, kindly teacher, Helen Cam accepted that the history of English law and of the medieval constitution was an austere discipline. But the best of her writing – though highly professional – is not austere; and her account of medieval Cambridge in the *Victoria County History* and accompanying articles are masterpieces of local history as it should be – genuinely local, yet expounded by a historian of the widest

---

[67] On Coulton, see pp. 276–70. [68] See p. 238.
[69] This is based on personal information. Much of the best of her work is distilled in Cam 1944; and see Cheney 1971.
[70] See esp. her introduction to Maitland 1957.
[71] Now represented by Lapsley 1951; for Lapsley's personal life see Newsome 1980, index.

vision.[72] In 1944 she concluded a defence of the study of medieval local history with a demonstration of its value in teaching us how to serve in a modern democracy, so that 'we need not. . . forget our village communities and local liberties in honouring the awe-inspiring obligations of world citizenship'.[73] For she was as devout a socialist as she was a scholar, and she greeted the election of a Labour MP for Cambridge in 1945 – for which she had ardently campaigned – with ecstasy. For many of my generation she was the very type of the dedicated woman don who won for Girton an honoured place in the academic spectrum of the colleges.

THE ADMISSION OF WOMEN

In the 1870s women attended lectures by informal arrangements with the lecturers, and the Girton students took the Previous examination – the Little-go – by a series of temporary arrangements with the university or the examiners.[74] It is ironical to recall that it was the very possibility of taking Cambridge exams which had been a major reason for Miss Davies choosing Cambridge as her academic home, though Cambridge was to prove the most reluctant of all British universities fully to accept the presence of women. By 1880 the informal successes of a few women students had shown that some at least could hold their own with men in tripos exams; and in 1880 a Syndicate was appointed to consider the admission of women to university examinations. To Miss Davies' annoyance and Dr Sidgwick's pleasure, it recommended that they be admitted to Little-go and honours exams, but not to the ordinary or pass degree – which Sidgwick reckoned a worthless academic exercise.[75] On 24 February 1881 the Senate voted in favour of these proposals by 398 votes to 32.[76] From 1882 on the women's results were published with the men's, on separate lists, yet recording their classes and their places among the wranglers;[77] and Newnham

[72] *VCH Cambs*, III; Cam 1944, chaps. 1–3.   [73] Cam 1944, p. xiv.
[74] For the shifts and anxieties this involved see esp. Bennett 1990, pp. 120, 138.
[75] Hamilton 1936, pp. 124–7; Phillips 1979, pp 17–19.
[76] *Reporter* 1880–1, p. 391; Phillips 1979, p. 18.
[77] Tanner 1917, pp. 541, 543, 646 etc.

celebrates the event with a Commemoration Feast. In 1896 Emily Davies, now approaching seventy, issued a new manifesto, 'Women in the universities of England and Scotland', which described what had been achieved and what was still to do.[78] To her alarm some Girton students organised public meetings and a demonstration to air the cause. A party of young men broke up the demonstration, and the police had to intervene; Miss Davies hastened from London to admonish her students to behave. But the university had woken up and appointed a Syndicate – a 'syndicate of peaceful men, dull men, perhaps the thirteen dullest men in the University', said Maitland, who was one of them – and in March 1897 debated the proposition that women be given the titles of degrees, or (as some had suggested) that the women form a separate university. In a celebrated speech F. W. Maitland laid low 'the Bletchley Junction Academy: . . . you wait there, but you do not wait there always. You change for Oxford and Cambridge'[79] – for down to the mid-twentieth century the LNWR, the LMS and British Rail recognised the link; and there was a line from Oxford to Cambridge with Bletchley at its centre. The grace to admit women to the titles of degrees was overwhelmingly defeated, by 1,707 to 661, a high poll revealing that passions had been aroused and MAs fetched in from far and wide to vote.[80] What is particularly striking is the force of undergraduate opinion, which was even more vociferous against any extension of women's privileges: 2,137 votes to 298. It could be that some senators voted against the grace since they wished for more; but the undergraduate vote seems unambiguous, and is very strange. As the years passed the colleges grew apace, but the place of women advanced slowly. In 1916–23 they were admitted to the MB examinations.[81] By the end of the Great War their unprivileged situation in both Oxford and Cambridge was widely felt to be inequitable, or scandalous. In 1920–1 Oxford argued the matter out and voted to admit them to the university; at the same epoch Cambridge came to the opposite conclusion. A Syndicate was formed in 1919, and in 1920 offered two rival

[78] Bennett 1990, p.213.
[79] *Reporter* 1896–7, pp. 749, 751. However, 'You would have to pay rent even for what I think to be the most suitable place, namely, the waiting room at Bletchley Station' (p.751).
[80] See p. 297; cf. Hewison 1983, p.27; Bennett 1990, p.214.
[81] *Reporter* 1896–7, p. 80; Hamilton 1936, p.170.

proposals – one, Report A, that women be admitted to full membership; the other, Report B, revived the notion of a separate women's university. As in 1897, the undergraduates had a trial run and voted by 2,329 to 884 against Report A.[82] In the Senate Report A was defeated by 904 votes to 712, and, soon after, Report B was brushed aside by 146 to 50.[83]. This outcome gravely embarrassed men of good will in Cambridge, and the Council of the Senate put forward two recommendations incorporating draft statutes for a full and formal vote by the Senate: that women be admitted to full membership (I), and that – in the event of I not being carried, they be admitted to the titles of degrees (II). Recommendation I had some sugar on the pill: the number of women students was to be limited to 500; they had all to be members of women's colleges or the equivalent; they would not become members of Senate. When the poll was taken on 20 October 1921, I was rejected by 908 votes to 694; II, conferring only titles of degrees, was passed by 1,011 to 369.[84] The result caused immense excitement. The Reverend Pussy Hart, MA of Corpus, vicar of Ixworth, cried out to the mob of undergraduates assembled outside the Senate House – 'Now go and tell Girton and Newnham'[85] – which they did, at least as far as Newnham, where they broke down the gates. The incident not unnaturally caused a revulsion of feeling: Pussy Hart was severely reprimanded, leading undergraduates set up a fund to repair the gates, and men of good will, in sorrow and shame, bided their time.

Rather a long time it proved to be. While this drama was being enacted, the Royal Commission on Oxford and Cambridge was drawing to the close of its deliberations; and it was greatly embarrassed by the failure of Cambridge to admit women. It was not Asquith's way to allow force or open compulsion into the decrees of the Commission; nor can we tell in detail what the views of the Commissioners were. Some may well have thought the sort of restrictions proposed by the Council of the Senate in 1921 good in themselves. There can be little doubt that the men

[82] CUL, CUA, V.C. Corr. XII. 20, 17.
[83] *Reporter* 1920–1, pp. 60–8, 395, 660; Hamilton 1936, pp. 178–9, gives 908 to 792 for the first vote. On all this see McWilliams-Tullberg 1975, pp. 57–62.
[84] *Reporter* 1921–2, pp. 46–50, 171. It is remarkable that in December 1920 E. D. Adrian and H. A. Hollond issued a fly-sheet against Report A (McWilliams-Tullberg 1975, p. 166).
[85] Howarth 1978, p. 42; Phillips 1979, pp. 150–1.

who drafted the Cambridge recommendations, led by G. M. Trevelyan and Sir Hugh Anderson, favoured the admission of women and thought the only practical way to encourage it was by further steps in the direction pointed by the failed Recommendation I of 1921. The Royal Commission recommended full admission but with all sorts of minor restrictions, including the specific prohibition of women in men's colleges. This has sometimes been thought to mean that the leaders of Cambridge opinion were really afraid of the infiltration of women into their colleges; and the women members of the Commission, including Miss Clough, principal of Newnham and niece of the first Miss Clough, naturally refused to subscribe to these proposals. Yet it is much more probable that Anderson and his colleagues thought the recommendations entirely nugatory – they had no notion that anyone would want to admit women or that women would ever want to be admitted to men's colleges – but they were the best they could do to meet the opposition which had so recently triumphed.[86] Nothing came of their proposals; and it is not at all clear why the women of Cambridge waited so long for their next campaign. Whatever the grounds, nothing was done until another World War produced a like reaction to the First. By 1947 it seemed a painful scandal that Cambridge still excluded women from degrees, even though in every other way – as students, examinees, examiners, members of faculties and so forth – they acted as if they were on the same footing as the men. In 1947 another Syndicate reported.[87] One brave fellow of Corpus spoke at the discussion: it was Bruce Dickins, the amiable, sardonic professor of Anglo-Saxon, who doubted if the women of Oxford had much advantage over those of Cambridge. He was, however, little heeded; and the grace was passed without a division, and women, led by the Queen, now Queen Mother, entered into degrees in 1948. In what measure women have achieved equality – and how they entered the colleges in spite of the statutes drafted in the 1920s in solemn obedience to the Royal Commission – is a story for another chapter.[88]

[86] See pp. 363–4, 526–33.
[87] *Reporter* 1946–7, pp. 1083–6; for the discussion, see *Reporter* 1947–8, pp. 295–6; for the grace approving the Report, ibid. p. 398.
[88] See pp. 526–33.

Women

In a celebrated passage in *A Room of One's Own* Virginia Woolf evoked the contrast between King's and Newnham.[89] She contrasted the flow of gold and silver to King's with the immense struggle for the bare necessities of life at Newnham. That was a fair contrast: King's was and is relatively rich; Newnham, in material resources, relatively poor. When she contrasted the ancient stone and the not so ancient red-brick, that too cannot be gainsaid. Yet red-brick can be ancient too; it is the supreme beauty of Cambridge; and there are many ugly college buildings built for men in Cambridge; and there were many men's colleges poorly endowed. Her final contrast is between an elegant lunch, of sole and partridge and exquisite sweet and wine, in a fellow's rooms in King's, with dinner in hall at Newnham. This comprised (or so she said) plain soup, 'beef with its attendant greens and potatoes – a homely trinity . . . prunes and custard followed'.[90] 'The visit of Miss Strachey's close friend Virginia Woolf[91] in 1929', wrote Mrs Duncan-Jones, who had been one of her student hosts,

> to read us a paper was a rather alarming occasion. As I remember it she was nearly an hour late; and dinner in Clough Hall, never a repast for gourmets, suffered considerably. Mrs Woolf also disconcerted us by bringing a husband and so upsetting our seating plan . . . Mrs Woolf was really very well disposed to us as a group of intellectual young women; but we found her formidable . . . It was disquieting to learn later . . . that Mrs Woolf had brought out a book . . . describing her Newnham dinner. Her purpose was, of course, to evoke pity for the poverty of the women's colleges; but at the time it made us, her hosts, decidedly uncomfortable.[92]

But Mrs Woolf did not compare like with like; had she taken the undergraduates of King's into her confidence, they might well have declared that their food was much more like Newnham's

---

[89] Woolf 1929/77, pp. 10–21. Neither college is named, but ibid., p. 10, has an unmistakable description of King's chapel; and for Newnham, see below.
[90] Woolf 1929/77, p.18.
[91] Miss Strachey, Lytton Strachey's sister, was the principal.
[92] Phillips 1979, p. 174.

than that enjoyed by their dons, only that they had to be content with two courses.[93]

As the menfolk of Cambridge saw the women gradually encroach upon them, they applied to them some legendary attributes. The women were said to be less imaginative. A. B. Ramsay, the master of Magdalene, is said to have claimed that he would vote for the most masculine-seeming poem in an important competition; but as the entries were anonymous, his choice fell on one from Newnham.[94] The women worked harder than the men (it was alleged) and reproduced dull learning in essays and exams; they all got II.1s, never firsts and so forth – this in spite of numerous distinguished firsts, led by Agnata Ramsay, top classic in 1887 (soon to be wife of the master of Trinity, Montagu Butler) and Philippa Fawcett, placed 'above the Senior Wrangler' in 1890. It was on the whole true that the women had had to work harder to get to Cambridge and came from schools in which work was prized more highly than sport – though the differences were sometimes more nuances than this would suggest. As to exam results, it was firmly believed by many women that their pupils were at a disadvantage; and anonymity was introduced, for example, in the History Tripos, though not till well after 1950. These legends are occasionally repeated even in the 1990s. But happily most of us no longer think it necessary to try to discover deep, inherent and inescapable divergences between academic women and academic men.

Another common topic to pass an idle hour has been the contrast between Newnham and Girton. There have been real differences: Newnham is nearer the centre, more accessible to visitors of either sex. This has been modified by the Wolfson Court of Girton, built midway between Girton and Cambridge, in Clarkson Road, in the early 1970s. Again, Miss Davies' corridors make for a different kind of social life from Miss Clough's villas. But it would be a very subtle anthropologist who defined the effects of this difference. 'Oral tradition', writes Dr Sutherland, 'no less to be neglected in a Cambridge college than in an African village, has it that Newnham was for governesses

---

[93] This is conjecture; but the catering in hall in King's in former times did not enjoy a high reputation.
[94] Elsie Duncan-Jones in Phillips 1979, p. 173.

while Girton was for ladies. Girton students were provided with both bedrooms and sitting-rooms, while Newnham students had only single bed-sitting rooms.' In early days Newnham did not insist on its students reading for a tripos and many came for less than three years.[95] But these differences sprang from Miss Davies' insistence that her college must be as like a man's college as possible: she aimed at total equality. And in the 1980s she seemed to have won; for Girton is now a mixed college like almost all the rest, while Newnham is still for women only. The tradition that Newnham was for governesses reflects a fundamental truth: the women's colleges were designed to prepare women for such professions as might be open to them. If Girton was for ladies, those who had studied and striven to make their mark in triposes would not expect to pass their days in the enforced idleness of Miss Austen's young women. *A Room of One's Own* is precisely what Jane Austen had never had.

Since 1870 Cambridge has passed from being a second-rate academy to one of the world's leading universities; and the arrival of women has been an essential feature of that transformation. Some men played a noble part in the story; Sidgwick Hall and Peile Hall in Newnham commemorate two of them.[96] But it owes a good deal more than is quite comfortable for a male commentator to observe to the women of Newnham and Girton, most of all perhaps to Emily Davies, who chose Cambridge almost by chance.

---

[95] Sutherland 1987, pp. 100, 102.   [96] On Peile, see pp. 59–61.

Chapter 10

THE GREAT WAR 1914–18

In 1909–10 there were 3,699 male undergraduates in residence; in the Michaelmas Term of 1914, only weeks after the outbreak of war, the numbers had fallen to 1,658; by 1915 they were 825, by the Easter Term, 1916, 575.[1] The numbers of women remained stable at about 400. In a great wave of popular enthusiasm undergraduates and college fellows alike rallied to the flag. Many went sorrowfully, pressed to the service by conscience or public opinion; but others were touched by the enthusiasm and the hysteria of the time. 'When the war was declared we were all very excited.' Thus Arthur Sanctuary, looking back from 1990 to 1914, when he had just completed four years of history and theology at Caius. 'We had a party to celebrate, which shows you how little we knew what it was going to be like. I joined the Wessex Division, Royal Field Artillery,' a Territorial unit which was drafted out to India to relieve a regiment of regulars.[2] In the autumn of 1914 a young Trinity graduate wrote to a friend in Cambridge 'that the front was like a first-rate club, as you met all your friends there; and he went on to name a host of young Trinity men'.[3] Its club-like character did not last; but Cambridge meanwhile was bereft of students. From 1917 there was conscription; not till the armistice was there any recovery in student numbers – in January 1919 to 2,635, in May to 3,844 – the largest number so far recorded.[4] During the war the university almost went into hibernation, with devastating effects on college

---

[1] *CUC* 1909–10, p. 1154; *VCH Cambs*, III, 287, citing *Reporter* 1916–17, p. 38; for rather different figures, see Howarth 1978, p. 25. The number of undergraduates recorded during the war in *CUC* are artificial: they make no difference between residents and those away on war service.
[2] *Caian* 1990, p. 88. [3] Parry 1926, p. 96.
[4] Howarth 1978, p. 25.

life and college finance. Out of a fellowship of twenty-seven at Caius, some of them of advanced age, seven joined the forces, and at least seven others engaged in war work of various kinds; even the master, much occupied in serving the college and the wider community, military and civil, of wartime Cambridge, worked for a time in the Ministries of Munitions and Agriculture.[5] But the women remained, and for a while there ensued a strange reversal of roles. This is how it appeared to a Newnham student, M. G. Woods (later Mrs Waterhouse):[6]

I went up in 1915 and sat my Tripos in 1918, so the First World War is the inescapable background of all memories. The preponderance of women in the classrooms made the salutation of 'Gentlemen' more ridiculous than ever. But the colleges housed soldiers doing courses, studying this and that, marching and counter-marching through the streets and the countryside. Working in the Library at Newnham you could hear them going by, singing the haunting songs of those years, which still have the power to twist the heart. 'There's a long, long trail awinding' always brings back that scene.

The days were so packed ... it is hard to realise that ... [my Cambridge career] only lasted three years. Our work and our play, our joys and our sorrows, lectures and tutorials, societies, debates and play-acting, hockey and lacrosse, cricket and tennis, swimming and boating (some of us fell in and some did not) filled every moment of time. Quite often we did not get enough to eat, but that was cheerfully accepted, and we somehow managed to have our winter cocoa-parties and our summer teas in the garden. Our multitudinous bicycles carried us in every direction over the Fenland, and we walked inevitably across the fields to Grantchester.

Which brings me to the point where Rupert Brooke can no longer be passed over. Nowadays opinions about him differ wildly. Everyone has his own, and I do not intend to give mine. But one thing must be said: Rupert Brooke expressed, as no one else has ever done, the mood and the atmosphere of those days. It was ignorant, if you like, for realisation of what modern war is came late to this nation. The strange exaltation, the burning patriotism, the enormous upsurge of the early days, were crystal-

[5] Venn, VI, 546–7; for H. K. Anderson, the master of Caius, see chaps. 11–12 below.
[6] Phillips 1979, pp. 103–5. On Rupert Brooke and Cambridge, see e.g. Marsh 1928, pp. xxiii–lvi; Chainey 1985, chap. 19.

lised in his verse. This should be recorded, because Brooke only wrote what everybody was feeling. He made his own generation articulate. This, I believe, was the root of his popularity and his cult. Disillusionment came later, but he cannot be blamed for that, nor did he survive to experience it.

I had the happiness of going back as a post-graduate, to keep term in the summer of 1919, and so in the end I saw it all as it ought to be.

Meanwhile Cambridge endured or enjoyed a military presence. The extent of it, as it impinged on Cambridge and Caius, was described with considerable relish by F. J. M. Stratton, who himself became an officer in the Royal Engineers, and was later senior tutor and professor of astrophysics – and a colonel in the Royal Signals in the Second World War:[7]

> As the first five divisions of the British Expeditionary Force passed across the channel to France and Belgium, the 6th Division, stationed in Ireland, was moved to the Cambridge area, to provide home defence while the Territorial Army was being mobilised. All the open spaces of the town were occupied, the encampments extending to the fields around as far as Grantchester; horses were picketed in quiet roads such as Adams Road. The officers of the 3rd Rifle Brigade who were encamped on Midsummer Common, were invited to become honorary members of the [Caius] Senior Combination Room and took their meals in College and dined at the High Table.[8]

When the 6th Division had departed, for a time military activity, in the town and in Caius, was confined to the OTC, which was extremely active. On 21 January 1915 Caius became the headquarters of the First Army, Central Force, and General Sir Bruce Hamilton and his headquarters staff of eighteen were billeted in Caius.[9] Trinity, meanwhile, became a hospital. 'We have a new Cambridge', wrote Henry Jackson on 18 October 1914,

> with 1700 men *in statu pupillari* instead of 3600. In September Nevile's Court and the Trinity backs were turned into a temporary hospital, with an operating theatre in one cloister, and beds in the other and in tents. There is now a permanent hospital on the

---

[7] For what follows, see Venn, vi, 541–9. [8] Venn, vi, 541–2.
[9] Venn, vi, 542. For the OTC, see Strachan 1976.

King's and Clare cricket ground.[10] Medical Colonels and Majors
and Captains dined in hall in khaki.[11]

The military hospital on the King's and Clare field – set in a
great array of huts – outlasted the war. For the rest, the First
Army passed elsewhere, to be followed by army staff officers:
staff courses were held in Clare and Caius in 1917. After the
armistice a number of American soldiers were settled in Cambridge awaiting transport home, and about 200 matriculated in
the Easter Term 1919.[12] Meanwhile arrangements were made
from January 1919 till 1922 for short courses for naval officers,
to give them a brief period of recovery from the stress of war
and expose them a little to the academic and more to the social
life of Cambridge.[13] 'I reached Caius ravenously hungry,' writes
one of those who came in 1920, 'and . . . being told that I could
sit anywhere I selected a comfortable chair and had a jolly good
meal after which I discovered that I had been dining with the
Fellows.'[14] While the war was on, news had come back from
the front of mounting casualties: over 2,000 Cambridge men
were killed and nearly 3,000 wounded.[15] College chapels and
other memorials record the melancholy tale of strife and
slaughter.

The ghastly experience was given a kind of heroic dimension,
especially by those who took no active part in it. The British
people as a whole was little prepared for it, and for many months
few realised that it would last for years, not weeks or months, and
involve such losses. Yet there had long been a number of leading
Cambridge dons who thought that preparation for war was an
essential part of college life. The University Rifle Volunteers –
the Corps as they became – were formed in 1859.[16] One of its
central characters was the admirable, pacific tutor and master of
Caius, the Reverend E. S. Roberts, commanding officer from
1889 to 1897 – and as fervent in recruiting men for the Corps as

[10] Where the University Library now stands: see p. 376. For the numbers of undergraduates, see above, n. 1.
[11] Parry 1926, p. 95.   [12] Venn, VI, 544–5, 548–9.
[13] Venn, VI, 481–504.   [14] *Caian* 1990, pp. 84–5.
[15] 2,162, 2,902, Howarth 1978, p. 16; Carey 1921; but these figures are based on information from colleges and cannot be precisely relied on. For difficulties in general in assessing casualties, see Winter 1986, pp. 66–76 and esp. for Oxford and Cambridge, pp. 92–3.
[16] CUA, CUR 64, fos. 1–5; Strachan 1976 (for its names, see ibid., Index, p. 276).

for the college boat club.[17] Roberts was no philistine: he was a cultivated scholar who believed that the boat club, and the patriotic preparations of the Rifle Volunteers, represented the wholesome side of college life – 'wholesome' was his more sophisticated version of Kingsley's 'muscular' Christianity.[18] In the hands of men like Roberts wars and rumours of war acquired a kind of romantic aura deeply puzzling to those who have experienced war as it actually is. Yet such was the mood of the 1910s that not even the horrors of the trenches – and the revulsion and cynicism they bred in many minds – entirely destroyed this image. When Earl Haig, who has sometimes been portrayed in recent literature as the mindless author of the massacres of the Somme and Passchendaele,[19] came in 1920 with Admiral Lord Jellicoe to receive honorary degrees, they were carried shoulder high by excited undergraduates, many of them veterans of the war.[20] One can understand that relief when peace came was an intoxicating experience; but that an academic throng should make a hero of the general who presided over the Somme seems today surprising.

There were other feelings, too, sometimes fighting within the same personalities who exalted Haig and Jellicoe. The actual experience of war had brought deep revulsion and left innumerable scars. These were all the more painful since there had been so little experience of war in this country or among the British for so long. The heroic quality of war was somehow familiar from the literature of military adventure throughout the Victorian and Edwardian ages. Its squalor was less generally appreciated; and the battles and skirmishes of recent wars, including the Boer War, had been fought in distant places. After 1914 this had to change. Something of the romantic appeal – its glory and melancholy – survived in the last poems of Rupert Brooke of King's; other war poets widened the spectrum to its furthest extent, to the depths of cynicism and despair. There were already many indeed in 1914 to whom war was anathema – or who refused to participate in killing, or who doubted the justice of the allied cause. It is often

17 Brooke 1985, pp. 254–6, and refs. p. 255 n. 115.
18 Venn, III, 306; Brooke 1985, p. 254.
19 Perhaps unfairly: see e.g. Middlebrook 1971, p. 290.
20 Howarth 1978, p. 24.

said that the role of the conscientious objector was far more difficult in 1914 than in 1939. But this is not wholly true. There were many indeed in 1914, including men and women normally sane, who were driven hysterical by the advent of war and regarded all pacifists as craven villains.[21] Nor was this all hysteria: one can well understand the feelings of parents and friends of soldiers at the front, who were witnessing the sacrifice of those closest to them 'for king and country' in what appeared a ceaseless slaughter, towards those who refused to expose themselves to such risks in the name of some high moral principle hardly intelligible to many of their fellow-countrymen. One can understand too why the lot of the conscientious objector could be extremely hard. But down to 1917 there was no conscription, so that it was open to them – if they had the moral courage – to refuse the allurements of the army, or to enlist as non-combatants. Thus F. R. Leavis[22] was a stretcher bearer on the western front. There were many such before conscription – after a long series of political battles – came slowly into force in 1916–17.

In both wars the most secure ground for refusal to enlist was a religious scruple – against war, against killing, whatever precisely it might be; for only fanatics wished to engage in religious persecution. It was never an easy ground, for those who did not share it often viewed with suspicion both the adequacy of the scruple and the sincerity of the objector. But it was more secure in the official and popular view alike than the equally firm and fervent moral grounds of agnostics like Leavis – more secure still than those of G. E. Moore and his like whose objection was essentially political.[23] Moore suffered great mental agony from his long quest for a clear answer to the question whether he should support or oppose the war. He was an agnostic; he saw no religious grounds for any opinion. He doubted very much whether it was right to settle the issues of 1914 by war, above all by a war so catastrophic. But this was not to say that war was wrong in all circumstances. As Paul Levy points out, Moore's position was courageously presented by Lytton Strachey – of all

---

[21] Nor was the current of opinion so different in 1939, when conscientious objectors needed great moral courage to sustain their lot – but popular reaction was (to put the matter a little crudely) much less hysterical than in the First World War.

[22] See pp. 448–50.   [23] For what follows see Levy 1979/1981, pp. 276–89.

the Apostolic disciples of Moore the one to whom one least looks for deep, clear-cut, courageous moral principles – in his defence before the Hampstead Tribunal in March 1916. 'I am convinced that the whole system by which it is sought to settle international disputes by force is profoundly evil; and that, so far as I am concerned, I should be doing wrong to take any active part in it.'[24] Strachey had to make public avowal of a deeply unpopular objection. Moore's suffering was real enough, but it was mostly inward. He was indeed an active member of more than one of the numerous societies which flourished in Cambridge and elsewhere dedicated to bringing the war to an end and resisting conscription, such as the Union of Democratic Control and the No Conscription Fellowship. Their members were called 'pacifists' in common parlance, though many of them were not pacifists in the senses in which we use the term today.[25] In this respect there was a profound difference between the two World Wars. In 1914 the enemy was Germany, which had been in many folk's eyes – especially in Cambridge – the homeland of learning and culture and the peaceful arts in the nineteenth century. In 1939 the enemy was Hitler, whose bestial doctrines were especially well known in Cambridge, for it had opened its gates in the 1930s to many Jews fleeing from his persecution.[26] Attempts have been made to dim the clarity of this sharp distinction: popular attitudes were doubtless full of nuances, and no opinion has ever been universally held. But it was much easier for a thoughtful person in 1939 to see the war as *necessary*; and at the same time the early introduction of conscription meant that the sacrifices of most of those who fought – though very real – were not voluntary.[27]

In 1942 the eminent mathematician G. H. Hardy, looking back from the Second World War to the First, wrote his fascinating account of the affair of Bertrand Russell's lectureship.[28] It was

---

[24] Quoted Levy 1979/1981, pp. 277-8.

[25] See esp. Hardy 1942, p. 3n on the common use of 'pacifist' in 1914–18.

[26] See pp. 505–6. The refugees included some persecuted for conscientious resistance to the Nazis not for Jewish descent.

[27] There were many volunteers in the early phases of the Second World War; but, considered as a whole, the British Army rapidly became a conscript army.

[28] Hardy 1942. To the reprint of 1970 C. D. Broad added a Foreword, noting in particular that after the publication of Hardy's booklet, the College Council re-elected Russell to a fellowship, and he was a fellow from 1944 till his death in 1970 (pp. vi–vii).

written with great depth of feeling carefully controlled: he attempted most strenuously to represent the story without *parti pris*. He set out to explain as dispassionately as he could how the Council of Trinity came to dismiss Bertrand Russell from his college lectureship in 1916. Opinion in Trinity was deeply divided; and I know of no evidence which reveals so sharply and clearly the spectrum of attitudes in Cambridge during the Great War.

Russell was already a lecturer before the war, but he had not been re-elected to a fellowship. This naturally seemed somewhat anomalous in view of his academic fame; but a move to elect him to a fellowship in 1915 foundered, because he hardened the opinion of those who disliked his political views by asking for leave of absence for the first two terms of his fellowship – in effect, to engage in political activity, in opposition to the war.[29] In 1916 one E. F. Everett was granted exemption from combatant service by the tribunals, that is to say he was to join the army but not to fight. Military service of any kind was against his conscience and he resisted orders by passive means; in due course he was court-martialled and sentenced to two years' hard labour – which was subsequently commuted to 112 days' detention. There presently appeared a leaflet expounding the case which was chiefly the work of Russell, but in the main a factual account. He was hauled into court for making 'statements likely to prejudice the recruiting and discipline of His Majesty's forces', found guilty and fined £100. The sentence was confirmed on appeal, and although he refused to pay his friends paid for him.[30] The appeal was heard on 29 June, and on 11 July eleven of the thirteen members of the Trinity College Council met and 'agreed unanimously that, since Mr Russell has been convicted under the Defence of the Realm Act . . . he be removed from his lectureship in the College'.[31] Protest was immediate and noisy, including such comments as D. S. Robertson's (the author was himself on military service): the refusal of the Council to distinguish what was dishonourable from what was illegal 'seems to me an inexpressible disaster to tolerance and liberty'.[32] Twenty-two

[29] Hardy 1942, pp. 25–31, esp. 27–8.   [30] Hardy 1942, pp. 31–40, esp. pp. 34, 40.
[31] Hardy 1942, pp. 40n, 41.   [32] Hardy 1942, p. 41.

fellows, representing many shades of opinion about the war, signed a protest.[33] Then, in 1918, Russell succeeded in having himself prosecuted once again, and on this occasion he was sentenced to six months' imprisonment, during which he 'wrote his *Introduction to Mathematical Philosophy* in Brixton Prison'.[34] None the less, once the war was over and the fellowship reassembled, twenty-seven fellows signed a memorial dated 28 November 1919 requesting that he be reinstated in his lectureship, and the Council concurred. In the event, Russell went on leave to China and Japan, and before he had returned he resigned his lectureship: his domestic affairs had reached a crisis which he evidently felt might cause scandal and embarrass some of those who had supported him.[35] Meanwhile, the memorial had been 'signed or supported by an absolute majority of the Society, by every Fellow under 45 except Laurence, Dykes and Ramanujan,[36] and by every Fellow who had served in the forces'.[37]

The division of opinion is very striking. The older fellows had all along been the most militant. The absence of younger fellows during the war had enhanced the natural tendency for the College Council to be a gathering of the aged. There had long been a number of fellows who supported the Union of Democratic Control – Hardy says four fellows were conscientious objectors, thirteen members of the UDC, though four of these were officers in the army.[38] Two members of the Council had supported Russell in 1915; but they were away from Cambridge before the critical meeting of 11 July 1916, which comprised eleven men united in support of the war effort and in condemnation of Russell.[39] Most fervent of all was the vice-master, Henry Jackson, now in his mid-seventies, still vigorous and vehement though in less liberal causes, perhaps, than in earlier days. He had two sons in the army, and felt with all the warmth and depth of an ardent nature that opposition to the war was wholly wrong –

---

[33] Hardy 1942, p. 42.   [34] Hardy 1942, p. 47.   [35] Hardy 1942, pp. 48–57.
[36] Ramanujan was a brilliant young Indian mathematician, who lay ill in India and was never sent it, Hardy 1942, p. 52n; cf. Hardy 1940b.
[37] Hardy 1942, p. 52; on pp. 59–60 he printed a full list of fellows, showing the signatories in italics.
[38] Hardy 1942, p. 8.
[39] Cf. esp. Hardy 1942, pp. 27, 41; but see p. 31n for evidence that one of them, the Reverend V. H. Stanton, Regius Professor of Divinity, had doubts about some of the proceedings in 1915.

and that the college he loved and had served with such devotion must not be polluted by contact with disloyalty.[40] The generation gap is particularly intriguing. No doubt the younger fellows who had served in the forces were inclined to be sensitive to the issues involved and had reason to understand some of the grounds on which a colleague might oppose war: the most notable pacifist in Cambridge between the wars, C. E. Raven, had been a serving chaplain converted to pacifism by his war experiences.[41] It was easier to feel fervent about the war if one had never seen a trench. But it probably went deeper than that. Somewhere in the moderate muscular Christianity of E. S. Roberts of Caius there had been an element of jingoism. Attitudes which the younger fellows of Trinity found repugnant in 1919 and would be merely embarrassing in the 1990s were still widely and deeply held: patriotism could still be seen as the loyalty which overrode all others.[42]

Meanwhile, in Trinity as elsewhere, the war ended with a marked military presence – army officers on short courses and a lively gathering of naval officers recovering from the experience of war.[43] When the armistice was signed on 11 November 1918 the bells of Great St Mary's broke out into discordant tumult, as their ropes were pulled by students with more zeal than knowledge, and the premises of C. K. Ogden – the brilliant eccentric under whose inspiration I. A. Richards was to lay essential foundations for the study of literature, and whose critical journalism throughout the war had angered the patriotic majority – were raided by a mob.[44] For almost all it was a period of intense relief, the passing of the war to end wars. For the university it opened an era of very rapid recovery; by the end of 1919 student numbers were above the level of 1914, and the urgent problems of academic organisation, of scientific progress, of the needs of the Library, came rapidly to life again.

[40] Cf. Hardy 1942, pp. 24–5; Parry 1926, pp. 93–113, esp. p. 99.
[41] See pp. 148–9.
[42] I hope I shall not be supposed to carp at patriotism: but in the 1990s it has to take its place in a very different hierarchy of claims and values from those generally admired in the 1930s and 1940s.
[43] See above, p. 334.
[44] On Ogden, Howarth 1978, pp. 19–20, 123; Ogden and Richards 1923.

Chapter 11

SIR HUGH ANDERSON, THE ASQUITH COMMISSION AND ITS SEQUEL

THE COMMISSIONERS

The Asquith Commission was set up in November 1919 and reported in 1922; by 1926 the process of reform was completed: Oxford and Cambridge had new constitutions and the statutes of both universities and all the colleges had been revised.[1] If we wish to understand Cambridge in the 1920s, and Cambridge now, we must grasp the meaning and achievement of the Commission. But to enter its counsels and purposes is peculiarly difficult; its archives are defective.[2] For the most part we must judge them by the outcome: by its fruits, and by its fruits alone, can it be known. When one contemplates the galaxy of talent which formed the Commission, it is especially tantalising; one would dearly like to know more of their debates.

The Commission comprised twenty-three persons, only two of them women: the principal of Somerville and the vice-principal of Newnham – Miss B. A. Clough, later principal. The Cambridge committee was presided over by Gerald Balfour, brother of Lord Balfour, whom he later succeeded, and of Mrs Sidgwick, and so brother-in-law of the late Henry Sidgwick. Besides Miss Clough, it included Sir Hugh Anderson, Sir Horace Darwin, Gwen Raverat's Uncle Horace, G. M. Trevelyan, already an eminent historian, later to be Regius Professor of Modern History and master of Trinity; and M. R. James, provost of Eton and

[1] Apart from the *Report of the Commission (RC 1922)* and the volume of *Appendices*, the chief sources for this chapter are the fragmentary archives in the Bodleian (see n. 2) and Maisie Anderson's 'Time to the Sound of Bells' (see below). In pursuit of the archives I have had generous help from John Prest.

[2] The most substantial fragments are: Oxford, Bodleian MS Asquith 139; Top. Oxon. b. 104–9. See below, pp. 350–3.

formerly of King's.[3] The Oxford committee included Lord Chalmers, a veteran civil servant, who suddenly became an undergraduate at Peterhouse in 1920, and by 1924 was master – a promotion hardly to be paralleled since the days of George Neville, brother of Warwick the Kingmaker, who was rapidly promoted from undergraduate to chancellor of Oxford in the 1450s.[4]

Horace Darwin was one of the 'benevolently Philistine' Darwins.

> Overtly, explicitly, they would have admitted that they knew nothing at all about music, very little about art, and not a great deal even about Literature, though they all loved reading. They were apt to regard the arts as the inessential ornaments of Life; unimportant matters. But this is a superficial view of them: in their scientific work they showed many of the characteristics of the creative artist: the sense of style, of proportion; the passionate love of their subject; and above all, the complete integrity and the willingness to take infinite trouble to perfect any piece of work . . . Uncle Horace [I am quoting Gwen Raverat] had not taken kindly to the classical and literary sides of his education; but he had a certain directness of perception, and delicacy of touch, which were very attractive . . . But his absorption in his dear machines always remained a barrier to me, for they are not at all in my line; though I liked to watch the affection in his face and the tender movements of his beautiful sensitive hands as he touched them.[5]

His monument is the Cambridge Instrument Company, and in all manner of ways he fructified the technical crafts of the Cambridge laboratories by his mechanical genius. M. R. James, scholar and dilettante, marked an opposite pole – literary, whimsical, unpractical, yet in his own way a great technician with medieval manuscripts.[6] We know a little of Sir Horace's contribution, nothing of James'. It is a sad loss not to know more of what passed in this remarkable gathering. But the indications are that the central figure in Oxford was T. B. Strong, dean of

---

[3] *RC 1922*, pp. 3–4.
[4] On Chalmers see *DNB 1931–40* (1949), pp. 154–5.
[5] Raverat 1952, pp. 188, 205.
[6] On him see Pfaff 1980. On p. 367 Pfaff quotes M. R. James referring to 'very dreary days' spent on the Commission's business. 'However a severe cold caught from some reformer came to deliver me.'

Christ Church, later bishop of Ripon, and in Cambridge Sir
Hugh Anderson. For Anderson we have an unorthodox source –
his daughter's reminiscences[7] – which tell us little directly of
policies, but a good deal of how the Commissioners worked and
the methods by which their findings were by measured steps
turned into statutes; and above all, an unforgettable portrait of
Hugh Anderson himself, the central creative figure in the story
we have to unfold. His activity covered so many regions of the
university in the 1920s she must be allowed some pages to reveal
his character and manner of work.

SIR HUGH ANDERSON

Hugh Anderson's daughter, Mary Desirée Anderson, was born in
1902, and from 1912 to 1928 she lived in the master's lodge at
Caius, while her father was master. She kept elaborate diaries,
and later in life she followed in Gwen Raverat's footsteps, and
described life in Cambridge in a set of enchanting memoirs.
Surrounded by the learning and culture of Cambridge, she was
given almost no formal education; but after her father's death she
became one of the earliest students at the Courtauld Institute in
London; she became a professional art historian and author of
delightful books on medieval sculpture – as well as three novels.
Through her work she met Trenchard Cox, whom she later
married – and who was himself in due course to be director of the
Birmingham Museum and Art Gallery and of the Victoria and
Albert. Lady Cox died in 1973, and it is through the generous
kindness of Sir Trenchard that her reminiscences were given to
her father's college.

> The cobbler's child is proverbially ill-shod and although Father
> was a firm supporter of advanced education for women the
> schooling given to his own daughter would be considered illegally
> inadequate today ... Mamma ... regarded it as her vocation in
> life to protect him from all minor family responsibilities, among
> which she probably included my education. One subject, how-

---

7 'Time to the Sound of Bells', now in Gonville and Caius College Archives. They are in process
of being serialised in *The Caian* (1988, pp. 94–109; 1989, pp. 69–84; 1990, pp. 89–106, so far) by
kind permission of Sir Trenchard Cox. The paragraph which follows is adapted from *Caian*
1988, p. 94.

ever, he taught me himself, the management of money. Before I was fifteen I had learnt how to buy and sell the securities which bought my minute dress allowance, and to reclaim my own income tax. Our first sessions were bewildering experiences, for he would cover sheets of paper with tiny, scribbled figures saying at frequent intervals: 'You see, you see.' And I didn't see, at all. Later, when the mathematical processes were no longer a mystery to me, I listened with keen interest to far-reaching reasons which he gave for his choice of investments ...

When I was seventeen Mamma told me that I could make my choice between a College education (if I could qualify for one) or freedom to travel abroad; we could not afford both. No attempt was made to see that my choice was based upon a reasoned balancing of the pros and cons, and I made my decision with far less serious thought than the matter deserved. On one side I saw the necessity for much agonised cramming of the compulsory subjects hitherto left out of my curriculum, if I was to have the chance of admittance to the University, and on the other, the care-free existence at the Lodge with the added excitement of travelling in the vacations. I never even considered that a total lack of qualifications would make it very difficult for me to earn a living, or even to achieve an interesting way of life. So I danced away the years when I might have gained a degree [in the Cambridge of the twenties, if women's opportunities for learning were limited, they could, by her account, dance almost every night of the week, anyway during term]. Such a choice would be criminal folly today and even then it was probably foolish, but I still enjoy in retrospect many experiences which I would otherwise have missed and even the moral of the tale is lacking for, as my life has turned out, I probably chose the more useful training.

She took considerable advantage of the opportunities of Cambridge – to attend lectures, to meet interesting people – and evidently learned more than she will quite allow.

In those days dons' daughters did not necessarily envisage a career unless they were particularly clever, or realised that they would have to earn their own living. [Many went to the Perse School, but] very few of my contemporaries went to College. Some of them started training as nurses, but most of these broke down under the strain of combining intensive study with heavy manual labour ... Several Cambridge girls acted as secretaries to their fathers and one friend of mine even saved her parent the trouble of signing his own letters by her skilled forgery. I wanted to do the same but Mamma vetoed the plan, saying that she was not going to listen to my grumbles all morning, as I hung about with nothing to do, if Father was at a meeting, and then soothe him in the evenings when I had gone to a dance and he wanted to dictate letters.

At the end of his life, for a while, she did act as his secretary;[8] but for most of the time 'I remained merely a "daughter at home" arranging flowers, writing menu cards for dinner parties and accompanying mamma when she went calling, with my name engraved below hers on the cards which she left when we were lucky enough to find people not at home' – it is astonishing how little had changed since the days of Jane Austen.

Hugh Kerr Anderson was the son of the founder of the Orient Line – his coat of arms was a charming convoy of ships.[9] As a young man he was a distinguished neurophysiologist, a fellow of Caius and a university lecturer. But he was also fascinated by college finance, and so was drawn into college and university administration; and in 1912 elected master of Caius. He was a strange mixture of parts – extremely diffident, yet assured of his own vocation; deeply devoted to his family, yet negligent of his daughter's upbringing; born to riches, yet believing himself on the edge of insolvency – Maisie has a vivid description of the annual rendering of accounts at Christmastime, and the gloom this gave to the festive season.[10] He was increasingly absorbed and immolated in the work of college and university; the most considerate of men – who yet relied on the tolerance of his wife and household to a scarcely credible degree. His wife's sole occupations were domestic; in the rambling master's lodge in the heart of the college they had butler, cook and ample domestic staff; and it was fortunate that it was so.

In most households there is one moment when their peculiar characteristics are most clearly displayed and with us it was at

---

8 But not during the sessions of the Royal Commission. These quotations are from Anderson 1988ff, chap. 7 (*Caian* 1989, pp. 73–4, 76–7). For her work as Anderson's secretary, see Anderson 1988ff, chap. 23.

9 On Anderson see Venn, VI, 514–28; *Caian* 37 (1929), 91–122; *Proc. of the Royal Society*, Series B, 104 (1929), Obituaries, pp. xx–xxv (W. B. Hardy and C. S. Sherrington); Brooke 1985, pp. 260–7.

10 Anderson 1988ff, chap. 15.

lunch-time. We never knew how many guests there would be, but we rarely ate alone. It was agreed, whether explicitly or through long custom I do not remember, that Father might invite one or two people to lunch without warning. Three extra? Well, we always had enough for them to eat but he would be warned that his luck might not hold next time and then be sent to make his peace with the servants. I never eavesdropped on his confessions to them but he never failed to win the forgiveness of our long-suffering maids. When, however, he arrived panting, touzled, and, for once, really apologetic, to say that he had invited five people to lunch and that they were following at a more leisurely pace from the meeting he had just left, then indeed Mamma protested indignantly, but somehow the guests were fed!

Warm, generous and involved; to him a meeting was a gathering of friends – or if it did not start so, so it must end; and it was the most natural thing in the world for them to adjourn for lunch. He evidently had great, and well-founded, faith in the efficacy of the lodge's hospitality to mellow differences and charm the memory.

It was therefore important to find out before the meal was actually served how many people were expecting to eat it. This was not easy, for Father was either out at a meeting, from which he might bring back any number of colleagues, or else holding one in the study, which we dared not disturb. Special techniques were evolved to deal with these different problems.

The master's study commands a view of the court through which he would normally return to the lodge if he had been elsewhere in Cambridge.

If the study was empty I kept watch from there until Father came into sight. If he was scuttling across the court alone, with his hat jammed down over his eyes, he might not have invited anyone. A Fellow of Caius walking with him was probably lunching in College, but anyone else was almost certainly coming to us and I would hurry away to give the warning. Observation was more difficult if the meeting was in the Lodge. In summer I could stroll nonchalantly in the garden and try to count the heads visible through the study windows, but in winter we could only listen outside the door and try to identify the voices.

The dining room of the Lodge was [and is] a pleasant room lit by three tall windows and on its green, panelled walls hung the portraits of former Masters. A pallid Reynolds looked down upon us with judicial detachment while a rubicund Opie always seemed ready to enjoy the party . . . Their painted eyes all seemed to rest upon their successor in office as the little man at the head of the table led the talk through every variation of tone and subject, from earnest debate to the wildest nonsense, or sat hunched in his chair, silently wrestling with the problems in mind.[11]

Thus lunch, every day; and every evening wife and daughter gathered with the master in his study – he to work, they to read; it was the nearest to a quiet time together that they ever enjoyed – save when they visited the master's other lodge at Heacham on the Norfolk coast; and even in the study friends and resident fellows would call from time to time, tearing a weary, yet ever a welcoming, master from his desk. The weekends were the busiest of all.

Sunday is not a day of rest for those who live in Master's Lodges! It was the day on which we did most of our official entertaining, as opposed to the casual open-house-at-any-time of the rest of the week. We generally had week-end guests: old Caians, past or future benefactors of the College, soldiers, sailors, doctors, lawyers, architects and leaders in various fields of industry, anyone in fact whose work had brought them, or was likely to bring them in touch with the University, and who had therefore made contact with Father . . .

Father broadcast invitations to stay, to anyone who approached him for help, but he was very unreliable in reporting their acceptance. Since Mamma was too scrupulous to pry into his correspondence it was not until I grew up that we had even the modicum of warning derived from my routine inspection of any letters lying about the study. Our spare rooms were therefore always kept ready and, if we saw an unfamiliar suitcase in the hall, we would welcome any stranger found in the study or ushered into the drawing room as a gladly awaited guest. But as our visitors often arrived wholly unheralded, we also became adepts at concealing surprise. I only remember one occasion when we must have betrayed ourselves . . . Having entertained a pleasant, but unexplained, guest to lunch, we were faintly surprised when he reappeared for tea, but . . . we once more bade him a friendly farewell and told him to come and see us again when he was next

[11] Anderson 1988ff, chap. 11 (*Caian* 1990, p. 99).

in Cambridge. It was not until we found him still in the house at seven o'clock that it dawned upon Mamma that he was staying with us, Father having given us no indication that he had invited him . . .

The company at [Sunday] Lunch was usually a queer cocktail of humanity, since pure chance determined its selection. We once sat down to lunch thirteen strong, of whom more than half were impromptu guests. Mamma had invited some shy Scottish undergraduates, whom she had been asked to befriend, and a French lector who knew too little English to join in general conversation but too much to be content to talk French. Lord Chalmers[12] had invited himself and, at the last minute, Father brought in a distinguished zoologist and his wife together with a man whom we learned afterwards was an expert on dress design. Our hearts sank as we looked round the party gathered before lunch, but their very incongruity made them mutually interesting and all went well.

Before our luncheon guests had gone the first undergraduates might begin to arrive. It was then the accepted convention that the men should call upon the dons of their College and more particularly the Master. I don't remember women students ever calling, even after we had entertained them, but we often had fifteen or twenty men to tea . . . This convention of calling seemed, no doubt, a tedious imposition to some of our visitors, and honesty compels me to admit that we also found it very heavy going when a solid phalanx of the pitilessly dumb occupied the chairs round the fire, too shy even to go, until the sound of the Chapel bell, at 6.45, released us all from this predicament. It did, however, create an opening for better acquaintance and our friendship with many Caians ripened term by term . . .

As a rule Father did not join the party till it had been under way for some time. Then he would stroll in and greet any man he knew with a word or two that showed he knew about their work and plans, before settling down to talk to any particular group. Then we would see the dour research student, who had steadfastly resisted all our attempts to get two consecutive words out of him, gradually unfold and begin to put forth ideas, till, from a corner where silence had lain as heavy as a pea-soup fog, would come laughter and the quick interchange of interested voices. Hardly ever, even at times of the greatest pressure, or when he was ill, did

12 See above, n. 4.

he fail to put in an appearance at the tea-party, but he liked to do so at his own time and we dreaded the appearance of guests who made it necessary that I should go down and summon him. That would sometimes provoke a storm of pent-up nervous irritation. He would pace up and down the study, saying that he was worked to death, and ill, and would have to sit up all night to make up for lost time.

'Let me say that I could not find you', I would plead, and the lie would have sat lightly on my conscience, but he would never allow it and, a few minutes later, he would enter the drawing room, smiling and apparently quite at leisure, eager to find out whether the visitor had seen everything and everybody he wanted to, or, if not, how he could be helped to do so . . .[13]

Of all the gifts which Father possessed, the one that I would have chosen to inherit was his extraordinary power of drawing interest from almost everyone he met, however dull they might appear to others. It was like the philosopher's stone of legendary alchemy, turning all things to gold. He had no leisure to read books, but he read The Times through every day and forgot nothing he had either seen or been told. Consequently he was never at a loss for the scrap of relevant knowledge which would encourage another person to develop a favourite theme. From this first response, Father would pick out the most significant aspect, often giving it a value which may not have been present in the speaker's mind, and this he did with such kindliness that even the shyest freshman gained confidence in his own ability to interest, and so became interesting. His power of identifying the subjects on which his guests could speak with authority and pleasure was uncanny. A specialised interest in the structure of snails' tongues is, to say the least of it, unusual, but it only took him a few minutes to discover this peculiarity in one of our guests and then he carried on the conversation as if this had always been one of his own particular studies . . .[14]

THE ROYAL COMMISSION

For the outward and the inward view of the Royal Commission – for its public aims and achievements and its manner of work – we have three substantial types of source. We have first

[13] Anderson 1988ff, chap. 13.   [14] Anderson 1988ff, chap. 14 *ad fin.*

the rather scanty archives of the Commission, preserved in the Bodleian, comprising many of the submissions of evidence; and the much fuller view of these given by the appendices to the published report. The archives also contain some valuable reports of discussions, especially with representatives of the Labour Party and others on means to open Oxford and Cambridge to more students from poorer homes; and on the relation of the governing bodies of the universities to outside authority.[15] Next we have the report itself and the recommendations of the Commission, and the statutes its successor, the Statutory Commission, laid down for the university;[16] and for the inward view we have the chapters of Maisie Anderson's reminiscences on the period of her father's life which was dominated by his role as the leading Commissioner for Cambridge and the central figure among the statute-makers. The first two are for the most part too formal to be a wholly satisfactory record; the third too informal. The surviving discussions are very interesting, but cover only a small part of the whole canvas. But with these we have to be content; until the British people learn the value of contemporary archives, we are likely to be similarly hampered in the study of much recent history.[17]

In the Commission's recommendations there were four major elements.

I. 'The government of the Universities'. There is much discussion under this head of the role and composition and shape of the Council of the Senate, the General Board of the Faculties and the Financial Board, which were refashioned as the Central Committees and so became the representative oligarchies[18] which ruled the university for the next sixty years or so. The Commissioners revealed their attitudes by discussing whether there should be lay representatives or government representatives on the Council. Lord Chalmers thought that it would be difficult to win government support without some sort of external

---

[15] Oxford, Bodleian MS Asquith 139 contains meetings of 2 July 1920, with representations of the Labour Party; 16 July 1920, in which relations with outside bodies were discussed and other matters; other discussions with witnesses are in Bodleian Top. Oxon. b. 109.

[16] *Reporter* 1925–6, 29 Jan. 1926 *ad fin*.

[17] Howarth 1978, p. 244, refers to notes on the Royal Commission in the custody of Tressilian Nicholas. Mr Nicholas assured me on more than one occasion that he never had such notes: for his recollections of the Statutory Commission, of which he was assistant secretary, see p. 369.

[18] See pp. 563–4.

control. Anderson saw the need for some kind of external control 'in place of the spasmodic reforms by commissions'; but his recipe – 'a Veto vested in the Chancellor' – savours of a *reductio ad absurdum*, since control is the one function a Chancellor may not by convention exercise in any university. Even though Anderson modified it by suggesting the possible addition of a Universities Committee of the Privy Council, the trend of the discussion was to emphasise the difficulty of checking the decisions of a large body of resident MAs by any element of outside representation. The end of the discussion was that the matter was dropped.[19] In their report the Commissioners cast a brief glance at the councils of modern universities; and then they rejected such suggestions on various specious grounds.[20] The most important of their recommendations led to the creation, or recreation – for every attempt was made by Commissioners and Statutory Commissioners alike to minimise or else disguise the revolutionary nature of their proposals – of the Regent House, or the House of Residents as it had been called in the discussions of 1908–11 and 1919–20.[21] The old Senate, the whole community of MAs who took the trouble to keep their names on the college books, was preserved but given only ritual functions such as electing the Chancellor, apart from a residual power to check the Regent House in the case of some disagreement in statute making – a residual power which has never been invoked.[22] The House of Residents was intended to comprise resident MAs actually engaged in the government, administration or teaching of the university. The Council's report of 1920 had recommended including resident MAs of ten years' standing and some others; but the Commission firmly set these aside if they were 'not engaged in teaching or administrative work'.[23] In the statute which eventually emerged the Regent House includes all those who are university officers engaged in teaching and administration, all fellows of colleges, and all members of faculties; and faculties have in practice been free to include in their membership all those who teach for them full or part-time – and those who have taught for them, since it was

[19] Oxford, Bodleian MS Asquith 139, fos. 158–60.
[20] *RC 1922*, pp. 72–3 and Appendix 2 B.I, pp. 84–5.
[21] *RC 1922*, pp. 59–60.   [22] *RC 1922*, pp. 65–6.
[23] *RC 1922*, pp. 60–1.

a common practice down to the Wass Report (1989) to leave retired members on the faculty lists. There has been a real liberality in this, but also some danger that the weight of opinion in the Regent House represented by its older members – many (though far from all) of them quite out of touch with current trends and problems – may tend to reinforce the opinion of those who hold that the Regent House is not a satisfactory instrument of government.[24]

II. 'Organisation of Teaching, Research Work, etc.' – which in practice comprised two main areas: (1) the establishment of faculties, Faculty Boards and teaching officers, and the effective payment of the teaching officers by the university; and (2) the reorganisation of fellowships in the colleges to meet the varied needs of teaching and research. The Commissioners' first concern, most emphatically expressed, was to ensure that university teachers had sufficient time for research and the instruction of 'advanced students' – that is to say for postgraduate students.[25] They were vigorously attempting to drag the ancient universities into the twentieth century: they recognised the distinction of much of the work done in both; they tactfully but firmly criticised the concentration of effort (especially in Oxford) on the routine teaching of undergraduates. To achieve their ends they prescribed the payment of adequate stipends, the reduction of the amount of tutorial work per teacher (again, primarily a revision of the traditional Oxford tutorial code), an increase in the number of university teachers, and a serious attempt to provide a period of apprenticeship in which an aspirant to the trade of university teacher could study, do research and travel. These aims led to a wide variety of measures, all of which contributed to foster learning and research, and some of which – in Cambridge – tended also to create a new and unintended schism between university and colleges. The Commission had been set up above all to justify and organise government grants to Oxford and Cambridge; and its laudable aim of increasing the stipends and the numbers of teachers was carefully formulated and given financial definition as one of the central planks in the Commission's platform. In Oxford the colleges in effect refused to surrender their grip on teaching appointments; there had always been a

---

[24] *Reporter* 1988–9, pp. 620–3.   [25] *RC 1922*, pp. 95–6.

much closer identity between college and university lecturers. This led to short-term financial difficulties;[26] and there was a long period after the Second World War when there were in fact many university appointments even in Oxford not attached to college fellowships. This separation has been brought to an end by the reforms of the post-Franks era of the 1960s and 70s.[27] In Cambridge the opposite has happened; the divorce has grown wider. The Cambridge Commissioners were evidently determined to maximise the effect of government grants by making university lectureships more clearly distinct from any college office. If one studies what survives of their discussions it seems fairly clear that they had no notion of separating university and college teachers: it was clearly assumed that, broadly speaking, the university would appoint teachers who had proved themselves in college teaching; that university and college lecturers would be the same people; and the salaries were assessed in the 1920s on this assumption.[28] The first lists of university lecturers drawn up by the Commissioners in the mid-1920s are in essence lists of the established teaching fellows in each subject.[29] Hitherto they had examined for the university when asked, for a suitable fee, and lectured for the university under a bizarre variety of *ad hoc* intercollegiate arrangements, for which they might or might not be paid from the fees of their students. The better off colleges compensated their teaching fellows for these capricious and inadequate rewards by offering higher stipends to college lecturers;[30] but the pattern of rewards was extremely confusing, and (as the Royal Commission reasonably observed) encouraged university teachers to seek financial support by other means, thus reducing their commitment to research.[31] Down to 1939 the stipends paid to university lecturers were modest; the reforms of the 1920s introduced regularity and sense into the system, but did not create, or attempt to create, a pattern of stipends which made the university lecturer independent of his college emoluments. It

---

[26] In Oxford the college tutor was paid almost entirely by the colleges until the inflation of the postwar decades compelled the introduction of realistic contributions by the university.

[27] I am told that all academic posts in Oxford are now joint college–university appointments.

[28] See esp. contributions by G. M. Trevelyan and Hugh Anderson to the discussion reported in Bodleian MS Asquith 139, fo. 165.

[29] *Reporter* 1925–6, pp. 582–4; *Reporter* 1926–7, pp. 105–10.

[30] See p. 282.   [31] *RC 1922*, p. 97.

was the changes of the postwar world – especially the revision of
university stipends nationwide in the 1950s and 60s and the great
expansion of the same era – which consecrated the divorce
between university and college, especially in the appointment of
teaching officers, which is so striking a feature of the Cambridge
scene in the late 1980s and early 1990s.[32] From the 1950s some
efforts – and from the early 60s very strenuous efforts – have been
made to heal the breach by finding college fellowships for an ever
increasing number of university teachers. But the divorce is still
manifest. In Oxford every university teaching office automatically has a fellowship attached to it; in Cambridge virtually
none.[33]

In spite of their strong emphasis on research, the Commissioners of 1922 proceeded rather hesitantly in their support of
study leave. They refused to propose the institutions 'of a
"Sabbatical Year" ' 'for reasons of public economy', but urged
that a fund be set up to help meritorious cases for leave.[34] In the
event, sabbatical leave was to be incorporated in the statutes of
1926 – one term in seven or one year in seven;[35] and it has slowly
spread about the academic world – America as in so many such
vital initiatives taking the lead, with the middle-aged universities
of Britain limping behind.[36] In recent years this vital provision,
without which many academic careers could never have taken
off, has been extended: for the humanities, the British Academy
has sponsored a scheme for two-year readerships which enables
more substantial periods of leave for academics in mid-career at
the height of their powers. But if we ask a wider question – how
have the wishes of the 1922 Commissioners fared? Has research
benefited from their prescriptions? – we enter a world of great
obscurity. The debate on the vocation of the university teacher –

---

[32] See p. 574.
[33] The changes of the 1920s following the recommendations of the Royal Commission specifically
abolished the ties which bound the Downing Professors of Law and Medicine to Downing.
Some close links remain – such as that between the Dixie Professor and Emmanuel College
which founded the chair – but it is just possible for a Dixie Professor to be a fellow of another
college in a way which would be virtually impossible in Oxford.
[34] *RC 1922*, p. 98.
[35] Statutes of 1926 (*Reporter* 29 Jan. 1926, p. 35), D.XII.5; one term after six, salary to be fixed by
the General Board.
[36] Some leave is a common practice, but not a right, nor funded, in most provincial universities
and most London colleges; a scheme similar to that in Oxford and Cambridge was established in
the new universities of the 60s.

between teaching and research – has gone steadily on; in the postwar world research won many victories, and it is rare today for appointments to be made, or for an academic to make progress in his career, without research publication of some substance.[37]

In 1972 the Committee of Vice-Chancellors and Principals of the Universities of the UK published the *Report of an Enquiry into the Use of Academic Staff Time*, which is the only attempt (so far as I know) that has ever been made to quantify the problem.[38] Many academics throughout the land were issued with little diaries which they were asked faithfully to keep – for one week during term, one in the vacation – and return with a precise account of how they spent every hour of the day; and in some cases of the night too, for nights spent away from home on academic duties could be counted as man hours of work. Those of us who helped to compile these diaries were constantly faced with the ambiguity of the questions we were asked. The aim was to separate out time spent on undergraduate teaching, on graduate course-work, graduate research, 'personal' research – with allowance made for 'unallocable internal time' and 'external professional time'. But all these categories overlapped in a way which many of us regarded as fatal. Group research in the natural sciences leads to eternal ambiguity between graduate and personal research. I was myself engaged in research on urban history at the time and especially on the history of London, which frequently spilled over into my undergraduate and graduate teaching – just as the undergraduate city walks and graduate seminars fructified my so-called 'personal' research. These problems could be solved by liberal use of 'unallocable' time, but that only served to fudge the results still more. When the data were transferred from the diaries to the report, further ambiguities emerged. There is a table showing the breakdown by discipline, and another by universities – but not the division of disciplines within each university; and this is a fundamental flaw. For a glance at the table of disciplines reminds us that education and clinical medicine are almost wholly taught to postgraduates in many places, and will tend to press down the percentage of time allotted to undergraduates for

[37] See pp. 512–16.
[38] Apart, that is, from a half-hearted attempt reported in the Robbins Report.

the whole institution. For Cambridge the percentage of staff time for undergraduate teaching and the like came to 32 per cent; for Oxford it was 31 per cent. These are suspiciously low figures compared with 47 per cent for Bedford College, 46 per cent for the University of East Anglia, and so forth; and there is little doubt that if the figures had been published for humanities alone the Oxbridge percentages would have been higher. Still, with all these qualifications made, it is the only statistical evidence we are ever likely to have. Here are the percentages for the whole country and for Cambridge and Oxford alone – I have added the 'mean hours per week over the working year' (i.e. excluding holiday periods, whatever that means) in brackets after the first set of figures.[39]

	All universities	Cambridge	Oxford
Undergraduate time	37 (18.5)	32	31
Graduate course-work time	5 (2.5)	3	5
Graduate research time	6 (3.0)	7	7
Personal research time	24 (12.0)	25	24
Unallocable internal time	18 (9.5)	20	20
External professional time	11 (5.5)	13	13

The total hours worked per week averaged at 50.5 – the 'mean number of weeks worked per year' at 47. I remember reflecting when I first saw these figures that, though the totals were perhaps respectable, there must be many idle academics still in the 1970s to account for them, since I knew that many (myself included) had returned figures greatly in excess of these.

Thus in the long run the aims of the Commissioners of 1922 were answered. However unreliable these figures may be, they indicate some sort of a balance between teaching and research which would have pleased the Commissioners. We cannot set them beside any comparable evidence from the 1920s or the 1980s – though we may guess that a similar enquiry in 1990 which took adequate account of the time spent handling the insatiable demands of central government would produce a less healthy

[39] These details are noted from a copy in my possession, pp. 9, 16–17.

distribution. We cannot allot causes to the pattern we observe with any precision; but all that we know of the development of the profession between 1922 and 1972 would suggest that if a little might be attributed to the Commissioners' efforts to improve the career structure and pay of the profession, much more should be attributed to the standards and attitudes of the profession itself.

The various disciplines and triposes were in some measure already managed by Boards of Studies, and in 1913 Oxford had established a group of Faculty Boards more tightly related to the needs and purposes of university teaching. The Commissioners recommended that Cambridge follow suit and laid down many prescriptions for their composition and their work.[40] They made the laudable observation that Faculty Boards ought to be more representative of the teachers of the subject than the existing boards, and then prescribed that they should not have more than sixteen members each. In the event, the Faculty Boards of the 1990s vary from 16 to 37, from boards in the smaller faculties which comprise a majority of the teachers in the subject and are truly representative, to those in the larger which are oligarchies.[41] The Commissioners were at considerable pains to lay down the ways in which the boards could manage lectures and exams and other regions of their work, and this is one of the sections of the report which has been most fully put into effect.

The Commissioners concluded their discussion of the faculties with a plea for the enlargement of research fellowships 'available for the endowment of young graduates'.[42] It had been often the practice for promising young scholars to be elected to fellowships immediately after graduation, and although enlightened colleges tried to allow them periods of study, they were often swept into a tide of teaching before they had completed research of any substance. This was the cause or the excuse of many a career, which might be exceedingly productive of good teaching but totally unproductive of original work. Many survived it; nor has the practice of instant promotion entirely died out. Professor Harold James was an undergraduate in Caius in 1978, a teaching fellow of Peterhouse before the year was out. A man of

[40] *RC 1922*, pp. 82–90; for Oxford see p. 80.
[41] *Ordinances of the University of Cambridge*, chap. 5.
[42] *RC 1922*, p. 93; cf. pp. 105–6.

exceptional stamina, he performed his teaching to admiration and yet completed a Ph.D. within two years; by 1986 he had departed for a chair in Princeton – a remarkable amalgam of the career patterns of the 1900s and the 1980s. In the 1920s the flow of graduate students was rising rapidly, and the Commissioners reasonably paid close attention to it. They observed, or foresaw, the pattern of the future, in which the research student (already in the 1920s often working for a Ph.D.), became a research fellow, then a university lecturer; and this became increasingly the norm in the 1930s and the postwar world. There have been many anomalies and overlaps: the war broke the pattern for a time, and it was still possible in the late 1940s for a young scholar to by-pass some of the stages now fairly firmly established – to proceed from the tripos to a research fellowship without embarking on a Ph.D., as I myself did; but by then I was something of a freak. With many qualifications and exceptions, the international pattern, with the doctorate as the universal basic qualification for higher posts, has been asserting itself in the last thirty years.

III. 'Accessibility of the Universities and Colleges to poor students.' This had been a major preoccupation of reformers in Oxford and Cambridge in the later nineteenth century, and had been a national issue already before the First World War. Many of the older colleges had been founded precisely to provide opportunities for 'poor scholars' and it was the poor alone who could not afford to enjoy them. The Commissioners of 1852 had from the highest motives frowned on closed scholarships and sizarships with 'menial duties attached'.[43] But these had been precisely the routes by which men of humble origin had entered the universities – and in earlier times no social stigma had attached to being a sizar; it was the normal way of reducing fees for a freshman. The late nineteenth century saw a vast expansion in secondary education, led and financed by the professional middle class; and most colleges in Oxford and Cambridge provided a standard of living which they could afford and the poor could not. Furthermore, scholarship money in the colleges of the 1920s was often paid to young men whose parents could well afford full fees – or might duplicate other sources of income. This was

---

[43] Cf. *RC 1922*, p. 131.

perhaps the region of university finance most open to public criticism in the first quarter of the twentieth century, and the Commissioners took infinite pains to reform it.[44] They had expert enquiry made into the efficiency of college administration – especially into the cost of catering; they looked closely at arrangements for non-collegiate students and for the various sources of support: state scholarships, local scholarships and the endowed scholarship funds of the colleges. These enquiries led them to recommend an increase in Local Scholarships which, slowly but surely, proved to be the answer to the financial problem in the end.[45]

Meanwhile, every effort was made to reduce the cost of living in college and increase the value of the scholarship funds. This was a major preoccupation of both the Royal and the Statutory Commissioners, as is very apparent from the bizarre system of college accounts which was devised by the Statutory Commissioners on lines laid down by the Commission – and revised on the advice of a committee of bursars[46] – and which is still prescribed in the University Statutes and still obeyed by the colleges. It is as different as possible from the accounts of a modern company. There is no attempt to determine whether the college finances as a whole are in a condition of profit or loss. In a sense it was a highly traditional instrument of college finance, for it was designed to determine not whether the college prospered but whether its money was being addressed to its proper purposes. The old college accounts had been designed to answer a complex variety of purposes and obligations, culminating in the element most precious to the fellows, the calculation of the sums which could reasonably be divided among them as their 'dividend'. The dividend was the ark of the covenant. It had its origin (roughly speaking) in the great inflation of the late sixteenth century. Fellows' stipends were based on fixed rents whose value fell with inflation; to compensate for this, entry fines for new tenancies and corn rents and various other dues were dealt out as dividends.[47] From its somewhat dubious origin the dividend

---

[44] Cf. the lengthy discussions recorded in the early sections of Bodleian MS Asquith 139.
[45] See p. 542.   [46] See p. 362.
[47] See esp. Howard 1935; Venn, IV, pt. 2 (1912, by E. J. Gross).

became (in the eyes of the fellows) the most respectable part of college finance; and it had this admirable consequence that the fellows took much more interest in the efficiency of the bursar's conduct of affairs than before or since the heyday of the dividend. The Statutory Commissioners of the 1920s were determined to see that college income was spent on college purposes. They were men of tradition, and so they embalmed the dividend without burying it; in a more radical era it would have been abolished. They ensured its survival but set limits to it;[48] even allowing that they worked at a time when there was no visible inflation,[49] they must have known that these limits made it no longer sufficient to support the fellowship – they took other steps to ensure that working fellows were rewarded for their work. But for all the care they showed for ancient practice, the new college accounts were clearly directed to new aims. These can be discerned by a brief glimpse at the main heads of account.

First comes the external revenue account; and although this gives some notion of the college's gross income from endowment, the account itself is geared, by its choice of exemptions, entirely to determine the amount of university tax the college has to pay: for support by the richer colleges for the university itself and for the poorer colleges was a substantial concern in the 1920s.[50] Characteristically, the external revenue account ends with a series of transfers: it is not the aim of these accounts to strike balances; at the point where we might expect them to do so they slip off to another account.

Next comes the internal revenue account, which covers college housekeeping – food, maintenance of buildings and so forth; and there is a serious attempt to balance this against fee income. Its purpose indeed is to ensure that fee income pays for what it should, and is fairly used. This involves a host of assumptions which are largely hidden in the accounts. How much of the cost of housekeeping can be attributed to endowment, how much is fairly laid on the day to day running cost supported by undergra-

---

[48] See below: some college statutes still allowed for the striking of a balance – an incredible feat in view of the form of college accounts prescribed by the Commissioners – but the fixed maxima now set on dividends made it a nugatory exercise.

[49] See p. 284.

[50] Strictly, for the university, though in practice it has been diverted to the colleges. *RC 1922*, pp. 203–10.

duate fees? This is equally evident in the tuition account, which covers in similar fashion the cost of education in the college – and again is balanced against the income from fees; balanced in a more precise sense, since the Statutory Commissioners enforced the rule that tuition fees should be determined so that the tuition accounts of each college were normally just about in balance.[51] So far, the general rule book is quite clear; but if one examines the accounts of individual colleges many ambiguities are revealed. To what extent is the library part of the general education of the college, paid for by the tuition funds, to what extent a proper claim on the endowment? What of the chaplain and some of the college officers?[52]

The endowment account at first sight seems the most straight-forward of all: it handles the major items of income not swept away in university tax, and the major items of expenditure not paid for out of fees. Its income comprises a major share of the endowment revenue not tied up in special trusts. But at every point, in practice, we encounter grey areas. We have observed some of its overlaps with the internal revenue and tuition accounts. Its income may include a surprising element of trust money – the share of the trusts which can legitimately be spent on payment of fellows and other general college purposes. Its income and much of its expenditure comprise transfers to or from other funds so that the balance struck at the end (not just a surplus, but a 'surplus transferred to General Capital Account') is no clear indication of college prosperity.

Two of the most significant transfers from the endowment account were to the Scholarship Fund and to general capital. A major purpose of the whole exercise was to identify possible surpluses in the endowment account for scholarships. Since the

---

[51] Thus the *King's* statutes read:
> The tutorial charges made to members of the College *in statu pupillari* shall be fixed, so far as is reasonably possible, so that the expenditure for educational purposes is met out of the Tuition Fund, except so far as it is charged on a special endowment, provided that, if those charges are fixed at such a sum that they cannot reasonably be raised, and the Tuition Fund is exhausted, the Governing Body may make payments from corporate revenue towards the stipends and pension contributions of Educational Officers. (*Statutes of King's College*, к.iii.2)

What follows is based on a survey of numerous college accounts, published annually in the *Reporter*.

[52] I omit the kitchen account, really a subsidiary of the internal revenue account.

advent of universal grants in the 1960s this function has been greatly diminished and a substantial purpose of the accounting system has fallen away; in this and many other regions it is really obsolete. But it is of its nature so obscure it is difficult to reform; and many a bursar has rejoiced in its obscurity – even to the point that a legend has arisen that it was devised by a committee of bursars to hide the truth from their colleagues. The Commission itself attributes it to Messrs W. B. Peat and Co., the accountants who advised the Commissioners – though admittedly after themselves taking advice from the colleges; and it was revised and put into effect by a Committee of the Statutory Commissioners chaired by Sir Hugh Anderson, which had received advice from the committee of bursars.[53]

The Commissioners finally ensured that some limits be set to the freedom of governing bodies to handle the college revenues by the provisions of the Universities and Colleges Estates Act of 1925 which govern the capital accounts.[54] First of all, the existing capital of the college which can be expressed as money – for no note is taken of buildings or assets – is called the corporate capital; there is no statement in the accounts of its total value, only of what has flowed in and out of it in the year; and this is to check that the college does not dip its fingers into the corporate capital, which is not permitted. It may borrow from it (as long as it repays what it borrows); it may give to or lend to it – but not diminish it. There is, however, another capital account, 'General Capital', in which prudent bursars may salt away their balances; to this may go the balance of the endowment account (or what is left after the numerous transfers have been transacted); and this may be freely used to cover deficits, or in happier times to pay for new projects. The accounts offer plenty of opportunity for building up reserves if colleges are so minded; the general capital is the general reserve. The other accounts are trust accounts, a reminder that college accounts could never, at the end of the day, be simple. For in some colleges these are numerous and complex, based on endowments made for specific purposes. From them a well-endowed college may pay many of its fellows; but they

---

[53] *RC 1922*, p. 194 and Appendix 16; for the Statutory Commissioners' Committee I am indebted to notes kindly provided by Mr Christopher Johnson.
[54] 15 George V, chap. 24, esp. c. 26.

cannot use the surplus for feasting or building, unless the terms of the trust permit it. Most of these trusts are quite modern, for the Commissioners of the 1850s were more ruthless and the older trusts were mostly wound up – not without reason, for, in the rare cases in which an ancient trust survives, it may perpetuate some very complex and useless provisions. A striking example is the Perse Trust, now in the main administered by Caius, from which relatively small sums have to be distributed to a galaxy of good purposes under provisions made in the early seventeenth century and only slightly modified in the nineteenth.[55]

Perhaps the most important of all the aims of the Commissioners in their treatment of college finance was to preserve the independence of the colleges – a very significant element in the attitudes and ethos of the 1920s. Government aid went to the university; the colleges looked after themselves. All the more care was therefore needed to ensure that they were free-standing, that even the poorer colleges could make ends meet. To this general principle there was an exception. 'We have no hesitation in recommending the payment of an annual grant from Public Funds for the benefit of the women's Colleges at both universities.' The grounds were that 'the funds available for women's education *as a whole* at Oxford and Cambridge are gravely insufficient . . .'[56] This was suggested as a temporary measure; the Commissioners looked forward to a day not far distant (as they hoped) when women would cease to be at a disadvantage. But the proposal was not implemented.

The sections of the Commissioners' Report on the place of women was an epilogue to the dramatic events of 1920–1, when Oxford succeeded and Cambridge failed to admit women to full membership of the university.[57] The Commissioners stated their unanimous wish to see women fully participate in the life of both universities, and left it to the Cambridge committee to state their views. They expressed indignation at the women's lack of status in words warm enough a little to disguise the ambiguity of their positive recommendations. There may have been a division of

---

[55] In 1852 the trustees were still the master and four senior fellows of Caius, *not* the college, so it escaped the reforms of the 1850s, to be swept up in the 1860s and 1870s: see pp. 73–6; Brooke 1985, p. 203.

[56] *RC 1922*, p. 171.   [57] See pp. 325–6.

opinion; there was evidently an urgent need to placate the opinion of Senate which had voted 904 to 712 against admitting women to full membership as recently as December 1920.[58] They urged that women be given full rights; but they also prescribed that women be not made Chancellor, Vice-Chancellor, proctor or head of department, and that their total numbers be limited by statute to 500; and they admitted that they were 'fairly' equally divided as to whether the admission of women should be effected by parliament or by the university. This was fatal; nothing was done, and the only consequence of the Commissioners' warmly expressed good intentions was a prohibition on the admission of women to men's colleges, which no-one at the time seriously proposed.

THE COMMISSIONERS AT WORK

There is a powerful irony in returning from the earnest (if ineffective) efforts for women's education of the Commission to Sir Hugh Anderson's neglected daughter. Although she was discreetly deaf to the business discussed in the master's lodge, and avoided discussing it in her reminiscences, she throws a rare shaft of light into the history of the Commissions by first quoting Sir Richard Glazebrook's account of Anderson's role – from a letter to *The Times* after his death – and then giving her own impressions. Here is Glazebrook:[59]

> That Sir Hugh Anderson took an important part of the work both of the Royal Commission and of the Statutory Commission which framed the new statutes for Cambridge, is generally known, but only those who were his colleagues on one, or both, of the Commissions can fully realise the magnitude of his share in that work. The general scheme of the new financial arrangements between the University and the Colleges was outlined in the report of the Royal Commission. It was he who, with infinite care and trouble, placed before the members of the latter body [the Statutory Commission] the data necessary to fill in the details of that scheme. The plan ultimately adopted was his, but he realised from the first that it must be worked out in cooperation

---

[58] *RC 1922*, p. 172; cf. pp. 172–5. For what follows, see above, pp. 325–7.
[59] *The Times* 1928, quoted Anderson 1988ff, chap. 22 and Venn VI, 520.

with the bursars and others versed in university finance. Many were the meetings and discussions in his study; the Master ever acute, but ever ready to consider most carefully the arguments of others and to assign to them their full weight. And thus, when some agreement had been reached, it was he who explained it in all its bearings to his colleagues, who prepared and wrote out in his own hand the sheets of figures needed to make clear the plan which he put forward as fair and equitable to College and University alike. Or again, in the intricate discussions which took place over the Faculty scheme, he was ever ready to assist. Were estimates needed to indicate how a plan would work out financially, Anderson provided them.[60] Was some criticism offered of his estimates, no trouble was too great for him, he would go through all his calculations again, modifying them where needed, though in most cases the result was only to show that he had been correct originally. Always quiet and unobtrusive, never rattled or flurried, silent until he felt sure, unless at times he spoke to point out his doubts and hesitations at a suggested course, he has died as he lived, a great son of the University, thinking only of its welfare, anxious to promote its interest as a place of learning and research.

Then Maisie Anderson takes up the story.

I heard little of what happened at sessions of the Royal Commission, and remember even less, although hour long discussions of the problems involved: pensions,[61] fellowships, provision of libraries, cost of living, College catering etc., flowed over my head at lunch or round the study fire. Only when Father talked of the personalities involved did I listen receptively. Once he described Asquith, Chairman of the Royal Commission, sitting crumpled in his chair, and apparently asleep, throughout a long session during which many witnesses gave conflicting evidence and yet, at the end of it, summing up the whole discussion with the most incisive lucidity . . . What I remember most vividly was the work of preparing for the various sessions, when the wide sheets of financial analyses, written in his own hand, were spread over the big table on which he worked . . . Papers were heaped on other

---

[60] Appendix 3 contains just such a record made by (or for) Anderson, one of the few original documents of his work for the Commission to survive.

[61] It is interesting that she places this first, and it was indeed a major preoccupation – to provide effective pensions and enable older staff to retire; it was not however the happiest region of the Commissioners' activities, for the old FSSU which emerged was in its early days woefully inadequate.

tables, on chairs, on the floor, the general confusion being made
worse by the genial gesture with which he swept them aside if
someone came in to consult him. At night the candles flickered on
his table . . . and his tired eyes seemed to grow paler as they moved
back and forth over the long columns of minutely written figures
. . . When, at last, the figures were marshalled in the form of
presentation which he had chosen, one might have expected that
he would leave the work of duplicating the statement to a
secretary, but no, that also he insisted on doing himself . . . I was
his only 'stooge' in the early days of the Commissions and my
capacity was limited to rolling off copies of documents after
Father had written the stencils.[62]

She goes on to give pencil sketches of some of the Commissioners who stayed in the lodge, which show how frequent were
visits from some Commissioners and how intense the work
which centred in Anderson's study – he was, as Asquith said of
him, '*the* business man of the University'[63] – which may reconcile us a little to the unbalanced nature of our evidence which
inevitably gives him too dominant a role. Some of the vignettes
are unforgettable. Lord Chalmers, the Oxford man who became
first an undergraduate then master of Peterhouse in these very
years, comes surprisingly to life as a co-mingler of weighty
phrases and subtle wit.

His slow, sagacious manner reminded me of the ponderous gait
and crafty watchfulness of a ceremonial elephant, such as he must
have ridden when he left the Treasury to become Governor of
Ceylon . . . He said, with the utmost gravity, that he was about to
give me a piece of advice on which he had based his own career.
'Never work between meals!'[64]

Her most significant portrait is of G. M. Trevelyan, evidently,
after Anderson, the most influential of the Cambridge Commissioners.[65] Trevelyan had left his Trinity fellowship in 1903 to
join the literary and political circles of London; and he had been a
tireless worker for the Liberal cause in the years which followed.
Doubtless this brought him to the notice of Asquith and helps to

[62] Anderson 1988ff, chap. 22.   [63] Asquith 1933, p. 141.
[64] Anderson 1988ff., chap. 22. Cf. above, n. 4.   [65] See pp. 127, 129.

account for his role in the Commission; and in Trevelyan's powerful mind an admiration for Cambridge which stopped well this side of idolatry – and an affection for Cambridge which he showed abundantly after his appointment as Regius Professor of Modern History in 1927 and as master of Trinity in 1940 – combined with critical sympathy and imaginative insight to make him a central figure in the Commission. He was 'the Great George' to the Andersons:

> I was frankly terrified of him when he first came to stay; a tall gaunt, iron-gray man with piercing eyes that seemed caged in behind his small steel-rimmed spectacles, and whose harsh voice cut through the superficialities of table talk like a saw-mill slicing rotten wood. Within a few days, however, fear had given way to liking for I discovered that the same grim jokes that amused us would make his grating laugh ring out 'like a duck that has quacked itself hoarse' as I impertinently remarked in my diary.[66]

Superficially, Trevelyan appears to be of the essence of the Cambridge establishment. In early days he was an Apostle, and a violent anti-clerical; he was a tireless fell-walker in the Cambridge tradition, and the National Trust owes much to him; and he rose to be Regius Professor and master of Trinity. But there was a fierce, if always amiable, independence which infuriated the more conventional Cambridge historians, for he never bowed to fashion – whether it be to J. B. Bury's cult of scientific history as a young man, or to the Namierisation of political history in his grey hairs. The result is that his essays on the poetry of history, his epic trilogy on Garibaldi (some of which has stood the test of critical enquiry better than more scientific rivals)[67] and his *England under Queen Anne* will still be read for many generations to come.

> When Father ... was there to stimulate good talk, George Trevelyan's conversation was enthralling ... But if Mamma and I were left alone with him, we tried out our modest conversational openings with trepidation. He had a way of snatching up a subject which did not interest him, like a terrier pouncing on a rat, and dropping it, stone dead, at the end of one sentence. It was

[66] Anderson 1988ff, chap. 22.
[67] See Mack Smith 1954. On Trevelyan see *DNB 1961–1970*, pp. 1015–17 (J. R. M. Butler), and especially Chadwick 1969; Plumb 1988, pp. 180–204, etc.

therefore with mixed feelings that we heard Father invite him to stay with us for a fortnight at Heacham[68] during the summer of 1921, while he was writing the Report of the Royal Commission.[69]

This is a tiresomely ambiguous and allusive reference of great historical interest; but from what follows it seems clear that it was Trevelyan who had the main responsibility for the Cambridge contribution to the final report.

> There was chaos in our home during that fortnight! Papers were thickly strewn over all the floors and the tables were covered with ink and glue. When he was not writing, the Great George strode up and down the garden, so deep in thought that he did not even notice that he was trampling straight through flower beds. When the current of his thought struck a snag, he would bark out requests for further information and Father would then work at feverish speed to produce what was needed. The new material would be absorbed at one gulp and fresh demands put forward until Father remarked pathetically that he felt like a chaffinch trying to satisfy a young cuckoo, and I drew a caricature of them both in this guise . . . Though alarming [GMT] was very lovable

and she describes him reading poetry, his rough voice stripping off the superficial music of the poems, but laying bare 'the skeleton of meaning' and deepening her understanding of them.

> Mamma never quite lost her shyness with him, but my avid interest overcame most of my fears and the last of them melted away after he had invited me to take a walk with him in Cambridge [in 1927], which included the deliberate crossing of every patch of the sacrosanct grass in Trinity, to proclaim his newly acquired Fellow's right of treading on it.[70]

With this patch-work view of the Commission at work we must be content. While Anderson constantly aided and inspired his colleagues to work in genial collaboration, the Statutory Commissioners completed what the Royal Commission had begun. Once again, we know little of the details of its work, for

---

[68] The handsome Queen Anne house which was at that time the master's country lodge.
[69] Anderson 1988ff, chap. 12.   [70] Ibid.

the *University Reporter*, so lavish in printing discussions of even the most trivial University Discussions, contains no reports of the discussions of the Commissions or their work,[71] but only formal announcements of the stages by which they completed their task. The secretary of the Statutory Commissioners was the Trinity lawyer H. A. Hollond, and to him fell the task of drafting, presumably the university statutes, certainly the statutes of all the colleges. A curious reader of college statutes as they emerged in 1926 might wonder at the amount of common language and common material they contain. In part this might be attributed to the general instructions which came from the Statutory Commissioners, in part to common traditional sources. But the main reason was explained to me in the last conversation I had with Hollond's assistant secretary, Tressilian Nicholas, the greatly respected doyen of Trinity fellows who died in 1989 at the respectable age of 101, with a memory for every period of his life remarkably fresh and vivid. The Statutory Commissioners insisted that all the new college statutes should be personally drafted by Hollond – though in all cases with due reference to the special needs and wishes of the college representatives – even to the point that a set of fully drafted statutes which emerged from one of the colleges was simply rejected.[72]

By the end of 1926 the university and all the colleges had received their new statutes, and the faculties could embark on their new careers.

---

[71] Except for the University Statutes, printed in *Reporter* 29 Jan. 1926.   [72] See n. 17.

Chapter 12

THE UNIVERSITY LIBRARY

On 7 May 1921 the Senate of the University of Cambridge agreed, by a modest vote of 121 to 73, that a new site be sought for the University Library.[1] In a formal sense, the senators approved a report from a Syndicate; but this was the gist and essence of its message; and few more important decisions have been made by that body in its long and chequered history. It was by no means the end of the debate: the anxious University Librarian, A. F. Scholfield, felt obliged in March 1924 to provide an elaborate defence of the decision, since many voices were being heard to question it.[2] Nor did anyone know how it was to be financed. Yet it came to pass. In 1926 officials of the Rockefeller Foundation visited Sir Hugh Anderson, the master of Caius, to discuss their liberal plans for financing the biological sciences – and went away half-committed to financing a new Library.[3] When Anderson died in 1928 Giles Gilbert Scott had produced plans for the Library, the site had been chosen, half the cost promised by the Rockefeller Foundation. In 1931 the first piles were driven and in 1934 King George V opened the new Library. In the years leading to 1972 it was successfully enlarged, and in the 1980s there were urgent plans to extend it again, of which the first fruits are visible in the early 90s. The University Library is the centre of study and research in Cambridge, the main key to its work and reputation in many fields – and in its galleries and coffee room much ardent learned discussion has

[1] *Reporter*, 1920–1, p. 959. This account is mainly based on the *Reporter* and on the archives of the Library (now CUA, CUL Archives), which Mr Nigel Hancock most kindly made available to me. For Maisie Anderson's reminiscences of Sir Hugh Anderson, see p. 343. For the extracts from the Rockefeller Foundation Archives, generously provided for my use, see n. 30.
[2] CUL Archives, 'History of the Library', IX (1924–39), no. 18 (a).
[3] See below, pp. 381–2.

taken place, and many marriages have been formed; its saga continues unabated. But the central events in its creation belong to the years 1920 to 1934.

Over the previous generation there had been countless schemes to improve the old University Library – which had come to occupy virtually the whole of the Old Schools – and to enlarge it. The story is full of irony, and a remarkable example of the way Cambridge and Oxford alternately copy one another and then choose the opposite courses. Cambridge had long been acutely aware that the Bodleian had more space, finer rooms and much richer collections of manuscripts and early printed books. The comparison had stirred many librarians, and many lovers of the Library, to emulation. Between 1867 and 1886 the genius of Henry Bradshaw had been directed – sometimes whimsically and ineffectively, but with a warmth of vision and a depth of scholarship new in the Cambridge Library – to make the collection worthy of a major university.[4] Meanwhile, after a long series of struggles and arguments, Cambridge had preserved its role as a copyright library, along with the British Museum, the Bodleian, and libraries in Scotland, Wales and Ireland. This and the vast expansion of learning of the late nineteenth and early twentieth centuries meant that it was flooded with books, and the readers were driven into smaller and smaller corners. The Bodleian naturally faced the crisis first, and began to burrow. In Cambridge there were schemes for modest new buildings, and for providing a roof over the eastern court – the main court of the original Old Schools. In 1901 the old Registrary, John Willis Clark, was actively canvassing support for this plan. Eventually it was put to the vote and Clark 'was intensely vexed when the Syndicate's proposals were non-placeted by nineteen votes'.[5] He regarded it as a major victory for the forces of darkness in Cambridge; but he battled on, and other ideas were discussed, including the excavation of underground stores in imitation of recent developments in Oxford. If the obscurantists had not won, if these schemes had matured, if the First World War had not given a large pause for reflection, the vote of 1921 might well

---

4 See McKitterick 1986, chaps. 17–19. For what follows, see McKitterick 1986, chap. 14.
5 Shipley 1913, p. 175.

have gone another way, and Cambridge might have struggled on with its hopelessly inadequate old Library. In Oxford the same debate took place over the first thirty years of the twentieth century. The Bodleian started with an enormous advantage which it never relinquished; and very naturally and properly there attached to Duke Humfrey and Bodley's splendid quadrangle a sentiment which could never quite attach itself to the Cambridge Library. So Oxford rejected all schemes for a new site or the provision of a major library elsewhere; and the 1930s saw the same Giles Gilbert Scott build the modest extension, the New Bodleian, which has helped to bind this great Library to its ancient ways – while Cambridge, which lost every battle except the last, has the finest working Library in Europe.

In 1902 an 'Extension Subsyndicate' had been formed to seek other means of enlarging the Library.[6] At first it comprised J. W. Clark, Mr Huddleston, censor of non-collegiate students, Mr Macaulay of King's, and the Reverend J. B. Lock, the formidable bursar of Caius. They considered many projects, including one suggested by a graduate of Pembroke in 1905 for stack rooms across the river joined to the Library by 'a double line of pneumatic tubes'.[7] In 1904–5 a young fellow of Caius, Hugh Anderson, a rising neurophysiologist, became deeply interested in college finance and so, intimate with Lock.[8] They belonged to a generation of fellows who dearly loved to see their college lined with timber, and in 1905 Lock and Anderson formed a generous partnership to buy the panelling from an old battleship and convert the fifteenth-century college library, then disused, into an Edwardian smoking room.[9] It may well have been out of this friendship that Anderson came first to be interested in the University Library. His daughter tells us that he was not a great reader himself;[10] yet he was to be the central figure in the making of the new Library. He enjoyed a first view of the Library Syndicate and the Extension Subsyndicate from January 1909 to

[6] CUL Archives, Minutes of Extension Subsyndicate.
[7] This letter of 20 October 1905 from C. A. Carus-Wilson is preserved in the same Minute Book.
[8] F. J. M. Stratton in Venn, VI, 516–17; cf. Brooke 1985, p. 266.
[9] Brooke 1985, pp. 253–4 and pls. 22–3.
[10] Anderson 1988ff, chap. 14; cf. chap. 7.

December 1912, when he was already master of Caius.[11] By then Anderson had evidently a deeply planted interest in the problem of the Library, which was to bear remarkable fruit in the 1920s.

In May 1914 the Subsyndicate proposed an underground bookstore of two floors, similar to that recently installed by the Bodleian, beneath the grass beside the Senate House.[12] The war prevented any action, but those who remained in Cambridge continued to ponder; and in 1917 J. B. Lock (a man devoted to the practical details of building operations) was authorised to consult Sindall's the builders about the practical possibility of putting underground stores under the courts of the Library.[13] Eventually, on 6 November 1918, the Subsyndicate produced its final report, recommending a whole series of daring measures – underground stores, a new bookstore on the west court, a reading room in the east court, and so forth.[14]

It seems to have been immediately recognised that these measures would prove immensely costly for a relatively modest return. So on 18 February 1920 the Library Syndicate itself – assuming that the 'cost of moving the whole library elsewhere renders such removal altogether impossible' – suggested to the university that a new building be set up on the south side of the Senate House yard.[15] There followed one of the most crucial debates in the history of the university. In their report the Library Syndicate had raised the possibility of moving part of the Library elsewhere – as the British Museum had recently moved the newspapers to Hendon; but it had dismissed the idea as unpractical and very inconvenient. Yet it was this possibility which most caught the attention of those who heard or read the report of the discussion.[16] Dr Giles, the master of Emmanuel and Vice-Chancellor, who had presided over the Extension Subsyndicate in 1918, could not be present, but a letter from him was read earnestly pressing for a long-term solution. The present Library

[11] CUL Archives, Minutes of CUL Syndicate, pp. 229, 231; Extension Subsyndicate 1909–11. Anderson is simply referred to as 'Dr Anderson', but reports in *Reporter* 1908–9, p. 1044; 1909–10, p. 1253, etc. are signed 'H. K. Anderson'.

[12] Ibid., Report to Library Syndicate, 6 May 1914.

[13] Ibid., 1917–18; Lock's practical interest also shows in a letter of 16 July 1906 on the basement of the Cockerell building preserved in the same minutes.

[14] Minutes of the Extension Subsyndicate, 6 Nov. 1918.

[15] Ibid., 18 Feb. 1920; *Reporter*, 1919–20, pp. 657–9.

[16] For what follows, *Reporter*, 1919–20, pp. 749–54.

was overcrowded; staff time in shifting books to make space was expensive; readers found the books 'in very unexpected places'. The Senate must decide on one of three courses – to build on another site, to build an underground chamber, or to build on the south side of Senate House yard. 'It is important that the scheme adopted should provide for a considerable time. Additions that provide only for a short period are much more expensive in the long run than a larger scheme providing for a longer period.' He then spoke very earnestly about the difficulties of dividing the Library; of the weakness of a much-canvassed suggestion to move the University Press and occupy its site for part of the Library; and finally – 'Whatever we do, we must do quickly.' The discussion was fluctuating and inconclusive, and towards the end came a desperate *cri de coeur* from Jenkinson, the University Librarian. The previous scheme, for burrowing and building in the east court, had been abandoned on grounds of expense. The new building, 'the scheme before them was therefore the only one left'. But it did not find favour, and it was increasingly evident that a full and serious investigation of alternative buildings or alternative sites was needed. On 22 June 1920 a new Syndicate 'to consider the needs of the Library for further accommodation and the means of satisfying them' was set up, comprising Dr Giles, Dr Pearce, the master of Corpus and Sir Geoffrey Butler of Corpus – the most strenuous opponents of the previous half-measures – Hugh Anderson, the Librarian and A. F. Scholfield, shortly to succeed as Librarian, and three other men much involved in the recent discussions.[17]

At their first meeting in July 1920 the Syndics prepared for bold measures. They readily agreed to Dr Pearce's suggestion that they minute their disapproval of all schemes for putting more buildings on the old site; and they agreed unanimously that it was 'desirable to secure a site for either an extension of the Library or a new home eventually for the whole Library'. Dr Pearce, Dr Anderson and two others were set to work to consider possible sites.[18] They briefly pondered an earlier idea for a building in front of King's, which was readily seen to be inadequate and

[17] *Reporter*, 1919–20, p. 126–8; CUL Archives, 'History of the Library', IX, no. 8.
[18] CUL Archives, Minute Book of Syndicate to Consider the Needs of the Library (henceforth 'Needs'), fo. 2, meeting of 27 July 1920.

unacceptable. They dismissed the Pitt Press and a site in Jesus Lane. Then they fastened on the Corpus cricket ground by Sidgwick Avenue, where the Sidgwick Site, the new arts complex of the 1960s and 1970s, was to lie, a space comprising three acres, which could be increased to four and a half if the college garden was thrown in.[19] Dr Pearce as master of Corpus did not sign the report and only spoke in the discussion to say that his college had not yet 'intervened' in the matter. Nor did they in the future.

When the discussion opened on 24 February 1921 Sir William Ridgeway, the Disney Professor of Archaeology and a fellow of Caius, rose to his feet; and a tremor might well have passed through the proponents of the report, for he was the prince of the non-placeters, a man who had led the opposition to every scheme for improving the lot of women in Cambridge and previous plans for the Library.[20] His speech was so comparatively urbane as to make me suspect that he and Anderson had been in conclave. He did indeed condemn earlier proposals in his most eloquent manner, observing that a building on the south side of Senate House yard 'would have destroyed for ever the finest academic view, not only in this country but in Europe'. He had formerly supported a scheme for building underground in imitation of Bodley; he had later urged that the Downing Site be used for a new Library – but he had not been listened to –

> he had himself been threatened. Now the spell was broken. The scales had fallen from the eyes of some of the supporters of the old plans, and they had before them a fine, statesmanlike scheme. He did not quite agree that the proposed site was the best that could be chosen. What he did want to emphasise was that the principle of the scheme was the true one. Once for all let the University make up its mind not to interfere with the ancient University, where everything that was good, and perhaps some things that were bad, had taken place from the thirteenth century . . . As to the site, it was of course no use crying over spilt milk. [The Downing Site had gone.] The question now was whether the site proposed on the Corpus ground was the best available for the purpose. He had looked round anxiously, and he was sorry to say

---

[19] *Reporter*, 1920–1, p. 628.
[20] See pp. 204–5; for this discussion see *Reporter*, 1920–1, pp. 732–6; cf. p. 622 for the date.

he could only see one other site – the playing field of King's and Clare which had been used for the First Eastern Hospital. If there was any chance of the University being able to acquire that in the near future, he believed that they would all urge strongly that that would be the more appropriate place, much more convenient, much more acceptable than the proposed site at Newnham.

On the plot he had named the University Library now stands. No doubt its merits were less obvious to those who viewed it in the early 1920s than they are now, since it had been covered with a hutted hospital, now temporary housing; but to those who knew west Cambridge well it could not fail to commend itself; and to Ridgeway goes the credit for this crucial proposal. True to his nature, he followed it with some swipes at Newnham – 'some people would think that the real centre of University activity and life would be in the region of Newnham' – but that was not very fair to Girton who would be better served by choosing the King's and Clare field – and with this Parthian shot he commended the report to the Senate.

Ridgeway was followed by an eloquent plea from Dr Cranage, later dean of Norwich, not to remove the Library from its old centre; he spoke warmly of the inconvenience of moving it to 'the suburbs'.[21] He was answered by Mr Forster Cooper of Trinity, a member of the Syndicate, who cited the experience of Harvard, where the decision had been made to bring the Library into a single new building, including 'no less than one hundred private rooms . . . for professors' (a clause not likely to commend itself in Cambridge, UK); a new building might take a very long time to complete, but they must plan for it. The master of Christ's 'said that Mr Forster Cooper spoke as a Paleontologist, to whom fifty years was but as a moment'. He had himself visited Harvard and pointed out that the new library there was in the centre of the university; he spoke strongly in support of Dr Cranage. The debate was wound up by Anderson.

He 'felt that the remarks of the master of Christ's called for an answer. He himself had been very much impressed' by the Vice-Chancellor's letter read in the former discussion. The Senate had to plan for a secure long-term future, not just for the twenty or

---

[21] On Cranage see *Who was Who 1951–60*, pp. 252–3.

thirty years which was all that they could foresee on the present site; although 'he shared the feeling that it would be a great loss to lose the central site', there was gain too for the university would recover its old buildings and have a centre for offices and 'dignified rooms for receiving guests, and other associations with past centuries'. The Syndicate had looked for a more central site and had not found it; hence its report which he hoped the Senate would accept.[22]

The vote was taken and the report approved. Dr Cranage and one or two others were added to the Syndicate on Library needs and it set to work again.[23] Within a few weeks it became apparent that Ridgeway's comments had borne fruit: King's and Clare put their heads together and let it be known that they were open to negotiation.[24] In May 1922 the Syndics formally reported in favour of the site and the university was asked to endorse the decision.

Meanwhile the Syndics were quietly engaged in seeking an architect.[25] They compiled a list of possible architects in June 1922, with Giles Gilbert Scott, who was already building the Memorial Court for Clare on the west side of Queen's Road, in front of the Library site, at its head; but they also proposed a competition. Plans were still going forward to this end when Sir Hugh Anderson (as he now was) mentioned that Lord Esher had visited the site, and the Vice-Chancellor put before the Syndics a letter sent by Lord Esher to the duke of Devonshire, which transports us for a moment into the world of the whig grandees of the eighteenth century.[26] Esher was a Cambridge graduate who had been much involved in earlier fund-raising for the university; he was a great man – a former head of the Office of Works – with much experience of building and fund-raising, very confident of his own opinion, used to getting his way, yet much respected.

---

[22] *Reporter*, 1920–1, pp. 735–6.
[23] *Reporter*, 1921–2, p. 1058; Dr Giles, formerly Vice-Chancellor, became a member in his own right; so did Sir Geoffrey Butler.
[24] 'Needs', fo. 6, report of meeting of 15 June 1921. The Needs Syndicate received this news in a letter from the secretary of the Financial Board, and replied that they had 'reason to believe' this was not so when they made their former report. From now on the site is effectively treated as settled. For the report of 16 May 1922, see *Reporter* 1921–2, pp. 978–80.
[25] For what follows, see 'Needs', fos. 11–21, esp. fo. 11 for the list of architects.
[26] For what follows, 'Needs', fos. 13–16. The date of Esher's letter is given as April 10 corrected to May 10; Esher's visit had taken place on 9 May (fo. 13).

'I went down to Cambridge yesterday', he wrote to Devonshire, who was High Steward of the university, on 10 May 1923,

inspected the site, examined certain sketch plans, and talked the whole matter over with the Vice-Chancellor, the Master of Caius, and others. The site is an excellent one, immediately behind the new buildings of Clare. The sketch plans are by a man called Mitchell . . . They will not do and would appeal to no one. We discussed the method of procedure, and it was resolved to ask you to join with all of us in approving the selection of [Giles] Gilbert Scott to make a plan and a design for the new Library. We were all of us opposed to a competition. The choice of Scott was decided by the fact that he was the architect of the new buildings at Clare, and as the new Library, if built, will be in close proximity to these buildings, there is an advantage in making the same architect responsible for both. Out of the £500 placed at the disposal of the Committee, it is proposed to pay Gilbert Scott a fixed fee for his plans, leaving the question of their acceptance or rejection open, to be decided when the plans and elevation are submitted . . . No one who cares for Cambridge and possesses an historical sense can do otherwise than regret the necessity of having to vacate the Old Library . . . The object of this letter is to obtain from you your approval of what we settled yesterday: that is to say
(1) The selection of Gilbert Scott to make sketch plans;
(2) Pay him out of the sum which has been placed in the hands of the committee.
Will you let me know your view on these two points?

The duke lent his approval, adding, 'I wish we could light on a substantial benefactor, but I think the idea will appeal to Cambridge men.' This proceeding, which seems to a modern reader used to orderly competitions and more open government remarkably high-handed, commended itself to the Syndicate; and they were also much impressed by the need for the new Library to live with the new Clare buildings. One anxious Syndic wrote to Lord Esher, and was reassured.

Dear Mr Forster Cooper,
    You can reassure anyone who appears to favour 'competition' by an argument from experience and authority – if these count for anything, which perhaps they do not.
    I say nothing about my own vicissitudes, when I was head of

the Office of Works. But I know that Lord Crawford, Sir Lionel Earle, Sir Aston Webb, Sir Reginald Blomfield, will bear me out in this, that we are more likely to get a satisfactory Library, both as to price and general design, if we fix upon our architect or architects, and work hand in hand with them from the inception of our plan.[27]

On 28 September 1923 Scott visited the Library and had his first recorded discussion with members of the Syndicate.[28] By such means the first consultation with Scott grew into an assumption in their minds that he was to be the architect; and although it was a while yet before the competition was formally abandoned, from this point on Anderson and some of his colleagues were quietly working to make Scott's plans acceptable. Doubtless they had interested Esher and the duke in their ideas with a view to an appeal; but not long after the wind was to blow from a new quarter.

Scott produced his first design in 1923–4; and of this some plans and charming sketches survive.[29] The Clare new buildings have a gateway and entrance with a modest touch of classical Georgian after the Adam mode in the shape of two pillars and an architrave, and the building is of blue-grey bricks. The first sketches of the Library show a long façade with a classical feature in the centre, an entrance with four pillars and an architrave, and with wings reminiscent of the orangeries of eighteenth-century mansions, the whole of blue-grey brick. It was similar in concept to the Clare building, but larger and more stately. Yet it is clear, if we examine both the original sketches and the final design, that Scott's imagination was fired by the brief he received for the *interior*; and although we do not know the brief in detail – only formal minutes survive, not the crucial conversations he had with the Committee and the Librarian – we can see that the idea of a monumental reading room, of long galleries to house the old cases of the Royal Collection, and the practical, convenient, accessible

27 'Needs', fos. 17–18.
28 CUL Archives, file of 'Letters of Sir G. G. Scott' – henceforth Scott file. 'Needs' (from this point unpaginated) records a formal meeting with Scott on 30 October 1923.
29 Now preserved in the Map Room. They comprise two watercolours by Cyril A. Farley, dated 1924, one of the façade, the other of the reading room; drawings of a virtually identical design, and an ink sketch of the façade signed by Scott. The Syndicate on Plans dated his first sketches to 1923 (*Reporter* 1928–9, p. 1038), but the watercolours are dated 1924.

Fig. 13 Sir Giles Scott's first design for the University Library: watercolour by
Cyril A. Farley, 1924

book-stacks, were already in his mind by 1924. It is clear that the brief was closely based on the tradition of the old Cambridge University Library: the books (old and new) must be accessible to the readers, and most of them readily borrowed. To this were added attractive and ample reading spaces.

In the early 1920s John D. Rockefeller, Junior, inaugurated an imaginative and beneficent scheme to endow and revivify the study of the biological and medical sciences in a variety of centres scattered over western Europe; and in 1922–3 Richard M. Pearce visited Europe specifically to discuss the development of medical research at a number of centres, and in October 1923 he came to Cambridge and stayed in the master's lodge at Caius. The outcome was a substantial endowment for pathology; and Anderson soon emerged as the chief negotiator for Cambridge. He and Pearce established a close working relationship; and when further emissaries from Rockefeller came to plan aid for other biological sciences in the summer of 1926, it was doubtless Anderson to whom they primarily looked for guidance. His daughter notes in her reminiscences that when the great men from New York came to Cambridge, she and her mother knew that something was afoot. The visit is ill-recorded; but it is evident that in the warm, beguiling company of Anderson they were inspired with the idea of helping fund a new University Library.[30] The chief negotiator in 1926 was Mr R. B. Fosdick, a central figure in the Foundation over many years; but he came on behalf of the International Educational Board – a limb of the Rockefeller Foundation specifically concerned with medical and biological sciences – and he evidently advised that negotiations carry on at a higher level.[31]

[30] What follows is mainly based on Rockefeller Foundation Archives, Record Group 1.1, Series 401A, 7, UC, P, 'Historical Record; University of Cambridge – Pathology, 1922–1929, 1933–1934'; and Series 401R, Box 64, Folder 850, 'IEB [*International Education Board*] and RF [*Rockefeller Foundation*] Appropriations to the University of Cambridge (1928–1933)'. I refer to them as *RF* 1 and *RF* 2. *RF* 2 is a dossier dated 29 March 1949 compiled from the archives for Mr R. B. Fosdick in preparation for Fosdick 1952, a general account of the history of the Rockefeller Foundation, which has a brief account of the endowment of the University Library on p. 263. I am deeply indebted to Mr Darwin H. Stapleton, director of the Rockefeller Archive and his colleague Mr Erwin Levold, who generously provided the University Archives with copies of these documents.

[31] *RF* 2 describes the visit and gives the detail which follows, but makes only occasional reference to Anderson. Maisie Anderson (1988ff, chap. 23) refers to the visits in very general terms, but she is quite specific that her father was chief negotiator; and this is amply confirmed by later tributes to him (see below). It is curious that neither in the memo prepared for Mr Fosdick nor in his book (Fosdick 1952) is there any indication of his central role. Fosdick clearly had

The outcome was that he carried back to New York a letter from the Chancellor of the university, Lord Balfour, to Mr Rockefeller Junior in person, dated 6 August 1926. 'Mr Rockefeller's reply was cordial, but non-committal.' He feared aid for one library might lead to other similar demands, and he did not care for Scott's plans. 'By the way', he wrote to Fosdick, 'the design for the library seems to me atrocious. I would hate to be a party to the erection of such a building in so beautiful a surrounding, but then that is a detail.'[32] None the less, over the two years which followed there somehow came to be growing confidence that Rockefeller aid would come. On 9 May 1927 a formal request was sent from Cambridge to Colonel Woods, Mr Rockefeller's aide: it was signed by Anderson, Scholfield the Librarian, and J. R. M. Butler of Trinity, with whom Woods had been in touch.[33] Advance was slow, but in February 1928 Mr Rockefeller transferred the Library project to the International Educational Board to be considered alongside grants for agriculture and biological sciences; and meanwhile in the same month another IEB emissary had a secret meeting with Anderson on the scientific programme in London to avoid 'unfounded rumours of a large Rockefeller benefaction'. The outcome of complex manoeuvres in Cambridge and New York was the integration of the Library project with the scientific subsidies: it seems that the benefactors wished the Library to be seen as part of the re-equipping of the sciences – perhaps to avoid giving the impression that they were eager to fund other library buildings.[34]

Meanwhile on 27 April 1927 Scholfield the Librarian had written to Scott a letter of consummate tact.

> After a long silence I am glad to be able to report that we seem to be a step nearer to realising our hopes of a new University Library. We have been able to bring our needs to the notice of certain persons who have interested themselves in the scheme, as

difficulty in winning Mr Rockefeller to support the Library, and may well have avoided saying (or forgotten) that he had spoken hopefully in Cambridge in August 1926. Yet unless he did so, the confidence with which Anderson and his colleagues proceeded is hard to understand – and so also is the successful outcome.

[32] *RF* 2, pp. 1–2.

[33] *RF* 2, pp. 3–4; for what follows, ibid. p. 5.

[34] This is the impression given by the rather confusing details noted in *RF* 2, pp. 5–8. This makes clear that the decision to make the grants was taken in the summer of 1928, but only formally confirmed in December 1928, shortly after Anderson's death.

set forth in the printed 'Appeal' ... and who we believe are
willing to give substantial help to the University.

Realising what our requirements are and how successfully your
proposed buildings meet them, they have made it clear that they
are ready to leave the University a perfectly free choice both as to
the general design and as to details of every description; so that
such criticisms as they had to offer, they offered the more frankly,
because there was no suggestion that we were bound to listen to
them, or else forfeit the support for which we hope!

Their criticism was confined to one point, and one only, viz.
the façade. It will surprise no one if in the circumstances we are
ready to be guided by their wishes, and are anxious to build
something which may evoke the enthusiasm of these potential
donors in a way which the designs before them do not.

One may say generally that the façade was thought not to be
sufficiently imposing, if regard be paid to the character, to the
ultimate size of the building, and its importance to the University.
Not that there is a want of dignity, but it is self-effacing, austere,
and with no trace of richness. And it was partly its modesty, so to
speak, partly its austerity that made it appear to our critics that
this new Library was alien in spirit to the rest of the aggregate of
buildings that make up the University of Cambridge. Partly too
the grey brick and dark red tiles looked discrepant and cold to
eyes accustomed to the red brick and green slates of St John's, of
Jesus, of Magdalene, or the mellow stone of King's and of Trinity
... A fresh design for the façade was asked for ...[35]

Scott replied at once saying that he would think the matter
over carefully; and by early June he was in Cambridge with new
designs, foreshadowing a building in reddish brick with a tower.
Thus was accomplished the transformation from a practical
Library with modest classical features to the Assyrian palace
which confronts us today. Throughout 1927 and 1928 the plans
for the new Library, the negotiations with the Rockefeller
Foundation and with the government and other bodies to
provide the rest of the money needed went steadily forward. A
new Building Syndicate was set up and in June 1928, with
Anderson in the chair, they debated the tower with Scott; at that
time a majority were against it, but gradually the tide turned –

[35] CUL Archives, Scott file, copy of letter 100/AL/27 of 27 April 1927. For what follows, see the
Scott file.

Fig. 14 The University Library: an artist's impression of 1931; a drawing by J. D. M. Harvey

and on 15 January 1929 (shortly after Anderson's death) it was saved by seven votes to three.[36] Meanwhile, on 30 October 1928 the university had discussed the decisive offer from Rockefeller, and with only one dissentient voice – a physicist disappointed to see so much money go to biology – it was greeted with a chorus of approval, and of thanks to the master of Caius.[37] At this moment of triumph Anderson was dangerously ill; he was taken to London for surgery. 'He never recovered consciousness after the operation and died on 2 November,' wrote his daughter. 'Although brilliant surgery removed the growth which would otherwise have killed him after months of agony, he had not the strength to survive. By nature magnificently spendthrift of himself, he never had to learn the pitiful precautions of a limited recovery.'[38]

In 1929 the final plans and estimates came before the university, and were approved.[39] Some voices were raised against its outward appearance – and an attempt was even made to non-placet the report; but there was surprisingly little argument about the tower and its effect on the sensitive sky-line of Cambridge. Probably most resident members of the university were too deeply conscious of the gift which providence had brought them to cavil. The Library was to cost £500,000: £320,000 for the building, the rest for maintenance, removal and essential endowment. The Rockefeller Foundation gave £250,000 to the Library: the Ministry of Agriculture and Fisheries and the Empire Marketing Board each gave £50,000; Lord Melchett (who chaired the appeal) and Mr Robert Mond gave £10,000 each; and when these and other lesser sums had been added together the university made up what was lacking from its own resources.[40] In 1930 the Rockefeller Foundation invited Scott and a group

---

[36] The new Syndicate was set up on 19 May 1928 (*Reporter* 1927–8, p. 996), and its minutes from 8 June 1928 to 20 Dec. 1929 are in 'Needs'.

[37] *Reporter* 1928–9, pp. 235–40; CUL Archives, 'History of the Library', IX, no. 239.

[38] Anderson 1988ff, chap. 23.

[39] For this and what follows, see *Reporter* 1928–9, pp. 1038–40; cf. ibid. pp. 162–6; *Reporter* 1927–8, pp. 664–5.

[40] See Rockefeller file, at end; cf. *Reporter* 1928–9, pp. 433–4. For what follows see *Cambridge University Library 1400–1934* (Cambridge, 1934), pp. 6–7. The Rockefeller Foundation Archives, Record Group 1.1; Series 401R, Box 64, Folder 848, contains a letter from Scott, dated 11 Nov. 1930, asking for more money; but in the event, it seems, financial stringency had to be met by economy in his design.

from Cambridge to tour the major libraries of America. Over the years Scott had a far more thorough briefing than has been accorded the architect of any other university building.

On 29 September 1931 the first of 1,200 ferro-concrete piles was driven into the ground.[41] Over the piles a raft was laid and over the raft the Library grew. In the winter of 1931–2 a four-year-old child was taken in a pushchair to view the driving of the piles; and on 22 October 1934, with many other schoolchildren, I stood on the pavement to watch King George V and Queen Mary drive past on their way to open the new Library. Meanwhile a mighty operation had been planned and executed to prepare the books for their removal and carry them across the Backs. In June and July 1934, over a period of eight weeks, 689 horse-drawn lorry loads carried 23,725 boxes of books – excluding bound copies of newspapers and elephant folios, which required separate treatment.[42]

The building and furnishing of the new Library went steadily forward, though not without tremors. The operation was in the hands of the Building Syndicate, over which presided, by chance, Anderson's successor as master of Caius, John Cameron – like him a canny Scot, though a much less outgoing personality, but deeply respected for his business acumen – and in the autumn of 1932 Cameron was faced by an ultimatum from the contractors: either the approach road must be instantly set in hand or their work would be seriously delayed.[43] So Cameron and his Syndics authorised the straight road which still runs from West Road to Burrell's Walk without any reference to the university – and were subsequently criticised, and exonerated, for doing so; alternative schemes for a meandering approach and a more picturesque landscaping had thus to be abandoned. When I am told our procedures preclude swift and urgent decisions I often think of John Cameron and the road past the front of the Library. In 1930–1 it had been suggested that some part of the Library

[41] CUL Archives, 'History of the University', IX, no. 416; Report of the Library Syndicate for 1931–2 and of the Syndicate for the building and equipment of the Library, 28 May 1932, *Reporter* 1932–3, pp. 1051, 1064, 1129.
[42] Ansell 1935; CUL Archives, 'History of the Library', IX, no. 513a. See also *Cambridge University Library 1400–1934* (Cambridge, 1934), prepared to celebrate the opening.
[43] CUL Archives, 'History of the Library', IX, nos. 421a–b; *Reporter* 1932–3, pp. 1156–7. On Cameron, see Venn, VI, 528–40; Brooke 1985, pp. 267–9.

should be associated with Anderson's name; and in May 1933 the Regent House approved the proposal that the special reading room for manuscripts and early printed books should be called the Anderson Room.[44] Subsequently doubts were raised: this was the scholar's room *par excellence*, and for all his crucial help in the making of the Library Anderson would never himself have used that particular room nor was he in that sense a scholar. By now the grace had passed; the title 'Anderson Room' was carved in stone, and such it still is; but the critics of its name have been justified by the failure of Librarians and Syndics for over half a century – until 1991 – to put any kind of notice in the room to explain its name. Meanwhile the meaning of the name has been known to only a tiny fraction of those who have used it.

This would not have troubled Anderson, who hated thanks almost as fanatically as Mr Jarndyce in *Bleak House*.[45] He would have felt well rewarded if the Library served its purpose. In a substantial sense there is no doubt of the answer: for those who seek ready access to large numbers of books, who like open access and some exercise in the pursuit of their quarry, it is a marvellous Library to work in. Its copyright status guarantees it all that is worth having published in this country, though it also gives it a character as a national library which sometimes sits uneasily with its function and financing as a University Library; and whether it has always bought the books it needs, whether it has developed in a way fully worthy of its founders future generations must tell. It has settled the question whether Cambridge should be eminent in science or in arts: it must be both. I can only add that for nearly fifty years – to me as a scholar – it has been a paradise.

[44] For this and what follows, see CUL Archives, 'History of the Library', IX, no. 417; *Reporter* 1932–3, p. 1072; CUL Archives, Library Syndicate Minutes, VII (1934–49), pp. 30–2; 'Index to Library Reports, etc.', fo. 46.
[45] Anderson 1988ff, chap. 23.

Chapter 13

THE DONS' RELIGION IN TWENTIETH-CENTURY CAMBRIDGE

My earlier studies of religion and religious learning dwelt mainly in the Establishment; in this chapter and the next I try to redress the balance by seeking out the contribution of all the churches – including the Anglican – but especially the free churches and the Roman Catholic Church – to religion and learning in Cambridge. I try first to observe something of the inwardness and the paradoxes of religious history by looking closely at how a group of leading churchmen interpreted the life and vocation of a Christian in twentieth-century Cambridge. My team comprises five laymen: Baron Anatole von Hügel the Catholic – brother of the more celebrated Baron Friedrich, the mystical modernist; T. R. Glover the Baptist; Alex Wood the Presbyterian; Bernard Manning, a Congregationalist who also drank deeply from the Methodist tradition; and Joseph Needham, the Marxist Anglo-Catholic Taoist. It may be objected that I have chosen an eccentric group, especially in my choice of Needham, who alone and rather strangely represents both the Anglican community and the living; and yet is in some eyes the one true nonconformist. But I hold him to be the most representative of all; for he is a man of paradoxes, of unlikely alliances – and it is through the pursuit of such alliances, of paradox and eccentricity that I have come to understand a little of the history of Cambridge in the last hundred years.[1]

When the Test Acts departed in 1871 Cardinal Manning – who knew Oxford only too well – declared that the ancient universities were no place for Catholics, and the formal prohibition

---

[1] I owe particular help in this chapter to David Thompson, but he is not to be blamed for the eccentricity of my choice.

(though not entirely effective) remained until his death in 1892.[2]
On 1 April 1895 a decree came out of Rome saying that the
situation had changed and Catholics might go to Oxford and
Cambridge until such time as a Catholic university could be
formed – but only so long as they attended some specially
arranged lectures by Catholic professors. By the happiest chance
one of the most eminent Catholic scholars in Britain, Dom Cuthbert Butler of Downside, took up residence at Cambridge in 1896
at the first Benet House, in Christ's, and gave the lectures a good
start.[3] Though the Catholic community never devised a system
of markers such as those who noted the presence of Anglican
youths in St John's chapel and elsewhere, the lectures were well
attended. Meanwhile the Catholic presence had been marked
already before 1896 in several striking ways. In the 1880s the one-
time ballerina Yolande Duvernay, now a rich widow, Mrs Lyne-
Stephens, made a treaty with Canon Scott, the Catholic parish
priest of Cambridge. They saw that the Catholic community
needed a more appropriate church, and foresaw that Catholic
students would presently return. So they built Our Lady and the
English Martyrs, a sort of late thirteenth-century gothic cathedral
completed in 1890 as a very ambitious parish church, and beside it
a presbytery in which Canon Scott looked forward to welcoming
the students.[4] Their arrival was preceded by a curious flutter in
the hierarchy. In 1895 the bishops set up the Universities'
Catholic Education Board to put the decree of Propaganda into
effect, and the Board appointed Edmund Nolan first chaplain; at
about the same moment the bishop of Northampton appointed
Canon Scott to be chaplain, and the two rivals set up house
together in the presbytery in Hills Road.[5] Meanwhile Baron
Anatole was helping larger plans to blossom. He had established a
Catholic presence in the university by becoming first curator of
the Museum of Archaeology and Anthropology in 1883, and he
has an honoured place in the history of the Downing Site and of

2 Couve de Murville and Jenkins 1983, chap. 6, esp. pp. 120–2.
3 Couve de Murville and Jenkins 1983, pp. 122–3.
4 Couve de Murville and Jenkins 1983, pp. 113–16.
5 Couve de Murville and Jenkins 1983, pp. 121–2.

Cambridge arch and anth.[6] He brought to Cambridge a skill in the handling of humankind learned from extensive anthropological field work in Fiji; and the mark of his years in the Pacific is both on the remarkable ethnological collections in the museum and on the Catholic community in Cambridge. He and his wife showed an early interest in the Catholic primary school recently established in Union Road;[7] and he was a prime mover in the petition to Rome to remove the ban on Catholic students in Cambridge. 'Always a visionary and a schemer' – as the authors of *Catholic Cambridge* describe him – he played a leading part in the foundation of St Edmund's as a house of study for priests and ordinands in 1896.[8] Over it was set Father Nolan, the Catholic chaplain, and in its chapel Dom Cuthbert Butler gave his lectures.[9] Dom Butler was a close friend of Baron Friedrich, and naturally an ally of Baron Anatole in his zeal for Catholic education in Cambridge. Dom Butler represented in Cambridge, as did the baron – and as did Lord Acton – the presence of the Catholic intellectual world, the type of man who could lead his fellow-Catholics back into the Cambridge fold. Butler formed a friendship with Professor Armitage Robinson which flowered exceedingly when Armitage Robinson (in later life) was dean of Wells; and so with John Peile, master of Christ's, which started the connection between Downside and the Catholic regulars and Christ's which has subsisted ever since.[10] And Butler above all opened a channel between two notable centres of ecclesiastical history hitherto remote and aloof from one another, Cambridge and Downside, and paved the way for the coming of David Knowles.

The number of Catholic students at first grew slowly: there were forty-five known to the chaplain in 1899.[11] When Father Nolan left Cambridge in 1902, the chaplaincy was split from St Edmund's and moved into the centre of Cambridge; in 1924 the ebullient Father Lopes acquired the Black Swan by the Guildhall

[6] Tanner 1917, pp. 229–31; cf. Thompson 1990. I am indebted to an unpublished history of the museum kindly lent me by David Phillipson; Cumming 1981: there is surviving correspondence in the museum and in CUL; cf. also von Hügel 1990.
[7] Couve de Murville and Jenkins 1983, pp. 118, 120.
[8] Couve de Murville and Jenkins 1983, p. 122.   [9] Ibid.
[10] Knowles 1963, pp. 299–303.
[11] Couve de Murville and Jenkins 1983, p. 123.

and faced the Catholic academic community in Cambridge (all 130 of them) with a bill for £12,500 to buy and restore the building as Fisher House. In this adventure he had a notable ally in Edward Bullough of Caius, future professor of Italian, who with his Italian wife – a daughter of Eleonora Duse – and aided by the brilliant artistic gifts of the architect H. C. Hughes – built the Italian villa which is now, by the generosity of the Bullough family, the nucleus of Blackfriars.[12] But the secure foundations of Catholic scholarship in Cambridge had been laid long before by Baron Anatole and Acton and Butler. In 1904 Cuthbert Butler celebrated the publication of the *Lausiac History* of Palladius, as is appropriately recounted by Butler's biographer, David Knowles, later to be the first monk since the Reformation to claim a Cambridge chair.

> To mark the occasion Dom Butler gave what he afterwards referred to as a 'garden-party' in the diminutive precincts of Benet House [then a tenement in the precincts of Christ's]. Melons were provided for the guests, among whom were most of the friends he had made in Cambridge, and the gathering thus accepting Benedictine hospitality, and numbering Presbyterian, Anglican, Jewish and agnostic scholars, caused no little astonishment to a distinguished French prelate who happened to be staying at Benet House.[13]   •

Next in age to Baron Anatole of my small gallery of devout laymen was T. R. Glover, son of a Baptist minister and for many years a leading figure in the Cambridge Baptist community.[14] He was a fellow of St John's from 1892, and apart from a five-year absence in Canada he remained a distinguished teacher of classics and ancient history in Cambridge till his retirement in 1939, and for nearly twenty years a much respected Public Orator. His *Conflict of Religions in the Early Roman Empire* (1909) had made accessible in a substantial and readable form the current learning on the religious climate in which the Christian Church first grew and flourished. His best-known book, *The Jesus of History* of 1917, represented for a generation the inheritance of a tradition

---

[12] Couve de Murville and Jenkins 1983, pp. 123, 126; on Bullough, see Brooke 1985, p. 243; Moriarty 1988, pp. 88–9.
[13] Knowles 1963, p. 303.
[14] On Glover, see esp. Wood 1953; and among his works, esp. Glover 1909, 1917, 1943.

of biblical scholarship which was already passing away. Like most historians who have worked seriously on the New Testament documents, he was not impressed by the scepticism of the more radical biblical critics, and it is a moving and thoughtful book, greatly superior to Seeley's *Ecce Homo* to which one naturally compares it. But the confident assertions of the age of Harnack were waning, and Glover's critical weapons were hardly sharp enough to resist the assaults of the Form Critics. In the *nachform-geschichtliche* world in which we live we can look back with respect at Glover's book; but I am not convinced that it will be reprinted.

His witness is of special interest to the historian of modern Cambridge on account of his *Cambridge Retrospect*.[15] In it he looked back with affection to the traditions and characters of an older Cambridge, especially to the classics lecturers of St John's of his youth. As the years roll by, the warmth cools a little, the sharp edge of criticism is felt. Some allowance must be made for an old man's mood. That said, he gives us the most reactionary criticism of the new university constitution of the 1920s and its spirit which I have encountered. 'For centuries the centre of academic life had been the College (and a very good centre too, with its diversities of types).' Now, for the benefit of the scientists, it was to be reorganised into faculties – it is intriguing that so experienced a historian does not seem to notice (as he has told us earlier) that we had faculties long before we had colleges; but it is indeed true that faculties as we know them now are creatures of the 1920s. 'Theorists, reformers, and science men had their way; and the men whose business was with history, language and literature were drastically herded into their several faculties.' Worse still, he quoted with gloomy assent 'the criticism that Cambridge after all was devoting herself chiefly to the production of professors. The newer ideal for a professor was devotion to "research", which is very well in scientific studies, but less obviously useful in literature ... The substitution of palaeography for philosophy among theologians simply ruins the subject.'[16]

The book was published in 1943; in 1949 I was elected to a

[15] Glover 1943.   [16] Glover 1943, pp. 110–11.

fellowship at Caius in a world in which it was rapidly coming to be dogma among the young – and not so young – that the genius of Cambridge lay in the union of research and teaching, in the exposure of undergraduates to minds constantly at work on the frontiers of knowledge. It was partly, but not wholly, that a new generation had come with the arrival of the postwar world; not wholly – for these two ideals of academic life had been disputing for preeminence ever since Professor Lightfoot and his fellow-Commissioners inspired those words, 'Education, religion, learning and research' in the act of 1877.

But I am straying from my theme; for the point is that this ardent Baptist was also a dyed-in-the-wool college man. 1871 had entirely passed away. Or perhaps not quite entirely; for Glover himself tells a delightful story of how he met Sir William Ridgeway – the eccentric professor of archaeology, charismatic teacher, devoted husband, yet hammer of academic women – in 1914. Ridgeway fell on his dissenting friend, and assured him that 'if the Kaiser would only promise to destroy the cathedrals on the conquest of England, the wicked dissenters would welcome him with open arms'. Glover did not voice his doubts about this improbable doctrine, but stemmed the flood by a seemingly innocent question on Ridgeway's view of F. M. Cornford's book on Greek Comedy. The Kaiser was forgotten, 'and the storm broke on the absent Cornford'.[17]

Glover was born in 1869, Alex Wood in 1879.[18] He came to Emmanuel not long after St Columba's had been built not far away; and he was a fellow of Emmanuel and an elder of St Columba's for most of his life. He was also an active member of the staff of the Cavendish Laboratory, an unpretentious, able physicist, who advanced knowledge of sound and acoustics. In close alliance with St Columba's, he and his wife played a leading role in the boys' clubs of Cambridge. For thirty years he was bursar of Westminster College and much involved in its affairs.[19] He was a Scotsman and a devoted member of the Church of Scotland. But he was also a leading figure in the Christian

---

[17] Glover 1943, pp. 76–7.
[18] For an outline of Wood's career, see *Who was Who 1941–1950*, p. 1256. The substance of what follows is based on Raven 1954.
[19] Knox n.d., p. 43.

community of Cambridge at large – in his admirable and amiable personality Christian engagement and charity flowed freely; and the Presbyterian church in Cambridge won a larger respect as a result. Not, however, from all; for Alex Wood had two other special devotions. He was a convinced pacifist, and a close friend and ally of Charles Raven in the pacifist cause between the wars; their intimacy went further back, indeed, to the time when they were young fellows of Emmanuel together and allies in the Chawner affair, natural partners too in exploring the relations of faith and science.[20] And Wood was a very active member of the Labour Party. In the 1920s he entered local politics and was soon a leading Labour councillor. Just as his work for the boys' clubs and for St Columba's spanned the gulf between gown and town, so his ardent – but extremely practical – socialism brought a new perspective into university politics in an age when Cambridge was still commonly represented in parliament by an MP well to the right of William Pitt. He remained to the end of his days a devoted college man, equally at home in the Emmanuel Parlour, the Cavendish, Westminster College, St Columba's and the Guildhall.

In 1967 Cheshunt College, the old Countess of Huntingdon Foundation long since incorporated into the Congregational Church, united with Westminster College; and in 1972 the parent communions became the United Reformed Church.[21] Meanwhile my fourth character, Bernard Manning, had represented a personal union of the Methodist heritage and the Congregationalist; and since he worshipped all his adult life in Jesus chapel, of the Anglican as well – though his practical ecumenism was tempered by an urbane and charitable, but very firm, assertion of his nonconformity. His grandfather was a Methodist.

'Come with me to John Wesley's own country: Lincolnshire,' cried Manning at the opening of his inspired essay on 'Hymns for the use of the people called Methodists'.

Come to the North Wolds, where from the Earl of Yarborough's woods at Pelham's Pillar you can see the line of the Humber and the North Sea, and the Dock Tower at Grimsby by day; and by

[20] Raven 1952, 1954 (and cf. Dillistone 1975, p. 235); cf. Emmanuel Coll. Archives, COL. 19.8.
[21] Orchard n.d.; Knox n.d., pp. 51–2. On Bernard Manning see Brittain 1942; and among his own works esp. Manning 1919, 1939, 1942.

night the lantern of the Spurn Lighthouse, the dull glow of Hull
on the north, the duller glow of Gainsborough on the west, and
between them the flaring furnaces of Scunthorpe. . .

And he gradually leads us through woods and meadows and
ploughed fields to where,

> in the hungry forties of the last century, in the ancient Roman
> town of Caistor, the Methodists built a new chapel, square and
> high and red, in a country of red bricks and curly red tiles . . . In
> that chapel it was my fortune to hear many sermons and to be
> bored by not a few.[22]

He goes on to describe how in desperation he sought solace in the
hymn books, and so acquired one of the great devotions of his
life, to the *Hymns of Wesley and Watts*.[23] He goes on too to
describe the other source of religious inspiration, the seventeenth-
century Congregationalist meeting house in which his father
ministered.

> There I found sermons less dull, for my father preached them;
> but the casual ministrations of strangers drove me to part II of Dr
> Barrett's *Hymnal*, where among 'Ancient Hymns of the Church'
> I found Irons's noble translation of the most moving of all
> medieval hymns, *Dies Irae*; and from the *Dies Irae*, not knowing
> what I did, I caught the infection of a love of medieval Christ-
> ianity. To boring sermons, then, I owe two of the best things
> that I know.[24]

The chief home of his early days was Ravenstonedale in
Westmorland, where his father was minister for a number of
years; but Caistor was his other home, and there he went to
school. His first year there was devastated by pneumonia, from
which he emerged with only one lung and permanent ill-health,
well disguised in later years by a cheerful, modest, uncomplaining
manner. A major scholarship and considerable parental sacrifice
enabled him to go to Jesus College, Cambridge, which was to be
his home for the rest of his life, though he was often in
Lincolnshire and was to set up a second home in Westmorland.[25]

[22] Manning 1942, p. 7.   [23] The title of Manning 1942.
[24] Manning 1942, p. 8.   [25] Brittain 1942, chaps. 1–2, and pp. 77, 83.

Jesus chapel is one of the great beauties of Cambridge: with something of the twelfth and much of the thirteenth and fifteenth centuries, it yet remains above all a monument to the genius of Pugin and William Morris and his partners. 'The Burne-Jones windows in the nave', said Manning, comparing them with Pugin's in the choir, 'are of another kind – natural, free, living. The skies around Adam and "Henock" [Enoch] are covered with racing clouds; one can feel the wind and smell the earth.'[26] He was a loyal, conformist, college man, and attended chapel; he was attracted by its beauty. He had too a natural sense of liturgy, and in spite of his free church ancestry – and his equal loyalty to the free churches – he had an affection for traditional Anglican liturgy and college worship such as few Anglicans of his generation felt. 'He reverenced' the Book of Common Prayer, wrote Freddy Brittain in his moving memoir of Manning, 'next to the Bible and Wesley's hymns';[27] he was naturally ecumenical. Being a layman (though he came near to ordination and studied at Cheshunt with that end in view)[28] he did not have to commit himself to forms and formularies as the clergy do. Living in the heart of the Anglican establishment, and being visibly a limb of it, he none the less delighted to remind Anglican and free church colleagues alike that he was a Calvinist and nonconformist. If he was constant in attending Jesus chapel, he was an assiduous member of the flock of Emmanuel Congregational church, proud of the long tradition of his own communion in Cambridge, whose 250th anniversary he helped to celebrate in 1937.[29] Emmanuel church had been rebuilt in the 1870s partly to celebrate the return of the free churches to the university, and like St Columba's it reflected the meeting of town and gown.[30] I can recall the days when Munsey and Mackintosh, silversmiths and ironmongers, sat near together in the centre of Cambridge (where Munsey still is). Miss Munsey and Miss Mackintosh both married in Emmanuel church young men they had met as undergraduates.[31] Among its most eminent members were the Keynes family. If Maynard Keynes was an outspoken agnostic, his mother, a daughter of the manse, was a

[26] Brittain 1942, p. 18.   [27] Brittain 1942, p. 19.
[28] Brittain 1942, pp. 47–9.   [29] Brittain 1942, p. 72.
[30] Pevsner 1970, pp. 231–2.
[31] For this and what follows, Binfield 1989, esp. pp. 409–10; for Maynard Keynes, esp. p. 15.

pillar of Emmanuel church before he was born and after his death; his father, University Registrary, came often to Emmanuel church in attendance on his wife. Emmanuel church had enjoyed the ministry of a remarkable preacher, P. T. Forsyth, in the 1890s – he has recently been brought to life by Clyde Binfield.[32] In Manning's day the minister was H. C. Carter, always one of his closest friends and his chief spiritual adviser.

In his early days at Jesus, Manning had the sympathy and help of a celebrated eccentric, the dean, Foakes-Jackson, known as Foakes officially in Jesus, Foakesie to irreverent juniors like my father. They were unlike in temperament, as Brittain underlined: 'Where Foakes-Jackson was exuberant, incalculable, and utterly careless of detail, Bernard Manning was quiet, methodical, and scrupulously accurate.'[33] But Foakes greatly helped Manning to find his feet in a college more celebrated for its bump suppers than its scholarship. What is remarkable is that Manning, good scholar that he was and physically incapable of lifting an oar, came in later life to be the heart and soul of the bump suppers.

In September 1912 Black Morgan, master of Jesus, died and was succeeded by Arthur Gray, perhaps the last of the great Victorian masters, for he was only 60 at his election and could look forward to thirty years of active headship.[34] In October 1912 Manning arrived as a freshman to a college already beginning to feel the chastening effect of Gray's determined rule.[35] Gray wished to prove that the boat club and the college were not identical, and he succeeded – aided it must be said by the caesura in men and mores of the First World War. But the boat club survived and flourished and the outer world did not see the great difference within. Anthony Mangan has accustomed us to the picture of late nineteenth-century Cambridge, ruled by arrogant, public school, rowing undergraduates, philistine in outlook and behaviour; and he has placed Jesus in the centre of the picture.[36] Nor has he spared Foakes-Jackson, whom he portrays as a complacent dean, ready to sacrifice everything for the credit of the boats.[37] Foakes, however, for all his oddity

[32] Binfield 1989.   [33] Brittain 1942, p. 17.
[34] Brittain 1942, pp. 14–15.   [35] Brittain 1942, pp. 11–16.
[36] Mangan 1984.
[37] Mangan 1984, esp. p. 61; on Foakes-Jackson see *DNB 1941–1950*, s. v. Jackson.

and high living, was a real scholar, who went off in 1916 to be professor at Union Seminary, New York, there to edit the early volumes of *The Beginnings of Christianity* with Kirsopp Lake. The truth, so far as one can discern it, is that there were a large number of good college men in Cambridge in the late nineteenth and early twentieth centuries – still indeed, in the mid and late twentieth century – to whom the chapel, the library and the boat house counted equally; the college was unthinkable without all three. This is abundantly clear in Bernard Manning.

He was, first of all, a more than competent scholar. After taking his degree, and aided by a Lightfoot Scholarship and wise counsel from Professor Gwatkin and Foakes, he set to work under the supervision of G. G. Coulton on the study which became the Thirlwall Prize and the book, *The People's Faith in the Time of Wyclif*.[38] The book itself shows Coulton's – and Wyclif's – influence in a surprisingly cold view of the state of fourteenth-century religion. Yet it is Manning's too, and one can glimpse afar the insight into religious sentiment and the imaginative and often enlightened perception which make his essays on the hymns of Wesley and Watts such masterpieces. Furthermore, the theme itself was original and exceedingly worth while: he anticipated by some forty years the apotheosis of medieval popular religion as a fashionable subject for research. With the aid of this book he achieved a fellowship, became a teacher of medieval history and a university lecturer; and he wrote two fine chapters for *The Cambridge Medieval History* – leaving none but happy memories with the much tried editors of that great work.[39] I never knew Bernard Manning, but my father's lamentation when he died, and the affection he felt for a man with whom he was never intimate, remain a vivid memory.

In due course he became increasingly devoted to college business. This never prevented him from doing his duty when his own and other churches called, or in lectures up and down the country. But a man with rather less than one whole lung had to watch his pace, and continued medieval research was the victim.

[38] Cf. Manning 1919, pp. ix–x; cf. Brittain 1942, p. 21.
[39] Vols. VII (1932), chaps. 15 ('England: Edward III and Richard II'), 16 ('Wyclif').

In its place, increasingly in later years, came the hymns for the use of the people called Methodists. 'I am inclined to read the whole preface to you,' said Manning, greatly daring, to the University Methodist Society:

> for, unwilling as I am to think ill of you, I believe that many of you have never read it. Never read it! Why, you have never seen it. The rascals who compiled your hymn-book in 1904 saw to that. They had the effrontery to refer to it as 'a celebrated preface' ('a preface' forsooth); and the wickedness to banish it from the book which you were to use for thirty years. They robbed you, in 1904, of what, as the children of John Wesley, you should regard as one of your priceless heirlooms. I use strong language, but that Preface is, to begin with, one of the noblest pieces of eighteenth-century prose extant: from its quaint opening words, 'For many years I have been importuned', to its moving conclusion, 'When Poetry thus keeps its place, as the handmaid of Piety, it shall attain, not a poor perishable wreath, but a crown that fadeth not away'.[40]

I myself rarely sing a hymn by either Wesley, nor survey the wondrous Cross with Isaac Watts, without thinking of Manning's marvellous book – though we may now study the religious sentiment of their world on the larger canvas of Gordon Rupp's delectable last book.[41]

Yet to many Manning was first and foremost the devoted college man. He was bursar of Jesus from 1920 to 1933, and senior tutor from 1933 till his death in 1941. As senior tutor he stood no nonsense, nor did he parade his office. He belonged to that generation of senior tutors – Francis Bennett of Caius and Donald Beves of King's were among them too – whom the undergraduates addressed by their Christian names to their face, as well as behind their backs.[42] It is strange to be reminded that we live in more formal times. He shared the affairs of the boat club with that eccentric genius Stephen Fairbairn. When bump supper night approached, Manning, who was assiduous on the towpath and greatly loved it, though he could never row, prepared a speech with the same delicate care which marked his

---

40 Manning 1942, p. 10.   41 Rupp 1986.
42 Brittain 1942, p. 64.

addresses on the Wesleys. Fairbairn meanwhile, the architect of innumerable watery triumphs, never went to bump supper, but sat alone dreaming, in Platonic fashion, of the idea of the perfect boat.[43] The boat club was not alone in Manning's affections. From 1925 he was senior treasurer of the Amalgamated Clubs, and rugger, soccer, hockey, cricket and tennis received a full share of his attention. He was an enthusiastic member of numberless college societies: the Jesuits, the Younger Brothers, the Alcock Society, the Red Herrings, and that arcane mystery the Roosters, which, if one could but penetrate its dotty rituals and debates, would reveal much of college life and sentiment of the 1930s and doubtless of later ages too.[44] He was the quintessential bachelor don; yet he never relinquished his links with the wider religious and scholarly world.

His *Essays in Orthodox Dissent* at once inspire and chill us.[45] For here was a man in whom Christian charity waxed very warm, who saw the good in almost every communion, and felt the lure of Anglican liturgy as few have felt it, who none the less looked at ecumenism with a sympathetic yet profoundly critical eye. The depth of his study of different traditions taught him caution. But that is not the last word, which perhaps may be reserved for his letter to Edward Wynn, fellow-historian and tutor of Pembroke, on his elevation to the bishopric of Ely.

> You know, I hope and am sure, what a solemn joy your news gives me; and you know how it will be followed by my unworthy prayers many, many times. We do not agree, I take it, on all points about episcopacy, and I am, I know, in some senses one of your 'separated brethren'; but we share a deep and affectionate reverence for the holy ministry, and neither of us would yield there to any man . . .[46]

Bernard Manning was born in 1892, Joseph Needham in 1900: he celebrated his ninetieth birthday on 9 December 1990. For one of his various Festschriften he was persuaded to write his own

---

[43] Brittain 1942, p. 66.
[44] Brittain 1942, pp. 58–9, 79.
[45] Manning 1939.
[46] Brittain 1942, p. 86.

Fig. 15 Portrait of Joseph Needham in Chinese costume, carrying the scientist's slide rule, by James Wood, in Gonville and Caius College

biography, a document at once moving and entertaining.[47] He was very much one of the young scientists of the 1920s, but 'he alone [the 'he' is Needham talking of Needham] started out as a

[47] Teich and Young 1973; it is cited here from Davies 1990, pp. 29–54, 'The Making of an Honorary Taoist'.

man of definite commitment to liturgical religion and alone has held to it throughout his life' – though he has been equally committed to communism.[48] When I sketched his role in a History of Caius published a few years ago, and submitted my draft to him, Joseph kindly but firmly rebuked me: 'You have not done justice to my lifelong commitment to socialism.'[49] Loyalty has been as much the keynote of his life as of Manning's. If Needham had not existed, the historian of Cambridge would have had to invent him – if he had the daring and imagination to do it – for he represents to a unique degree the combination of the cosmopolitan and the parochial so characteristic of Cambridge in the mid and late twentieth century. When I was first a fellow of Caius in 1949 he had already had twenty-five years in the fellowship, but was regarded as eccentric and unsound by some of the senior fellows; and when he modestly asked for an additional room in 1956 to house his rapidly growing and unique collection of Chinese literature, it was observed that to give two keeping rooms to a fellow who did so little college teaching was unheard of. But a few of us felt very strongly that the values for which a college stood were at stake; and a committee was set up of the dean, the senior tutor and Mr Brooke (then 28), which recommended that he be given a second room – and thus, I like to think, I earned a small niche in the history of scholarship.[50] Thus too his books were united for the first time – though they have since gone on to ampler premises and now live in the charming pagoda in Sylvester Road, the Needham Research Institute. Joseph meanwhile has enjoyed a double apotheosis, as holder of the Order of the Brilliant Star and every other mark of recognition in China, and as president and master and senior fellow of Caius. It is alleged that during meetings of the College Council his attention would sometimes be focussed on China while the discussion meandered about him; but noone doubted his dedication. There is a list of Exequies of his devising – days on which we should remember the benefactors of the college, which included everyone who had given money to the college since 1348; and there is a fine set of blue silk vestments in

[48] Davies 1990, p. 30.   [49] See now Brooke 1985, pp. 277, 280–1, 300–1.
[50] Brooke 1985, pp. 300–1.

the college chapel, which he presented when he had completed sixty years as a fellow.

The vestments recall another of his loyalties, to Thaxted.

> Thaxted [he wrote] had long been notable for three things: a very thorough-going Christian socialism, a great musical tradition . . . and . . . a liturgical beauty learnedly yet informally based on medieval English precedents. Thus for forty years the clerks of Thaxted, first under Conrad Noel and then under Jack Putterill, have formed a group of friends drawn from all walks of life devoted to the coming of the Kingdom on earth, the celebration of the holy liturgy, and one another.

> Here this doctrine of the Kingdom of God was of particular importance. Joseph Needham formed at that time the conviction, never afterwards abandoned, that it should be regarded as a realm of justice and comradeship on earth, to be brought about by the efforts of men throughout the centuries, not primarily as some mystical body existing already, or some spiritual state to be expected somewhere else in the future. Gradually this became linked up in his mind with a conviction of the essential unity of cosmological, organic, and social evolution, in which the idea of human progress, with all due reservations, would find its place. Parallel with this was the conviction that the Christian must take Marxism extremely seriously, such doctrines as historical materialism and the class struggle being perhaps recognition of the ways in which God has worked during the evolution of society . . . The necessity of faith in the irrational seemed more and more pointless when everything that we know of evolution and history indicated a continuous process or plan of salvation which humanity was working out, and this was the reason why later on he came to feel so much sympathy not only with the emergent evolutionists such as Lloyd Morgan and Samuel Alexander, but even more with the religious form of the same thing, represented by Teilhard de Chardin.[51]

Joseph Needham was an undergraduate at Caius just after the First World War, and joined the brilliant circle of Cambridge biochemists directed by Gowland Hopkins.[52] Among his colleagues was Dorothy Moyle, soon to be his first wife and an FRS in her own right; and later in the 1930s Lu Gwei-Djen, one of the

---

[51] Davies 1990, pp. 39–40.
[52] For an outline of his career, see Davies 1990, pp. 10–20.

group of Chinese students who first opened his eyes to the meaning of Chinese science (after Dorothy's death the second Mrs Needham). He has been a fellow of Caius since 1924, and was in his day lecturer and reader in biochemistry. In this sense it has been a life of extreme stability; yet his mind and influence have spread over the world on a magic carpet out of the Arabian Nights. In the 1940s he was a cultural attaché in China, and soon after the war he formed the idea which has blossomed in his massive history of *Science and Civilization in China*, whose volumes noone can number, and which is now an international enterprise involving scholars in every quarter of the globe.

It is evident enough that he had a quite unusual capacity to absorb influences the most diverse in character. Very early he had sat at the feet of E. W. Barnes in the Temple church and heard the call to unite Christianity and scientific enquiry; this and the rationalist element in his theology – strange companion to his romantic Anglo-Catholicism – are among many persistent threads in the elaborate skein of his thought. A different thread, equally persistent, has been his optimistic Marxism. In 1947, as the nations prepared for Cold War, Joseph issued a volume of essays entitled *History is on our Side*. It is the most dated of his books, yet it contains much doctrine which he has never repudiated. He has been a man of large frame and immense intellectual energy, with the most ample memory of any man I have ever encountered, and an equal capacity to hold together in a single generous grasp ideas and ideologies which we lesser folk find incompatible: Marxism, Christianity and Taoism. The paradoxical nature of his assertion that a high church Anglican can happily be an honorary Taoist may well obscure the deeper truths which underpin his whole intellectual world: that Europe and its thought and culture and ideologies cannot claim the arrogant monopoly that too many Europeans have taken for granted; that all the world's great cultures have much to teach each other – China and the west above all. And secondly, that the natural sciences and theology and religious thought have a single aim, the pursuit of truth, and must be allies in it, however difficult it may be to see the path of reconciliation.

Among my group of Christian laymen, Needham stands out as the one who will hold a massive place in the history of scholarship – yet rather in the history of science and of oriental civilisation than of theology. None have been profound or original theologians. Anatole von Hügel aptly represents the meeting of the Catholic and Cambridge intellectual worlds. Glover, Wood and Manning all reveal how much Cambridge owes to the free churches, and in a variety of intriguing and subtle ways. For all were laymen devoted to a variety of the activities – teaching, learning, social life and politics, and above all religion – which make up the life of Cambridge; and they illustrate how deep the influence of religion still has been in the secularised world of the twentieth-century university. Needham started from a more conventional, Anglican base; but his adventures have carried the experience of Cambridge far beyond the confines of any Christian tradition, and that has made him a controversial figure within and without the university. He received no recognition out of Whitehall until 1992, but copious honours from China and from Cambridge – in particular his election as master of Caius and the conferment by the university of the Honorary Litt.D.

Joseph Needham is hardly a Victorian figure; yet he is the only one of the characters we have been exploring who could have held office in Cambridge before 1871, or (if the law were strictly applied) have been an undergraduate before 1856. The repeal of the Test Acts has had a rich legacy: we shall explore it further in the next chapter. For a final comment, let us invoke the great agnostic F. W. Maitland – the disciple of Henry Sidgwick, the intimate friend of Leslie Stephen – on the Catholic, Lord Acton.

> Those who sat or stood in the crowded Divinity School can never forget the majestic act of pardon and oblivion which was the preface of the inaugural lecture [as Regius Professor of Modern History, in 1895]. 'At three colleges [said Acton] I applied for admission and, as things then were, I was refused by all. Here, from the first, I vainly fixed my hopes, and here, in a happier hour, after five and forty years, they are at last fulfilled.' . . . [To which Maitland:] Intolerance is a foolish thing, and an apology based upon unintended consequences is an apology of just the sort that aroused Lord Acton's indignation. Still to some of his hearers must have occurred the thought: – 'Were you not the gainer by our churlishness? Had Cambridge then received you, no doubt

you would have been a very learned man and by this time Regius Professor. But would you have been quite such a master of contemporary history, quite such an impartial judge of modern England, so European, so supernational, so catholic, so liberal, so wise, so Olympian, so serene?' And even now, I cannot but think, the pride and sorrow with which Cambridge writes Acton's name on the roll of her illustrious dead is not unalloyed by an uncomfortable suspicion that just those qualities that were most distinctive of his work and most admirable, are but exotic flowers in our Cambridge garland. An effective resolve that never hereafter shall there be cause for such an abatement of our pride is the debt that we owe to his memory. Meanwhile a little remorse will do us no harm. The pardon was freely granted. We have yet to earn it.[53]

[53] Maitland 1911, III, 520–1.

Chapter 14

RELIGION AND LEARNING:
C. H. DODD AND DAVID KNOWLES

The battle of the university tests in the 1860s was a real battle, fought over issues that with imaginative sympathy we can appreciate still. Yet noone can doubt that the growth of Cambridge into a major international university would have been impossible if the tests had not been abolished. They went in 1871, the year after the Chancellor, the duke of Devonshire, had taken the first initiatives which were to lead to the building of the old Cavendish Laboratory. Can one imagine the sensational successes of the Cavendish in the century which followed had all the university officers which served it been compelled to some measure of assent to the 39 Articles? How would Cambridge economics, or the finances of King's, have fared if the abrasive agnosticism of Maynard Keynes had driven him from his home city and college never to return?

This chapter is an essay in hagiography – a study of two of the scholars who most deeply influenced my own outlook on life and scholarship, both of whom I knew over a period of thirty years, both of whom extend the reflections of the last chapter. Dodd was a Congregationalist – United Reformed as we should say today – throughout his life, though deeply ecumenical in his outlook; he is said to have been the first free church minister for whom Westminster Abbey provided a memorial service.[1] Knowles was born, or anyway baptised, a Roman Catholic – for his father was under instruction at the time, and his mother was not received till some years later. He was a devout Catholic

---

[1] Dillistone 1977, p. 238. In what follows I am deeply indebted to Dillistone's admirable biography. For Knowles see esp. Brooke et al. 1991; Morey 1979. This chapter perhaps needs some apology: it may seem out of scale in the book. But it was a conviction that a vital element in the history of Cambridge – the personal impact of its leading scholars – would otherwise be missing which inspired its writing.

throughout his life and a monk for most of it, even though in conflict with authority for many years; but theologically he was conservative and became something of a figurehead among conservative Catholics in the age of the Vatican Council and *Humanae Vitae*. Neither of them could have held office in Cambridge before 1871 – nor indeed for a while after; for Cardinal Manning did all he could to keep Catholics, and especially the religious, out of the ancient universities long after 1871;[2] and even in 1947 Knowles was the first monk since the Reformation to hold a chair in Cambridge. Dodd first came to Cambridge to the Norris-Hulse Chair of Divinity in 1935, at the moment when it was released from its Anglican chains. The tests had in fact survived for divinity degrees until 1913–14, and for chairs until 1935 – the remaining chairs were only released in the 1950s and 1970s.[3]

The strength of Cambridge as a centre of academic excellence owes an immense debt to the students and scholars who have brought the assumptions and traditions of distant places to enlarge its visions and enrich its resources. I do not mean distant in space alone, though Ernest Rutherford the New Zealander may remind us that this is true in a quite literal sense. In their different ways the Pen-y-Bryn Congregational chapel and the schools of Wrexham in which Dodd was brought up, and the abbey church at Downside which fostered David Knowles, were as remote from Cambridge as the New Zealand bush in which Rutherford was born. It is often said – with obvious truth within certain limits – that Cambridge in the late nineteenth and early twentieth centuries was predominantly recruited from public schools and from the middle classes.[4] It is doubtless true numerically; it is profoundly true of the football clubs; but one has only to contemplate what Cambridge would have been without J. J. Thomson, or Rutherford, or James Chadwick, or C. H. Dodd, to perceive that it is not the whole truth. Knowles had been to a public school; none the less – and even though his father was a cultivated man of wide interests – his background was truly less

[2] See pp. 388–9.
[3] *Reporter* 1912–13, pp. 42, 982; 1913–14, pp. 1007–8; Dillistone 1977, p. 145; *Reporter* 1956–7, pp. 204, 339 (Lady Margaret Chair); *Reporter* 1976–7, pp. 440, 1018.
[4] See pp. 247–50.

408

C. H. Dodd

academic than Dodd's. Not only were Dodd's parents teachers, but he was one of four highly intelligent brothers, all of whom won university scholarships, three of them in Oxford.

C. H. DODD

Dodd combined in a quite exceptional degree scholarship and simplicity. Simplicity is one of the subtlest of human virtues. In a great scholar it is sometimes founded on a strange alliance between a natural simplicity and the opposite – an extreme sophistication of mind produced by the endless nuances of serious academic study. So it was in Dodd. By background and early conviction and practice he was half-preacher half-scholar. In his first book, *The Meaning of Paul for Today* (1920), the preacher and perhaps the teacher are most in evidence – though the quality of mind and diction has something already of the purity and strength which mark his later books. But in his later years, especially after his move to Cambridge – and under the influence (one gathers) of the New Testament Seminar in which his mind was constantly matched by those of David Daube, Charlie Moule and many others living and no longer living – the subtlety and the nuances were refined, the learning deepened and sharpened. He was a good talker and a supremely good listener; a tiny, bird-like person, sharp and quick, precise and enchanting, warm and kind. He spoke with authority and assurance, qualities which maddened some of those who thought his approach to the gospels fundamentally wrong; but he was ready to the end of his days to listen to criticism and refine his tools. I recall a visit to him when he was approaching 90 and busy correcting minor inconsistencies in the NEB.

Dodd won a double first in Classical Mods and Greats at Oxford, and spent the next three years, from 1906 to 1909, partly in research, mainly in training for the ministry at Mansfield College, Oxford, one of the principal monuments to the era of liberation for the free churches. He went to Berlin to study ancient coins, and sat at the feet of Wilamowitz and Harnack – like so many British scholars of his generation, he was deeply influenced by contemporary German learning: to spend only one term in Germany and encounter both Harnack and Wila-

409

mowitz was an exceptional stroke of fortune. Dodd's first aim was to be a minister, but he had laid very deep scholarly foundations. From Mansfield he went to Warwick for some years of pastoral work, deeply fulfilling a part of his vocation. In 1915 he returned to Mansfield, and from then on combined teaching in the theological college with increasing involvement in the university until 1930, when he left for the Rylands Chair in Manchester – moving on to Cambridge in 1935. His early years in Oxford were full of personal anxiety, only resolved by his marriage in 1925.[5] The ambiguity in his vocation, and his years of turmoil, help to explain perhaps a late maturity. His first major book, *The Bible and the Greeks*, was published in 1935 – and from then on his creativity never flagged until he crowned his life work with his life of Jesus, *The Founder of Christianity*, in 1971, when he was 87.

Dodd was a man of very wide interests. He could write at length on the current philosophical views of history; he could plunge not only into Latin and Greek but several oriental languages, so that the greatest of his books, *The Interpretation of the Fourth Gospel*, is often tough going for the ignorant – though deeply exciting and satisfying too. F. W. Dillistone, at the end of his marvellously urbane and sympathetic yet penetrating book on Dodd, places him first and foremost as an expert on words and language: 'however valuable his historical researches have been for Christian apologists, it is as philologist that he stands supreme among New Testament scholars of this century'.[6] He has often been called 'a prince among exegetes'; and the patient skill with which he directed the New English Bible was rewarded – at least for the New Testament – in a unique instrument for the modern understanding of these ancient texts, if not for their recitation in church (unique for a time, that is, since it now has a godchild in the Revised English Bible).

Dodd was an immortal among New Testament scholars, and it would be absurd and paradoxical to claim him wholly for another trade. But one reason why we filled our shelves with Dodd's books in preference to those of even his greatest rivals was that he was a historian of genius. By this I mean first and foremost

---

[5] For all these details see Dillistone 1977, esp. pp. 54–5 (visit to Germany), 65–76 (Warwick), 76–101 (Oxford), 78–83, 90–8 (crisis and marriage).
[6] Dillistone 1977, p. 228.

that he practised the craft of a historian with a clear head, a cool judgement and an incisive imagination. His methods were equally at variance with the fundamentalist who thinks God's word has been plainly laid before us, and the dogmatic theologians to whom the historical uncertainties of New Testament criticism are anathema. Dodd was deeply interested in the philosophy of history, but his accounts of it were relatively naive – what abides is the deep conviction based on the experience of a lifetime spent in the study of historical texts that the scepticism of Rudolf Bultmann and his disciples, to take the most eminent examples, was gravely exaggerated. It was not an easy path to tread. The scholarly world was in plain reaction against the confident search for the historical Jesus of earlier generations. Even when Dodd was sitting at the feet of Harnack – the supreme exponent of the Jesus of history – Albert Schweitzer was mercilessly exposing the subjective consequences of *The Quest of the Historical Jesus*. From this there were various escape routes. The fundamentalist hides his head in the desert of obscurantism, and tries to forget that scholarship exists. Theologians of many different schools have urged that the New Testament is a theological book, that we seek history in it mistakenly – we should seek only the teaching of Jesus and the Christ of faith – the present encounter, not the uncertain historical events of 2,000 years ago. Dillistone prints a fascinating account of an informal debate between Dodd and Paul Tillich at Union Theological Seminary in 1950, in which Tillich expounded his conviction that faith cannot depend on historical enquiry at all – even if it affirms that there is a historical reality somewhere in its heart; while Dodd asserted that the Christian must both rest his faith on a historical figure and on the 'risk of faith' that he was the Christ.[7] Throughout his books Dodd was able to show, again and again, that historical enquiry can lead to reasonable and lucid historical reconstruction. It was precisely the calm assurance with which he presented his enquiries which so maddened those who disagreed with him – scholars who took a more radically sceptical view of the possibility of the historical reconstruction of the life of Jesus found the Dodd line, as I have heard it called, a brilliant, misleading, tendentious rearguard

---

7 Dillistone 1977, pp. 241–3 (by Langdon Gilbey).

action before the whole position crumbled and the scholarly world admitted that it knew nothing certain of the life of Jesus.

The chronic weakness of older attempts to reconstruct the historical Jesus had been to separate the historical from the theological context of the New Testament; and this brought a reaction in which baby and bathwater disappeared instantly together. Even those with a deep assurance of the fundamental historicity of the gospels have to safeguard themselves by saying in and out of season that the gospels are not biographies. But what is a biography? The gospels are statements about the divine order, manifestos of good news; they are every inch theological in that sense of the term. But if it be a prime function of a biography – as many have thought – not to chronicle every trivial detail of a life, but to portray that life in vivid and truthful colours, then they must hold their place among the masterpieces of the world's biographical literature, whatever else they are. By the same token, the New Testament literature now holds its own among historians the most secular as well as the most sacred as a collection of authentic historical documents of fundamental importance for the understanding of the ancient world. The historical aspect – to use a phrase of Dodd's – is inescapable. It will not go away.

There is ample space for disagreement. The discussions, arguments, battles of the last 150 years have taught us that study of the historical Jesus can be advanced by Christian, Jew, agnostic and atheist alike; they have taught us equally that there is space still for a very wide divergence of view on the date and authenticity of many of the documents. The great impact which Dodd made as lecturer and author on my generation of historians was that – though we recognised he was much more than a historian, that he had absorbed to the full the theological and philological inheritance of his world – yet his work was a model of historical enquiry, rich in instruction for any student of the craft, all the more so because he never departed from sound canons of historical judgement. He may often have been wrong: that is another matter. But he was a model historian; and his maturer writings were composed in a scholarly language of jewelled precision – not vivid or electric or colourful, but a wonderful instrument of precise scholarly expression.

C. H. Dodd

Let me illustrate this briefly from *The Parables of the Kingdom* of 1935, *The Apostolic Preaching and its Developments* of 1936, and *Historical Tradition in the Fourth Gospel* of 1963.

The first two books show the deep influence on Dodd – as on all New Testament critics of his age and ours – of form criticism. Under the influence of Dibelius and Bultmann, the endless sifting of minute problems of literary dependence in the synoptic record was set aside and attention focussed on the nature and transmission, on the *form*, of oral stories, myths and legends. The shape in which stories and sayings and parables are passed on was closely studied – and sometimes almost totally invented. But the outcome was a kind of historical criticism vital to the gospels and of great importance to a much wider historical circle. It has been applied with telling effect by Raoul Manselli and my wife in particular to the early stories about St Francis of Assisi.[8] Much form criticism has been rigid and lifeless and expelled most of the living history out of the stories and pericopes it investigated. Much more has had the opposite effect, of helping in the vivid imaginative reconstruction of the making of a historical source. But the most delicate issue – though the one least regarded in much form critical research – is the effect of Jesus and Francis themselves on the stories which were told about them. Twenty years after the death of St Francis a group of his companions produced a collection of extremely vivid and telling stories about the saint to illustrate his life, his principles and his intentions; at least that is my wife's view, to which I subscribe – for in Franciscan as in Christian origins every major issue is highly controversial.[9] What is generally agreed is that these stories were produced partly to present a point of view, to be a political manifesto (to state the matter crudely) of what the Franciscan Order should be and how it should live; partly they were an act of direct and genuine devotion to a great saint and a dear friend. The two elements are inseparable. By the same token the young Church produced the gospels and the gospels produced the young Church. *The Parables of the Kingdom* attempted to disentangle elements in the parables due to later interpretation, or adaptation to the problems and situations of early Christian life – to the *Sitz*

[8] Manselli 1980; Brooke, R. B., 1967, p. 194; Brooke, R. B., 1982, pp. 666–76.
[9] See Brooke, R. B., 1970/1990.

im Leben. It is a most exciting piece of detective work, as fresh and alive as when it was written. In such a field and on such a theme it raises many doubts and has been subjected to many criticisms. The parables he selects most brilliantly – and sometimes altogether too neatly – support his particular view of Jesus' teaching on the Kingdom of God as something which had arrived – of realised eschatology. Of the parables themselves he takes too simple a view. His basic idea of them as stories to light up a situation – to point a lesson, not allegories of complex meaning – is profoundly true, but many have thought that he missed something of the variety and the nuances of Jesus' use of them.[10] For the historian, his selection is unfortunate, since it excludes from view the Parable of the Good Samaritan, which is of all the parables the one in which there is most reason to think we have something like the original context in St Luke's account of it. For the great saying 'Go, and do thou likewise' with which it ends is peculiarly subtle and effective: it is not an answer to the question Jesus had been asked, but it cuts deep through and under the whole situation which the story reveals. Nothing is sure, nothing is certain in synoptic criticism; but it is at least possible that substantial stories have survived with their context relatively intact.

   The Parables of the Kingdom, by a shrewd and lively mingling of literary criticism, source criticism and form criticism, poses question after question of deep fascination historically and theologically alike. In *The Apostolic Preaching and its Developments* Dodd looked with a microscope at the earliest forms in which the Christian message was delivered, and sought a pattern or patterns in the primitive *kerygma*, the message of the Apostles; and he attempted to show the way in which it provided the frame, not only for the message but for the gospels themselves when they came to be written. He excavated the Church before the gospel, even, in a sense, the gospel before the gospel. It had been widely assumed before he wrote that the speeches in Acts, for example, were free compositions like speeches in innumerable historical writers – even of the most veridical character – from Thucydides to the seventeenth century. Dodd showed that this need not be so; he provided cogent grounds for believing it was not so. Not all

[10] E.g. Drury 1985; but I find it hard to accept John Drury's view that the Good Samaritan and its context were in effect of St Luke's creation.

his readers were convinced; there is no unanimity in this or any field of New Testament criticism. But no serious student of the subject can fail to read and ponder Dodd's argument.

In *The Interpretation of the Fourth Gospel* Dodd laid out in rich and ample detail the evidence he had gathered to explain the intellectual background, assumptions, motifs and so forth of John. He has no discussion of its value as historical narrative – save for some fascinating hints in an appendix. These he expanded into *Historical Tradition in the Fourth Gospel*, perhaps the most controversial of all his books. He starts by briefly surveying the endless debate on the authorship of the gospel. He allows that 'the external evidence for the apostle John son of Zebedee as author of the Fourth Gospel is relatively strong. From the closing decades of the second century the tradition is firm'[11] – but he proceeds to canvas with characteristic lucid brevity the difficulties and uncertainties of this evidence. He then looks at the internal evidence, and faces the baffling problem which – after generations of intense and subtle criticism – cannot be evaded, that the author of the fourth gospel shows much direct personal knowledge of the events he describes, but both in narrative and in theological exposition a capacity to interpret and embroider which makes the distinction between history and interpretation peculiarly difficult to trace.[12] Dodd himself had built up in his earlier book a picture of the intellectual background of the author of the fourth gospel which made it very difficult for him to believe it was the work of a Galilean fisherman. But he was strongly persuaded that the claims to knowledge – that 'this is vouched for by an eyewitness, whose evidence is to be trusted' was not an invention of the evangelist.[13] The issue of authorship as such was secondary; what mattered was to disentangle, so far as historical criticism permits the enterprise, history from interpretation, historical tradition from embroidery. For Dodd the primary task in studying the fourth gospel had been its meaning; *The Interpretation of the Fourth Gospel* is the first and larger and more important book. But he was a historian to whom facts and events mattered as well as

11 Dodd 1963, pp. 10–11.
12 Robinson 1985 discusses in depth the evidence for an early date and close dependence on an eyewitness; among the many responses to his book, J. V. M. Sturdy is preparing a study which argues for a date well into the second century.
13 John 19: 35; cf. Dodd 1963, pp. 14, 134 n. 1.

ideas; and so he embarked on one of the most delicate critical adventures a historian can undertake.

Dodd had been brought up in a world in which all but the very conservative took it for granted that the synoptic gospels told us what was known of the life of Jesus, that the fourth gospel was a pious embroidery; and that – though views of its date varied widely – it was later than the other gospels and presupposed knowledge of them, even occasionally quoted them. Belief in a very late date received a salutary shock when the palaeographers argued that a tiny fragment of papyrus in the John Rylands Library in Manchester contained a portion of the fourth gospel thought by some to have been written very early in the second century at latest; but palaeographical evidence cannot bear so much weight – it could be of the mid-second century. Meanwhile some scholars have argued for a much earlier date than used to be fashionable.[14] To Dodd all this was secondary: his prime concern was with the tradition and material available to the evangelist. In a prolonged enquiry of the greatest intricacy – a sustained argument of great brilliance – he suggested that where the fourth gospel and the synoptics use the same material, the indications are always that John had independent access to it not dependent on any surviving gospel; and that the author of the fourth gospel did indeed have access to early strands of historical tradition; that when he contradicts Mark, for instance, on the date of the Last Supper – Mark seems to make it clear that it was the paschal meal itself, John states precisely that it was the eve of the passover – he did so because he followed an independent tradition, not for any esoteric or theological motive.[15] Many of the experts, I understand, are not convinced that John is independent of the synoptics; many would reckon that Dodd's reconstruction of the historical tradition behind the fourth gospel was highly speculative. It remains for me one of the most exciting pieces of historical detection which I know: and a part of the excitement for a scholar lies in the marvellous precision of Dodd's scholarly language. The most rarefied arguments are plainly and economically expounded.

[14] On the papyrus see esp. Roberts 1936, 1938. For an early date for the gospel, see esp. Robinson 1985; cf. Robinson 1976, chap. 9.
[15] Dodd 1963, pp. 109–12.

C. H. Dodd

Dodd's scholarship was international. To it Pen-y-Bryn, Oxford, Berlin and the whole world of ecumenical endeavour had paid their tribute money. It was fitting that F. C. Burkitt's chair, freed at last from the Anglican chain, should offer Dodd a base for the best years of his working life; and he found companionship among the scholars of Cambridge to add depth and dimension to his work. That his influence was deeply felt not only among theologians and experts on the ancient world but on those with wider or different historical interests I can testify myself. But in the context of university history his towering achievements raise fundamental questions. Between 1860 and 1960 there has been much advance. If we look at the Cavendish or at numerous other laboratories, if we look at the study of medieval history or the New Testament, we witness a story of scholarly progress in which Cambridge has played a distinguished role. But modern science is capable of indefinite expansion; we have no serious grounds, I understand, for supposing that the pace of advance will slacken – unless we are all buried under the mountain of bureaucratic processing with which our culture threatens us in every field. But the future is not quite so open in some of the scholarly fields which have been most fruitful hitherto. It is not that the mine is worked out – the Cairo Genizah has many secrets yet to yield, and we cannot tell how many similar stores of ancient learning may not emerge to enrich our knowledge of the context of the New Testament and the early Church. It is not that the fundamental questions are settled – far from it. The problem is that modern scholarship has thriven on new ideas; and in some fundamental regions of study these can become, in the nature of the case, more difficult to compass. While the writings of scholars such as C. H. Dodd may inspire whole generations to fresh and exciting adventures in biblical criticism, they may also lead the experts themselves to despair. It cannot be supposed that the history of New Testament criticism has before it the same boundless horizon as nuclear physics. Yet it has shown, in its best exponents, an extraordinary resilience: whole new schools of New Testament criticism have arisen in the short time since Dodd laid down his pen.[16]

[16] See Neill and Wright 1988, chap. 9.

Religion and learning

DOM DAVID KNOWLES

In a very different way Dom David Knowles also illustrates the inspiring and silencing qualities of great scholarship, and equally the enrichment of the religious and academic tradition of Cambridge by the widening of its religious horizons. Knowles delighted to tell the story of G. M. Trevelyan giving thanks at the party given by the History Faculty to celebrate his 80th birthday. By then Dom David himself was Regius Professor, and Trevelyan – after expounding his ancient friendship with his own successor Sir James Butler – proceeded with the ominous words 'David Knowles comes from another tradition'. It was indeed so; in younger days Trevelyan, agnostic, anti-clerical, would have been horrified to find a monk in his chair;[17] but he had mellowed; and he had also found much common ground with the new Regius – and he proceeded to a most friendly welcome to him. They both loved great narrative history; they both deeply admired Macaulay; they were romantics. But it was very true that Dom David came from a different tradition.

He had read classics at Christ's in the early 1920s; but that apart his whole formation had been within his own religious order. He had been a boy at Downside, a monk when he was just 18. Following the normal practice of the day he performed his novitiate before going on to higher study – which meant the Classics Tripos at Cambridge and a period of theological study at Sant'Anselmo in Rome. As a young monk he saw something of the great Catholic medievalist Edmund Bishop, who was a frequent visitor at Downside, and he learned more from his books and his fame in the community; he was among a galaxy of scholars which included the abbot, Cuthbert Butler, and several of his own generation such as Dom Hugh Connolly and Dom Adrian Morey. Downside, with its fine library and its brilliant group of scholars, was like a Maurist cell from the age of Dom Mabillon; and it was here that he was formed as a scholar and historian. At first it seemed a wayward path: the young monk who knew nothing of war wrote a book on *The American Civil War* (1926).[18] He was deeply read in imaginative and historical

---

[17] See p. 129. For all that follows see esp. Brooke et al. 1991; Morey 1979.
[18] See Brooke et al. 1991, pp. 11–14; Green 1989.

literature, and still at this stage regarded them much alike: it was, by his own account, the reviews and reactions to this first book which showed him the dedication needed for original history. In 1929 he began collecting systematic materials for a major work on medieval English monastic history. Meanwhile a zeal for reform at Downside led to his being set at the head of a group of young monks who sought leave to make a new foundation. The scheme failed and his colleagues submitted to authority. Dom David himself – for all that he was a devout and conservative Catholic all his days, and always in his own eyes true to his vocation as a monk – found total submission impossible. He lived for several years at Ealing, then a priory of Downside, almost in limbo – enjoying meanwhile the leisure needed to encompass his *Monastic Order in England, 940–1216*. In 1939 the book was in the press, but its author at the depth of his personal crisis. In 1914 he was clothed as a monk; in 1939 he left his community and lived the rest of his life under the devoted care of the Swedish doctor Elizabeth Kornerup – retaining in his own eyes the monasticism of the spirit, and eventually submitting to a formal reconciliation with Downside which left him free to live outside the cloister.

In 1944 he was elected to a teaching fellowship at Peterhouse, and early in 1947 he became professor of medieval history. He became a leader in the History Faculty without having served any apprenticeship there. Even in the 1930s his work had been known to Z. N. Brooke and other leading medievalists. *The Monastic Order* was published in the year of doom 1940: 500 copies were printed by a nervous University Press, partly at Knowles' expense, and the type was broken up. It had quickly to be reassembled, and since the easing of paper restrictions after the war it has usually been in print. It made an immediate and deep impression, so that he was much discussed by Cambridge medievalists, Zachary Brooke, Philip Grierson and Munia Postan (later Sir Michael Postan); his quality became known to Herbert Butterfield in Peterhouse, on whose initiative he was elected.[19] Thus in a mind and personality of exceptional quality the remarkable scholarly tradition of Downside was grafted into Cambridge.

[19] See esp. Roger Lovatt in Brooke et al. 1991, pp. 82–5.

The study of English monasticism at Downside had been founded by the notorious Dom Aidan Gasquet, later cardinal; and monastic history had flourished in Cambridge before Dom David came in the eccentric lectures and writings of G. G. Coulton. It is worth dwelling for a moment on these forebears, if such they may be figuratively called. In 1956 David Knowles gave the Creighton Lecture in the University of London and chose as his theme 'Cardinal Gasquet as an historian'.[20] It is one of the most entertaining of his occasional writings, and by contrast revealing of some of his own concerns and values.

> Gasquet's inaccuracies in his early books were many, but they could be numbered. But from *c.*1900 Gasquet's pages crawl with errors and slips ... Towards the end of his life, indeed, Gasquet's capacity for carelessness amounted almost to genius. He could refer, in a tribute to Edmund Bishop (of all places), to Gibbon's *Rise and Fall*, and he could print a stanza of *In Memoriam* in five or six lines of type without any ascertainable metre or rhyme.[21]

Gasquet was no scholar; and yet in his earlier days he had done industrious and useful work on medieval monastic history and the dissolution of the monasteries. He had even helped and inspired Edmund Bishop – a friendship and an alliance between scholarship exquisite and deplorable of the most unlikely character. If one were to ask – who had laid the foundations of the great building Dom David himself was to erect? – one would have had to say, Dom Gasquet. But they were such as needed to be totally excavated; Gasquet's work inspired better scholars to start afresh. In a characteristic phrase, Dom David observed that 'In Gasquet's case the triumphal car had a good start, but Vengeance came limping after in the person of George Gordon Coulton.'[22] Coulton was one of the remarkable characters of Cambridge and of the medieval world of his day. He was compounded of genuine learning and extreme prejudice: though never a soldier he was a relentless militarist; though personally kind and friendly to many individual Catholics, he hated the Roman Catholic Church with remorseless hatred. He was deeply learned and had an extraordinary knowledge of medieval life and

[20] Knowles 1963, chap. 11.   [21] Knowles 1963, p. 254.
[22] Knowles 1963, pp. 257–8.

of medieval religion; he could write with warmth and insight about St Benedict and St Francis. But he pursued less worthy monks and friars as if he was a medieval reformer desperate to improve them; and his books are gatherings of fragments, sometimes enchanting, often maddening, arranged almost at random. Academic recognition came late: he struggled for many years on inadequate salaries in inferior posts; but in the end he became a university lecturer in English, a fellow of St John's and of the British Academy.[23] His achievement was to bring vividly before his many readers, and generations of undergraduates, a wide range of medieval sources. The sources were fresh and often brilliantly chosen; but among the lilies thorns grew – he never ceased to parade his prejudices. While still unknown and unrecognised, Coulton found errors in the work of Dom Gasquet; and he noted how, as the errors mounted, Gasquet climbed the hierarchy. The church was rewarding him for his bad scholarship (so Coulton thought); it was all part of the sinister world of Roman Catholic politics. In correcting Gasquet's errors, Coulton 'was almost invariably right' – but he quite misjudged the man.

> The Gasquet he attacked – the suave, polished, successful hierocrat, lying for the sake of his Church and rewarded for so doing – was to that extent so much a caricature of the real Gasquet – patriotic, 'broad-brow', often indiscreet, often critical of persons and policies within the Church – that it diverted many of Gasquet's friends and apologists from meeting or admitting the detailed charges.[24]

In *The Monastic Order* Dom David achieved what was denied both to Gasquet and to Coulton. It is a work of precise and penetrating scholarship: like C. H. Dodd, Dom David worked from the sources, was always at his best when he was closest to them. He was not infallible, and he trusted too much to a remarkable memory; but it is a work of fine scholarship both in its appreciation of detail and in its extraordinary power to evoke the atmosphere and inspiration of a monastery or an ideal. It is partly based on a comprehensive catalogue of medieval religious houses which he published separately, to replace the haphazard compilation of Gasquet, partly on systematic notes of heads of

[23] On Coulton see esp. Coulton 1943; Campion 1948; above, pp. 276–7.
[24] Knowles 1963, p. 259.

religious houses.[25] Above all, it is a most shapely, well organised book – great in narrative as well as in analysis; the model which Coulton may have aspired to, but never approached. It was characteristic of Coulton that he welcomed the book and spoke warmly of the author; and in an enthusiastic letter to H. P. Morrison, then head of Nelson's the publishers, he united the two young Downside scholars – as he thought of them, though Knowles was little short of 50 when he wrote – David Knowles and Adrian Morey as 'Dom Adrian Knowles'.[26]

Thus Knowles brought to Cambridge his remarkable gifts as scholar and author; and his reputation swiftly grew and spread, until in 1954 he was translated to the Regius Professorship by Winston Churchill. But what precisely was it that he brought to Cambridge 'from another tradition'? The study of the medieval church had long flourished – one of those who most warmly welcomed him was Zachary Brooke, his predecessor as professor of medieval history, author of *The English Church and the Papacy*, a classic of Cambridge research and exposition; and Coulton had long made it known as a place where monastic history might prosper.

It has been the prerogative of Regius Professors of Modern History at Cambridge to bring their special view of history into the limelight. To Acton history was the judgement seat, a source of moral understanding; to Bury it was a science – no less and no more; to Trevelyan, in plain reaction against the drier tendencies of the scientific historian, it had an element of poetry in it which was of its essence. Dom David never preached or prophesied in quite this way, though his inaugural as Regius, on 'The historian and character',[27] paraded human nature before his audience with a wit and point and width of learning which laid proper emphasis on personality and character in whose portrayal he himself excelled. He was a small, quiet man of intimate charm – but also reserved, introverted, inward-looking; and he taught more by example than by precept. For noisy preaching he had no use. Three elements in his work – his style, his subtlety of exposition,

[25] Knowles 1940b, replaced in its turn by Knowles and Hadcock, see esp. edn of 1971. The notebooks of heads, much revised, became Knowles, Brooke and London 1972.
[26] Letter of 23 March 1945 temporarily in my possession.
[27] Knowles 1963, chap. 1.

and his high seriousness – will illustrate an influence which ran deeper and wider than can easily be expounded.

He brought back the idea that historical prose can be a work of art, or at least of high craftsmanship. His style, personal, charged with literary echoes, rich and varied – alternating austere exposition and romantic evocation – opened windows into a new world of scholarly language, of the use of style as an instrument of scholarship. He has been thought self-indulgent in his use of jewelled prose; but one of his most striking characteristics was the restraint with which he used his effects.

The Monastic Order brought him fame and office; and it was continued in three volumes of *The Religious Orders in England*, the third of which carried the story to the dissolution of the monasteries and even a little beyond. The scholarly world had waited with eager anticipation to see what Dom David would make of the dissolution: here was the acid test of his fair-mindedness; where Gasquet had wept and Coulton triumphed, could Dom David, the monk, be impartial? It must first of all be said that many think that Dom David, the reforming monk, was at the end of the day more severe than Coulton in his judgements of his confrères. With a few heroic exceptions, the religious of Henry VIII's time accepted the breach with Rome, accepted the royal supremacy – even outwardly accepted their own dismissal, especially when they were amply pensioned – with extraordinary passivity. Knowles sees every side of the question, and uses his literary skills brilliantly to bring every point to the fore; he allows, and emphasises, how much devotion and suffering may be hidden from our gaze by the failure of evidence; he pays tribute to the heroism of the Carthusians; but his judgement on religious who could surrender their papal allegiance so swiftly and silently is exceedingly severe – though expressed with a marvellous restraint which covers even the carefully chosen words he allots to Henry VIII and Thomas Cromwell. Of Cromwell's visitors he speaks with a nice mixture of evocation and burlesque:

> As they rode over the rainswept English countryside in the late summer of 1535 the life of some eight hundred religious families, great and small, was continuing, at least in external show, to follow the rhythm that had endured for centuries and that had been familiar to Englishmen from the very dawn of national

history. From the grey turrets and lichened gables, set among the red roofs of a town or framed by the ricks and elms of the open country, bells still rang to Mattins and Mass, and the habits, white or black, still crossed the great courtyard or passed down the village street. When, five years later, their work was done, nettles and the fire-weed were springing from the dust, and the ruins of Hailes and Roche and Jervaulx were already beginning to wear the mantle of silence that covers them to-day.[28]

Contrast the following, which hovers on the borders of burlesque, as he deploys Cromwell's visitors, Layton and Legh, and paints them with subtle strokes:

> The abbot of Bruton who, after some initial unpleasantness, had succeeded in giving a fairly favourable impression to Layton, had a disagreeable shock a few days later when Legh arrived at the gate with a written commission. Some plain speaking followed, for the abbot, having already parted with a substantial fee and a venerable relic, in addition to hearing the comments of his canons on his régime, had no desire for a repetition of the experience within a fortnight. Nevertheless, he was only in part successful in avoiding it, for Legh, though refraining from a formal visitation, demanded to see Layton's *comperta* and proceeded to stiffen up his injunctions.[29]

Throughout the book it is abundantly clear that great issues were at stake; history is not a trivial subject – certainly not the history of the Church. The religious life itself may become trivial in the hands of a man like Prior More of Worcester, whose comfortable existence down to the eve of the dissolution is most penetratingly and gracefully, and entertainingly, portrayed.[30] But it is a way of life which can express some of the deepest spiritual urges of mankind. A study by Father David left no room for frivolous or trumpery judgements of high matters.

When he retired, the university gave him the honorary degree of Doctor of Divinity. The Doctorate of Letters he already had; divinity was suited to his cloth and his habit; it underlined his special role as a Benedictine Regius Professor. It also reflected the Cambridge tradition that the history of the Church, of monasti-

---

[28] Knowles 1948–59, III, p. 274.   [29] Knowles 1948–59, III, p. 281.
[30] Knowles 1948–59, III, chap. ix.

cism and of the spiritual life, are a fully accepted part of theology
– even if the Faculty of Divinity itself had paid scant attention
hitherto to the medieval centuries. But there was a special
appropriateness, since one of his major gifts to Cambridge had
been to implant the study of medieval theology. He was not alone
in this: in their different ways Donald Mackinnon, Thomas
Gilbey and Walter Ullmann were expounding aspects of medieval thought, and Kenelm Foster the depths of the thought world
of Dante. One could multiply examples. Dom David mounted a
successful course of lectures on medieval thought which inspired a
number of younger scholars who were to devote their scholarly
lives to its pursuit – David Luscombe and Gordon Leff among
them. These lectures issued in his book *The Evolution of Medieval
Thought* – not the most original or profound of his books; but one
which reflects the heritage he brought to Cambridge, in which
Catholic theology and scholastic thought – and, be it said, the
history of the universities themselves – were presented in a broad
historical context, as the heirs of Greek philosophy and early
Christian thought and devotion; and as a living world of ideas
worthy of study by historian and theologian alike.

At the end of his life C. H. Dodd was awarded a prestigious
prize for his last book, *The Founder of Christianity*; and David
Knowles was one of the panel which awarded the prize. The two
men came of very different traditions; but the large room of
Cambridge scholarship – and a deep devotion to Jesus – gave
them much common ground too. In their very different ways
both proved in their lives and their scholarship how fruitful and
necessary it is to walk on the boundaries which attempt to divide
history and theology.

Cambridge is a microcosm of the intellectual and academic
world, and much of the interest of our story lies in the way it
reflects a larger saga in a wider realm. But it was not perhaps the
academy Dom David would most have liked to serve. In 1941 he
thus described the Christian humanism of Rievaulx in the twelfth
century:

> Here indeed, far from the familiar centres of European life, is the
> quintessence of the humanism of the twelfth century; Ailred, the
> novice-master and teacher, surrounded by a small group of finely

educated young minds absorbed in living debates – Ailred, the friend and guide, learning recollection and true charity from his contact with others – Ailred the abbot, in middle age and in premature old age brought on by long and sharp illness, the centre of an ever shifting gathering of his sons to whom he, with his old charm intensified by suffering and sanctity, was all things to all, now discussing the nature of the soul in a dialogue left unfinished at his death, now counselling an illiterate lay-brother with equal care, while around him the fixed life of choir and farm-work, of changeless routine and sparing diet, went on unchanged.[31]

[31] Knowles 1963, p. 26.

Chapter 15

A DIVERSITY OF DISCIPLINES

PROLOGUE: ON PHILOLOGY AND ORIENTAL STUDIES

The gravest problem I have encountered in planning this book has been to instil order and discipline into the triposes and departments almost beyond counting which have flourished in recent generations in Cambridge. I have tried to command by dividing them; a number have been the themes of chapters 5, 6 and 7. Some which remain had a prehistory – even a distinguished prehistory – before 1920; some were invented later, a few much later than that. To have handled them all together would have given author and readers indigestion. The situation of some in this chapter is arbitrary; but I fancy the observant reader will find some of the reasons for my choice in every case. The book is drawing on; I have in relatively brief compass to do justice to many disciplines and to the learning and culture of modern Cambridge – to the study of German and Russian and radio astronomy and music, to the Fitzwilliam Museum and Kettle's Yard. It is a formidable task, and I shall fail in it; but my hope is to inspire future scholars with some insights into how to do it better. It cannot be done really well till more of these institutions and disciplines have turned to and studied their own past.

English and modern languages, as we now know them, are triposes born in the First World War; they flourished in the student boom which followed it, and have remained giants ever since. Their prehistory is perhaps the most obscure passage in the history of Cambridge disciplines; and it was closely interwoven with the development of oriental studies.

In many German universities, to this day, a large range of the humanities is gathered under the generic title 'Philologie'; and although the term is wider than the English 'philology', its use reflects the immense prestige of philology as a scientific study in the wake of the triumphs of the brothers Grimm in the early and mid-nineteenth century. They are famous for the study of literature – of fairy tales at least – as well as of language; but in scientific circles it was language, philology, which achieved universal respectability and imitation. Philology is a highly specialised field, of the deepest fascination to a relatively restricted body of students. It played a notable role in late nineteenth-century Cambridge, partly in response to the wider appeal of Philologie; partly because of the presence of a group of linguistic scholars of exceptional gifts – Edward Cowell, Edward Palmer, Robert Bensly, W. W. Skeat and the classical philologists John Peile and Peter Giles; partly because the call of empire seemed to make a knowledge of oriental languages an essential ingredient in a forward-looking university, and there was pressure from some students, especially women students, to open the languages and culture of Europe for their contemplation.

There had long been some provision for the teaching of oriental languages: a Regius Professor of Hebrew since the sixteenth century, a professor and reader (sometimes two professors) of Arabic since 1632 and 1724 respectively.[1] The first major step forward came with the establishment of the chair of Sanskrit in 1867, with Edward Cowell in it.[2] He had matriculated as a maltster in Ipswich, then become a mature student in Oxford, and rapidly made a name for himself as an orientalist, with a particular knowledge of Sanskrit and Persian. Between 1856 and 1864 he played a leading role in Calcutta University and became principal of Sanskrit College there; and in 1867 he was elected professor of Sanskrit in Cambridge. He was a brilliant teacher whose influence was felt among all the young philologists of Cambridge – not only students of Sanskrit, but English philologists in the making like W. W. Skeat, and classics such as E. S. Roberts, future master of Caius and one of the supporters of medieval and modern languages, and J. S. Reid, Roberts' close

[1] Tanner 1917, pp. 76–7, 81–2, 89–90. The Lord Almoner's chair was sometimes reckoned a professorship, normally a readership (for its peculiar history, see Clark 1900, pp. 238–41).
[2] On Cowell, see Tanner 1917, p. 100; *DNB*; Bury 1952, pp. 100, 221–3; Brooke 1985, p. 234.

friend, later professor of ancient history.[3] Among his closest colleagues was John Peile, later master of Christ's, a classical philologist who had taught Sanskrit before Cowell's arrival. Cowell was also a notable figure in Corpus, where he became a professorial fellow and a kind of symbol of the academic standards of a college; round him were to gather in his later years the young fellows who wished to see Corpus less of an evangelical seminary, more of a home of learning.[4]

One of Cowell's first duties as professor was to examine a young candidate for a fellowship of St John's, Edward Palmer. Palmer had been born in Cambridge and was a pupil at the Perse; but his real education started in and around London where he picked up Romany, Italian and French and developed a remarkable taste for dialect and patois. He came to Cambridge as a mature student and scraped a third in classics. But in 1860 he encountered there a Hebrew scholar and an Arab, who taught him a love for oriental languages. By 1867 he was ready to face Professor Cowell. 'I undertook to examine him', said Cowell, 'in Persian and Hindustani, as I felt that my knowledge of Arabic was too slight' – though Arabic was Palmer's chief accomplishment; and the outcome was a fellowship at St John's.[5] Palmer failed to get the senior Arabic professorship in 1870 – William Wright, who brought the learning of St Andrew's, Halle, Leiden and Dublin to Cambridge, was preferred – but he was appointed to the Lord Almoner's readership in the next year. He taught oriental languages to students aiming for the Indian Civil Service, and made a considerable name for himself as an explorer of the near east. But he felt stifled in the academic atmosphere of Cambridge, and for this and domestic reasons – his first wife was an invalid – he spent more and more time elsewhere. Whether his lien with the university would have survived we cannot tell, for in 1882 he was sent by the government on a secret mission among the Bedouin of the Arabian desert, and after some remarkably successful adventures he was caught and murdered by a robber gang. Yet his short career had helped to set a mark on oriental studies in Cambridge. His work had revealed the need for

---

3 Brooke 1985, p. 234.   4 See pp. 50–1.
5 Clark 1900, pp. 219–20. On Palmer, see ibid., pp. 201–81; *DNB*.

language teaching, especially for those aspiring to the Indian Civil Service. The imperial theme had inspired Jowett and his colleagues in Oxford to unite in Classical Greats two Victorian aspirations: the cult of classics and the call to service of the empire. In Cambridge the practical needs of empire were met in some measure by provision of language courses; and it seemed a logical step to offer a tripos for the abler students. Two indeed were set up: one in Semitic languages, first examined in 1878, another in Indian languages in the next year. The examiners for the former included William Wright and Robert Bensly of Caius; for the latter Edward Cowell and John Peile; for both, Palmer.[6] Bensly was to hold the Lord Almoner's readership at the end of his life; but his most notable achievement for oriental studies in Cambridge was in the University Library, where he established the oriental collections on a new footing between 1864 and 1876.[7]

The examiners for these two triposes had a modest task. Four examiners commonly sat in judgement on one or two candidates only; in 1890 the candidates for the Semitic Languages Tripos equalled the examiners in number, but one fell sick; in 1886 four candidates sat the Indian Languages Tripos, all of them Indians; four again in 1889, five in 1892, three of them Indians.[8] These triposes were caviare to future civil servants, who took other degrees; and they were rapidly abandoned. Palmer's students were keen to learn the languages of the middle east, but not to take a tripos in them. From 1895 the Oriental Languages Tripos took their place, but in this too there were commonly more examiners than candidates. None the less, oriental languages – now oriental studies – have flourished modestly since, an essential element in a great university with any pretension to a wide view of the world and its languages and cultures. The faculty (as it now is) has expanded and contracted over the years, but held its own; it has formed valuable alliances with theology and history in particular; it has fostered Centres for Middle Eastern and South Asian Studies; it has spread further east into Mongolia and China and Japan. It has formed an alliance of great distinction with the

---

[6] Tanner 1917, pp. 938–45. On Bensly see *DNB*.
[7] McKitterick 1986, pp. 628–9, etc.
[8] For the details, see Tanner 1917, pp. 938–50.

eminent sinologist Joseph Needham, and helped him to build a noble shrine to his learning in the Needham Research Institute in the gardens of Robinson College.[9] Characteristic of the intervening generations, in the early twentieth century, was the work of F. C. Burkitt, whose home came to be in the Divinity Faculty and the Norrisian Chair, and is perhaps best remembered as an inspired New Testament scholar; but much of his most significant work lay among Syriac texts, and he was exceptionally proficient in the languages of the ancient near east.

FROM MEDIEVAL AND MODERN TO MODERN AND MEDIEVAL LANGUAGES

Meanwhile Edward Cowell and his disciples also helped to inspire the study of European languages. The same mingling of a need for the study of languages, including English, with the esoteric learning of a coterie of scholars helps to explain the difficult birth of MML. Liberal minded teachers and scholars saw clearly the need for Cambridge to look more kindly on modern studies, and not only in the natural sciences. In 1867 William Bateson, the enlightened master of St John's, had helped Edward Palmer to a fellowship. In the 1880s men like E. S. Roberts of Caius – himself a fervent classic – gave strong backing to the formation of a tripos in medieval and modern languages.[10] More traditional classicists cried out against such trumpery nonsense, spoon-feeding for travellers and couriers. Nor did the colleges give much help at first: it took two generations for teaching fellows in modern languages to penetrate many of the older colleges. Significantly, the lead came from the women, whose example encouraged their supporters and stiffened their opponents in the arguments which preceded the birth of MML. In the first year of medieval and modern languages, 1886, three men and three women took the tripos; in the second three women and two men; and between the two years three women and no men secured firsts. In due course MML won more male support; but in its early years the women usually led the men in numbers and

<hr/>

[9] See pp. 400–5; for Burkitt (below), see pp. 146–7.
[10] *Caian* 1912, Special Number, pp. 19–20.

quality. By 1910 there were 33 women and 29 men in the list.[11] The rise and success of MML was one of the first and most remarkable consequences of the opening of exams to women in the early 1880s.

But of what did it consist? The early exam papers make it clear that it was indeed medieval before modern, especially in English. Thus in 1894 there was a paper on Shakespeare and another on modern English authors; but a whole group of Old and Middle English with a strong philological and linguistic bias, though Chaucer had a paper to himself. The papers in French and other languages were chiefly practical – proses and translations abounded; literature had a place, but it was secondary.[12] Only slowly over the years did the history and culture of Europe – later to be central to MML – penetrate these exam papers. The emphasis was on language and, especially in English, the bias was medieval.

The most eminent figure in MML in its early days was Walter William Skeat of Christ's, first Elrington and Bosworth Professor of Anglo-Saxon from 1878 till his death in 1912.[13] Skeat was a brilliant philologist of wide learning whose prestige kept Old and Middle English in the forefront of MML while he lived. In 1910–11 a serious attempt was made to establish English literature as a major field of academic study in Cambridge – as it was already in most other universities in the land – by the founding of the King Edward VII Chair, and was promptly neutralised by the appointment of an elderly classic, A. W. Verrall.[14] He died the next year and Sir Arthur Quiller-Couch reigned in his stead.[15]

In 1916 the Great War was at its height and rebellion brewing in Ireland; in the same year three conspirators – Sir Arthur Quiller-Couch (Q), H. M. Chadwick, Skeat's successor as professor of Anglo-Saxon, and the Reverend H. F. Stewart, the leading teacher of French – plotted the dismemberment of MML. To its consequences for the English Tripos we shall presently return. In modern languages, as in English, there was strong

[11] Tanner 1917, pp. 951–71.
[12] *Cambridge University Examination Papers*, 1894–5, esp. pp. 341–53. For a detailed account of the development of the syllabus of MML, see Tillyard 1958, pp. 27–38.
[13] On Skeat, see p. 444.   [14] On Verrall, see *DNB*.
[15] On Q, see below, pp. 445–8.

pressure from within and without the cabal for a wider study of literature; with it went an impulse to study the culture and history of the European countries whose languages held a place in Cambridge teaching. In the same year 1916 a Prime Minister's Committee was set up to ponder the present and future of modern languages in British schools and universities; it recommended in 1918 a major expansion of chairs and lectureships, especially in Oxford and Cambridge.[16] It was an extremely propitious time for the start of the new-style MML. It still took a while for it to establish itself as a major academic discipline in the Cambridge scene; but there were many portents of a better future already in the 1920s. In 1918, at a meeting in Cambridge, the Modern Humanities Research Association was formed. In 1919 the Serena Fund gave money which made it possible to appoint a professor of Italian, and the Drapers' Company agreed to fund (for a number of years) the Drapers Professorship of French.[17] It was symptomatic of the current state of academic Italian that the first professor had no degree; but Thomas Okey was *sui generis*, and by great good fortune has told us his own story in *A Basketful of Memories* (1930) – his progress from the craft of basket-making in the east end of London, via Toynbee Hall, the WEA and the opportunities these contacts opened to be a guide and leader on expeditions to Italy, to the accolade of a Cambridge chair when he was 66. Prior, the first professor of French, was a less notable character, though an earnest proponent of his subject; H. F. Stewart, the creator of the new MML, remained the central figure in the teaching of French for many years. He was a clerical don at St John's, later dean of Trinity and a DD, devoted especially to Pascal: one of his later books was characteristically called *The Heart of Pascal* (1945). Equally characteristic was his collaboration with his close friend and colleague Arthur Tilley, which issued in standard textbooks on seventeenth and eighteenth-century French literature.

Other languages were also coming to the fore, some of them represented by native speakers of their tongues – most notably

[16] Charlton 1987–8. I owe this reference, and much help in this region, to Professor D. G. Charlton and Professor Peter Bayley.
[17] For what follows, see Howarth 1978, pp. 114–16; on Okey, Brooke 1985, pp. 283–4 and refs., esp. to Okey 1930.

German, in which Karl Breul from Berlin, who had taught German in Cambridge since 1900, became first Schröder Professor in 1910.[18] But the most significant figure in German and Italian was Edward Bullough, who combined Lancashire descent with an upbringing in Switzerland and Germany, and gave a European dimension to the teaching, first of German, then of Italian in Cambridge. To him language, literature, art and religion were indivisible elements in the culture of the lands he studied, and he laid a special mark on MML by his example and his teaching. He had taken the initiative in 1916 in the moves which led to the reform of the old MML, and quickly won the support of Stewart and Chadwick. His influence spread beyond his faculty: Michael Oakeshott, historian and philosopher, used to recall with particular gratitude his lectures on aesthetics.[19] His taste is happily reflected in the Italian villa he and his Italian wife inspired the architect H. C. Hughes to design for them, now the nucleus of Blackfriars. The Bulloughs were devout Catholics, and he played something of the role among the Catholic academic community that Baron Anatole von Hügel and Lord Acton had played in an earlier generation. He became professor of Italian in 1933, but died in 1934: his widow gave the house to the Dominican Friars; and it was appropriate that one of his most distinguished pupils should be Father Kenelm Foster, OP, for many years resident in Blackfriars and university lecturer in Italian, whose deep understanding of medieval thought helped to make him a charismatic lecturer on Dante.

Many other languages and cultures have been represented in modern MML: they have included Scandinavian languages, Dutch, and especially Spanish – in recent times represented by a small but distinguished group of leading experts in Spanish literature. They now include linguistics, a fashionable field with close links in English and philosophy; it may yet prove the cuckoo in MML's nest that English was before 1919. Medieval French, German, Italian and Spanish have flourished; and with them medieval Latin, a remarkable example of the shifting

[18] Tanner 1917, pp. 110–11.
[19] I owe this to a personal communication. On Bullough see Brooke 1985, p. 243 and refs.; Moriarty 1988, p. 89 (with portrait on p. 88); Stopp 1986. For his initiative in 1916, see Tillyard 1958, p. 54. For help in this area, I am much indebted to Dr Elisabeth Stopp.

frontiers of modern humanities. It was taught for many years by a celebrated Cambridge character, Freddy Brittain of Jesus; when he was succeeded by Peter Dronke an enthusiastic amateur gave way to a scholar who was to become one of the leading professionals in Britain. There is no 'department' of medieval Latin in Cambridge or elsewhere in the island. Yet it has deep roots in Cambridge now, in English, history and classics as well as in modern languages. Peter Dronke has a personal chair; Michael Lapidge is professor of Anglo-Saxon; Michael Reeve, the professor of Latin, is an expert on medieval as well as classical Latin; Marjorie Chibnall, a distinguished medieval historian, has been the leader among a group of editors of medieval historical texts, and one of the history professors was for twenty-eight years a general editor of the Oxford Medieval Texts.

The rise of modern languages in the 1920s and 30s reflects a movement on the national stage. A dramatic mirror of a similar movement can be seen in the history of Russian and Slavonic studies. These were represented before the Great War already by Sir Ellis Minns, college lecturer in Pembroke and later Disney Professor of Archaeology, and the university lecturer A. P. Goudy.[20] With Goudy's departure in the later 1930s there entered the Cambridge scene one of the outstanding characters of mid-twentieth-century Cambridge, Dame Elizabeth Hill – still actively at work in her 90s.[21] She was born in Russia in 1900; her father was a hereditary Baltic merchant of English extraction, trading between London and St Petersburg; but she is by descent as much Russian as English, was nurtured by Russian nurses and English governesses, and lived till she was 17 in the cosmopolitan world of the rich merchant families of St Petersburg. The Russian Revolution sped her family to England and near-destitution. After a considerable struggle she was able to study at the School of Slavonic Studies in London and became deeply and passionately interested in the culture, literature and social history of Russia as well as its language. She had to combine work for a Ph.D. on the development of the Russian analytic novel to Dostoevsky and Tolstoy with active breadwinning, by lecturing and coaching.

---

[20] Clark 1989, pp. 30–4; Tanner 1917, pp. 127–8.
[21] I owe what follows to two fascinating interviews with Dame Lisa, kindly arranged for me by Ian Roberts. For dates etc., see *Who's Who*.

Her first full-time academic post was the Cambridge lectureship, which she won in 1936. By the time she retired in 1968 as professor of Slavonic studies she was a leading figure of the Cambridge establishment. Not so in 1936, when she first enquired what might be the duties of a lecturer in Slavonic studies. The Cambridge scene was totally unfamiliar and it was noone's special duty to explain it to her. Those within were kind and wished to help; but being Cambridge men, they took the strange divorce of university and college for granted. They explained to her that college teaching was for the colleges – and it was many years before she became a fellow of Girton. As for lectures, 'the Reporter will tell you'; but it took her much anxious enquiry to learn that the *Reporter* was a journal not a person. The duties were few, the classes small. But the Second World War and the Russian alliance gave her an extraordinary opportunity to alter all this. From the start she opened her Russian classes to all who would come; and she used the special needs and encounters of wartime to develop an offshore operation – Russian classes for all who needed them, backed by but not part of the university. After the war these classes grew to immense proportions: she taught and arranged the teaching of thousands of students. The contacts and resources this brought her enabled her to build up Slavonic studies within the university too. It was the personal achievement of a teacher of genius; and it came on the crest of a wave. The need for Russian teaching in the late 1940s was manifest, and enhanced by the onset of the Cold War. Yet the scale of the need, or the fashion, did not last; and by the time she retired in the late 1960s the British universities, for the practical demands of the day, were over-provided with Russian teachers. Slavonic studies have continued to thrive in Cambridge, but modestly; the great offshore operation was born and retired with her. It is in a way a solitary drama in the history of MML; but it vividly illustrates the latent, potential relation which exists between university teaching and the chances and changes of the wider world.

PHILOSOPHY AND ENGLISH

English and philosophy are among the largest and the smallest schools in Cambridge in the late twentieth century, and likely to remain so. The devotees of the Philosophy Tripos have been a tiny coterie gathering at the feet of major prophets like Moore and Wittgenstein; while the English Faculty has attracted a great multitude of adherents, as if to hear a team of revivalist preachers. Neither faculty would welcome the analogy. Moore (after a brief flirtation with an evangelical revivalist group in his youth)[22] was sublimely indifferent to religion, though a deeply moral man much committed to ethics – and the faculty has played its part in the flight from metaphysics and faith so characteristic of early and mid-twentieth-century British philosophy. The English Faculty meanwhile has rather prided itself on eschewing Christian charity. The *University Reporter* for 1981 showed that the rancour of the Leavis era still lived: a marvellously obscure debate on the issues dividing the faculty – which would take the skill of Hercule Poirot to make plain – none the less sometimes rose to heights of polemical eloquence so that one might almost believe that Milton had returned to Cambridge.[23]

Philosophy

The Moral Sciences Tripos was founded in 1851 and had its first *annus mirabilis* in 1872, when William Cunningham, later a powerful combination of economic historian and archdeacon of Ely, and F. W. Maitland were linked in first place in the first class, and Henry Sidgwick was one of the examiners.[24] The numbers were never large and tended to sink rather than to rise: in 1905 the candidates outnumbered the examiners by the narrowest margin, five men and one woman – in both parts combined – to four examiners. After the war the numbers grew a little, but have never risen high: 36 achieved honours in part II philosophy in 1991, 187 in English.[25] These figures form an extraordinary contrast both to those in Oxford and to the fame of the Cambridge philosophers. In Oxford, philosophy was securely attached to Classical Greats in the mid-nineteenth century, and to politics and economics (as PPE) in 1920. Greats

---

[22] Levy 1979/81, pp. 39–41.   [23] *Reporter* 1980–1, pp. 330–62.
[24] See pp. 14, 16–18, 216–24, 232, 236.
[25] Tanner 1917, pp. 703, 709, 731; *Reporter* 1990–1, Special No. 17, p. 18.

and PPE have commanded high figures throughout the mid and late twentieth century, and most of the candidates have done some, many of them much philosophy. None the less it has become in both places – and elsewhere too – a very esoteric science, concerned with precise meanings and logic, dominated for a time by logical positivism which tended to drive away all metaphysics and narrow the field of thought to the logic of scientific statements. There has been some reaction in recent years; even Hegelian idealism has staged a come-back and the Cambridge Hegelian Michael Oakeshott, who taught history in Cambridge and politics in London, has come to be recognised as a master of a kind of philosophy no longer wholly despised or ignored.[26]

Yet there is a startling truth in the assertion that the history of British philosophy in the first half of the twentieth century has its centre in Cambridge, in Russell and Moore, brilliant native products of Cambridge and Trinity, and Wittgenstein, who was twice transplanted from Austria to Trinity, as a young student from 1912 to 1914, and as a mature sage from 1930 to 1951, when he died. Nor were they isolated figures. Between 1894 and 1904 Moore was at the centre of the Cambridge Apostles, radiating influence on Russell, J. M. Keynes, Lowes Dickinson, G. M. Trevelyan, E. M. Forster, and the Stracheys; and he soon became the guru of Bloomsbury, though he held aloof from its wit and its morals.

In 1894 Russell introduced Moore to the Apostles and he thus described Moore's debut.[27]

> The scene was ... perfectly wonderful and unprecedented ... He looked like Newton and Satan rolled into one, each at the supreme moment of his life. I had said (we were discussing the Cambridge education) that our training up has produced such a profound scepticism about everything that many of us are unfitted for practical life: Moore said that there was the one great gain from education: at least, he said, we are not so far unfitted as to be unable to earn our bread: we should therefore spread scepticism until at last everybody knows that we can know absolutely nothing.

[26] On Oakeshott, see pp. 236–7.
[27] In a letter to his fiancée Alys Pearsall Smith in Levy 1979/81, pp. 125–6.

Then Moore dissolved in laughter: and this light-hearted quality flits in and out of his many communications to the Apostles, mingling with enormous enthusiasm for discussion, for probing into the meaning of things, and the deeper seriousness and integrity which were to become the special marks of the mature philosopher.

In 1903 Moore published his *Principia Ethica*, which was heralded by his disciples as the dawn of reason. It is not easy quite to grasp the excitement which it caused. In the preface he explains that he has 'endeavoured to write "Prolegomena to any future Ethics that can possibly pretend to be scientific". In other words, I have endeavoured to discover what are the fundamental principles of ethical reasoning . . .' He sets out to investigate the nature of 'good' and 'the good', and to demonstrate the folly of previous attempts. On naturalistic ethics he observes (in a chapter summary) 'Mr [Herbert] Spencer is in utter confusion with regard to the fundamental principles of Ethics'; on hedonism and utilitarianism, he observes of the latter 'as a doctrine of the end to be pursued, it is finally refuted by the refutation of hedonism'; on metaphysical ethics he observes of the idealists, 'like Green . . . that their ethical reasonings have no value whatsoever', and so pursues his own study of 'Ethics in relation to conduct' and 'The Ideal'.[28] Towards the end he shows his caste of mind in these revealing sentences:

> The practice of asking what things are virtues or duties, without distinguishing *what these terms mean* [italics mine]; the practice of asking what ought to be here and now, without distinguishing whether as means or end – for its own sake or for that of its results; the search for one single *criterion* of right or wrong, without the recognition that in order to discover a criterion we must first know what things *are* right and wrong; and the neglect of the principle of 'organic unities' – these sources of error have hitherto been almost universally prevalent in Ethics. The conscious endeavour to avoid them all, and apply to all the ordinary objects of ethical judgment these two questions and these only: Has it intrinsic value? and Is it a means to the best possible? – this attempt, so far as I know, is entirely new; and its results, when compared with those habitual to moral philosophers, are certainly

---

[28] Summarised in Moore 1903, pp. ix, xiii–xxvii.

sufficiently surprising: that to Common Sense they will not appear so strange, I venture to hope and believe.[29]

In his celebrated paper 'A Defence of Common Sense' he listed a number of truisms, evident facts about man and his life on earth.[30] To call him a philosopher of common-sense is perhaps to underestimate the subtlety and depth of his thought; yet his assurance that if a philosopher contradicted what all of us really know to be true he must be talking nonsense lies at the root of much of his thinking. In the basic propositions of science and morality he believed; he thought they were real; thus he was a realist. He was not against metaphysics; in principle he approved of it; but in practice he felt no need for it. He was not the radical sceptic that he had represented himself to the Apostles in 1894; but he was profoundly sceptical of all that did not fall within his own experience of reality. He had lost interest in the Christian faith before he came to Trinity; and in Cambridge he mingled with men to whom Christianity was of no interest save as a dying superstition. In early days he was a fervent admirer of M'Taggart, ten years his senior in the Apostles and the Trinity fellowship, a Hegelian who propounded an idealist philosophy of diabolical complexity. But in due course Moore freed himself from the spell and joined Russell in explaining his ground in 'The refutation of idealism', a characteristic paper whose simplicity takes the breath away.[31] Moore's greatness lay (as Geoffrey Warnock says) in his *character*.[32] Moore had a quality of simplicity such as one commonly finds in people of exceptional intellectual gifts. He saw that clarity and precision should be of the essence of philosophical enquiry, and found that they were not. He constantly probed the meaning of what was said to him, of his own thoughts, of philosophical propositions. He naturally enjoyed the company of intellectual friends, whether at meetings of the Apostles or in the reading parties which he organised over many years. The power of his mind and personality was such that he was the centre and inspiration of these groups. Yet this was not in the least the result of egoism or natural assertiveness: he was mild

[29] Moore 1903, pp. 223–4.   [30] Moore 1925.
[31] Moore 1903a.   [32] Warnock 1958, pp. 12–13.

and modest, with a love of simple things and of children – when he married in his forties he was often seen pushing a pram; he was a celebrated Father Christmas at children's parties. But when the excitement of an intellectual chase was upon him, he was irresistible. And his disciples carried his influence to other disciplines: Maynard Keynes most notably to economics and I. A. Richards to English – *The Meaning of Meaning*[33] is a heroic application of Moore's search for precision and understanding to language and literature.

Keynes was equally, perhaps more deeply, influenced by Bertrand Russell, for his first major book, *Probability*, was a brilliant essay in mathematical logic, a field reopened by Russell's work with A. N. Whitehead, *Principia Mathematica*.[34] This was an attempt to deduce the elements of mathematics from the most basic and self-evident principles, a procedure which reappears in many of Russell's philosophical adventures. 'The point of philosophy is to start with something so simple as not to seem worth stating, and to end with something so paradoxical that no one will believe it.'[35] This highly characteristic utterance provides a clue to the curious puzzle of Russell's relations with Moore. In the 1890s they were close friends: Russell brought Moore to the Apostles, and was soon swallowing a deep draught of Moore's influence. Both felt the need for precision, the appeal to scientific fact. The word 'scientific' plays a significant role in the preface to Moore's *Principia* and is the heart and core of Russell's early work. Original as they were, in this respect they were the children of fashion. In the same year that Moore's *Principia* was published J. B. Bury observed in his inaugural lecture as Regius Professor of Modern History that history was 'simply a science, no less and no more'.[36] It is perhaps significant that the Apostle of this era who seems to have been least congenial to Moore was G. M. Trevelyan, who was to become a leader in the protest against Bury's scientific history, to revive the notion that Clio was a muse, and history inseparable from poetry.[37]

[33] Ogden and Richards 1923.
[34] Keynes 1921; Whitehead and Russell 1910–13. For Moore's and Russell's influence on Keynes, see Harrod 1951, pp. 75–81, 651–6.
[35] Russell 1956, p. 193, quoted in Warnock 1958, p. 33.
[36] Bury 1903, p. 42.
[37] Trevelyan 1913; cf. Levy 1979/81, pp. 186–7.

Thus far, Russell and Moore travelled together, and they met constantly and discussed their pursuits and interests. But in course of time, and especially in 1903, Moore's diaries reveal a growing distaste for Russell's company and conversation.[38] In part this may have arisen from Russell's personal life and treatment of his first wife; but it may rather be due to their different caste of mind – that Moore, searching for what was simple, direct, in a sense obvious, found Russell's love of paradox surpassingly tiresome. Mutual respect and admiration survived this crisis; but they tended to go their own separate paths. Moore, after a spell in Edinburgh and London, from 1904 to 1911, returned to Cambridge to spend the rest of his days as lecturer and (from 1925) professor. Russell roamed the world, though his home was most often in London. For a time he held a lectureship in Trinity from which he was ejected after a court case and a fine for his opposition to government in the First World War – to be briefly reinstated by the urgent demand of most of the fellows of Trinity, comprising some who had conscientious scruples about the war and many who had not, and including all those who had served in the forces.[39]

Wittgenstein's first book, the *Tractatus Logico-Philosophicus*, published in German in 1920 and in English in 1922, represented, among other things, an extremely rigorous development of a major strand in Russell's thinking: reality, at its roots, comprises logical atoms; Wittgenstein attempts to explore the ways in which human language can express and search out these basic truths. Once it was published Wittgenstein came increasingly to think he had reduced logical atomism *ad absurdum*. However that may be, nothing can be more absurd than for a mere historian to try to penetrate Wittgenstein's later thought; yet its effect had profound historical consequences. F. H. Bradley, the eminent Oxford idealist whom Moore and Russell had attacked, laid his philosophy on the obscure foundation of 'The Absolute', and a portrait of Mr Bradley's absolute once appeared in *Mind*, portraying it, like the Bellman's chart, as a total and absolute blank. By the same token, Wittgenstein came to think that the logical consequence of his earlier teaching had been that no meaningful

[38] Levy 1979/81, pp. 204–7, 249–50, etc.
[39] See pp. 337–40; Hardy 1942, esp. pp. 57, 59–60.

propositions at all could be made about the 'logical atoms'; the rest is silence. But the reason for this was not that philosophers must inevitably talk nonsense or keep quiet – but that he and they had misconceived the nature of language.[40] As Sir Geoffrey Warnock has said:

> Wittgenstein . . . does *not* suggest that philosophical problems are all 'about language'. Of course they are not; they are about knowledge, memory, truth, space and time, perception and innumerable other things. What he suggests is that, though thus not *about* language, they spring *from* language; they show themselves in distorted uses of language; they reveal confusion as to the uses of language; they are to be solved (or removed) by our coming to see and to employ our language properly.[41]

In other words, Wittgenstein had come to see that language was something much richer, more varied, more complex, more subtle than the scientific instrument he and Russell had sought in vain in the 1910s.

From this perception – which Wittgenstein was only one of many to grasp in the second quarter of the twentieth century – was to spring the study of linguistics and its exceedingly uneasy alliance with the study of literature. Philosophy in Cambridge continued to flourish as the haven of a few men and women prepared to think clearly and deeply for themselves, heirs in some sense of the extraordinary heritage of the three men of genius who made Cambridge for a brief space the centre of the world in the study of philosophy.

English

It is curious to reflect, looking back from the 1990s, that the coming of modern English literature to Cambridge as an academic discipline might have been delayed almost as long as the admission of women. One of many winds of change blowing in the opening years of the twentieth century was the demand for a degree in English.[42] But the view was also widely held that

[40] Wittgenstein 1953; Ayer 1936; for a perceptive summary exceptionally helpful to the non-specialist, see Warnock 1958, chap. 6.
[41] Warnock 1958, p. 89.
[42] Fundamental for what follows is Tillyard 1958; and there is a brief account in Howarth 1978, pp. 116–24. I owe much to the guidance of Nicholas Brooke.

A diversity of disciplines

English literature was the possession of all cultivated men and women, and that it must above all be saved from becoming a specialism and preserved from the experts. This view may still be held, for all I know; it was certainly powerful in Cambridge till well past the middle of the century. In the early 1950s, for example, when the tripos was well established and already popular, English was entrenched in some colleges, scarcely provided for in others: in Jesus E. M. W. Tillyard was master, A. P. Rossiter director of studies, and there was an assistant college lecturer besides; meanwhile in Caius there was no teaching fellow in English until the late 1950s. It was not that Caius was a philistine college; far from it. But among the most cultivated of the fellows was E. K. Bennett, whose special field was German literature, and who was prepared to contemplate the thought that he might have an English colleague one day; but who deprecated the invasion of literature by professional critics – yet none the less gave great encouragement to undergraduates studying English.[43] In German literature some expertise was wholly acceptable so long as it did not obscure the natural taste and appreciation of reader and student; but English literature was in truth (as he saw it) a common heritage. The English Tripos had to make its way against the powerful opposition of its natural friends.

We have seen that English was a part of medieval and modern languages down to the 1910s. The study of Anglo-Saxon and English philology was already well established. To say nothing of Abraham Whelock, the notable seventeenth-century eccentric, who had been reader in Arabic and Anglo-Saxon, it flourished exceedingly under W. W. Skeat, first Elrington and Bosworth Professor of Anglo-Saxon. Skeat had relatively few pupils, but some of them were eminent; as a scholar he was internationally famous and immensely productive. Some of his Anglo-Saxon editions are still used, and his texts of Chaucer and Langland held the field till the 1950s and 60s. But his successor, H. M. Chadwick, one of the notable polymaths of Cambridge history, resisted from the start any alliance with *belles lettres*. English language and literature had a modest home under the wing of modern and medieval languages, and Chadwick (who in middle

---

[43] On Bennett see Moriarty 1988, p. 90; Brooke 1985, pp. 273–4.

444

life lost his earlier enchantment with philology) looked increasingly toward archaeology and anthropology as a natural ally. A formal link between Anglo-Saxon and arch and anth took place in 1928.[44] It was a logical extension of Chadwick's own interests: he had been a profound philologist; he became an anthropologist and historian, and devoted two major books to Anglo-Saxon history and institutions; his later work comprised a brilliant combination of literature, history, philology, anthropology and archaeology in *The Heroic Age* (1912) and *The Growth of Literature* (1932–40) – the last in collaboration with his wife, Nora Kershaw Chadwick, a scholar of like versatility particularly interested in Celtic literature and history. Nora Chadwick was notably kind to young scholars, and bequeathed the residue of her estate for funds and lectureships in the university and in Newnham to support the disciplines at the centre of her interests. But the alliance of Anglo-Saxon and archaeology suited the professor and not the students; and in the 1960s Professor Dorothy Whitelock led the Saxon flock back into the English fold. There it forms a cell of its own, the Department of Anglo-Saxon, Norse and Celtic, with a great deal of medieval Latin and history besides, of high academic distinction; a modest companion to the mighty English Faculty, but attracting an enthusiastic group of students to its own independent tripos. Some study of Anglo-Saxon and Middle English literature has always been an option within the English Tripos, but never an inescapable part of it, as it once was in most other schools of English.

In 1910–12 Sir Harold Harmsworth, later Lord Rothermere, founded the King Edward VII Professorship of English Literature, requiring that it be 'treated on literary and critical rather than on philological and linguistic lines'.[45] It was to be a crown appointment, like the less ancient Regius chairs; and the first professor was the respected classical scholar A. W. Verrall. The entry of literary criticism could be expected to proceed at a dignified slow march. Verrall died in 1912, and from 1912 to 1944 Q – Sir Arthur Quiller-Couch – was King Edward VII Professor. Q was

[44] On Skeat see *DNB*; Tillyard 1958, pp. 23–5; above, p. 432; on Whelock, Oates 1986, chaps. 7–8. On Chadwick see *DNB*; Navarro 1947; Tillyard 1958, pp. 15–17, 69–76, 110, 112–16. On the transfer of Anglo-Saxon to arch and anth (1926–8) see Tillyard 1958, pp. 110, 112–16; *Reporter* 1927–8, pp. 621–2, 701 (no. 9).

[45] *Reporter* 1910–11, pp. 264–6, 405–7, etc., quoted in Howarth 1978, p. 117.

a Cornishman who had settled in Fowey in 1892 and remained there till his death in 1944, sallying forth in term time to lecture in Cambridge. He was well known as a novelist and author of essays on literary style, and *The Oxford Book of English Verse* of 1900 made him a household name. He was Liberal in politics and conservative in his tastes; he believed in 'the old sense of decorum, propriety and ceremony in human relationships as in literature', in Basil Willey's words. 'He always lectured in correct morning dress', wrote T. E. B. Howarth, 'but was equally meticulous sartorially in donning a suit of emphatic checks and a brown bowler hat and brown leather gaiters for his not infrequent leisure occasions.'[46] He did not live to see the formal admission of women to the university, and pretended till the end of his days that he was addressing only men. Q was a dilettante of considerable panache; and his coming was characteristically welcomed by A. C. Benson, who saw in him a man of congenial tastes and caste of mind, and knew from within Cambridge how genuine was the call for an English Tripos, for a formal vehicle, that is, of literary study.

In 1916–17 H. M. Chadwick and H. F. Stewart, chairman of the Board of Medieval and Modern Languages – under which English had hitherto nestled – aided Q to devise the English Tripos. It was a strange alliance of divergent interests and characters who found none the less a common aim. Stewart wished to rescue modern languages from the grip of philology and the neighbourhood of English, which was threatening to overwhelm its companions. Q sought elbow room for the study of English literature. Chadwick sought to free Anglo-Saxon studies from both. He wished to avoid having to teach the language to growing numbers of reluctant conscripts: unlike most Saxonists of his day he wished to avoid making Anglo-Saxon compulsory for students of English. In the end he was to seek a haven for his flock within archaeology and anthropology, the disciplines most congenial to him. The study of English literature seemed no discipline at all to old-fashioned classics; but the allies who met in Chadwick's garden in 1916–17 were determined to make a tripos out of the study of English literature. It was not long before it

---

[46] Willey 1968, p. 20; Howarth 1978, p. 83; cf. Willey 1968, pp. 15–20; Tillyard 1958, pp. 65–70.

began to gather that element of comparative literature – including its very characteristic paper on tragedy – and of philosophy which have been two of its marks; and most characteristic of all, the practical criticism paper in which all candidates have to comment on extracts drawn from the whole gamut of English literature, and to place and date them. It is a striking irony that English, despised by many in its birth for being without depth or discipline, provided a critical menu of width and penetration which made most other humane disciplines – history for example – look shallow and amateurish.[47] It is stranger still that it was Q himself, when reform was again under way in 1925–6, who suggested the paper on the English moralists, which brought intellectual history into the tripos. But in a truer sense it was I. A. Richards who brought the element of intellectual history, the depth of thought, the influence of philosophy which has penetrated many parts of it, and who devised the paper on practical criticism. He conducted crucial experiments in criticism and lectured on its theory. Tillyard describes the way in which he himself – 'the political factotum' of English studies in the early and mid-1920s – and Richards and Mansfield Forbes, the eccentric, charismatic fellow of Clare who was perhaps the most creative teacher in the faculty in early days, worked with Chadwick and Q to build and reform the new tripos.[48] Richards left Cambridge in the late 1920s and devoted some years to the development of Ogden's 'World Language', Basic English, settling in America as a better base than England for his plans; he only returned to live in Cambridge once more in old age. Meanwhile some of his ideas returned to Europe to help develop linguistics in the 1950s, and his work was carried on by his most notable pupil, William Empson, himself the teacher of A. P. Rossiter, both of whom spent part of their formative years working with Richards in the far east.

After the Great War the English Tripos rapidly recruited men

---

47 For the reform of the English Tripos see esp. Tillyard 1958, pp. 103–9. History has in recent years added to its excellent special subjects a sheaf of 'specified subjects' in part II in which there is a great deal of serious history; and there are a few papers faintly inter-disciplinary. But the History Faculty has always refused to embark on serious inter-disciplinary study akin to tragedy, or on professional testing of historical competence akin to practical criticism.

48 Tillyard 1958, esp. p. 81. On Richards, see esp. Ogden and Richards 1923; Richards 1929; Richards 1990, and esp. Richard Luckett's introduction. For what follows I am indebted to Nicholas Brooke.

and women of wide-ranging ability and interest, including Richards and Forbes and the redoubtable F. R. Leavis. Tillyard and Willey gave the study of English a solid historical background; Tillyard's books included *The Elizabethan World Picture*, a presentation of sixteenth-century *mentalités* admired in its day, and Willey likewise provided background studies of practical help to students of literature.[49] The pioneers of the English Faculty represented a spectrum of talent and interest; but they tended to start with the assumption that literature was either a branch of history or of *belles lettres*. What this could mean is vividly portrayed by Maisie Anderson who, as part of her very informal education, was sent to Benson and Q for criticism of her early attempts at poetry.[50] Both gave her kind and interesting advice, but the basic assumption that both conveyed to her was that poetry is first and foremost literary music. In the course of the 1920s and 30s such views were widely challenged; first by Richards and his disciples, but in the long run by none more forcefully than F. R. Leavis, who laid a special mark on the English Faculty still visible in the 1980s.

This is perhaps most clearly revealed in the volumes of Leavis' collected essays, mostly reprinted from *Scrutiny*, especially in *The Common Pursuit*.[51] The unsuspecting reader might readily assume he was summoned to the pursuit of Leavis' many enemies. There is a chapter entitled 'In defence of Milton' which tells us a little about Tillyard, much about Leavis, almost nothing about Milton; it is a sustained polemic against a close colleague.[52] There is another chapter little concerned with literature on 'Keynes, Lawrence and Cambridge'.[53] It is a comment on Keynes' *Two Memoirs*,[54] in which he looked back on D. H. Lawrence's visit to Cambridge in the heyday 'of the Cambridge–Bloomsbury ethos'.[55] He found a 'civilization' based on a religion – essentially the agnosticism of Moore dressed in the fashions of Blooms-

---

[49] Tillyard 1943; Willey 1940, 1962.
[50] Anderson 1988ff, chap. 8 (*Caian* 1989, pp. 81–3).
[51] Leavis 1984, first published in 1952.
[52] Hayman 1976, pp. 7, 53, alleges that Tillyard had used all his influence to prevent Leavis achieving a permanent lectureship. The truth of this I do not know.
[53] Leavis 1984, pp. 255–60. [54] Keynes 1949.
[55] Leavis 1984, p. 257.

bury[56] – which Lawrence thought essentially frivolous, and repulsive. Thus Leavis:

> Of course, Keynes criticises the 'religion' for deficiencies and errors. But he can't see that, 'seriously' as it took itself, to be inimical to the development of any real seriousness was its essence. Articulateness and unreality cultivated together; callowness disguised from itself in articulateness; conceit casing itself safely in a confirmed sense of high sophistication; the uncertainty as to whether one is serious or not taken for ironic poise: who has not at some time observed the process?[57]

His violent and contorted prose has the quality of a windswept tree in winter. However one may sympathise with such a view of Bloomsbury, violence breeds violence, not the pursuit of truth. Yet alongside these pieces of eloquent polemic the book shelters some of the most powerful critical studies of the age, on Hopkins and Swift and Pope.

Leavis combined an instinct for martyrdom with a deep and genuine devotion to literature and the creative world in which it lived.[58] He set out to teach a rising generation the deeper and wider values of literary culture. In 1927 he won temporary recognition in a probationary university lectureship. In 1929 he married his pupil Queenie Roth, who shared something of his penetrating insight and love of polemic, and helped to draw his attention increasingly to the novel as the vehicle of serious thought. But the lectureship was not renewed and it was only in 1932 that he became director of studies in Downing – one of a group of college posts which kept him rather precariously in Cambridge for the rest of his days. In the same year *Scrutiny* was founded and soon became the vehicle for his prophetic utterances. His major books came later: he began his career above all as a teacher; and he instilled into generations of students his wholehearted devotion to creative literature – to the best, for only the best truly deserved the total attention of the critic. Only in the best could one discern the riches of human creativity and the

---

[56] Leavis acknowledges the stature of Moore but does not absolve him from exerting what he regards as a pernicious influence.

[57] Leavis 1984, p. 257.

[58] For a general study see Hayman 1976. What follows is mainly based on Leavis 1948, 1970, 1984, 1986.

cultural values which the critic must above all discover and rescue from the philistine world of popular literature and journalism by which he was surrounded. More than that: criticism involves a very close and penetrating study of texts; only so can the creative author's use of language and style be united at a deep level with the study of his or her meaning and ideas; for poetry as literary music was anathema to Leavis. He sought great utterance – creative thought as well as creative language; the two were inseparable. Current studies of language by philosophers were of little use to him, for they could not explain the range and subtlety of literary effects which were of the essence of creative writers' use of language.[59] He eschewed literary theory, to the impoverishment of Cambridge. In 1948 he expounded his views of what most deeply mattered in literature in *The Great Tradition*, a study of a small group of novelists who were really worth the closest attention: George Eliot, Henry James and Joseph Conrad. Many others, like Thomas Hardy, were consigned to oblivion; a select few, like Jane Austen and Dickens, were allowed a modest place in Leavis' paradise. Dickens later had a larger share of attention in the book Leavis published with his wife in 1970; but in *The Great Tradition* he is there on sufferance, as the author of *Hard Times*, a singular illustration of the insight and perversity which mark all his work – and have so often been combined in the character of a creative teacher. By a strange mixture of dogma and perceptive insight Leavis made the world, or anyway Cambridge, safe for a really professional mode of literary criticism – and very unsafe for the litterateur and the dilettante. No doubt something was lost in the process. And it is a paradox that the Cambridge English School eschewed one most obvious element of mental discipline – the study of language and Anglo-Saxon – and yet became a very distinguished centre for the disciplined study of literature. For this I. A. Richards had prepared the way, but Leavis must have some share of the credit.

Some share – but not the whole; for in the years just before and after the Second World War the English Faculty became large and diverse, and rich in talent among undergraduates and dons alike; in a true perspective many of the younger generation

---

[59] On Leavis and language, see Bell 1988. For his wayward friendship with Wittgenstein, Hayman 1976, p. 18.

contributed to its growth. Leavis helped to give criticism a sense of depth and purpose; he also bequeathed a tradition of noisy polemic, still abundantly alive in the debates of 1981. But to gain a juster view of its quality in the middle years of the century, one must seek out some of the less dramatic figures of the faculty, such as A. P. Rossiter.

> Cambridge was for learning, for scholarship; not to be made paying or practical; not to cater for the career, but to shape full men, heedless of money and business as in the middle ages. Yet never reactionary from a timid fear of development: a home of the spirit of man seeking truth where alone it can be found: in the study of the widest body of human knowledge without consideration of creed or place or time.[60]

Thus the young Rossiter – or at least the leading character in his early novel, *Poor Scholars*. Like Leavis, he believed profoundly that the study of literature enriched the whole of life; but unlike Leavis he was only for a short time a central figure in the English Faculty. He came back to Cambridge after teaching in Durham in the mid-1940s, and died sadly and prematurely in a motor-cycle accident in 1957. He lives a little in his edition of *Woodstock* (1946), the play which lies behind Shakespeare's *Richard II*, and *English Drama from Early Times to the Elizabethans* (1950), which is marked by an inspiring sense of historical continuity: it is rare for a Shakespearean critic to be equally at home in the Middle Ages. But he lives above all in his lectures on Shakespeare, *Angel with Horns*, published with devoted care by Graham Storey after his death.[61] He made large demands on his audience, but evidently to good purpose. The lectures 'undoubtedly owed much of their effect', writes Storey,

> to their delivery: Rossiter was a born lecturer, with a manner entirely his own, and (as those who heard his broadcast talks, 'Our Living Language', will remember) a passionate belief in the effectiveness of the spoken word. But their more enduring appeal came from another source – from a mixture of allusiveness and

---

[60] Rossiter 1932, p. 354, quoted by Peter Holland in Rossiter 1989, p. xi. For my knowledge of A. P. Rossiter I am indebted to Nicholas Brooke, and to a perceptive lecture, alas unpublished, by Graham Storey. But they are not responsible for what follows.
[61] 1st edn 1961; reissued with introduction by Peter Holland in Rossiter 1989.

closeness to contemporary life that was always exciting and often – as it was meant to be – disturbing. Through Shakespeare he invariably forced his listeners to reconsider their own attitudes to living.[62]

In the final lecture Rossiter compared Shakespeare with Wordsworth: in the former he finds depth and complexity and insight and ambivalence in understanding man and nature which is at once deeply disturbing and deeply satisfying; in Wordsworth a blinkered, inadequate view even of the nature he loved, even before he fell away 'from paganism and towards Anglican orthodoxy, in the shape of the mid-nineteenth century belief in a providential Creator who has devised Nature as an educational convenience'.[63] After contemplating the immense range and depth of Shakespeare's insight into human nature, he takes us, with Lear, into the storm.

'Think now not of Nature as something comfortably in our English pockets: but of the awesomeness of great storms, great floods, earthquakes, fires; of great mountains ... as icy hells of murderous wind, shaking thunders of avalanche' – Rossiter spoke of what he knew: he was an expert climber. Then he confronts us with Wordsworth's happy vision of Nature – noting however that the young Wordsworth perceived a little of her harsher edges; noting with characteristic sensitivity the cultural differences between 1600 and 1800; but crushing Wordsworth in the end. 'There is no "Heart of Darkness" in him. Thus I admire him at his best; but I cannot persuade him far into the mountains – not even into his own mountains, small enough in all conscience.'[64]

With the sure grasp of a mountaineer, Rossiter also climbed the ridge which separates – or unites – the criticism of literature and of art. In his seminal lecture on the ambivalence in the History plays he notes 'something remarkable in the grotesque, Hieronymus-Bosch-like sarcastically-comic scenes of Cade's rebellion' in *2 Henry VI*; adding a note: 'I mean such Bosch paintings as *Ecce Homo* and the Veronica picture, where the mob is not only grotesque – absurd and half diabolic – but also presents

[62] Storey in Rossiter 1989, p. vii.   [63] Rossiter 1989, p. 310.
[64] Rossiter 1989, pp. 304, 310.

itself as a kind of hydra . . . A European tradition is shared by the Flemish painters and Shakespeare.'[65]

Ambivalence was a key word for him; and the power and subtlety and complexity of his mind were exceptionally well endowed with the gifts needed to penetrate the depths and ambiguities and complexities of Shakespeare. In his hands the Histories begin to make intelligible sense and the problem plays to handle some of the most perplexing problems of human experience. And the tragedies? At least they are rescued from Aristotle and Bradley; we are made to think anew what tragedy might mean to us and to Shakespeare; we are given unforgettable insights into Hamlet's moods, Othello's jealousy and Lear's madness. In the end, perhaps, they become a little too like the problem plays. At least, I personally find the lecture on *Measure for Measure* the most satisfying of all: here Rossiter, in true Shakespearean vein, makes rings round us – every moment of optimism or hope is answered with a deeper vision of the ambivalent nature of justice and love and sex – though human values survive. At the end he trails his coat.

> I can imagine *Measure for Measure* being read, for its humanity, its keen and subtle inquisition into man's nature (into justice and truth, sex and love), by humans in a remote future to whom all the Gospel references belong to a bygone myth . . . no nearer to them than the Gods in Euripides. And I can imagine it holding them none the less, as *we* can be held by the human tangles of the Greek problem-playwright.[66]

We may smile at the quip about the gospel, but the passage is a sad reminder that his death may have robbed us – not only of wider ranging studies of English literature – but of original studies of Bosch and Bruegel, of Euripides and Sophocles, which would have shown how much the best critical study of literature has to offer to the art historian and the classic.

Human affairs do not proceed in a tidy fashion, as Rossiter well knew. In the thirty years since his death others have

---

[65] Rossiter 1989, p. 58, with reference to his exceedingly penetrating study of Bruegel in Rossiter 1948–9.

[66] Rossiter 1989, p. 170. Ironically, by stripping the play of the spurious Christian interpretations once fashionable, Rossiter helped to make it much more interesting to theologians of the late twentieth century.

followed him in this ecumenical endeavour,[67] but the barriers between the disciplines have not grown less; nor – since Leavis retired in 1962 – have the polemics declined. The debate of 1981 was as fierce and opaque as anything in the Leavis era.[68] But its themes were different. On the one hand were the supporters of established standards of literary enquiry, for Cambridge has enjoyed a number of the most eminent critics of the intervening decades; on the other stood those to whom new modes of enquiry, whether politically motivated – by the urge to see the Marxist interpretation of literary modes prevail – or by the rising tide of linguistic theory and structuralism, destructuralism and poststructuralism.[69] The threads are not distinct; every skein was twisted; and in the midst – partly hidden by the smoke but at times only too manifest – were personal animosities such as had fanned the flames in the 1930s. To an observer from a neighbouring wood two positive comments spring to mind. First, however repugnant polemic may be, the debate of 1981 was the outward and visible sign of life and vigour: whatever else the English Faculty may have been, it was not moribund. The other is that the critical triumphs of the 1950s had left behind somewhat the study of language: that the rise of linguistics and the intimate, if sometimes very uneasy, alliance of literature and language in any English School was likely sooner or later to bring new and searching problems. Indeed, the criticism of the 1950s bred doubts in discerning minds about many current views of the nature and function of language, and sent the experts seeking ever deeper for the roots of the subtleties and ambiguities which Rossiter and his colleagues had brought to light. In the 1960s and 70s these enquiries became mingled with new studies of language, with their roots in philosophy and psychology, philology and animal behaviour. From these, new ideas and problems were bound to come to give new shape and direction to the study of English.

---

[67] E.g. N. S. Brooke 1990, pp. 22–34.
[68] *Reporter* 1980–1, pp. 330–62.
[69] For an 'introduction' to the jargon and the perplexities of the poststructuralist world, see Leitch 1983.

ART, ARCHITECTURE AND MUSIC IN CAMBRIDGE

If English literature came relatively late to Cambridge – once the home of many poets – as an academic discipline, the history of art came later still. *Kunstgeschichte*, so deeply entrenched in Basel or Vienna or Munich in the nineteenth century, and in many places in America in the twentieth, was very slow to reach Britain. When the UGC set up an Arts Sub-Committee in the mid-1960s to give expert advice on the humanities, it contained at first no art historian, and it was a professor of English and a professor of history who were instructed to report on its role in the age of university expansion.[70] Their first recommendation was the addition of an art historian to the sub-committee; but the episode was symptomatic. There were a number of small departments of art and art history about the land, and it was a growth area in one at least of the new universities; but the one great academic centre was the Courtauld Institute of the University of London, and even the Courtauld was only a generation old. With such encouragement as the University Grants Committee could give, art history expanded very rapidly in the 1960s and 70s. It had already been established at Cambridge as a modest, shoe-string operation. Even in the 60s it could not hope to command large resources, nor penetrate very deeply into the colleges. It had the advantage of an exceptionally fine university museum, the Fitz-william, on its doorstep; and it could seek a measure of alliance with the well-established School of Architecture. The pattern established by Michael Jaffé of King's, later director of the Fitzwilliam, and continued by his successor, the medievalist George Henderson, was to expand the resources of a tiny staff by inviting a galaxy of guest lecturers: thus their students, and a wider circle, can enjoy lectures from almost every notable figure in the history of art and architecture in Britain, and occasionally from elsewhere. They also took advantage of the tripos system to recruit from other disciplines: art history is a part II for students bred elsewhere, or an interval of humane culture for those deep in medical sciences. They live modestly in Scroope Terrace, conve-niently close to the Fitzwilliam Museum; but occasional lectures in art history – especially those given or arranged by Patrick

70 The late Professor Philip Brockbank and myself.

Boyde, professor of Italian – have been among the most popular in modern Cambridge.

A Faculty of Fine Arts, containing a School of Architecture, was formed in 1926, and there had been exams in architecture long before that. But the School sprang to new life in the 1950s and 60s, under its dynamic and fashionable professor, Sir Leslie Martin. It has bred many of the leading British architects of our day, and it has laid its mark on the face of Cambridge: future generations will judge with what result. In 1839, when Scroope Terrace was built, the southern end of Trumpington Street was a fashionable part of residential Cambridge: it has now been swallowed by Peterhouse, the Fitzwilliam, and the Engineering Lab, which replaces Scroope House and much else. But Scroope Terrace itself houses history of art and the School of Architecture in fine terraced houses of the late 1830s as unlike as could be the products of the school itself. As a reminder of this truth, there lie behind it two new buildings of the 1950s and 60s. The first is by Colin St John Wilson, who was Martin's colleague and was to be his successor, thus described by Tim Rawle:

> This small building is an excellent example of the modular architecture of this era, employing mathematical relationships developed for mass-produced schools and housing. It could be classified as 'architects' architecture' as its aesthetic values were, at the time, probably very unappealing to the man in the street. Booth and Taylor sum this up perfectly. 'To the architect this building exudes geometric refinement. He will study the golden section, the modular relationships of shelf to blackboard to window. He will rejoice over the purity of the structure. The layman sees almost exactly the opposite: the deliberate (and very attractive) crudity of the massive brickwork, the rough-shuttered concrete and the self-consciously massive pulpit, which juts out into the lecture room and turns out to be merely a table for the slide projector.' Located to the south of the extension is a Buckminster Fuller-type geodesic dome. This was built in 1958–62 and designed by David Crohan, another lecturer at the School. It is used for teaching . . . and research into the levels of daylight in buildings with the use of models. Based on Archimedes' truncated icosahedron, it is constructed of two surfaces: an outer skin of anodised aluminium, and an inner skin of translucent plastic. Between these two skins are 184 fluorescent lamps which provide

the light source which is diffused through the inner plastic layer, creating an artificial 'sky' for use in experiments. The dome was also built by students at the School.[71]

Martin and Wilson were for many years partners, and their presence is felt in Peterhouse, and in Harvey Court for Caius in West Road; in 1969–70 Martin and another partner converted a group of slum dwellings behind Northampton Street into Kettle's Yard; and in the 1970s Martin laid his hand on the other end of West Road in the new Music School, which – however it may seem in the future as architecture – is one of the most notable additions to the cultural life of Cambridge of the late twentieth century.

Music and drama are now so inescapable a part of Cambridge life that it is hard to realise how little this was true between the early or mid-seventeenth century – the close of the first great age of Cambridge music, masques, madrigals and plays – and the late nineteenth, when they revived. The professorship of music was set up in 1684, but it was a non-resident, honorific post, which made little impact on Cambridge until the election of C. V. Stanford in 1887.[72] CUMS, the Cambridge University Musical Society, is younger than the University Boat Club – it was founded in 1843–4.[73] Music played an occasional role between 1650 and 1850; and a small number of colleges maintained choirs and choral services. King's, St John's and Trinity not only had choral music written into their statutes, but read and obeyed them. But they were the exceptions: until the very late nineteenth century most services were said, or at best enlivened by occasional hymns. From the 1880s on new traditions were quickly established. It was a notable age in British music, when choirs and music societies were forming or flourishing in many places. Its mark in modern Cambridge is the sheer variety and accomplishment of university and college societies and choirs; and it has been the breeding ground of much varied talent.

Sir Charles Stanford is the central figure in the revival of music in Cambridge. He became conductor of CUMS in 1875, still in

[71] Rawle 1985, p. 194, quoting Taylor and Booth 1970, p. 59. For what follows, see Rawle 1985, pp. 200, 202.
[72] Tanner 1917, p. 85. For what follows, see esp. Knight 1980.
[73] Knight 1980, p. 65.

his early twenties, professor of composition and orchestral playing in the Royal College of Music in London in 1883, professor of music in Cambridge from 1887 – and held both positions till his death in 1924. In his later years he was rarely seen in Cambridge: legend had it that he 'only gave one lecture a year and gave it in the Cambridge railway station'.[74] But in the crucial years between 1887 and 1914 he was a dominant figure in Cambridge music, temperamental, noisy, 'a lovable, powerful and enthralling mind' as the most eminent of his pupils, Ralph Vaughan Williams, said of him.[75] His contacts greatly enriched the music of the city: Joachim, the sublime violinist, was his friend and a frequent visitor to Cambridge.[76] Music in Cambridge has never been a monopoly of the university: in the 1950s and 60s, for example, one of its main centres lay in CCAT, the College of Arts and Technology, under the inspired direction of Norman Hearn.[77] In earlier days Stanford vied with Dr A. H. Mann, organist of King's, founder of the Festival Choir, lineal ancestor of the Cambridge Philharmonic Society, for the talent of town as well as gown. Mann was an amiable eccentric who looked with a beady eye on much modern music, and loved to watch trains at Bletchley. But he was the creative figure in the modern tradition of choral singing in King's. In early days he was much involved in college teaching, and Stanford accused him of laying hands on 'every respectably voiced undergraduate ... he can' for his choir, and so starving CUMS of talent. Gradually the rift healed, and in 1901 the two choirs combined for a joint programme featuring Brahms' *German Requiem* as a memorial to Queen Victoria. After the Great War, as Stanford became more and more remote, Mann's influence had its apogee. In 1918 he first conducted the King's Christmas Eve Carol Service, and continued to conduct it until 1928, when it was first broadcast; he died in 1929.[78] Meanwhile choral music was also reviving in St John's – which has since rivalled King's in building a preparatory school round its choir – and Trinity, its traditional homes, and elsewhere. Stanford had been succeeded by Charles Wood –

[74] Knight 1980, pp. 107–8. On Stanford, see *DNB*; Knight 1980, pp. 72–108 passim.
[75] Knight 1980, p. 84.   [76] Knight 1980, p. 77.
[77] Knight 1980, pp. 126–33.
[78] Knight 1980, pp. 84–8, 107–8.

briefly, for he died in 1926 – the founder of a notable music tradition in a lesser college than King's, in Caius, where his memory and some of his enchanting church music survive. Wood too was a character, remembered for the accuracy with which he aimed *Songs of Zion* at the head of an inattentive chorister, and for his report on the young Vaughan Williams in which he despaired of him 'as a composer'.[79] It is curious to reflect that Stanford himself – an immensely prolific composer of a wide range of music – is now chiefly remembered, like Wood, for his church music.

In 1936 the Arts Theatre opened, and the event marked an epoch in Cambridge drama. The Footlights, the ADC (Amateur Dramatic Company), the Marlowe Society, the Greek play, had flourished long before; and the tiny Festival Theatre had fostered some remarkable professional talent in the 1920s and 30s. But the Arts Theatre provided a permanent home for Cambridge theatre, Marlowe and the Footlights included, and for travelling drama, previews of London productions, opera and ballet – such as can accommodate themselves to a small stage. Maynard Keynes 'was in every sense responsible', wrote his biographer, 'for the idea, for the execution, and for the finance'.[80] Lady Keynes, the great ballerina Lydia Lopokova, had fostered his love of the theatre, and – though not so inspired as an actress – took leading parts in Ibsen's *Doll's House* and *Master Builder* in the opening season. The lien with King's has always been intimate, and for those of us brought up in the 1940s and 50s the Arts Theatre is indelibly linked with George Rylands, who gave the Marlowe its tradition of clear diction in rendering Shakespeare's English, and played roles both congruous – Lear or Macbeth – and incongruous, like Caliban; and Donald Beves, a noted comic actor who led troupes of undergraduates to entertain the forces in wartime, and was an inimitable Pandarus and a less admirable Macduff. The cultural traditions of Cambridge were united on the eve of war in 1939 in J. T. Sheppard's *Antigone*, strikingly accompanied by music composed for the occasion by Patrick Hadley.[81] Sheppard was at his best in comedy; but the *Antigone* in Greek is deeply moving

[79] Knight 1980, pp. 86, 97–8. On Wood, see also Brooke 1985, pp. 242–4.
[80] Harrod 1951, p. 473.   [81] For Sheppard, see pp. 125–6.

even if only half-understood. Hadley was at the threshold of a distinguished career in Cambridge, as precentor of Caius and later professor of music. He was a delectable character, warm, outspoken, indiscreet, and no administrator; but he contrived in the 1950s to preside over the early years of the Music Tripos, devised by his colleagues, and to see music as a fully professional subject in the Cambridge curriculum.[82] He had lost a leg in the Great War, and in the teething troubles of the tripos was heard to say that the results were the worst casualty list since the battle of the Somme.

Professional and amateur have also been inextricably woven into the history of Cambridge's museums and art galleries. The original endowment in 1815–16 by Lord Fitzwilliam was an amazing stroke of fortune, and the building devised to house his benefactions no less amazing. But at the turn of the century its director was M. R. James, scholar and dilettante, who regarded it as a pleasant hobby, a part-time job; the days of professional staffing of museums lay in the future. Among its earliest treasures was a fine collection of manuscripts, subsequently much enhanced; and this James catalogued with his usual combination of deep scholarly flair and inadvertence.[83] But arranging, cataloguing, improving the collections fell into abeyance. A new dawn came when James was succeeded in 1908 by Sydney Cockerell.

Cockerell was a showman and a beggar of genius, under whose inspired direction the museum was transformed and its collections immensely enriched. The Marley and the Courtauld Galleries of 1924–36 are his monument – as well as to the benefactors he ensnared. There were many stories of his methods, often invented by himself. Maisie Anderson, later to be wife of a distinguished director of the V and A, first encountered the breed in friendship with Cockerell.

> Sometimes he would laughingly describe his somewhat piratical methods of extorting gifts for the Museum, and one day he pointed out a small spiral staircase near his office as 'the oubliette down which I throw people who won't give me what I want.' Surely no pirate ever left such a beautiful memorial as the Fitzwilliam Museum became under his highly idiosyncratic direction.[84]

---

[82] Knight 1980, p. 122.   [83] On James, see esp. Pfaff 1980.
[84] Anderson 1988ff, chap. 7 (*Caian* 1989, p. 78).

Fig. 16 Drawing of M. R. James, by William Strang, in the
Fitzwilliam Museum

Under Cockerell and his successors it has become a major centre of academic research as well as the delight of those visitors fortunate enough to find the galleries they seek open – for in recent years the financial stringency imposed by government has prevented its being open as constantly as it ought to be. It has become a centre internationally admired for its paintings and drawings, its illuminated manuscripts, its classical and medieval coins, its ceramics, its remarkable collection of antiquities, Egyptian, Cypriote, Greek and medieval. It has entered the world of conservation in the most professional manner in the Hamilton Kerr Institute based in Whittlesford, which was endowed by a legacy from a former MP for Cambridge and philanthropist, and which conserves and restores pictures with admirable expertise. One among the museum's most spectacular resources is its collection of medieval coins. In large measure this comprises the collection of Professor Philip Grierson of Caius, who

> has made a modest inheritance and the income of a university professor work quite outside the rules of economics to such purpose that, having parted with half his collection – the Byzantine coins – to the great American Institute, Dumbarton Oaks in Washington, he still possesses the finest representative collection of medieval coins from western Europe that has yet been known.[85]

His coins are housed in the Fitzwilliam and will become part of its own collections in due time, in the Department of Coins and Medals whose Keeper, Mark Blackburn, has been at work for a number of years with Philip Grierson himself on *Medieval European Coinage*, which, when complete, will be a vast manual of medieval numismatics as well as a catalogue of the resources of the Fitzwilliam. The one gap in Grierson's collection, deliberately made, has been in British coins; for these the Fitzwilliam, partly from its own collections, partly because it has been able to acquire the collection of the late Christopher Blunt, has itself an exceptionally fine cabinet.

As a collection of artefacts the Fitzwilliam has a partner or rival in the Museum of Arch and Anth;[86] as a picture gallery it has

---

[85] Brooke 1985, p. 298; cf. Grierson and Blackburn 1986.   [86] See pp. 201–5.

been supplemented in recent decades by the highly personal collection in Kettle's Yard. It was created by Jim Ede, a dedicated connoisseur, who generously presented it to the university in the late 1970s to be preserved and to grow as he had created it. He has also given us his own account of its making.[87] When he was an assistant at the Tate in the 1920s he met Ben Nicholson and his wife; and their friendship, and Nicholson's pictures, which he saw as heirs to a great tradition set in 'the everyday world of the twenties and thirties', inspired him to the idea of 'somehow creating a *living place* where works of art could be enjoyed' in a domestic setting, 'where young people could be at home unhampered by the greater austerity of the museum or public art gallery, and where an informality might infuse an underlying formality'. He planned to provide a home full of beautiful things, of which the pictures would form a natural and integral part. Thus his house and pictures will live on, combining old cottages and new extensions, on the slopes behind Northampton Street, with space for passing exhibitions; the aging, but eternally young Jim Ede's artistic mission to the undergraduates – a timely reminder to elderly dons that the university was founded by young men, for the young.

EDUCATION AND EXTRA-MURAL STUDIES

The Local Examinations and Schools Examinations Syndicates have long provided crucial links between the university and the schools; they are an inherent part of the university, among the most profitable of its undertakings. But they are in essence an offshore operation, a part of the national examination system, and by that token to enter their history deeply would lead us far astray. This omission is one of many: and it is to be regretted, since the Syndicates have played a crucial role in the history of British education. In a similar fashion extra-mural studies and adult education – continuing education as it is now called – deserve a chapter they do not receive. Outward looking Cambridge dons played a significant part in the various movements to spread adult education about the land in the nineteenth century; and it was from one of the most imaginative of these that

[87] Ede 1984. The quotations are from Ede's earlier account quoted in Rawle 1985, pp. 202–3.

came the schemes for lectures for women out of which Newnham sprang.[88] Extension lectures and extra-mural lectures rose and fell and rose again in the late nineteenth and early twentieth centuries; and these and public lectures of every kind have been one of the most important services the university has offered the wider public; it is in this sense that they follow naturally from the museums.

Closely related has been the history of teacher training, of the Department of Education. Courses began in 1879: the Faculty of Education was set up in 1968.[89] 1968 represents a crucial stage in the vast expansion of teacher training in the university in the 1960s and 70s. A part of the story comprises the gathering into the university community of the two well-established colleges of education in Cambridge. Homerton had been founded in 1731 to train nonconformist ministers; it had been a training college for teachers since 1852; it came to Cambridge to occupy the deserted buildings of Cavendish College in 1895. Hughes Hall was founded in 1885 under the inspiration of Cheltenham Ladies' College and Newnham, where Miss Hughes, the foundress, had studied; from the start its students went to the university's lectures, though otherwise its links with the university only became formal after the Second World War.[90] Closer bonds with the two Colleges of Education help to explain the rapid growth of the faculty and department in the second half of the twentieth century. But the department itself grew out of a third, the Day Training College founded in 1891.

The formation of a Syndicate and the planning of a regular series of lectures came in response to requests from far and wide that the universities in general, and Cambridge in particular, should help in the training of secondary school teachers.[91] In 1890–1 the Education Department in Whitehall responded to the many suggestions it received by encouraging the formation of day training colleges; and one such was set up in Cambridge, with Oscar Browning as Principal.[92]

[88] See p. 303.
[89] What follows is based on Peter Searby's admirably clear account in Searby 1982.
[90] For the integration of Homerton and Hughes Hall into the university, see p. 576; and for Cavendish College, pp. 91–3.
[91] Searby 1982, p. 5.
[92] Searby 1982, pp. 11–12. On the OB, see pp. 36–7.

The Cambridge Day Training College brought out the best in the O.B. From one point of view he was the quintessence of Eton and King's; he erected name-dropping into a fine art and loved to mingle the great and the humble in his parties. The young Ernest Rutherford was not the only visitor to think him 'snobby'.[93] But he was a devoted teacher with a supreme delight in the company of the young: his enjoyment of the fashionable Victorian sentimental friendship had cost him his post at Eton. Yet it was not just self-indulgence, but grew from a deep interest in young people; and a warm sympathy which embraced the genuinely poor as well as the gilded 'poor scholars' from Eton. The desire to find a way into Cambridge for more of the poorer aspirants was a powerful urge among many reformers of the late nineteenth century;[94] and Browning saw the Day Training College as a means to two ends: to train teachers and to provide a Cambridge education for the less well off. Under his direction, from 1891 to 1909, it flourished; many notable names, including Henry Thirkill, later master of Clare, J. H. Clapham of King's, the economic historian, and Lytton Strachey, owed it some training (in Strachey's case ineffective) as teachers.[95] Many poor students recognised the debt they owed to the O.B. But his fatal mingling of egoism and inefficiency – his love of tortuous administration that did not quite work – made life increasingly difficult for colleagues who had to excuse his methods and endure his petulance in committee. In an extremely perceptive and sympathetic appreciation of Browning and his work for the College, Peter Searby admits that 'he was . . . often egotistical, with a frail sense of his own talents or his effect on others. His relationship with colleagues was sometimes warm and affectionate, but often also frictional.'[96] When he was past seventy his attention to the task became intermittent and trouble with his colleagues grew worse. In 1909 he was firmly told to resign.[97] He retired in high dudgeon to Italy, there to hold court to his friends and pupils till his death. 'I called on the OB in Rome,' Sir Frank Adcock of King's, later professor of ancient history, used to say, 'on his eightieth birthday, an event which

---

[93] See p. 36.   [94] See p. 96.
[95] Searby 1982, pp. 18, 23, 34.   [96] Searby 1982, p. 8.
[97] Searby 1982, p. 27.

happened annually for many years.' Meanwhile the Day Training College lived on; but from the 1920s its function as the home for poor boys steadily declined, and its principals lacked Browning's flair. Still, it survived, to be converted into a university department in 1939. 'It is ironic', writes Searby, '... that the university decided to replace a man incompetent at teacher training with one uninterested in it.'[98] Sir Will Spens, master of Corpus, had been a prime mover in setting up a professorship of education, and he played a leading role in choosing the first professor. It was a puzzling role, for G. R. Owst was an HMI who believed fervently in the value of medieval studies and not at all in education – anyway in the theory of education. He came to Cambridge to be a scholar among scholars, to carry on his admirable work on medieval sermons; and he lectured on the history of education to his students.[99] But he did little else for them; and the morale of the department suffered accordingly. The real expansion and entry into the modern world came after his retirement in 1959.

The department has 'grown several times in size' since 1959; the faculty has grown around it; it has added to the Postgraduate Certificate – now extensively recast to allow a much wider range of alternatives, while still combining courses theoretical and practical – an Education Tripos, for which it works in harness with Homerton.[100] This is the local version of the B.Ed. degree which sprang up everywhere in the 1970s. All this has been made possible by the work of a devoted group of pioneers, by the formation of a much larger group of university teachers in education over the last thirty years, and by the integration with the colleges of education, which has gone steadily forward in spite of the ups and downs of government policy and stop–go in the world of educational training. Hence the enrolment of the old colleges of education among the new colleges or approved societies of the university in the 1970s and 80s.[101]

[98] Searby 1982, p. 37.
[99] This is partly based on personal information from the late Professor Owst: in two periods when he was on leave in the early 1950s I gave his lectures for him. But see esp. Searby 1982, p. 37.
[100] Searby 1982, esp. pp. 37–8.
[101] See p. 576.

ECONOMICS AND SOCIAL SCIENCES

If history of art is a small discipline in Cambridge and education a relatively modest presence, there is nothing modest about economics. There was no false modesty in Alfred Marshall, creator of the Economics Tripos and a dominant figure in British economics at the turn of the century, nor about Maynard Keynes, the mandarin of political economy – that is, of economics applied to politics – in the years between the wars, who led the subject to perilous heights from base camps in Cambridge and Bloomsbury. Marshall had been professor of political economy from 1884 to his retirement in 1908; Keynes refused any university office. He was a fellow of King's, second bursar from 1920, first bursar from 1926.[102] King's meant much to him, and so did the Cambridge establishment from which he sprang. But he was equally a man of Bloomsbury, of the City, of Whitehall; a politician – not one who yearned for a place in parliament or the cabinet; but the creator of a higher office, of economic wizard advising cabinets. Towards the end of his life he was economic envoy to the States. It was an extraordinary mixture, and Keynes was a man of miraculous talents; his achievements turned British economics, and especially Cambridge, in a new direction.

A part of the secret of their enormous success lay in the Mathematical Tripos from which both sprang; their mathematics gave a deep permanency to much of their work, and underpinned their flights of theory. Marshall was a man of powerful mind; of some originality and of great authority – irrespective of how much of his doctrine was new. He reigned at a time when the natural sciences had their greatest dominance over Cambridge academics – when J. B. Bury was asserting that history was a science, when G. E. Moore was equating philosophical and scientific method.[103] Marshall assumed that the deposit of economic doctrine which he had inherited and modified – which he and his followers regarded as classical, or neo-classical economics – was established knowledge, an unassailable fortress of learning. His business was to impart it, and to extend it. The extraordinary thing is that Keynes, a very faithful disciple who acknowledged

102 Harrod 1951, pp. 286–7, 371n; cf. pp. 388–90.
103 See p. 441.

the deepest of debts to Marshall, believed in this doctrine while at the same time destroying many of its foundations.[104]

Marshall added a good deal to the classical doctrine he inherited. He is celebrated for new-refining the principles of marginal value, and especially of equilibration. 'The higgling of the market', in Peter Clarke's summary, 'is axiomatically capable of finding a point at which supply and demand are brought into equilibrium.'[105] His best writing is underpinned by mathematical insight of a high order.[106] But what perhaps most surprises the modern reader of Marshall's works is his fervent belief that economics will serve the good of mankind. In early life he held a lectureship at St John's in moral sciences; he taught philosophy; and it was only through the modest place economics held in the Moral Sciences Tripos that he first came to teach it.[107] In due course he came to reckon poverty and the need and opportunity to combat it the deepest motive for the economist. In the peroration to his inaugural lecture he looked forward to increasing

> the numbers of those whom Cambridge, the great mother of strong men [he was a devout believer in university sport], sends out into the world with cool heads but warm hearts, willing to give some at least of their best powers to grappling with the social suffering around them; resolved not to rest content till they have done what in them lies to discover how far it is possible to open up to all the material means of a refined and noble life.[108]

A cynic might observe that the numbers he thus sent out were not great. Even in his later years, when he had rescued economics (as he saw it) from its small share in the moral sciences, and created the Economics Tripos, numbers were few. Five men and five women were examined in part I in 1905, and even by 1910 only 18 took part I and 12 part II.[109] It was in the 1920s and 1930s that it became a giant among triposes; and its growth at that epoch

---

[104] Alfred Marshall has been deeply studied in recent years: I am especially indebted to Reisman 1990. On Keynes, I have made particular use of Harrod 1951 and Clarke 1988.
[105] Clarke 1988, p. 22.
[106] Reisman 1990, e.g. pp. 106–7, 126.
[107] Reisman 1990, pp. 6–7.
[108] Quoted in Reisman 1990, p. 77, cf. p. 209; and in general, cf. ibid. chaps. 4–5.
[109] Tanner 1917, pp. 981–6.

owed more, perhaps, to the prestige it had won from the work of Keynes than from the imperious self-confidence of Marshall. Yet Marshall remains an impressive pioneer: by his teaching, his writings and his immense influence over the leaders in the field he set new standards in British economics.

The inheritance of Maynard Keynes was complex. He sprang from the Cambridge establishment; his family are central to its intellectual aristocracy.[110] His father taught economics and was for many years a deeply respected University Registrary; his mother was a leader in local politics. She was a pious evangelical, a Congregationalist, and Maynard rebelled early against her religion.[111] He was an Apostle, much under the influence of Moore and Russell; a man of Bloomsbury, sharing its homosexual pleasures and deep concern for human relations.[112] But in the long run he retained or recovered a remarkable respect for the values of Edwardian Cambridge, something even of its moral earnestness. Above all he remained devoted to King's, and kept his hand on its finances throughout his later career. No doubt his was a very complex character; but one important key to his career is the desire to hold together an academic and a political life; and he shrewdly perceived that this was not most effectively achieved by entering politics – nor even by remaining a civil servant after the exigencies of the Great War were over – but in combining an academic base in Cambridge with money-making in the City and giving advice – or public criticism – to the lords of the Treasury. One of the most brilliant recent studies of Keynes, Peter Clarke's *Keynesian Revolution in the Making* (1988), is the work of a leading Cambridge historian. But Cambridge has only a small place in the book; one spends far more time in the political labyrinth; and one tends to meet Marshall's successor, the formidable Professor A. C. Pigou, more often in London committees than in Cambridge. This was partly due to Pigou's reticence in Cambridge: as Sir Austin Robinson has said of him, 'We talked climbing. We talked cricket' – but never economics.[113] Yet it also lay in the nature of Keynes' work in the

---

[110] See p. 275.   [111] See pp. 369–70.
[112] Cf. e.g. Clarke 1988, p. 11.
[113] Quoted in Clarke 1988, p. 177.

1920s. He spent the week in London; the weekend, commonly a long weekend, in Cambridge.[114]

Intellectually, he had absorbed many of the influences flowing in Cambridge in his early life, especially among the Apostles. This is strikingly illustrated by his first major book, a study in mathematical philosophy, *A Treatise on Probability*, long in the making, eventually published in 1921.[115] He acknowledged the help of a group of Cambridge philosophers: the logician W. E. Johnson who had been a friend in his early years, but above all Moore and Russell, his apostolic preceptors. In the book itself the influence of Russell is the more apparent; indeed his inspiration, and the methods of Whitehead and Russell's *Principia Mathematica*, pervade it. It was to win profound criticism from the most original Cambridge mathematical philosopher of the 1920s, F. P. Ramsey. It illustrates the width of Keynes' interests; his extraordinary intellectual self-confidence, and the depth of his knowledge of mathematics.

The Keynesian revolution was preceded by *The Economic Consequences of the Peace* (1919), a political pamphlet – or tour de force of political and economic journalism – of great brilliance, which assured his fame. It was heralded in *A Treatise on Money* in 1930, and consummated in *The General Theory of Employment, Interest and Money* in 1936. Peter Clarke's study of it 'tells the story of an argument. The argument arose out of the performance of the British economy in the period of depression between the two World Wars.' It was about policy, and 'it naturally involved assessing what it was administratively feasible and technically sensible for government to attempt'. It was about politics, 'challenging the conventional view of the economic role of the state'. It was 'about economic theory, as the analysis of unemployment itself emerged as a professionally contentious matter'.[116] In the course of it so much that is familiar in public discussions of economics emerged – unemployment, inflation, wages, investment, savings, balance of trade, and all the techniques to harmonise their various claims and threats; above all the relation of money and monetary theory to political activity, and

[114] Clarke 1988, pp. 18–19.   [115] See esp. Harrod 1951, pp. 651–6.
[116] Clarke 1988, p. 3 and passim.

the techniques of controlling money supply and inflation (how-ever abstract a concern in the mainly deflationary 1920s and 30s).[117] All these were aired and set on new foundations. In the last forty years political and economic discussions have been full of the words 'post-Keynesian' and 'neo-Keynesian': we have been for ever adjured to escape the grip of Keynes or bring him back to life. The only point of general agreement is that he made serious economics the stuff of politics, for weal or for woe. These books are great works of academic economics, and in that sense products of Cambridge. They are parts of a political argument, and in that sense London-bred. They are the works of an intellectual giant who changed the course of rivers, academic and political.

A fuller account of the Cambridge Economics Faculty would pay tribute to the distinguished role of economic history in Cambridge economics, from Cunningham to Postan and beyond. It would have much to say of Marshall's successor, Pigou, a traditional economist who yet issued a notable study of *The Economics of Welfare* (1920) and *The Theory of Unemployment* (1933); of Keynes' many allies, disciples and rivals in Cambridge, especially Professor D. H. Robertson, Keynes' friend and one of the most acute of his critics. It would make mention of Sir John Hicks, the eminent economic theorist, who spent part of his early career in Cambridge before going on to Oxford; it would say much of Sir Richard Stone of Caius and King's, who was a central figure in providing a rational framework for national economic statistics and indices. It would bring economic theory and other aspects of the science into the 1980s with Partha Dasgupta. It would give ample space to the remarkable School of Applied Economics, in which Phyllis Deane and her colleagues have filled large books with valuable and meaningful statistics. More recently Cambridge has entered accounting with the aid of the Price Waterhouse Chair.

As it is, we have hardly done justice to the immense com-plexity of modern economic science, nor to its increasingly mathematical complexion. Furthermore, Cambridge economics have also sometimes been deeply involved in politics. In a

---

[117] See p. 284.

measure this links the faculty to political science, for its official title is the Faculty of Economics and Politics, like that of its big brother, LSE. But it also means politics in a less academic sense: advising and criticising governments, forecasting, following political alignments of various hues. And this is the legacy of Keynes.[118]

In recent decades economics has had a modest companion in land economy. This grew up under the wing of the once flourishing School of Agriculture, which between the wars gave birth to an estate management branch, which taught the science and administered the university's properties. Since the Second World War land economy has survived as a vestigial reminder of agriculture and become a course in its own right, and the administration Department of Estate Management, its twin, has grown enormously. It has to handle the management of the university's buildings and properties, and their immense extension in the 1960s and 70s has given it enormously enhanced responsibilities.[119]

Economics in Marshall's day grew out of moral sciences. In the 1960s and 70s it has been in closer alliance – or rivalry – with the other social sciences. The development of sociology was one of the marked features of academic change in the 1960s. Not unnaturally Cambridge was a little slow to join this bandwagon: it encountered opposition from academic traditionalists and passive resistance from many colleges. But it had some deep roots in Cambridge already, and not only among the economists. Political science has had a distinguished chair since 1927; and men of such eminence in the history of political ideas as Quentin Skinner and John Dunn naturally span the space between the History Faculty and the social sciences. A group of these have, over the last three decades, formed SPS, social and political sciences, and this has slowly grown into a fully fledged tripos, in which social studies, politics and economics mingle. A future history of Cambridge will have to give a larger space to this – and especially to the advance of politics and political ideas; and it is likely to set beside it what may prove the fastest growing subject of the 1990s, management studies. This is indeed a child of

---

[118] For his cultural legacy, see p. 459.   [119] See Todd-Jones 1989.

engineering, and management studies have been a component in Cambridge engineering since 1954. But it has achieved a life of its own very recently. In 1990 came massive endowments from Guinness plc and from Mr Paul Judge, an eminent business man who studied management as part of the Engineering Tripos when he was an undergraduate at Trinity. His immensely generous endowment will carry on deep into the 1990s, and belongs to the history of the future. Meanwhile the Judge Institute has been formed for the furtherance of management sciences.[120]

GEOGRAPHY AND HPS − HISTORY AND PHILOSOPHY OF SCIENCE

Poised between the humanities and the sciences − and both closely related to the social sciences with which they are sometimes numbered − are the old discipline of geography and the young HPS.[121] Geography began on a shoe-string in Cambridge in 1888, after a long campaign by the Royal Geographical Society to win recognition in Oxford and Cambridge. But as a fully-fledged tripos and a substantial department it was effectively founded after the Great War. In a sense it had a romantic, or rather tragic, origin. Towards the end of March 1912 Captain Scott and his companions perished in the antarctic snow. At their base camp − and so among the survivors − was a group of able young geographers and the like, among them Frank Debenham. After the war, when the opportunity came, Debenham gathered some of the survivors of Scott's expedition and other young scientists to help him found an institute in Cambridge in Scott's memory. Debenham was able to join the existing group of geographers, led by Philip Lake, then reader; and from 1927 Debenham combined the posts of head of the Department of Geography (as reader, later professor) and director of the Scott Polar Research Institute. The Institute now lives apart, in the modest yet monumental building by Sir Herbert Baker provided for it in the early 1930s; but in the 1920s it greatly helped to provide the creative stimulus for geography, still in Cambridge a young discipline with its way

---

[120] See Watson 1991, a brief account by the founder of management studies in their new form, Stephen Watson, Peat Marwick Professor of Management Studies.
[121] On Cambridge geography, see Balchin 1988; Stoddart 1989.

to make. Both in its origins in Cambridge and under the inspiration of Debenham and his first colleagues its bias was towards physical geography. In some universities it has been a social science, in some almost an art; but in Cambridge it has retained close links with the natural sciences, while spreading its interests over many academic regions. In more recent times Sir Clifford Darby has mapped Domesday England and led a team which studied Domesday England in great depth, while some of his younger colleagues plotted other aspects of medieval Britain. It has been a very notable centre of historical geography, and appropriately fostered, and has retained close links with, aerial photography.[122]

Visitors from afar to a Cambridge college commonly ask what disciplines are studied within it; for they assume that a college is the outward face of a university department. The natives explain that this is not so; that in each college students may be working on any or all of the Cambridge courses. But there are undoubtedly local concentrations of talent, and some colleges in which such a general statement fails to match the facts. One such is St Catharine's. In 1917 J. A. Steers took the diploma in geography from St Catharine's, and he was one of the first to take the new tripos on his return from war service. In 1922 he joined the staff of the department, and he succeeded Frank Debenham as professor on his retirement in 1949. His benign and dominant influence made St Catharine's – not the only, for there have been notable pockets of geographers elsewhere – the leading college in Cambridge for the subject, with a galaxy of geographers among its scholars and fellows.[123]

The history and philosophy of science impinged on the Cambridge scene as the personal interest of a group of scholars, some scientists, some historians, some neither, who first promoted courses of lectures, and then seminars. Among these were Joseph Needham, biochemist turned historian of science and Sinologist, Charles Raven, theologian and naturalist, and Herbert Butterfield, professor of modern history.[124] In 1944 Mr Robert

---

[122] See p. 176.   [123] See esp. Balchin 1988.
[124] See pp. 148, 236–7, 400–5. There is a brief and helpful account of HPS in Hoskin 1990; but he makes no mention of Butterfield, whose contribution was substantial, and whose lectures were published as Butterfield 1949.

Whipple gave his collection of books and instruments and an endowment, on the understanding that they would be properly cared for. Such gifts concentrate the mind; and over the years the resources of Cambridge have steadily grown – the substantial collection of Darwin papers in the University Library is a particularly important example. Efforts began to be made to find space for HPS in the Natural Sciences Tripos. There was considerable opposition: some thought the philosophy of science a bogus, intrusive subject; others thought history dead, that true science lay ahead not in the past. There was also a flowing argument whether a scientific or a historical training is the more desirable foundation for a historian of science – an argument without an end, though a historian must confess that historical imagination is rarely an adequate substitute for first-hand experience in a lab. The Syndicate revising the tripos recommended the rejection of HPS; but the Regent House non-placeted this rejection, and so, a little shakily at first, HPS crept into the syllabus. It was put on its feet by a succession of distinguished scholars – A. R. Hall, Gerd Buchdahl, Michael Hoskin, Mary Hesse among them. In 1971 the Wellcome Trust recognised Cambridge as a suitable place for one of its units in the history of medicine. HPS has slowly won its place as an independent department under the General Board; it is now 'easily the largest in the UK'; and although this may not mean all that it might seem, since history of science came late and slowly to this island – almost as slowly as history of art – the combination of HPS, with a secure place now in the Natural Sciences Tripos and 'fifty-odd M.Phil. and Ph.D. students', and the Wellcome Unit, with the oriental splendour of the Needham Institute, makes Cambridge a centre of international standing in this field.[125]

ENGINEERING

'In 1943 the Engineering Department was staffed by 24 lecturers' and two professors. 'In 1986 there were 120 teaching staff, of whom 15 were professors', a change which 'was part of the general explosion of the physical sciences in the period after World War II', but also owed much, very much, to J. F. Baker,

[125] The quotations are from Hoskin 1990, p. 50.

later Lord Baker of Windrush, who came back to Cambridge in 1943 and presided over the school for twenty-five years.[126] I am quoting Jacques Heyman's memoir of Baker, the chief architect of the Engineering School as we know it. But the school had in a real sense been founded long ago by Robert Willis, a very notable mechanical engineer and architectural historian. Now the wheel has come full cycle, and Heyman himself, Baker's disciple and successor, is not only an eminent civil engineer but the saviour of a number of great medieval churches and a fellow of the Society of Antiquaries.

We frequently encounter the name of Robert Willis in this book. He was the uncle of John Willis Clark, the Registrary and recorder of so much in the Cambridge of his day; he was the friend of Whewell; he was the grand master of architectural history – of the English cathedrals and above all, chief author of Willis and Clark's *Architectural History of the University of Cambridge and of the Colleges of Cambridge and Eton.*[127] Willis was not the first man to teach engineering in Cambridge: Isaac Milner introduced mechanical principles into his lectures from 1783 on.[128] But Willis' teaching of engineering science as Jacksonian Professor between 1837 and his death in 1875 established it as an element in the Cambridge scientific tradition; and when he died 'the University woke up to the fact that he had effectively established an engineering school, and this was given formal recognition in the same year', 1875.[129] His successor, James Stuart, had spent his early years commuting between Trinity, where he was a fellow and assistant tutor, and his father's linen mill at Balgonie in Fife; and he remained a man of wide interests, deeply involved in practical engineering. He built up courses, provided workshops, largely at his own expense, and was the effective creator of engineering as a practical science. He had, however, a fatal weakness for politics; and as he grew in stature as a Liberal MP – and a very radical one, who believed in votes for women – he became increasingly remote from Cambridge and his workshop. Eventually in 1889–90 he resigned; and James Ewing,

---

[126] Heyman 1987, pp. 3–4. In what follows I am particularly indebted to Heyman 1987, and have learned much too from Heyman 1990; for the rest my account is chiefly based on Hilken 1967.
[127] Willis and Clark 1886/1988.   [128] Hilken 1967, p. 1.
[129] Heyman 1990, p. 43.

another Scot, sprung from a Dundee manse, took up the reins.[130] His early career had been divided between Scotland and Japan, and he came as a comparative stranger to Cambridge, but quickly made his mark. In the early 1890s Ewing created the Mechanical Sciences Tripos, which was first examined in 1894. He and his colleagues had much ado to rescue engineering from the doldrums of Stuart's last years, and in the first year there were only 7 candidates. By 1910 the numbers had risen to 35.[131] In the 1920s and 30s there were normally about 500 undergraduate students of engineering; in 1991, 327 took Engineering part IA, 324 part IB, 146 part II – but this takes no account of the 78 who had opted for manufacturing engineering, a tripos established in the early 1980s under government initiative, nor the 97 who have transferred to electrical and information sciences, that new creation which symbolises the technological revolution of our day; still less the 232 full-time and 91 part-time postgraduate students; nor the students of materials science and metallurgy or chemical engineering, which have stood for many years poised between engineering and chemistry.[132]

The phases in the history of the Department of Engineering in Cambridge are quite faithfully reflected in its buildings. In 1893–4 Stuart's makeshift workshops were replaced by a substantial building to record the advent of Ewing and the tripos, built along Free School Lane to the south of the old Cavendish, designed by an active local architect, W. C. Marshall, also author of the Botany School and Leckhampton House, 'a spacious red-brick Tudor villa of 1881', now part of Corpus' fine postgraduate complex.[133] After the Great War a substantial expansion was foreseen, and the workshops and equipment needed to be brought into the twentieth century. The new professor, C. E. Inglis, set to work with great energy to transform the tripos and the buildings. By 1920 he had plans and an appeal committee of which Lord Esher was a central figure.[134] What seemed a large site

[130] On Stuart and Ewing see Hilken 1967, chaps. 3 and 4.

[131] Tanner 1917, pp. 972–80.

[132] For the current triposes see Heyman 1990. The figures for the 1920s and 30s are from Hilken 1967, p. 164, for 1991 from *Reporter* 1990–1, Special No. 17, Student Numbers, pp. 8, 18. For the relation of management studies to engineering see p. 473.

[133] Pevsner 1970, pp. 65, 206, 208.

[134] Hilken 1967, pp. 155–6. Esher's involvement in the engineering appeal doubtless explains his role in the discussions about the University Library: see above, pp. 377–9.

was acquired, on land long ago conveyed to Caius (or Gonville Hall, as it was then) under a legacy from the Lady Anne Scroope; its centre was called Scroope House, set back beside Scroope Terrace in Trumpington Street, and behind Scroope House the Inglis building grew, designed by F. W. Troup. The first stage was financed by a great Indian engineer, Sir Dorabji Tata, a graduate of Caius. Troup's first campaign produced 'some low, utilitarian brick buildings'; he added something 'of a more ambitious plan' in 1930–1.[135] The Engineering Department had expanded; but the original Inglis building would now seem only a small part of the laboratories, which grew into a vast complex in the age of Baker, between 1946 and 1966. 'The total result of this growth', says Pevsner a little unkindly, 'is regrettably bitty'[136] – but it is an impressive monument to a great imperialist. As buildings, their chief interest lies, not in their architecture, but – appropriately enough – in their structural design.

Baker's most notable contribution to engineering science was the development of 'the plastic theory'. 'The revolutionary idea of plastic theory', writes Jacques Heyman,

> is very simple. We require our buildings to stand up, so that we can use them safely. The conventional designer, the elastic designer, attempts to calculate the actual state of the structure, so that he can assure himself that the building is safe. The plastic designer makes a trivial inversion of the design statement: instead of requiring a building to stand up, he requires it not to fall down. The question the plastic designer asks is then not how a building comports itself under its loading, but rather how it could possibly collapse under an overload. This collapse concept involves com-pletely different calculations, referring to permanent plastic defor-mations rather than hypothetical elastic states . . . And it turns out, as a technical matter, that plastic calculations give a far more accurate representation of reality than elastic calculations.[137]

Baker had begun to develop the studies leading to this doctrine some years before he returned to Cambridge. Its full deployment was the centre of his own and of his group's research in the late 1940s and early 50s. A vital element in the development of plastic

---

[135] Pevsner 1970, pp. 211–12.
[136] Pevsner 1970, p. 212; Hilken 1967, pp. 187–99.
[137] Heyman 1987, pp. 10–11.

theory was his collaboration with W. Prager, a German refugee established in the 1940s at Brown University in Providence, Rhode Island.

Prager and Baker were very different men, and never established a close relationship; at their first meeting, however, they realised that each had much to offer the other. Baker had a wealth of practical knowledge and Prager could supply the framework of mathematical support. [And so they planned exchanges of staff and research findings.] Baker had always tackled his problems head on. The assault on the mountain took place on a broad front, with painstaking uniform moves forward. If the work was held up at one point, then other work was delayed until the block had been cleared. Prager, on the other hand, would pursue any important road that went in the right direction, and would leave unscaled peaks behind him, unsolved problems, perhaps to be returned to later. It would sometimes happen that, viewed from behind, the unscaled peak was seen to be irrelevant to the progress of the work or alternatively, a previously hidden path to the summit would be revealed ... The Cambridge team, once in possession of the underlying principles, could begin to establish a rounded account of the engineering theory of plasticity; and the American workers developed a powerful mathematical framework for that theory, which they pushed forward in areas of practical importance.[138]

By the time the second stage of his building scheme – of the Baker building, as it is now called – was in preparation, Baker and his colleagues had not only developed the theory but had great confidence in it.

The steel work of Stage IIA is of particular interest [writes Mr Hilken] as it was designed by the plastic method by Professor Baker and his team, Dr M. R. Horne and Dr J. Heyman. The main beam–to–stanchion connections were welded on site, seating brackets being provided on the stanchions and special lamps holding the beams in contact with the flanges during welding. Butt welds between the beam flanges and the stanchion and fillet welds on either side of the beam web enabled the joints to transmit the full plastic moment of the beam. This method of construction resulted in a saving of weight of 20 per cent for the main members

[138] Heyman 1987, pp. 13–14.

and enabled beam depths in the centre wing to be reduced to 14 inches instead of the 20 inches which would have been required in the orthodox method of construction.[139]

This was completed in 1956. In the early 1960s plans were laid for the north wing, also

> of considerable technical interest as it is designed on a further development of the plastic theory. Research on the behaviour of composite steel and concrete structures started in the department in 1961 under Mr R. P. Johnson ... [and] the north wing provided an excellent opportunity for trying out the first results ... Seven different designs were produced, four by Mr Johnson and Dr Heyman on the composite plastic theory and three by the Consulting Engineers ... One of the plastic-composite designs, with the concrete floor slabs connected by welded studs to a rigid-jointed frame, proved to be the cheapest and gave a floor construction only 25 inches thick – 6 inches less than the corresponding figure for a traditional steel structure ... This design was ... adopted, and the north wing is believed to be the first plastic-composite structure to be erected in this country.[140]

Similarly, when the rebuilding of the Inglis building was undertaken in the mid-1960s, the steel frame was designed by Heyman and Johnson.

Baker 'took immense pains with the appointment of his staff; he was quick to terminate employment of those who did not meet his high standards, in a way that is not possible in these more bureaucratic times; and he gave unstinting support to those he thought of as his team.'[141] He was very much a man of the lab, but saved from contempt of the college system by his own devotion to Clare, where he had been an undergraduate and was for many years a professorial fellow. 'Baker had an extraordinary energy ... He could be tactless – complaints in the Common Room about levels of surtax did not always receive sympathy from struggling junior lecturers. He was sometimes prickly ... and the family, and friends, had occasionally to smooth over some temporary misunderstanding.' So much Professor Heyman admits in his very sympathetic memoir.[142] Lord Baker enjoyed

---

[139] Hilken 1967, p. 192.
[140] Hilken 1967, pp. 193–4; for what follows, ibid. p. 198.
[141] Heyman 1987, p. 3.   [142] Heyman 1987, pp. 14–15.

the House of Lords and his many committees and links with industry; he was not a humble man. But he valued good colleagues and was valued by them. He was straightforward and unpompous with his staff. One of his leading technicians has told me of the respect in which he was held: they knew he was a great man, but he was without airs or affectation; they knew where they were with him. It is hard to imagine where Cambridge engineering would have been without him.

Yet as so often in these impressionistic surveys of complex scientific disciplines we falsify the picture by concentrating on one element in it. Civil engineering has had great prestige in Cambridge; but the Engineering School has many mansions. In the age of the electronic revolution, electrical and information sciences have a large role to play; and a glance at the rooms in the Baker building – or at the specialisms in part II of the tripos – is a reminder of the many branches of the subject, stretching out into neighbouring disciplines, including fluid mechanics, dynamics, economics, aspects of materials science and aspects of physics and maths. Furthermore, engineering principles in recent years have been much applied to the working of the human body and to animals, and in biotechnology – though on the Downing Site – engineers and biologists are involved. Within the building one may find soil mechanics, electrical sciences, electronics, structures research, mechanics, metrology, thermodynamics, aeronautics – and fatigue.[143]

Heyman concludes his memoir of Lord Baker with a moving reference to his old age – when despite some sadness and sorrow,

> he was still buoyant – he had, after all, made a great voyage, he had achieved his fleece, and he knew it to be gold. It is just possible that even Baker did not know how pure the gold was. He had constructed a theory, the plastic theory, as he thought to discuss the behaviour of steel frames. It turns out that the theory is universal, and can be applied to any material that is used for building. The new theory of general structural design is applicable to the medieval cathedral and to the skyscraper. The simple intellectual inversion, which seems a truism, was finally proved to be absolute.[144]

[143] Hilken 1967, p. 195. On aeronautics, see Haslam 1977.
[144] Heyman 1987, p. 15.

A diversity of disciplines

Appropriately enough, Jacques Heyman, as head of the Department of Engineering, presides over a structure as complex and intellectually demanding as a gothic cathedral.

MATHEMATICS

To the layman's eye, mathematics is as elusive as the Cheshire Cat. Most notable advances in applied maths turn into something else. Sir George Stokes was a leader in the path which led to the Cavendish. His successor as Lucasian Professor of Applied Mathematics, Sir Joseph Larmor, is remembered for work on the electron and for bringing Rutherford back to Cambridge. The present holder of the Lucasian Chair, Stephen Hawking, is celebrated the world over for his study of black holes and the origin of the universe – that is to say, for astronomy and cosmology.[145] Outstanding work in physics has taken place in the Department of Applied Mathematics and Theoretical Physics, and scientists have flitted this way and that between the department and the Cavendish. As I write, the General Board has just issued a report establishing a G. I. Taylor Professorship of Fluid Mechanics from 1992.

> Sir Geoffrey Taylor, former Royal Society Research Professor and Fellow of Trinity College, spent over sixty years until his death in 1975 carrying out research on the mechanics of fluids and solids. He made particularly outstanding contributions to the understanding and application of basic Fluid Mechanics and is widely regarded as one of the founders of the study of that subject in its present form . . . Building on the foundations laid by Taylor, the Department of Applied Mathematics and Theoretical Physics has established an outstanding international reputation for its work in the field . . .

The report describes the varieties of work in the department, 'including applications in acoustics, dynamical meteorology, oceanography, theoretical geophysics, astrophysical fluid dynamics, microhydrodynamics, colloid science, and aerodynamics'.[146] Yet this is only one branch of mathematics. In a true

---

[145] See pp. 152–3, 185–6, 490–1.   [146] *Reporter* 1990–1, p. 950.

sense it is the mother of all sciences, especially in Cambridge, where so many were founded by wranglers in the Mathematical Tripos. Most of the disciplines in the following pages are based in a measure large or small on mathematics; and it could be said that the rest of the chapter explores the field – which has played its part in the history of the Cavendish in chapter 6.

Pure mathematics is equally diverse, even if not equally chameleon-like: it does not constantly reappear under other scientific labels – even if apparently innocent labels, like the theory of games, may turn out to describe territory hotly disputed between maths and philosophy, and even if it has been found useful in the interpretation of physical and biological phenomena. But modern pure maths is like the Tower of Babel: it is an impressive and coherent structure, but those who build it talk many languages not mutually intelligible. A pure mathematician working in a particular speciality may have to travel from Cambridge to California to find a colleague with whom he can meaningfully discuss it. The historian is hopelessly bemused by the complexity of the labels and the obscurity of mathematical language. By the mercy of providence, however, one of the most eminent of Cambridge mathematicians, G. H. Hardy, Sadleirian Professor and fellow of Trinity, devoted a part of his later years to *A Mathematician's Apology*.[147]

Hardy took part II mathematics in 1900 and was instantly elected a fellow of Trinity.

> I wrote a great deal during the next ten years [and became an FRS], but very little of importance; there are not more than four or five papers which I can still remember with some satisfaction. The real crises of my career came ten or twelve years later, in 1911, when I began my long collaboration with Littlewood [J. E. Littlewood was to be a fellow of Trinity till his death in 1977], and in 1913, when I discovered Ramanujan.[148]

Hardy and Littlewood explored extensive new territories in mathematical analysis and especially on the theory of numbers. 'The Hardy–Littlewood researches', wrote C. P. Snow, 'domi-

---

[147] Hardy 1940/67, first published when he was in his 60s and feeling the loss of mathematical creativity.
[148] Hardy 1940/67, pp. 147–8; cf. C. P. Snow, ibid. pp. 27–8. For Littlewood, see also *DNB 1971–80*, pp. 510–11 (J. C. Burkill).

nated English pure mathematics, and much of world pure mathematics, for a generation.'[149] Since the early stages of the collaboration were conducted in their rooms in Trinity, they are undocumented; but there is little doubt that they quickly found that their qualities were complementary – 'Hardy, with his combination of remorseless clarity and intellectual panache ... Littlewood imaginative, powerful, humorous.'[150] The collaboration with Ramanujan had a more romantic origin. He was a humble, impoverished clerk in Madras, whose hobby was mathematics, and who was inspired to send a sheaf of his mathematical speculations to Hardy. In a celebrated scene, Hardy and Littlewood meditated on the curious mixture of old truth, new error and brilliant invention, and decided that Ramanujan must be an essentially self-taught mathematical genius. With the help of other fellows of Trinity Hardy made contact with Ramanujan and arranged for him to come to Cambridge. At first his religious principles forbade overseas adventure – for he and his wife and mother were strict Brahmins; but the goddess of Namakkal appeared to the mother in a dream and made the way plain.[151] His arrival opened another brilliant collaboration, but a brief one, for Ramanujan died of tuberculosis in 1920; Hardy ensured that the fruits of his work were carefully harvested.[152] From 1919–20 to 1931 Hardy was a professor in Oxford, enjoying the more intimate common room of New College, collaborating with Littlewood from afar; and in 1931 he returned to the Sadleirian Chair in Cambridge[153] to spend his declining years in Trinity – declining, since he felt the failure of creative power; and in his sadness enchanted posterity by *A Mathematician's Apology*, first published in his early 60s in 1940. In it he explored the nature of research and the qualities of 'real' mathematics. Of the respectable motives for research he noted three:

> The first (without which the rest must come to nothing) is intellectual curiosity, desire to know the truth. Then professional pride, anxiety to be satisfied with one's performance, the shame

[149] Hardy 1940/67, p. 28.   [150] Ibid. p. 33.
[151] Ibid. pp. 30–5; for what follows, ibid. pp. 35–8; cf. Thomson 1936, pp. 310–14.
[152] Hardy 1940b.
[153] Snow in Hardy 1940/67, pp. 40–3.

that overcomes any self-respecting craftsman when his work is unworthy of his talent. Finally ambition, desire for reputation, and the position, even the power and the money, which it brings.

But he scouted the notion that it could be done for the good of mankind. 'If a mathematician, or a chemist, or even a physiologist, were to tell me that the driving force in his work had been the desire to benefit humanity, then I should not believe him (nor should I think the better of him if I did).'[154] Hardy kept a photograph of Lenin in his rooms, and was at one time president of the Association of Scientific Workers; part of him was far from being an ivory-tower professor, and the book is full of shrewd insight into his own mind. It is abundantly true that the creative scholar cannot be diverted by the immediate needs of mankind; but it is palpably false that he cannot be inspired by them.

In another, allied respect Hardy's book is misleading. He draws too sharp a line between mathematics pure and applied. He almost seems to say that when maths is applied to some practical task it becomes dull and unreal. This set him a problem; for he fervently believed that 'real' mathematics, that beautiful, creative work of craftsmanship to which his life had been primarily dedicated, was no game. He sharply contrasted it with chess – in a manner hardly fair to the depths and subtleties of a chess master's mind.[155] He sought *significance* in a mathematical idea, by which he meant not its practical consequences, but its 'natural and illuminating' connection 'with a large complex of other mathematical ideas'.[156] In one aside, he seems prophetic; for (doubtless a little with his tongue in his cheek) he observes that pure maths is more useful than applied, 'for what is useful above all is *technique*, and mathematical technique is taught mainly through pure mathematics'.[157] While the modern applied mathematician would doubtless deny the force of his 'mainly', it is indeed the case that much pure mathematics of one generation has proved the foundation of many sciences in another, precisely because of the range and precision of its techniques. It is also true that between the outlook of a research team based in a university and one based

---

[154] Hardy 1940/67, p. 79. For what follows see Snow, ibid. pp. 41–3.
[155] Hardy 1940/67, pp. 88–9, 112–13.
[156] Ibid. p. 89.   [157] Ibid. p. 134.

in business, however enlightened, there must commonly be a difference which can sometimes become a chasm; for practical, commercial ends must play a larger role. None the less, there has been much fruitful cooperation between the sectors, and this distinction is not that between mathematics pure and applied. Hardy much overstated his case; yet the layman is eternally grateful that one great mathematician at least has expounded his craft without recourse to a mountain (however beautiful) of symbols and numbers.

RADIO ASTRONOMY AND COSMOLOGY

'"Imaginary" universes', wrote Hardy, 'are so much more beautiful than this stupidly constructed "real" universe; and most of the finest products of an applied mathematician's fancy must be rejected, as soon as they have been created, for the brutal but sufficient reason that they do not fit the facts.'[158] Applied mathematics was thus a dispiriting affair, since the universe was so absurdly constructed. He wrote some years before two of the most spectacular scientific developments of the mid and late twentieth century: the development of radio astronomy, and the cosmological deductions of Stephen Hawking. Sir Martin Ryle, the central figure in the creation of radio astronomy in Cambridge, devised machines which would read signals from galaxies too distant to be observed by even the most powerful visual telescopes: he was developing observational astronomy in a way which owed much to advanced mathematical techniques. Stephen Hawking is an applied mathematician, currently Lucasian Professor: by taking thought, by the application of largely theoretical techniques to the universe, he greatly added to the depth of our knowledge of black holes, and has passed on to survey the whole structure of the universe. Radio astronomy is one of the most remarkable offshoots of the Cavendish; Hawking has described himself as a theoretical physicist and his work owes much to physics and astronomy, but it is now conducted from Newton's chair in applied mathematics.

Astronomy in Cambridge had a respectable prehistory, in

[158] Ibid. p. 135.

the old Observatory of 1822–3 and the researches of men like Sir George Darwin – pictured at work in his study on the 'Pear shaped Figure of Equilibrium' by his daughter Gwen Raverat – who summed up his scientific work as the study of the tides and the moon: 'what can be more romantic than the tides or the moon?'[159] There had also been a tradition of solar physics, fostered by men like F. J. M. Stratton, which blossomed into the Institute of Astronomy, created by Sir Fred Hoyle. But it was radio astronomy above all which made Cambridge a notable centre of the science after the Second World War, and which explains the migration of the Royal Observatory from Greenwich to Cambridge in the 1980s. In the 1930s and 40s it was in the capable hands of J. A. Ratcliffe. In 1939 Ratcliffe examined in Oxford, and so the young Martin Ryle came to his attention – and to the Cavendish. During the war Ryle worked on radar; and his adventures included the planning of the spoof invasion fleet which deceived the Germans in 1944 as to the direction of the allied attack on Normandy.[160] His work on radar gave him valuable experience about the effect of radio signals from the sun.[161] In 1945 he returned to Cambridge.

While Ryle was developing radio astronomy in Cambridge in the late 1940s he and his team paid little attention to rapid advances in the science in Australia or at Jodrell Bank near Manchester: it was only later that the results were pooled – not without friction between Cambridge and Australia – and the full impact of their discoveries made apparent.[162] Ryle had exceptional scientific insight and set to work at an ideal moment for rapid progress. His radio telescopes developed the principle of aperture synthesis: 'the underlying principle is the relation between an angular distribution of brightness, i.e. the sky, and the complex correlation across a wavefront, i.e. the output of a pair of aerials used as an interferometer'.[163] In due course, with the timely aid of Mullard Ltd, the Mullard Radio Astronomy Observatory was set up at Lord's Bridge beside the old LMS

[159] Raverat 1952, pp. 185, 187–8.
[160] Graham-Smith 1986, pp. 499–506. What follows is based on Graham-Smith 1986 and Hewish 1990. I am much indebted to the advice of Professor Antony Hewish FRS.
[161] Ex inf. Antony Hewish.   [162] Graham-Smith 1986, pp. 508, 514–15.
[163] Ibid. pp. 508–9.

railway line to Bedford and Bletchley.[164] The station was eventually converted into a lecture room and a stretch of track relaid to enable the great telescopes – or synthesis interferometers – to be constructed on much longer baselines. The results could be enhanced by comparing signals received further and further away, on even greater baselines, and recently interferometers have been connected via computers across the world. The development of computer science has greatly enhanced the interpretation of the signals; and by what is basically a very sophisticated form of observation our knowledge of the universe and its history has been much advanced. There have been many remarkable results by the way: thus Antony Hewish and his pupil Jocelyn Bell discovered the pulsars, the neutron stars, a short step from the theoretical black holes; and this work – for which Hewish received the Nobel Prize for physics with Ryle in 1974 – helped to make it possible for Hawking's work on black holes, based on the deductions of a brilliant theorist, to be taken seriously.[165]

Modern views of the universe stem above all from Einstein's statements of general relativity in 1905 and the discovery in the 1920s that the universe was expanding. In the 1950s two theories held the field to explain the fundamental nature of the universe and its creation. They were represented in Cambridge by Fred Hoyle, Hermann Bondi and Thomas Gold, who propounded the steady-state view of the universe, involving the continuing and continuous creation of matter, and by Ryle, who held firmly to the view (originally propounded by Lemaître and Gamow) that the universe had been created in a moment, at the big bang. 'The idea [of steady state] was that as the galaxies moved away from each other, new galaxies were continually forming in the gaps in between, from new matter that was being continually created.'[166] Ryle was convinced that his discoveries and calculations made this theory impossible, and battle ensued. Hoyle and Ryle were notable champions; neither was a peacemaker. For the time at least, in the eyes of those most able to judge, victory lay with Ryle. The last word on him in Sir Francis Graham-Smith's

---

[164] Ibid. p. 513.
[165] Cf. ibid. p. 514; I owe the explanation to Antony Hewish.
[166] Hawking 1988, p. 47: my summary is based on Hawking's lucid exposition.

Fig. 17 The Mullard Radio Astronomy Observatory, Lord's Bridge

admirable memoir lies with Owen Chadwick: 'a *rare* personality, of exceptional sensitivity of mind, fears and anxieties, care and compassion, humour and anger'.[167] The bizarre telescopes – remarkable examples of modern art and technology, now copied throughout the world – still receive their signals from galaxies

[167] Graham-Smith 1986, p. 519.

489

undreamed of, infinitely more remote in space and time than anything imagined before the middle of the twentieth century.

This story has an epilogue, however. In the 1980s Stephen Hawking emerged from his black holes to present to one of the largest audiences which a single scientific book has enjoyed, his *Brief History of Time* (1988). He starts by expounding the history and meaning of the idea of the big bang.

> The general theory of relativity . . . predicts that there is a point in the universe where the theory itself breaks down. Such a point is an example of what mathematicians call a singularity. In fact, all our theories of science are formulated on the assumption that space–time is smooth and nearly flat, so that they break down at the big bang singularity, where the curvature of space–time is infinite.

But 'mathematics cannot really handle infinite numbers'; in such a situation the laws of science themselves break down; hence the singularity of the big bang.[168] Hawking's work with Roger Penrose in the late 1960s showed that the black holes represent dying stars, and he argued that there must be 'a singularity of infinite density and space–time curvature within a black hole. This is rather like the big bang at the beginning of time, only it would be an end of time for the collapsing body . . .'[169] In the course of the book he seeks to draw the quantum theory into his cosmological speculations; and by a process of argument most carefully explained, yet truly beyond the comprehension of many of his readers, he proceeds to outline a new theory of the universe. Among the various principles invoked is 'Einstein's idea that the gravitational field is represented by curved space–time'; this was applied to particles. But if it be applied on a cosmic scale, 'the analogue of the history of a particle is now a complete curved space–time that represents the history of the whole universe'.[170] In this speculation time is imaginary, and the singularities can be made to disappear; yet perhaps in the end it is the imaginary time which is real, not the finite times in which we live – and so the universe may ultimately be free of singularities, and the big bang no longer be needed. If this be so, the universe was not created; it

---

[168] Hawking 1988, pp. 20–1, 46.   [169] Hawking 1988, p. 88.
[170] Hawking 1988, p. 135.

just exists. 'But if the universe is completely self-contained, with no singularities or boundaries, and completely described by a unified theory, that has profound implications for the role of God as Creator.'[171] If this be taken to mean that the big bang was not the act of creation described in figurative language in Genesis, we may agree. If it be taken to mean that the unified theory truly explains all our experience of the universe, including the genius of Hawking, we may disagree; for all his intellectual stature, he is a theoretical physicist, not a philosopher or a theologian.

COMPUTERS AND COMPUTER SCIENCE

If we return from the most distant regions of the universe to life on earth, we must observe the very obvious fact that our lives and studies have been most profoundly affected by the technological revolutions of our time – in communications, in radio and television, above all, in computers. The computer affects Cambridge in all manner of likely and unlikely ways. Project Granta, an attempt to provide the university and all its institutions and colleges with a computer network to prepare it for the 21st century, has led to much excavation; and this has been one of the major stimuli in the formation and work of the Cambridge Archaeological Unit, to ensure that archaeological deposits are harvested, not destroyed or lost.[172] This book has been written with the aid of modest personal computers; no historian is exempt from their influence. At a deeper level the computer has spelt a revolution in mathematics itself – making possible calculations which would have been beyond the horizons of mankind hitherto, and providing novel sophistication in a thousand mathematical techniques. By the same token it has penetrated into the heart of every science and most of the humanities, opening new fields of research, offering greatly improved precision in many more. It is based on technology and has brought technology into every corner of the university, including the most ancient rooms of the oldest colleges. In that sense it is most intimately linked with engineering and is part of the expansion from the largest of all university departments. But it is also the product of maths, for

[171] Hawking 1988, p. 174.   [172] See p. 202.

its first and most fundamental aim was to mechanise mathematical processes. It is not all gain: the love of numbers is sometimes beyond the love of truth. Most statistics presented to the wider public have an element of phoney in them. But this is the common price of scientific advance.

Deeper still is the study of computer science itself, of the forms and patterns and models of the techniques which have so rapidly evolved. At its most refined this is a branch of philosophy; at its most raw it is a branch of linguistics, since the advance of computers has brought in its train an array of new languages.

All this has happened in just over forty years. There is a considerable prehistory, in which the Cambridge mathematician Charles Babbage (1792–1871) has an honourable place. His analytical engine was a device for solving problems mechanically, but owing to technical difficulties it was never quite finished. Computers which could perform elaborate calculations were developed in the 1940s. But the great step forward was to devise a machine with a built-in programme – with a memory, that is, which gives instructions to the machine on the sequence of its activities. From this all else has stemmed; and yet it only happened just over forty years ago. In May 1949 the EDSAC ran in Cambridge; and it was the first of its kind. Its history has been delightfully told by its chief inventor, Maurice Wilkes, in his *Memoirs of a Computer Pioneer*.[173] The rest of the story is highly technical, beyond the grasp of the historian as yet; when the history of Cambridge science is retold fifty years hence, it will lie at the heart of the tale.

SOME BIOLOGICAL SCIENCES

Prologue: zoology and veterinary science

To students in school and to scientists contemplating the roots of their disciplines biology is a very real presence. In Cambridge it has two faculty boards and no department; it has a professor, who sits in the prestigious Quick Chair of Biology, but he may be an entomologist or a pathologist by trade. In the Natural Sciences Tripos biology is a major and visible element; in the labs it

[173] Wilkes 1985.

disappears behind a galaxy of other labels. Some of these we have inspected in chapter 6; here we gather another sheaf to illustrate some of the exciting developments in which Cambridge biologists have been involved. The most perplexing of these sciences to the historian is zoology, still one of the most active and extensive of departments. But what is it? The study of animals. That wears an antique look; yet it houses within it groups and units dealing with molecular embryology, insect neurophysiology and pharmacology, and under its umbrella sub-departments and field stations flourish in applied entomology and animal behaviour. And these are but the limbs and outward flourishes of a department which studies animals by every means and under every aspect known to humankind, from the flight of birds, a favourite theme of its celebrated head in the 1930s and 40s, Sir James Gray, to the study of cells, one of its central interests, but a whole world of study in itself.

Outside zoology, animals have played a part in many biological and medical sciences. At the turn of the century Sir Clifford Allbutt, Regius Professor of Physic, stated eloquently the case for comparative study of the diseases of plants and animals with those of man; and in 1901 the professor of pathology, G. S. Woodhead, bought land on Milton Road for the study of the diseases of farm animals. From this grew an Institute of Animal Pathology established in 1920, in whose management agriculture, biochemistry, pathology and parasitology met and mingled; and since 1949 there has been a Veterinary School.[174] The Vet School grew out of a government report, and has been bedevilled by government reports: first by the Swann Report of the early 1970s, headed by an eminent product of the Cambridge Zoology Department, then Vice-Chancellor of Edinburgh, Sir Michael Swann, later Lord Swann. The consequence of this report was a threat of closure. After a reprieve another report in the late 1980s threatened closure again. This too has been reversed, and one cannot but echo the exasperated words of the Vet School's former head, Professor Spratling: 'Is it too much to hope that the Veterinary School will . . . be left to do its proper work, trying to realise the dreams of Woodhead and Allbutt?'[175]

[174] For the Institute and the Vet School see Spratling 1989.
[175] Spratling 1989, p. 52.

A diversity of disciplines

By way of illustration of the sciences of man and of animals, I have selected three of the most notable Cambridge scientists of the mid-twentieth century: Sir Ronald Fisher the geneticist – whose science may lead us into molecular biology, Sir Frederic Bartlett the psychologist, and Sir Vincent Wigglesworth, insect physiologist, for many years Quick Professor of Biology.

Sir Ronald Fisher and genetics

An outstanding example of the effects of mathematics on other sciences – especially on the biological sciences and particularly on genetics – can be seen in the work of Sir Ronald Fisher.[176] After the Mathematical Tripos in Cambridge he became a professional statistician: he worked for a time with the Mercantile and General Investment Company. Projecting the expectation of life of the company's clients stimulated an early interest in the relations of statistics and inheritance; and in 1917 he wrote a paper propounding a new solution of one of the fundamental problems of genetics. The biometricians argued that the correlations between parents and children proved the existence of blending inheritance; the Mendelians denied its existence and attributed the correlations to the control of individual genes. Fisher argued, in Charles Goodhart's words, that the correlations

> could best be explained on the assumption that the characters involved were controlled not by single Mendelian genes (the existence of which, or at any rate their importance, was not accepted by the biometricians) but by large numbers of them working together in concert. The Royal Society, wishing to be quite fair, referred this paper, so it is said, both to the leading biometrician and also to the leading Mendelian geneticist for their opinions. Agreeing in this as in nothing before, they unanimously advised its rejection and the paper was later published at the author's expense in the *Transactions of the Royal Society of Edinburgh*. It is now regarded as a landmark in evolutionary theory and Fisher's synthesis of the Mendelian and biometrical points of view, as later developed in his classic book *The Genetical Theory of Natural Selection* (1930), is universally accepted.[177]

[176] On Fisher, see Box 1978, and the excellent short account in Goodhart 1990 (first published 1962); cf. Brooke 1985, pp. 297–8.
[177] Goodhart 1990, p. 70.

The book illustrates the extraordinary width of his interests, for in it he propounds historical and sociological theories of great originality. His genetical interpretation of the fall of the Roman empire long passed unnoticed by professional historians, though it penetrated far more deeply into some of the real problems of major social and cultural change than did current historical fashions. As has been said elsewhere,

> it has now attracted the attention of historians – after a long interval – and been challenged; and it did not escape notice among his irreverent junior colleagues that it was part of an elaborate argument for the benefits of providing handsome allowances to members of the middle-class intellectual elite who, like himself, had large families of children.[178]

From 1919 he was statistician to the Rothamsted Experimental Station, working on agricultural research; and here he applied his mathematical skills to redesigning such experiments. From this sprang what were perhaps his two most influential books, *Statistical Methods for Research Workers* (1925) and *The Design of Experiments* (1935); for they can be and have been used in almost every region of scientific research, and some whole regions of study have had to be abandoned or profoundly modified under the impact of his exposition of their statistical failings. *The Design of Experiments* is deceptively simple, and so can be enjoyed and relished by a scholar who has hardly any acquaintance with a lab: like much of Fisher's best work, it is succinct and elegant and subtle; it has to be very carefully studied for the full message to be conveyed. It has ensured the diffusion of sound statistical method to every scientist who will listen; but its effective use requires extremely hard thought, an intellectual discipline terrifying to contemplate from without – characteristic of much of the best scientific enquiry, but not of all professional scientists. Much more can be said about the design of experiments today: Fisher's was the first, not the last word on some points; but his book remains a classic. It sits in judgement on all and every experimental scientist, and sets them standards they must seek to achieve.

---

[178] Brooke 1985, p. 298.

A diversity of disciplines

But what has this to do with Cambridge? First of all, Fisher is an exceptional example of the range of talent attracted to the Maths Tripos in the years before the Great War, and the skills it helped to provide. Further, his work at Rothamsted was noted and admired by many in Cambridge. Most important, he returned to Cambridge to succeed the notable Mendelian pioneer R. C. Punnett as Arthur Balfour Professor of Genetics in 1943. In the chair he did much important work on a wide range of genetical themes.

> In particular he became a pioneer in the field of human genetics . . . Fisher's mathematical insight enabled him to make full use of all the medical and other statistics available, and it is largely due to his work that human genetics is now one of the most rewarding lines of study, of great importance not only to evolutionary and genetical theory, but also in its practical applications to the problems of disease and medicine.[179]

His width of interest and brilliant conversation also made him a central figure in the intellectual life of the Caius Combination Room, where he was a professorial fellow and for a time president; and more occasionally he addressed gatherings of undergraduates, for he enjoyed discussion with the young. 'Fisher could be provoking and petty; but warm and friendly too; and young men of whatever discipline who came into contact with him were given a unique revelation of the nature of science and the range and power of the human mind.'[180] The young fellows of Caius used to gather round to help him solve crossword puzzles; for he loved puzzles of every kind, from the ancient Greek mathematical puzzle, of the sieve of Eratosthenes, which he was the first satisfactorily to explain, to the problem of Rhesus blood groups. By pure thought he resolved one of the most tangled and important of the medical problems of the 1940s, and 'the essential correctness of Fisher's scheme has now been confirmed by the discovery of all the possible rarer chromosome types, long after he had predicted their existence on theoretical grounds.'[181]

[179] Goodhart 1990, pp. 71–2.   [180] Brooke 1985, p. 298.
[181] Goodhart 1990, pp. 71–2.

Some biological sciences

Molecular biology

Some of the most celebrated events in the history of genetics in Cambridge in recent decades have taken place in the molecular biology labs old and new. The new lab in the precincts of the new Addenbrooke's Hospital was and is financed by the Medical Research Council; it is not part of the university. Yet it is an inherent part of Cambridge and has the closest links with university departments and (for some of its staff) with the colleges; it would be absurd pedantry to pass it by. For its story is not only fascinating and famous, but a parable of the history of modern science. The most celebrated of its discoveries, the double helix – the structure of DNA – has been told in vivid colours by the two notable personalities who made the discovery, James Watson and Francis Crick; it has been told in great detail by a historian of science, Robert Olby.[182] But for the lay reader, the ideal introduction was the special number of the *New Scientist* of 21 May 1987, celebrating the fortieth birthday of the molecular biology lab.[183]

Max Perutz came to Cambridge from Vienna to work on crystallography with the eminent eccentric J. D. Bernal in the Cavendish in 1936. Bernal was the founder of what later came to be called molecular biology in Cambridge, a prophetic, flamboyant figure.[184] Hitler's invasion of Austria in 1938, Perutz tells us, 'changed my status overnight, from a guest to a refugee'.[185] The same year saw Bernal move away to Birkbeck College in London. After some hesitation Perutz called on the Cavendish Professor, Sir Lawrence Bragg. Bragg saw the value of Perutz's x-ray photos of haemoglobin and recognised the possibility of 'extending x-ray analysis to the giant molecules of the living cell'; and gave him a fellowship with the aid of a grant from the Rockefeller Foundation – which played a crucial role in the foundation of molecular biology; it is said that its director of natural sciences, Warren Weaver, first coined the phrase 'molecular biology' in 1938.[186] After the end of the war Perutz began to

[182] Watson 1968; Crick 1988; Olby 1974.
[183] I owe knowledge of this to my son, Philip Brooke.
[184] Olby 1974, chap. 16, esp. p. 249.
[185] All this is based on Perutz's own delightful account in *New Scientist* 21 May 1987, pp. 38–41.
[186] Ibid. p. 40.

497

gather disciples, but still had no permanent post. Bragg's attempt to provide a university office failed: 'I was a chemist working in the Physics Department on what was in fact a biological problem. What could one do with such a misfit?' At this crisis Perutz's other patron David Keilin, the biochemist and professor of biology, suggested to Bragg an approach to the Medical Research Council, and the MRC Unit for the Study of the Molecular Structure of Biological Systems was born in 1947; it was given the name molecular biology nine years later.

> The year 1953 became the *annus mirabilis*. The Queen was crowned; Everest was climbed; DNA was solved ... and I [Perutz] found a method of deciphering the X-ray diffraction patterns of crystalline proteins ... It seemed to me that the focus of structural research in biology had shifted to Cambridge. My job was to keep it there, but this proved difficult.[187]

In the same year 1953 Bragg went to be director of the Royal Institution in London and Nevill Mott came from Bristol to succeed him; space in the Cavendish was desperately short and Mott determined to be rid of Perutz and his group – not because he did not appreciate their work, but because they were not, and would not become, physicists.[188] In 1958 Perutz was ready for a new approach to the MRC; and the outcome, after much anxiety, was the stately lab amid new Addenbrooke's – now a jewel in the crown of MRC and Cambridge. In 1962 Perutz had his reward: the MRC lab was formally opened, and the leaders of his team received Nobel Prizes for their work – Perutz himself and his first disciple, John Kendrew, for chemistry, for their studies of haemoglobin and myoglobin; Watson, Crick and Maurice Wilkins in medicine 'for their discoveries concerning the molecular structures of nucleic acid and its significance for information transfer in living material',[189] in other words, for devising the celebrated model of the double helix, an object even more ingenious and fantastic than themselves. The double helix stole the limelight; but Perutz's role was crucial. 'A chemist working in the Physics Department on ... a biological problem',

---

[187] Ibid.   [188] Cf. Mott's own account in Mott 1986, p. 110.
[189] Crick 1988, pp. 51–2.

going, that is , to the very roots of scientific enquiry, where all the sciences meet and mingle: and more than that, a shrewd and kindly man, able to gather and inspire and tolerate a very diverse gathering of lively minds and divergent personalities.

But this is only the Cambridge story, which is part of an immensely complex international ferment of research partly explained, and in depth, by Robert Olby.[190] He examines the role of the 'informational' school, founded by Niels Bohr and Max Delbrück in Denmark and Germany, developed by Delbrück and his disciples in CalTech. They were physicists seeking some of the relations between the laws of physics and the basis of life, of biology. The Cambridge school had been inspired by structural crystallography in the first instance, and came to be known as the 'structural' school, bringing chemistry as well as physics to the study of fundamental problems in biology. Into these deep waters we cannot penetrate: Perutz made Cambridge a principal centre of structural research, but only because it was a focus of international interest; in some respects the MRC lab is nearer to CalTech than to the Senate House; with triposes and examination structures it has little to do.

Sir Frederic Bartlett and psychology

Experimental psychology in Cambridge was effectively the creation of one remarkable scientist, F. C. Bartlett. Its prehistory was closely allied to anthropology.[191] W. H. R. Rivers had been established as a lecturer in psychology under the inspiration of Sir Michael Foster, and psychology had for a time links with physiology and medicine. But Rivers and his pupil C. S. Myers had both been to the Torres Straits and become enthusiasts for social anthropology, so early psychology had an ethnological and sociological direction too. It was this which first caught the attention of the young Frederic Bartlett, seeking learning in Cambridge after a London MA in philosophy in which sociology and ethics had played the leading role.[192] From social studies

---

[190] Olby 1974, esp. chaps. 15 and 16.   [191] See p. 204.

[192] This and all that follows is based on Broadbent 1970. I am most grateful to Dr Denis Bartlett, Sir Frederic's son, for generously providing me with a copy of this memoir.

Bartlett was led to psychology by Rivers; and when the Great War took Rivers and Myers away to medical service in the army, Bartlett, who was rejected on medical grounds for military service, was left in charge of the lab. After the war Rivers and Myers returned much occupied with new and wider concerns: Rivers in seeking medical recognition of mental illness such as 'shell-shock', Myers in industrial psychology; and in 1922 Rivers died and Myers departed to found the National Institute of Industrial Psychology. From then on Bartlett directed the lab in name as well as fact; and from 1931 he was professor of experimental psychology. In effect he created the subject in Britain. 'The teaching system thus established by the 1930s', wrote D. E. Broadbent, 'produced a brilliant crop of students who, after the Second World War, held the lion's share of the Professorships of Psychology in Britain; and . . . quite a number elsewhere in the Commonwealth'.[193]

Bartlett's insight was displayed over a wide range; but what set him apart was the depth and penetration – and experimental ingenuity – which altered some fundamental conceptions of what the human brain can do and how it works. In 1932, after long gestation, he published one of his best-known books, *Remembering*, in which 'he emphasised . . . the selective and constructive character both of perception and of memory', and explained the way the mind constructs what it believes it is remembering: all familiar doctrine now, so that we forget how original it once was. Most important was

> the sharp contrast between *Remembering* and much other psychology of the time. In America [where psychology had flourished much more than in Britain in earlier generations] the early forms of behaviourism were restricted to chains of elementary stimulus – response links; in Europe, the Gestaltists thought of experience as determined by field-forces in the brain, comparable to those governing distribution of charge on a conductor. Neither party allowed for anything so complex as the mixed and hierarchical levels of processing which Bartlett was discussing; nor for the intimate links of social structure and of individual psychology.[194]

[193] Broadbent 1970, p. 3.   [194] Broadbent 1970, pp. 3–5.

In the 1940s Bartlett was deeply influenced by a young colleague, Kenneth Craik, who sadly died in a car accident in 1945 – but not before he had opened the mind of the master to new approaches and perceptions. Bartlett was also much involved in advising the air force on the pressures and possibilities of the human mind in flight. From these stimuli he developed a new interest in the nature of skill, which called out the deepest, most subtle and most inspired of his teaching and research. Broadbent quotes one of the postwar generation: 'We had driven tanks, laid artillery barrages, one of us had flown over Hiroshima. But Bartlett taught *us* about skill.'

> The views he was putting forward have been published only in ... articles, and probably never formed a complete system. Indeed that was their strength, because they were a flexible method rather than a rigid dogma. The key concept was that of skill: the ability of men to produce for each new situation a fresh and yet perfectly adapted sequence of movements. No prewar model comparing the brain to a telephone switchboard could cope with such facts. Rather they require a subtle and hierarchically organised system which could predict the future, launch actions at appropriate times, handle local difficulties by peripheral closed-loop sub-systems, remember for brief periods the stage reached in a continuous process, monitor its own level of performance and adjust to inadequacies, and so on.[195]

After his retirement he explored a space between 'the data and the answer' in his study of *Thinking* (1958). There were striking gaps in his equipment: he took little interest in animal studies or in evolution; nor did he follow Rivers in combining psychology with physiology – in these directions his science has made enormous advances since his death. But modern psychologists are seeking to explain quite a different kind of machine from earlier models: the human brain is known to be a much deeper, subtler instrument as a result of his enquiries.

I recall as a child being taken to his lab, to play a few of the games they had there, as he disingenuously explained. In fact he was testing me for left-handedness, and the letter he subsequently wrote to my mother on whether I should be encouraged to write

[195] Broadbent 1970, p. 6.

with my right hand (which proved a lost cause in any case) was a model of calm and sensible advice at a time when such issues were rousing fervour and heat. His deadpan manner hid a brilliant ingenuity; and his informality, friendly welcome, and exceptional capacity to listen helped to make him a brilliant teacher – and to forward his research.

> His weekly lecture-discussions were a festive performance which nobody would have dreamed of missing, so that every corner of the small room was crammed. Out of hours, the staff and students might meet for tennis at his house: mixed with discussion with the Professor and Lady Bartlett, herself one of the earliest members of the laboratory ... Some of the stories about his handling of departmental paperwork are, one hopes, apocryphal; but there is no doubt that to him people were always more important than forms, timetables, or academic syllabuses.[196]

Doubtless the tennis helped him to study human skills at many different levels – just as cricket played a leading role in *Thinking*. Human kindliness and scientific insight were close allies – without any impairment of his warm humanity.

Sir Vincent Wigglesworth

In the zoology laboratory one could still in 1991 encounter Sir Vincent Wigglesworth hard at work on the insects who have been his friends since he was five. He is now well over 90, and thinking of retirement; but his mind is as clear and penetrating as ever – that is to say, a great deal clearer than the mind of almost anyone else one knows – and the twinkle in his eye undiminished. His friendship with the insects is of a peculiar sort. He has studied them with insight, subtlety, and deep respect – few have spoken with more authority or understanding of the social organisation of many insect communities, and he is never patronising to them. Yet he can be brusque with them. In commending the study of insects to the Royal Society as 'a medium for the study of physiology' he observed that 'the insect is tolerant of much greater insults than can be borne by mammals. Some insects can survive decapitation for a year or more; many can support

[196] Broadbent 1970, p. 7.

502

complete anoxia for several hours; or can be kept narcotized with pure carbon dioxide for long periods.'[197] Though acutely aware of the dangers of DDT and other modern insecticides, he has brought his expertise time and again to help control the more outrageous activities of insects, from spreading malaria to damaging crops. 'It is a commonplace that insects are the chief competitors with man for the domination of this planet.'[198] Yet he is their friend in a very true sense, ever seeking new knowledge of their physiology and of their habits.

It might have been logical to end this survey of recent scientific enquiry with some more of the studies that reach, with modern genetics, to the roots of life itself. But I have chosen rather a great scientist who has penetrated problems of unusual depth and complexity and yet retained the capacity to explain his thoughts in simple (even if often deceptively simple) language. He tells the story of how a Third Programme producer sent back a script he had prepared asking for 'something more profound. I replied that I could not promise to write a script that was profound, but if that would be more acceptable, I could easily make it more obscure.'[199] I have deliberately given his science no title: he is a doctor of medicine, an insect physiologist, a celebrated entomologist, an eminent zoologist, an emeritus professor of biology.

Vincent Wigglesworth came up to Caius in 1919 after brief war service, already deeply interested in insects. 'By the age of five I was keeping a large collection of caterpillars and other insects, and spending hours and hours watching them.'[200] In Cambridge he began research in biochemistry under Sir Gowland Hopkins, and then completed his medical training in London. 'When Patrick A. Buxton was appointed by the London School of Hygiene and Tropical Medicine in 1926 to head their Department of Medical Entomology' he set up a new and vital lectureship in insect physiology to which Wigglesworth was appointed, 'with opportunity for extensive travel ... and with abundant time for research'. Seventeen years later he was made director of the Agricultural Research Council's new Unit of Insect Physiology. 'So once again I was able to undertake world-wide travel – to

[197] Wigglesworth 1976, p. 104.   [198] Wigglesworth 1976, p. 7.
[199] Wigglesworth 1976, p. 202.   [200] Wigglesworth 1979, p. 31.

learn the elements of agricultural entomology.'[201] In 1946 he returned to Cambridge and to Caius as Quick Professor of Biology. Some of the most readable of his lectures and essays have been gathered in *Insects and the Life of Man* (1976), a delightful revelation of a humane scientist of exceptional width of interest and insight. They range from some fairly sharp glances at Wordsworth's views on science to the technical study of 'The epidermal cell', appropriately published in the Festschrift for the eminent Cambridge zoologist, Sir James Gray[202] – appropriately, since the cell in various forms has been the basic unit of study of the zoologist in recent times, and for many scientists prepared to look at something larger than an atom or a molecule. It describes the amazing complexity of function of a small and apparently simple element in a blood-sucking bug, *Rhodnius prolixus*, and the extraordinarily bold and subtle experiments devised to discover them.

Through all these papers, including those apparently concerned with the practical use of insecticides, runs a deep belief in the value of basic scientific research. One element in his faith is eloquently expressed in a famous passage which bears repetition.

> Man is an arrogant animal. In the euphoric state engendered by her Centenary in 1969, even *Nature* was betrayed into claiming that 'the directions of scientific advance are no longer left to chance but, rather, are charted almost deliberately in advance'. In his famous address to the combined Darwin Centenary and International Congress of Zoology in the Albert Hall in 1958, Julian Huxley assured us that man was no longer subject to natural selection. As one who does not believe any of these things I hold that there are still unexpected discoveries to be made, and that there is still room for the enquiring mind and the untrammelled researches of the experimental biologist.[203]

---

[201] Wigglesworth 1976, p. 1. For his later career, see Brooke 1985, p. 296; Wigglesworth 1979.
[202] Wigglesworth 1976, chaps. 16, 13.
[203] Wigglesworth 1976, p. 194, quoted in Brooke 1985, p. 296.

Chapter 16

THE SECOND WORLD WAR

The war of 1939 had a tragic prelude in Hitler's persecution of the Jews. There had long been a distinguished Jewish community in Cambridge, playing a distinctive role in the life of the city and university. It was greatly enhanced by the arrival of Jewish refugees from Germany and Austria and other parts of Europe contaminated by Hitler's influence in the mid and late 1930s. Some were of the Jewish faith, some Jewish in culture or heredity; all were equally victims of a terrible persecution. But to Britain and to Cambridge in particular they brought the rich fruits of continental Jewish culture and intellect. Efforts were made to find homes and occupation for them by many Cambridge citizens, Jewish and non-Jewish. Some of the most distinguished Cambridge academics of that era were among them: men such as Ernst Chain, the biochemist, who took a Cambridge Ph.D. in 1935 and went on to be professor in Imperial College and Nobel laureate; Max Perutz from Austria, who came to visit and stayed a refugee, later founding the molecular biology laboratory and also going on to a Nobel Prize; David Daube, Roman lawyer and rabbinic scholar, who after some years in Cambridge, including distinguished service in C. H. Dodd's New Testament seminar, went on to eminent legal chairs in Aberdeen, Oxford, Berkeley and Constance; or Peter Bauer, an emigré from Hungary in the 1930s, later an eminent economist in Cambridge and LSE, now a peer; or Walter Ullmann, the Austrian jurist who became a brilliant teacher (and professor) of medieval history in Cambridge, after fleeing from Austria for refusing to submit to Nazi pressure and under faint suspicion of distant

Jewish ancestry.[1] Hitler gave Britain and Europe a decade of crisis and war, of terror and conflict; but he also gave Britain an offering of the finest fruit of Jewish and continental learning and scholarship.

The Second World War seems at first sight a much less dramatic caesura than the First. Conscription came early, but at first it was only applied to men of twenty or more, and university teachers formed a reserved occupation. Many in practice joined the forces, or a ministry; a notable contingent was recruited for the celebrated intelligence think-tank at Bletchley.[2] But many remained: there was nothing comparable to the flight of the young to the recruiting offices in the Great War. None the less it formed a boundary almost equally important in the history of the university. Appointments, especially to chairs, were frozen, new projects put on ice; there was a long pause which concentrated the minds of the university's leaders, so that the late 1940s and 50s saw new ideas and new developments flow swiftly in. The war ended in 1945, and at first all the energies of those who had stayed and of those who were returning were concentrated on coping with a large influx of students old and new; but in 1947 a new era was heralded by the decision to admit women to the university.

In the early years of the war students came to study the whole range of university subjects for up to two years before they were called up. Throughout the war medical students and students of some scientific subjects were allowed to complete their studies; it was only in its closing phases that women were recruited in any large numbers, and women students were little affected. As in the First World War, Girton and Newnham remained full; other colleges remained for a while rather more than half full. Some college buildings were requisitioned for offices evacuated from London. Thus St Michael's Court in Caius, across Trinity Street from the older courts, was claimed by the Lord Chancellor for his Master in Lunacy: the staff of his department were politely termed 'our friends across the road', less politely 'the Lunatics'.

---

[1] For what follows see esp. Raphael Loewe, 'Cambridge Jewry: the first hundred years', in Frankel and Miller 1989, pp. 13–37, 167–299. Professor Loewe's father, Herbert Loewe, was reader in rabbinics at Cambridge and a leading figure among those who helped the refugees. For Max Perutz, see pp. 497–9; for Lord Bauer, Brooke 1985, p. 299.

[2] Bennett 1979, 1989. In this chapter I am particularly indebted to the account by F. J. M. Stratton in Venn, VI, 550–4.

The academic community was enlarged and enriched by two colleges from London, Bedford College and the London School of Economics. These enhanced still further the proportion of women students in Cambridge, since Bedford was still for women only and LSE was mixed; and the close proximity of a segment of London University was a sharp reminder to some that the women of Girton and Newnham were not full members of the University of Cambridge, over sixty years after women had been admitted to the University of London.[3] The fellows who stayed in Cambridge had many added burdens. They had to cover syllabuses and supervise students far beyond their prewar quotas. They had to take a lead in organising fire-watching for the colleges and university buildings: a new community of the rooftops and fire-watching posts rapidly developed. Cambridge was wholly blacked out at night. Ornamental posts and chains were removed from college courts – not primarily, as has commonly been supposed, to provide scrap metal for the war effort, but to remove unnecessary hazards to men moving round the courts in the dark.[4] After a while an auxiliary army, the Local Defence Volunteers, was formed in Cambridge as throughout the land, which grew into the Home Guard. It was led by men of the calibre of Hugh Heywood, dean of Caius and a veteran of the First World War, when he had been a notable army chaplain.[5] A few bombs fell on Cambridge and caused some casualties, but its buildings received only minor scars: to students from London and other cities in the front line it seemed a haven of peace. In 1940 it had its share of the agonies and panic of that year of doom. Some dons sent their children across the Atlantic or to distant parts of Britain. Regional Commissioners were set up by Churchill's government to prepare for crisis measures in case of invasion: Cambridge and East Anglia were ruled for a time from the master's lodge at Corpus by Sir Will Spens.[6] In June 1940 he prevailed on the heads of the colleges to disperse the university immediately examinations were finished. Only medical students and those who could help in the defence of

3 Gillian Sutherland in Thompson 1990, pp. 35–56.
4 Stratton in Venn, VI, 552.
5 Stratton in Venn, VI, 552; *Caian* 1987, pp. 102–8.
6 Bury 1952, p. 166.

Cambridge stayed, such as 'signallers of the STC [the Senior Training Corps], who were in charge of the communications of the local Home Guard, gunners and sappers who were selected as most suitable for guarding aerodromes and local buildings – the Post Office, the Regional Commissioner's office, etc. Their activities did not pass off entirely without injury to the public.'[7]

For much of the war few or no academic appointments were made. But the active scientific departments could not live without some measure of recruitment; and a particularly urgent need was felt when Sir Gowland Hopkins retired in 1943. The university authorities felt that the time had come to look forward as well as backward; that the immense reputation of Hopkins and his department could not be allowed to wither away by their default. So they took steps to fill the chair, first offering it to the most brilliant star among British chemists under forty, Alexander Todd, then professor in Manchester; and when Todd declined, they appointed Charles Chibnall, an older man, also of exceptional talent, to steer biochemistry into the postwar world. In 1944 the university turned to filling the chair of organic chemistry, vacant since the death of Sir William Pope in 1939. They turned once more to Todd, and offered him a more entrancing prospect.[8] Hopkins had presided over a diffuse but thriving empire, which would have offered little scope for Todd's particular methods of departmental management. Organic chemistry in Cambridge was in the shadows, and the university, with extraordinary faith since the war was far from over, offered Todd ample resources for its reconstruction. So he came.[9] Thus was the silence broken, and boards of electors began once more to gather, even though most vacant chairs had to wait till the end of the war. By a special providence – attributed at the time to Sir John Clapham – the chair of medieval history was brought out of wraps, so that Zachary Brooke, who had led the teaching in the subject since the foundation of the Junior Historians in 1911,

---

[7] Stratton in Venn, VI, 552.

[8] For all this see Todd 1983, pp. 61–73. The first initiative towards filling chairs took place late in 1942, led by Sir John Clapham (*Reporter* 1942–3, pp. 207–10); for the chair of medieval history, see *Reporter* 1943–4, p. 198.

[9] See pp. 264–5.

could be elected (to his own surprise) while he still had a few years to go before retirement.[10]

These were but the first preambles to greater changes to come. The war ended in 1945, but it was several years before rationing was abolished or postwar planning could seriously begin. Meanwhile the summer of 1945 saw the people of Cambridge looking both back and forward. On 8 May 1945 a bonfire was lit on Midsummer Common to mark – more quietly and decorously than in 1918 – the end of the war in Europe. Among those who gathered round it was Mrs J. S. Reid, widow of the professor of ancient history, now 100 years of age; and as she watched the flames she recalled another such celebration in 1856 when she was a child to mark the end of the Crimean War.[11] In the course of that summer was held the first general election since 1935, and the electors of Cambridge mirrored the national mood by electing a Labour MP for the first time. Six years of socialist government inaugurated the very different world of postwar Britain. The war had helped to speed growing equality, or aspiration to equality, in British society; and this meant a much enhanced demand for higher education. This was not, however, a party matter; for it may well be that Cambridge was more directly affected by R. A. Butler's Education Act of 1944, which set the pattern for secondary education for the next twenty years or so, than by any or all of the acts of the Labour government; and the expansion of demand for university places – and the growing prestige of scientific education – went on quite irrespective of which party was in power.[12]

In their different ways, Oxford and Cambridge faced the expansion of the postwar world with institutions ill-prepared for change. In Oxford, the dominance of the colleges in the teaching structure – which had been confirmed by the Commission of the 1920s – made the introduction of new disciplines and shifts in the balance of the old cumbersome and painful. In Cambridge change was easier; but the separation of college and university decreed by the same Commissioners meant that the consequence of change was to make the separation a divorce. It was possible to establish a

[10] Two years only, as it sadly proved, for Brooke died in October 1946.
[11] Stratton in Venn, VI, 553–4.
[12] See pp. 541–6, 559–62.

flourishing Veterinary School as a university department;[13] impossible to find most of its staff college fellowships. By the late 1950s nearly half the academic staff of the university had no fellowships. It is often said that the colleges and the university have grown much closer together in the thirty years from 1960 to 1990, and in the sense that a much larger proportion of university staff have fellowships – 84 per cent of UTOs instead of little over 50 per cent – this is true.[14] But the great gulf was the product, not of any long tradition, but mainly of the 1950s.

The pattern of future change must be explored in the history of the leading disciplines and of the new colleges of the postwar world. Meanwhile, the harbinger of perhaps the greatest change of all – the conversion of Cambridge from a male university with two women's colleges to one which is mixed – came swiftly when the war had ceased. In 1946 L. P. Wilkinson and F. L. Lucas of King's submitted a Memorial to the university bearing 142 signatures. A syndicate was set up which proceeded with measured steps to recommend the admission of women to the university, subject still to a limitation in numbers. There was a little discussion on the proposal, but it passed the Regent House without a vote. The war was over, and eighty years had passed since Miss Davies had chosen Cambridge because she despaired of the admission of women to London.[15]

[13] See p. 493.
[14] See McCrum 1989, p. 33. UTOs are University Teaching Officers.
[15] See p. 308; Bertram 1989, pp. 3–4.

Chapter 17

THE UNIVERSITY AND THE
WORLD 1945–1990:
A COSMOPOLITAN SOCIETY

In the aftermath of the Second World War the British universities were swept into a tide of discussion and change: it was widely
agreed that they must be fitted out to grasp new needs, challenges
and opportunities; it was only the nature of these on which there
was divergent opinion. The late 1940s saw a rapid revival, the 50s
and early 60s a dramatic expansion of the British universities –
often associated with the Robbins Report of 1963 which in fact
came towards the end, not the beginning, of the process. In the
early 1960s the island was full of anxious parents – or so the
politicians thought – who wanted to see their offspring at
university; and it was notorious that the opportunity to get there
was less than in almost any other of the world's richer nations. So
for a time university expansion was front-line political news, and
university funding grew at a rapid pace. Then came a check.
Probably it would have come in any case; it was a rare and
unnatural event for higher education to command so much
attention, and particularly votes; and the euphoria which followed Robbins almost immediately received douches of cold
water from the Treasury. But harassed ministers and treasury
officials seeking grounds for cutting back on university spending
found an unlikely ally in the student throng. All over the world
students rose in revolt in 1967–8; and even in Britain, where the
riots were least violent and most of the demonstrations were
peaceable – even in Britain, where the police did not shoot live
bullets at students (as in the United States) and never used
machines guns (as in Mexico),[1] there was riot sufficient to rouse

---

[1] See Caute 1988, pp. 344 (machine guns in Mexico); 396 (firing in USA); cf. p. 191 (reports of
CS gas in France). This chapter is largely based on personal experience and can of its nature only
be sparsely annotated.

public opinion against the students. Too much had been done for them, it was said; they demanded higher education as of right and expected to run it themselves; they had long hair, ill-fitting, tattered clothes, sang hideous songs and rarely washed. The student uprising – whether one views it as a great surge of human idealism or a sordid outflow of human violence – was a godsend to those who handled the country's finances. The brakes were steadily applied throughout the 1970s, and the way prepared for the savage cuts (as they seem to those within the universities) or more modest expansion (as some ministers believe) of the 1980s.

I ANTHROPOLOGY

Research

The political outline of the relations of the universities and the world in the period 1950–90 is relatively simple, but it is unintelligible unless we first rehearse what I describe as the anthropology of the university scene in the same period. I traverse familiar ground; yet much of it has not been studied in depth, and it is particularly noticeable that the flurry of books and articles which heralded the anniversary of 1968 in 1988 were much stronger in narrative than in analysis.[2] We are not much further forward in understanding that strange and powerful movement than we were when the winds of it blew over us in the late 1960s.

The university scene of the late 1940s and 50s was still in large measure dominated by the dons. The mature ex-servicemen who formed so large a part of the community did not come to rule the university but to study – to enjoy a brief but often earnest break between the army and their career. They could not be treated as schoolboys; but they did not expect to be consulted on how college and faculty conducted their affairs. Out of their number appeared a large new generation of young dons, eager to return to academic work, ardent in their ideal of academic life. For many research took on a new meaning. To those who joined this élite in the early 1950s it was dogma that the prime function of the university was to foster learning and research. This was not

---

[2] This is true of Caute 1988, which I have found very useful for facts and events; less true of Fraser et al. 1988.

thought to be inimical to education, for the young, if they were worth teaching and seized their opportunities, would learn more from contact with the best minds in Cambridge – with those who were trampling on the boundaries of human knowledge – than from old, tired teachers. Not all the young dons took this view; they hardly could, for the war had cut many off from all possibility of research, and it was especially true of the younger arts dons that they had to catch up with reading and revive their interest in new knowledge as best they could. It was also the case that university and college posts had to be (or anyway were) filled with some speed; and although most appointments were of men of the highest intelligence and capacity, they had not, in the nature of the case, the paper qualifications – the Ph.Ds in some cases, the articles and books in many more – which would be necessary for their successors today. There was still indeed much difference of opinion as to the precise role of research. Older university teachers advised their pupils not to start Ph.Ds[3] – or not to bother to complete them if they did. Learn the arts of research by all means; but establish yourself first as a teacher; make your mark in the lecture room and in supervisions; time enough to write your books later on. Some were given, and some took this advice. For others, especially the natural scientists, this was topsy-turvy: a young man must learn to be productive or he would never master the art of writing and publishing. His career would depend on research, so it must come first. Let him establish himself in research, win a university post – then go early to a chair in a provincial university where he would have wider opportunities to gain experience and do service and (so it was fondly imagined) have more time to advance his own work.

Cambridge still retained many older teachers who had never aspired to research; and in some fields they have been recruited in more recent times. Many of them were pillars of the establishment still in the 1940s and 50s, and apart from occasional murmurs about the need to preserve their supposed 'amateur status' – or cracks at the Ph.D. mentality[4] – they could live on happily in a changing world. Opinion among their juniors was

[3] I believe that I was one of the last to receive this advice, as late as 1950, because I had already been elected to a research fellowship at Caius.
[4] See p. 280.

often hard on them, and often quite unjustly. It is true that if you sought the really idle Cambridge don you were most likely to find him among the older, established, 'good teachers' who had settled into posts in the 1920s and 1930s. But one could also find some of the hardest worked of all dons among the same cohorts. Yet the ideal of the don as a man of peculiar mental agility who would not reveal in the Combination Room where his true intellectual interests lay had departed altogether, though perhaps not in all societies with equal speed. In Caius in the early and mid-1950s it was regarded as of the essence to talk shop and to enjoy the extraordinary mental stimulus (for a young arts fellow) of some of the world's most eminent scientists. Not all conversation was at this level: the most trivial as well as the most profound was frequently to be encountered. But there were no embargos on academic or religious or political themes. It was in this sense that Cambridge and its Combination Rooms were centres of intellectual advance and academic distinction in which many powerful common values were founded.

There was still much variety, much misunderstanding, much difference of opinion; and it is very easy in contemplating such societies to find opinion far more uniform than it truly was. None the less, the assumption that research was the heart of the matter – closely linked to the very questionable assumption that the best research man made the best university teacher – was something like dogma to many of us. It was like dogma above all in this that it was based on assumption not on evidence.

The cult of research was far from new. The word itself had entered the college statutes in the 1870s and 80s and powerful voices had cried out then in Cambridge, as in Oxford, that research and its professors should guide the fortunes of the university.[5] But equally powerful voices kept such ideas in check. There was no body of teachers with quite so much authority in Cambridge as the tutors of Oxford.[6] The Cambridge tutors of the 1880s were a relatively small band, many of them not deeply concerned in teaching, struggling with the winds of change, leading or gently resisting the reform which was converting Cambridge colleges into teaching institutions once

---

[5] See pp. 24–6.   [6] See Engel 1983, pp. 45–9, 77–81, 122–55.

again. In the process many notable teachers, some tutors, some not, invested heavily in commitment to an ideal of education very close to that of their Oxford colleagues. Some of them were men of learning; and a number of the most notable tutors still in the 1920s and 1930s were men of academic eminence. Almost every conceivable variety of situation can be illustrated some-where among the colleges. Thus in Caius the tutors of the 1910s and early 20s were eminent scholars and scientists who rose to chairs in Oxford and Cambridge; they were replaced (in the main) by clever teachers, able men with no pretension to research. In the 1930s Emmanuel, which in an earlier epoch had fostered Gowland Hopkins, one of the supreme geniuses of Cambridge science, was under the sway of Edward Welbourne, the very type of the college man, a devoted teacher and tutor, of exceedingly ingenious and original mind, deeply suspicious of research and the Ph.D.[7] Welbourne and a number of his kind survived the Second World War, and he was elected master of Emmanuel in 1951. The teachers and administrators of Caius were still in the saddle when Sir James Chadwick came back to be master in 1948. But the younger fellows chafed under their sway, and in the early 1950s rebelled in the name of academic standards, research and academic democracy – by which they meant, a more democratic government by the fellows of the college; they had no thought of student participation.[8]

The cult of research carried some remarkable corollaries. Beside the polarisation of teaching and research came the division between research and administration. Should the officials who ran the college – and especially the bursars and domestic bursars – be academics who could combine a full appreciation of their academic colleagues' standards with a modicum of professional zeal? – or should they be professional men with no academic stake but some training in estate management or finance? As their colleagues contemplated men like Keynes in the role of college bursar, it was evident that more than a modicum of expertise might be found in the most eminent of academic bursars. Many of the most successful bursars of the mid-twentieth century were also successful academics. But here and there among them,

---

[7] See p. 280.
[8] For the movement known as the 'Peasants' Revolt' in Caius, see Brooke 1985, pp. 272–4.

already, were professional men from other walks of life, who could show by intuitive sympathy as full an understanding of the academic point of view as those who actually performed both roles. Yet again there were cases of argument and friction in which the professional interests of bursars – whether they were academics by background or not – fell into conflict with the aims and purposes of their academic colleagues. Broadly, the argument was inconclusive until the flood-tide of bureaucracy in the 1980s made an element of professional bursars in the administration of colleges a common and accepted feature of Cambridge life.

Religion, exams and sport: intellectual élitism

After mammon, the fervour for research helped to set religion in perspective. Religion was still officially among the purposes of college and university alike; and the period between 1945 and the early 1960s saw college chapels – or some of them at least – more flourishing than for many a decade, with more communicants probably than they had ever had before.[9] This was a part of the postwar world, but it also owed much to an exceptionally talented generation of college deans and chaplains, many of whom could hold their own (to put it at the least) with their most scientific, most agnostic colleagues; and this bred a mutual respect which canonised the place of religion in the colleges as it had developed since 1871. For many, probably a large majority of college fellows, religion was irrelevant or at best an interest for other folk; for the religious, it was a part of their faith that there should be none of the discrimination in college or university which had made Cambridge a scandal and a byeword before 1871. The faith must find its own way, if at all, and scholars of every discipline and every creed or none could work together and talk the common language of scholarly discourse as it were in a large Combination Room. They could talk together and respect each other's views without discomfort. This was a very heartening situation for most of us; but it left an impassable – or almost impassable – divide between Christians prepared to accept modern learning, historical and scientific, wherever it led them, and the fundamentalists. This is not a denominational divide –

9   See pp. 120–1.

Roman Catholics welcoming modern scholarship have been numerous in recent decades as well as Protestants. There are many Catholic fundamentalists too; but the numerical strength of the fundamentalists in Cambridge (which has been great and is thought to be steadily increasing) lies among conservative Protestants of all the persuasions who gather in CICCU.[10]

In the 1940s and 1950s the pressure for places in Cambridge steadily mounted – not always in a purely numerical sense, but in relation to the standards which had to be attained for admission. This has gone firmly on – with variants in different disciplines and colleges – ever since. Cambridge has become by the sheer force of competition much more intellectually élitist. There was a sharp reaction in the 1960s, when the new winds and the new universities inspired a very healthy eclecticism among young aspirants. If the bright promise of the British university world of the 1960s had been fulfilled – if cuts and selectivity exercises had not followed – then the British universities would have remained much more equal than they had been hitherto, and one cannot but think it would have been for the health of the whole community, and not least for Oxford and Cambridge themselves, had it been so. But the fact is, they are *intellectually* extremely élitist; and although there are plenty of idle and unintellectual students in them today, the general assumption is that everyone has come to take a degree, and as good a one as he or she can get – an aim and purpose which would greatly have startled and amused many of their predecessors in the 1920s and 1930s. This is a movement quite distinct from the cult of research, yet obviously having a certain affinity with it: the reputation of Oxford and Cambridge has been sustained on twin foundations – they have exceptionally high academic standards, both for the academic staff and for the undergraduates. This has carried many corollaries with it, of which two immediately stand out.

With an increased concern for examinations and their results has gone an almost inevitable decline in sport. A newcomer to a Cambridge Combination Room in the 1920s was startled to find the eminent academics about him discussing their applicants almost entirely in terms of rugger.[11] Some of these were men

---

[10] See pp. 132–3.   [11] See Brooke 1985, p. 284.

who would gain good results in the tripos; the first who also had a blue was no great rarity. But there were many for whom a real conflict arose, and others for whom there was none. Even in the 1940s one occasionally met men who had come to Cambridge entirely on account of their athletic prowess, and who shone brilliantly on the football field but looked out of place in the college court. They were by then a set of dinosaurs. This is not to say that sport has disappeared from the Cambridge scene – far from it. The Boat Club Dinner is commonly one of the central events – and certainly one of the noisiest and most destructive – in a college year; a visitor to the river Cam would never guess that any decline had taken place – an impression now strengthened by the energy and success of the much increased participation of women in rowing. But a close inspection of the playing fields shows that they have somewhat declined in extent and use over recent decades in spite of increasing numbers of students; and the captains of sport, though still persons of authority, are no longer the mandarins in undergraduate society – before whom young and old alike bowed down – that they were fifty years ago.

Cosmopolitan Cambridge

The growth of research has had another and a very different kind of consequence. True research knows no frontiers. One might think that the study of medieval English history was not likely to flourish outside English-speaking countries; but even that is no longer true – as witness a whole seminar of Japanese research students who spent some weeks in Cambridge not long ago being grounded in the techniques of English palaeography and documentary research. For the sciences the point is obvious: never since 1870 has the Cavendish been prepared to pay much attention to national frontiers. It was for men like the New Zealander Ernest Rutherford that the university degree regulations were turned upside down in the 1890s so that places and posts were no longer confined to 'men with a degree' – which meant Cambridge, Oxford and Trinity College, Dublin.[12] Cambridge is full of paradox: it became totally cosmopolitan in the

---

[12] Which are still the only universities whose degrees are fully recognised in Cambridge, i.e. which can be 'incorporated' by those who have posts there.

late nineteenth century with scarcely a qualm while retaining every possible vestige of the parish pump which was compatible with a university of international standing. The Cambridge degree is the supreme symbol of this duality: Cambridge welcomes students from every corner of the globe, of every nationality, race, colour, religion and persuasion. But it still only fully recognises the degrees of Cambridge, Oxford and Trinity College, Dublin. More creditable to Cambridge is the story of the Mond Laboratory, built in the 1930s specifically for the Russian physicist Peter Kapitza; it was no British chauvinism, but the jealousy of Stalin, which prevented him from working there.[13]

Student attitudes

This cosmopolitanism has bred international standards of scholarship and research and helped to raise and sustain the academic standards of almost all the disciplines which flourish in Cambridge. It has brought a stream of visitors from many parts of the globe, and frequent interchange. One could explore many byeways and backwaters in the general tide of cosmopolitan exchange and influence over the last hundred years – the fashion for doing honour to international potentates which made the lists of honorary degrees exceptionally long in the late nineteenth century; the fashion for rich Indians and others under the British Raj to seek education in England which made Cambridge a breeding ground for the movements fostering Indian independence in the 1920s and 30s; and so forth.[14] Since the Second World War the tide of international visitors has flowed freely, first and foremost in the laboratories and among the visiting scholars – but also in increasing numbers who have made Cambridge their home; next in a very great and increasing number of postgraduate students; finally and less conspicuously among the undergraduates.[15]

With these international exchanges has come a much wider

[13] See pp. 188–91.
[14] A notable alumnus was Pandit Nehru, the politician.
[15] Undergraduates from overseas – i.e. those domiciled outside Britain – numbered 568 out of a total of 10,243 in 1989–90; overseas postgraduates 1,022 out of 2,975 (*Reporter* 1989–90, Special No. 18, pp. 5, 14). In the History Faculty 60 research students were admitted in 1989–90: 27 from the UK, 33 from overseas (*ex inf.* Faculty of History Degree Committee Office).

acceptance of international standards – a democratisation of fashion and manner of life. The fact is very clear; the explanation lies deep in the unexplored labyrinth of modern student society. No doubt the presence of large numbers of overseas students – and the extensive travels of many British students – help to explain the rapid waves of fashion from distant places which have flowed into Britain in recent decades. It has been plausibly suggested that in a single large student demonstration somewhere in this island in the late 60s or early 70s one might find some whose mission was student government of the universities, some the end of American intervention in Vietnam, some an improvement in the college food, some the wearing of long hair. Length of hair has been an issue between old and young in every century since the eleventh (at least);[16] college food has certainly been a burning issue in the last two centuries, and doubtless long before; student demonstrations of various kinds are well recorded from the earliest days of Cambridge.[17] But Vietnam and university government were really something new. One can find many earlier instances of students rallying to international good causes; and the students of the 60s felt no more deeply about Vietnam than those of the 30s had about Spain or those of the 40s about the Jewish Holocaust, as news of it slowly trickled through from the Nazi empire. But the solidarity which British students felt and showed for their colleagues in the States represented something much wider than the issue involved: it was a kind of trade union movement, in which the standards, aims, aspirations, ideals and taboos of a segment of international society came – so far as those of student age were concerned – to permeate a whole age group.

Like many such statements, this is at once profoundly true and very misleading. First let us glimpse the truth, and observe the very remarkable difference in student attitudes between 1926 and 1968. In the brief whirlwind of the General Strike, when vast numbers of working folk, in what seemed like desperation, sought common action to secure their ends, the instinctive response of great numbers of students was to support the government, not the strikers – to man the buses and the trains, to

[16] Cf. St Anselm, archbishop of Canterbury 1093–1109, as reported by Eadmer, *Historia Novorum* (ed. M. Rule, Rolls Series, London, 1884), p. 48.
[17] Cobban 1988, esp. pp. 406–8.

join in a great adventure palpably aimed to beat the strike and reassert the rule of government, and the standards of the social groups to which they belonged. Doubtless there were many who felt differently; but what is remarkable is the large number who had no inhibition about demonstrating public support for authority.[18] In 1968 there were also doubtless very many students to whom the riots and disruptions were repugnant. There were a few prepared publicly to say so. But there was an acute reluctance to give any overt support to authority: the most moderate of students, if brought face to face with university authorities, showed little enthusiasm for offering them succour. Some of the students were perhaps intimidated by their colleagues; but it would be superficial to attribute much to fear in a situation so full of zeal and idealism. It was rather that they were inspired by a deep and powerful sense of solidarity; they accepted often by instinct the methods and standards of the trade union in the face of management, even though this was wholly alien to the traditional relationship of the student and university worlds. Student participation in the breaking of the General Strike of 1926 seems infinitely remote – an event of a former century – viewed from the standpoint of 1968.

'Trade union' attitudes among the dons, and student action

Yet it is precisely in what I have called the trade union attitude that my generalisation is most misleading. For it was not only the students who had come to adopt the attitudes, methods and assumptions of trade unionists. Let me be clear what I am saying, for I am walking in a minefield. My purpose is neither to condemn nor to applaud these attitudes, but to describe them. I confess that I personally find it much easier to admire the methods of trade unions when they are genuinely engaged in protecting the underprivileged against exploitative employers; I find it very hard to accept that either students or university teachers are underprivileged. Yet I most readily accept that my younger colleagues face problems from which I have been exempt – and also that there is a genuine age gap here. It is not

[18] Howarth 1978, pp. 148–50.

only the students, but their teachers, who have become union-ised; and this is part of the world in which we live. I have been a member of the Association of University Teachers for nearly forty years, and seen it change its nature and its function out of all recognition. It was a docile professional association – a very necessary support for junior staff in the very undemocratic provincial universities of the 1940s and 50s, but in little else resembling a trade union. Now it is not only a fully fledged union but its General Secretary can storm the holy of holies and sit on the TUC General Council; and the profession meanwhile is a great deal less downtrodden than forty years ago, even if its members face new and alarming threats and challenges. I recall observing about twenty years ago, when the airline pilots of British Airways staged a strike over their pay, that the traditional method of the oppressed working class had been fully adopted by the prosperous middle class. Of course, these terms are meaning-less today; but the pilots were earning – before the strike began and no doubt with good reason – far more than most professional men in Britain. Their action was a very clear signal both that the old class[19] arrangements had disappeared altogether and that the tastes and standards and attitudes of the old trade unions had been adopted by the professions, or at least by some of them. It is as difficult for those of us who were brought up in the forties – for whom professional standards could not possibly include such violent and anti-social methods of asserting our needs as strike action – to appreciate what seems wholly natural and inescapable to those only a decade or two younger than ourselves, as for the attitudes of the students in 1926 to be grasped by their successors in 1968. Here then is a genuine case of a generation gap. If we wish to understand what happened in 1968 it is peculiarly necessary for the old to feel some sense of the international, universal loyalty – the bond of common ideals and hopes and fears – that inspired the students, and for the young to realise that their actions and demands rode roughshod over professional standards, traditions and etiquettes greatly treasured by former generations of teachers and students alike.

On 13 November 1968 the House of Commons set up a Select Committee of a number of its members to survey the educational

[19] See pp. 240–2.

scene, and they turned at once to student relations in the universities and other institutions of higher education. Whey they reported in July 1969 they observed: 'Although we received little evidence to suggest that unrest in British universities and colleges owes much to international inspiration, it would nevertheless be unrealistic to ignore the fact that student disquiet is world wide or that there are common factors.'[20] In fairness to the group of highly intelligent men who formed the committee it must be conceded that little was known still in the summer of 1969 about the exact chronology and extent of student unrest, and even now, after all the extensive research which has been devoted to its elucidation, the nature of the movement is little understood. The relation of student unrest to the political events of a turbulent world makes real understanding extremely complicated.[21] In 1967–8 the Cultural Revolution in China was in full swing and there were revolutionary movements in Paris and Prague; 1967 witnessed the Six Day War between Israel and the Arabs; the Vietnam War had entered a peculiarly violent and controversial phase. Such events form a kind of smoke-screen obscuring the clear lines of the student revolts. Furthermore, they were accompanied by a political movement which noone doubts had international links and agencies, the movement commonly referred to as that of the New Left. So far as we can at present discern, this greatly influenced the tactics and the timing of student revolts in many parts of the world, including Britain, without being itself a deep explanation of the nature or aims of student unrest itself.

Let us put it another way. What was so exceedingly confusing to even moderately sympathetic university teachers in the late 60s and early 70s was that student leaders appeared to be promoting a mixture of very liberal and less liberal causes by fascist methods in the name of Marx or Trotsky or Mao or Che Guevara or Marcuse or some other unlikely deity of the old or new left. The liberal principle most widely diffused was that students should be treated as adults – they were voters in the wider community by now, why not in the more intellectually advanced community of the university? They should be consulted, they should discuss

---

[20] *Report from the Select Committee on Education and Science, Session 1968–69, Student Relations,* I, London, 1969, p. 40.
[21] For what follows see esp. Caute 1988.

their courses, their lectures, their teachers with members of the faculty. Most universities came rapidly to accept a much larger student participation than had existed hitherto, with student members of councils and senates and faculty boards; and most university teachers readily came to value the enhanced advice of students. Many problems remain. Student generations are short; the courses they plan are studied by a new generation, sometimes with new ideas. But few would doubt that these changes have improved communications between teachers and students.

Some student action was politically motivated, and the fascist methods were never in these years far from the surface. If a party of activists wished to carry a meeting, they organised a filibuster until only the rump of their own supporters was left, when an overwhelming vote in their favour could be carried – or if this proved difficult another meeting could be called at an impossible time to which only their supporters were willing to come. Then they confronted the university administration, 'mandated' to insist on concessions, some of which might be reasonable, some outrageous. The more extreme student politicians wanted either to reduce the university to anarchy or to run it entirely themselves; and they were delighted to meet resistance since a kind of martyrdom was one of their principal aims. They were only frustrated by the tactics advocated by Sir Eric Ashby, Vice-Chancellor of Cambridge in the years 1967–9 – 'aggressive tolerance'.

> This meant refusing to respond to provocation with force, while vigorously launching an intellectual counter-offensive through fact-sheets, news-bulletins, and statements from 'young members of staff known to have liberal views'. This would ensure that tolerance looked like an act of conviction rather than weakness. If the students demanded an amnesty ... the best thing was to get all the ... deans and chaplains to join forces to quote Martin Luther King, Jr, on accepting the legal consequences of civil disobedience. The whole purpose, wrote Ashby and his co-author Mary Anderson, 'was to cut the demonstrators down to size, so that they appeared to be adolescents seeking a painless martyrdom ...'[22]

[22] Caute 1988, pp. 342–3, quoting Ashby and Anderson 1970, pp. 136–7.

In many cases the demonstrations were in support of national or international political causes. In France the student rebellion of May 1968 – followed by widespread industrial action – nearly toppled the regime of General de Gaulle, and the rioters were dispersed by police using CS gas and other unpleasant weapons. In Mexico in 1968 the students were fired on by machine guns.[23] In May 1970 the Ohio National Guard opened fire on students demonstrating against the invasion of Cambodia. Violent clashes between students and police or troops occurred in many other countries, especially in Japan and on the continent of Europe. Britain by comparison seems peaceful, but many observers, not all of them wholly ignorant, were roused to anger by student demonstrations. The students were supported out of high taxation; they should be working – instead of which they were talking, demonstrating, thumbing lifts; they claimed poverty but drank more than many tax-payers could afford. The high seriousness of many students was scarcely intelligible to wide spectra of public opinion. There were numerous demonstrations, sit-ins, confrontations, campaigns; the LSE in London was subject for months if not years to a dual system of government, its director and Council of Management on the one hand, the student junta on the other. In Cambridge there was much rumour of war and one ugly incident: while the Greek colonels ruled their unhappy country, the Greek Tourist Board held a dinner in the Garden House Hotel in 1970, and a large party of students held a noisy and violent demonstration at its gate and in its garden.[24] More characteristic of the role of Cambridge in the student riots was the debate at the Union in October 1968 on the morality of violence. In spite of the eloquence of a leading LSE activist, 'the Union rejected violence by a majority of more than three hundred'.[25] 'But [a few months later] the cocky voice of ultra-Jacobinism was heard from Jeff Olstead, Secretary of Queens' College Union ... deriding "the whimpering of the so-called 'moderates'" who "will presumably exhibit the same bovine capacity when released into the greater and sicker society of this country".'[26] So the voice of the New Left was heard in

---

[23] Caute 1988, pp. 191, 344, 396.   [24] See below, pp. 557–9.
[25] Caute 1988, p. 312.   [26] Caute 1988, p. 325.

Cambridge; and in some of the scuffles in university and college alike its methods were tested. John Twigg has chronicled in exemplary detail the efforts of the students of Queens' to win a share in the management of the college; but while bringing out most effectively the genuine idealism which inspired many of the students, he has done less than justice to the perversity of some of their tactics and the firmness and sense of some of the tutorial measures taken. This has called out a tremendous rejoinder from one of the former tutors of Queens', and it is greatly to be hoped that more such dialogues will elicit the story of student unrest from both sides before the tutors have retired to another world and the students grown too forgetful of their youth.[27]

The role of women

The barrier between the aims of the New Left and the liberal opinions of many of their allies is most dramatically revealed in the attitude to women's liberation. In this the New Left had notoriously little interest. A few women were involved in the leadership of the New Left, and the student rebellions had vital consequences for the role of women; but this was a bye-product not sought by the leading activists of 1968 who were for the most part unashamed male chauvinists, though some later recanted.[28] None the less, the chief consequence of the movement in Cambridge was the attempt to find a new role for women there. In Oxford and Cambridge the hard-line politics and the violence had only a slight or brief impact; and participation in university government has still not made advances to compare with what was achieved in many other campuses. The clearest reason for this is an odd one. Oxford and Cambridge are academic democracies: whereas in the provincial universities the students could find a place in the infinite hierarchy of committees by which the university was run, in Oxford and Cambridge they were in the end frustrated by the authority of Convocation and Regent House, bodies which by definition consisted wholly of teachers and administrators, and of the whole body of the university academic staff. They have also suffered from the inevitable

---

[27] Twigg 1987, pp. 404–33; Bowett 1988.
[28] Cf. Caute 1988, chap. 13, esp. p. 236.

weakness of student politicians in British universities. The exceptionally short courses which students take in Britain mean that continuity is difficult to obtain; the generations pass with great rapidity; there is much less place – except in a few exceptional institutions like LSE – for the long-term professional student politician.

But Oxford and Cambridge had one great peculiarity still in the 1960s: they were male universities. There were indeed distinguished colleges of women attached to them; and since 1948 Cambridge had recognised that the women were full members of the university. But in every other university in the land women entered on the same terms as men; all places were open equally to both. Yet in Oxford and Cambridge, where admissions were (and are) still governed by the colleges, a woman applicant had only a one in ten chance against a man.[29] Furthermore, they were still in large measure segregated; down to the early 1950s all the women were either in Girton, deliberately planted at a safe distance from any male college, or Newnham, much nearer the centre, but still a world of its own. In the aftermath of the Second World War there was a considerable stir of interest in this anomalous situation: it could not be right – in the eyes of men and women alike of liberal views – and it was peculiarly galling that it should happen in Cambridge, which in other spheres claimed, or would like to claim, international esteem as the home of liberal academic principles. First of all came the movement to found another college, and New Hall was the fruit of this fervour in the early 1950s – though still modest in scale and endowment.[30] The 1950s and 1960s saw the growth of a dining society of academic women which came to form a small women's college for underprivileged women academics and mature women students, Lucy Cavendish College. Meanwhile the other new undergraduate college of this era, on a very much larger scale, was for men only: Churchill College discriminated in favour of science but not of women.[31] From the early and mid-1960s new graduate colleges began to spring up, inspired by other needs, and they

---

[29] In 1968–9 among undergraduates women comprised 10.9%, among postgraduates 14.4%; in 1989 the figures were 41% and 32.2% respectively (*Reporter* 1989–90, Special No. 18, p. 4).
[30] See p. 570.   [31] See pp. 568–9.

were mixed foundations in which women had an equal role with men from the start.[32] The first mixed colleges were Darwin and University Colleges and Clare Hall. These facts underline a curiously persistent feature of Cambridge history: the recruitment of the rank and file of undergraduates seems often strangely different from that of the academic élite; certainly, the graduate colleges reflected the role of Cambridge in the wider world more naturally by 1970 than the men's colleges.

Meanwhile the demand for the admission of women to the men's colleges came very slowly. In the 1920s the possibility had seemed so remote that the Royal Commission – really wishing to see women have a fuller place in the university at large, and so seeking for minor concessions to throw to the old guard – recommended specifically that women be not admitted to men's colleges, and a number of colleges included a statute to this effect in the new constitutions of the 1920s.[33] This was an innovation: college statutes had not troubled hitherto to specify that women were excluded – to the older statute makers it was axiomatic, a law of nature. Thus ironically many colleges saddled themselves with statutes in the 1920s which they found incumbrances in the 1970s. But not before. There was a rustling in the trees in the mid-1960s when New College, Oxford announced that it would admit women; it seemed a strange novelty, possibly a portent; hardly more. But it went away. Then in the late 1960s the Cambridge students made the admission of women a major plank in their programmes of reform.[34]

It would be superficial to attribute the movement solely to student pressure, for the late 1960s and 70s saw a period of intense discussion and introspection by the men's and women's colleges alike as to their role and destiny; and a fundamental change in the nature of Oxford and Cambridge came to pass with extraordinary rapidity. It did not appear rapid to impatient students who came and went while the dons deliberated; nor to the liberal-minded fellows of some colleges who watched their colleagues debating the same issue time and again over a period of eight or ten years. But in comparison with many other changes over the

[32] See pp. 576–82.   [33] *RC 1922*, p. 175.
[34] In contrast to the leaders of the international student movement: see n. 28.

seven or eight centuries of Cambridge history it came in a flash. In 1969 no men's college could admit women to membership, nor any women's college men; by 1987 all the men's colleges had become mixed societies – in principle at least;[35] Girton was mixed, Newnham still for women only, New Hall for women undergraduates with men permitted as fellows and postgraduates. The different nuances reflect the complexities of the debate.

Just as the 1960s had seen the unionisation of society, so it had also seen a new mingling of the sexes. The expansion of the 60s involved a higher proportion of women than before.[36] Very many of the schools in this country were already mixed, and in home and school an ever-increasing number of Cambridge students had learned a natural relationship between the sexes which seemed strangely violated when they entered the segregated colleges of Cambridge. No doubt the issue was not new, nor were the complaints; but the outcome was a radically new sentiment. The ethos of the 60s did not allow the students to accept dictation from ancient walls or paternalist tutors; they demanded their own way of life. It was the age of the permissive society; and tutors found it increasingly difficult to exercise any kind of control over or inquisition into the social habits and sexual mores of their charges. In Girton in the 1940s there were still checks of a kind on male visitors and on the movements of the Girton students. By then they were much resented and easily bye-passed; in men's colleges they only consisted of gate hours – it was still the practice down to the 1960s to forbid visitors (and especially female visitors) after 10 or 11 or 12 according to the arcane local regulations. Student rebellion in the late 1960s swept these restrictions away and by 1970 the tutors of the male colleges at least could no longer be sure of the sex of all those who slept within their portals. There was still some attempt at control for a decade or more after this; but since contraceptive machines became a normal feature of once male colleges in the 1980s – whatever private advice tutors and chaplains may still give to undergraduates – it is no longer claimed that they have any control over the relations between the sexes. This is a part of a

---

[35] The first woman fellow of King's was elected in 1970 (*CUC* 1971–2, p. 243). For the rest see n. 38.
[36] Cf. Carswell 1985, pp. 166–7.

very complex change of attitudes and practices which we only
partly understand: we can hardly hope fully to grasp something
which goes so deeply into the intimacies and private worlds of
every individual. Social surveys of sexual practices, for example,
are largely worthless, partly because so many of those whose
witness would be most significant are reticent, or disinclined at
least to tell the truth;[37] and partly because of the very complex
nature of the phenomenon itself. In the 1950s and early 60s it
seemed as if the age of marriage was going down as a younger
generation arose more mature in its sexual habits. But one of the
most powerful winds which blew in the 60s and 70s was the
reaction against marriage, in favour of more informal relationships in which the woman in particular is not enslaved by old-
fashioned legal bonds. Statistically there is no way one can clearly
distinguish between companionate partnership which is the fruit
of a very highly thought out and deeply valued morality and
living together which is the equivalent of mere promiscuity. They
are socially and morally at opposite poles, yet both in their ways
the natural products of the ethos of the 60s. It is crucial to accept –
if we wish to understand the profound changes of these decades –
that the motives for the infinite variety of new forms of
cohabitation which became an essential part (as they saw it) of the
life of folk of student age in the 60s and 70s had and have both
deeply conscientious and extremely irresponsible elements. For
our present purpose, it is the basic fact which tells: in 1960 it was
an easy matter to fill men's and women's colleges alike; by 1970
the appeal of Cambridge was gravely diminished in the eyes of
applicants by the single-sex arrangements in the colleges. The
most powerful anxieties were felt in Girton, hampered (as its
fellowship reckoned) both by its remote site and by its rejection
of male society. An appeal was launched which enabled the
building in the early 1970s of Wolfson Court in Clarkson Road –
midway between the college and the centre of the town – to the
stupefaction of old Girtonians who had bicycled the full distance
to and from the college several times a day in their time. Soon

---

[37] I do not doubt that many are prepared to describe their experiences accurately; but it takes only
a relatively small minority who do not to render statistics meaningless – and we have no control
to establish that it is a minority. There is perhaps no region of human experience in which men
and women are less inclined to tell the truth.

after, the process began which made Girton and the men's colleges, after much heated argument, mixed.[38]

Conservatives argued that this was a major change in the whole nature of the society which must not be undertaken in a hurry; that it was right that somewhere in the British university system there should remain havens of celibacy for those who wished for it; and that ancient colleges should not bow to winds of fashion. Those who supported the admission of women often did so because they could see no grounds against it – men and women mingled in every other university; why should they not in Cambridge if they wished to? But the argument which told most heavily (so it seems) with those who were at first disinclined for change, and with those who needed convincing, was that once a few colleges had gone mixed the quality of applicants to the all-male colleges plummeted. It is not possible to quote precise figures or to enter deeply into this argument; the crucial point is that it was widely believed both in Oxford and Cambridge that it was so, and that carefully thought out and documented arguments were produced to convince wavering fellowships that their colleges were suffering.[39] The argument can be seen under many aspects; and it might be fairer to put it as it was put to me by a leading Oxford tutor: he saw it, not as the pressure of this or that popular movement or request, but as a move dictated by natural justice if one wished to make Oxford more attractive to a wider spectrum of applicants. The public schoolboys might be used to single-sex schools and accept single-sex colleges (though in fact they were often the most vociferous for change); it was less reasonable to expect those from mixed schools and especially from comprehensives to do so. Such were the arguments, very much abbreviated. But it is not quite true to say that the issue of co-residence was confined to Oxford and Cambridge; for halls of

[38] King's and Churchill from 1972; Sidney from 1976; Girton, Trinity and Trinity Hall from 1977; eight more in 1978 and two in 1979; the rest followed more slowly; Magdalene completed the mixing of the men's colleges in 1987 (these details are from *The World of Learning 1989*, p. 1442; I have corrected Caius from 1978 to 1979, when the first women were admitted: it is not clear in all cases whether the years relate to change of statute or actual admission). Newnham, New Hall and Lucy Cavendish are still for women only, save that New Hall has some male fellows. The graduate colleges and Robinson (founded 1977) were mixed from the start.

[39] This was an important element in discussions in Caius in 1977. The fullest account in print of a campaign for 'co-residence' is in Twigg 1987, chap. 29.

residence in modern universities had normally been single-sex down to the late 1960s. In the mid-1960s Liverpool University, where great trouble had been taken to weld the residential halls into the structure of university society and to plan a notable expansion of them, a large scheme of new halls on the Carnatic site was begun. The idea was to have central dining halls and common rooms, but blocks of residence in which men and women would be housed separately at night. To this the students made very strong objections – and this was for Liverpool an entirely novel problem.[40] In the late 1960s similar arguments throve in most universities in the land: the issue in Oxford and Cambridge was deeper and more acute, but was in its essence – here as throughout the movements we have been surveying – universal to British universities and much related to wider national and international movements of opinion.

Thus Cambridge has been converted from a male university with two distinguished female colleges within it – as it was in 1948 – to a mixed university. Or has it? The number of women undergraduates has gone up from 900 in 1968–9 to over 4,000, and there is little doubt that opportunities for women to enter as students have been greatly enhanced.[41] The proportion of women – roughly two to three, 4,000 to 6,000 – is still below the national average for such institutions and it is growing very slowly. Nor is it clear to what extent this is due to any resistance there may still be in some ex-men's colleges to allow the proportion of women to increase to anything like equality with men (if there is such resistance, as is often denied), and to what extent it is due to diffidence or reluctance on the part of women applicants – or to a dearth of applicants who have been prepared in their schools to raise current Cambridge admission standards. All these factors may play a part; the historian must remain a little agnostic of current explanations. But what is much clearer is that the admission of women has done little for the female don. The number of women fellows in Girton has grown only from about 37 to 42 in a fellowship of about 74; but most men's colleges have so far elected exceedingly few women. Most of us who have observed the

---

[40] Most of the halls are now mixed: Kelly 1981, pp. 334–5.
[41] *Reporter* 1989–90, Special No. 18, p. 4.

electoral process do not believe that this is mainly, or perhaps in any significant measure, due to male prejudice. One cannot penetrate the human heart; there are indications that prejudice can work in the other direction – that many appointing committees have been troubled by the inadequate numbers and inadequate opportunities for women and have tried to do something to rectify it. Some colleges have overtly sought women tutors. But in most academic appointments any open discussion of the issue is hampered by the Sex Discrimination Act which forbids discrimination in favour of women as much as in favour of men; there is little doubt in my mind that it has been, however ironically, a very powerful factor in checking the increase in women fellows in the colleges once male. Notoriously, women have hitherto been more affected than men by the interruption of career prospects by bringing up children, and by the movement of a partner to a job elsewhere. Whatever the explanation, the total number of women fellows in mixed colleges had, by 1 October 1985, reached only 147 (9.4 per cent), out of 1,556; the women's colleges raised the total to 241 out of 1,654.[42] These are eloquent figures: they tell of a movement to find an adequate place for women among the teachers of Cambridge which has failed.

Bureaucracy

The last of my very selective list of fundamental marks of the society from which the university of the 1980s has sprung is bureaucracy. As with the admission of women there is a point in time when the whole atmosphere of the university's relations with central government and the wider world changed, and the grip of bureaucracy was felt as never before. Needless to say, it was not something wholly new. I recall in 1967 the then Keeper of Public Records observing that in the previous forty years, during which he had been an official of the Public Record Office, the mileage of records – in one of the oldest and richest historical archives in the world – had doubled; and that was before the advent of postwar forms and restrictions, and of nationalised

---

[42] These figures are taken from Whitehead 1987, p. 111. There is a very helpful discussion of these problems in the *CUWAG Report*.

industries, had impinged on the PRO itself. The pace of increase has been very rapid, never more so than in the 1980s. With squeamish phrases Mrs Thatcher's government talked of deregulation, while a thick coating of bureaucratic control settled on every side of the national life. It would be superficial to blame this or any other government; it is part of the culture in which we live. One might expect to find rebellion against it among students, but it was first among students that I became aware of its more bizarre and rococo expressions. Over the last twenty years I have seen a succession of constitutional documents, for students' unions and societies in Liverpool, London and Cambridge, sometimes (not always) drawn up by scholarly postgraduates with a very close attention to the detailed effect of what they are composing; but whether intelligible or unintelligible, useful or useless, one and all were of immense length and complexity. There are many good features in these documents, and much of them truly reflect responsible attitudes on the part of those who drafted them – if a certain naivety in supposing that the rank and file of students and dons can ever read or master all that they have written. They have been paid the compliment of imitation by heads of department and tutors, and Cambridge college regulations have grown into substantial booklets.

One might think that company law, the law of the market place, would be a region exempt from complicated regulations under a government dedicated to fostering market forces. But no region of British law has grown more in detail and complexity than company law. Even so mundane a reflection of it as an insurance policy, which occupied one side of a modest sheet of paper forty years ago, now demands a complete booklet of numerous pages, some of them occupied with tiny print. The very possibility of proliferating this kind of literature at reasonable cost owes much to the computer revolution, the full consequences of which we have yet to see. One might have supposed that the advent of computers would mean a decline in the use of paper: that the memory can be mechanised and stored and need not be spilt out as formerly in acres of typescript. So far, the opposite has happened – the ease of reproduction and the dangers of relying on computers alone have led to a vast increase in the quantity of printouts, xerox copies and what-have-you, to the use of square miles of paper where acres formerly served.

It will be seen that I have used the word bureaucracy in a variety of senses, especially two: in the sense that more and more of the details of our lives have been covered by regulations, and that more and more paper flows inexorably across our desks. They are closely connected. There is a benevolent and high-minded element in all this, which is also part of our culture. The growing complexity of company operations has led to all manner of devices to protect the public from the chicanery of defaulting business men; the result is an immense heap of new company law. It has been increasingly perceived that university staff and students alike live mainly on the public purse; and there has been a demand – entirely reasonable in itself – that they should account more fully for the way they spend public money. Hence an infinite quantity of returns and reports and forms. There has also been a tightening of the public purse. Since 1979 the government grants to universities have been adjusted (mostly in effect downwards) every few months, sometimes every few weeks, according to the fundamental laws of public spending, as currently interpreted. This has involved both a ceaseless process of recalculation and readjustment, and also some wholly new procedures – such as relativity exercises in the universities to determine the quality of work done in different faculties and departments, and so their entitlement to shrinking funds. Once again, this is not a purely financial tool: it corresponds to something deeper in the culture, or anyway in the attitude of the Conservative government of the 1980s. For it has been accompanied by an insistence that university staff engage in various kinds of appraisal of one another – a process, in so far as it involves no more than some rather more active pastoral work in departments than used to be the norm, to which few would object, but one which has been mounted as an immensely complex bureaucratic exercise involving a whole new world of files and forms.

It is easy to admire or to condemn the vast growth of modern administration; but that is not my purpose. Evidently enough, it has a positive side: it often reflects a more professional attitude to all manner of processes rather carelessly performed in former times. Thus academic appointments which forty or fifty years ago might be very informal affairs conducted with very modest paper-work can now be formidable exercises in which mountains of paper unroll, first discussing the need for the appointment and whether the university (which has to pay for the paper and the paper-work) will have the money left to pay the salary; this may be closely argued in a hierarchy of committees, all costly in staff time, and then the real work of advertising, collecting references, short-listing and interviewing begins. Even so, there are still heights for British academic appointing committees to scale. In America a tenure track appointment may involve months of preparation: visits by candidates, who give lectures and conduct seminars and meet the faculty; numerous references and a very long process of elimination and selection. For major chairs in the US this may be followed by letters of enquiry to almost every expert in the field in the world. The contrast with older methods, which often involved old-boy networks and private patronage, or at the least the very informal passage of information, is striking. The new mode is more professional, more searching, more thorough and more fair. But for those who administer it it is immensely time-consuming; and forests have to be felled to provide the paper.

The change is quite a profound one in our culture, and the examples show that it is world-wide. In the 1940s F. J. E. Raby retired from the Ministry of Works, and in the 1950s Sir Charles Clay retired from the post of Librarian of the House of Lords. Both were greatly admired, experienced, able officials. Both were men of very quick and acute mind who worked fast. Raby was able to produce massive works of scholarship on medieval Latin verse, some of which were written (so it was plausibly reported) at his desk in the Ministry. Charles Clay edited many volumes of *Early Yorkshire Charters* – models of precise and accurate scholarship; and some of the research for them was conducted during his working hours as Librarian.[43] In neither case was there any dereliction of duty, nor ground for criticism; it was the way of their world in their day and generation. The pace of administration in a ministry or a library has so much grown that at least two men are probably engaged full-time in doing what they performed so admirably in shorter hours; very likely more.

[43] Brooke 1980, pp. 322–3.

The working academic is in a measure cushioned from the effects of this bureaucratic explosion by the parallel growth of a large class of professional administrators, and by his vacations.[44] For many natural scientists term-time and vacation are much alike, with experiments constantly rolling and postgraduate students needing constant supervision; and for them the tension between research, teaching and administration is often much stronger than for their arts colleagues. But for the university teachers in the arts the vacation alone enables their pattern of life to survive; for it is a strange irony that the demands of administration have made research in term-time almost impossible at just the same epoch that research has finally become a necessity, a categorical imperative, if the teacher and his faculty are to survive.

The system has marked out some folk as its martyrs, and an obvious example are the archaeologists. There is an element in the discipline which is very ancient; but in all essentials it is a very young discipline demanding scientific and technical and historical skills only brought together in recent years.[45] It is at once science, social science and arts; and it is extremely expensive. An academic archaeologist must spend his or her vacations, or a substantial part of them, in the field, trowel in hand, or at least directing an army of excavators. One must spend one's terms in the normal teaching and administration of a university. But one has two other tasks to perform, both immensely time-consuming. One must publish one's excavation or – notoriously – one's findings may be lost or destroyed and the excavator fall under the ultimate condemnation of his or her colleagues. But if one's standards are high and one's excavation important, publication involves a major collaborative exercise with armies of experts; if one reckons to complete one's report before one breaks the soil again one may lose all contact with original research in the field. But an excavation is also surrounded by administration: one must obtain the necessary permissions and approvals, which involve not only formal approaches to English Heritage but informal sounding of a

---

[44] I am aware that much less than justice is done in this book to university and college staff, and especially to the administrators, clerks and secretaries, without whom a modern university could not survive. Their history has yet to be written.

[45] See pp. 205–8.

galaxy of local bodies reasonably jealous of their territory and anxious to know what the latest excavation is about, and how it relates to their own plans. One must write a sheaf of letters to bodies which may supply funds for the excavation; not just proforma letters, for special forms and questionnaires are often demanded by the committees which distribute funds; and whether they provide the cash in thousands or hundreds or tens, they expect detailed reports on how the money has been spent. In the last twenty years all this has grown enormously: the cost of scientific archaeology has escalated, everyone has become much more meticulous, and excavation has been subjected to much more precise legal regulation. All this is very necessary, say the archaeologists themselves, and it is certainly a self-imposed martyrdom; the mushroom growth of amateur archaeology had threatened our heritage; legal sanctions alone will serve to protect it. But it is very hard for archaeologists, surrounded by the paperwork their profession and their creed have created, to engage in original scholarly and creative meditation, to see any wood among their trees. In spite of this we have witnessed a remarkably creative era in original archaeological thought.

If we had time and knowledge and understanding, we could pursue this discussion much further and into much greater depth; this much must suffice to show how great and how varied are the changes in social attitude which underlie the new world of the university, and of Cambridge in particular, in the late twentieth century. In the same epoch it has been exposed to political winds of a new force and complexity.

II POLITICS

In the seventeenth century many major appointments in Cambridge were settled in or near the royal court. In the eighteenth century the court itself withdrew to a distance; but the strings of patronage and the university's activities were closely watched by leading politicians. The duke of Newcastle as Chancellor of Cambridge in the middle of the century exercised an extraordinary influence of a very direct kind such as no modern government in Britain has ever thought to imitate.[46] At the end of the

---

[46] See Winstanley 1922.

century, when the young Mr Pitt was MP for the University of
Cambridge, he was a frequent visitor to Cambridge and a central
figure of the university establishment.[47] The Victorians used
more indirect methods: they set up Royal Commissions, and the
Royal Commissions continued down to the 1920s. There have
been no more since and the historian of the future who sees only
the surface of events might think that an era of public intervention in Cambridge had come to an end. The truth is that the
methods have changed. The Royal Commission of the 1920s
contained several serving Cambridge academics; it was determined to bring change, but by peaceful sympathy not by
external regulation.[48] The Robbins Committee of the early
1960s contained no university officers from Cambridge, and it
ostensibly washed its hands of the ancient universities.[49] One of
its prime purposes was to bring greater equality among British
universities and it spoke harsh things of Oxford and Cambridge;
it told them in plain language to set their own houses in order.
In the event both of the ancient universities greatly benefited
from the ampler funds and the new winds of the 1960s, and
Oxford took the opportunity for fundamental reform: the
Franks Report is a noble monument of that era;[50] beside its
incisive and richly documented proposals for restructuring,
Cambridge's Bridges Report and Graves Report seem like the
tinkering of mechanics, though each helped in its way in a vital
area of change.[51] But the tone of the Robbins Report was a
harbinger of worse to come; since 1979 all British universities,
like Victorian children, have been reminded of their financial
dependence on the parent government, kept on tiptoe wonder-
ing when and how the next blow will fall; and if ever there is a
modest check in the downward spiral of university grants it is
accompanied by a fearsome inquisition or 'selectivity exercise',
or by a stern injunction to new measures of change – the
introduction of assessments for all staff, or of differential salaries
for some.

In exploring the labyrinth of university politics since the

[47] Cf. Brooke 1985, p. 210.   [48] See chap. 11.
[49] Carswell 1985, chaps. 3–4, esp. pp. 39, 42.   [50] Franks 1966.
[51] For Bridges (Lord) see *Reporter* 1961–2, pp. 1073–150; for Graves (W. W.), *Reporter* 1967–8,
    pp. 333–67.

Second World War – politics in the sense of the relation of Cambridge and its fellows to central government – we are exceedingly fortunate to have the guidance of John Carswell, whose lucid book *Government and the Universities in Britain: Programme and Performance 1960–1980*[52] combines urbane presentation by a skilled and experienced historian with the inner knowledge of a former civil servant who witnessed the events he describes from the heart of the Treasury, the DES and the UGC.

He opens by looking back to the 1930s.

> Despite, or perhaps because of, Britain having proportionately fewer university students than any country in Western Europe (let alone the United States) its universities achieved an extraordinary power over the feelings and outlook of those who studied in them . . . I have met many of that generation who repudiated their schooldays with horror and disgust, but none – even the most radical – who really wanted to subvert or destroy the university world he had known[53]

– a circumstance he reckons had important influence in the postwar world. 'In 1937 there were twenty-one universities [in Great Britain] . . . as against forty-four today' – though he goes on to explain in a footnote and an appendix that 'counting universities is a specialised art' and that the total today might be 43 or 46 if one made slightly different distinctions, or 52 if one counted the institutions on the UGC (now UFC) grant list (since the colleges of the University of Wales are there treated as separate entities), or 54 if one included Northern Ireland.[54] In the 1930s there were roughly 50,000 students in British universities, a quarter in London, a quarter in Oxford and Cambridge (5,023 and 5,931 in 1938–9),[55] a quarter in Scotland and a quarter in red-brick – the modern or civic or provincial universities. The civic universities were still very much part of their local communities, their Councils peopled by proud and generous patricians, their students in considerable measure drawn from the local communities. Cambridge by contrast had a much wider catchment area; and of the 5,000 or less overseas students in the

---

[52] Carswell 1985.   [53] Carswell 1985, pp. 2–3.
[54] Carswell 1985, pp. 3, 176. For what follows, see ibid. pp. 3–4.
[55] *UGC Returns 1938–9*, p. 7.

land 70 per cent were in London, Oxford and Cambridge.[56] In Oxford and Cambridge alone arts students predominated – in Oxford 80 per cent, in Cambridge 70 per cent of the total in 1935; elsewhere they comprised roughly half.[57] Since the Royal Commission of the 1920s there had been a steady flow of government funds into Oxford and Cambridge as well as into the other universities; but the total sums issued by the Treasury to the UGC amounted only to about £2,000,000 in the mid-1930s; that is, 'barely a third of total university income, the rest being made up from fees, endowments, and . . . grants from local authorities'.[58] 'In 1937 . . . the UGC was a highly respectable backwater of Whitehall', more than half of whose members were over 80.[59]

From the 1920s to 1939 prices were relatively stable or declining;[60] in the 1940s inflation began to climb, and by 1946 the UGC grant perforce had come to represent more than half the income of the universities. But the real turning point came with the appointment of Sir Keith (later Lord) Murray as chairman of the UGC in 1953.

> In manner large, benevolent, persuasive, in action almost inexhaustible, he was a convinced and consistent expansionist . . . Between 1935 and 1961 the number of university students more than doubled – from 51,000 to 113,000 . . . In 1956, his third year of chairmanship, Murray's capital programme was £3.8 million: for 1963, his last, it was £30.0 million with a promise that it would be still more. No fewer than seven new universities emerged during his chairmanship . . . [and] Dundee was severed from St Andrews, Newcastle from Durham, adding two more . . .[61]

To cap it all, he was the architect of UCCA, the central clearing house for applications. And it was in the same epoch, though the fruit of a different committee, that the system of students' grants was reformed.

In the 1920s it had been a major concern of the Commissioners

---

[56] Carswell 1985, p. 4. But in the 1990s the majority of Cambridge undergraduates come from within a hundred miles or so.
[57] Carswell 1985, pp. 8–9.   [58] Carswell 1985, p. 11.
[59] Carswell 1985, pp. 12–13.   [60] See p. 284.
[61] Carswell 1985, pp. 14–15.

and of those who revised college statutes to make the most of scholarship funds and seek ways of making Cambridge more accessible to those from poorer homes. There were already before the war state and county scholarships which enabled a fair number of undergraduates to enter Cambridge without seeking any substantial support from their parents.[62] From 1945 there were a large number of war veterans on special grants; and as the old system settled down to a peacetime regime in the 1950s, it could be said that although some local authorities were 'more generous than others . . . on the whole very few of those who had secured places at universities were refused support if they lacked other resources'.[63] In 1958 a committee chaired by Sir Colin Anderson was set up to clarify and bring into the light of day a system which had grown up piecemeal over many years. They found that about 90 per cent of those offered places already qualified for support – and they were happily at work before the great expansion of the 1960s and were hardly aware of its shadow. So they recommended that the whole system be replaced by something much simpler: every British subject offered a place at university should be entitled to receive a grant; the committee was divided as to whether there should be a parental means test. In the event, their findings, with the addition of a parental contribution, were accepted in the early 1960s and have been in force ever since. What was hailed as a superlative simplification of law and administration in 1960 – and has been the simplest and, in conception if not in practice, for all students and most parents the most satisfactory system of grants in the world[64] – is now under a cloud, for in the 1980s and 90s simple administration is no longer in fashion, and a great many expensive accountants have been set to work to count the cost. The basic arrangements seem likely to survive for the time being; but from 1990–1 a very complex system of supplementary loans has been attached to them. The event of 1960 took a little time fully to impinge on Cambridge. It was soon observed that the old system of entrance scholarships simply duplicated what the state would now provide; and

---

[62] See p. 359.   [63] Carswell 1985, p. 24.

[64] Not wholly satisfactory, because the *level* of the grant has often seemed arbitrarily low; but the system retained until recently the merit of extreme simplicity. The introduction of loans has brought it into the bureaucratic world of the 1990s.

gradually entrance scholarships were abolished and scholarships altogether became honorary save for those in real financial need. But all colleges still have statutory arrangements and a system of accounts devised in the 1920s on the assumption that scholarship funds were an essential limb of every college's finances. They have been slow to change partly because the system of college accounts is so obscure that the full meaning of it is often not grasped;[65] and it may well be that in the 1990s the colleges will find new and urgent uses for their scholarship funds once more.

Meanwhile by the early 1960s the UGC under Murray's guidance had proposed and won the campaign for the foundation of seven new universities. These grew and flourished in the early and mid-1960s in the era of Robbins and are often supposed to be fruits of Robbins. But indeed they were Murray's children.[66] The Robbins Report of 1963 recommended that six more be founded, and among other grandiose arrangements, that ten colleges of advanced technology grow into universities. The ten CATs duly became universities. But of the six, only one came to pass, at Stirling.[67]

Under the benign and powerful leadership of Lord Robbins, the celebrated economist and the dominating leader of LSE, the Robbins Committee, between 1961 and 1963, played a unique and beneficent role in the history of higher education. It was not a Royal Commission since the universities had long and hideous memories of earlier Royal Commissions, and Sir Keith Murray, one of its principal architects, is said to have feared that it would be transformed into a standing Commission and challenge the UGC.[68] So it was the Prime Minister's Committee. The Anderson Committee had said that every British citizen for whom a place could be found should receive a grant. The core of the message of the Robbins Report of 1963 was that places should be found for all who were qualified; and this liberal doctrine has been (in deed or word) the basic principle of British higher education ever since. It has left two kinds of ambiguity. The first is financial. Anderson gave support to grants, which were to pay

---

[65] See pp.359–63.   [66] See esp. Carswell 1985, p. 18.
[67] Carswell 1985, pp. 60–3.   [68] Carswell 1985, p. 27 and n. 1.

fees and maintenance; Robbins to grants which supported the universities directly. But it is obvious that these two are closely intertwined; that in practice Cambridge University is supported both by government grants and by student fees – and the colleges wholly by fees and their own endowments. Anderson, further-more, related to British students; what of those from overseas? Robbins recommended that fees be raised so that a larger element of support would come from overseas students. This was at first successfully resisted; but the issue has been a bone of contention over the intervening decades, and in due course overseas students' fees have been greatly enlarged by government fiat.[69] The whole issue is now in the melting pot. The only thing one can say with confidence is that any division is arbitrary – anyone seriously engaged in handling university costs on the ground, so to speak, knows well that all attempts to divide and allocate the cost of universities to this cause and that – to research, teaching, adminis-tration and what-have-you – are wholly arbitrary.[70] A very obvious example is library costs, especially in a national library, such as the CUL. It can be confidently said that in the 1960s and 70s senior university staff, and the members of the UGC and its sub-committees, had a fairly clear notion of the nature of the costs with which they were concerned. Since the recent attempts to shift the balance between fees and grants, and schemes and rumours of schemes to undermine the current system altogether, all such clarity has departed; the grounds of funding have grown more complicated; more research funding has been channelled through the research councils; administration has won the first battles – who will win the war is yet to see.

It must be accepted that the arguments of principle in this field are themselves extremely complex. To some, the raising of fees for any students is repugnant since it tends to militate against those from poorer homes, whether the homes be in Britain or Viet-nam. For others, fees which fail to reflect anything like the true cost of education distort the funding arrangements and lead to open and hidden subsidies to overseas students at the expense of

---

[69] Carswell 1985, pp. 110–18.

[70] E.g. the actual division of time and cost of a professor's salary between teaching and research cannot be defined with any precision; nor can the cost e.g. of meetings of the General Board in which considerable quantities of academic time, and so salary, are spent.

the British tax-payer.[71] In the event, fees have risen very sharply, and elaborate arrangements have been made to mitigate the effects for at least a fair number of overseas students. The only certain consequence is an immense amount of complex administration; the true cost of supporting overseas students – and the costs in international good will and academic reputation of not doing so – can never be precisely measured.

Throughout this period and down to the 1970s the UGC in theory planned its grants to the universities by quinquennia, five-year blocks. If the system had worked, the universities would have had long periods of peaceful development in which they knew how much or how little they could spend. In practice the quinquennial system sprung a leak as soon as it was buffeted by substantial expansion in the late 1950s and early 1960s, and sank without trace in the era of rapid inflation of the 1970s. A period of particular dislocation followed the Robbins Report. It appeared at the time to a head of department in a civic university that our plans and estimates had to be revised every six months:[72] first to take account of the new requests coming forward for university expansion, then of the cooler reality of the government grant aimed to support it. Carswell speaks in awed tones of the revision of the quinquennial settlement of 1962–7 to allow for expansion, and of the 'huge capital programme covering eighteen months from April 1964 ... pushed through against passionate Treasury resistance';[73] but within the universities bracing themselves for unparalleled expansion the aid and support they received from the government always seemed inadequate. Cambridge was a little cushioned from these storms, since its expansion was bound to be more measured, controlled by the limits of its colleges. None the less, the university enjoyed to the full the benefits of the new level of grants of the mid-1960s, and felt the pressures for expansion of the Robbins era. The effects can be seen in staff and student numbers: academic staff, 31 December 1970, 938; undergraduates, 1968–9, 8,271; postgraduates, 2,145; 1990–1, academic staff, 31 December 1990, 1,527;

---

[71] But see Carswell 1985, chap. 9, on money. It is striking, however, that the number of overseas students has mounted, not fallen.
[72] I was professor of medieval history at Liverpool from 1956 to 1967.
[73] Carswell 1985, p. 57.

The university and the world

undergraduates, 1989–90, 10,243; postgraduates, 2,975.[74] It can be seen also in the changing face of west Cambridge. The arts faculties had already settled on the Sidgwick Avenue site in the mid-1950s, and looked forward to a new campus as portrayed in Sir Hugh Casson's enchanting water-colour sketches. If the reality has been more sober than the prospect, that is partly due to the failure of imagination on the part of the architects and the academics who briefed them; partly to the need to make the buildings conform to the economies demanded by the UGC when it made grants for buildings. John Carswell asserts of this period that 'building standards were generous';[75] but those of us who struggled to fit together cost limits and reasonable standards of accommodation in that era thought differently; and the immense sums which have had to be spent in the 1980s restoring some of the buildings of the 1960s has suggested to some eyes more expert than mine that false economies were made.[76] To those of us who use these buildings in the 1980s and 90s the most serious shortcomings seem to arise from the space between users and architects. The lecture block on the Sidgwick site comprises lecture rooms which are devoid of the special features of design which make so many lecture rooms of the 60s and 70s in other universities convenient and comfortable for all who use them; and they signally lack provision for the disabled. The History Faculty building is a special case.[77] James Stirling produced in the years 1964–8 the most original, the most controversial, the most admired and the most hated building in modern Cambridge.[78] The original cost was relatively modest; the cost of repairing and restoring it in the 1980s and 90s has been prodigious; and the end is not yet. Architectural students from every corner of the globe have flocked to Cambridge in recent years – not to visit King's

74 The years are chosen as those most clearly represented and analysed in the annual special issues on Student Numbers in the *Reporter* – see 1989–90, p. 4; the figures for staff have kindly been provided by Dr J. Pickles and Mr F. J. Thompson.
75 Carswell 1985, p. 63.
76 A distinguished American architect viewing the History Faculty building at Cambridge (see below) commented that he would have reckoned more expensive materials appropriate for such a design.
77 Professor Sir Geoffrey Elton, who was much involved in its planning, has told me that the notion that it had been reoriented owing to problems about land tenure is substantially correct; but the story often repeated that it had to be designed to meet a very swift deadline is not true.
78 Cf. e.g. Pevsner 1970, pp. 217–18; Brooke, Highfield and Swaan 1988, pp. 322–3.

chapel but to admire and study the Stirling building. Yet in the early 1980s the university seriously debated whether to repair it or demolish it. Whatever one's view of it aesthetically – and it is hard not to admire it, impossible to feel that it makes any concession or contribution to its immediate neighbourhood – it is a monument to the history of a notable faculty. In various forms the History Board and the History Tripos go back to the 1870s.[79] But it was only after 1926 that the History Faculty Board became the master of Cambridge history in the modern sense; and even then it was composed of fellows of colleges who taught in their college rooms. As late as the 1950s, if one asked – when the Faculty Board was not actually in session – where is the Faculty of History? – one good answer was: 'in a typist's bureau in Green Street', where the only permanent member of its staff was at work, half the day, ordering its affairs. The History Faculty building provided at last a framework for a genuine institution, fitted to a university dominated by the faculties; fitted also a little, it must be admitted, to the bureaucratic systems of the 1980s, since it houses the faculty's Secretariat, and the members of the university administrative staff who clarify the faculty's needs and actions with admirable zeal and skill, and guide it through the bureaucratic labyrinth. Its building marks a great change; and it is in several quite different senses a remarkable monument to the movements of the 1960s. The other great monuments of the same era are the scientific laboratories much further west – along the Coton footpath for cyclists, off the Madingley Road for the car. The explosion of scientific teaching and research at last determined the university, guided by the Deer Report of 1966, to abandon the infilling of the Downing Site, or the search for other central spaces such as the chemistry laboratories had occupied in the 1950s.[80] The vets had already colonised some of the land on the western horizon near the University Farm (1954–5), and theoretical astronomy and geology and geophysics had made a start in the mid-1960s.[81] After 1966 the new Cavendish Laboratory was built in this region, making it a scientific nucleus as vital as the Downing Site itself.[82]

---

[79] See pp. 228–32.   [80] See pp. 200–1; Rawle 1985, p. 202.
[81] On the Veterinary School see Spratling 1989.   [82] See p. 193.

Fig. 18 The Backs from the air: in the foreground the History Faculty, with Caius' Harvey Court beyond and Queens' new building in the distance – from the west (taken in 1980 before the third phase of the Queens' building)

The Robbins era brought much change, but no major restructuring to Cambridge. It brought new ideas, and a major initiative to reconcile university and colleges in a human sense so as to provide fellowships for the very numerous university officers who had little contact with the colleges; a major initiative too to provide adequately in the colleges for the postgraduates and research workers who had come to form a much more substantial part of the academic community than before – especially by the foundation of new colleges.[83] In Oxford it witnessed the era of

[83] See pp. 573–82.

Fig. 19 The Backs from the air (1975): the Queens' new building (before the third phase), Harvey Court and the History Faculty from the south-east

Franks: a major report (1966) leading to substantial change in the structure of the university and a serious attempt to heal the breach which rapid growth had brought there too between college and university. In Cambridge the Bridges Report (1962) helped to provide fellowships for the underprivileged and inspire the founding of graduate colleges and similar moves; the Graves Report (1967) tightened the screws in the central committees and administration.[84] But the Cambridge tradition, unlike the Oxford, has been to tinker; and this seems to be continuing in the

[84] See n. 51.

549

Wass Report (1989) and its aftermath.[85] I myself left Cambridge in 1956 to return in 1977. Among the admirable fare provided at the orientation session for new staff when I returned was a lecture on the relations between colleges and university by one of the most experienced of Cambridge tutors. I could not detect a single word that he uttered which would not have been as true in 1956 as in 1977. Cambridge was in many ways a very different place; it was larger, the faculties and the labs were much stronger; the place of women had been transformed; new colleges had been founded and a great number of homeless staff provided with fellowships. But the structures were still – to an astonishing degree – firmly in place.

The colleges remain the home of the undergraduates – and in a sense of the whole community. This meant that any expansion in the Robbins era had to be accepted by the colleges as well as by the university. There was much discussion in the colleges as to the effect on their community life of any expansion, and especially of a rapid and extensive one; and it was evident enough that there were limits to what was possible. Within those limits Cambridge colleges responded generously; but it involved extensive building. In the 1960s some colleges reckoned that too many of their undergraduates had to live out - most aimed to provide them with two out of three years in college sets; and any expansion of numbers must involve new building. In the 1970s the old established lodging houses tended to disappear and 'living out' came to mean living in college hostels scattered about the town, often old lodging houses adapted to new purposes. These changes reflected changing attitudes; above all, the emancipated students and the motherly lodging-house keepers came to agree ill together. Old restrictions were irksome and contrary to the new ethos; the lodging-house keepers cared nothing for novelty and were not prepared to have lodgers who came and went at all hours with all manner of company. So both social change and expansion have compelled the colleges to provide more accommodation themselves; and the consequences of this can be seen in a notable era of college building, which expanded the campuses of many colleges and has in the long run drastically diminished what

---

[85] See below, pp. 564–6.

had been some of the most desirable regions of Cambridge domestic dwelling.[86] Some colleges had already begun their expansion in the 1950s and early 60s. Queens' appealed to its alumni in 1957 for support for Basil Spence's imaginative Erasmus building, which was completed in 1960.[87] A richer college like Caius was able to build its Harvey Court in 1960–2 from its own resources. But the greater expansion of the mid and late 1960s owed much to a remarkable benefactor, Sir Humphrey Cripps, who financed the first stages of a vast expansion in St John's (1963–7),[88] provided an ample extension to Selwyn – a college which could have done little from its own resources – and has made possible over the last two decades a much more ambitious extension of Queens' than the college could have planned by any other means. The alumni have helped to furnish the rooms and in other costs; but Cripps has provided the building. By such means some colleges have been able to meet the demands for expansion without sacrificing the standard of living of the inmates.

It is often alleged that the rapid expansion of the 1960s led to a dilution of quality, both of staff and of students. It is certainly the case that many of us in the provincial universities in the early 1960s, as we contemplated the demands which would be made for more postgraduates leading to more academic staff, wondered if it were possible to maintain the quality of the recruits; and it has often been alleged that we did not. Here is a characteristic statement from a shrewd observer: 'There would be an appreciable margin of staff recruited at a lower standard occupying posts for the next forty years; and long before that it would become more difficult than it had ever been for the most brilliant graduates to obtain posts.'[89] The second part of the prophecy has been most fearfully fulfilled: rapid expansion followed by stagnation followed by contraction has produced just such a consequence. But the first is in my view very misleading. Such impressions are subjective, and my own – based on experience in three contrasting universities and observation in many more – is

---

[86] See p. 281.   [87] Twigg 1987, pp. 373–6.
[88] Rawle 1985, p. 135.
[89] Carswell 1985, p. 49.

Fig. 20 St John's College, new buildings of the nineteenth and twentieth centuries, and the Backs: taken in 1970, before the Fisher building of the 1980s

very different. Mistakes were made and the quality of appointments has varied; that has been true in all epochs; it is misleading to exaggerate the quality of the appointments of the 1940s and 1950s. After 1945 numerous appointments were made with great rapidity. The 1960s were a creative era in the British universities and this inspired unusual efforts; it also offered unusual opportunities; and the academic profession – with higher public esteem (for a short time), better pay, much more mobility, much more opportunity for creative work in founding new universities and refurbishing old ones, and better funds for research – was attractive in a way it had not been before and has not been since.

A close examination of the qualifications of entrants to the profession in the 1960s – at least in my own field – does not suggest any notable reduction of quality in the 1960s; rather the reverse. A part of the malaise in the universities in the 80s and 90s is due to the desperate shortage of opportunity in many fields for the best young recruits. But there is much malaise of a different kind: there are many posts, including many chairs, in British universities unfilled, even a few in Cambridge. This is because the academic profession has become much less attractive for all sorts of reasons in which morale and esteem play an important part. In some subjects, such as law and mathematics, there are powerful attractions outside the academic world; in all, the attraction of business, or of some better paid profession, is much greater than in the 60s. There is a basic problem of finance: a young lecturer cannot afford to buy a house in Cambridge on his current salary – nor, be it said, can a professor coming from a less prosperous region hope to buy a house of comparable amenity. There are many grounds for anxiety today in the profession unaffected by the survival of the dinosaurs of the 60s. And although the Robbins Report and the movements of the 1960s made serious and very successful efforts to create a new equality among British universities, it led to no diminution of the traditional standards of Cambridge. To those of us who felt that the efforts to make British universities more equal in esteem and achievement was one of the most creative aspects of the 1960s it was a tragedy to see the revival of class distinctions among universities in the 1980s; in this perspective the whole selectivity exercise is anathema.

The selectivity exercise is the end product of the slow and steady erosion of university independence since 1963. From the first the universities had to pay a penalty for their short-lived prosperity. The old UGC had been a gentle buffer state; the universities were left very much alone to pursue their destinies. By a normal convention the Public Accounts Committee was not interested in university accounts since the government grants amounted to less than half their income; and as this margin was reached and passed a strenuous resistance was mounted against any such interference, supported by the Robbins Committee itself. But from then on it was an anomaly, and in 1965 the committee once again sought access to the universities, and 'the walls of Jericho fell'.[90] Meanwhile the old Ministry of Education had been expanded and extended, and then replaced by the Department of Education and Science, with a Secretary of State and two ministers under him for education and for science; the UGC was subjected to more continual scrutiny; and the DES – while uttering squeamish phrases about university autonomy – sought to undermine it. In 1967 the Secretary of State announced 'an assumed fee income' for overseas students, assumed that is in any grant allocations.[91] The UGC and the universities were not consulted; the age of direct government had come. At the time this announcement sounded like the last trumpet; looking back it seems almost inevitable that the scale of government funding of the 1960s should lead to increased intervention. But the fear that more, much more, was to come, was only too precisely fulfilled. The DES has since used the issue of fees and their levels as an occasion for intervening in the minutest details of university and college finance. In the 1920s college statutes were devised to ensure that students' fees should be set so that the tutorial account – which provides for the educational activities of each college – could be normally in balance. Since the late 1970s fees are determined by the DES, in negotiation with the colleges, and these clauses have become almost nugatory.

The freedom of action of the UGC has been eroded also from another angle. One of the great anxieties of the 1960s was to increase the number of students studying science and technology; and in this region, so far as the universities were concerned, may be said to lie one of the great failures of that epoch. But serious attempts were made to provide funds for research where they were genuinely needed, and under an act of 1965 the Science Research Council and its sisters for medicine, agriculture, the natural environment – and eventually for the social sciences – were set up to replace the old Department of Scientific and Industrial Research.[92] Only the humanities were forgotten; and they received some compensation as arrangements were made for the British Academy to handle government grants in this region. Whether that rather geriatric body is ideally suited to this task has

---

[90] Carswell 1985, p. 86.   [91] Carswell 1985, p. 106.
[92] Carswell 1985, pp. 58–9.

been and is the subject of debate; an aging FBA can only say that the Academy is not, and cannot pretend to be, representative of the younger echelons of the profession; but it has a record in collecting and administering funds which compares rather favourably with the variable fortunes of the SSRC, now ESRC. These research councils cannot indeed claim to be representative in any truer sense than the UGC or the UFC. They are managed by committees of academics who reflect a range of interest and skill; they live under constant pressure from the government and the DES. They are for ever threatened with reform. To maximise their utility and justify their existence they have grown increasingly dictatorial towards the universities. In the 1980s they have attempted to reorganise the whole system of university research: universities which allow their research students to take many years to complete their doctorates are liable to find themselves under penalties, losing the right to receive student grants at all. This is a peremptory solution to the old debate whether a Ph.D. should be a finished piece of work or simply the product of three years' research or so. I personally see all sorts of grounds for preferring the second solution, and to that extent am on the side of the research councils; but their arbitrary dealings have destroyed a major pillar of university autonomy.

Such were some of the more distant consequences of the heady years 1963–5. But we have strayed far ahead. For at that time, though all of us involved in university administration realised that we were bound to years of intensive hard work, and although the wiser heads among our elders constantly warned us that we should be sold down the river in the end by the politicians, we lived in a world of expansion and hope, and creativity.

Into this hopeful world there broke with the minimum of warning the student rebellions of 1967–8. The Commons Committee found little evidence of international influence on the British students; and John Twigg, in his searching study of student rebellion in Queens' College, Cambridge, says that 'The suddenness and vehemence of the protest [in 1968] suggests strongly that there had been a good deal of discontent simmering in the College for some time.'[93] But for those of us who witnessed it – in my

---

[93] Above, pp. 522–3; Twigg 1987, pp. 406–7.

case in Liverpool and London – the lack of preparation and warning was one of its most marked features; and if, looking back twenty years later, we examine the timing of the revolt in different quarters of the globe, there can be little doubt that revolt in Britain and in Cambridge was a response to an international movement.[94] Student insurrection first appeared in Britain in the LSE in 1966.[95] At that time in Liverpool activist students were demanding a say in the management of halls of residence, and perhaps in university affairs more widely. We pay the bills, ran the argument, we have a right to a say in the management. As a substantial political claim, this was a novelty; and not a very attractive one to those of us who really paid the bills through our taxes. A much more plausible argument lay in the new awareness of adulthood which was a genuine part of the ethos of the 60s. And to those of us who had been campaigning in undemocratic universities for junior academic staff to have a greater share in decision-making, the sudden overweening demands of the students had an ironic ring, especially in those rather numerous cases when they won a measure of assent from university establishments which had shown little interest in junior staff. But in the course of 1967–8 many academics of moderately liberal opinions, as well as those of the left who were drawn into the overtly political elements in the strife, came to feel and utter a measure of support for many of the students' demands. In due course staff–student committees were set up within departments and student observers established on many if not most of the committees governing universities. In the present state of knowledge Cambridge appears to have been exceptionally slow to accept these measures.[96] A Student Representative Council was formed about 1964 and converted into an Assembly in 1969; in 1970 the Cambridge Students' Union was born. There was much argu-

---

[94] See above, pp. 523–6.   [95] Caute 1988, p. 302.
[96] A Consultation Committee of 7 senior members, 2 graduates, 7 undergraduates, was formed in 1968 (for this and the genesis of CSU see *Devlin Report, Reporter* 1972–3, Special No. 12, pp. 8–15). Students became members of Faculty Boards – save for 'reserved business', i.e. mainly confidential and financial items – under Statute c.III of 1973–4 (*Reporter* 1973–4, pp. 338, 1000); final approval 4 Dec. 1974 (*Reporter* 1974–5, pp. 428–9). They entered College Councils etc. piecemeal in the 1970s and 80s: see below. In Caius they were occasionally invited to discuss agenda of mutual interest in the 1970s; student observers only became a normal element in College Council meetings in the 1980s.

ment and much consultation; and many staff–student committees
or meetings were held. In the course of these much of the
structure of traditional discipline, from gate hours to guest rules,
from the wearing of gowns to attendance at formal hall, were
eroded or abolished. But the Cambridge colleges, like ancient
Athens or modern Switzerland, were democracies rather strictly
defined; they had and have governing bodies of fellows; there was
no customary or statutory place for wider democracy. Thus in
Queens', for all the furore of argument between 1968 and 1970, it
was not until 1977–8 that student observers were established on
the governing body;[97] some colleges had them earlier, some later;
but here as elsewhere the oligarchical university bodies, and
especially the faculties, were more readily adapted to an active
student presence than the colleges.

In February 1970 the Greek Tourist Board held a 'Greek
Week' in Cambridge in wintry weather culminating in a Greek
dinner in the Garden House Hotel on Friday the 13th.[98] The riot
which ensued was the one outbreak of serious violence in
Cambridge in the wake of the student uprisings of 1968. A party
of about 200 students, observed by several dons, picketed the
entrance to the hotel, supported by a loud-speaker in a conve-
niently placed fellow's room in Peterhouse. When dinner was
under way they passed into the garden, walked through the snow,
hammered on the windows, and jumped on the roof. When a
member of the hotel staff turned a hose on them, snowballs gave
place to stones and bricks. In the riot which ensued a great deal of
damage was done, two policemen were injured, and Dr Charles
Goodhart, deputy proctor, was hit on the head by a brick and had
to retire to hospital. This assault shocked many of the demonstrators – most of whom had apparently set out aiming at
peaceful protest – and reaction in the crowd and police trun-
cheons brought the riot to an end.

The incident was brief and discreditable; but the circumstances
and the reactions vividly reflect the state of opinion and the

[97] Twigg 1987, p. 431.
[98] This is based on an admirably clear and accurate account given me by Charles Goodhart, who
also generously lent me his file of correspondence and press cuttings, containing the less clear
and less accurate newspaper accounts. The details of students sentenced are from *The Times* and
The Daily Telegraph of 4 July 1970. Professor Owen Chadwick's denial of 'the evil influence' of
senior on junior members was reported in *The Daily Telegraph*, 7 July 1970.

conflicting attitudes of the late 60s and early 70s. Not unnaturally the university authorities were more sensitive than the civic community to the danger involved in the Greek dinner. The Greek regime of that era seemed to many a revival of the fascism which the Second World War had been fought to quell; and left-wing activists found an echoing response in the minds of many young students of a variety of political views. Some young dons, and a small number of older ones, including a Danish couple who remembered Hitler's occupation, joined in revulsion against a celebration which seemed to condone an evil regime. Of all this the proctors were aware: they warned the police and turned out in force themselves. At the outset only two policemen were present, and by the time a force of seventy had been collected from a wide area round Cambridge the demonstration had got out of hand. There is little evidence that professional agitators from afar were among the crowd; but a minority of activists among the demonstrators carried 'mole fuses' (sulphur candles for attacking moles), which they lit and threw into the restaurant, turning the event into an ugly riot.

In the sequel many of the students were deeply ashamed, and Dr Goodhart received heartfelt messages of sympathy from young as well as old. Six students were convicted of riotous or unlawful assembly and sent to prison for up to eighteen months by Mr Justice Melford Stephenson – and two more to Borstal; and the judge observed that these sentences – reckoned severe by some cool observers – would have been sharper but that a group of dons had been an evil influence upon them. This was denied by the dons, who were loyally supported by the Vice-Chancellor, Professor Owen Chadwick, who was deeply shocked, but rejected the charge that senior members had corrupted the young. Further afield, Conservative critics condemned the affair and all the neutral witnesses without making any visible attempt to understand the feelings which had inspired it; and Socialists, within and without the student community, continued to regard the Greek Tourist Board and the hotel as limbs of a fascist beast. Political alignment is rarely the path to mutual understanding.

The incident left bitter memories. There had been a number of other demos and sit-ins and expressions of solidarity with LSE. None was so violent as the Garden House affair; and the unpreparedness of the police in February 1970 – however unimaginative it seems to us – illustrates the underlying confidence of the civic authorities that Cambridge students were noisy but not dangerous. This view passed away for a while in 1970, and Cambridge became regarded as one of those homes of idle layabouts whose notoriety seemed to some to justify the sharp reaction of Conservative politicians against the generosity to the universities and their students inspired by the Macmillan government in the early 1960s.

In February 1972 a mass meeting was held in the Faculty of Economics to protest against the General Board's refusal to accept some proposed liberalisation of the economics exam programme. The protesters proceeded to occupy the Old Schools; a court of enquiry was set up, chaired by the High Steward of the university, the eminent retired judge Lord Devlin; and the *Devlin Report* surveyed existing measures for student participation and proposed some new ones. Since about 1964 there had been a Student Representative Council – refurbished in 1969 as an Assembly; and in 1970 replaced by the Cambridge Students' Union. The Union Society was, and is, a prestigious debating society whose presidency has led on to thrones in Westminster and Lambeth. In contrast the CSU, now CUSU, is in the image of the student guilds and unions which have long been an integral part of the modern universities, and also a pressure group. Consultative committees began to grow up in the late 1960s and early 1970s; and the *Devlin Report* urged some form of student representation on university bodies.[99] In the sequel they came to be represented on faculty boards and by observers on the Council of the Senate – all for business not reserved on the grounds that it was confidential to senior members.

In 1972 the thinking of the post-Robbins era and the new look of the 1970s met in a striking amalgam in the White Paper *Education: a Framework for Expansion*, which was among the first fruits of Mrs Thatcher's term as Secretary of State for Education and Science. Its projections for students participating in higher education were firmly based on the Robbins principle of free access for the qualified; its arithmetic went far beyond Robbins

---

[99] See n. 96 and *Devlin Report* (ibid.), esp. pp. 8–9, 11–15, 18–19, 76–7.

and produced a total (supposedly for 1981) of 750,000 students in higher education compared with Robbins' figure of 558,000. But it envisaged two major differences. Ever since a celebrated speech by the Labour Secretary of State, Anthony Crosland, in 1965, it had been accepted government doctrine that higher education had two sectors, the first the universities, the second the polytechnics and colleges of further education. The future of the polytechnics was still fairly obscure in 1972, but it was assumed (not entirely correctly) that higher education would in the short or long run be much cheaper in polys than in universities. There was also a determined, if at first modest, effort to cut university costs: the 'unit' cost of a student was reckoned to be cut from £1,070 to about £1,000 in the second year of the new quinquennium (1973–4).[100] The Treasury and the civil servants in the DES and the UGC seem to have taken note of the element of extravagance in these projections, and in retrospect John Carswell, who lays great stress on the effect of student rebellion in damping public enthusiasm for higher education, reckons the projected student numbers needlessly high.[101] Within the universities it was the economies which were most apparent; they hardly amounted to a foretaste of the 1980s, but throughout the 70s universities felt a braking effect: the expansion of the mid-1960s had accustomed them to expanding finance and to planning which depended on some measure of expansion and freedom of manoeuvre. This steadily disappeared in the growing stringency and the galloping inflation of the 70s. Already by the end of 1973 the government had leaned on the UGC to tell the universities to prepare for cuts in student numbers and finance; and although the losses were partially restored in 1974,[102] it was only too apparent within the universities that they lived in a more stringent world. Meanwhile the independence of the UGC was further eroded by a series of ministerial decisions on the level of fees. It was not till after 1979 that it was determined that overseas students should pay a fee supposed to represent the full cost of their places; but the system of levers which would eventually bring the fees to that peak was now firmly in place.[103]

---

[100] Carswell 1985, pp. 139–42.   [101] Carswell 1985, pp. 140–1.
[102] Carswell 1985, p. 147.   [103] Carswell 1985, p. 155.

One crucial prop of the Robbins era remained. It was accepted doctrine, so far as my personal observation went – both as a long-serving member of the UGC Arts Sub-Committee in the 1960s and early 1970s and from conversation with full members of the UGC – that however much the government might put on the brakes, there would be no actual cuts. The level of UGC spending in real terms would be preserved. This was based on a curious mixture of wishful thinking and the give-and-take of political discussion over the later 1960s and early 1970s. It may indeed have been a fantasy of some members of the UGC. But it was deeply held and widely assumed. In 1979 there came to power a government with no respect for such assumptions – radical in its outlook, deliberately seeking to eradicate hopes and fantasies and presuppositions which prevented *de fundo* rethinking of public expenditure. Mrs Thatcher and her colleagues were wedded first and last to the attack on inflation, and to the doctrine that public expenditure is a major component in inflation; they also aimed at radical cuts in taxation. From 1979 on grants to universities could no longer be settled by leisurely discussions preceding quinquennial settlements. Indeed the quinquennia had been largely fictional since 1963, first because of the rapid reappraisals of the Robbins era, then because of the inflation of the 1970s. After 1979 they were swept from the drawing boards; every few months the government made new prognostications from its current studies of the crystal ball of what can be spared, what is appropriate, for the next few months in the universities. It would be quite misleading to say that the policies of 1979 and after have reflected a lack of care or concern for higher education; it seems from what has consistently occurred, that it is simply that all such considerations must be subordinated to the central aim which has justified a decade of radical 'conservative' government, which involves cuts in public spending all over the board. But there has been more to it than this. First of all, it has been a radical government indeed; that is to say it has deliberately forgotten its predecessors. It was a Conservative government in 1963 which welcomed the Robbins Report and took the first steps to give it life and being. The wiser heads in the universities were sceptical – the politicians, they said, will betray us. But the universities responded magnificently to the challenge – they had indeed little alternative if they wished to answer crying public needs, to play their share in the aspirations of the decade, and to receive any part of the rewards the government was offering. None the less, they ignored the warning signs and threw themselves into an immensely complex and difficult operation – not with perfect success, but in a creative mood which succeeded beyond what many of us had thought conceivable in 1963. It was peculiarly galling to find a Conservative government in the 1980s appearing most precisely to fulfil the gloomiest predictions of 1963. But as historians we must reject such thoughts: the links between the political party which governed and fell from power in 1963 and the party which has ruled since 1979 are tenuous.

Furthermore, Mrs Thatcher and her ministers developed in the 1980s the doctrine that all the established professions needed reform. They tackled the teachers, the doctors, and (greatly daring) the lawyers; they would have tackled the Church if they could. Naturally university teachers have not been exempt. Let us ponder three limbs in the government's onslaught on the universities. First it is evidently reckoned that many university teachers are not very good at their job: the insistence on appraisals, and on bonuses for the more active or efficient, are the outward sign of this principle.[104] Next, their salary structure takes too little account of market forces. The universities complain that they cannot compete with the universities of America when they appoint to posts in certain disciplines. The answer is plain – they should keep funds in reserve for such appointments, not try to pay all academics equally. Third, they do not conduct their affairs efficiently. In modern government, questions need to be asked and answered with great promptitude; one cannot wait for the cumbersome round of university committees – least of all for the traditional Cambridge ritual of consultations and committees and boards, ending in a report to the Regent House which must then be discussed and graced and possibly voted on. This kind of criticism took material shape in the Jarratt Report of 1985, whose main findings the universities have been adjured (a stronger word would be appropriate) to implement.[105] This was

---

[104] See p. 535.
[105] The Committee of Vice-Chancellors and Principals' *Report of the Steering Committee for Efficiency Studies in Universities*, 1985 (chairman, Sir A. Jarratt).

severely critical of the slow-moving hierarchy of committees in
most British universities and propounded a much more managerial style, with more power delegated to smaller bodies and in the
hands of senior executives. It is a trumpet call for the managerial
university, and has been answered in many places. In the modern
universities in the 1930s – still in large measure in the 1950s – great
power resided in the hands of vice-chancellors and university
councils; and heads of departments commonly enjoyed dictatorial powers. It is a similar pattern which Jarratt and its advocates
have reimposed on many universities in the 1980s. The chief
difference seems to me a much franker acknowledgement of
oligarchy; under the colourable pretext that the university's
policies have to respond with great rapidity to every call – and
every cut – dictated by the UGC or the UFC or the DES, a
greater concentration of decision-making than ever before has
been gathered into the hands of vice-chancellors and small
oligarchies of senior professors and administrators. At the same
time some of the hierarchy of committees has been pruned. The
Jarratt Report claimed to be the first in a series of 'Efficiency
Studies', and when I first read it I naively sought in it a definition
of 'efficiency'. There is none. It is simply assumed that efficiency
in a university is identical with efficiency in a business concern or
a government department. I can understand this simple confusion
arising in the minds of the experienced business men who formed
a part of the committee; but it was a strange and striking feature
of the 1980s that it should have imposed itself on the majority of
the Jarratt Committee who were academic administrators. I can
only repeat that the managerial university as I knew it in
Liverpool in the 1950s was the most inefficient model I have
encountered, since a large proportion of a highly trained and able
staff could not participate in management or government.

In Cambridge we live in a world a little apart. The pressures
fall on Cambridge as on all other universities, but movement is
slower. A democratic university finds it more difficult to adjust to
managerial models than the hierarchical. But it is only a half truth
to call Cambridge democratic. The growing power of the central
committees, especially of the Council of the Senate and the
General Board, has brought a strongly undemocratic element into
university life, and an ever-growing tension between administra-

tors and committees on the one hand and the Regent House on the other. This was one of many grounds for growing dissatisfaction in the mid and late 1980s with current structures, and a large number of members of the Regent House signed a request for a formal investigation into the government of the university which issued in the establishment of the Wass Committee – under the chairmanship of Sir Douglas Wass – which reported in 1989.[106] It has recommended much detailed restructuring of central committees; some concentration of power in the hands of the Council of the Senate, some decentralisation and delegation of matters of lesser moment. Above all it recommends that a long-term Vice-Chancellor be appointed, and that the wings of the Regent House be clipped: that many matters of urgent university business be handled wholly by the Council or some lesser authority; that the Regent House should only be able to debate issues not specifically laid before it if a hundred signatures be collected (in place of the present ten). The Wass Committee was also asked to investigate the relations of the colleges and the university; but here it contented itself with fairly numerous minor suggestions and an earnest adjuration to the colleges to do it themselves.

We are now deep in the realms of current politics, and the historian must lay down his pen. By the end of 1991 many of the proposals of Wass have been accepted: some restructuring of central committees and other changes have been set in motion, and the Regent House has decided, by a large majority, to have a 'long-term' Vice-Chancellor; it has settled his or her term as five years renewable to seven. In recent centuries the Vice-Chancellor had always (in fact) been a head of house: between the sixteenth and the nineteenth centuries he presided over the central committee of the university, the meeting of heads; and after the reforms of the mid-nineteenth century, he continued to preside over the Council of the Senate, on which the heads were strongly represented – as well as over every other syndicate and committee he had a mind to. But he always remained the head of his college; and in recent generations he has reigned for two years, no less and no more. This has been a crucial element in binding colleges and university together; but it has been widely held in

[106] *Reporter* 1988–9, pp. 613–46.

recent years that it weakens the links of the university and the world; and in particular, that Cambridge cannot play its full role in the Committee of Vice-Chancellors and Principals, now a crucial organ of university government in the nation at large, since its representative changes too frequently. In response to this view, Oxford changed the term of its Vice-Chancellor from two to four years after the Franks Report of 1966, while still reserving the office to heads of house. From 1 October 1992 Cambridge will have a Vice-Chancellor who cannot be a head of house, though he may be a fellow. The pace of change has been happily mitigated by the choice of Sir David Williams, who has long been a head of house, has already served three years as Vice-Chancellor, and will serve four more. It can be held that this reflects long and deep thought about the relation of Cambridge and the modern world; but there is no evidence either in the Wass Report or elsewhere that its effects on the relations between the colleges and the university have been deeply considered. That is the central feature of the strange constitution of the University of Cambridge, and may well be a central issue of shifting debate in the decade to come.

Meanwhile, another major new feature of the constitution was by no means in such accord with the recommendations of Wass. It has been observed that since 1570 the Caput, and since the mid-nineteenth century the Council of the Senate, have had absolute control (in law) over the framing of proposals to be placed before the Senate or the Regent House. A statute is now in the making, in accordance with the wishes of the Regent House, to allow a certain number (not yet finally settled) of members of the Regent House to initiate proposals, so to speak, from the floor of the House.

Many other changes signal the radical world of the 1980s and 1990s. Perhaps as important as Wass in the present and immediate future is the immense effort in fund-raising, set in movement by the Cambridge Foundation and the University Development Office.

Yet it is doubtful whether a future historian looking back on this era will be more struck by the changes or the continuities of Cambridge life. As a final illustration of these continuities – to set some of the changes in perspective – the supreme office in the university hierarchy, that of Chancellor, has altered little, if at all. The days when the university was ruled by the Chancellor, be he Thomas Cromwell or Lord Burleigh, have departed long ago; so has the era of the duke of Newcastle, who in the mid-eighteenth century manipulated Cambridge politics like a microcosm of Westminster. Recent Chancellors have reflected the role of Cambridge and its image in the world: Smuts, the great international statesman; Marshal of the Royal Air Force Lord Tedder, the war hero; Lord Adrian, supreme in his day among Cambridge physiologists, symbol of its academic standards. The Chancellor reigns, he no longer rules: his function is largely ceremonial – but not entirely, for, since the days of Prince Albert, he has been often a benevolent public figure deeply interested in the welfare of his charge. And that is very clearly the inheritance of the present Chancellor, Prince Philip, duke of Edinburgh. His wife is Queen; and he plays a role in Cambridge which is a microcosm of hers in Britain at large, dedicated, involved, concerned; but government lies elsewhere. Thus at the summit of the university, as in the colleges, old patterns survive.

Chapter 18

THE NEW COLLEGES

FITZWILLIAM AND CHURCHILL

In 1800 Cambridge acquired its seventeenth college; and in the 1870s and 1880s it was widely held there were too many: schemes for amalgamation were aired, and two nearly succeeded; meanwhile Girton, Newnham and Selwyn were founded.[1] Between the early 1950s and the late 1980s seven more were founded or won recognition, and there are four other societies, not yet full colleges, which have achieved status in the university in these decades. In part this reflects expansion of numbers: the older colleges could not absorb, or thought they could not absorb, the growing numbers; new homes were needed for them. But expansion took many forms: there were more university teachers, more postgraduates, more undergraduates. In the late nineteenth century the anxious search for ways to bring young men to Cambridge who could not afford the normal fees had led to the formation of Fitzwilliam House as a centre for non-collegiate students, and Selwyn College for poor Anglicans.[2] In the 1950s the old financial pressures had weakened: it was becoming easier for the less well off to get grants; the special character of Selwyn hampered its full acceptance within the Cambridge framework. Both colleges began to tread the path to full collegiate status. For Selwyn this meant a great expansion and new buildings. For Fitzwilliam it made possible the move to a new site in Huntingdon Road. Here Sir Denys Lasdun and Richard MacCormac have designed a group of buildings recognisably collegiate, of dark brown engineering brick, returning, like

[1] See pp. 93–5, chap. 9.
[2] See p. 92. On Fitzwilliam House and college, see Grave 1983.

567

most of the modern collegiate buildings, to the old conventional pattern of staircases, not corridors, as the guiding domestic principle. In 1966 Fitzwilliam received its royal charter as a full college. Meanwhile it had become accepted doctrine that the special need of the postwar universities was to expand in science and technology; and Churchill College was founded to meet this, yet also to commemorate the architect of British survival in the war with a college of traditional pattern and of substantial size.

In the mid-1950s Winston Churchill came to regret that he had done so little to meet Lord Cherwell's urgent demands for more technologists.[3] Sir John Colville, his private secretary, Lord Cherwell and others worked on this, and Colville devised a scheme for an English equivalent of MIT, the Massachusetts Institute of Technology, reviving an idea which had won a good deal of support some years earlier. Colville consulted Lord Todd, who 'pointed out that it was the people in an institution like MIT that mattered'; that Oxford and Cambridge still tended to attract 'the best brains'; that there was already a large engineering school in Cambridge, and that one might found a new college concentrating on science and technology, which could be a centre for research and links with industry. Todd, the great scientist who was also a deeply committed Tory politician, was a natural catalyst – one of several, no doubt – in the curious transformation of Winston Churchill into an apostle of science and technology in Cambridge. One of those Todd brought in to join the discussion was Sir John Cockcroft, the eminent nuclear physicist.[4] In 1958 a public announcement was made that the college was to be founded as a monument to Churchill's heroic achievements; Churchill himself appointed Cockcroft the first master; and a highly successful appeal was launched. As senior tutor of the new college, J. S. Morrison, later to be first president of Wolfson, had his first taste of founding new colleges.[5] He was a classical scholar helping to found a college predominantly scientific and technological; but Morrison is adept at harnessing divergent elements in the traditions of Cambridge. In more recent years he

---

[3] Gilbert 1988, p. 1131; for what follows, see ibid. pp. 1263, 1267–8, 1284, 1352; Todd 1983, pp. 143–8; Morrison 1991.

[4] Todd 1983, p. 144. Cockcroft was appointed first master by the founder; thereafter it was to be a crown appointment. Cf. Oliphant and Penney 1968, pp. 183–6.

[5] Morrison 1991, esp. pp. 79–84.

has set the Cambridge tradition of rowing to work to explain the nature of the ancient Greek trireme; in Churchill he helped to unite old and new concepts of a Cambridge college.

Churchill himself took a keen interest in the progress of the college. 'I have a letter here from a woman', he announced one day, 'a very interesting letter. She says we ought to have women in the college. Seems quite a good idea – why don't we have women in the college?' He was told that if so he might have to return some of the money collected for the appeal, and he pursued the idea no further;[6] it was only a flash of summer lightning. The idea of a mixed college still seemed remote in the later 1950s.

Meanwhile the college was a grand Churchillian conception, aping Trinity in the extent of its campus – 42 acres – and the scale of its buildings, whose design crowned the career of Richard Sheppard.[7] It had copied Trinity too in the curious provision that its future masters be chosen by the crown. It aimed to comprise 60 fellows (at that date a prodigious number: there are now 100) and 540 students. From the first there were many postgraduates – there are now 200 of them – and there was soon ample provision of flats for visiting scholars. Churchill was designed to combine the old world of college courts and staircases, of hall and Combination Rooms, with a bias, novel for Cambridge, towards science and industry. Like the best of the continental Technische Hochschulen, or like the California Institute of Technology, it has an element of the humanities, wide in range and distinction. Thus Churchill combined a number of the impulses of the 1950s and 60s; and it was to be one of the first men's colleges to admit women; but not till 1972. Till then, they had to seek their salvation elsewhere.

NEW HALL AND LUCY CAVENDISH

As in the 1860s and 70s, so in the era after the Second World War a common movement to improve the lot of women in Cambridge led, not to the foundation of a single college, but of two. It

---

6 Todd 1983, pp. 146–7. Lady Churchill is said to have supported the plea for women (Oliphant and Penney 1968, p. 185).

7 Pevsner 1970, pp. 183–6; Rawle 1985, pp. 156–7.

is fair to say that the relations between the dining club which was eventually to found Lucy Cavendish and the association which sponsored New Hall were much closer than between Newnham and Girton. Kate Bertram, second president of Lucy Cavendish, was for twelve years secretary of the New Hall Association.[8] The difference between the two foundations is of great interest to the student of Cambridge history, for it reflects in a fascinating way Cambridge attitudes and the special problems of the 1950s and 60s. New Hall was founded by a committee; Lucy Cavendish grew out of a dining club. The new men's colleges reflect similar aspects of Cambridge life: Wolfson College was founded by the activity of university bodies; Darwin College was planned at an informal meeting of a committee of college bursars; Clare Hall grew up within the womb of Clare College.[9] The Women's Dining Club reflected already in the 1950s the needs and anxieties which were to be the main impulses among the men of Cambridge behind the new foundations of the 1960s. There was a significant and growing number of women who held university posts, or did some college teaching, and so were members of the Regent House, but who had no fellowships. They formed a dining club; and among their aims was the advancement of women's education, and to promote the foundation of a new college for women. Their hope indeed was that the new college would grow organically out of the Dining Group – that some or most or all of them would become its fellows; this was designated the 'guild principle' for the new foundation. Meanwhile another group had been formed in which the old women's colleges and some sympathetic males were represented – and also in due course some of the diners. They made an informal approach to the Vice-Chancellor, and then held a series of meetings to promote the cause. This group was led by Dame Myra Curtis, principal of Newnham, and believed in what was a little unkindly called the 'civil service' approach to founding the new college: committees were formed, meetings were held; the approval of the university was won, and New Hall was founded. Its first president came from Girton: Dame Rosemary Murray had been

---

[8] For this, and all that follows, see esp. Bertram 1989 (esp. p. 12); Murray 1980 (a reference I owe to the kindness of the president of New Hall).
[9] See below, pp. 576–82.

a much respected tutor in Girton, and was to be not only New Hall's first leader, but the first woman Vice-Chancellor of Cambridge. New Hall was modest in size at first, straitened in means and in living quarters. But it was supported by widespread enthusiasm for the extension of opportunities for women in Cambridge; and in the 1960s, aided by the Wolfson and Nuffield foundations and a widespread appeal, the college was able to move from a Darwin house in Silver Street to an ample site, also the Darwins', in Huntingdon Road generously given by the family. Here Chamberlin, Powell and Bon, creators of the Barbican in London, erected (in Tim Rawle's words) a 'white-skinned' complex with a domed hall, reflecting their view of 'the feminine aura' of the 1960s, as Champneys had done in Newnham in the 1870s.[10]

The central figures in the Dining Group were Margaret Braithwaite, philosopher and wife of the King's philosopher Richard Braithwaite, author of the titles 'the civil service principle' for the manner of the founding of New Hall, and 'the guild principle' for that of Lucy Cavendish; Dr Anna Bidder, zoologist, later first president of Lucy Cavendish, whose father provided the noble gift which first made possible the funding of the college, and a handsome legacy of mature vintage wine which made the husbands of some of the Dining Group – generously allowed to share in it – trust that it would remain a dining group for ever; and Dr Kathleen Wood-Legh. Kay Wood-Legh was the heroic figure in the founding of Lucy Cavendish.[11] She had been blind from childhood, and can never have seen a medieval manuscript; yet she became a distinguished medieval historian, and she deliberately chose fields of work where insight and imagination could be no substitute for detailed research. She even edited a medieval text, the account book of two chantry priests – *A Small Household of the Fifteenth Century* (1950). She had a succession of intelligent and devoted assistants, most of them German students; one of these she taught palaeography, and with some expert help the pair of them made a transcript, which Richard Vaughan and I checked for her with the manuscript. We found little amiss; it

---

[10] See esp. Rawle 1985, pp. 154–5.
[11] With Kay Wood-Legh my wife, who was a member of the Dining Group *c.*1953–6, and I enjoyed long friendship. What follows is personal reminiscence: see also Bertram 1989, p. 13.

was an achievement I would hardly otherwise have credited. Kay was devoted heart and soul to the Dining Group, and gave constant reminders by phone to its members to attend; to her dogged determination the success of the venture probably owes most of all.

When New Hall was founded it seemed to some members of the Dining Group that its work was finished; more wished to continue dining; a few held firm to an alternative view of what a college should be. And so it was that in the wake of the Bridges Report, and the Council of the Senate's report on 'Societies for Graduates' which followed it, the Dining Group applied for recognition as a collegiate society.[12] The guild principle implied that a part of its function was to convert the underprivileged women academics who dined together into the fellows of a college. They aimed also to help older women from any background to seek an academic qualification. The application in 1963 was unsuccessful: the scheme was not sufficiently advanced to win recognition, but the door was not firmly closed. By 1965 a scheme and a trust had been formed; the Council of the Senate could now recommend acceptance of Lucy Cavendish as an approved society. It had also found a name: it is called after the wife of Lord Frederick Cavendish, son of the founder of the Cavendish Laboratory, who was herself celebrated for her work for women's education.[13] Like New Hall, it entered life in Silver Street, but it rapidly moved to houses kindly made available by Magdalene. From 1966 to 1971 Lucy Cavendish, like the other new colleges of the 1960s, was a graduate society; in 1970 it began to admit students for the Bachelor of Education degree; in 1971 it was at last permitted to receive up to fifty mature women as undergraduates.[14] In 1969–70 it had moved into the first of the group of houses in Lady Margaret Road which still form its

[12] See below; Bertram 1989, pp. 27–8.

[13] Bertram 1989, pp. 28–34. There are three categories of foundation recognised by the university since the 1960s: fully fledged colleges, self-governing, self-supporting, though tied to the university by many legal bonds; approved foundations, which are almost colleges, and may receive grants from the College's Fund, but have restricted rights – their heads could not be vice-chancellors, for example (but see p. 565); and approved societies, which are societies in which students may live and work, but whose academic character and/or financial basis is not sufficient as yet to allow them to be approved foundations (Statutes G and H of the university). Lucy Cavendish became an approved foundation in 1984 (Bertram 1989, p. 78).

[14] Bertram 1989, p. 58. For Lucy Cavendish in the 1980s and 90s, see now Warburton 1990.

nucleus. In the 70s and 80s it grew in buildings and stature, though still a small society of fellows, postgraduates and up to fifty undergraduates: the limit has now been lifted. It represents, in its origins and its students, underprivileged segments of British intellectual society. Its struggles for recognition, and its survival, reflect the ambivalence of Cambridge. It came into existence amid much criticism from those who thought a group of ambitious women were providing themselves with fellowships; later on, its application for enhanced status in the 1980s came near to failure. Yet this modest college survived; it fulfils a need to provide for women who missed the opportunity for higher education at the normal student age, and seems set for a secure future. In the same period the University of London merged into larger institutions two of its most flourishing smaller colleges – Bedford and Westfield, both founded for women, though mixed long since. Bedford went south to join Royal Holloway (another one-time women's college) and Westfield east to join Queen Mary – and abandoned the buildings generous benefactors had provided for them. That the rise of Lucy Cavendish was possible at all was due to the anxieties and the euphoria, and the generosity, of the 1960s.

THE BRIDGES REPORT

By 1960 the university was taking stock of what had happened since 1945. There had been a rapid expansion, and more, much more, was to come. There were more undergraduates, and the colleges were full of new building schemes to house them. But, relatively speaking, the expansion was much greater in staff – academic and non-academic – visiting scholars and postgraduate students. They were, furthermore, the least catered for in the old collegiate structure. Colleges were the homes of undergraduates and a small group of fellows, mostly involved in teaching or tutoring them. The thirteen fellows of C. P. Snow's *The Masters* (1951), or similar communities in the tales of college murders popular in that epoch, were in number not uncharacteristic of the smaller colleges. Of the older colleges Peterhouse has now the smallest fellowship, of 31; more than half are over fifty; most are two or three times their size in 1945. The postgraduates from outside Cambridge found it difficult to feel at home in student communities essentially undergraduate. The non-academic staff had always been the least privileged element in university society; they had grown enormously since 1945, especially in two regions: the great increase in scientific laboratories and research multiplied technicians and technical support of all kinds; and the new office techniques and the new bureaucracy bred administrators in and out of the Old Schools, and secretaries everywhere. In a more democratic age, their role and their plight came to be much more regarded. Even in the colleges their numbers were growing: if the gyps and bedmakers and boots declined, the administrative and library staffs grew rapidly. But the group to whom the colleges were least hospitable were the academic staff who were not fellows. By 1961–2 these comprised 45 per cent of the academic staff of the university. The separation of university and colleges devised by the Commissioners of the 1920s had – quite contrary to their expectation or wish – become a divorce. Lord Ashby's table illustrates some of these points quite dramatically.[15]

	1928–9	1961–2
UTOs (University Teaching Officers)	372	946
UTOs without fellowships	109	433
Percentage of UTOs without fellowships	29	46
Research students (approx.)	204	916[16]
Visiting scholars in science	?	144

By the mid-1950s there was serious anxiety for the plight of the outsiders. The Cambridge branch of the Association of University Teachers boldly led a public discussion; but the AUT was to the old Cambridge don an alien body – as much suspected of left-wing tendencies as it was to be accused of right-wing domination by the insurgent young academics of the 1960s. It won some sympathy but carried little weight. But by 1960 new winds were blowing, passions were running high, and a major university committee, with eminent outside members under the chairmanship of Lord Bridges, reported on the measures to be taken to close the gap between university and colleges.

[15] Ashby 1976, p. 2, based on *Bridges Report, Reporter* 13 March 1962, pp. 1138–41.
[16] The figure for all postgraduates was considerably higher; by the late 1960s it was well over 2,000.

The members of the Bridges Committee were concerned to provide fellowships for UTOs and a home for all university staff and postgraduates. Their monument is the University Centre (1964–7), designed by Howell, Killick, Partridge and Amis, 'the most successful and the least mannered' of their buildings, though it manifests their 'passion for canting and chamfering'.[17] In 1950 one of the finest rooms in the Old Schools had been reopened as a meeting place for the Regent House, the University Combination Room; but its facilities and its scope had perforce to remain limited. The University Centre provides a large cafeteria, restaurant, meeting rooms and bar for the whole graduate community, staff and students, and fills one of the most urgent needs of a modern university. This apart, the Bridges Syndicate may be said to have ushered in the age of the graduate colleges. 'We should ... like to see a Graduate College come into existence,' they said – a deliberately modest statement it seems, for Ashby himself (vice-chairman of the committee) glossed it later by saying 'the syndicate did not propose specifically that new Colleges should be created'.[18] Not *specifically*, perhaps, because they were much concerned that the existing colleges should not evade their responsibilities: their chief recommendation was that the colleges should attempt over the next few years to absorb all tenured UTOs and assistant directors of research. The colleges made squeamish noises; they did not as a whole fulfil the target, so that some said the Bridges Report had failed; but many within them caught the mood, and new developments followed. The proportion of university teaching officers who are fellows of colleges has risen steeply, from little more than 50 per cent in 1960 to 84 per cent in 1989.[19]

HUGHES HALL, HOMERTON, ST EDMUND'S, WOLFSON, DARWIN AND CLARE HALL

The Bridges Report included an appendix by Michael McCrum, later master of Corpus, and F. G. Young, later first master of Darwin, outlining the shape a graduate college might take. The

17 Pevsner 1970, pp. 209–10; Rawle 1985, p. 194.
18 *Bridges Report*, p. 1107; Ashby 1976, p. 3.
19 McCrum 1989, p. 13.

idea that new colleges might provide fellowships particularly appealed to those anxious to help, but not keen to see the older college fellowships expand beyond reason – or beyond the walls of their Combination Rooms – both concepts very variously interpreted. In the course of the 1960s a variety of ideas led to the formation of three new colleges, and the transformation of two old societies into new ones. Hughes Hall had been founded to train women graduates, and its main thrust still lies in the training of teachers; but since it achieved new status in 1965 it has contained within its fellowship and postgraduate community a variety of other disciplines besides and, from the 1970s, men as well as women.[20] Homerton College, the large college of education which moved to Cambridge in the 1890s, and took over the buildings of Cavendish College, is still wholly dedicated to education. It comprises a multitude of undergraduates and postgraduates studying for university education courses, and has been an approved society since 1977. St Edmund's had been founded as a Roman Catholic house of studies, and still has many Catholic links and a Catholic chapel; but since 1965 it has been a graduate college – now, like Lucy Cavendish, including also some mature undergraduates – welcoming members of all communions and of none.[21]

The most ambitious attempt to provide fellowships for UTOs, in fields where older colleges could see little teaching need, was University College, now Wolfson College, deliberately set up by the university to this end. In August 1963 the Council of the Senate appointed a committee to investigate the case, and it reported in favour of a graduate college in March 1964. The idea was already mooted that half the fellowship should be UTOs without fellowship, elected by seniority, and that it should be mixed; but that the total fellowship should not exceed sixty. This was modified by the second report of April 1965, which included a draft statute removing the upper limit, reserving fellowships of

[20] See Bottrall 1985 and p. 464. It became an approved society in 1965, an approved foundation in 1985. For Homerton, see pp. 93, 464.

[21] An approved society since 1965, an approved foundation since 1975. In addition, the theological colleges train many students, most of them graduates – some of them both graduates and students of the Theological Tripos. These have to be registered as members of full colleges; but the links between the Federation of Theological Colleges and the university are close, and becoming closer.

half the total, so long as it was not less than thirty, for the disinherited UTOs. On this report the trust deed was based and by 9 July 1965 J. S. Morrison, then senior tutor of Churchill, was appointed first president.[22] By then Darwin College was already under way, but it was still widely felt that the university itself should take an initiative, quite apart from the more private ventures already in the wind. In 1964–5, as Morrison himself has written, 'my peace was shattered by a request from the then Vice-Chancellor, John Boys-Smith, to call upon him in St John's'. A Board of Trustees was being set up for a new college under the baton of Professor Owen Chadwick, master of Selwyn – who in a variety of parts, and in particular as chairman of the University College trustees, trustee of Robinson and entrepreneur of many other liberal ventures, has played something of the role in the Cambridge of the 60s and 70s that Sir Hugh Anderson played in the 1920s. The plan 'attacked the problem of the postgraduates as well as that of the non-Fellows ... The statutory provision laid down that half the Fellows should be freely elected ... but the other half should come by seniority from ... the outcasts or in some proud cases the self-exiled from Collegiate society.'[23] This vital provision has done more than anything else to close the gap between college high tables and the university staff – this, and the general expansion of colleges and fellowships.[24] Morrison set to work to create a society in which fellows and graduates, wives and husbands freely mingled, to attract overseas visitors and – a speciality of his new college – 'to bring people at a middle stage of their careers in industry, banking, and the various public services ... to Cambridge for a term to experience the refreshment of pursuing some intellectual interest ...'[25] In due course he was able to put it to the Wolfson Trustees, who had just founded Wolfson College at Oxford, that they might have 'a Wolfson College at Cambridge as well'.[26] Thus in 1973 University College was able to record its gratitude to the Wolfson Foundation, which in large measure financed its buildings, by changing its

---

[22] *Reporter* 1962–3, p. 2102; *Reporter* 1963–4, pp. 1120–8, 1822, 1843–8, 1925; *Reporter* 1964–5, pp. 1618–27, 1841–4, 1850–1, 1950, 2162, 2303. I owe much help in this region to Graeme Rennie.
[23] Morrison 1991, pp. 84–5.   [24] See p. 575.
[25] Morrison 1991, p. 87.   [26] Morrison 1991, p. 88.

Fig. 21 Wolfson College, façade

name to Wolfson College. This great building programme enabled it to welcome and to house a substantial postgraduate
community, and in essence it is a graduate college. But it includes
a limited number of mature undergraduates and a considerable
leavening of folk on short courses of various kinds. These form a
kind of offshore operation, with little relation to the university,
but making the college a more distinctive reflection of the wider
community – as visitors to its guest nights are liable to discover
when they enquire of their neighbours where they are from and
receive such replies as 'from a bank in Madrid' or 'from Scotland
Yard'. Yet the prime function and most remarkable feature of the
college is to provide fellowships: it has well over eighty fellows,
many of them leading members of the administrative staff, or of
research institutes attached to the university, or of rare
specialities.

Perhaps the most characteristic of the new colleges of the 1960s
are Darwin College and Clare Hall. After the publication of the

Bridges Report, John Bradfield, senior bursar of Trinity, informally proposed to his colleagues in St John's, Caius and King's that the four colleges might found a college of fellows.[27] By a happy chance the four bursars were confined to a railway carriage held up outside Cambridge station by a benevolent signalman for a considerable time in mid-1962; and they whiled away the time pursuing the idea, to the point of agreeing to propose it to their colleges. Lord Adrian, master of Trinity, urged the addition of postgraduates to fellows; and – after the withdrawal of King's, which found other ways of contributing to the creative ideas of the 1960s, including the formation of its own Research Centre – the three colleges united to provide finance and backing for the first stages in the new foundation. It was Bradfield, once again, through a fellow of Trinity connected to the Darwins, who opened the negotiations which led to the acquisition of the Darwin houses in Silver Street – celebrated already as the scene of Gwen Raverat's *Period Piece* (1952), later to be supplemented on the college's behalf by Mrs Raverat's sister, Lady Keynes, in *The House by the River* (1976/84). In this romantic setting the college grew up; and its early struggles and the development of its buildings were financed by the Rayne Foundation, as the result of further efforts by Dr Bradfield. It has come to comprise, not only the 40 fellows and the 40 students proposed by the founding colleges, but in 1990–1 41 fellows, 10 research fellows and 277 postgraduate students (and 165 not full-time), with a number of visiting scholars besides.

In the centre of Clare Hall there is a remarkable picture of its three founders: Lord Ashby, Richard Eden and Sir Brian Pippard.[28] In the 1960s, Ashby was master of Clare College, Eden and Pippard both fellows; Eden worked in the Department of Applied Mathematics – he subsequently moved to the Cavendish, and later still became professor of energy studies; Pippard was already a leader in experimental physics, working on the plans for the new Cavendish, later to be Cavendish Professor. The 1960s were creative years in all British universities, and

---

[27] Bradfield 1989, p. 15. What follows is based on Bradfield 1989 and Young 1967. I am much indebted to Elisabeth Leedham-Green for generous help on the founding of Darwin.

[28] By Bob Tulloch (1984). What follows is based on Ashby 1976 and other documents generously made available to me by Richard Eden, and on discussions with him.

Cambridge had its share in labs and faculties as well as in the colleges. In this new world Lord Ashby, the master of Clare, played a leading role. He had been vice-chairman of the Bridges Syndicate, and its leading spokesman within the university. The panache of his advocacy and the example he set helped to inspire, or to shame, other colleges to play their part in providing for the underprivileged and the dispossessed. The dining table in the Clare lodge was a natural meeting place of groups and committees in the 1960s as the Caius lodge had been in the 1920s. His charm and his wide experience of university affairs in and out of Cambridge combined with a readiness to listen to the ideas of his younger colleagues – to adopt and adapt them, and to hold ceaseless talks with his colleagues when the progress of the scheme demanded it. Although he had been a professional vice-chancellor, he had a deep and instinctive understanding of the role of head of house; and he always insisted that the ideas he was supporting were other men's, and worked to bring to fruition the persuasion of the majority among his fellows. He is also evidently a man of exceptional powers of persuasion. It was natural for his college to embark in 1962–3 on the imaginative discussion of possible ways of meeting the needs of the day; but after some months of talk no end was in sight. John Northam, the senior tutor of Clare, returned from leave in the summer of 1963, and urged that the various schemes were not sufficiently radical; that what was needed was 'a new society', basically a satellite of Clare College, but self-contained. It was a device to increase the fellowship without affecting the SCR of Clare. On 1 November he and the master took a walk on the Coton footpath, 'and we both concluded that the College must soon be brought to jump the fence'.[29] They also agreed that they both wanted to find a way to increase the fellowship and to provide for visiting scholars. A variety of drafts was prepared for a crucial meeting to be held on 11 January 1964. On 6 and 7 January Richard Eden – in the short intervals of two days' consulting at Harwell – prepared yet another draft, which incorporated Northam's and Ashby's basic principles, and a good deal more. This 'Proposal for an Institute for Advanced Study having Special Relations with

[29] Ashby 1976, p. 5.

Clare College' reveals in its title one of its major sources: the Institute for Advanced Study at Princeton, at which Eden had been a frequent visitor. It is crisp and brief, and allows for all the categories under discussion: fellows, visiting fellows, research fellows – of more than one kind, for postdocs and advanced research students and postgraduate students. It was grasped with both hands by the master and approved in principle, without dissent, by the governing body of Clare College – though possible differences were turned aside by the decision to go ahead also with plans to house more research students. In the spring, armed with a memo by Eden which is at all points prophetic of Clare Hall as we know it, the master set off for America in search of financial support. In the event the college gave the site and £450,000, and the endowment was substantially enlarged by grants from the Old Dominion Foundation and the Ford Foundation. By a happy chance, the college had recently acquired the house in Herschel Road which Clare Hall has now replaced. The university needed a substantial plot of land behind the University Library; and a triangular conveyance was arranged whereby St John's received the Divinity School from the university and Clare the house in Herschel Road from St John's.[30] Eden's proposal had envisaged a dining room and common room in which the whole community could meet and mingle, especially at lunch time; a reading room, ten studies and fifteen flats. He also envisaged a further expansion of up to 30 permanent fellows, 60 visiting fellows and so forth: there are now 24 fellows, 12 research fellows and 43 visiting fellows;[31] and the buildings have grown pretty much as he foresaw. On 15 June 1964 the first five fellows were nominated. On 16 June Ashby characteristically leaped on his bicycle and visited, and persuaded, the five elect. As the community took shape, so it acquired independence: by the end of 1964 it was agreed that the new society must be a separate college. It had grown out of Clare, and its origin was preserved in its name, Clare Hall – the name of Clare College itself in earlier days, an inspiring reminder of its history and a source of endless

---

[30] The university kept a 25-year lease of the Divinity School, and it was assumed that by then a new Divinity building would have been built. This has not yet happened, and the Faculty of Divinity is still the tenant of St John's.
[31] *Reporter* 1990–1, Special No. 4, p. 6.

confusion to the Post Office. On 15 June 1965 Pippard was chosen – and agreed – to be first president, and the new college was accepted as an approved foundation early in 1966.

Clare Hall may keep the name of its mother; but in every other respect it is a new creation of the 1960s. Like most of the new colleges, it has made its own traditions; it is informal, sociable, outward looking. It was open to women as well as to men from the start; and by an instant tradition formed in early days, the husbands and wives of fellows and members are as much at home as their spouses. The visitor is as much a part of the community as the older fellows.

ROBINSON COLLEGE

In the late 60s and early 70s there was a debate in many male colleges whether to admit women. In Caius the debate was complicated by anxiety about the growing size of the college, and the issue whether it should not follow Clare's example and become two. The opposition to the admission of women was strong, and a group of three professorial fellows – 'i tre professori'[32] – proposed a compromise: that Caius remain for men, but found a new, mixed college. Meanwhile, the college became aware that David Robinson, a citizen of Cambridge of great wealth founded on television rentals, and a race-horse owner based on Newmarket, had in mind a substantial endowment in Cambridge. The college offered land in Barton Road or Madingley Road for the site of a new college if Robinson would build and endow it. Neither site satisfied the benefactor, and he turned to the university and discussed his plans with successive Vice-Chancellors, Owen Chadwick and Jack Linnett, masters of Selwyn and Sidney. Chadwick at first suggested to him that he might endow professorships; in due course Linnett, having taken extensive counsel, turned his mind back to a college. He followed Linnett's advice, and a body of trustees was set up with Linnett as chairman, till his early death in 1975, and Chadwick as an

---

[32] Charles Brink, Kennedy Professor of Latin, Geoffrey Lampe, Regius Professor of Divinity, and Edward Parkes, Professor of Engineering – later Sir Edward Parkes, chairman of the UGC, and Vice-Chancellor of Leeds. What follows is chiefly based on information most kindly provided by Charles Brink, the warden of Robinson and Martin Brett. See also *Cambridge University Reporter*, Supplement 1976–80, p. 121.

experienced member. David Robinson himself chose the present site, nearer to the University Library and the centre of Cambridge than those offered by Caius, having a charming natural garden with the Bin brook flowing through its midst. The contribution of Caius now took a different form: Charles Brink and Joseph Needham (master of Caius) became trustees; and after Linnett's death Brink became chairman, and remained so till the college received its charter in 1985; in due course two fellows of Caius joined the fellowship of Robinson. A friendly tussle ensued between David Robinson's view of a college and that of the academic trustees. To him it was first and foremost a splendid building, with hall, chapel, and Combination Rooms. The trustees valued some or all of these elements in the idea of a college; but to them it had to be first and foremost a centre of teaching and research. Sir David Robinson was amiable, generous, old-fashioned: he was ready in the end to spend large sums on the buildings, imaginatively designed by a Scottish firm of architects, Gillespie, Kidd and Coia, to mingle modern shapes and masses with the traditional red-brick of Cambridge – it is lavishly coated with expensive and beautiful Dorset bricks.[33] But he gave funds much more reluctantly to endow fellowships and research. The idea took legal form in 1973; the first students – 6 postgraduates – were admitted in 1977; between 1977 and 1980 the main buildings went up; and in 1979 120 undergraduates were admitted. Meanwhile an academic community had been forming, with Professor Lord Lewis, an eminent chemist, appointed in 1975 as warden, to set standards of academic excellence and humane fellowship; and the college was created by a triangular dialogue between Robinson, the trustees and the fellowship. In 1985 it received a royal charter and was recognised as a college, and warden and fellows ruled as in other colleges. The graduate societies of the 1960s had been founded partly to meet obvious immediate needs. Although Robinson College could provide more fellowships and graduate places – could be the first undergraduate college actually to be founded for both men and women – it grew from the wishes of its founders: not only of Robinson, though his was a powerful voice, but of the trustees

[33] Rawle 1985, p. 163.

Fig. 22 Robinson College, 1977–80, by Gillespie, Kidd and Coia

and the warden and fellows; and to the historian it has given a fascinating insight into how such triangles are formed and operate. For every college, with all due differences allowed, must have been founded by similar dialogues, often very ill-recorded. But if the undergraduate element in Robinson was not at first a response to an obvious challenge, it rapidly became so; for in the early 1990s, in face of national need and government pressure, Cambridge has expanded, and some colleges have grown beyond their resources in buildings and teachers; Robinson has become indispensable.

Chapter 19

EPILOGUE

Many conclusions could be drawn from this study; most would be premature. One certain fact is that the University of Cambridge has grown more complex – in its disciplines and activities prodigiously more complex – since 1870. I have had to be highly selective. Some enterprises have been omitted because I lacked a reliable guide; others because the guides were too good, and I could not usefully compete with them. A conspicuous example is the Cambridge University Press. It has already been portrayed in a fine history by Michael Black and an admirable exhibition guide by David McKitterick;[1] a much more detailed history by David McKitterick is on the way, and a short history by Michael Black has recently been published.

I have attempted to sketch something of the character of every college and many disciplines. Such an enterprise forces one to ask the question, should not the historian of literary or scientific studies be an expert on literature or science? The issue is complicated. Historical insight and sympathy are more important than esoteric knowledge in writing the history of any discipline. But they are not the monopoly of professional historians. Someone with a deep understanding of literary criticism could write an admirable history of the English Faculty; a team of scientists could bring to the recent history of science in Cambridge a whole battery of knowledge. What the expert may tend to lack is a wider perspective. That perspective is not easy to describe; for it is more, much more, than the history of Cambridge. I have tried to put the history of the sciences, the social sciences and the humanities into the perspective of Cambridge

[1] Black 1984, McKitterick 1984.

585

Epilogue

history,[2] to view them as elements in the history of one university. Time and again, however, they refuse to be caught in this straitjacket. At one epoch or another the history of the Cavendish has been the history of physics, so it is said; and even if that is an exaggeration, the Cavendish has time and again burst the narrow bounds of Cambridge and Cambridgeshire; just as in astronomy Ryle and Hewish and Hawking have made the universe their parish.[3] The Cambridge perspective, none the less, has great importance in the history of science. In that sense the viewpoint of a historian who has never worked in a lab may help to explain elements in the story opaque to the working scientist – though only if he remembers that the enterprise of science, the excitement of discovery, the drudgery and the cameraderie of the lab, the loneliness of life with a computer, can only be known to him in part if he enters imaginatively into a world now so specialised that communication between disciplines grows ever more difficult.

It is, however, this kind of communication which is most vital to any definition of a university: it can hardly claim nowadays to be a place of universal knowledge, but its *raison d'être* in large measure is to be a place where the professors and students of many disciplines talk to one another. In the late nineteenth century many thought that the future of the sciences lay in Cambridge, the future of the arts in Oxford. 'My boy, you are to be a scientist. I have entered you for Trinity College, Cambridge,'

---

[2] I have deliberately not distinguished arts, humanities and social sciences in my text. The boundaries between social sciences and humanities are drawn in various ways, and classifications differ endlessly; the divergence of views was nicely illustrated when the faculties set to work to give names to the Councils of the Schools which were erected in the 1980s to act as buffers between faculty boards and the General Board. In the end the long established groups of faculties took the following names: 1, 'The School of Arts and Humanities', comprising the Faculties of Architecture and the History of Art, Classics, Divinity, English, Modern and Medieval Languages, Music, Oriental Studies and Philosophy. 2, 'The School of Humanities and Social Sciences', comprising the Faculties of Archaeology and Anthropology, Economics and Politics, Education, History, Law, Social and Political Sciences, and the Departments of the History and Philosophy of Science and Land Economy. 3, 'The School of Physical Sciences', comprising the Faculties of Engineering, Earth Sciences and Geography, Mathematics, Physics and Chemistry, the Department of Chemical Engineering, the Computer Laboratory, the Research Centre in Superconductivity, the Judge Institute for Management Studies and the Isaac Newton Institute for Mathematical Science. 4, 'The School of Biological Sciences', comprising the Faculties of Biology A and B and Clinical Medicine, the Department of Clinical Veterinary Medicine, the Wellcome Trust and Cancer Research Campaign Institute of Cancer, and Developmental Biology.

[3] See pp. 486–91.

Epilogue

said the headmaster to Tressilian Nicholas in 1906–7.[4] Why then has Cambridge remained a leading centre for the humanities as well as the sciences, while Oxford has itself become over the same period a very notable centre for the sciences? The answer is very simple: we do not know. Much more research into this and other universities is needed if we are really to grasp the way in which the various academic regions of Cambridge came to develop. But if I were content to leave it there, much of this book would never have been written. Some ideas at least we may have as to how the arts and the sciences came to grow as they did.

In the beginning, in 1870, there were triposes in mathematics and classics and moral sciences and law; theology was soon to follow. Half the undergraduates, meanwhile, took general degrees in a mixture of this and that. The traditional strength of mathematics was insecurely based, however, for the colleges had largely to recruit from schools in which classical teaching was on the whole stronger than mathematical, and the sciences little regarded. Undergraduate demand played its part. As the colleges came to appoint more lecturers, they naturally attended, then as now, to teaching needs, that is to what the undergraduates wanted to study. Thus Cambridge rapidly acquired a very flourishing medical school, partly – perhaps mainly – because the budding physicians of the late nineteenth century saw Cambridge as a thriving home for basic medical science, which could be happily combined with college life and rugger and rowing. For the best clinical teaching one went to seek the great names of the profession, who had naturally gathered in London, a city more disease-ridden than Cambridge. This abbreviates a complex tale, but there is much substance in it. The basic sciences they needed included chemistry and biology; and chemistry in great measure – and the biological sciences in part – throve in late nineteenth-century Cambridge by providing basic courses for numerous students, most of them medical. Research came later. In physics the story was the other way round. Theoretical physics had long been a part of the Mathematical Tripos and Cambridge boasted theoretical physicists, like Sir George Stokes, of great eminence. The arrival of experimental science with the Cavendish introduced a revolution led by the labs and the professors. This is not

4 See p. 155.

the whole story – college labs, for example, preceded and for a generation accompanied the university's provision – but what happened is unintelligible without the genius of Clerk Maxwell and J. J. Thomson, or without Thomson's capacity to attract from afar and to keep for a space students of talent, including Ernest Rutherford. Some leaders of reform from within the colleges, furthermore, were deeply interested in the growth of science: Coutts Trotter, vice-master of Trinity, is one example, S. G. Phear, tutor and master of Emmanuel, is another.[5] Cornford, the classic, uttered angry words about the Adullamites who lived in caves near Downing Street – that is, in the new buildings of the New Museums and Downing Sites – in 1908,[6] and most of the Adullamites were scientists. But not all – law and social anthropology flourished in their caves at that time; and though feuds in the Senate House and the Combination Rooms were frequent and noisy, within the colleges arts and sciences were often at peace. E. S. Roberts of Caius was a classic and fostered classical teaching in Caius; but he was equally the patron of medical and scientific studies, for he presided benignly over one of the few colleges in which the scientists won an early predominance.[7] His successor as master, Hugh Anderson, was a neurophysiologist, dedicated throughout life to fostering the growth of medical and biological sciences especially, even though his own research had ceased long since. But he had inherited from his predecessor a broad view of the needs of a university.[8] This the college system may reasonably be said to foster, so long as we are not so parochial as to doubt that it exists elsewhere. It was very noticeable that in the creative 1960s, when government grants were relatively generous, they were used by many universities to foster a broad spectrum of disciplines, based on a liberal sense of what a university should be – a school of many arts and sciences; and that in the harsh financial climes of the 70s and 80s many universities have found their horizons narrowed by economic compulsion or government fiat. As a young man Hugh Anderson had been brought to realise – not from his own reading, for

---

[5] See pp. 58, 70, 155–6. For chemistry and physics, see pp. 173–201.
[6] See pp. 90–1.   [7] See Brooke 1985, p. 310.
[8] On Anderson, see chaps. 11–12.

though his house was full of books he rarely read them, but from the intuitive sympathy of a man in whom the virtues of the college system enjoyed a kind of apotheosis – that the deepest need of his colleagues in the arts was for a new library; and he devoted some of the best energies of his later years to planning and plotting for the University Library.

If we ask again, why did Cambridge remain a great centre of the arts as well as the sciences, a part of the answer will more truly be that it became so in this period by an inspiration similar to that for the sciences, stemming from theologians like Lightfoot and Hort, lawyers and historians like Maitland, classics like Housman, and so forth.[9] A part of the answer will be sought in student demand, especially among the women, to whom the Faculties of History, Modern Languages and English owe much: the women were not tied to traditional disciplines, and though one woman might top the Mathematical Tripos and another the Classical, most flourished in new disciplines and fostered their provision.[10] But the women were relatively few in number, and it was the big battalions of men who made the large arts triposes into giants. If we take a wider view, and ask what it was that has attracted so many graduate students of the arts to Cambridge from afar, one answer must be, the University Library. It has not been a universal panacea, for students have been attracted in equal numbers to Oxford and London; reputation depends on a wide variety of cooperant factors. Many scholars still prefer the Bodleian, with its great collections of manuscripts and the fifteenth-century aura of Duke Humfry in which to view them. There are some who prefer the British Museum or the British Library, more richly stored as it is than any of its rivals. But the Cambridge University Library of 1934 offered open access, plentiful space, a well-run tea room, and rich resources; it is the largest open-access library in Europe.[11] It is that which has given it wide fame; and that is one of the major elements in the survival of Cambridge as a leading centre of the arts in the second half of the twentieth century.

If we scan the contents of the University Library – or, more

---

[9] See chaps. 5, 7.   [10] See pp. 229, 428, 431.
[11] On the Library, see chap. 12.

modestly, the lists of books published by the University Press – and ponder the major creations of Cambridge dons over the last hundred years, it is striking how many we can find whose authors have crossed the boundaries of major disciplines. It was a combination of mathematics and natural sciences with classics which prepared Fenton Hort for his leading role in the Revised Version of the Bible and his textual introduction to the Greek New Testament of 1881.[12] 1886 witnessed Willis and Clark's incomparable *Architectual History of the University of Cambridge and of the Colleges of Cambridge and Eton*, a book more admired than read, perhaps, in its early life, since it remained in print till 1967; but now secure of immortality, not only from the notable revival of interest in architectural history of recent years but because the Press reprinted it in 1988.[13] Robert Willis (1800–75) was a notable engineer, a giant in the prehistory of Cambridge engineering; but he was also an architectural historian of genius, bringing the notion of precise measurement to a foggy discipline and combining with it a firm conviction that all kinds of history should be rooted in documents. John Willis Clark, Robert Willis' nephew, was one of the notable characters of Cambridge history: by origin a classic who devoted many years to the Zoological Museum, of which he was superintendent, and who edited *The Life and Letters* of the great geologist Adam Sedgwick.[14] He was a fellow of Trinity, University Registrary, up to his elbows in every good cause in the university, lively, quixotic, irascible, universally loved.[15] His generous character is especially well reflected in his own reminiscences of his Cambridge friends.[16] He devoted many years to completing his uncle's masterpiece, and took extraordinary pains to follow every path that Willis had opened. It is easy now to see its imperfections: neither was a historian by training, and Clark drew splendid maps of Cambridge topography without any real grasp of the techniques of historical topography.[17] But it has a lasting quality rare in Cambridge scholarship in the humanities in the period between

[12] See pp. 10–12.
[13] With a new introduction by David Watkin; on Willis and Clark see also McKitterick 1984, p. 121; on Willis see Brooke 1985, pp. 203–5 and refs.; above, pp. 2–3, 476, etc.
[14] Clark and Hughes 1890.   [15] See esp. Shipley 1913.
[16] In Clark 1900.   [17] See esp. Hall and Lovatt 1989.

about 1850 and 1886 when it was written. The same immortal quality attaches to the works of F. W. Maitland, student of philosophy turned lawyer and legal historian, who published book after book in the austere black binding of the day in the 1890s and the early 1900s, all of them still avidly read.[18] Very characteristic of the intellectual achievement of Cambridge in the Edwardian years was G. E. Moore's *Principia Ethica* (1903) – itself the work of a professional philosopher – expounding the didache of the Cambridge Apostles of that era.[19] It was to be followed by the *Principia Mathematica* of A. N. Whitehead and Bertrand Russell (1910–13), which made mathematics a philosophical art and philosophy a mathematical science.[20]

If we look forward to the late twentieth century – pausing briefly to observe that the darkest year of the Second World War was illuminated by David Knowles' *Monastic Order in England* (1940), the work of a monk and classic turned historian and soon to be a fellow of Peterhouse and a Cambridge professor[21] – we may dwell for a moment on two striking cases in which arts and sciences mingle. In 1954 there emerged the first of many volumes of Joseph Needham's *Science and Civilization in China*, the work of a biochemist of immensely capacious mind and memory who turned to China and to history in his middle years. It is not only a masterpiece in the history of science; in it two of the world's great civilisations enter into dialogue together. In 1965 came two of the three volumes of *Anglo-Saxon Architecture* (1965–78) by H. M. Taylor and his first wife, Joan: a model of patience and precision, in which an applied mathematician, also a revered administrator – University Treasurer and Secretary-General of the Faculties in Cambridge, and Vice-Chancellor in Keele – spent his scanty spare time over many years, with his wife, measuring and describing a host of surviving monuments, lending much needed precision to a complex field.[22] Harold Taylor has sometimes claimed to be an amateur, and his work may be a happy reminder that the best Cambridge scholarship does not always need a lab or a faculty for

[18] See pp. 221–4.
[19] McKitterick 1984, p. 128; see pp. 439–40.
[20] McKitterick 1984, p. 138.
[21] See pp. 419–23 passim.
[22] McKitterick 1984, pp. 164, 169.

its support; he has been a true successor to Robert Willis. One and all of these examples illustrate what a university is: a large room in which men and women of diverse intellectual backgrounds, of different disciplines – of many faiths and cultures – meet and share their learning and their insights.

FELLOWS AND UNDERGRADUATES OF THE MEN'S COLLEGES, 1869–1919

The figures are based on the *Cambridge University Calendar*. A selective check with the lists in *CUC* shows occasional discrepancies, either due to slips by the tutors who had to provide all the information, or to the coming and going of students in the course of the year. Categories of fellowship changed a great deal over the years, and it is sometimes difficult to be sure one has the correct total: I have tried to include all categories, e.g. research fellows, but not bye-fellows.

	1869–70		1879–80		1889–90	
	F	U	F	U	F	U
Christ's	14	94	13	121	15	146
Clare	16	70	18	123	14	171
Corpus Christi	12	141	10	122	12	95
Downing	6	33	6	80	6	78
Emmanuel	14	88	12	82	13	143
Fitzwilliam (non-collegiate)		18		185		143
Gonville and Caius	30	113	29	162	20	200
Jesus	14	104	12	216	14	199
King's	53	23	43	71	47	87
Magdalene	5	59	6	64	5	60
Pembroke	12	44	13	122	13	131
Peterhouse	11	59	10	57	11	82
Queens'	15	51	15	45	8	79
St Catharine's	8	42	8	57	4	51
St John's	54	361	55	354	55	274
Selwyn	–		(founded 1882)		–	119
Sidney Sussex	8	57	10	46	9	52

	1869–70		1879–80		1889–90	
	F	U	F	U	F	U
Trinity	56	548	60	567	61	621
Trinity Hall	12	114	13	179	12	227
Total undergraduates		2,019		2,653		3,020[1]

Note: F = Fellows; U = undergraduates. I have not included heads of house who add one to all these totals.

[1] The figures add up to 2,958 because I have not included Cavendish College and Ayerst Hall (founded in 1882 and 1884) to provide for less well-off students: both were short-lived. See pp. 91–3.

	1900–1		1909–10		1919	
	F	U	F	U	F	U
Christ's	15	168	14	208	15	340
Clare	15	183	15	219	12	219
Corpus Christi	11	59	11	106	10	95
Downing	6	52	6	140	7	132
Emmanuel	14	177	16	229	16	286
Fitzwilliam (non-collegiate)	–	108	–	97	–	158
Gonville and Caius	26	222	27	313	28	475
Jesus	16	112	13	187	13	202
King's	46	143	47	175	38	188
Magdalene	3	48	7	91	7	142
Pembroke	14	226	13	256	12	392
Peterhouse	10	55	8	79	8	128
Queens'	8	98	8	184	8	221
St Catharine's	6	73	6	104	5	122
St John's	44	237	46	253	44	347
Selwyn	–	84	–	122	6	112
Sidney Sussex	10	72	10	91	11	182
Trinity	65	676	64	700	58	704
Trinity Hall	13	190	13	145	10	132
Total undergraduates		2,983[1]		3,699		4,577[2]

[1] 2,985 in *CUC*.
[2] 4,582 in *CUC*.

Appendices

In 1919 the figures were inflated by students returning from war service – and possibly by some not yet in residence: the figures give an approximate idea of the maximum colleges could hold – sometimes (one gathers) rather more than they could hold.

Appendix 2

STUDENT NUMBERS BY COLLEGE, 1990–1

| | Undergraduates Full-time | | | Postgraduates | | | | | |
| | | | | Full-time | | | Not full-time | | |
	Men	Women	Total	Men	Women	Total	Men	Women	Total
Christ's	264	132	396	44	20	64	30	15	45
Churchill	323	101	424	141	35	176	72	16	88
Clare	247	168	415	59	25	84	25	20	45
Clare Hall	4	–	4	57	24	81	39	27	66
Corpus Christi	176	75	251	67	29	96	30	11	41
Darwin	12	–	12	194	83	277	106	59	165
Downing	248	141	389	30	9	39	13	2	15
Emmanuel	292	148	440	66	30	96	38	19	57
Fitzwilliam	309	132	441	56	7	63	20	5	25
Girton	284	252	536	35	23	58	28	11	39
Gonville and Caius	304	172	476	79	28	107	26	13	39
Homerton	19	266	285	64	113	177	–	–	–
Hughes Hall	12	1	13	107	96	203	18	5	23
Jesus	291	168	459	74	26	100	47	18	65
King's	233	167	400	78	32	110	58	18	76
Lucy Cavendish	–	60	60	–	17	17	–	14	14
Magdalene	230	117	347	50	22	72	20	2	22
New Hall	–	316	316	–	41	41	–	22	22
Newnham	–	420	420	–	47	47	–	40	40
Pembroke	246	117	363	55	29	84	35	11	46
Peterhouse	162	62	224	42	3	45	22	3	25
Queens'	289	180	469	102	59	161	43	19	62
Robinson	283	127	410	45	10	55	16	6	22
St Catharine's	258	171	429	64	21	85	22	7	29
St Edmund's	22	7	29	74	26	100	35	8	43
St John's	420	178	598	103	34	137	59	26	85
Selwyn	224	138	362	45	18	63	20	9	29

Appendices

	Undergraduates Full-time			Postgraduates					
				Full-time			Not full-time		
	Men	Women	Total	Men	Women	Total	Men	Women	Total
Sidney Sussex	192	129	321	33	11	44	20	7	27
Trinity	536	156	692	123	42	165	70	29	99
Trinity Hall	202	120	322	66	29	95	27	13	40
Wolfson	39	40	79	170	59	229	84	33	117
Total	6,121	4,261	10,382	2,123	1,048	3,171	1,023	488	1,511

Source: Reporter 1990–1, Special No. 17, p. 10.

Appendix 3

COLLEGE INCOMES, *c.* 1926

This list is simply intended to give a rough idea of the relative wealth of the colleges midway through the period of the book. The figures are taken from CUL, CUA Comm. B.8.2, from a small collection of notes by or for Sir Hugh Anderson when he was preparing to implement the new constitution of 1926 (see chap. 11). They comprise the revised assessment for university taxation; and these figures are 'gross taxable income', i.e. before the allowances were deducted for scholarships etc., and not including income from trusts which were not liable to tax. Like all such figures, they have a spurious air of precision; but they probably give a not too misleading account of relative incomes. Girton, Newnham and Selwyn, not being then fully fledged colleges of the university, are not included (see pp. 94, 327).

Trinity	£68,577
St John's	£48,832
King's	£41,803
Gonville and Caius	£29,495
Sidney Sussex	£17,096
Emmanuel	£16,101
Christ's	£15,344
Clare	£14,815
Jesus	£13,693
Corpus Christi	£12,043
Peterhouse	£11,277
Pembroke	£8,754
Queens'	£7,536
Trinity Hall	£6,764
St Catharine's	£6,388
Downing	£5,560
Magdalene	£5,372

Appendix 4

A NOTE ON SCHOOLS

On pp. 247–9 I emphasised the difficulty of comparing the school backgrounds of the undergraduates of different generations, and I quoted some figures for Caius from Brooke 1985, p. 309. Much more work needs to be done before more general figures can be hazarded; and it would be especially interesting to study relations of colleges with particular schools. Meanwhile a brief survey of the three other colleges whose records for the late nineteenth century are most accessible in print shows that there was considerable variety in the sources of recruitment. The names applied to different types of school, and the problems which arise in devising figures, are explained in Brooke 1985, pp. 308–9. In Trinity, the numbers coming from the small group of 'Clarendon' public schools (see p. 245n) were so great that I have separated them from the other public schools (all but St Paul's were boarding schools). For Peterhouse, no details of schools seem to be available before 1876, and as it was a very small college, I took the sample 1876–9; for Christ's and Trinity I sampled the single year 1879.

Christ's, entry for 1879 (Peile 1910–13, II, 665–71)

From other universities, etc.	2
Public boarding schools	13
Public day schools	4
Grammar schools etc.	9
Private schools or tuition	5
Overseas	2
Unknown	3
Total in sample	38

Appendices

Peterhouse, entry for 1876–9 (Walker 1912, pp. 547–57)

From other universities etc.	8
Public boarding schools	8
Public day schools	13
Grammar schools, etc.	16
Private schools or tuition	4
Overseas	2
Unknown	14
Total in sample	65

Trinity, entry for 1879 (Ball and Venn 1913, pp. 599–623)

From other universities, etc.	2
Clarendon schools	91
Other public boarding schools	46
Other public day schools	7
Grammar schools etc.	11
Private schools or tuition	28
Overseas	2
Not known	4
Total in sample	191

With these figures we can compare the analysis based on a much larger sample, rather differently designed, by Dr Peter Searby (Searby 1982–3, p. 114).

Matriculants in Cambridge colleges, 1876–90: their previous schooling

	Total of matriculants	% from 22 leading public schools		% from 42 lesser public schools		% from 100 fringe public schools		% from other schools educated privately or abroad		% schooling not known	
Cavendish	358	12	(42)	12.5	(45)	7	(25)	11	(40)	57.5	(206)
Caius	881	30	(266)	19	(169)	18.5	(162)	30.5	(267)	2	(17)
Christ's	713	21	(152)	16	(112)	21	(152)	38	(270)	4	(27)
King's	416	54	(223)	15	(64)	8	(34)	21	(88)	2	(7)
Peterhouse	400	16	(65)	19	(77)	21	(84)	40	(159)	4	(15)
Trinity	2,740	68	(1,871)	8	(214)	8.5	(229)	14	(386)	1.5	(40)

PROFESSIONS AND STATUS OF CAMBRIDGE STUDENTS

I have discussed the very difficult problems of producing meaningful figures or statements about the social status and professional
background or foreground of Cambridge students on pp. 249–52.
The best material is provided by the University Careers Service
(formerly the Appointments Board) in their annual reports in the
Reporter; but this is only detailed for recent generations. Some
attempt was made to quantify the professions of fathers and
students at Caius between 1886 and 1971 in Brooke 1985,
pp. 311–15. Caius is exceptionally well documented, but even
there the exercise is full of hazards: professions are often ill-
defined in the documents, and later information is sometimes
scanty. In some other colleges research is in progress; and a
selective, detailed survey covering the whole university, such as
has been undertaken for *The History of the University of Oxford*,
would yield extremely valuable results – but be very difficult
indeed to undertake. Meanwhile I print tables from two pieces of
research which give interesting information.

1. From Anderson and Schnaper 1952, pp. 3–4, 6, 16–17, as
extracted for Cambridge in Twigg 1987, p. 463. This analyses the
social composition of the Cambridge student body from a sample
ranging over the whole period 1752–1886, and the result of a
survey taken of the generation of students leaving in 1937–8 of
fathers' professions and those the sons hoped to enter.

Appendices

1752–1886

	Father's status (%)	Son's status (%)
Nobles	7.2	4.7
Gentry	25.5	5.8
Clergy	32.6	54.3
Military	6.0	4.5
Law	5.3	11.2
Medicine	6.0	3.5
Government	1.5	1.6
Business	9.4	3.9
Academic	3.3	9.1
Plebeian	3.2	1.4

1937–8

	Father's occupation (%)	Son's occupation (%)
Commerce	32.5	17.8
Scientific business	13.7	11.5
Government	8.3	9.8
Clergy	7.4	6.2
Military	7.0	8.4
Law	6.6	10.4
Medicine	8.1	11.2
Architecture	0.8	1.6
Teaching	6.9	15.2
Research	–	4.1
Misc.	6.5	3.8

Appendices

2. From *VCH Cambs*, III, 288: an analysis of 446 pass men who matriculated in 1903–7.

Profession	Percentage
Holy orders	25
Barristers and solicitors	16
Business (other than engineering)	13
Engineers	11
Medical profession	9
Regular army	6
Teaching	5
Government service at home and abroad	4
Farmers and planters	3
Other vocations	8

BIBLIOGRAPHICAL REFERENCES

Ackerman, R., 1987, *J. G. Frazer: his Life and Work*, Cambridge, 1987

Allen, P., 1978, *The Cambridge Apostles: the Early Years*, Cambridge, 1978

Amos, M. S., n. d., 'Reminiscences for my children', n. d. (see p. 287n)

Anderson, C. A. and Schnaper, M., 1952, *School and Society in England: Social Backgrounds of Oxford and Cambridge Students*, Washington, 1952

Anderson, M., 1988ff, 'Time to the Sound of Bells' (see p. 343: publ. in *The Caian*, 1988 –)

Annan, N., 1951/1984, *Leslie Stephen*, London, 1951; 2nd edn, *Leslie Stephen the Godless Victorian*, 1984

1990, *Our Age*, London, 1990

Ansell, E., 1935, 'The move of the Cambridge University Library', *Library Association Record*, March 1935, pp. 1–6

Anstruther, I., 1983, *Oscar Browning: a Biography*, London, 1983

Ashby, E., 1976, 'The founding of Clare Hall', typescript, 1976

Ashby, E. and Anderson, M., 1970, *The Rise of the Student Estate in Britain*, London, 1970

Asquith, H. H., 1933, *H.H.A.: Letters of the Earl of Oxford and Asquith to a Friend: First Series, 1915–1922*, London, 1933

Atcheson, D. B., 1986, 'A charmed life: a biographical memoir of my grandfather Tressilian Charles Nicholas', Dissertation for MA, Bard College, Annandale-on-Hudson, 1986 (cited by the author's permission)

Austen Leigh, W., 1906, *Augustus Austen Leigh*, London, 1906

Ayer, F., 1936, *Language, Truth and Logic*, edn of Oxford, 1936

Badash, L., 1985, *Kapitza, Rutherford, and the Kremlin*, New Haven, 1985

Bailey, S. J., 1955, 'Percy Henry Winfield, 1878–1953', *PBA* 41 (1955), 329–37

Balchin, W. G. V., 1988, 'One hundred years of geography in Cambridge: a St Catharine's view', *Cambridge*, 23 (1988), 39–53

Ball, W. W. Rouse and Venn, J. A., 1913, *Admissions to Trinity College, Cambridge*, v, London, 1913

Banks, J. A., 1954, *Prosperity and Parenthood*, London, 1954

Barker, E., 1953, *Age and Youth*, Oxford, 1953

Bibliographical references

Barnes, W. E., ed., 1924, *In Memoriam: Adolphus William Ward, Master of Peterhouse*, Cambridge, 1924

Barrett, C. K., 1959, *Westcott as Commentator* (Westcott Memorial Lecture, 1958), Cambridge, 1959

Bell, H. E., 1965, *Maitland: a Critical Examination and Assessment*, London, 1965

Bell, M., 1988, *F. R. Leavis*, London, 1988

Bennett, D., 1990, *Emily Davies and the Liberation of Women, 1830–1921*, London, 1990

Bennett, H. S., 1947, 'George Gordon Coulton, 1858–1947', *PBA* 33 (1947), 267–81

Bennett, R. F., 1979, *Ultra in the West*, London, 1979
  1989, *Ultra and Mediterranean Strategy, 1941–1945*, London, 1989

Benson, A. C., 1907, *From a College Window*, London, 1907, cited from the 9th impression, 4th edn
  1911, *The Leaves of the Tree: Studies in Biography*, London, 1911
  see also Lubbock

Bertram, C. K., 1989, *Lucy Cavendish College, Cambridge: a History of the Early Years*, Cambridge, 1989

Bicknell, P., 1982, 'The development of the College buildings', in *Aspects of Downing History*, Downing College Association, 1982, pp. 2–18

Bill, E. G. W. and Mason, J. F. A., 1970, *Christ Church and Reform, 1850–1867*, Oxford, 1970

Binfield, C., 1989, 'Principal when pastor: P. T. Forsyth, 1876–1901', *Studies in Church History* 26 (1989), 397–414

Bingham, C., 1987, *The History of Royal Holloway College, 1886–1986*, London, 1987

Black, M., 1984, *Cambridge University Press, 1584–1984*, Cambridge, 1984

BMFRS: Biographical Memoirs of Fellows of the Royal Society

Boag, J. W. and Shoenberg, D., 1988, 'Letters from Kapitza to his mother, 1921–27', *Notes and Records of the Royal Society of London*, 42 (1988), 205–28

Boag, J. W., Rubinin, P. E. and Shoenberg, D., 1990, *Kapitza in Cambridge and Moscow*, Amsterdam, 1990

Bottrall, M., 1985, *Hughes Hall 1885–1985*, Cambridge, 1985

Bowett, D., 1988, 'Queens' 1960–1980: some personal recollections', *Queens' College Record 1988*, pp. 12–13

Box, J. F., 1978, *R. A. Fisher: the Life of a Scientist*, New York, 1978

Boys Smith, J. S., *Memories of St John's College, Cambridge, 1919–1969*, Cambridge, 1983

Bradbrook, M. C., 1969, *'That Infidel Place': a Short History of Girton College 1869–1969*, London, 1969

Bibliographical references

Bradfield, J. R. G., 1989, 'Reminiscences of the early days of Darwin College', *Darwin College Magazine*, 4 (1989), 15–17

Bridges Report, 13 March 1962: *Reporter* 1961–2, pp. 1073–152

Briggs, A., 1983 (first publ. 1967), 'The language of "class" in early nineteenth-century England', in *History and Class*, ed. R. S. Neale (Oxford, 1983), pp. 2–29

Brink, C. O., 1986, *English Classical Scholarship: Historical Reflections on Bentley, Porson, and Housman*, Cambridge, 1986

Brittain, F., 1942, *Bernard Lord Manning*, Cambridge, 1942

Broadbent, D. E., 1970, 'Frederic Charles Bartlett, 1886–1969', *BMFRS* 16 (1970), 1–13

Brooke, C. N. L., 1980, 'Charles Clay', *PBA* 64 (1980), 311–40
  1985, *A History of Gonville and Caius College*, Woodbridge, 1985

Brooke, C. N. L., Highfield, J. R. L. and Swaan, W., 1988, *Oxford and Cambridge*, Cambridge, 1988

Brooke, C. N. L., Lovatt, R., Luscombe, D. and Sillem, A., 1991, *David Knowles Remembered*, Cambridge, 1991

Brooke, N. S., 1990, *The Tragedy of Macbeth*, The Oxford Shakespeare, Oxford, 1990

Brooke, R. B., 1967, 'The lives of St Francis', in *Latin Biography*, ed. T. A. Dorey (London, 1967), pp. 177–98
  ed. and trans., 1970/1990, *Scripta Leonis, Rufini et Angeli sociorum S. Francisci*, Oxford Medieval Texts, Oxford, 1970, corr. repr. 1990
  1982, 'Recent work on St Francis of Assisi', *Analecta Bollandiana*, 100 (1982), 653–76

Browne, G. F., 1915, *The Recollections of a Bishop*, London, 1915

Buchan, J., 1898, *Brasenose College*, London, 1898

Buckland, W. W., 1912, *Elementary Principles of Roman Private Law*, Cambridge, 1912
  1921–3, 'F. W. Maitland', *Cambridge Law Journal*, 1 (1921–3), 279–301
  1925, *Manual of Roman Private Law*, Cambridge, 1925
  1963, *A Text-book of Roman Law from Augustus to Justinian* (1st edn, 1921), 3rd edn, ed. P. Stein, Cambridge, 1963

Buckland, W. W. and McNair, A. D., 1936, *Roman Law and Common Law*, Cambridge, 1936

Bullock, F. W. B., 1941–53, *The History of Ridley Hall, Cambridge*, 2 vols., Cambridge, 1941–53

Burnaby, J., 1953, *Education, Religion, Learning and Research* (Inaugural Lecture), Cambridge, 1953

Bury, J. B., 1903, *An Inaugural Lecture*, Cambridge, 1903

Bury, (J.) P. (T.), 1952, *The College of Corpus Christi and of the Blessed Virgin Mary: a History from 1822 to 1952*, Cambridge, 1952

Bibliographical references

Butterfield, H., 1948, *Lord Acton*, Historical Association Pamphlet G9, London, 1948

1949, *The Origins of Modern Science*, London, 1949

Buxton, J. and Williams, P., eds., 1979, *New College, Oxford, 1379–1979*, Oxford, 1979

Caine, B., 1988, *Destined to be Wives: the Sisters of Beatrice Webb*, Oxford, 1986, cited from edn of 1988

Cam, H. M., 1944, *Liberties and Communities in Medieval England*, Cambridge, 1944

ed., 1957, *Selected Historical Essays of F. W. Maitland*, Cambridge, 1957

Campion, S. (Mary Coulton), 1948, *Father: a Portrait of G. G. Coulton at Home*, London, 1948

Cannon, J. et al., 1988, *The Blackwell Dictionary of Historians*, Oxford, 1988

Carey, G. V., ed., 1921, *The War List of the University of Cambridge, 1914–1918*, Cambridge, 1921

Carey, H., 1984, *Mansfield Forbes and his Cambridge*, Cambridge, 1984

Carswell, J., 1985, *Government and the Universities in Britain: Programme and Performance 1960–1980*, Cambridge, 1985

Casey, J., 1991, 'Michael Oakeshott, 1901–1990', *The Caian* 1991, pp. 97–103

Caute, J., 1988, *Sixty-Eight: the Year of the Barricades*, London, 1988

Cavendish 1910: A History of the Cavendish Laboratory, 1871–1910, London, 1910

Chadwick, H., 1961, *The Vindication of Christianity in Westcott's Thought* (Westcott Memorial Lecture, 1960), Cambridge, 1961

Chadwick, H. M. 1912, *The Heroic Age*, Cambridge, 1912

Chadwick, H. M. and N. K., 1932–40, *The Growth of Literature*, 3 vols., Cambridge, 1932–40

Chadwick, (W.) O., 1963, *Westcott and the University* (Westcott Memorial Lecture, 1962), Cambridge, 1963

1969, *Freedom and the Historian* (Inaugural Lecture), Cambridge, 1969

1970, *The Victorian Church*, II, London, 1970

1973, *Selwyn College 1882–1973: a Short History*, Cambridge (1973)

1975, 'Charles Kingsley at Cambridge', *Historical Journal*, 18, 2 (1975), 303–25

1978, *Catholicism and History: the Opening of the Vatican Archives*, Cambridge, 1978

1987, 'Acton and Butterfield', *Journal of Ecclesiastical History*, 38 (1987), 386–405

1990, *Michael Ramsey, a Life*, Oxford, 1990

Chainey, G., 1985, *A Literary History of Cambridge*, Cambridge, 1985

Chapman, R. W., ed., 1952, *Jane Austen's Letters*, 2nd edn, London, 1952

Bibliographical references

Charlton, D. G., 1987–8, 'French studies: a report to the Prime Minister (in 1918)', *French Studies Bulletin*, 25 (1987–8), 10–16

Chawner, W., 1909a, *Prove all Things*, Cambridge, 1909
1909b, *A Supplement to a Paper entitled Prove all Things*, Cambridge, 1909
1911, *Truthfulness in Religion*, Cambridge, 1911

Cheney, C. R., 1971, 'Helen Maud Cam, 1885–1968', *PBA* 55 (1971 for 1969), 293–309

Clare College 1326–1926, 2 vols., Cambridge, 1926

Clark, G., 1989, *Prehistory at Cambridge and Beyond*, Cambridge, 1989

Clark, J. W., 1900, *Old Friends at Cambridge and Elsewhere*, London, 1900
1904, *Endowments of the University of Cambridge*, Cambridge, 1904

Clark, J. W. and Hughes, T. McK., 1890, *The Life and Letters of Adam Sedgwick*, 2 vols., Cambridge, 1890

Clarke, P., 1988, *The Keynesian Revolution in the Making*, Oxford, 1988

Clough, B. A., 1897, *A Memoir of Anne Jemima Clough*, London, 1897

Cobban, A. B., 1988, *The Medieval English Universities: Oxford and Cambridge to c. 1500*, Aldershot, 1988

Cohen, Lord Cohen of Birkenhead, 1958, *Sherrington, Physiologist, Philosopher and Poet* (Sherrington Lectures, IV), Liverpool, 1958

Collinson, P., McKitterick, D. and Leedham-Green, E., 1991, *Andrew Perne: Quatercentenary Studies*, Cambridge Bibliographical Society, Cambridge, 1991

Cornford, F. M., 1908, *Microcosmographia Academica*, Cambridge, 1908, cited also from the edn of 1987

Coulton, G. G., 1943, *Fourscore Years*, London, 1943

Couve de Murville, M. N. L. and Jenkins, P., 1983, *Catholic Cambridge*, London, 1983

Cowling, M., 1979, 'Herbert Butterfield, 1900–1979', *PBA* 65 (1979), 595–609

Cox, M., 1983, *M. R. James: an Informal Portrait*, Oxford, 1983

Crawley, C. W., 1970, 'Sir George Prothero and his circle', *Transactions of the Royal Historical Society*, 5th Series, 20 (1970), 101–27
1976, *Trinity Hall: the History of a Cambridge College, 1350–1975*, Cambridge, 1976

Creighton, L., 1904, *Life and Letters of Mandell Creighton*, 2 vols., London, 1904

Crick, F., 1988, *What Mad Pursuit: a Personal View of Scientific Discovery*, London, 1988

Crook, A. C., 1980, *From the Foundation to Gilbert Scott: a History of the Buildings of St John's College, Cambridge, 1511–1885*, Cambridge, 1980

Crook, J. M., 1987, *The Dilemma of Style*, London, 1987

Crowther, J. G., 1974, *The Cavendish Laboratory 1874–1974*, London, 1974

CUA: Cambridge University Archives (in CUL)

CUC: Cambridge University Calendar (cited by year)

Bibliographical references

CUL: Cambridge University Library

Cumming, Joan, 1981, 'Cambridge University Museum of Archaeology and Anthropology: a history' (typescript), 1981

Cupitt, D., 1970–1, 'The Chawner affair', *Emmanuel College Magazine*, 53 (1970–1), 5–11

CUWAG Report: The *CUWAG Report on the Numbers and Status of Academic Women in the University of Cambridge* (The Survey Committee of the Cambridge University Women's Action Group), 1988

Davies, M., ed., 1990, *A Selection from the Writings of Joseph Needham*, Lewes, 1990

Deane, P. and Cole, W. A., *British Economic Growth 1688–1959*, Cambridge, 1967

Devlin Report: Reporter 1972–3, Special No. 12, 14 February 1973

Dillistone, F. W., 1975, *Charles Raven*, London, 1975

  1977, *C. H. Dodd, Interpreter of the New Testament*, London, 1977

DNB: *Dictionary of National Biography*

Dodd, C., 1983, *The Oxford and Cambridge Boat Race*, London, 1983

Dodd, C. H., 1920, *The Meaning of Paul for Today*, London, 1920

  1935, *The Parables of the Kingdom*, London, 1935

  1936, *The Apostolic Preaching and its Developments*, London, 1936

  1953, *The Interpretation of the Fourth Gospel*, Cambridge, 1953

  1963, *Historical Tradition in the Fourth Gospel*, Cambridge, 1963

  1970, *The Founder of Christianity*, New York, 1970 (London, 1971)

Drury, J., 1985, *The Parables of the Gospels: History and Allegory*, London, 1985

DSB: *Dictionary of Scientific Biography*, ed. C. C. Gillespie, 16 vols., New York, 1970–80

Dunbabin, J., 1975, 'Oxford and Cambridge college finances, 1871–1913', *Economic History Review*, 2nd Series, 28 (1975), 631–47

  1976, 'Oxford college finances, 1871–1913: a reply', *Economic History Review*, 2nd Series, 29 (1976), 446–9

Ebin, V. and Swallow, D. A., 1984, *The Proper Study of Mankind ... Great Anthropological Collections in Cambridge* (Exhibition Catalogue), Cambridge, 1984

Ede, J., 1984, *A Way of Life: Kettle's Yard*, Cambridge, 1984

Eden, G. R. and MacDonald, F. C., ed., 1932, *Lightfoot of Durham: Memories and Appreciations*, Cambridge, 1932

Edwards, A., 1989, 'Viewpoint', *Cambridge Review*, 110 (1989), 172–6

Edwards, K., 1967, *The English Secular Cathedrals in the Middle Ages*, 2nd edn, Manchester, 1967

Elton, G. R., 1984, 'Herbert Butterfield and the study of history', *Historical Journal*, 27, 3 (1984), 729–43

  1986, *F. W. Maitland*, London, 1986

Bibliographical references

Engel, A., 1976, 'Oxford college finances, 1871–1913: a comment', *Economic History Review*, 2nd Series, 29 (1976), 437–445

1983, *From Clergyman to Don: the Rise of the Academic Profession in Nineteenth-Century Oxford*, Oxford, 1983

Fairbairn, S., 1931, *Fairbairn of Jesus*, London, 1931

Fifoot, C. H. S., ed., 1965, *The Letters of Frederic William Maitland*, Cambridge, 1965

1971, *Frederic William Maitland: a Life*, Cambridge, Mass., 1971

Fisher, H. A. L., 1910, *Frederick* [sic] *William Maitland, Downing Professor of the Laws of England: a Biographical Sketch*, Cambridge, 1910

Fletcher, S., 1980, *Feminists and Bureaucrats: a Study in the Development of Girls' Education in the Nineteenth Century*, Cambridge, 1980

Forster, E. M., 1907, *The Longest Journey*, London, 1907

1934, *Goldsworthy Lowes Dickinson*, London, 1934

Fosdick, R. B., 1952, *The Story of the Rockefeller Foundation*, London, 1952

Fowler, L. and H., 1984, *Cambridge Commemorated: an Anthology of University Life*, Cambridge, 1984

Frankel, W. and Miller, H., eds., 1989, *Gown and Tallith: in Commemoration of the Fiftieth Anniversary of the Founding of the Cambridge University Jewish Society*, London, 1989

Franks, O., 1966, *University of Oxford: Report of Commission of Inquiry* (Chairman, Lord Franks), 2 vols., Oxford, 1966

Fraser, R. et al., 1988, *A Student Generation in Revolt*, London, 1988

French, S., 1978, *The History of Downing College*, Cambridge, 1978

Furbank, P. N., 1977–8, *E. M. Forster: A Life*, 2 vols, London, 1977–8

Garland, M. M., 1980, *Cambridge before Darwin: the Ideal of a Liberal Education*, Cambridge, 1980

Geison, M. F., 1978, *Michael Foster and the Cambridge School of Physiology*, Princeton, 1978

Gilbert, M., 1980, *Winston Churchill*, VIII, *'Never Despair'*, *1945–1965*, London, 1988

Girouard, M., 1977/1984, *Sweetness and Light: the 'Queen Anne' Movement, 1860–1900*, Oxford, 1977, cited from edn of New Haven, 1984

Glover, T. R., 1909, *The Conflict of Religions in the Early Roman Empire*, London, 1909

1917, *The Jesus of History*, London, 1917

1943, *Cambridge Retrospect*, Cambridge, 1943

Godwin, H., 1985, *Cambridge and Clare*, Cambridge, 1985

Gooch, G. P., 1939, 'Harold Temperley, 1879–1939', *PBA* 25 (1939), 355–93

Goodhart, C. B., 1990, 'Sir Ronald Aylmer Fisher, Sc.D., F.R.S.', *The Caian* 1990, pp. 68–73

Gow, A. S. F., 1936, *A. E. Housman*, New York and Cambridge, 1936

Bibliographical references

Gowing, M. M., 1964, *Britain and Atomic Energy 1939–45*, London, 1964

Graham-Smith, F., 1986, 'Martin Ryle, 27 September 1918 – 14 October 1984', *BMFRS* 32 (1986), 495–524

Grave, W. W., 1983, *Fitzwilliam College, Cambridge, 1869–1969*, Cambridge, 1983

Grave Report: Reporter 1967–8, pp. 333–68

Gray, A. and Brittain, F., 1979, *A History of Jesus College, Cambridge*, London, 1979

Gray, P., 1988, 'An interview with Professor P. Gray, Master of Gonville and Caius College' (by Edward Timms), *The Caian* 1988, 19–47

Green, B., 1989, 'David Knowles's first book', *Downside Review*, 107 (1989), 79–85

Green, V. H. H., 1957, *Oxford Common Room: a Study of Lincoln College and Mark Pattison*, London, 1957

1964, *Religion at Oxford and Cambridge*, London, 1964

1979, *The Commonwealth of Lincoln College, 1427–1977*, Oxford, 1979

Greenway, D., 1985, 'The false *Institutio* of St Osmund', in *Tradition and Change: Essays in Honour of Marjorie Chibnall*, ed. D. Greenway, C. Holdsworth and J. Sayers (Cambridge, 1985), pp. 77–101

Grey, G. W., 1941, *Education on an International Scale: a History of the International Education Board, 1923–1938*, New York, 1941

Grierson, P., 1946, 'Z. N. Brooke, 1883–1946', *The Caian* 51, 3 (1946), 95–105

Grierson, P. and Blackburn, M., 1986, *Medieval European Coinage*, I, Cambridge, 1986

Haig, A. G. L., 1984, *The Victorian Church*, London, 1984

1986, 'The Church, the universities and learning in later Victorian England', *Historical Journal*, 29, 1 (1986), 187–201

Hall, C. P. and Lovatt, R., 1989, 'The site and foundation of Peterhouse', *Proceedings of the Cambridge Antiquarian Society*, 78 (1989), 5–46

Hamilton, M. A., 1936, *Newnham: an Informal Biography*, London, 1936

Hammond, N. G. L., 1968, 'Frank Ezra Adcock', *PBA* 54 (1968), 425–34

Hardy, G. H., 1940/1967, *A Mathematician's Apology*, Cambridge, 1940, cited from edn of 1967, with Preface by C. P. Snow

1940b, *Ramanujan: Twelve Lectures on Subjects Suggested by his Life and Work*, Cambridge, 1940

1942, *Bertrand Russell and Trinity*, Cambridge, 1942

Harman, P. M., ed., 1985, *Wranglers and Physicists: Studies in Cambridge Physics in the Nineteenth Century*, Manchester, 1985

Harrod, R. F., 1951, *The Life of John Maynard Keynes*, London, 1951

Harte, N. B., 1979, *The Admission of Women to University College London: a Centenary Lecture* (delivered 1978), London, 1979

1986, *The University of London, 1836–1986*, London, 1986

Haslam, J. A. G., 'An account of the conduct and development of research in flight' [1921–39], unpubl. paper in CUA, CUR 39.54.16, Cambridge, 1977

Hawking, S. W., 1988, *A Brief History of Time*, London, 1988

Hayman, R., 1976, *Leavis*, London, 1976

Helmholz, R. H., 1990, *Roman Canon Law in Reformation England*, Cambridge, 1990

Henson, H. Hensley, 1889, 'Oxford and its Professors', *Edinburgh Review*, 170 (1889), 303–27

Hewish, A., 1990, 'A Cambridge view of the universe', *Cambridge*, 27 (1990), 51–6

Hewison, R., 1983, *Footlights: a Hundred Years of Cambridge Comedy*, London, 1983

Heyman, J., 1987, 'John Fleetwood Baker, Baron Baker of Windrush', *BMFRS* 33 (1987), 3–20

  1990, 'Cambridge University Engineering Department new four-year course', *Cambridge*, 27 (1990), 43–6

Hilken, T. J. N., 1967, *Engineering at Cambridge University 1783–1965*, Cambridge, 1967

Hinchliff, P., 1987, *Benjamin Jowett and the Christian Religion*, Oxford, 1987

Holt, C. D., 1987, *Letters from Newnham College, 1889–1892*, ed. E. O. Cockburn, 3rd edn, Cambridge, 1987

Hort, A. F., 1896, *Life and Letters of Fenton John Anthony Hort*, 2 vols., London, 1896

Hoskin, M., 1990, 'History and Philosophy of Science in Cambridge', *Cambridge* 26 (1990), 46–50

Housman, A. E., ed., 1903–30, *M. Manilii Astronomicon, Liber Primus . . . Liber Quintus*, London, 1903–30, 2nd edn, Cambridge, 1937

  ed., 1905, *D. Iunii Iuuenalis Saturae*, London, 1905

  ed., 1926, *M. Annaei Lucani Belli Ciuilis Libri Decem*, Oxford, 1926

  1933, *The Name and Nature of Poetry*, Cambridge, 1933

  1971, *The Letters of A. E. Housman*, ed. H. Maas, London, 1971

Howard, H. F., 1935, *An Account of the Finances of the College of St John the Evangelist in the University of Cambridge, 1511–1926*, Cambridge, 1935

Howarth, J. and Curthoys, M., 1987, 'The political economy of women's higher education in late nineteenth and early twentieth-century Britain', *Historical Research*, 60 (1987), 208–31

Howarth, T. E. B., 1978, *Cambridge between Two Wars*, London, 1978

Hulbert, J., 1975, *The Little Woman's always Right*, London, 1975

James, M. R., 1907–8, *A Descriptive Catalogue of the Manuscripts in the Library of Gonville and Caius College*, 2 vols., Cambridge, 1907–8 (and *Supplement*, 1914)

James, M. R., Brooke, C. N. L. and Mynors, R. A. B., eds., 1983, *Walter*

Bibliographical references

Map: De Nugis Curialium, Courtiers' Trifles, Oxford Medieval Texts, Oxford, 1983

Jebb, C., 1907a, Life and Letters of Sir Richard Claverhouse Jebb, Cambridge, 1907

Jebb, R. C., 1907b, Essays and Addresses, Cambridge, 1907

Jenkins, H. and Jones, D. C., 1950, 'Social class of Cambridge University alumni of the 18th and 19th centuries', British Journal of Sociology, 1 (1950), 93–116

Jones, J., 1988, Balliol College: a History, 1263–1939, Oxford, 1988

Jones, W. H. S., 1936, A History of St Catharine's College, Cambridge, Cambridge, 1936

Kelly, T., 1981, For Advancement of Learning: the University of Liverpool, 1881–1981, Liverpool, 1981

Keynes, J. M., 1921, A Treatise on Probability, London, 1921, new edn, 1951
    1949, Two Memoirs, with notes by D. Garnett, London, 1949

Keynes, M. E., 1976/1984, A House by the River: Newnham Grange to Darwin College, Cambridge, 1976, cited from edn of 1984

King's Statutes 1952: Statutes of King's College in the University of Cambridge 1926–1952, Cambridge, 1952

Kitson Clark, G., 1973, 'A hundred years of the teaching of history at Cambridge, 1873–1973', Historical Journal, 16, 3 (1973), 535–53

Knight, F., 1980, Cambridge Music from the Middle Ages to Modern Times, Cambridge, 1980

Knowles, M. D., 1940/1963, The Monastic Order in England 940–1216, Cambridge, 1940, 2nd edn, 1963
    1940b, The Religious Houses of Medieval England, London, 1940
    1948–59, The Religious Orders in England, 3 vols., Cambridge, 1948–59
    1963, The Historian and Character and other Essays, Cambridge, 1963

Knowles, M. D., Brooke, C. N. L. and London, V. C. M., 1972, Heads of Religious Houses, England and Wales, 940–1216, Cambridge, 1972

Knowles, M. D. and Hadcock, R. N., 1971, Medieval Religious Houses, England and Wales, 2nd edn, London, 1971

Knox, R. Buick, n.d., Westminster College, Cambridge, Cambridge, n.d.

Langham, I., 1982, The Building of British Social Anthropology, Dordrecht, 1982

Lapsley, G. T., 1951, Crown, Community and Parliament, ed. H. M. Cam and G. Barraclough, Oxford, 1951

Larsen, E., 1962, The Cavendish Laboratory: Nursery of Genius, London, 1962

Lawson, F. H., 1968, The Oxford Law School, Oxford, 1968

Leavis, F. R., 1948, The Great Tradition: George Eliot, Henry James, Joseph Conrad, London, 1948
    1984, The Common Pursuit, London, 1952, cited from edn of 1984
    1986, Valuation in Criticism and other Essays, ed. G. Singh, Cambridge, 1986

613

Bibliographical references

Leavis, F. R. and Q. D., 1970, *Dickens the Novelist*, London, 1970

Leitch, V. B., 1983, *Deconstructive Criticism; an Advanced Introduction*, London, 1983

Leslie, S., 1923, *Mark Sykes; His Life and Letters*, London, 1923

Levy, P., 1979/1981, *Moore: G. E. Moore and the Cambridge Apostles*, London, 1979, 2nd edn, 1981

Lightfoot, J. B., 1868, *St Paul's Epistle to the Philippians*, London, 1868

1869, *St Paul's Epistle to the Galatians*, London, 1865, cited from edn of 1869

1889, *Essays on the Work entitled Supernatural Religion*, London, 1889

Liscombe, R. W., 1980, *William Wilkins 1778–1839*, Cambridge, 1980

Lowes Dickinson, G., 1973, *The Autobiography and other Unpublished Writings*, ed. D. Proctor, London, 1973

Lubbock, P., ed., 1926, *The Diary of Arthur Christopher Benson*, London, 1926

McCrum, M., 1989, 'Address to the Regent House of the retiring Vice-Chancellor, Mr M. W. McCrum, October 1989', *Cambridge*, 25 (1989), 9–21

McKitterick, D., 1984, *Four Hundred Years of University Printing and Publishing in Cambridge, 1584–1984* (Exhibition Catalogue), Cambridge, 1984

1986, *Cambridge University Library: a History*, II, *The Eighteenth and Nineteenth Centuries*, Cambridge, 1986 (vol. I is Oates 1986)

Mack Smith, D., 1954, *Cavour and Garibaldi: 1860*, Cambridge, 1954

McLachlan, J. O., 1947–9, 'The origins and early development of the teaching of history at Cambridge, 1873–1973', *Cambridge Historical Journal*, 9 (1947–9), 78–105

MacLeod, R., ed., 1982, *Days of Judgement: Science, Examinations and the Organization of Knowledge in Victorian England*, Driffield, 1982

MacLeod, R. and Moseley, R., 1979, 'Father and daughters: reflections on women, science and Victorian Cambridge', *History of Education*, 8 (1979), 321–33

1980, 'The "naturals" and Victorian Cambridge: reflections on the anatomy of an elite, 1851–1914', *Oxford Review of Education*, 6 (1980), 177–95

McNair, A. D. and Duff, P. W., 1947, 'William Warwick Buckland, 1859–1946', *PBA* 33 (1947), 283–91

McWilliams-Tullberg, R., 1975, *Women at Cambridge*, Cambridge, 1975

Maitland, E., 1957, *F. W. Maitland, a Child's-eye View*, Selden Society, London, 1957

Maitland, F. W., 1897, *Domesday Book and Beyond: Three Essays*, Cambridge, 1897

1898a, *Township and Borough*, Cambridge, 1898

1898b, *Roman Canon Law in the Church of England*, London, 1898

1906, *The Life and Letters of Leslie Stephen*, 2 vols., London, 1906

1911, *The Collected Papers of Frederic William Maitland*, ed. H. A. L. Fisher, 3 vols., Cambridge, 1911

1957, *Selected Historical Essays*, ed. H. M. Cam, Cambridge, 1957

Malden, H. E., 1902, *Trinity Hall*, London, 1902

Mangan, J. A., 1984, '"Oars and the man": pleasure and purpose in Victorian and Edwardian Cambridge', *History of Higher Education Journal*, 1984, pp. 52–77

Manning, B. L., 1919, *The People's Faith in the Time of Wyclif*, Cambridge, 1919

1939, *Essays in Orthodox Dissent*, London, 1939

1942, *The Hymns of Wesley and Watts*, London, 1942

Manselli, R., 1980, *Nos qui cum eo fuimus: contributo alla questione francescana*, Rome, 1980

Manton, J., 1965, *Elizabeth Garrett Anderson*, London, 1965

Marsh, E., ed., 1928, *The Collected Poems of Rupert Brooke: with a Memoir*, 2nd edn, London, 1928

Massey, H. and Feather, N., 1976, 'James Chadwick, 20 October 1891 – 24 July 1974', *BMFRS* 22 (1976), 11–70

Megarry, R. E. and Wade, H. W. R., 1957, *The Law of Real Property*, 1st edn, London, 1957

Middlebrook, M., 1971, *The First Day on the Somme*, London, 1971

Miller, E., 1961, *Portrait of a College; a History of the College of St John the Evangelist, Cambridge*, Cambridge, 1961

1983, 'Michael Moissey Postan, 1899–1981', *PBA* 69 (1983), 543–57

Milsom, S. F. C., 1980, 'F. W. Maitland', *PBA* 66 (1980), 265–81

Mitchell, B., 1971, *Abstract of British Historical Statistics*, Cambridge, 1971

Moore, G. E., 1903, *Principia Ethica*, Cambridge, 1903

1903a, 'The refutation of idealism' (1903), in Moore 1922, pp. 1–30

1922, *Philosophical Studies*, London, 1922, repr. 1960

1925, 'In defence of common sense', in Moore 1959, pp. 32–59

1959, *Philosophical Papers*, London, 1959

Moorman, M., 1957, *William Wordsworth, a Biography*, 1, *The Early Years 1770–1803*, Oxford, 1957

1980, *George Macaulay Trevelyan*, London, 1980

[Moralee, D., ed.,] 1980, *A Hundred Years of Cambridge Physics*, 2nd edn, Cambridge, 1980

Morey, A., 1979, *Dom David Knowles: a Memoir*, London, 1979

Moriarty, M., 1988, 'Modern Languages in Caius', *The Caian* 1988, pp. 87–93

Morris, C., 1989, *King's College: a Short History*, Cambridge, 1989

Morrison, J. S., 1991, 'A tale of three colleges', *Cambridge*, 28 (1991), 78–89

Mott, N., 1986, *A Life in Science*, London, 1986

Mullinger, J. B., 1911, *The University of Cambridge from the Election of*

Bibliographical references

    Buckingham to the Chancellorship in 1626 to the Decline of the Platonist Movement, Cambridge, 1911

Murray, K. M. E., 1977, *Caught in the Web of Words: James A. H. Murray and the 'Oxford English Dictionary'*, New Haven, 1977

Murray, R., 1980, *New Hall 1954–1972: The Making of a College*, Cambridge, 1980

Navarro, J. M. de, 'Hector Munro Chadwick, 1870–1947', *PBA* 33 (1947), 307–30

Needham, J., 1947, *History is on our Side*, New York, 1947

Needham, J. et al., 1954– , *Science and Civilization in China*, 1– , Cambridge, 1954–

Needham, J. and Baldwin, E., eds., 1949, *Hopkins and Biochemistry 1865–1947*, Cambridge, 1949

Neill, S. C. and Wright, T., 1988, *The Interpretation of the New Testament, 1861–1986*, 2nd edn, London, 1988

Newsome, D., 1966, *The Parting of Friends*, London, 1966

    1980, *On the Edge of Paradise: A. C. Benson: the Diarist*, London, 1980

    1984, 'Two Emmanuel historians', *Emmanuel College Magazine, Quatercentenary Issue*, 1984, pp. 104–14

Oates, J. C. T., 1954, *Catalogue of the Fifteenth-Century Printed Books in the University Library, Cambridge*, Cambridge, 1954

    1986, *Cambridge University Library: a History*, I, *From the Beginnings to the Copyright Act of Queen Anne*, Cambridge, 1986 (vol. II is McKitterick 1986)

Ogden, C. K. and Richards, I. A., 1923, *The Meaning of Meaning*, London, 1923

Okey, T., 1930, *A Basketful of Memories*, London, 1930

Olby, R., 1974, *The Path to the Double Helix*, London, 1974

Oliphant, M. L. E. and Lord Penney, 1968, 'John Douglas Cockcroft, 1897–1967', *BMFRS* 14 (1968), 141–88

Orchard, S., n.d., 'Cheshunt College 1768–1968', *Cheshunt College*, n.d., pp. 4–18

Ordinances . . . see Statutes

Owen, D. M., 1988, *Cambridge University Archives: a Classified List*, Cambridge, 1988

Page, N., 1983, *A. E. Housman: a Critical Biography*, London, 1983

Parry, R. St J., 1926, *Henry Jackson, O.M.*, Cambridge, 1926

Patrick, G. A., 1988, *F. J. A. Hort, Eminent Victorian*, Sheffield, 1988

PBA: Proceedings of the British Academy

Peacock, S. J., 1988, *Jane Ellen Harrison: the Mask and the Self*, New Haven, 1988

Peile, J., 1900, *Christ's College*, London, 1900

Bibliographical references

1910–13, *Biographical Register of Christ's College, 1505–1905*, 2 vols., Cambridge, 1910–13

Perkin, H., 1969, *The Origins of Modern English Society, 1780–1880*, London, 1969

1989, *The Rise of Professional Society: England since 1880*, London, 1989

Pevsner, N., 1970, *The Buildings of England: Cambridgeshire*, 2nd edn, Harmondsworth, 1970

Pfaff, R. W., 1980, *Montague Rhodes James*, London, 1980

Phillips, A., ed., 1979, *A Newnham Anthology*, Cambridge, 1979, cited from 2nd edn, 1988

Plumb, J., 1988, *The Making of a Historian, Collected Essays*, New York and London, 1988

Pollard, S., 1955–6, 'Barrow-in-Furness and the seventh Duke of Devonshire', *Economic History Review*, 2nd Series, 8 (1955–6), 213–21

Pollock, F. and Maitland, F. W., 1895, *The History of English Law before the Time of Edward I*, 2 vols., Cambridge, 1895, 2nd edn, 1898

Pollock, J. C., 1953, *A Cambridge Movement*, London, 1953

Porter, H. C., 1987, 'May Week', *Cambridge*, 20 (1987), 45–52

1988, 'Cambridge Commencements', *Cambridge*, 22 (1988), 21–6

Porter, R., 1982, 'The Natural Sciences Tripos and the "Cambridge School of Geology", 1850–1914', *History of the Universities*, 2 (1982), 193–216

Power, E., 1922, *Medieval English Nunneries*, Cambridge, 1922

1941, *The Wool Trade in English Medieval History*, Oxford, 1941

Powicke, F. M., 1955, *Modern Historians and the Study of History*, London, 1955

Prothero, G. W., 1888, *A Memoir of Henry Bradshaw*, London, 1888

Quiggin, A. H., 1942, *Haddon the Head-Hunter*, Cambridge, 1942

Rackham, O., 1975, *Hayley Wood: its History and Ecology*, Cambridge, 1975

Ratcliff, E. C., 1935, 'Francis Crawford Burkitt', *Journal of Theological Studies*, 36 (1935), 225–54, 337–46

Raven, C. E., 1923, *Apollinarianism*, Cambridge, 1923

1928a, *A Wanderer's Way*, London, 1928

1928b, *Women and Holy Orders*, Cambridge, 1928

1931, *Musings and Memories*, London, 1931

1942, *John Ray, Naturalist: his Life and Works*, Cambridge, 1942

1947, *English Naturalists from Neckam to Ray*, Cambridge, 1947

1954, 'Alex Wood – a memoir', in A. Wood and F. Oldham, *Thomas Young, Natural Philosopher, 1773–1829*, (Cambridge, 1954), pp. ix–xvi

Raverat, G., 1952, *Period Piece: a Cambridge Childhood*, London, 1952

Rawle, T., *Cambridge Architecture*, London, 1985

RC 1852: Report of Her Majesty's Commissioners appointed to inquire into the . . . University and Colleges of Cambridge, 1852

RC *1874*: *Report of the Commissioners appointed to inquire into the property and income of the Universities of Oxford and Cambridge,* 3 vols., 1874

RC *1922*: *Royal Commission on Oxford and Cambridge Universities Report* (Cmd. 1588), 1922

RCHM *Cambridge*: *Royal Commission on Historical Monuments for England, City of Cambridge,* 2 parts, London, 1959

Reisman, D., 1990, *Alfred Marshall's Mission,* London, 1990

Reporter: Cambridge University Reporter

Rich, E. E., ed., 1973, *St Catharine's College, Cambridge, 1473–1973,* London, 1973

Richards, I. A., 1929, *Practical Criticism,* London, 1929

1990, *Selected Letters,* ed. J. Constable, with introd. by R. Luckett, Oxford, 1990

Ridgeway, W., 1892, *The Origin of Metallic Currency and Weight Standards,* Cambridge, 1892

1905, *The Origin and Influence of the Thoroughbred Horse,* Cambridge, 1905

1910, *The Origin of Tragedy,* Cambridge, 1910

Roach, J. P. C., 1959, 'The University of Cambridge', *VCH Cambs.,* III (1959), 150–312

1986, *A History of Secondary Education in England, 1800–1870,* London, 1986

Roberts, C. H., 1936, 'An unpublished fragment of the Fourth Gospel in the John Rylands Library', *Bulletin of the John Rylands Library,* 20 (1936), 45–55

ed., 1938, *Catalogue of the Greek and Latin Papyri in the John Rylands Library, Manchester,* III, Manchester, 1938

Roberts, G. K., 1980, 'The liberally-educated chemist: Chemistry in the Cambridge Natural Sciences Tripos, 1851–1914', *Historical Studies in the Physical Sciences,* 2,1 (1980), 157–83

Robinson, J. Armitage, 1903, *St Paul's Epistle to the Ephesians,* 1st edn, London, 1903

1921, *Somerset Historical Essays,* London, 1921

1923, *The Times of St Dunstan,* Oxford, 1923

Robinson, J. A. T., 1976, *Re-dating the New Testament,* London, 1976

1981, *Joseph Barber Lightfoot,* Durham, 1981

1985, *The Priority of John,* ed. J. F. Coakley, London, 1985

Robson, R., 1967, 'Trinity College in the age of Peel', in *Ideas and Institutions of Victorian England: Essays in Honour of George Kitson Clark,* ed. R. Robson, London, 1967, pp. 312–35

Robson, R. and Cannon, W. F., 1964, 'William Whewell, F.R.S.', *Notes and Records of the Royal Society of London,* 19 (1964), 168–91

Romilly, J., 1967, *Romilly's Cambridge Diary 1832–42,* ed. J. P. T. Bury, Cambridge, 1967

Bibliographical references

Rook, A., ed., 1971, *Cambridge and its Contribution to Medicine*, London, 1971

Rossiter, A. P., 1932, *Poor Scholars: a Novel*, London, 1932

    1948–9, 'Bruegel's ambivalences', *Cambridge Journal*, 2 (1948–9), 131–47

    1989, *Angel with Horns*, ed. G. Storey, 1st edn, 1961, cited from 2nd edn, with introd. by P. Holland, London, 1989

Rothblatt, S., 1981, *The Revolution of the Dons: Cambridge and Society in Victorian England*, 2nd edn, Cambridge, 1981

RSO: Royal Society Obituaries

Rupp, (E.) G., 1977, *Just Men: Historical Pieces*, London, 1977

    1981, 'A Cambridge centenary: the Selwyn Divinity School, 1879–1979', *Historical Journal*, 24,2 (1981), 417–28

    1986, *Religion in England 1688–1791*, Oxford, 1986

Russell, B., 1956, *Logic and Knowledge*, ed. R. C. Marsh, London, 1956

Rutherford, E., 1904, *Radio-Activity*, Cambridge, 1904

St John's Statutes 1948: Statutes for the College of Saint John the Evangelist in the University of Cambridge, edn of Cambridge, 1948

Sanctuary, A., 1990, 'Arthur Sanctuary, born 1891', ed. Mr and Mrs W. D. Harrap, *The Caian* 1990, pp. 86–8

Schneewind, J. B., 1977, *Sidgwick's Ethics and Victorian Moral Philosophy*, Oxford, 1977

Scott, A. C., 1927, *The History of the Caius College Boat Club 1827-1927*, Cambridge, 1927 (= *The Caian* 35)

Scott-Giles, C. W., 1975, *Sidney Sussex College: a Short History*, Cambridge, 1975

Searby, P., 1982, *The Training of Teachers in Cambridge University: the First Sixty Years, 1879–1939*, Cambridge, 1982

    1982–3, 'A failure at Cambridge: Cavendish College, 1877–1892', *Proceedings of the Cambridge Antiquarian Society*, 72 (1982–3, publ. 1984), 106–20

Shipley, A. E., 1913, *'J', A Memoir of John Willis Clark*, London, 1913

Shrosbree, C., 1988, *Public Schools and Private Education: the Clarendon Commission 1861–64 and the Public Schools Acts*, Manchester, 1988

Shuckburgh, E. S., 1904, *Emmanuel College*, London, 1904

Sicca, C. M., 1987, *Committed to Classicism: the Building of Downing College, Cambridge*, Cambridge, 1987

Sidgwick, A. and E. M., 1906, *Henry Sidgwick, a Memoir*, London, 1906

Sidgwick, E., 1938, *Mrs Henry Sidgwick*, London, 1938

Slee, P. R. H., 1986, *Learning and a Liberal Education: the Study of Modern History in the Universities of Oxford, Cambridge and Manchester, 1800–1914*, Manchester, 1986

    1987, 'Professor Soffer's "History at Oxford"', *Historical Journal*, 30 (1987), 933–42

Smith, A. L., 1908, *Frederic William Maitland: Two Lectures and a Bibliography*, Oxford, 1908

Snow, C. P., 1951, *The Masters*, London, 1951

1967, *Varieties of Men*, London, 1967

1981, *The Physicists*, London, 1981

Soffer, R., 1987a, 'Nation, duty, character and confidence: history at Oxford, 1850–1914', *Historical Journal*, 30, 1 (1987), 77–104

1987b, 'The modern university and national values, 1850–1930', *Historical Research*, 60 (1987), 166–87

1988, 'The development of disciplines in the modern English university', *Historical Journal*, 31 (1988), 933–46

Sondheimer, J., n.d., *History of the British Federation of University Women, 1907–1957*, London, n.d.

Spratling, F. R., 1989, 'Veterinary Medicine in Cambridge', *Cambridge*, 25 (1989), 49–53

Squibb, G. D., 1972, *Founder's Kin*, Oxford, 1972

1977, *Doctor's Commons: a History of the College of Advocates and Doctors of Law*, Oxford, 1977

Statutes and Ordinances of the University of Cambridge, various editions. (For *Statutes* of Colleges, see *King's College, St John's College*, etc.)

Stedman Jones, G., 1976, 'From historical sociology to theoretical history', *British Journal of Sociology*, 27 (1976), 295–305; repr. in *History and Class*, ed. R. S. Neale (Oxford, 1983), pp. 73–85

Stein, P., 1992, 'Maine and legal education', in Maine centenary volume, ed. A. Diamond, forthcoming, Cambridge, 1992

Steinberg, J., 1976, *Why Switzerland?*, Cambridge, 1976

Steiner, W. A., 1991, 'The Squire Law Library of the University of Cambridge', *Bibliothek und Recht-international. Festschrift Ralph Lansky* (Hamburg, 1991), pp. 243–94

Steiner, Z., 1977, *Britain and the Origins of the First World War*, London, 1977

Stephen, B., 1927, *Emily Davies and Girton College*, London, 1927

Stephen, L., 1865, *Sketches from Cambridge*, London, 1865

1885, *Life of Henry Fawcett*, 2nd edn, London, 1885

1893, *An Agnostic's Apology and other Essays*, London, 1893

Stewart, H. F., 1945, *The Heart of Pascal*, Cambridge, 1945

Stewart, J., 1959, *Jane Ellen Harrison: a Portrait from Letters*, London, 1959

Stoddart, D. R., 1989, 'A hundred years of Geography at Oxford and Cambridge, II. A hundred years of Geography at Cambridge', *Geographical Journal*, 155 (1989), 24–32

Stokes, R., 1984, *Henry Bradshaw, 1831–1886*, Metuchen, NJ, 1984

Stopp, E., 1986, 'The Cambridge setting', in 'The mind in love: the world of

Bibliographical references

Kenelm Foster, O.P., friar, scholar and preacher, 1910–1986', *New Blackfriars*, 67 (1986), 401–56, at 407–13

Strachan, H., 1976, *History of the Cambridge University Officers' Training Corps*, Speldhurst, 1976

Stubbings, F., 1977, *Emmanuel College Chapel, 1677–1977*, Cambridge, 1977

    1983, *Forty-Nine Lives: an Anthology of Portraits of Emmanuel Men*, Cambridge, 1983

    1984–5, 'Who was Chapman?', *Emmanuel College Magazine*, 67 (1984–5), 17–21

Sutcliffe, P., 1978, *Oxford University Press: an Informal History*, Oxford, 1978

Sutherland, G., 1987, 'The movement for the higher education of women: its social and intellectual context in England, *c*.1840–80', in *Political and Social Change in Modern Britain: Essays presented to A. F. Thompson*, ed. P. J. Waller (Brighton, 1987), pp. 91–116

    1990, 'The plainest principles of justice: the University of London and the higher education of women', in Thompson 1990, pp. 35–56

Sweeney, G., 1982, *St Edmund's House, Cambridge: the First Eighty Years: a History*, Cambridge, 1982

Symonds, R., 1982, 'Oxford and India', in *Oxford and the Idea of Commonwealth: Essays presented to Sir Edgar Williams*, ed. F. Maddon and D. K. Fieldhouse (London, 1982), pp. 49–72

    1986, *Oxford and Empire: the Last Lost Cause?*, London, 1986

Szreter, S. R. S., 1984, 'The genesis of the Registrar-General's social classification of occupations', *British Journal of Sociology*, 35 (1984), 522–46

Tabor, D., 1969, 'Frank Philip Bowden, 1903–1968', *BMFRS* 15 (1969), 1–38

Tait, J., 1987, review of Maitland 1897 in *English Historical Review*, 12 (1897), 768–77

Tanner, J. R., ed., 1917, *The Historical Register of the University of Cambridge*, Cambridge, 1917

Tatlow, T. T., 1933, *The Story of the Student Christian Movement of Great Britain and Ireland*, London, 1933

Taylor, H. M. and J., 1965–78, *Anglo-Saxon Architecture*, 3 vols., Cambridge, 1965–78

Taylor, N. and Booth, P., 1970, *New Cambridge Architecture*, 3rd edn, London, 1970

Taylor, T. F., 1991, *J. Armitage Robinson*, Cambridge, 1991

Teich, M. and Young, R., 1973, *Changing Perspectives in the History of Science: Essays in Honour of Joseph Needham*, London, 1973

Temperley, H. W. V., ed., 1920–4, *A History of the Peace Conference of Paris*, 6 vols., London, 1920–4

Thistlethwaite, N., 1983, *The Organs of Cambridge*, Oxford, 1983

Bibliographical references

Thompson, D. M., 1992, 'Lightfoot as Victorian churchman', *The Lightfoot Centenary Lectures*, ed. J. D. G. Dunn, *Durham University Journal*, Extra No. (1992), pp. 3–21

Thompson, F. M. L., ed., 1990, *The University of London and the World of Learning, 1836–1986*, London, 1990

Thompson, M. W., 1990, *The Cambridge Antiquarian Society, 1840–1990*, Cambridge, 1990

Thomson, J. J., 1903, *The Conduction of Electricity through Gases*, Cambridge, 1903
  1936, *Recollections and Reflections*, London, 1936

Tibbatts, G. K., 1988, *The Oratory of the Good Shepherd*, Windsor, 1988

Tillyard, E. M. W., 1943, *The Elizabethan World Picture*, London, 1943
  1958, *The Muse Unchained*, London, 1958

Todd, A., 1983, *A Time to Remember: the Autobiography of a Chemist*, Cambridge, 1983

Todd-Jones, D. J., 1989, 'The University's Estate Management and Building Service: its history and development', *Cambridge*, 25 (1989), 76–82

Trevelyan, G. M., 1913, *Clio a Muse and other Essays*, London, 1913
  1943, *An Autobiography and other Essays*, London, 1943

Truscot, B., 1943, *Redbrick University*, London, 1943

Twigg, J., 1987, *A History of Queens' College, Cambridge, 1448–1986*, Woodbridge, 1987

Ullmann, E., 1990, *Walter Ullmann: a Tale of Two Cultures*, Cambridge, 1990

Underwood, M. G., 1990, 'Restructuring a household', *Eagle* 72 (1990), 9–18

Vaughan, R., 1958, *Matthew Paris*, Cambridge Studies in Medieval Life and Thought, New Series, 6, Cambridge, 1958

VCH Cambs: The Victoria History of the Counties of England: a History of the County of Cambridge and Isle of Ely, III, ed. J. P. C. Roach, London, 1959

Venn: Venn, J. et al., *Biographical History of Gonville and Caius College*, 7 vols., Cambridge, 1897–1978

Venn, *Alumni*: Venn, J. and J. A., eds., *Alumni Cantabrigienses*, 2 parts (to 1751, 1752–1900), 4 + 6 vols., Cambridge, 1922–54

Venn, J., 1901, *Caius College*, London, 1901
  1913, *Early Collegiate Life*, Cambridge, 1913

Ventris, M. and Chadwick, J., 1956, *Documents in Mycenaean Greek*, Cambridge, 1956

von Hügel, A., 1990, *The Fiji Journals of Baron Anatole von Hügel, 1875–77*, ed. J. Roth and S. Hooper, Suva and Cambridge, 1990

Wade, E. C. S., 1976, 'Arnold Duncan McNair, 1885–1975', *PBA* 62 (1976), 507–12

Wade, E. C. S. and Phillips, G. G., 1931, *Constitutional Law*, 1st edn, London, 1931

Bibliographical references

Wade, H. W. R., 1961, *Administrative Law*, 1st edn, Oxford, 1961

Walker, T. A., 1912, *Admissions to Peterhouse or S. Peter's College in the University of Cambridge*, Cambridge, 1912

Walters, S. M., 1981, *The Shaping of Cambridge Botany*, Cambridge, 1981

Warburton, Dame Anne, 1990, 'Lucy at 25', *Cambridge*, 27 (1990), 67–70

Warnock, G. J., 1958, *English Philosophy since 1900*, London, 1958

Watkin, D., 1989, *The Architecture of Basil Champneys*, Cambridge, 1989

Watson, J. D., 1968, *The Double Helix*, London, 1968

Watson, S., 1991, 'Developing Management Studies in Cambridge: the Judge Institute of Management Studies', *Cambridge*, 28 (1991), 32–5

Weatherall, M., 1990, '1814–1989' in J. Geyer-Kordesch, M. Weatherall and H. Kaminga, *The History of Medicine in Cambridge* (Exhibition pamphlet), Cambridge, 1990, pp. 29–71

Welch, E., ed., 1990, *Cheshunt College: the Early Years*, Hertfordshire Record Publications, 6, 1990

Westcott, A., 1903, *Life and Letters of Brooke Foss Westcott*, 2 vols., London, 1903

Westcott, B. F., 1887, *Social Aspects of Christianity*, London, 1887

1901, *Lessons from Work*, London, 1901

1903, *Christian Social Union Addresses*, London, 1903

Westcott, B. F. and Hort, F. J. A., 1881, *The New Testament in Greek*, Cambridge, 2 vols., 1881

White, J. F., 1962, *The Cambridge Movement*, Cambridge, 1962

Whitehead, A. N. and Russell, B., 1910–13, *Principia Mathematica*, Cambridge, 2 vols., 1910–13

Whitehead, J., 1987, 'Why so few? Women academics in the University of Cambridge', *Cambridge Review* 108 (1987), 107–15

Whiteside, D. T., et al., eds., 1967–91, *The Mathematical Papers of Sir Isaac Newton*, Cambridge, 1967–91

Whitney, J. P., 1919, *The Study of Ecclesiastical History To-day: an Inaugural Address*, Cambridge, 1919

Wigglesworth, V. B., 1976, *Insects and the Life of Man*, London, 1976

1979, 'Interview with Sir Vincent Wigglesworth' (by E. Timms), *The Caian* 1979, pp. 31–44

Wilamowitz, 1985, *Wilamowitz nach 50 Jahren*, ed. W. M. Calder III et al., Darmstadt, 1985

Wilkes, M. V., 1985, *Memoirs of a Computer Pioneer*, Cambridge, Mass., 1985

Wilkinson, (L.) P., 1969, *John Tressider Sheppard, Kt., M.B.E., 1881–1968*, Cambridge, 1969

1980a, *A Century of King's, 1873–1972*, Cambridge, 1980

1980b, *Kingsmen of a Century: 1873–1972*, Cambridge, 1980

Bibliographical references

Willey, B., 1940, *The Eighteenth Century Background*, Cambridge, 1940
    1962, *The Seventeenth Century Background*, Cambridge, 1962
    1968, *Cambridge and Other Memories, 1920–1953*, London, 1968
Williams, Glanville, 1985, 'The Lords and impossible attempts', *Cambridge Law Journal* (1985), 33–83
Williamson, R., ed., 1987, *The Making of Physicists*, Bristol, 1987
Willis, R., 1845a, *The Architectural History of Canterbury Cathedral*, London, 1845
    1845b, 'The architectural history of Winchester Cathedral', in *Proceedings at the Annual Meeting of the Archaeological Institute of Great Britain and Ireland at Winchester, September 1845*, London, 1846, repr. by Friends of Winchester Cathedral, 1980
    1869, *The Architectural History of the Conventual Buildings of the Monastery of Christ Church, in Canterbury*, London, 1869
Willis, R. and Clark, J. W., 1886/1988, *The Architectural History of the University of Cambridge and of the Colleges of Cambridge and Eton*, 3 vols., Cambridge, 1886, repr. with introduction by D. Watkin, 1988
Wilson, D., 1983, *Rutherford: Simple Genius*, London, 1983
Winfield, P. H., 1937, *A Textbook of the Law of Tort*, 1st edn, London, 1937
Winstanley, D. A., 1922, *The University of Cambridge in the Eighteenth Century*, Cambridge, 1922
    1935, *Unreformed Cambridge*, Cambridge, 1935
    1940, *Early Victorian Cambridge*, Cambridge, 1940
    1947, *Later Victorian Cambridge*, Cambridge, 1947
Winter, J., 1986, *The Great War and the British People*, London, 1986
Wittgenstein, L., 1953, *Philosophical Investigations*, with English trans. by G. E. M. Anscombe, Oxford, 1953
Wood, H. G., 1953, *Terrot Reavely Glover: a Biography*, Cambridge, 1953
Woodward, E. L., 1942, *Short Journey*, London, 1942
Woolf, V., 1929/1977, *A Room of One's Own*, London, 1929, cited from edn of 1977
Wormell, D., 1980, *Sir John Seeley and the Uses of History*, Cambridge, 1980
Young, F. G., 1967, *Darwin College 1963–66, and the University of Cambridge*, Cambridge, 1967

INDEX

University of Cambridge institutions are indexed under University of Cambridge; colleges, disciplines and faculties separately. Numbers in italics refer to pages with illustrations. Offices such as Chancellor, etc. refer to Cambridge unless otherwise specified.

Abraham, Bishop C. J., 93
accounts, 282–7, *and see* University of Cambridge: colleges, accounts and finance
Acton, Lord, Regius Professor of Modern History, 54, 218, 390–1, 422, 434; and German scholarship, 234; and history in Cambridge, 229, 232–4, 237; and Maitland, 405–6
Adams, Mrs, 305
Adams, J. C., 174n
ADC (Amateur Dramatic Club), 299, 459
Adcock, Sir Frank, professor of ancient history, 216, 465
Addenbrooke's Hospital, 14, 165, 167–73, 191, 497–8
Addyman, P., 208
administration, 545, *and see* bureaucracy
Adrian, Anne, Mrs Keynes, 275
Adrian, E. D., Lord Adrian, master of Trinity, professor of physiology, Vice-Chancellor and Chancellor, 275, 566, 579
Adullamites, the, 90–1, 588
aerial photography, 176, *192*, 208, 474
aeronautics, 481
Africa, and archaeology, 207
African Studies, Centre of, 208
agnostics, agnosticism, 13, 105, 113, 121–31, 146, 293, 336, 405, 407, 418, 517; and Sidgwick, 14–18
agricultural depression, 67, 74, 76, 78–80, 181
Agricultural Research Council, 503
agriculture, 91, 472
Ailred, St, abbot of Rievaulx, 425–6

Albert, Prince, Chancellor, 566
Alcock, John, bishop of Ely, founder of Jesus, 38
Alexander, Samuel, 403
Alexandra, Queen, 64
Alfred, King, 223
All Souls College, Oxford, 179
Allbutt, Sir Clifford, Regius Professor of Physic, 97–8, 167–8, 170, 493
Alps, 10, 62, 291
America, North, 581; and Maitland, 218, 220, 224; and physics, 180; American Civil War, 254; *and see* USA
Amos, Sir Maurice, 287–9
Anderson, C. A., and Schnaper, M., 249
Anderson, Sir Colin, and the Anderson Committee, 542–4
Anderson, Elizabeth Garrett, 244, 307–8
Anderson, H. K., Sir Hugh, master of Gonville and Caius, 170, 276, 327, 366, 577, 588; his achievements, 588–9; his character and career, 343–9; and Gowland Hopkins, 196–7; and Royal Commission, 1919–22, and Statutory Commission, 341–3, 353n, 362, 364–8; and the University Library, 370, 372–87; the Anderson Room, 387; his war work, 332
Anderson, Lady, wife of Sir Hugh, 48, 306, 343–9 passim, 368
Anderson, Maisie (Mary Desirée), Lady Cox, 341n, 343, 350; her reminiscences quoted, 48, 343–9, 364–8, 460; on Benson and Quiller-Couch, 448; on Gowland Hopkins, 196–7; on the

Index

Rockefeller Foundation and the University Library, 370n, 381
Anderson, Mary, 524
Anglicanism, chaps. 4–5; devotion and tradition, 9, 93–4; high church, 50–1; 403–5; *and see* evangelicalism
Anglo-Saxon, study of, 64, 432, 444–6, 450; and Norse and Celtic, 445
animal behaviour, 493
Annan, N., Lord Annan, 122
Annesley, F., master of Downing, 55
Anselm, St, archbishop of Canterbury, 520n
anthropology, physical, 201; social, 201–5; Anthropological Studies, Board of, 204
Apostles, the, 9–10, 15, 35, 127–9, 438–41, 469–70, *and see* Moore; Trevelyan
Arabia, Arabic, 428–9; Arabs, 523
archaeology, archaeologists, 201–9, 537–8; Archaeological Unit, Cambridge, 202, 491; the new archaeology, 207
archaeology and anthropology faculty and tripos, 163, 201–9, 499–500
architecture, 455–7
archives, xx
Aristophanes, 126
Aristotle, 71–2, 453
Arnold, Thomas, 9, 92
Artillery, Royal Field, Wessex Division, 331
arts, 541
Arts Theatre, 459
Ashby, Sir Eric, Lord Ashby, master of Clare, 574–5, 579; and Clare Hall, 580–2; as Vice-Chancellor, 524
Asquith, H. H., Lord Asquith (Earl of Oxford and Asquith), 96, 98, 213, 326, 341, 365–6
Association of Scientific Workers, 485
astronomy, 486–90, 547
Athens, ancient, 557
Atkinson, E., master of Clare, 63
atom, and Rutherford, 187; atom bomb, 177, 190–1
Austen, Edward, 246n
Austen, James, 246n
Austen, Jane, 243–4, 246, 330, 345, 450; her father, 145
Austen Leigh, Augustus, provost of King's, 34–5, 37, 40, 128, 260, 273; election as provost, 293; and chapel attendance, 115
Austen Leigh, Edward, 35, 273–4
Austin, Lord, 176–7
Austin Friars, precinct of, 153
Australia, and radio astronomy, 487

Austria, 497, 505–6
Austria-Hungary, 235
AUT (Association of University Teachers), 522, 574
Ayerst Hall, 594

Babbage, C., 492
Babington, C. C., professor of botany, 161
Bailey, Professor D. R. Shackleton, 215
Baker, Sir Herbert, 473
Baker, Professor J., 217n, 224n
Baker, J. F., Lord Baker, professor of engineering, 475–6, 478–81
Balfour, A. J., Lord Balfour, prime minister and Chancellor of Cambridge, 15, 112, 178, 218, 314, 382
Balfour, Eleanor, *see* Sidgwick
Balfour, Gerald, later Lord Balfour, 341
Balliol College, Oxford, 83–5, 106, 252n; master, *see* Jowett
Banks, A. L., professor of human ecology, 172
Baptists, 165, *and see* Glover
Barker, Sir Ernest, professor of political science, 251–2
Barnes, E. W., 404
Barnes, W. E., 52, 53n
Barth, Karl, 150
Bartlett, D., 499n
Bartlett, Sir Frederic, professor of psychology, 494, 499–502; his wife, Mary, Lady Bartlett, 502
Bateson, Mary, 318, 320–1
Bateson, William, master of St John's, 9, 68–9, 259, 326, 431; and St John's chapel, 107; as Royal Commissioner, 88
Bauer, Professor P. T., Lord Bauer, 505
Baur, F. C., 122
Bayley, Professor P., 433n
Beagle, The, 160
Beard, Charles, 102
Beaufort, Lady Margaret, countess of Richmond, 59
Becquerel, 184
Bedford, 488
Beerbohm, Max, 36, 48
Belgium, 333
Bell, Jocelyn, 488
Bellingham, Emily, 300
Bendall, S., 123n
Benedict, St, 421
Benet House, 60, 389, 391
Benians, E. A., later master of St John's, 236
Bennett, E. K. ('Francis'), senior tutor (and president) of Gonville and Caius, 399, 444

Index

Bensly, R., 428, 430
Benson, A. C., fellow, later master of
  Magdalene, 46–9, 89, 95n, 446, 448; 47;
  quoted 96, 273; on Westcott, 136–7
Benson, E. W., archbishop of Canterbury,
  15–16, 48, 134
Bentham, J., 18
Bentley, Richard, master of Trinity, xv, 5,
  211–12, 214–15
Berkhamsted School, headmaster of, 155,
  586–7
Berlin, 169, 220, 417
Bernal, J. D., 497
Bernard of Clairvaux, St, 313
Bertram, Kate, president of Lucy Cavendish,
  570
Bethune-Baker, J. F., 146–7
Beves, Donald, senior tutor of King's, 399,
  459
Bible, biblical scholarship, 12, 121, chaps. 5,
  14, and see Dodd; Hort; Lightfoot;
  Westcott; and Darwin, 15; Revised
  Version of the Bible, 1, 12, 139, 590
Bidder, Anna, president of Lucy Cavendish,
  571
Biddle, M., 208
Binfield, C., 397
biochemistry, 170–1, 194, and see Hopkins
biology, 492–504; developmental, 586n;
  biological sciences and Rockefeller, 381
Birdwood, Lord, master of Peterhouse, 262
Birkbeck Lectures, xviii, 277
Birmingham, 96; bishop of, see Gore; King
  Edward's School, 134; Museum and Art
  Gallery, 343
Bishop, E., 418, 420
Black, Michael, 585
Blackburn, M., 462
Blackett, P. M. S., Lord Blackett, professor
  at Birkbeck College, London, and
  Manchester, 188
Blackfriars, Cambridge, 391, 434
black holes, 482, 486, 488, 490
Blackwell, E., 308
Bletchley, 459, 488, 506; 'Bletchley Junction
  Academy', 325
Blomfield, Sir Arthur, 94, 142
Blomfield, Sir Reginald, 379
Blunt, C., 462
Board of Education, later Ministry, later
  Department of Education and Science,
  97–8; President, see Fisher, H. A. L.
Boards of Studies, 357
Bodichon, Mme (Barbara Leigh-Smith),
  307–8, 316

Bodley, G. F., 107, 109–11
Bohr, Niels, 188, 499
Bondi, Sir Hermann, 488
Bonney, T.G., 117, 158; professor at
  University College London, 159
Born, M., 188
boroughs, medieval, 222–4
Bosch, Hieronymus, 452–3
botany (now plant sciences), xv, 91, 156,
  160–4, 477; and archaeology, 201
Bowden, P., 193, 195, 265
Boyde, P., professor of Italian, 455–6
Boys-Smith, J., master of St John's, 577
Bradbrook, Professor, mistress of Girton, 311
Bradfield, J., senior bursar of Trinity, 579
Bradley, Professor A. C., 25, 453
Bradley, F. H., 442
Bradshaw, Henry, University Librarian,
  fellow of King's, 33, 35; and the
  University Library, 272–4, 371
Bragg, Sir Lawrence, Cavendish Professor,
  176, 191, 497–8
Braithwaite, Margaret, 571
Braithwaite, Professor Richard, 571
Brasenose College, Oxford, 38, 78
Braybrooke, Lord, 45–6, 258, and see Neville,
  Latimer
Brentano, R., on Maitland, 224n
Brereton, J., 92–3
Bresslau, H., 234
Brett, M., 582n
Breul, K., Schröder Professor of German,
  434
Bridges, Lord, and the Bridges Report, 539,
  549, 572–5
Brink, C., professor of Latin, and Robinson
  College, 582n, 583
Bristol University, 29, 266
British Academy, 60, 72, 354, 554
British Council of Churches, 149
British Expeditionary Force (1914), 333
Brittain, F., 38, 396, 435
Broad, Professor C. D., 337n
Broadbent, D. E., 500–1
Brockbank, Professor P., 455n
Brogan, Sir Denis, professor of political
  science, 54, 238
Brooke, C. N. L., Dixie Professor, 402, 455n,
  571
Brooke, Professor N. S., 443n, 447n, 451n
Brooke, Philip, 497n
Brooke, Rosalind B., 301n, 413
Brooke, Rupert, 127, 129, 332–3, 335
Brooke, Z. N., fellow of Caius, professor of
  medieval history, 40, 205n, 222, 226n,

231, 234–6, 284, 508–9; and Jack
Hulbert, 299; and David Knowles, 419,
422; and Bernard Manning, 398; his
wife, Rosa G. Brooke, and their
accounts, 282–7
Browne, E. H., Norrisian Professor of
Divinity, bishop of Ely and Winchester,
4, 141
Browne, G. F., 134
Browning, Oscar, the OB, 34, 36–7, 49, 89,
219; and the Day Training College,
464–6
Bruegel, Pieter the elder, 453
Bruton, abbot of, 424
Buchan, John, on Brasenose, 38
Buchdahl, G., 475
Buchman, F., 133
Buckingham, duke of, Chancellor, 258
Buckland, W. W., Regius Professor of Civil
Law, 218, 227; and his books, 225–6; as
senior tutor and president of Gonville
and Caius, 40, 225–6
Buckminster-Fuller geodesic dome, 456
Bullard, Sir Edward, 159
Bullough, R., professor of Italian, 40, 434;
and his wife and family, 391
Bultmann, Rudolf, 411, 413
bureaucracy, 533–8
Burgon, J. W., dean of Chichester, 12
Burkitt, F. C., Norrisian and Norris-Hulse
Professor of Divinity, 142, 146–7, 417,
431
Burleigh, Lord, Chancellor, 566
Burnaby, J., Regius Professor of Divinity, 104
Burne-Jones, E., 107, 396
Bury, J. B., Regius Professor of Modern
History, 235, 367, 422, 441, 467
Bury, P. T. B., 49
Butler, Dom Cuthbert, monk and abbot of
Downside, 389–91, 418
Butler, Sir Geoffrey, 377n
Butler, H. Montagu, master of Trinity, 71,
132; his wife Agnata (Ramsay), 329
Butler, J. R. M., Sir James, Regius Professor
of Modern History, 382, 418
Butler, R. A., Lord Butler, master of
Trinity, 262–3; and Education Act of
1944, 509
Butterfield, Sir Herbert, professor of modern
history, Regius Professor of Modern
History, master of Peterhouse, 54, 207,
236–9, 419
Buxton, P. A., 503

Cade, Jack, 452

Cairo Genizah, 135, 417
Caistor (Lincs.), 395
Caius, John, 104
Caius College, *see* Gonville and Caius College
Calcutta University, 428
Caldwell, R. T., master of Corpus, 51
California, 483; California Institute of
Technology, CalTech, 199, 499, 569
Calvinism, 104
Cam, Helen, and Girton, 222, 321–4; and
Harvard, 323
Cambrian Revolution, 158
Cambridge city: guild of thegns, 223; mayor
of, 4; MP for, 324; in *VCH*, 323
streets, bridge, houses etc.: Adams Rd, 281,
333; the Backs, *548–9, 552*; Barton Rd,
582; Bin Brook, 583; Brookside, 281;
Burrell's Walk, 386; Chesterton Lane
and Castle Brae, 144; Chesterton Rd,
292; Clarkson Rd, 284, 530; Downing
St, 375; Fisher House, 390–1; Free
School Lane, 153, 477; Garden House
Hotel, 525, 557–9; Grange Rd, 281, 284;
Green St, 547; Harvey Rd, 281–2;
Henry Martyn Hall, 132; Herschel Rd,
281, 581; Hills Rd, 389; Huntingdon
Rd, 567; Jesus Lane, 375; Lady Margaret
Rd, 572; Lensfield Rd, 265; Madingley
Rd, 281, 547, 582; Magdalene Bridge,
253; Merton Hall and School of
Pythagoras, 303; Midsummer Common,
333, 509; Mill Rd, 287; Milton Rd, 284,
493; Newnham Grange, 275–6;
Northampton St, 457, 463; Parker's
Piece, 291; Queen's Rd, 377; Regent St,
2; St Peter's Terrace, 7, 281; Scroope
House and Terrace, 455–6, 478;
Sidgwick Avenue, 254, 314, 375, 546;
Silver St, 579; Springfield, 254; Sylvester
Rd, 281, 402; Trinity St, 506;
Trumpington Rd, 160; Trumpington St,
456; West Rd, 225, 386, 457;
Wilberforce Rd, 281–5
theatres: *see under individual theatres*
Cambridge Antiquarian Society, 202–3
Cambridge Architectural Society, 109
Cambridge Camden Society, 106, 109
Cambridge College of Arts and Technology
(CCAT), 458
Cambridge Foundation, 565
Cambridge Group for the History of
Population and Social Structure
(ESRC), 238
Cambridge Historical Society and *Journal*
(now *Historical Journal*), 236

Index

Cambridge Instrument Co., 342
Cambridge Law Club, 217
Cambridge Magazine, 97
Cambridge Medieval History, 234, 398
Cambridge Modern History, 54, 233
Cambridge Philharmonic Society, 458
Cambridge Philosophical Society, 160
Cambridge University, *see* University of
    Cambridge
Cambridge University Bill (1856), 99
Cambridge University Musical Society
    (CUMS), 298, 457–8
Cambridge University Press (CUP), 200–1,
    419, 585, 590–1
Cambridge University Students' Union, *see*
    University of Cambridge, institutions
Cameron, Mrs F., 255, 306
Cameron, J., master of Gonville and Caius,
    255, 386; his wife, *see* Cameron,
    Mrs F.
Campion, W. M., tutor and president of
    Queens', 57, 110–11, 173
Canada, 183, 391
Canary Islands, 221, 225
Canterbury, archbishops of, *see* Anselm;
    Benson; Longley; Whitgift
Carswell, J., 540, 545–6, 560
Carter, H. C., 397
Carthusians, and the dissolution of the
    monasteries, 423
Cartmel, 174–5
Cartmell, J., master of Christ's, 60, 87
Cartwright, Dame Mary, mistress of Girton,
    321; *322*
Carus-Wilson, C. A., 372n
Cass, Sir Geoffrey, 201
Casson, Sir Hugh, 546
Catholic community in Cambridge, 203,
    388–91, 405, 407, 418–26; Benet House,
    60; Chaplaincy, 133; and Christ's, 60;
    and St Edmund's, 576; Roman
    Catholicism, 517; and Selwyn, 94n
Cavendish, Lord Frederick and Lady Lucy,
    572, *and see* Lucy Cavendish College
Cavendish College, 91–3, 95, 464, 576
Cavendish Laboratory, *see* physics
    department and Cavendish Laboratory
Cayley, A., 69
CCAT, *see* Cambridge College of Arts and
    Technology
celibacy, 10, 31, 62–3, 88, 134, *and see*
    marriage
Chadwick, H. M., professor of Anglo-Saxon,
    64, 202, 432, 434, 444–7
Chadwick, Henry, chaplain of Queens', dean

of Christ Church, Regius Professor of
    Divinity (Oxford and Cambridge),
    master of Peterhouse, 120–1, 142
Chadwick, Sir James, master of Gonville and
    Caius, 176–7, 179–80, 186, 188–91, 408,
    515; as professor of physics at Liverpool,
    190
Chadwick, Mrs N. K., 64, 445
Chadwick, W. Owen, Dixie Professor,
    Regius Professor of Modern History,
    master of Selwyn, 94, 139–40, 142–3,
    237, 489, 582; as dean of Trinity Hall,
    120–1; as Vice-Chancellor, 557n, 558
Chain, Ernst, 505
Chalmers, Lord, master of Peterhouse, 262,
    342, 348, 350, 366
Chamberlain, Powell and Bon, 571
Champneys, Basil, and Divinity School, 142,
    315; and Manchester, John Rylands
    Library, 315; and Newnham, 142, 314–
    15, 571
Chancery, Court of, and Downing, 54–5
Chapman, A. T., 9, 58, 87
Charles I, King, 258
Charlton, Professor D. G., 433n
Chaucer, 274, 444
Chawner, William, senior tutor and master
    of Emmanuel, 123–6, 186–7, 260, 394;
    his pamphlets, 124, 131
Cheltenham College, 247
Cheltenham Ladies' College, 464
chemistry, xvii, 194–201; biochemistry,
    195–9, inorganic and physical, 201;
    organic, 199–201; labs, 264–5
Cherwell, Lord, 568
Cheshunt College, 143, 394, 396
Chibnall, A. C., professor of biochemistry,
    508
Chibnall, M. M., 435
Chichester, dean of, *see* Burgon
Childe, Gordon, 206
China, 180, 339, 405, 430, 591; and Joseph
    Needham, 402–4; Cultural Revolution,
    523
Christ Church, Oxford, 99; dean of, 260n,
    and see Chadwick, Henry; Heaton;
    Strong; dean and canon professors, 86;
    cathedral, 86
Christian, E., Downing Professor, 210
Christian humanism, 425–6
Christian socialism, 403
Christ's College, 59–61, 121, 161, 376, 418,
    bursar, *see* Phillips; masters, *see* Cartmell,
    Peile, Raven, Todd; tutors, *see* Gunson,
    Putt; vice-master, 266

numbers of students, 41; scheme to
amalgamate with Emmanuel, 9, 44, 58,
61, 86–7, 259; and Downside, 390–1;
and schools, 93, 599

Christ's Hospital, 245

Church of England, chaps. 4–5; and religious
tests, 99–106; *and see* Anglicanism;
clergy; religion

Churchill, Lady, 569n

Churchill, Sir Winston, 149, 422, 507, 568–9

Churchill College, 188, 200, 527, 531n;
foundation, 568–9; master, *see*
Cockcroft; senior tutor, *see* Morrison,
J. S.

Clapham, J. H., Sir John, professor of
economic history, 115, 229, 236, 465;
and King's, 33

Clapham Grammar School, 277

Clare College, 63–4, 447, 480; dean, *see*
Robinson; masters, *see* Ashby; Atkinson;
Mollison; Thirkill; Wilson; master's
lodge, 580; senior tutor, *see* Northam;
cricket ground, *see* King's; fellows'
garden, 64, Memorial Court, 377–8
and Clare Hall, 570, 579–82; numbers of
students, 41

Clare Hall, 193, 256, 528; foundation, 570,
578–82; president, *see* Pippard

Clarendon Commission (1861–4), Clarendon
Schools, 245–8, 599–600

Clark, Grahame, Disney Professor and master
of Peterhouse, 162, 202, 206–8

Clark, J. W., University Registrary, 2, 165,
252, 260, 304n, 590; and Luard, 4–7; and
Museum of Archaeology and
Anthropology, 203; and Museum of
Zoology, 204; and University Library,
371–2

Clark, Professor V. M., 200

Clark, Professor William, and his wife, 252

Clarke; D., 206–7

Clarke, Professor Peter, 468–9

Clark Kennedy, A., 171

class, concept of, 240–1, 244, 251; 'gentility',
243–4, 246–7

classics, classical faculty and tripos, 147, 207,
210–16, 295

Clay, Sir Charles, Librarian of the House of
Lords, 536

Cleese, John, 300

clergy, Anglican, 242, 247, 249–50; 'country
clergy', 290, 297; and schools, 91

Clerk Maxwell, James, Cavendish Professor,
10, 13, 31, 69, 80, 176, 178, 180–1, 184,
588

Clifton, Professor R. B., 80

Clio, 236, 441

Clough, Anne Jemima, principal of
Newnham, 2, 262, 303–4, 310–14, 329

Clough, Arthur Hugh, poet and principal of
University Hall, London, 303

Clough, B. A., vice-principal and principal of
Newnham, 327, 341

coaches, private, 53, 71, 76, 83, 173, 267–81,
294

Cockcroft, Sir John, master of Churchill,
188, 568

Cockerell, Sydney, director of the
Fitzwilliam Museum, 460, 462

coins, 204–5, 462

Cole, L., 171

Cole, S. W., 198

Colonial Service, 204

Colville, Sir John, 568

computers and computer science, 491–2, 534;
EDSAC, 492

Comte, Auguste, 167

Congregationalists (United Reformed
Church), 469; *and see* Emmanuel
Congregational Church; Dodd;
Manning, Bernard L.

Connolly, Dom Hugh, 418

Conrad, Joseph, 450

conscientious objectors, 336, 339

Constable, Professor W. G., 297

Constantine the Great, 123

Cookson, H. W., master of Peterhouse, 53; as
Vice-Chancellor, 53

Cooper, Forster, 376, 378

Cornford, F. M., Laurence Professor of
Ancient Philosophy, 393; his
Microcosmographia Academica, 90, 111–12,
275

Cornford, Mrs Frances (Frances Darwin),
130–1, 275

Corn Rent Act (1576), 74

Corpus Christi College, 49–51, 83–4, 171,
326–7, 374, 429; dean, *see* Pearce;
masters, *see* Caldwell; McCrum; Pearce;
Perowne; Pulling; Spens; master's lodge,
507; tutor, 51
cricket ground, 375; Leckhampton House,
477; and Selwyn, 94, 132

Corrie, G. E., master of Jesus, 39

Cory, R., 161

cosmology, 482, 490–1

Coton footpath, 547, 580

Coulton, G. G., 276–7, 323, 398, 420–3

Counter-Reformation, 280

Countess of Huntingdon's Connexion, 394

Index

Cowell, E. B., professor of Sanskrit, 51, 428–31
Cox, Sir Trenchard, 343, *see also* Anderson, Maisie
Cranage, D. H. S., dean of Norwich, 376
Crawford, Lord, 379
Crawford, O. G. S., 208
Crawley, C., 62
Creighton, Mrs L., 254, 257
Creighton, M., fellow of Merton and Emmanuel, Dixie Professor, bishop of London, 59, 146, 231, 246n, 254, 257, 318
Crick, Francis, 497–8
Cripps, Henry William, 226, 246n
Cripps, Sir Humphrey, and his benefactions, 95, 551
Crofts, Ellen, wife of Francis Darwin, 130, 256, 275
Crohan, David, 456
Cromwell, Thomas, Chancellor, 423–4, 566
Crosland, Anthony, 560
Cumberland, Cumbria, 59–60
CUMS, *see* Cambridge University Music Society
Cunningham, William, archdeacon of Ely, 232, 236, 322, 437, 471
CUP, *see* Cambridge University Press
Curie, Marie and Pierre, 184
Currey, W. E., 'Pat', 71
Curtis, Dame Myra, principal of Newnham, 570
CVCP (Committee of Vice-Chancellors and Principals), 355, 565; *Report* of 1972, 355
CWICCU, *see under* religious societies

Daniel, Glyn, Disney Professor, 206
Dante, 425, 434
Darby, H. C., Sir Clifford, professor of geography, 474
Darwin family, 274–7, 288n, 579
Darwin, Charles, 158, 160–1, 204, 275; *Origin of Species*, 2, 10, 15, 121–2; Darwin centenary, 504; Darwin papers, 475
Darwin, Sir Charles (grandson), master of Christ's, at Manchester, 185, 275
Darwin, Sir Francis, 129–30, 161, 256, 275; his wives, *see* Crofts; Maitland
Darwin, Sir George, professor of astronomy, 130, 275–6, 487
Darwin, Sir Horace, 275, 341–2
Darwin College, 22, 528; foundation of, 570, 575, 577–9; masters *see* Finley; Young; and the Darwins, 275
Dasgupta, Partha, professor of economics, 471

Daube, David, 409, 505
Davies, Emily, and foundation of Girton, 302–11, 315–18, 510; her later career, 324–5; personality and achievement, 306–8, 329–30; and London, 307, 311–12, 317; retires, 317–18
Davies, Llewellyn, vicar of Marylebone, 307
Day Training College, 464–6
Dean, H. R., professor of pathology, master of Trinity Hall, 170–1
Deane, Professor Phyllis, 471
Debenham, F., professor of geography, 473–4
Deer Report (1966), 547
degrees, 293–7; ordinary (general, pass, poll), 270, 309, 324, 587; Previous exam, 309, 324
Delbrück, Max, 499
democracy, 563–4
Denmark, and physics, 499
Department of Education and Science, DES, 540, 554–5, 560, 563
Department of Scientific and Industrial Research, DSIR, 554
Derby, bishop of, *see* Pearce
Devlin, Lord, High Steward, and Devlin Report, 559
Devonshire, 7th duke of, William Cavendish, Chancellor, and the Cavendish Laboratory, 1–2, 86–7, 92, 174–5, 407
Devonshire, 9th duke, High Steward, 377–9
Dibelius, M., 413
Dickens, Charles, 450; *Bleak House*, 54, 301, 387
Dickins, B., professor of Anglo-Saxon, 327
Dictionary of National Biography, 122
Dies Irae, 395
Dillistone, F. W., 410–11
Dining Club, *see* Lucy Cavendish College
Dirac, P. A. M., Lucasian Professor, 188
divinity faculty, *see* theology
Dixie, Sir Wolstan, 59
DNA, 497–8
Dodd, C. H., Norris-Hulse Professor of Divinity, 142, 407–17, 421, 425; *Apostolic Preaching*, 413–15; *Historical Tradition in the Fourth Gospel*, 413, 415–16; *Interpretation of the Fourth Gospel*, 410, 415; *Parables of the Kingdom*, 413–14; his New Testament seminar, 409, 505
Dodgson, C. (Lewis Carroll), 85
Domesday Book, 474
Dominican friars, 434
Donaldson, S., master of Magdalene, 46
Donne, John, 279

Downing, Sir George, 54
Downing College, 54–6, 121, 265, 279, 449;
   foundation, 54–5; bursar and tutor, *see*
   Perkins; masters, *see* Annesley; Hill
college laboratory, 86n; and Downing Site,
   90–1, 154
   Downing Professorships, 210; Professors, of
   Law, *see* Christian, Maitland, Wade; of
   Medicine, *see* Howard; Latham
   number of students, 43
Downside Abbey and School, 389–91,
   418–20; abbot, *see* Butler
Drapers' Company, 433
Dronke, Professor P., 435
Drury, J., 414
Dublin, Trinity College, degrees of, 518–19;
   Library, 371; Royal Commission on, 95
Duff, P., 225
Dunbabin, J., 78
Duncan-Jones, Mrs E., 328
Dundee, 477; University of, 541
Dunn, Professor J., 472
Dunn, Sir William, 171, 194
Durham, 140; bishop of, *see* Henson;
   Lightfoot; Westcott; University of, 451,
   541
Durnford, Sir Walter, provost of King's,
   251n
Dutch, 434
Dykes, F. J., 339

Earle, Sir Lionel, 379
earth sciences, 152, 157–60, 159n, 160, *and see*
   geology
Easterling, J., 117n
economics, applied, 471
   and politics, faculty and tripos, 296–7,
   467–72; Special Board for, 97
ecumenism, 49, 119, 394, 400
Ede, Jim, 463
Eden, Richard, professor of energy studies,
   192, 579–81
Edinburgh, National Library of Scotland,
   371; University, 168, 199, 442
Education, Ministry of, 554, *and see*
   Department of Education and Science
education, religion, learning and research,
   103–4, 393
education department, faculty and tripos,
   463–6
Edward the Confessor, Lives of, 5
Egypt, 287n; Egyptologists, 207
Einstein, 188, 488, 490
Eliot, George, 85, 122, 302–3, 450;
   Middlemarch, 167–8

Elizabeth II, Queen, 566
Elizabeth, Queen, the Queen Mother, 149,
   327
Elton, G. R., Sir Geoffrey, Regius Professor
   of Modern History, 237, 546n
Ely, 284; bishop of, 4, *and see* Alcock;
   Browne; Wynn; cathedral, 86; canonry
   and professorship, 86
Emeleus, Professor H. J., 201
Emmanuel College, 57–9, 123–6, 141, 196,
   393–4, 515; masters, 262, *and see*
   Chawner; Giles; Phear; Welbourne;
   senior tutors, *see* Chawner; Phear;
   Welbourne
   archives, 126; chapel windows, 9;
   Chapman's garden, 58; parlour, 394
   and Chawner affair, 123–6; and Dixie
   Chair, 58–9, 140, 268n; and Goulding
   Brown, 278–81; and Hort, 10, 12, 58–9,
   69; plan to merge with Christ's, 44, 58,
   61, 86–7, 259
Emmanuel Congregational Church, 396–7
Empire Marketing Board, 385
Empson, W., 447
energy research group, 192
Engel, A. J., 8, 84
engineering: department and lab, 90, 456,
   475–82, 568; tripos (formerly mechanical
   sciences), 296, 473, 477; electrical, 477
English, 277, 279, 427, 431–3, 437, 443–54,
   585; tripos, 49, 446–54
English Heritage, 537–8
English Historical Review, 224, 231
Ephesians, Epistle to the, 146
Eratosthenes, sieve of, 496
Esher, Lord, 377–9, 477
Essex, James, 108
estate management, 472
Eton College, 245n, 260; provost, *see* James;
   and King's, 30, 33–4, 36–7, 251, 260–1,
   273, 465; and Magdalene, 46–7, 49
Euripides, 453
evangelicalism, evangelicals, 8, 49–50, 84, 261,
   271, 307, *and see* religious societies,
   CICCU
Everett, E. F., 338
Ewart, M., 315n
Ewing, Professor Sir James, 476–7
Exeter, bishop of, *see* Ryle

faculties, faculty boards, 30, 351–2, 357, 365,
   369, 392, 559; and Schools, 586n; *and see*
   under individual subjects
Fairbairn, S., 39, 399–400
Fanshawe, H., 51

Index

Faraday, 181
Farley, C. A., 379, *380*
Fawcett, Henry, fellow of Trinity Hall and
    politician, 62–3, 305, 316
Fawcett, Mrs Millicent (Millicent Garrett),
    305, 307, 316
Fawcett, Philippa, 329
Fawcett, W. M., 142, 176
Fenland, 332; Fenland Research Committee,
    162–3, 207
Ferrers, N., master of Gonville and Caius,
    261
Festival Theatre, 459
Fiji, 202–3, 390
Finley, Sir Moses, professor of ancient
    history, master of Darwin, 216
Fisher, H. A. L., 78; as Vice-Chancellor of
    Sheffield, 98; as President of the Board
    of Education, 98, 178
Fisher, R. A., Sir Ronald, Arthur Balfour
    Professor of Genetics, 494–6
Fisher, St John, 59, 219; as president of
    Queens' and founder of St John's, 107–8
Fitzmaurice, Lord Edmund, 51
Fitzwilliam, Viscount, 460
Fitzwilliam House, 567; College, 567–8
Fitzwilliam Museum, 47, 153, 197, 427,
    455–6, 460–2; director, *see* Cockerell, Jaffé,
    James; Hamilton Kerr Institute, 462
Flemish painting, 452–3
Fletcher, Sir Walter Morley, 196, 198
Foakes-Jackson, F. J., dean of Jesus, 39, 397–8
Footlights, 291, 299–300, 459
Forbes, Mansfield (Manny), 64, 447–8
Ford Foundation, 581
form criticism, 413
Fosdick, R. B., 381–2
Forster, E. M., 33, 37, 126, 438
Forsyth, P. T., 397
Foster, Kenelm, OP, 425, 434
Foster, Sir Michael, professor of physiology,
    13, 155–7, 159, 164–5, 169, 499; and
    Allbutt, 168; and Botanic Gardens, 161;
    and Gowland Hopkins, 170–1, 194–5
France, 174, 333; student rebellion in, 525;
    French historical scholarship, 234
Francis, St, and Franciscan Order, 413, 421
Franks, Lord, and Franks Report, 268n, 539,
    and see Oxford, University of
Frazer, J. G., Sir James, and the *Golden
    Bough*, 204–5
free churches, 100, 112, 293, 405, chaps.
    13–14
Freeman, Professor E. A., 219
French, S., 56

Froude, J. A., 219
fundamentalism, fundamentalists, 123, 132–3,
    411, 516–17
Furness, Furness Abbey, Furness Railway,
    175

Galatia, Galatians and Gauls, 135–6
Galilee, Galilean fishermen, 415
Gamble, J. G., 317
Gardiner, W., 64
Gardner, Alice, 318, 320
Garrett, *see* Anderson, Elizabeth; Fawcett
Garrod, Dorothy, Disney Professor, 206
Gaskell, J. F., 171
Gasquet, Dom Aidan, Cardinal, 420–3
Gathercole, P., curator of the Museum of
    Arch and Anth, 203
Geison, M. F., 164
Geldart, T. C., master of Trinity Hall, 62
General Strike, 520–1
Genesis, 121, 491
genetics, 200, *and see* DNA; Fisher
geodesy, 152, 159
geography, 473; historical, 474; physical,
    473–4
geology, xv, 121–2, 152, 156–60, 163, 547;
    and archaeology, 201; Geological
    Survey, 157
geophysics, 152, 159, 547
George V, King, 370, 386
German, 434, 444
Germany, 36, 231, 337, 434; Jewish refugees
    from, 505; labs in, 174; Lände, 26
German universities, 25, 60, 84–5, 240,
    427–9; scholarship, 84, 165; classical, 214;
    historical, 6, 232–5, 239; and medicine,
    168; and physics, 178, 499; and
    physiology, 164; and theology, 142, 212,
    409
Gibson, Mrs, 144
Gilbert and Sullivan, *Iolanthe* and *Princess Ida*,
    300
Gilbey, Thomas, OP, 425
Giles, P., master of Emmanuel, Vice-
    Chancellor, 373–4, 376; as philologist,
    428
Gill, Eric, 176, 191; *192*
Gillespie, Kidd and Coia, 583–4
Gilson, A. R., 264
Girton College, 287n, 298, 375; *312*;
    foundation at Hitchin, 2, 302–4, 309–10;
    early history, 2, 252, 296, 302–11, 567;
    in late 19th and early 20th cents., 316–
    24; and debates of 1896–7, 325; and
    World War II, 506; in mid-20th cent.,

Index

527, 529, 570; benefactions, 316–17; and
celibacy and married fellows, 256;
admission of men, 531n, 532; its council,
317–18; mistresses, *see* Bradbrook,
Cartwright, Davies, Jones, Welsh
architecture, 312, 315; chapel, 310–11;
Emily Davies Court, *312*; garden and
grounds, 311; lab, 316; library, 310–11,
316; Wolfson Court, 329, 530
and the education of women, 324–7; and
professionalism, 105; and Dame E. Hill,
436; and E. Power, 256; and C. Skeel,
229

Giry, A., 234

Gladstone, W. E., 93–4, 233; and act of 1871,
100

Glasgow, University, 199; professor, *see*
Thomson; University of Strathclyde,
Chancellor of, *see* Todd

Glastonbury, abbot's kitchen, 81

Glazebrook, Sir Richard, 364–5

Glover, T. R. (Baptist), fellow of St John's,
Public Orator, 388, 391–3, 405; his
Cambridge Retrospect, 392; *Conflict of
Religions*, 391; *Jesus of History*, 391

Godwin, Sir Harry, professor of botany,
162–4: Godwin Laboratory, 163–4

Godwin, Margaret, 162

Gold, T., 488

Gonville and Caius College, 8, 39–41, 55, 66,
147, 347–8, 372, 438, 462, 599; College
Council, 29; student observers on, 556n;
deans, 114, *and see* Heaton; Heywood;
Montefiore; masters, 104, *and see*
Anderson, H. K.; Cameron; Chadwick,
Sir James; Ferrers; Mott; Needham;
Roberts; Wade; portrait of Joseph
Needham, *401*; master's lodge, 343–9,
381, 580; presidents, *see* Bennett;
Buckland; Venn; tutors, 515, *and see*
Bennett; Buckland; McNair
chapel, 106, 119; Combination Rooms, 41,
372; hall, 76; Harvey Court, 457, 551;
548–9; lab, 86n; library, 319; senior
tutor's house, 31; Tree Court, 76
admission of women, 531n; benefactors,
347; and education, religion, learning
and research, 103; and historians, 230–1;
marriage of fellows, 305; medical
students, 41; numbers of students, 41;
'Peasants' Revolt', 515; Perse Feast and
Trust, 73–4, 363; poll men, 294;
professions of Caians and parents,
249–50; and Robinson College, 582–3;
and schools, 248–9; and urban

development, 79; and World War I,
332–4; II, 506; in 1950s, 514
and Allbutt, 167; and Z. N. Brooke,
230–1, 235, 282; and Fisher, 494–6; and
Grierson, 462; and Hadley, 460; and the
Hulberts, 299; and Paget, 165–6; and
Quiggin, 319; and Ridgeway, 375–6; and
A. Sanctuary, 331; and Anne Scroope,
478; and Stone, 472; and Tata, 478; and
Venn, 305; and Wigglesworth, 502–4;
and Charles Wood, 116, 459
boat club, 40, 114; and Fenner's, 291

Gooch, G. P., 229

Goodenough Report on medical education,
172

Goodhart, Charles, 557–8

Goody, Professor J., 205

Gordon, Sir Arthur, 202–3

Gore, Charles, bishop of Birmingham (later
Oxford), and university reform, 96–8

Göttingen, 60

Goudy, A. P., 435

Goulding Brown, B., 278–81

Graham-Smith, Sir Francis, 488–9

Granta, 293

Grantchester, 332–3

Graves Report, 539, 549

Gray, A., master of Jesus, 38–9, 397

Gray, Sir James, professor of zoology, 33,
493, 504

Gray, Thomas, Regius Professor of Modern
History, 228

Great St Mary's, 4–7; bells of, 340

Great War, *see* World War I

Greece, Greeks, ancient, 269; archaeology,
319–20; maths, 496; philosophy, 425;
religion, 320; tragedy, 453; trireme, 569;
language, New Testament and patristic,
136

Greek colonels and Tourist Board, 525,
527–8, 557–8

Green, G. E., 230–1

Green, T. H., 439

Greenwich, 487

Greenwood, L. H. G., 125

Gregory VII, Pope, 234

Grierson, Professor P., 419, 462; Grierson and
Blackburn, *Medieval European Coinage*,
462

Grimm brothers, 428

Gross, E. J., 74

Groves, General, 177

Gunson, W. M., tutor of Christ's, 60

Gwatkin, H. M., Dixie Professor, 124, 146–7,
219, 398

Index

Haddon, A. C., 204
Hadley, P., professor of music, 459–60
Hague, International Court, see McNair
Haig, A. G. L., 143–5
Haig, Sir Douglas, Earl Haig, 335
Hall, A. R., 475
Hamilton, General Sir Bruce, 333
Hamilton, Walter, master of Magdalene, 46
Hancock, N., 370n
Harcourt, Sir W. G. G. Vernon, Whewell
    Professor of International Law, later
    chancellor of the exchequer, 4
Hardy, G. H., fellow of Trinity, professor at
    Oxford, then Sadleirian Professor of
    Pure Mathematics, 69, 117, 153; quoted,
    118–19; *A Mathematician's Apology*,
    483–6; and the Russell case, 337–40
Hardy, Sir William, 151
Harland, B., 158n, 159n
Harnack, A., 139, 392, 409–11
Harris, J. Rendel, 64
Harrison, Jane, 319–20; *321*
Harrow School, 138, 245n
Hart, J. H. A., 147
Hart, Pussy, 326
Harvard University, 201, 298n, 323; Widener
    Library, 376
Harvey, J. D. M., *384*
Harwood, Sir Busick, Downing Professor of
    Medicine, 167
Haviland, J., Regius Professor of Physic, 166
Hawking, Stephen, Lucasian Professor, 482,
    486, 488, 490–1, 586
Hayley Wood, 164
Heacham (Norfolk), 347, 368
Head, F. W. fellow of Emmanuel, archbishop
    of Melbourne, 124
Hearn, N., 458
Heaton, E. W., later dean of Christ Church,
    as dean of Gonville and Caius, 121
Hebrew scholarship, 429; and Sidgwick, 15;
    and see Kennett
Hegel, Hegelians, 127, 237, 438, 440
Heisenberg, W. K., 188, 262
Heitland, W. E., 69
helix, double, 497–8
Henderson, Professor G., 455
Henry VI, King, and King's, 30, 104
Henry VII, King, 104
Henry VIII, King, 61, 104, 423
Henry I, king of Germany, Henry the
    Fowler, 223
Henslow, J. S., professor of botany, 160
Henson, H. Hensley, later bishop of Hereford
    and Durham, 79

Herbert, George, 78
Hereford, bishop of, see Henson
Heretics, Society of, 126
Hertz, H., 178
Hesse, Professor M., 475
Hewish, Professor A., 488, 586
Heyman, J., professor of engineering, 476,
    478–82
Heywood, Hugh, dean of Gonville and
    Caius, 507
Hicks, Sir John, professor of economics,
    Oxford, 471
Hilken, T. J. N., 479–80
Hill, A., master of Downing, 55–6, 97
Hill, Professor Dame Elizabeth, 435–6
Hindustani, 429
history: building, 229, 546–7, *548–9*; tripos,
    54, 210–11, 218, 228–38, 296, 329, 547,
    and archaeology, Board of, 219n;
    Lightfoot Scholarship, 398
historians and history faculty, 59, 218–19,
    227–39, 419, 447n, 472, 547
history and philosophy of science, 473–5
history of art, 455–6
Hitler, 149, 497, 558
Holker Hall, 174–5
Holland, Peter, 451n
Hollond, Professor Harry, Secretary of the
    Statutory Commissioners, 256, 369
Hollond, Marjorie (Marjorie Tappen), 256
Holloway, Thomas, 316
Holt, Catherine, 313–14, 316
Holt, George, 102
Holy Sepulchre, church of the, 106
Home Guard, 507–8
Homerton College, 93, 464, 576
Hopkins, Sir Frederick Gowland, professor of
    biochemistry, xvii, 156, 171, 195–9, 503,
    508; *197*; and Emmanuel, 196, 515; and
    Trinity, 70; and Foster, 195; and the
    Needhams, 403
Hopkins, Lady, 196
Hopkins, Keith, professor of ancient history,
    216
Hopkins, William, 53, 83, 180–1
Horace, 14, 214
Horne, M. R., 479
Hort, A. F. (son of F. J. A.), 58n, 138
Hort, Fenton J. A., fellow of Trinity and
    Emmanuel, Hulsean and Lady Margaret
    Professor of Divinity, 7, 9–13, 85, 89,
    105, 135–40; and Bradshaw, 263–4; and
    Council of Senate etc., 259; and
    Emmanuel, 9, 58–9, 87; and Dixie
    Chair, 11, 140; and Natural Sciences

Tripos, 156; and Revised Version, 139, 589–90; at St Hippolyts, 309; and Trinity, 69; his Life by his son, 138; his death, 146
Hoskin, M., 475
House of Commons, Select Committee, 522
House of Lords, 96, 200, 227, 295, 481; Librarian, *see* Clay
Housman, A. E., Kennedy Professor of Latin, 211–16; as professor at University College, London, 213; his *Manilius*, 212–13; his *Name and Nature of Poetry*, 213
Howard, H. F., 74
Howarth, T. E. B., 47, 446
Howell, Killick, Partridge and Amis, 575
Hoyle, Professor Sir Fred, 487–8
Huddleston, T. F. C., 372
Hügel, Baron Anatole von, curator of the Museum of Arch and Anth, 203, 388–91, 405, 434
Hügel, Baroness von, 390
Hügel, Baron Friedrich von, 203, 388, 390
Hughes, Miss, and Hughes Hall, 464
Hughes, H. C., and Hughes and Bicknell, 176, 190, 285, 391, 434
Hughes, T. McKenny, professor of geology, 64, 156–7, 159
Hughes Hall, 464, 576
Hulbert, Claude and Jack, 299
Humanae Vitae, 408
Humfrey, Charles, 252, 304n
Humphry, Sir George, professor of human anatomy and surgery, 166, 169, 173
Huntingdon, countess of, 143
Huxley, Julian, 504
Huxley, T. H., 165
Hyam, Ronald, 113

Ibsen, 459
India, Indians, 60, 152, 205, 243, 339n, 430, 519
Indian Civil Service, 67, 204–5, 244, 429–30
Inglis, C. E., 477–8
insects, 493, 502–4
Inter-Varsity Fellowship, 132
Ireland, 272, 274, 333
Irons, W. J., 395
Italian, 433–4
Italy, 317, 465

Jackson, Henry, vice-master of Trinity, Regius Professor of Greek, 60–1, 70–3, 117–19, 214, 259–60; his two sons, 339; and Maitland, 55, 218; and Russell case,

339–40; and Trinity College, Dublin, 95–6; on World War I, 333–4
Jackson, H. A., 71n
Jackson, T. G., 203
Jaffé, Professor M., director of the Fitzwilliam Museum, 455
James, Professor Harold, 357
James, Henry, 188, 450
James, M. R., director of the Fitzwilliam Museum, provost of King's and Eton, 33, 37, 48, 89, 251n, 341, 460; *461*; and Royal Commission III, 342
Jameson, F. J., tutor of St Catharine's, 42–3
Japan, Japanese, 180, 339, 430, 477, 518; student riots in, 525
Jarratt, Sir A., and Jarratt Report (1985), 562–3
Jebb, Sir Richard, MP, Regius Professor of Greek, 69, 71, 214, 254–5, 275
Jebb, Caroline, Lady Jebb, 'Aunt Cara', 214, 254–5, 275
Jeffreys, Sir Harold, 159
Jellicoe, Admiral Lord, 335
Jenkinson, F. J. H., University Librarian, 374
Jenkinson, Sir Hilary, 235
Jennings, Sir Ivor, 227
Jesus College, 37–9, 107, 383, 435; bursar and senior tutor, *see* Manning; deans, *see* Foakes-Jackson; Morgan; masters, *see* Corrie; Gray; Morgan; Renfrew; Tillyard
chapel (formerly church of nuns of St Radegund), 106–7, 109, 394, 396, 398
boat club, 397–400; *The Chanticlere*, 38; societies, esp. the Roosters, 400; student numbers, 41
Jesus and the Gospels, 15, 411–17; his family, 136
Jews, 112, 293, 337; Jewish community in Cambridge, 505–6; Jewish Holocaust, 520
Joachim, J., 458
John, St, son of Zebedee, and the Fourth Gospel, 415–16
John, Augustus, *321*
John Bonnett Laboratory, 171
Johnson, C., 362n
Johnson, R. P., 480
Johnson, W. E., 470
Johnston, M., 159n
Joliot-Curies (F. Joliot and I. Joliot-Curie), 189
Jones, Constance, mistress of Girton, 317–18
Jones, W. H. S., 42–3
Jowett, Benjamin, tutor and master of

Index

Balliol, 84, 106, 212–13, 244, 430
Judge, Paul, 473
Junior Historians, Society of, 230–2, 235–6, 239, 508

Kapitza, Peter, 176, 188–91, 519; Kapitza Club, 190
Kapp, E., *197*
Keble College, Oxford, 93
Keele, University of, Vice-Chancellor, *see* Taylor, H. M.
Keilin, D., Quick Professor of Biology, 498
Kelvin, Lord, *see* Thomson, Sir William
Kendall, J., 167n
Kendrew, Professor J., 498
Kennedy, Benjamin Hall, 305, 316
Kennett, R. H., Regius Professor of Hebrew, 110
Kenny, *Cases on Criminal Law*, 217, 227
Kerr, Sir Hamilton, MP, 462
Kettle's Yard, 427, 457, 463
Keynes, family, 275, 469
Keynes, Sir Geoffrey, 275
Keynes, J. M., Lord Keynes, 16n, 33, 129, 275, 396, 407, 438, 441; bursar of King's, 467, 469, 515; as agnostic, 127–8; and Arts Theatre, 459; his books, 470–1; and Cambridge economics, 467–72; and D. H. Lawrence, 448–9; on Sidgwick, 15; and USA, 467
Keynes, Lady, Lydia Lopokova, 459
Keynes, J. N., University Registrary, 275, 316, 396–7, 469
Keynes, Mrs J. N., 396–7, 469
Keynes, Lady, Margaret Darwin, 275, 287n, 579
King's College, 33–7, 269, 383, 407; bursar, *see* Keynes; fellows, 69, 510; governing body, 361n; provosts, 28n, 258, *and see* Austen Leigh; Durnford; James; Leach; Okes; Sheppard; Thackeray; senior tutor, *see* Beves; statutes, 260, 361n
chapel, 34, 104, 107, 119, 125, 546–7; choir, 475; Christmas Eve Carol Service, 126, 458; music, and A. H. Mann, 458
Gibbs and Wilkins buildings, 272; King's and Clare playing fields, 334, 376–8
admission of women, 531n; and Eton, *see* Eton; and *Granta*, 293; and History Tripos, 228–9; plan to merge with St Catharine's, 44–5, 86; mission debate, 128–9; numbers of students, 41; and Henry Bradshaw, 272–3; and Oscar Browning, 89, 465–6; Clapham, 229, 465; and M. R. James, 89; and W. F.

Reddaway, 229; and E. G. Selwyn, 51; and Sir Richard Stone, 471; and Virginia Woolf, 328–9
Kingsley, Charles, Regius Professor of Modern History, 1, 11, 114, 210, 291, 335
Kirkpatrick, A. F., master of Selwyn, 95
Knowles, Dom David, professor of medieval history and Regius Professor of Modern History, 208, 407–8, 418–26, 591; his *Monastic Order in England*, 419, 421, 423, 591; his *Religious Orders in England*, 423–4; and Downside, 390–1; and Peterhouse, 207, 238; and Trevelyan, 129, 418
Knox-Shaw, T., University Treasurer and master of Sidney, 29
Kornerup, E., 419

Labour Party, 350, 394
Lachmann, K. K. F. W., 214–15
Lake, Kirsopp, 398
Lake, P., 473
Lampe, G. W. H., Regius Professor of Divinity, 582n
Lamprecht, K., 235
Lancashire, 252, 316, 434
land economy, 472
Langland, William, 444
Lapidge, M., professor of Anglo-Saxon, 435
Lapsley, G., 89, 222, 279, 323
Larmor, Sir Joseph, Lucasian Professor, 153, 185–6
Lasdun, Sir Denys, 567
Laslett, P., 238
Latham, H., senior tutor and master of Trinity Hall, 62–3
Latham, P. W., Downing Professor of Medicine, 168
Latin, medieval, 216, 434–5, 536
Laurence, R. V., 339
law: faculty and tripos, 54–5, 90–1, 210–11, 216–27, 296; and history tripos, 295–6
Law, canon, 61; company, 534–5; English, 217–24; German, 217; Roman, 61, 210, 217–18, 225–6
Lawrence, D. H., 448–9
Layton, Richard, 424
Leach, Professor Sir Edmund, provost of King's, 205
leave, sabbatical, 354
Leavis, F. R., 336, 437, 448–51; *The Great Tradition*, 450; and *Scrutiny*, 449
Leavis, Mrs Q., Queenie Roth, 449–50
Leedham-Green, E., 579n

Leeds University, 323, *and see* Manchester, Victoria University of Manchester, Liverpool and Leeds; Vice-Chancellor, *see* Parkes

Leff, G., 425

Legh, Thomas, 424

Leigh, *see* Austen Leigh

Lendrum (later Vesey), W. T., 147

Lenin, 180, 485

Leslie, Shane, 38

Levold, E., 381n

Levy, P., 336

Lewis, J., Professor Lord, warden of Robinson, 201, 582n, 583

Lewis, Mrs, 144

Lichfield, bishop of, *see* Selwyn

Liddon, H. P., Oxford professor and Chancellor of St Paul's, 140

Lightfoot, J. B., fellow of Trinity, Hulsean and Lady Margaret Professor of Divinity and canon of St Paul's, bishop of Durham, 1, 9, 12, 69–70, 85, 105, 134–40, 589; and Council of Senate, 259; on *Galatians*, 135–6, 140; and Liverpool, 24–5, 85, 102, 134; and Maitland, 222n; and religious tests, 70, 100; and Sidgwick, 16, 134; and Statutory Commission, 393; Scholarship, 140, 398 and St Paul's, 140; at Durham, 135, 140, 145

Linacre lecture, 198

Lincoln College, Oxford, rector, *see* Pattison

linguistics, 443, 447, 454, 492

Linnett, J., master of Sidney, Vice-Chancellor, 582

Little St Mary's, 107

Littlewood, Professor J. E., 483–4

Liveing, G. D., professor of chemistry, 69, 156, 173, 195

Liverpool, city, 25–6, 102; Council of Education, 24–5; Lord Mayor, 26; Town Hall, 26; and the Holts, 313; and Newnham, 316; Royal Institution, 134; Unitarians in, 102

University College and university, 26, 102–3, 304n, 532, 534, 545n, 556, 563; Court, Council and Senate, 26; Vice-Chancellor, 26, *and see* McNair; Carnatic Halls, 532; King Alfred Chair of English, 25; and Chadwick, 190; and J. G. Frazer, 204; and Lightfoot, 24–5, 85, 102; and theology, 103

Llewellyn Davies, T., 289

Lock, J. B., bursar of Gonville and Caius, 8, 372–3

Loewe, Herbert, 506

Loewe, Professor Raphael, 506

London, bishop, *see* Creighton

Bloomsbury, 122, 438, 448–9, 467, 469; Buckingham Palace, 64; the City, and Keynes, 467, 469; citizens (10th cent.), 223; Doctors' Commons, 61–2; Downing St, 301; East End, 251; Hendon, 373; history of, 355

hospitals: clinical studies in, 168–73, 587; Guy's, 195; London, 171; St Bartholomew's, 166, 169, 264; St George's, 167, 179; St Mary's, 169; St Thomas's, 169

Inns of Court, 105, 210, 216–17; Lincoln's Inn, 220

institutions, societies etc.: Albert Hall, 504; British Museum (and British Library), 21, 371, 373, 589; King's College mission, 35; other college missions, 132; Patent Office, 213; Public Record Office, 220, 235, 533–4; Public Records, Keeper of, 533–4; Royal College of Music, 458; Royal Institution, 182, 187, 498; Toynbee Hall, 433; Whitehall, 464, 467, 469, 541

Marylebone, vicar of, *see* Davies

St Paul's Cathedral, 139; canon, *see* Lightfoot; Chancellor, *see* Liddon

Temple Church, 404

University, Colleges and Schools, 534, 541, 556–7; admission of women, 308, 507, 510; as collegiate university, 21, 354n; Bedford College, 22, 356, 373 (*and see* Royal Holloway, below); in Cambridge, 507; Birkbeck College, 188, 497; Courtauld Institute, 297, 343, 455; Creighton Lecture, 420; Imperial College, as Royal School of Mines, 165; as IC, 21, 165, 184, 199, 201, 505; Institute of Archaeology, 205; Institute of Historical Research, 21; King's College, 21, 251; London School of Economics, 205, 237–8, 256, 323, 438, 472, 525, 527, 556, 558, *and see* Bauer; Oakeshott; Power; LSE in Cambridge, 256, 323, 507; Queen Mary College (now Queen Mary and Westfield), 264, 573; Royal Holloway College (now Royal Holloway and Bedford New College), 316, 573; School of Hygiene and Tropical Medicine, 21, 503; School of Slavonic and East European Studies, 435; University College, 21, 159, 165, 288; professor of Latin, *see* Housman;

University Court, 21, 30; University Hall, *see* Clough; Warburg Institute, 21; Westfield College (see Queen Mary College, above), 21n, 22, 229, 573

Westminster Abbey, 4, 139, 407; dean, *see* Robinson; Stanley; Jerusalem Chamber, 12

other references: Anderson in, 385; and E. Davies, 307, 310, 312, 317; and the Hill family, 435; and Keynes, 469–71; and Moore, 442; and E. Palmer, 429; and Pigou, 469

Longley, Charles, archbishop of Canterbury, 99–100

Lopes, Father, 390

Lopokova, *see* Keynes

Lord's Bridge, Mullard Observatory at, 191, 487–9

Lowes Dickinson, G., 127–8, 438

Lu, Gwei-Djen, Mrs Needham, 404

Luard, H. R., University Registrary, vicar of Great St Mary's, fellow of Trinity, 4–8, 70, 180

Lubenow, Professor W., 127n

Lucas, F. L., 510

Lucy Cavendish College, 53n, 527, 570–3, 576; presidents, *see* Bertram; Bidder; the 'Dining Group' and the foundation of the college, 570, 572

Lunacy, Commissioners in, 506

Luscombe, Professor D., 425

Lyell, Sir Charles, 121–2

Lynch, R. I., 161

Lyne-Stephens, Mrs Y., Yolande Duvernay, 389

Lyon, T. H., 120

Lyttleton, A., master of Selwyn, 93–4

Mabillon, Dom J., 418

Macaulay, T. B., Lord Macaulay, 237, 418

Macaulay, W. H., 372

MacCormac, Richard, 567

McCrum, M., master of Corpus, 575

Mackinnon, Professor Donald, 425

Mackintosh, Miss, 396

McKitterick, D., 273n, 585

MacLeod, Professor R., 155–6

Macmillan, Harold, and his government, 559

McNair, A. D., Lord McNair, fellow and tutor of Gonville and Caius, Vice-Chancellor of Liverpool, president of the International Court, the Hague, and the European Court, Strasbourg, 40, 225–6

Macpherson, W. J., 284n

McTaggart, J. M. E., 118–19, 127, 131, 440

Magdalen College, Oxford, 78

Magdalene College, 44–9, 89, 96, 229, 383; masters, *see* Benson; Donaldson; Hamilton; Neville, Latimer; Ramsay; Willink

chapel, 106, 113; admission of women, 45, 531n

Maine, Sir Henry, master of Trinity Hall, 62, 218

Maitland, Mrs Florence, later Lady Darwin, 275

Maitland, F. W., Downing Professor, 2, 103, 187, 211, 216–24, 227, 323; apostle and agnostic, 13, 127; and Trinity, 6; Moral Sciences Tripos, 437; and Downing, 55–6; and Council of the Senate, 259; his death, 98

his books, 221–6, 591; *Domesday Book and Beyond*, 221–4; *History of English Law* (with Pollock), 221, 226; in Canary Islands, 225; and history in Cambridge, 228–9; and law, 216–24, 227; legacy, 236 and admission of women, 325; on Acton, 405–6; on Mary Bateson, 318, 320–1; on Sidgwick, 14, 16–18; on Stephen, 122

Maitland, S. R., 6

Malinowski, B. K., 205

management studies and Judge Institute, 472–3

Manchester, 303; John Rylands Library, 315, 416; Manchester Grammar School, 252; Owens College, 13, 32, 101–2, 303, 304n; professor in, *see* Ward

Victoria University of Manchester, Liverpool and Leeds; and University of Manchester, 32, 101–2, 303–4; and chemistry, 199, 264; History school, 224, 232, 239; and physics, 180, 185, 187–8, 199; professors, *see* Rutherford; Schuster; Rylands Chair, 410

Mangan, J. A., 38, 397

Manhattan project, 171

Manilius, 212–13, 215

Mann, A. H., 458

Manning, Bernard L. (Congregationalist), 388, 394–400, 402, 405; fellow, senior tutor and bursar of Jesus, 394–400; his books, 395, 398, 400

Manning, H. E., Cardinal, 388, 408

Manselli, P., 413

Mansfield College, Oxford, 409–10, 417

Marlborough College, 246–7

Marlow Society, 459

marriage, married fellows, 5, 10, 31, 62–3,

71–2, 260, 262, 278; marriage as partnership, 257, 305

Marsh, F. H., professor of surgery, master of Downing, 169

Marshall, Alfred, professor of political economy, 219, 467–72; and his wife, 316

Marshall, W. C., 477

Martin, Sir Leslie, professor of architecture, 456–7

Marx, 241, 523; Marxism, 403–4; Marxist, interpretation of literature, 454; of prehistory, 206

Massachusetts Institute of Technology, MIT, 568

materials science and metallurgy, 477

mathematics, xv, 271, 482–6; applied, 152–3, 482–3; and theoretical physics, 482–3, 485–6; pure, 152, 483–6

maths tripos, 5, 9–10, 101, 151–4, 157, 183, 243, 294–5, 309, 467, 483, 494, 496, 587

Maudsley, A., 203

Maurice, Professor F. D., 7, 9, 11, 227–8, 307

Maxwell, *see* Clerk Maxwell

Mayor, J. E. B., professor of Latin, University Librarian, 69

May Week, 291, 298–300; May Races, 298

mechanical sciences, *see* engineering

Medical Research Council, 196; MRC Molecular Biology Laboratory and Unit, xvii, 191–2, 265, 497–9

medical school, 54–5, 90, 154, 156–7, 165–73, 587; clinical, 166–7, 169, 172–3, 586n

medical sciences: and Rockefeller, 381; tripos, 171–2

medieval and modern languages tripos (old MML), 296, 318, 427–8, 431–4

Melchett, Lord, 385

Mendel, Mendelians, 494, 496

Merton College, Oxford, 78, 251

Methodists, 399; Methodist heritage, 394–6, 399–400

Mexico, student revolts in, 511

Middle Eastern Studies, Centre for, 430

Mill, James and J. S., 18

Miller, E., 68, 116–17

Miller, Jonathan, 300

Milner, Isaac, president of Queens', 476

Milsom, Professor S. F. C., 227

Milton, J., 437, 448

Ministry of Agriculture and Fisheries, 385

Minns, Sir Ellis, Disney Professor, 66n, 206, 435

Modern and medieval languages tripos (new MML), 427, 433–6

Modern Churchman's Union, 150

molecular biology, 200, 497–9; molecular science, 200

Mollison, W. L., master of Clare, 63

Mond, Robert, 385

Montefiore, Bishop Hugh, as dean of Gonville and Caius, 121

Monumenta Germaniae Historica, 234

Moore, G. E., 16n, 144, 289, 437–41, 448, 449n, 467, 591; as agnostic, 127–8; *Principia Ethica*, 19, 129, 439–41, 591; and Keynes, 469–70; Sidgwick on, 19; and World War I, 336

Moorman, Bishop J. R. H., 129

Moorman, Mrs Mary, and her Life of Wordsworth, 129

moral sciences (later philosophy) tripos 10, 16, 220, 228, 295, 437–43, 469

More, William, prior of Worcester cathedral priory, 424

Morey, Dom Adrian, 418, 422

Morgan, E. H., 'Red Morgan', dean of Jesus, 38–9

Morgan, H. A., 'Black Morgan', master of Jesus, 38–9, 397

Morgan, Lloyd, 403

Morris, C., 261

Morris, William, 107, 396

Morrison, H. P., 422

Morrison, J. S., senior tutor of Churchill, 568–9; president of Wolfson, 577

Moseley, H., 185

Moseley, R., 155–6

Mott, Sir Nevill, Cavendish Professor, master of Gonville and Caius, 29, 176, 191–3, 264–6, 498

Moule, C. F. D., Lady Margaret Professor of Divinity, 409

Mullard Ltd, 487

Munich, 233, 455

Murray, Sir Keith, Lord Murray, chairman of the UGC, 541–3

Murray, Dame Rosemary, president of New Hall, Vice-Chancellor, 570–1

muscular Christianity, 40, 114, 291

music, 457–60; School, 457

Myers, C. S., 204

National Health Service, 172

National Institute of Industrial Psychology, 500

National Trust, 367

natural sciences tripos, 153, 156–7, 171, 295, 475, 492

Nazis, 505–6, 520

Needham, Joseph, master of Gonville and

Index

Caius, 151, 388, 400–5, 474–5; *401; Science and Civilization in China*, 404, 591; his first wife, Dorothy Moyle, 403–4; his second, *see* Lu; Needham Research Institute, 402, 431, 475; and Robinson College, 583

Neill, Bishop Stephen, 121

neutron, 190

Neville, George, Chancellor of Oxford, 342

Neville, Latimer, later Lord Braybrooke, master of Magdalene, 44–5

Newcastle, duke of, Chancellor, 538, 566

Newcastle, University of Durham in, 304n; University of Newcastle, 541

New College, Oxford, 33, 91, 98, 484, 528; chapel, 107

New English Bible, 409–10

New Hall, 72, 527, 529, 531n, 570–2; president, *see* Murray; New Hall Association, 570

New Left, 523, 525–6

Newman, J. H., 106

Newnham College, 252, 287n, 296, 298, 375, 531n, 567, 571; foundation and early history, 2, 302–5, 311–16, 464, 570; benefactions, 316; in late 19th and early 20th cents., 318–21; and World War I, 332–3; II, 506; in mid-20th cent., 527, 529; council of, 317–18; principals, *see* Clough, Curtis, Sidgwick, Strachey architecture, 142, 314–15; absence of chapel, 101; Clough Hall, 328; gates (1921), 116; Library, 332; Peile Hall, 59, 330; Sidgwick Hall, 330; *315*; and admission of women to University, 324–7; Commemoration Feast, 325; and History Tripos, 229; married fellows, 256; and professionalism, 105 and Nora Chadwick, 445; Peile, J., 59, 259; and Virginia Woolf, 328–30

Newsome, D., on Goulding Brown and Welbourne, 278–81

Newton, A., professor of zoology, 4, 46

Newton, Isaac, Lucasian Professor, 438, 486; age of, 52

New York, xv, 381; Union Seminary, 398, 411

New Zealand, 178, 280, 408; bishop of, *see* Selwyn; Dominion of, 93

Nicholas, Tressilian, 155, 158, 350n, 369, 586–7

Nicholson, Ben, 463

Nicholson, Sir William, 47

Niebuhr, Reinhold, 150

Nineham, D., Regius Professor of Divinity, 125n

Nobel Prizes, 32, 80, 182, 200, 266, 488, 498, 505

Nolan, Father E., Catholic chaplain, 389–90

Norrish, Professor R. G. W., 201

Northam, J., senior tutor of Clare, 580

North Sea, and archaeology, 207

Norwich, bishop of, 4; cathedral, canonry and St Catharine's, 85n; dean, *see* Cranage; University, *see* University of East Anglia

Nuffield, Lord, 177

Nuffield Foundation, 571

Oakeshott, M., fellow of Caius, professor at LSE, 236–7, 434, 438

Odling, Professor W., 80

Office of Works, 377, 379

Official Trustee of Charitable Funds, 74

Ogden, C. K., 126–7, 340, 447

Okes, R., provost of King's, 260–1

Okey, T., professor of Italian, 41, 251, 433

Olby, R., 497–9

Old Dominion Foundation, 581

oligarchy, as an element in university government, 350, 563–4

Olstead, J., 525

Oratory of the Good Shepherd, 133

Oriel College, Oxford, 83, 106

oriental languages and studies, 296, 428–31; Semitic and Indian languages triposes, 296, 430

Our Lady and the English Martyrs, 389

Owst, G. R., professor of education, 466

Oxford, Archaeological Unit, 202 bishop of, *see* Gore city, North Oxford, 78, 292

Oxford, University of, 25, 92, 97, 99–100, 101, 143–4, 240, 242, 244, 247, 352, 389, 517; college fellowships etc. and the university, 20, 22, 268–9, 316, 352–4; corn rents, 74; tutors and college teaching, 22–3, 76, 79–80, 83–5, 356, 514–15; 'from clergyman to don', 84; professors, 23, 268, *and see* Hardy, G. H.; Hicks; Powicke institutions: the Bodleian Library, 350, 371–3, 375, 589; New Bodleian, 372; Botanic Garden, 160; Clarendon Laboratory, 173; Congregation, 24, 30; Convocation, 526; degrees, 518–19; Examination School, 203; examining boards, 308; faculty boards, 357; Radcliffe Infirmary, 231; Romanes Lecture, 234

Index

(Oxford, University of, *cont.*)
officials: Chancellor, *see* Neville, George; Vice-Chancellor, 565
schools and disciplines: arts and sciences in, 154–5, 541, 586–7; botany, 161–2; chemistry and physics in, 80–1, 184; classics, 212–14; Greats and PPE, 212–13, 231, 243, 437–8; geography, 473; history, 230, 232; modern languages, 433; theology, 139; graduate students, 589; research, 103, 514; sabbatical leave, 354
19th cent. reformers, 358; the three parties, 85; and hegemony of Balliol, 84–5; admission of women, 302, 325, 327, 363, 527, 531; and Royal Commission III, chap. 11 passim; and World War II, 509; and Robbins Report, 539; and Franks Report, 539, 548–9, 565; and CVCP Report of 1972, 356
and Barker, 251; and Helen Cam, 323; and Cowell, 428; and A. J. Engel, 8; and H. A. L. Fisher, 178; and Gladstone, 100; and Jowett, 212–13, 430; and Liddon, 140; and Maitland, 219–20, 224; and Nicholas family, 155; and Nuffield, 177; and Pattison, 212–13; and M. Ryle, 487; and Sherrington, 80; and Rebecca Squire, 224; and Todd, 199–200
Oxford and Cambridge Act of 1877, 44, 86; of 1923, 20
Oxford Group, 133
Oxford Medieval Texts, 435
Oxford Movement, 109

Pacific ethnological material, 202–3
pacifism, 148–9, 338–40, 394
Page, T. E., 69
Paget, Sir George, Regius Professor of Physic, 166–8, 173
palaeobotany, 162–4
Paley, W., 105, 309n
Palladius, *Lausiac History*, 391
Palmer, E., 428–31
Paris, 169, 523; École des Chartes, 234
Paris, Matthew, 6–7
Parkes, Professor Sir Edward, Vice-Chancellor of Leeds, 582n
Parry, R. St John, 71
Pascal, 433
Passchendaele, battle of, 335
Pattison, Mark, rector of Lincoln, 85, 212–13
Pearce, E. C., dean and master of Corpus, later bishop of Derby, 50–1, 374–5
Pearce, Richard M., 170, 381
Pearsall Smith, Alys, Mrs B. Russell, 438, 442

Peat, W. B., and Co, 362
Peile, J., master of Christ's, 59–61, 87, 259, 428–9; as Vice-Chancellor, 61; as college historian, 59; and Downside, 390; and Newnham, 59, 330, *and see* Newnham College
Peile, Mrs J., 305
Peill, J. N., 56–7
Pembroke College, 65–7, 372, 400; chapel, 107; library, 65; masters, *see* Power; Searle; Stokes; senior tutor, *see* Searle; student numbers, 41, 49
Penrose, Roger, 490
Pen-y-Bryn, 408, 417
Perkins, John, bursar and tutor of Downing, 56
permissive society, the, 529–30
Perne, Andrew, master of Peterhouse, 53
Perowne, E. H., master of Corpus, 8, 10, 43, 49–52, 83, 87, 180, 261–2
Perry, Bishop C., formerly bishop of Melbourne, 144
Perse, Stephen, 73; Perse Trust and fellows (of Caius), 73–4, 76, 363
Perse School, 73
  Perse Boys', 286
  Perse Girls', 344
Persian, 428–9
Perutz, Max, 497–9, 505
Peskett, A. G., 46
Peterhouse, 52–4, 251, 456, 573; masters, *see* Birdwood; Butterfield; Chalmers; Cookson; Perne; Porter; Temperley; Ward
  chapel, 107; Fen Court, 285; Museum of Classical Archaeology in, 203; 20th cent. buildings, 457
  numbers of students, 43; historians, 238, 357, 419; and schools, 93, 248, 599–600
Pevsner, Sir N., 478
Ph.D. degree, 178–9, 280, 358, 513, 515, 555
Phear, S. G., senior tutor and master of Emmanuel, 9, 58, 86, 173, 260, 588
Phelps, R., master of Sidney, 52, 83, 87, 261n
Philip, Prince, duke of Edinburgh, Chancellor, 566
Phillips, C. K., bursar of Christ's, 267
Phillips, G., president of Queens', 56–7
Phillips, G. C., 227
Phillipson, D., curator of the Museum of Arch and Anth, 202n
philology, 60, 210, 427–30, 444, 446
philosophy, *see* moral sciences
physics, department and Cavendish Laboratory, 2, 19, 58, 86, 89–90, 103,

Index

142, 153, 156, 173–91, 222, 266, 393–4,
407, 417, 482–3, 498, 518, 572, 579;
Austin wing, 176–7; Mond Lab, 176,
190–1, 519, 586–7; new Cavendish, 177,
191–4, 228–9, 547, 579; Rayleigh wing,
182
physiology, 89, 157, 164–5
Pigou, A. C., professor of political economy,
469, 471
Pippard, Sir Brian, Cavendish Professor,
president of Clare Hall, 176–7, 193, 265,
579–81
Pitt, H. G., 113
Pitt, William, 394, 539
plant sciences, *see* botany
plastic theory, 478–81
Plato, 71–2, 212–14; Platonists, 128
Plumb, Professor J. H., Sir John, 237
pollen analysis, 162–3
Pollock, J. C., 131
Pollock and Maitland, *see* Maitland
Poole, R. L., 222
Pope, Sir William, professor of organic
chemistry, 195, 508
Porson, R., Regius Professor of Greek, 2, 5
Porter, J., master of Peterhouse, 53
Porter, R., 157–8
Postan, M. M., Sir Michael (Munia),
professor of economic history, 54, 207,
236–8, 256, 323, 419, 471
Power, Eileen, fellow of Girton, professor at
LSE, wife of M. M. Postan, 235, 238,
256, 321–2
Power, John, master of Pembroke, 66–7
Powicke, Sir F. M., Regius Professor of
Modern History, Oxford, 227
Prager, Professor W., 479
Prest, J., 341
Previté-Orton, C. W., professor of medieval
history, 222, 234, 236
Prime Minister's Committee (on teaching of
modern languages), 433; *and see* Robbins
Committee
Princeton, Institute for Advanced Study, 581
Prior, O. H., professor of French, 433
professions, professionalism, 242–52; and
clergy, 105, 145, *and see* clergy; and
women, 105, 304; in late 20th cent., 522
Prothero, G. W., Sir George, 36
Providence, Rhode Island, Brown
University, 479
psychology, 204; experimental, 499–502; *and
see* Bartlett
Public Accounts Committee, 553
Pugin, A., 106–7, 396

Pulling, J., master of Corpus, 49–50
Punnett, R. C. Arthur Balfour Professor of
Genetics, 496
Putt, G., senior tutor of Christ's, 267

quantum theory, 188, 490
Quaternary Research, Godwin Lab for,
163–4
'Queen Anne' style, 314–15
Queens' College, 56–7, 467–8, 526, 555, 557;
presidents, *see* Campion; Fisher, St John;
Milner; Phillips, G.; Ryle, H. E.; Venn,
J. A.; tutors, *see* Campion; Wright
chapel, old, 110; new, 109–11; and Henry
Chadwick, 120–1; Old Court, 108;
Cripps buildings and Sir Humphrey
Cripps, 95, 551; 548–9; Erasmus building,
551
numbers of students, 41, 44; Queens'
College Union, 525–6
Quiggin, E. C., 319; Mrs Quiggin, 319
Quiller-Couch, Sir Arthur, 'Q', King Edward
VII Professor, 432, 445–8

Raby, F. J. E., 536
Rackham, O., 164
radio astronomy, 191, 486–90
radiocarbon dating, 163
Radley, warden of, *see* Selwyn College
Ramanujan, S., 339, 483–4
Ramsay, A. B., master of Magdalene, 46–7,
262, 329
Ramsey, A. S., 46
Ramsey, F. P., 470
Ramsey, Bishop Ian, and Christ's, 121
Ramsey, Michael, archbishop of Canterbury,
46
Ratcliffe, J. A., 487
Rathbone, William, 25, 102
Raven, C. E., dean of Emmanuel, Regius
Professor of Divinity, master of Christ's,
146–50, 266; and Emmanuel, 123–6, 131,
148; as historian of science, 148, 474; and
pacificism, 148–9, 340, 394
Raverat, Mrs Gwen, 214, 343, 487, 579;
quoted, 130–1, 254, 274–6; on Horace
Darwin, 341–2
Rawle, T., 456–7, 571
Ray, John, 148
Rayleigh, J. W. Strutt, Lord Rayleigh,
Cavendish Professor, Chancellor, 19, 31,
69, 80, 176, 180, 182, 255, 305, 314
Rayleigh, Lady, Miss Balfour, 19, 180
Rayne Foundation, 579
Reddaway, W. F., 229

Reeve, M., professor of Latin, 435
Registrar General, social statistics of, 242, 244
Reid, J. S., professor of ancient history, 230, 428
Reid, Mrs J. S., 509
religion, xviii, 516–17 and chaps. 4, 5, 13–14 passim; religious tests, abolition of (1871), 99–106, 112, 117, 121, 137, 139, 165, 247, 261, 388, 405, 407; religious tests and Liverpool University, 102
religious societies: Church Missionary Union, 132; Church Society, 144; CICCU, 110, 132–3, 144, 517; Confraternity of the Holy Trinity (Sanctae Trinitatis Confraternitas), 132, 144; CWICCU, 132; free church chaplaincies, 133; Methodist Society, 399
Renfrew, A. C., Lord Renfrew, Disney Professor, master of Jesus, 208
research, 77, 155–6, 179, 278, 280–1, 484, 512–16, 552; Glover on, 392–3; Royal Commission III and, 352–6 passim; selectivity exercises, 553
Revolution of the Dons, The (Rothblatt 1981), 278, 281
Reyner, G. F., 117
Richards, I. A., 340, 441, 447–8, 450
Richmond, countess of, *see* Beaufort
Ridgeway, Sir William, fellow of Gonville and Caius, Disney Professor, 204, 206, 230, 321; and Glover, 393; and government aid, 97; and the Ph.D., 178; and the University Library, 375–6
Ridley Hall, 144
Rievaulx, abbot of, *see* Ailred
Rifle Brigade, 3rd, 333
Ripon, bishop of, *see* Strong
Rivers, W. H. R., 204, 499, 501
Roach, J. P. C., 66n
Robbins, Lord, 543–4; Robbins Committee (Prime Minister's Committee) and Report, 355n, 511, 539, 543–5, 548, 550, 553, 559, 561; and Oxford and Cambridge, 539
Roberts, E. S., senior tutor and master of Gonville and Caius, 2, 40, 59, 262, 278, 292n, 340, 588; as classic and philologist, 59, 428; as clergyman, 8; and compulsory chapel, 114–15; marriage, 254; and his house, 31; and Rifle Volunteers, 51, 334–5
Roberts, Ian, 435
Robertson, Professor D. H., 471
Robertson, D. S., 338
Robinson, Sir Austin, 469

Robinson, C. K., master of St Catharine's, formerly bursar, 42–3
Robinson, Sir David, 582–3
Robinson, John, as dean of Clare, 121
Robinson, Professor Joseph Armitage, later dean of Westminster and Wells, 11, 146, 390
Robinson, Sir Robert, 200
Robinson College, 531n, 577, 582–4; *584*; fellows, 584; warden, 584, *and see* Lewis students, 583–4;
and Needham Research Institute, 431
Roby, H. J., 69
Rockefeller, John D., Jr, 179, 381–2
Rockefeller Foundation, 90, 169–70, 199, 370, 381–5, 497; Archives, 370n, 381n; International Education Board, 170, 381–2
Rolleston, Sir Humphrey, Regius Professor of Physic, 171–2
Rolls Series, 5–6
Rome, abbey of Sant' Anselmo, 418; Acton in, 233; ancient, Roman empire, 495; O. Browning in, 465
Church of, and Vatican, 423; Archives, 233; First Vatican Council, 233; Second Vatican Council, 408; Decree of Propaganda, 389
Romilly, J., diaries of, 252
Röntgen, 184
Rosebery, Lord, 233
Rossiter, A. P., 444, 447, 451–4; *Angel with Horns*, 451
Rothamsted Experimental Station, 495–6
Rothblatt, S., 8
Rothermere, Lord, Sir Harold Harmsworth, 445
Round Church, *see* Holy Sepulchre, church of the
Routh, E. J., 173
Roy, G. R., professor of pathology, 169
Royal Commission on Inns of Court (1850s), 217
Royal Commissions on Oxford and Cambridge, 55, 75, 539, 543; I (1852), 3, 27, 33, 56, 69, 75, 261, 358, 363
II (1874), 82–9 passim, 169; and Statutory Commission, 44–5, 50, 55, 79, 85–6
III (1922) (Asquith Commission), preparation for (1907–14), 96–8; the Commission, xx, 2, 20, 98, chap. 11 passim; commissioners, 341–3, 364–9, 539; Cambridge Committee, 341–2, 509, 574; Oxford committee, 342–3; writing of report, 367–8; recommendations, 170,

Index

263, 282, 349–65, 541–2; on women,
326–7, 363–4; Statutory Commissioners,
350–1, 359–62, 369
Royal Commission on Trinity College,
Dublin, 95
Royal Engineers, 333
Royal Geographical Society, 473
Royal Observatory, 487
Royal Signals, 333
Royal Society, 190, 494, 502; professor, *see*
Taylor
Rugby School, 9, 245n
Rupp, E. Gordon, Dixie Professor, 11, 141–
2, 399
Russell, Bertrand, Earl Russell, 19, 118–19,
127, 129, 144, 289, 438–43; and Keynes,
469–70; his Trinity lectureship, 72,
337–40
Russia, 238; and Kapitza, 176, 180, 189;
Russian and Slavonic studies and Dame
E. Hill, 435–6
Rutherford, Ernest, Lord Rutherford,
professor at Montreal and Manchester,
Cavendish Professor, 153, 176, 179–80,
184–91, 199, 588; and New Zealand,
178, 186, 408, 518; and O. Browning,
36, 465; and Larmor, 153, 185–6, 482;
and Trinity, 69
Rutherford, Lady, 186
Rylands, George, 459
Ryle, H. E., president of Queens', bishop of
Exeter, 110
Ryle, Professor Sir Martin, 486–9, 586

St Andrew's University, 21, 429, 541
St Catharine's College, 41–4, 51; bursar, 43;
masters, 85n, *and see* Robinson; plan to
merge with King's, 44–5, 86; and
geography, 474
St Columba's Church, 393
St Edmund's College, formerly House, 390,
576
St John, hospital of, 107
St John's College, 59, 67–9, 227, 577; fellows,
69, 108; masters, 28 *and see* Bateson,
Benians, Boys-Smith; master's lodge,
258; finances, 74–5
archives, 116; buildings, 109, 383; of 19th-
20th cents., 552; chapel, 66, 76, 106–10,
116–17, 119, 389; choir, 107, 457–8;
Cripps building, 95, 551; lab, 86n; New
Court, 76
and archaeology, 206; and classics, 68; and
the Lady Margaret Chair, 141; and the
Divinity School, 142; and maths, 68;

and moral sciences, 295; scholars and
exhibitioners, 68n; student numbers, 32,
41, 67, 295; and urban development, 79,
284
and T. G. Bonney, 158–9; and W. G.
Constable, 297; and G. G. Coulton,
276–7; and T. R. Glover, 391; and
J. H. A. Hart, 147; and A. Marshall,
468; and E. Palmer, 429; and H. F.
Stewart, 433
St John's College, Oxford, 78
St Joseph, Professor J. K. S., 208
St Michael's Church, 107
St Paul's School, 245n, 248
St Petersburg, 435
St Radegund's Priory, 106
Salisbury, Lord, 314
Salter, F. R., 229
Saltmarsh, J., 33n
Salvin, A., 90, 106, 153
Sanctuary, A., 231, 331
Sanger, C., 289
Sanskrit studies, 60, 428–9
Savigny, F. K. von, 220
Scalands (Sussex), 307–8
Scaliger, 212–13
Scandinavian languages, 434
Schneewind, J. S., 18–19
Scholfield, A. F., University Librarian, 370,
374, 382–3
schools, 91–2, 245–9, 599–600; Anglican, 124;
comprehensive, 248–9; for girls, 286;
grammar, 247–9; informal, 145; public,
38, 41, 77, 240, 243, 245–9, 289, 291,
408, 599–600; fees, 285–6; secondary
education, 245–9; schoolmasters, 250;
and see under individual schools
Schuster, Sir Arthur, professor of physics,
Manchester, 185
Schweitzer, A., 147, 411
SCM (Student Christian Movement), 132–3
Scotland, Church of, 393; universities of, 21,
240; Scottish metaphysics, 181
Scott, Canon, 389
Scott, George Gilbert, 66
Scott, Sir Gilbert, 66, 108, 142
Scott, Sir Giles G., and Clare, 377–9; and
New Bodleian, 372; and the University
Library, 370, 377–86
Scroope, Lady Anne, 478
Scrutiny, 448–9
Searby, Peter, 92–3, 465–6, 599
Searle, C. E., senior tutor and master of
Pembroke, 66–7
Sedgwick, A., professor of geology, 2–4, 152,

156, 158, 590; and Cambridge
    Philosophical Society, 160
Seeley, J. R., Sir John, Regius Professor of
    Modern History, 210, 230–2, 309; and
    Christ's, 60; and Caius, 230; his *Ecce
    Homo*, 231, 392
Selden Society, 221
Selwyn, E. G., fellow of Corpus, 51, 132;
    later warden of Radley and dean of
    Winchester, 51
Selwyn, G. A., bishop of New Zealand and
    Lichfield, 93, 141
Selwyn, William, Lady Margaret Professor,
    108, 141; and Divinity School, 93,
    141–2
Selwyn College, 92–5, 567; *94*; masters, *see*
    Chadwick; W. Owen; Kirkpatrick;
    Lyttleton
    court, 94; Cripps building, 95, 551; hall, 95
Senior Training Corps, 508
Serena Fund, 433
Seward, A. C., Sir Albert, professor of
    botany, 162
Sex Discrimination Act, 533
Shakespeare, W., 25, 432, 451–3; and
    Marlowe Society, 459; and Rossiter,
    452–3
Sheffield University, Vice-Chancellor, *see*
    Fisher
Sheppard, J. T., Sir John, fellow and provost
    of King's, 35, 125–7, 129, 459
Sheppard, Richard, 569
Sherrington, Professor Sir Charles, 80n
Shilleto, Richard, 53
Shippea Hill, 163
Shoenberg, Professor David, 189–90
Shrewsbury School, 68, 245n
Sidgwick, A., brother of Henry Sidgwick,
    17
Sidgwick, Mrs Eleanor, Eleanor Balfour,
    vice-principal and principal of
    Newnham, 14, 182, 255, 315–16, 341;
    marriage to Henry Sidgwick, 305; and
    Peile, 59; and Rayleigh and the
    Cavendish, 19, 180, 305; and Society for
    Psychical Research, 15
Sidgwick, Henry, fellow of Trinity,
    Knightbridge Professor of Moral
    Philosophy, founder of Newnham,
    13–19, 88–9, 137n, 144, 165, 180, 221,
    437; foundation of Newnham, 302–4,
    311–14, 319; marriage, 305; account of
    him by Maitland, 14, 16–18; *Memoir* of
    him, 17; and Apostles, 127; and Trinity,
    70–1; resigns fellowship, 16, 70, 100, 165

and E. W. Benson, his brother-in-law, 15,
    134; and Emily Davies, 306–7, 309–10;
    and Maitland, 14, 16–18, 220, 405; and
    Peile, 59–61; on L. Stephen, 122
Sidney Sussex College, 51–2, 58; masters, *see*
    Knox-Shaw; Linnett; Phelps
    new chapel, 119; *120*
    and maths, 52; numbers of students, 43, 52;
    admission of women, 53[n]
sizars, 78
Skeat, W. W., professor of Anglo-Saxon, 60,
    428, 432, 444
Skeel, Professor Caroline, 229
Skinner, Q., professor of political science, 472
Slee, P., 228
Smith, A. L., 219–20
Smuts, J. C., Field Marshal, Chancellor, 149,
    566
Snow, C. P., 181, 188, 262, 573; on
    Chadwick, 186; on Hardy and
    Littlewood, 117, 483–4; *The Masters*,
    148–9
social sciences, *see* SPS
Society for the Prevention of Cruelty to
    Undergraduates, 112
Society for Psychical Research, 15, 274
Society of Antiquaries, 476
Society of St Francis, 133
Somerville College, principal of, 341
Somme, battle of the, 335, 460
Sophocles, 453; *Oedipus Coloneus*, 126
Southward, W. T., tutor of St Catharine's, 43
Spain, Spanish Civil War, 520
Spence, Sir Basil, 551
Spencer, Stanley, *322*
Spens, Sir Will, master of Corpus, 51, 466,
    507
sport, 41, 63n, 115, 159, 288, 290–3, 468,
    517–18; and women, 329
Spratling, Professor F. R., 493
Spratt, A. W., dean and tutor of St
    Catharine's, 43
SPS and social sciences, 467, 472–3
Squire, Rebecca Flower, 224
SRC, Science Research Council (formerly
    DSIR; later SERC), 554
Stalin, 180, 519
Stanford, C. V., Sir Charles, professor of
    music, 457
Stanley, A. P., dean of Westminster, 4
Stanley, Lady of Alderley, 311, 316
Stanton, A. H., 145n
Stanton, V. H., Regius Professor of Divinity,
    339n
Stanton, W. H., 246n

Index

Stapleton, D. H., 381n
Steers, J. A., professor of geography, 474
Stein, Baron K., 231
Stein, Peter, Regius Professor of Civil Law, 217n, 218
Steiner, W., 224n
Stephen, Leslie, fellow and tutor of Trinity Hall, 62, 105, 121–3, 221n, 291–2; quoted, 101, 261, 270–2, 290; and heads of house, 261; and Maitland, 405; and sport, 272, 291–2; Leslie Stephen Lecture, 213
Stephenson, Mr Justice Melford, 558
Stewart, H. F., 432–4, 446
Stirling, James, 229, 546
Stoeber, Elias, 211–12
Stokes, G. G., Sir George, Lucasian Professor, master of Pembroke, 67, 152–3, 173, 181, 482, 587
Stone, Sir Richard, 471
Stopp, Elisabeth, 434n
Storey, Graham, 451
Strachey family, 438
Strachey, G. Lytton, 16n, 336–7, 465
Strachey, Miss J. P; principal of Newnham, 328
Strang, William, 461
Strasbourg, 212; European Court, see McNair
Stratton, Professor F. J. M., 333, 487
Strauss, D. F., 122
Strong, T. B., dean of Christ Church, later bishop of Ripon, 342–3
structuralism, 206, 454
Stuart, Professor James, MP, 476
Stubbings, F., 87n, 123, 125n
Stubbs, William, 6, 220, 222
students, attitudes, of (1945–90), 519–21; background of, 240–52; grants, see Anderson, C.; loans, 542; and professions, 601; poll men, 294; reading men and rowing men, 287–90, 293; rebellion and representation, 511, 523–6, 555–60
postgraduate, 178–9, 352, 519, 537, 567, 589; overseas, 544, 560
superconductivity, 193
Sutherland, Gillian, 301n, 304, 306, 316, 329
Sutton, John, 106–7
Swann, Sir Michael, Lord Swann, and the Swann Report (on veterinary education), 493
Swete, H. B., Regius Professor of Divinity, 146, 221n
Switzerland, 33, 557; Swiss Alps, 195
Syriac, 146, 431
Szreter, S., 241n

Tait, Professor J., 224
Taoism, 404; Taoist paradox, 198
Tansley, A. G., Professor Sir Arthur, 162
Tata, Sir Dorabji, 478
Taylor, G. I., Sir Geoffrey, Royal Society Professor, 482
Taylor, H. M., University Treasurer and Secretary-General of the faculties, Vice-Chancellor of Keele, 164, 208–9, 591–2
Taylor, Mrs Joan, 208–9, 591–2
Taylor, Samuel, 52
Tedder, Lord, Chancellor, 566
Teilhard de Chardin, 403
Temperley, H., professor of modern history, master of Peterhouse, 54, 235–6, 239
Tennyson, In Memoriam, 420; The Princess, 300
Territorial Army, 333
textual criticism, 137–8, 140; and see Housman
Thackeray, Mr, 167
Thackeray, G., provost of King's, 33
Thatcher, Mrs M., as secretary of state for education and science, 559; as prime minister, 534, 561–2
Thaxted, 403
theological colleges, 143–5, 576n; and see under individual colleges
theology, xv, chaps. 5, 14 passim; divinity faculty and school, 140–2, 148, 425, 576n, and see under University of Cambridge, buildings and sites; tripos, 10–11, 105, 295; New Testament seminar, 409, 505
Thirkill, Sir Henry, master of Clare, 63–4, 262, 465
Thompson, A. Hamilton, 323
Thompson, David, 134n, 137n, 388n
Thompson, F. J., 546n
Thompson, W. H., master of Trinity, 70–1, 259–60
Thomson, J. J., Cavendish Professor, master of Trinity, 13, 31–2, 80, 153, 176, 180, 183–7, 222, 408, 588; as master, 69, 183–5; on government aid, 97; and the Ph.D., 178; on Rayleigh, 182
Thomson, Sir William, Lord Kelvin, professor at Glasgow, fellow of Peterhouse, 53, 180–1, 187
Tilley, A., 433
Tilley, C. E., professor of mineralogy and petrology, 159
Tillich, Paul, 411
Tillyard, E. M. W., master of Jesus, 444, 447–8

Times, The, 349, 364–5
Todd, Alexander, Lord Todd, professor of
    organic chemistry, xvii, 156, 195,
    199–201, 508, 568; master of Christ's,
    29n, 200–1, 264–7; Chancellor of
    Strathclyde, 201
Todhunter, Isaac, 83, 271
Tomkinson, H., 310
topology, 152
Torres Straits, 204, 499
tort, 218, 227
Tout, Professor T. F., 224, 232
Townsend, Professor Sir John, 184
trade unions, 521–2; TUC, 522
Treasury, the, 511, 540, 560
Trent, Council of, 280
Trevelyan, G. M., Regius Professor of
    Modern History, master of Trinity, 127,
    129, 236, 285, 327, 365, 422, 438, 441;
    early career 366–7; and Royal
    Commission III, 341, 353n, 366–9; his
    books, 367; and Knowles, 229, 418
Trevelyan, R. C., 129
Trinity College, 69–73, 368; bursars, *see*
    Bradfield; Nicholas; College Council,
    and Russell case, 338–40; fellows, 2–3,
    69, 369; masters, 46, 281, *and see* Adrian;
    Butler, H. Montagu; Butler, R. A.;
    Thompson, W. H.; Thomson, J. J;
    Trevelyan, G. M; Whewell; Whitgift;
    master's lodge, 4, 258; the seniority, 68;
    vice-masters, *see* Jackson, Henry;
    Trotter; Walker
  buildings, 383; campus, 569; chapel, 9, 112,
    117, 119, 129; choir, 107, 457–8; and
    religious tests, 100; Great Court, 72;
    Nevile's Court, 72, 333; Senior
    Combination Room, 4, 72, 255;
    Whewell's Court, 3
  boat club, 298; college teachers, and
    teachers, 68, 70–1, 76–7, 83, 319;
    classical tutors, 17; praelectorships, 71,
    165; foundation of Darwin College, 579;
    gentlemen commoners, 70; and History
    Tripos, 228–9; and Moral Sciences
    Tripos, 295; and nobility, 295; numbers
    of students, 32, 41, 67, 295; and schools,
    599–600; and theology, 7; admission of
    women, 531n; and World War I, 331,
    333–4
  and M. Amos, 288; and the Apostles, 438;
    and F. Cooper, 376; and Devonshire,
    175; and Foster, 155, 165; and Frazer,
    204; and Gooch, 229; and Goulding
    Brown, 279; and Hardy, 483–4; and

Hopkins, 196; and Hort, 9–10; and
    Housman, 72–3; and Jackson, 70–3, 215;
    and Paul Judge, 473; and Lapsley, 89;
    and Lightfoot, 85, 134; and Littlewood,
    483–4; and Luard, 5; and M'Taggart,
    440; and Maitland, 6, 56, 219; and
    Moore, 440; and Stephen Neill, 121; and
    T. Nicholas, 155; and Ramanujan,
    483–4; and Russell, 337–40; and
    Sidgwick, 1, 16; and H. F. Stewart, 433;
    and G. I. Taylor, 482; and Westcott,
    138; and Wittgenstein, 438
Trinity College, Oxford, 96
Trinity Hall, 61–3, 104–5, 120–1, 217–18,
    291–2, 305, 531n; masters, *see* Dean,
    Geldart, Latham, Maine; tutors, *see*
    Latham, Stephen
  chapel, 106; and law, 61–2; and urban
    development, 79
triposes, 293–7; *and see under individual subjects*
Trotter, Coutts, vice-master of Trinity, 13,
    70, 155–6, 165, 174, 588; proposal to
    abolish office of heads, 87, 259, 261
Troup, F. W., 478
Twigg, J., 57, 109–11, 526, 555
Twistleton-Wykeham-Fiennes family, 245–6

UCCA, 541
UFC, University Funding Council, 173, 540,
    555, 563
UGC, University Grants Committee, 21n,
    173, 540–1, 543–4, 546, 553–5, 560–1,
    563; chairman, *see* Murray; Arts Sub-
    Committee, 230, 455, 561
Ullmann, Professor W., 425, 505–6
Underwood, M., 116n
Union of Democratic Control, 337, 339
Union Road Primary School, 390
Unitarians, 102, 124, 316
United Reformed Church, 394–400; *and see*
    Cheshunt College, Dodd
Union Society, 159, 291, 559
universities, *passim*: *see esp.* University of
    Cambridge; Oxford; civic, 84, 124–5,
    and see Liverpool; Manchester; new
    (1960s), 543, 552; in 1945–90,
    anthropology of, 512–38; and political
    history, 538–66
Universities and Colleges Estates Act (1925),
    362
Universities Catholic Education Board, 389
University Boat Club, 151, 290, 457
University Careers Service, *see* University of
    Cambridge, institutions
University Library: old, 153, 173n, 225, 319,

Index

340, 370–1, 378, 381, 430, 581, 589; and
Henry Bradshaw, 273–4; new, 90, 175,
182, 229, 284, chap. 12, 544; Cairo
Genizah, 135; copyright status, 371, 387;
Darwin papers, 475; manuscripts,
catalogue of, 5; Royal Collection, 379
Anderson Room, 387
Keynes Room, 275
Reading Room, 379
Syndicate and Subsyndicates, 371–8, 383,
386
University Archives, xx, 5, 381n
University Rifle Volunteers (later OTC,
etc.), 333–5
University of Cambridge, buildings and sites
(for labs, *see under individual subjects*):
Arts School, 90, 176; Botanic Gardens
(old and new), 153–4, 160–1; Cavendish
Laboratory, *see* physics; Cockerell
Building (formerly in old University
Library), 173, 225, 373n; Divinity
School, Selwyn, 7, 93, 108, 581;
Downing Site, 90–1, 154, 159, 161, 174,
224–5, 481, 547, 588; Examination
School, 90; Fenner's Cricket Ground,
291; Mullard Radio Astronomy
Observatory, 487–9; *489*; Museum of
Archaeology and Anthropology
(formerly Museum of Ethnology, etc.),
389–90, 462; curators, *see* Gathercole;
Hügel; Phillipson; Museum of Classical
Archaeology, 203; New Museums Site,
90, 153–5, 174, 177, 191, 588;
Observatory, 153, 487; Old Schools, 91,
141, 153, 225, 371, 574–5; Pitt Press,
374–5; Scott Polar Research Institute,
473; Sedgwick Geological Museum, 91,
157, 159, 173; Senate House, 97, 116,
270, 291n; Senate House Yard, 334–5;
Sidgwick Site, 225, 546; University
Combination Room, 575; University
Farm, 547; Whipple Museum, 474–5;
Zoological Museum, 203, 590; curator,
see Clark, J. W.; *and see* Fitzwilliam
Museum
colleges: *see under individual colleges*;
accounts and finance, 73–82, 359–63,
598; boat clubs and boat houses, 291–2;
bursars, 362; chambers, 78; chapels, 101,
104, 106–11, 516; compulsory chapel,
111–21, 124–5; Colleges' Committee, 27;
fellows, fellowships, 30–1, 267–81, 354,
574–6, 578; economics of livelihood,
281–7; fellowship dividends, 74–7, 83,

282, 359–60; heads, 85, 87, 257–67, 270,
564; proposal to abolish, 87, 259, 261;
labs, 86, 588; libraries, 291, 319;
medieval colleges, 104; new colleges,
chap. 18; and the poor, 92; and schools,
599–600; SCRs, 514; societies, 400;
students and schools, 240–52; student
numbers, 593–7; teaching, supervision,
34, 70–2, 76–7, 79–80, 82–4, 156, 278,
280–1, 296, 319, 352; tutors, 22, 31,
84–5, 113–15, 270–2, 313
disciplines – degrees, departments, faculties,
laboratories and triposes: *see under
individual subjects*; departments, and
schools, 586n; *and see* degrees; faculties;
triposes
institutions: Board of Graduate Studies
(formerly Board of Research Studies),
178; Caput, 27, 258; Commencement,
298–9; constitution of the university,
20–32, chap. 11, 563–6; Council of the
Senate, xvi, 12, 22n, 27, 30, 61, 134,
258, 326, 350, 559, 563–5; Councils of
the Schools of Arts and Humanities, of
Biological Sciences, of Humanities and
Social Sciences, of Physical Sciences, xvi,
586n; CUSU, Cambridge University
Students' Union (formerly Students'
Representative Assembly and Council,
then CSU), 291n, 534, 556, 559;
Development Office, 565; Financial
Board, 350; General Board, xvi, 22, 29–
30, 265, 350, 475, 544n, 563; Local
Examinations and School Examination
Syndicates, 308, 463–4; McDonald
Institute for Archaeological Research,
208; Regent House, xvi, 24, 28n, 30, 97,
172, 278, 297, 351–2, 387, 475, 562,
564–5, 570, 575; Senate, 24, 30, 98, 258,
290, 297, 326, 351, 370, 376–7, 526, 565;
University Statutes, 56, 359; University
Careers Service, 601; Wellcome Trust
and Cancer Research Campaign Institute
of Cancer, 586n; *and see* faculties
libraries: Seeley Library, 279; Squire Law
Library, 90, 224–5; *and see* University
Library
officers, officials: assistant directors of
research (ADRs), 575; Chancellors, 28,
270, 565–6, *and see* Adrian, Albert,
Balfour, Buckingham, Burleigh,
Cromwell, Devonshire, Newcastle,
Philip, Rayleigh, Smuts, Tedder; esquire
bedells, 28, 270; high stewards, *see*

(University of Cambridge, officers, *cont.*)
Devlin; Devonshire; Librarians, *see*
Jenkinson; Scholfield; proctors, 28
professors, chairs, 23, 31–2; of anatomy, *see*
Humphry; ancient history, *see* Adcock;
Finley; Hopkins; Reid; Anglo-Saxon,
Elrington and Bosworth chair, 432, *and*
see Chadwick, H. M.; Dickins; Lapidge;
Skeat; Whitelock; Arabic, 428; and Lord
Almoner's chair or readership, 428n, 429;
architecture, *see* Martin; Wilson, C. St J.;
Arthur Balfour Professor of Genetics, *see*
Fisher, R. A.; Punnett; astronomy, *see*
Darwin; botany, 160, *and see* Babington;
Godwin; Henslow; Seward; Ward;
Cavendish Professors of Physics, 263, *and*
see Bragg; Clerk Maxwell; Mott;
Pippard; Rayleigh; Rutherford;
Thomson, J. J.; chemistry, *see* Chibnall;
Emeleus; Hopkins, Sir Frederick
Gowland; Lewis; Liveing; Pope; Todd;
Disney Professors of Archaeology, *see*
Clark, Grahame; Daniel; Garrod; Minns;
Renfrew; Ridgeway; Dixie Professorship
of Ecclesiastical History, 9, 11, 59, 140,
354n, *and see* Creighton; Gwatkin; Rupp;
Downing Professors, 354n, of Law, *see*
Christian; Maitland; of medicine, *see*
Harwood; Latham; economic history, *see*
Clapham; Postan; economics, *see*
Dasgupta; Robertson; *and see below*
political economy; Ely chair of divinity,
86; energy studies, *see* Eden; engineering
(formerly mechanism and applied
mechanics, mechanical sciences), *see*
Baker, J. F.; Heyman; Inglis; Stuart;
French, Drapers' Professor, *see* Bayley;
Prior; geography, *see* Darby; Debenham;
Steers; geology, *see* Hughes, T.
McKenny; G. I. Taylor chair, 482;
history of art, *see* Henderson; Jaffé;
Hulsean Professor of Divinity (later
Norris-Hulse), *see* Hort; human ecology,
see Banks; Italian, *see* Boyde; Bullough;
Okey; King Edward VII Professor of
English literature, 432, 445, *and see*
Quiller-Couch; Verrall; Willey;
Knightbridge Professor of Moral
Philosophy, *see* Sidgwick; Lady Margaret
Professorship of Divinity, 141, *and see*
Moule; Selwyn; Latin, Kennedy
Professorship, *see* Brink; Housman;
Reeve; Laurence Professor of Ancient
Philosophy, *see* Cornford; Lucasian
Professorship of Applied Mathematics,
see Dirac; Hawking; Larmor; Newton;
Stokes; medieval history, 284, *and see*
Brooke; Knowles; Previté-Orton;
mineralogy and petrology, *see* Tilley;
modern history, *see* Butterfield;
Temperley; music, *see* Hadley; Stanford;
Wood; Norrisian and Norris-Hulse
Professors of Divinity, *see* Browne,
E. H.; Burkitt; Dodd; pathology, *see*
Dean; Roy; Woodhead; Peat Marwick
Professor of Accounting, 473;
physiology, 169, *and see* Adrian, E. D.;
Foster, Sir Michael; political economy,
see Marshall, Alfred; Pigou; political
science, *see* Barker; Brogan; Skinner;
Price Waterhouse Chair of Accounting,
471; psychology, *see* Bartlett; Quick
Professors of Biology, 492, *and see*
Keilin; Wigglesworth; Regius Professors
of Civil Law, 210, *and see* Buckland;
Duff; Stein; Regius Professors of
Divinity, 86, 282, 339n, *and see*
Burnaby; Lampe; Nineham; Swete;
Westcott; Regius Professors of Greek,
86, *and see* Jackson, Henry; Jebb; Porson;
Regius Professor of Hebrew, *see*
Kennett; Regius Professors of Modern
History, 228, *and see* Acton; Bury;
Butler, J. R. M.; Chadwick, W. Owen;
Elton; Gray; Kingsley; Knowles; Seeley;
Trevelyan; Regius Professors of Physic,
168, *and see* Allbutt; Haviland; Paget;
Rolleston; Whitby; Rouse Ball
Professors of law, *see* Wade; Williams;
Winfield; Sanskrit, 428, *and see* Cowell;
Schröder Professor of German, *see*
Breul; surgery, *see* Haviland; Marsh;
Sadleirian Professor of Pure
Mathematics, *see* Hardy, G. H.;
Whewell Professor of International Law,
see Harcourt; zoology, *see* Gray, Sir
James; Newton; Public Orator, 29, *and*
see Glover; Registrary, 28–9, 270, *and see*
Clark, J. W.; Keynes; Luard; Secretary-
General of the faculties, 28–9, 266, *and*
see Taylor; Treasurers, 28–9, *and see*
Knox-Shaw; Taylor, H. M.; Wilson;
university teaching officers (UTOs), esp.
university lecturers, 353–7, 574–6, 578;
Vice-Chancellors, 27–9, 174, 261, 270,
378, 564, 570, *and see* Adrian; Boys-
Smith; Chadwick, W. Owen; Giles;
Linnett; Murray; Whewell; Williams
societies and other bodies, *see under separate*
entries and under religious societies

Index

women in Cambridge, chap. 9 passim,
526–33, *and see* Girton College; Lucy
Cavendish College; New Hall;
Newnham College; admission to
university, 324–7, 364, 506, 510; *and see*
women
University of East Anglia, Norwich, 356
university teachers, 250; attitudes (1945–90),
521–6; *and see* AUT
USA, 447; libraries of, 386; universities, 354,
536, 562; and nuclear physics, 177; and
atom bomb, 190; psychology in, 500;
and students revolts, 511

Vaughan, Professor R., 571
Vaughan Williams, R., 458–9
Venn, John, president of Gonville and Caius,
xv–xvii, xx, 40, 59, 82–3, 114, 145, 173
Venn, Mrs J., 305
Venn, J. A., president of Queens', 145
Verrall, A. W., King Edward VII Professor,
69, 127, 432, 445
Versailles, Peace Conference, 235
veterinary school and science, 492–3, 510
Victoria and Albert Museum, 343, 460
Victoria University, *see* Manchester, Victoria
University of Manchester, Liverpool and
Leeds
Vienna, 169, 455, 497
Vietnam, 520, 523, 544
Vines, S., 161
Vinogradoff, Professor Paul, 220
Virginia, governor of, 293
vitamins, 195, 198, 200

Wace, H., 69
Wade, E. C. S., Downing Professor, 227
Wade, Sir William, Rouse Ball Professor,
master of Gonville and Caius, 227
Wadham College, Oxford, 155
Walker, R., vice-master of Trinity, 160
Walton, E. T. S., 188
Ward, Sir Adolphus, professor at Owens
College, Manchester, Vice-Chancellor of
the Victoria University, master of
Peterhouse, 53–4, 233
Ward, Marshall, professor of botany, 161–2
Warnock, Sir Geoffrey, 440, 443
Warwick, 410; University of, 200
Washington, Dumbarton Oaks Institute, 462
Wass, Sir Douglas, and Wass Report, 29,
550, 564–5
Waterhouse, A., and Girton, 312; and
Gonville and Caius, 66, 76; and Jesus,
66; and Pembroke, 65–7

Waterhouse, Mrs M. G., M. G. Woods,
332–3
Watson, James, 497–8
Watson, S., Peat Marwick Professor, 473n
Watts, Isaac, 396–400
Wavell, A., Major the (2nd) Earl Wavell,
314n
Welbourne, Edward, tutor and master of
Emmanuel, 262, 278–81, 515
Wellcome Trust, 475
Wells, archdeacons of, 146; dean of, *see*
Robinson, Professor Joseph Armitage
Welsh, Miss, mistress of Girton, 311, 317
Wesley, Charles and John, 394, 396–400
Wesley House, 144
Westcott, B. F., Regius Professor of Divinity,
bishop of Durham, 1, 7, 86, 105, 134–
41; as canon of Peterborough, 139, and
Westminster, 139; his commentaries,
140; as bishop, 138, 146
and Hort, 10–12, 274; and Trinity chapel, 9
Westcott House (formerly Clergy Training
School), 140, 144
Westcott, Mrs B. F., 138
Westminster College, 144, 393–4
Wheeler, R. E. M., Sir Mortimer, 205
Whelock, A., 444
Whewell, W., master of Trinity, xv, 3, 71,
152, 260, 476; as Vice-Chancellor, 116
Whipple, Robert, and Whipple Museum,
474–5
Whitby, Sir Lionel, Regius Professor of
Physic, 172
Whitcut, Mrs Janet, 287n
Whitehead, A. N., 441, 470
Whitelock, Dorothy, professor of Anglo-
Saxon, 202, 445
Whitgift, John, master of Trinity, archbishop
of Canterbury, 104
Whittlesford, 462
Wigglesworth, Sir Vincent, Quick Professor
of Biology, 494, 502–4; *Insects and the
Life of Man*, 504
Wilamowitz-Moellendorf, U. von, 214,
409–10
Wilberforce, Robert, 106
Wilkes, Maurice, 492
Wilkins, William, 55, 265
Wilkinson, L. P., 510
Willcox, M. A., 316
Willey, Basil, King Edward VII Professor,
446, 448
Williams, Sir David, Vice-Chancellor, Rouse
Ball Professor, president of Wolfson,
565

Index

Williams, Professor Glanville, 227

Willink, Lord, master of Magdalene, 46

Willis, Robert, Jacksonian Professor, fellow of Gonville and Caius, 2–3, 153–4, 252, 592; and the engineering school, 476; his marriage, 304n; Willis and Clark, *Architectural History*, 3, 203, 476, 590; his sister, Mrs Clark, 252

Willis, Mrs R., 252

Wilson, C. St J., professor of architecture, 456–7

Wilson, C. T. R., 184

Wilson, David (biographer of Rutherford), 186–7

Wilson, David (curator of Aerial Photography), 208

Wilson, G. H., University Treasurer and master of Clare, 29, 63

Wilson, Harold, 263

Winchester, bishop of, *see* Browne; cathedral, dean of, *see* Selwyn, E. G.; Winchester College, 47, 71n, 91, 245–7

Winfield, Sir Percy, Rouse Ball Professor, 227

Winkoff, H., 317

Winstanley, D. A., 50, 294–5

Wittgenstein, L., 437–8, 442–3

Wolfson College, formerly University College, 256, 528, 570–1, 576–8; presidents, *see* Morrison; Williams

Wolfson College, Oxford, 577

women, in Cambridge, xix, 59, chap. 9 passim, esp. 324–7, 526–33, 589; womens' education, 247, 301, 343–4, 464 and chap. 9 passim; in parliament, 301; and marriage, 530, 582; as dons' wives, 252–7, 274–6, 304–5; and professions, 242–5; academic, 252; ordination of, 148–9; admission to university and degrees, 149, 324–7, 375; and student opinion, 291, 297–300, 363–4; admission to colleges, 297, 531–2; co-residence in modern universities, 531–2;
and MML, 428, 431; *and see* Girton College, Lucy Cavendish College, New Hall, Newnham College

Wood, Alex (Church of Scotland), 388, 393–4, 405

Wood, Charles, professor of music, 116, 458–9

Wood, J. S., 116

Wood, James, *401*

Woodard, Nathaniel, and Woodard Schools, 247

Woodhead, G. S., professor of pathology, 493

Woods, Colonel, 382

Woods, George, 121

Woodward, Professor R. B., 201

Woolf, Virginia, and Leonard, 328; *A Room of One's Own*, 328–30

Worcester cathedral priory, prior, *see* More

Worcester College, Oxford, 113–14

Wordsworth, William, 53, 290–1, 452, 504

World Wars, and Cambridge, xix; World War I (the Great War, 1914–18), 113, 119, 131–2, 170, 283, 331–40, 397, 442, 469, 500; and Cavendish Lab, 186; chaplains in, 506; and Junior Historians, 230; and T. Nicholas, 155; recruiting in, 506; and Temperley, 235; and University Library, 371; and women, 325, 327, 506; *and see* Russell II (1939–45), 505–10, 558, 591; and atom bomb, 191; and India, 205; and professorships, 264; Regional Commissioners, 507; and teaching of Russian, 436; and women, 327; aftermath, 149, 511

wrangler, senior, 71, 151, 173

Wren, Sir Christopher, 95n

Wren, Bishop Matthew, 107

Wright, Arthur, tutor of Queens', 57, 110–11

Wright, W., 429–30

Wyclif, 398

Wycliffe Hall, Oxford, 144

Wynn, Edward, bishop of Ely, 400

X-rays, 184

Yarborough, earl of, 394

Young, F. G., master of Darwin, 575

zoology, 492–3, 502–4